THE ITALIAN CONCEPTION
OF INTERNATIONAL LAW

By ANGELO PIERO SERENI

THE LAWBOOK EXCHANGE, LTD.
Clark, New Jersey

ISBN-13: 978-1-58477-974-2 (cloth)
ISBN-10: 1-58477-974-8 (cloth)
ISBN-13: 978-1-58477-985-8 (paperback)
ISBN-10: 1-58477-985-3 (paperback)

Lawbook Exchange edition 2009

THE LAWBOOK EXCHANGE, LTD.

33 Terminal Avenue
Clark, New Jersey 07066-1321

*Please see our website for a selection of our other publications
and fine facsimile reprints of classic works of legal history:*
www.lawbookexchange.com

Library of Congress Cataloging-in-Publication Data

Sereni, Angelo Piero, 1908-
 The Italian conception of international law / by Angelo Piero Sereni.
    p. cm.
 Originally published: New York : Columbia University Press, 1943.
 Includes bibliographical references and index.
 ISBN-13: 978-1-58477-974-2 (cloth : alk. paper)
 ISBN-10: 1-58477-974-8 (cloth : alk. paper)
 1. Law--Italy--History. 2. International law--Italy--History. 3. Italy--
Foreign relations. I. Title.
 KKH120.S47 2009
 341.0945--dc22   2009015554

Printed in the United States of America on acid-free paper

THE ITALIAN CONCEPTION
OF INTERNATIONAL LAW

By ANGELO PIERO SERENI

1943

COLUMBIA UNIVERSITY PRESS

NEW YORK · MORNINGSIDE HEIGHTS

TO PAOLA

FOREWORD

THIS BOOK is an attempt at a systematic and comprehensive account of the development of international law in Italy from its origin until the intervention of that country in the Second World War. The subject has been considered in its relationship to the general development of international law. In view of the importance of Italy's contribution to this branch of the law, it is hoped that the book will furnish useful material to the scholar who will undertake the hard but indispensable task of writing a general history of the law of nations. Emphasis has been laid on those theories and institutions which are of present interest. It has been found advisable also to give particular attention to certain institutions, such as reprisals, which are now obsolete but had original and important developments in Italy in the past centuries.

No previous attempt has been made to write a history of international law in Italy. For this reason the main purpose of this book is to give a general outline of the subject as a guide for further studies on particular periods and institutions. For those who intend to proceed to a more detailed analysis of some special topics, abundant bibliographical material is offered.

The book has also a political purpose. It is intended to show that a deeply rooted love for justice and freedom pervades the writings of all the greatest international lawyers of Italy, from Bartolus and Gentili to Mancini and most of the contemporary authors. The chapters on fascism are intended to show that its theory and practice in the field of international law and relations, as in all other fields, were an obvious deviation from the best Italian tradition. They also are intended to prove that a silent but efficient resistance against fascist influence in the field of international law has been maintained by most of the Italian scholars. The chapters on fascism were written in 1940–1941. Recent events substantiate these theses of the book. They also prove that the feelings of the overwhelming majority of the Italian people coincide with those of Italy's international lawyers. In his Message to the Congress, September 17, 1943, President Roosevelt acknowledged the unconquerable love of liberty of the Italian people.

The unmistakably sincere welcome given to the Allied troops by the Italian people has proved conclusively that, even in a country which had lived for a generation under a complete dictatorship—with all of its propaganda, censorship and suppression of free speech and discussion—the love of liberty was unconquerable.

It has also proved conclusively that this war was not waged by the people of Italy of their own choice. All of Mussolini's propaganda machine could not make them love Hitler or hate us. The less said about the feelings toward Mussolini the better.

At this tragic hour of their national life the Italian people will find some solace in these memorable words from the head of a great nation, which will be understood by them to constitute a solemn and generous commitment as to the future of their country.

I wish to extend a word of thanks to all who helped me in my effort. Professors Joseph P. Chamberlain and Philip C. Jessup, of Columbia University, and Professor Manley O. Hudson, of Harvard University, gave me constant encouragement while my work was in progress. I am especially indebted to Professor Edwin M. Borchard, of Yale University, and Dr. George A. Finch, director of the Division of International Law of the Carnegie Endowment for International Peace, for reading the manuscript and being instrumental in obtaining its publication. The financial burden of the publication has been borne by the Carnegie Endowment for International Peace, Division of International Law. In expressing my gratitude to the Carnegie Endowment, I also wish to point out that an analysis of the works of many authors (such as Giovanni da Legnano, Belli, and Gentili) considered in my book has been made possible only through the publication of their works by the Endowment. Miss Marie S. Klooz, of Washington, D.C., Mrs. Ernestine Minciotti and Miss Rachel Minciotti, of New York City, were of assistance in the preparation of the English manuscript. I wish to express my deepest appreciation and gratitude to Miss Ida M. Lynn, of the Columbia University Press, who edited the manuscript and supervised the production and indexing of the book with exceptional ability and inexhaustible patience.

ANGELO PIERO SERENI

New York
September 22, 1943

CONTENTS

Part One: The Renaissance

Part Two: The Period of Foreign Ascendancy

BIBLIOGRAPHICAL ABBREVIATIONS

Am. J. Int. L.	American Journal of International Law.
Foro it.	Foro italiano.
Gazz. uff.	Gazzetta ufficiale del Regno d'Italia.
Giur. it.	Giurisprudenza italiana.
Mon. trib.	Monitore dei tribunali.
Perm. Ct. Int. Jus., Publ.	Publications of the Permanent Court of International Justice.
Ser. A.	Series A—Judgments.
Ser. B.	Series B—Advisory Opinions.
Ser. A/B.	Series A/B—Cumulative Series of Judgments, and Advisory Opinions Given after 1931.
Ser. C.	Series C—Acts and Documents Relating to Judgments and Advisory Opinions.
Ser. D.	Series D—Collection of Texts Governing the Jurisdiction of the Court.
Ser. E.	Series E—Annual Reports.
Racc. uff. leggi e decr.	Raccolta ufficiale delle leggi e dei decreti del Regno d'Italia.
Rec. des cours	Académie de droit international de la Haye. Recueil des cours.
Rep. Foro it.	Repertorio del Foro italiano.
Rep. Giur. it.	Repertorio della Giurisprudenza italiana.
Rev. dr. int. et lég. comp.	Revue de droit international et de législation comparée.
Rev. gén. dr. int. publ.	Revue générale de droit international public.
Riv. dir. int.	Rivista di diritto internazionale.
Ziletti, *Tractatus*	Ziletti, F. Tractatus universi juris (1584).

PART ONE

The Renaissance

Chapter 1: THE BIRTH OF THE ITALIAN NATION

THE first contribution of Italy to international law dates from the middle of the twelfth century, when the Italian nation originated. Politically Italy was still divided into a mosaic of organizations, often struggling among themselves. But under the twofold influence of the Roman traditions and institutions and of the Roman Catholic Church, the peoples living in Italy since the days of Rome were at that time blended with the later settlers, invaders of German origin from the other side of the Alps, Greeks, Normans, and Saracens, who came by sea during the Middle Ages. United by a common language, common usages, culture, and ideals, the Italian nation emerged and drew the richness and vitality of its civilization from the diversity of its component races. The period of political, economic, and cultural decadence which followed the barbaric invasions and the fall of the Roman Empire had ended at last. Italy had been freed from the bonds of the feudal system.

The twelfth century began a period of extraordinary greatness and prosperity, perhaps the most glorious in Italy's history, the Renaissance, also known with particular regard to its politico-legal aspects as "the period of autonomies." This period lasted until the middle of the sixteenth century, when, following the Peace of Château-Cambrésis, 1559, Italy fell under foreign domination—first of Spain; then of Austria.

FACTORS CONTRIBUTING TO THE EARLY DEVELOPMENT OF INTERNATIONAL LAW IN ITALY

Since the first developments of international law in Italy are intimately connected with the geographic, economic, religious, cultural, and political factors on which the greatness of Italy during the Renaissance is founded, a brief survey of these factors is necessary.

At the beginning of the Renaissance America and Australia were still undiscovered, and Africa and Asia were barely known to Europe. The whole civilized world, Christian and Moslem, was concentrated around the Mediterranean. Italy, flung across the midst of this sea, was destined to be the center of world civilization during that period. She fulfilled her natural function of equilibrium, acting as liaison between the various peoples who lived on the shores of the Mediterranean, a bridge for the traffic among the countries of northern Europe, the Spanish peninsula, the Balkans, Africa, and the East.

The economic and social conditions of Italy permitted her to enjoy to the full the advantages of this exceptional geographic situation. Even though the Italians had not attained political unity, they already constituted from the ethnic point of view one of the largest and most homogeneous groups of Europe. The large numbers and the rapid increase of the population made it possible for the Italian states to pursue a foreign policy of military and demographic expansion without affecting the density of the population within the mother country.

In every part of the peninsula large urban communities grew up. In the fourteenth century Milan, Florence, and Venice each had more than one hundred thousand inhabitants—a huge population for that period. The fields, generally very fertile, were efficiently irrigated and cultivated. There were numerous ways of communication which were safe and convenient enough for that time. Natural ports offered easy approach and safe refuge to the small ships, and various Alpine passes united Italy with the rest of Europe.

Under the leadership of an enterprising bourgeoisie and by means of expert artisan guilds, Italy became one of the greatest commercial and manufacturing centers. From the Alpine regions and Sardinia came raw metals; from the Adriatic and Tuscany, salt; from France, Germany, and Flanders, coarse cloths; from the northern countries, furs; from England and Africa, raw wool; from the Orient, dyes, leather, and spices (such as drugs, perfumes, and medicines) ; from Sicily, Africa, and the Black Sea, grain. Italy was the center for the exchange of products between Europe and the Orient. Many commodities, such as fine cloths, embossed leather, arms, silks, crystal, Venetian glass, perfumes, and drugs, were processed in Italy and then re-exported. The Italians became the foremost bankers in Europe. They engaged in the most important financial transactions of the period. Florentines, Siennese, and Lombards made loans to popes and sovereigns and opened agencies in London, France, and the Orient. The florin of Florence and the ducat of Venice were symbols of security and financial stability.[1]

Propelled by the dynamics of commercial expansion, Italian maritime republics soon reached the forefront of Mediterranean sea trade. Amalfi and Pisa at the beginning of the Renaissance and subsequently Genoa and Venice surpassed Barcelona and the towns in the south of France in

[1] See Bonfante, *Lezioni di storia del commercio*, Vol. I; Depping, *Histoire du commerce entre le Levant et l'Europe*; Doren, *Storia economica dell'Italia* (Italian translation by Luzzatto) ; Heyd, *Histoire du commerce du Levant au moyen âge*; Schaube, *Handelsgeschichte der lateinischen Völker des Mittelmeergebiets bis zum Ende der Kreuzzüge*; Yver, *Le Commerce et les marchands dans l'Italie méridionale*. For a rapid survey of the participation of Italians in commerce at the beginning of the Renaissance see Sapori, "Il Commercio internazionale del medioevo," 9 Archivio di studi corporativi (1938), 281 ff.

Mediterranean trade. Italian navigators sailed through the straits of Gibraltar, traded with Holland, England, and the Hanseatic towns, pushed on to the Azores, and followed the western coast of Africa.

Commercial competition and the spirit of adventure favored military enterprises against rival Italian towns, the Balkan princes, and the Infidels. The beginning of the Renaissance coincided with the period of the Crusades. For the Italian cities, which furnished the greater part of the means of transportation and were therefore entitled to a large share of the booty, the Crusades represented lucrative commercial enterprises. This explains the preponderance of Italian influence in such expeditions and in the military religious policy of the Levant in general. Hence "the key to the history of the Near East lies in the rivalry of the Italian towns for commercial supremacy." [2]

The fact that Rome was the seat of the papacy conferred upon Italy notable advantages. Until the unity of the Christian world was shattered by the Reformation, the Pope remained the spiritual leader of all Europe. To Rome came all who had relations with the Vatican, such as ecclesiastics and sovereigns, pilgrims and scholars, artists and adventurers. Thus Rome became the greatest intellectual and artistic center of the Christian world. Huge sums poured into Rome from all Christendom in the form of voluntary offerings and payment of indulgences. This revenue, which was invested almost exclusively in the Italian peninsula, helped to increase the economic prosperity of the country.

Among the many aspects of the artistic and cultural revival upon which the fame of the Italian Renaissance rests, the flowering of legal studies and especially the revival of Roman law must here be taken into consideration, since they played an important role in the development of international law.[3] During the dark period of the Middle Ages, Roman traditions, kept alive by the Church and the Empire, were never extinguished in Europe.[4] Latin was still the language of the ecclesiastic and the scholar. Roman law itself survived in Italy to some extent. Common law, which regulated relations among peoples of Roman civilization, was in substance Roman law adapted to new times. Roman legal influence may also be found in the codification of laws of barbarians who settled in Italy during the Middle Ages. But the Roman law of the classical

[2] Fisher, *A History of Europe*, p. 239.

[3] For the history of Italian law see Besta, *Il diritto publico italiano*; Calisse, *Storia del diritto italiano* (*A History of Italian Law*); Del Giudice, ed., *Storia del diritto italiano*; A. Pertile, *Storia del diritto italiano*; Giuseppe Salvioli, *Storia del diritto italiano*; Sclopis, *Storia della legislazione italiana*; Solmi, *Storia del diritto italiano*.

[4] On the influence of ancient Rome over medieval Italy see Graf, *Roma nelle immaginazioni e nelle memorie del medioevo*, and Novati, *L'influsso del pensiero latino sopra la civiltà italiana del medioevo*.

period was almost unknown during the Middle Ages, because of the general decadence of studies, the scarcity of available sources, and the lack of interest in a legal system which was no longer in force.

During the Middle Ages there did not exist in Italy a uniform system of law. The Lombards, the Franks, and other German invaders continued to live in accordance with their own laws. The Germanic conception of law as personal, each individual being governed by his own national law, was a strong obstacle to the unification of the law. Nor was the need for a uniform law felt in Italy as long as the separation of ethnic groups existed and while the economic relations between the various regions of the peninsula and between Italy and other countries were not well developed. At the beginning of the Renaissance several factors contributed to the revival of the study and practice of Roman law. First, the love for classical antiquity in all its aspects led humanists to seek out the texts of Roman law and to interpret them. There were, however, practical reasons which especially contributed to the revival of Roman law. The birth of an Italian nation created the need of a uniform law common to all the inhabitants of the country. This law could not logically be based on German laws, which were considered too rudimentary and foreign to the customs of the majority of Italians. Instead it seemed natural to base the new legal institutions on the ancient law of Rome, toward which, during the Renaissance, the Italian communes looked as toward a common mother. Because of the simplicity, the clarity, and the complete elaboration of its institutions, which were grounded upon generally recognized principles of justice, fair dealing, and common sense, and because of its tendency to universality, Roman law easily became the basis of the new legal institutions of the Renaissance, destined to satisfy the exigencies of a rapid and intense traffic among peoples of different customs and civilizations. Another factor contributing to the revived fortune of Roman law during the Renaissance is the peculiar tendency of the law of this period to base the validity and authority of new principles on pre-existing rules. New rules adequate to the needs of the time were not introduced through the enactment of new laws but by way of reference to Roman texts, which were more or less arbitrarily construed in order to deduce from them principles adequate to new exigencies, which in reality were new laws.

The center of the study of the Roman law was Bologna, whence the teaching of law spread to the rest of Italy, to France, and subsequently to most of Europe. At Bologna arose the school of glossators (1100–1250), so-called because the study of jurisprudence came to be perfected chiefly by means of marginal notes, *glossae*, on the Roman texts. According to tradition the founder of this school was the half-legendary Irnerius (d. 1130?) who was followed by the "four doctors": "Bulgarus, *os aureum;* Martinus, *copia legum;* Hugo, *mens legum;* Jacobus, *id quod ego.*" Azo and Accursius were also famous. Even greater were the post-glossators; the most prominent among them were Cino da Pistoia (1270–1336), Bartolus of Sassoferrato (1313–1357), and his disciple Baldus degli Ubaldi (1327–1400). These scholars developed a systematic study of Roman law, succeeded in elaborating new principles and general doctrines and favored developing from the old Roman trunk new legal institutions.[5] These Italian jurisconsults were not only men of science. They took part in the management of public affairs, administered justice, were consulted as lawyers—lived, in short, the life of their times and were therefore inclined to understand and satisfy its needs. To the experience which they had gained in practice, these men united a sense of equity and legal precision proper to Roman law, in which they were educated and whose spirit they had imbibed.[6]

POLITICAL DEVELOPMENT OF THE ITALIAN STATES DURING THE RENAISSANCE

At the beginning of the Renaissance Italian political life was dominated by the conflict between the pope and the emperor. As heirs of the spiritual and the temporal traditions of Rome, respectively, they struggled for supremacy over Italy in an epoch in which the dominion of Italy meant the dominion of the world. Neither, however, succeeded in this ambitious design: the pope, to use the incisive phrase of Machiavelli, although too weak to effect the unification of Italy, was strong enough to prevent others from accomplishing it; [7] the emperor was opposed by the Italians, inasmuch as he represented the interests of the hated Germans. At the beginning of the Renaissance Emperor Frederick Barbarossa, defeated at Legnano, 1176, by the League of Lombard Communes, was forced to renounce, by the Peace of Constance, 1183, several rights over the Italian cities. Taking advantage of the conflict between the pope and the emperor and leaning now toward the one and now toward the other, the Italian communes succeeded in snatching greater concessions and privileges and in reducing to a not much more than nominal allegiance their dependence on the pope and the emperor, establishing themselves as free and autonomous. As a result, the Renaissance is called the period of autonomies. While they were emancipating themselves from the pope and the emperor, the Italian cities struggled among themselves

---

[5] The fundamental work on the history of Roman law in the Middle Ages is still Savigny, *Geschichte des römischen Rechtes im Mittelalter,* 2d ed. For a general outline of the revival of legal science in Italy in the Middle Ages, in the works of doctrine, see Engelmann, *Die Wiedergeburt der Rechtskultur in Italien durch die wissenschaftliche Lehre.*
[6] See Lainé, *Introduction au droit international privé,* I, 99, and Anzilotti, *Corso di diritto internazionale,* p. 35.
[7] See *Discorsi sulla Prima Deca di Tito Livio,* Book 1, ch. 12.

for supremacy. The larger communes such as Florence in Tuscany, Milan in Lombardy, Venice in Venetia, ended by absorbing the smaller. But the interminable struggles exhausted the people of the Italian cities, who surrendered their political liberty and trusted the government to one ruling family or to aristocratic oligarchies on condition that peace and order might be assured. Thus there arose in Italian cities the *Signorie* (lordships), such as that of the Medici at Florence, the Sforza at Milan, and others who, having succeeded in their more immediate objectives, endeavored toward the end of the Renaissance to build up large political organizations of an absolute character, namely, independent and hereditary principalities. At the same time the great Italian duchies of Venice and Genoa were set up, and in southern Italy the Kingdom of Naples. The struggle between the communes for hegemony in a single region were followed by the struggles between the *Signorie* and between the principalities and duchies for hegemony in the Italian peninsula. As soon as it became reasonably apparent that one of the contenders was well on the way toward supremacy, the other powers immediately coalesced against him in order to defend their independence. The principle of balance of power thus became the fundamental political canon of the Italian states during the Renaissance. Guicciardini says in his *History of Italy* that Lorenzo de' Medici, who was the foremost supporter of this principle, together with the Florentines, considered it necessary to oppose the aggrandizement of the principal powers of Italy and to maintain an exact equilibrium of forces as much for the safety of the Florentine republic as for the guarantee of his own authority.

Strange as it may seem, the disorganization and political division of the peninsula did not immediately exercise an unfavorable influence on Italian life in the Renaissance. In the first place, political disunity was not exclusively an Italian phenomenon. In this period no European state had yet attained unity. France, Spain, and England, not to mention Germany, were deep in the struggle for political unification, thrown into disorder by external wars and domestic quarrels, both religious and social. In the second place, it was this very lack of central power that made possible the fecund development of so many small Italian cities in that period. At the beginning of the Renaissance every Italian town was a little state, desirous of participating in international life on the basis of its own commerce and industry. A fruitful competition between town and town grew up, stimulating the energies of citizens and favoring individual initiative, not only in the mercantile but also in cultural and artistic fields. This explains why there was in no part of Italy a province closed to the great currents of international life and why all the Italian centers, no matter how small, were then able to effect so notable a creative effort in the fields of economic, artistic, and intellectual endeavor.

Other important reasons for the intensity of international relations were the small size of Italian states, which often consisted, especially at the beginning of the Renaissance, of single cities, and the frequent migrations of persons from one state to another. Not only economic and commercial relations but often even those of a personal and familial character could not easily be exhausted within the ambit of a single state, but, instead, generally assumed an international aspect.

From what precedes it appears that the greatness of Italy during the Renaissance was above all due to the development of its international relations.[8] This intense international life favored the precocious development in Italy of institutions of international law. It also gave to Italian states the direct sensation of belonging to an international community and explains why there arose earlier in Italy than in any other country a practical as well as theoretical interest in problems of international law. In undertaking a detailed examination of the Italian contribution to international law during the Renaissance it is convenient for reasons of method to examine doctrine independently of practice. Precedence will be accorded to the practice of international law for the reason that it assumed greater importance than the theory during this period. However, the contribution made by Italy to the development of the doctrines of international law during the Renaissance was far from negligible.

[8] On the reasons why international relations and the theory of balance of power originated in Italy earlier than in any other part of Europe see some interesting observations in Butler and Maccoby, *The Development of International Law*, p. 35.

Chapter II: PEACEFUL INTERCOURSE OF THE ITALIAN STATES

IN ORDER to point out the essential characteristics of the peaceful intercourse of the Italian states during the Renaissance the following analysis is divided into three sections: (*a*) intercourse on the European continent; (*b*) intercourse with the countries overseas; (*c*) maritime intercourse.

INTERCOURSE ON THE EUROPEAN CONTINENT

By the Peace of Constance, of 1183, Emperor Frederick Barbarossa was compelled to relinquish in favor of the cities of northern Italy a number of imperial prerogatives. Yet he still maintained some imperial power over them. For centuries the Peace of Constance continued to be the formal law regulating the relations between the empire and the Italian cities. Actually, however, there soon broke out a bitter struggle between the emperor, who endeavored to regain his former privileges, and the communes, who sought for the extension of their autonomy. After alternate successes and defeats and after often passing through phases of tragedy, the struggle ended with the victory of the communes. Toward the end of the thirteenth century—that is, more than two centuries earlier than the Reformation, which according to some writers marked the rise of independent states in Europe—the Italian city-states had already gained the most complete autonomy. The city-state, the free commune vested with the effective power and almost all the formal attributes of the modern state had become at the beginning of the fourteenth century the basis of the Italian political and legal organization.[1] The communes appointed their own *podestà* (mayors), enacted laws and took care of their enforcement, administered justice, levied tributes, and coined money. The communes were also autonomous in the matter of foreign relations. They exercised the diplomatic protection of their subjects abroad, concluded treaties, sent diplomatic missions, had their own armies, fought wars, and concluded peace. "It is not a question whether some of their rights were legally exercised and others were usurped from the emperor. The fact is that they came continually and actually to be exercised." [2] Both in their mutual relations and in their relations with foreign states and with the emperor, Italian states of the Renaissance

---

[1] See Ercole, *Dal comune al principato*, p. 209. [2] See *ibid.*, p. 240.

acted as autonomous entities not subject to any superior power; in other words, they acted as subjects of international law.

At the same time, the Italian city-state clearly established its own powers over dependent persons and territory. As to power over persons, citizenship became especially relevant. Generally only citizens of a state were entitled to its diplomatic protection. The benefits obtained through treaties concerned only the citizens of the contracting parties. In many Italian states conflicts of laws regarding the status and capacity of persons and the distribution of personal property were governed by the national law of the persons concerned. Various incapacities applied to foreigners.[3] Consequently, in almost all Italian states precise and minute rules from the beginning established the distinction between a citizen and a foreigner, the means of acquiring and the causes for losing citizenship.[4]

As for power over territory, the very geographic configuration of Italy, by which natural boundaries could be easily traced, and the small size of the Italian states both enabled exact determination of the frontiers between the different states. The situation then differed from that of almost all other parts of Europe, where at that time the frontiers were badly defined, uncertain, and generally fluctuating.[5] Numerous treaties and arbitrations established frontiers between bordering states, settled boundary disputes, and regulated transfers of territory. Sometimes mixed commissions were appointed to ascertain boundaries. One such commission was set up in 1201 between Novara and Vercelli. In a number of towns there were magistrates charged with maintaining the boundaries.[6] It was agreed that the territory of a state included its territorial waters as well, but the extent of territorial waters was a somewhat controversial question. Foreign influence within the territory of a state was normally not tolerated. There ensued the early development of and in general the rigorous observance of the right of asylum for political refugees.[7]

---

[3] On the legal status of foreigners in the Italian states during that period see Morpurgo, "Sulla condizione giuridica dei forestieri in Italia nei secoli di mezzo," 8–9 Archivio giuridico 248–89, 255–88.

[4] On the means of acquiring citizenship in the Italian city-states, on the legal effects of such acquisition, and on the legal problems arising from double citizenship see Bonolis, "La concessione di cittadinanza e i suoi effetti," in *Questioni di diritto internazionale in alcuni consigli inediti di Baldo degli Ubaldi*, pp. 7–63. The laws of the Italian states classified foreigners in various categories, to which different rights were recognized; the same applied also to citizens. In attributing citizenship the Italian states often followed the principle of *jus sanguinis*, by which in principle he is a citizen who is a son of a citizen, wherever born. See Catellani, *Il diritto internazionale privato e i suoi recenti progressi*, I, 282; Saredo, *Saggio sulla storia del diritto internazionale privato*, p. 80.

[5] On the indefiniteness of the frontiers in almost all Europe at this time see P. de Lapradelle, *La Frontière*, pp. 13–14, 19–20, 24–26; and Vollenhoven, *The Law of Peace*, p. 39.

[6] In the statutes of Bologna, 1245–1267, the provision was enacted that the mayor with the *procuratori del comune* had to visit at least once a year the boundaries between Bologna and Modena and suggest the necessary repairs.

[7] When in 1500 Venice was forced by the political pressure of France to surrender Cardinal

The intense international activity of the Italian states during the Renaissance resulted in the conclusion of numerous treaties among themselves and also with the cities of southern France and Dalmatia, which were bound to Italy by close economic and cultural ties.[8] Some of these treaties had a political character, being treaties of alliance, peace, and truce. But contrary to current opinion most of them were concluded for the purpose of promoting economic and commercial intercourse and to protect citizens abroad. From the end of the twelfth century there were frequent treaties dealing with commercial matters in which each contracting party granted to the citizens and to the merchandise of the other contracting party commercial facilities and privileges, tariff concessions, and the right of free passage. The heavier the traffic of a state, the greater was the number of treaties it concluded on these matters. For instance, Florence, then one of the principal Italian economic centers, concluded in a short period of time the following treaties: with Lucca, in 1184, a promise not to institute or increase reciprocal duties except in the amount agreed upon by the contracting parties; with Faenza, in 1204, reduction of duties in favor of Florence; with Bologna, in 1220, reduction of duties; with Siena, in 1176 and in 1245, agreements to fix duties through arbitration and tariff exemption of merchandise in transit.[9] The treaty of 1193 between Bologna and Ferrara is one of the first examples of stabilizing tariff duties by treaty. In order to settle any doubts which may have arisen as to the kinds of merchandise covered by these duties, a mixed commission of representatives of the two cities was set up in Ferrara in 1194.

Numerous treaties were concluded to assure the liberty and safety of communications, which were indispensable for the regular flow of commerce. In 1156 Bologna and Modena entered under solemn oath into a reciprocal agreement to provide for the safety of communications between both cities. Similar treaties were concluded by great leagues of cities, for example, by the Lombard League, in 1174, with Bologna, Modena, Reggio, Parma, and Mantua, and in 1191 by the League of Pavia, Como, Lodi, and Bergamo with the Marquis of Monferrato.[10] Treaties were concluded to assure the protection of merchants and goods in transit, such as the treaty between Pavia and Vercelli of December 20, 1165, and for the erection of warehouses and inns to be endowed

---

Ascanio Sforza, who had sought political refuge from Milan in the territory of the Venetian Republic, the fact created a sensation in Italy because of its novelty.

[8] On treaties of peace and alliance between Italian towns the study of Muratori, "De Civitatum italicarum foederibus ac pacibus, dissertatio quadragesima," in *Antiquitates italicae medii aevi*, IV, 337 ff., is still useful.

[9] See Rapisardi Mirabelli, *Storia dei trattati*, p. 128; Arias, *I trattati commerciali della repubblica fiorentina*.

[10] For more detailed information see Schaube, *Handelsgeschichte der lateinischen Völker*.

with special prerogatives. One of the first examples of treaties for freedom of river navigation is the *Pactum Ferrariae de tenenda aqua Padi
omnibus aperta*, June 8, 1171, relative to the Po River, by which Ferrara
promised Venice, Bologna, Mantua, Milan, Modena, and Ravenna to
"aperire aquam Padi libere omnibus hominibus et apertam omnibus
hominibus eam tenere nec ullo tempore eam claudere et hoc observare
bona fide et sine fraude ulla." [11] Numerous treaties for the safety of
land and river traffic were entered into by Venice: with Verona, September 21, 1192, guaranteeing safety of transit on the Adige and compensation for the damage that Venetians might suffer on this route; with
Mantua, July 12, 1257, offering a similar guarantee for traffic on the Po;
with Milan, December 10, 1268, promising to keep the roads in its territory open and safe.

The minute division of territory, the intense traveling, the frequent
migrations, and the intermingling of territories often gave rise to problems of private international law and international penal law. For their
solution numerous agreements were concluded. A number of treaties
of extradition, negotiated at the beginning of the Renaissance, contained
provisions very similar to those of modern treaties on the same matter.
Between 1191 and 1227 Venice concluded treaties of extradition with
Ferrara, Verona, Treviso, Padua, Cervia, and Bologna. A 1218 extradition treaty between Venice and Genoa was renewed in 1308. A treaty
of extradition was entered into in 1293 by Ferrara and Mantua.[12] These
treaties differed from contemporary treaties in that extradition of debtors
was occasionally stipulated; for example, in the extradition treaty between Venice and Verona, 1306. The reason is that under certain conditions insolvency was considered a crime in many Italian states. Sometimes extradition treaties were also concluded with states beyond the
Alps. One such treaty, dating from 1376, between Charles V of France
and Amadeus of Savoy, has been preserved.[13] Jurisdictional questions
and conflict of law concerning penal matters were also often settled by
means of treaties. Treaties concluded September 5, 1143, by Genoa and
Pisa with the Count of Toulouse and Saint Gilles laid down the rule
that crimes such as theft or adultery and crimes against the person were
to be punished at the place where the crime occurred and in accordance

---

[11] The text of the treaty has been published by F. Rey, 11 Rev. gén. dr. int. publ. (1904)
192–199.

[12] See Neumeyer, *Die gemeinrechtliche Entwicklung*, II, 54. See also Kohler, "Beiträge zum
internationalen Strafrecht," 4 Zeitschrift für internationales Recht (1894) 225–238, and 5,
(1895) 232–249. It seems that, in the absence of international conventions on the matter,
extradition was not permitted between Italian states. See Bartolus, in Lege D. 47, 12, 9 (lege
sepulchri violati) n. 3; "Consuetudinem Italiae secundum quam remissio non fit." Cf. also
Bartolus in Lege D. 1, 18, 3 (lege praeses provinciae).

[13] See text in Kohler, *Internationales Strafrecht*, p. 150.

with the laws there in force at the time.[14] Several treaties regulated the recognition of foreign judgments in civil and penal matters and of decrees in bankruptcy.[15] Numerous treaties were concluded for the protection of the rights of citizens abroad. These treaties assured to these citizens the enjoyment of civil rights, the free exercise of trade, the right of applying to the local courts and the exemption from the law of escheat.[16] Special proceedings were agreed upon in order to expedite the distribution of decedent estates and the collection of debts of citizens abroad.[17]

The rules established by treaty constituted only one of the classes of international rules binding the Italian cities. Aside from the written rules there also existed a considerable number of unwritten rules, which were nevertheless equally binding. Those rules concerned especially the duty of granting a minimum standard of treatment to foreigners and the obligation of recognizing the validity, within certain limits, of foreign laws, judgments, contracts, and wills. These rules, which were in substance based on the principles of Roman law adapted to new times, originally constituted the common law of Italy or, more exactly, the common law of the Italian portion of the Holy Roman Empire. Therefore this law was not, in its inception, international law: that is, a law in force among independent entities, but municipal law of the empire, which Italian cities had to apply, inasmuch as they were subordinate to it. With the waning of Imperial authority, the validity of this law common to Italian cities did not come to an end. The foundation of its authority however was based no longer upon the superiority of the empire, but upon the free consent of Italian towns, which tacitly agreed among themselves that their relations should continue to be based upon this law. "When the Emperor was no longer recognized as superior, his place was taken by the law." [18] Moreover it came to be agreed that this law was to be in force not only in the relations between Italian cities which had been part of the empire but also in their relations with countries and peoples

[14] For various other examples see Neumeyer, *Die gemeinrechtliche Entwicklung*, II, 54; Meili, *Die hauptsachlichsten Entwicklungsperioden des internationalen Strafrechts*; Cybichowski, "La compétence des tribunaux à raison d'infractions commises hors du territoire," 12 Rec. des cours (1926) 272.

[15] See Meili, *Die geschichtliche Entwicklung des internationalen Konkursrechts*.

[16] On the law of escheat in Italy see Saredo, *Saggio sulla storia del diritto internazionale privato*, p. 137, and Fusinato, "Albinaggio," in *Digesto italiano*, VII, 630 ff.

[17] According to Rapisardi Mirabelli, *Storia dei trattati*, p. 129, one of the oldest Italian treaties establishing a special procedure to be followed in case of litigations between citizens of the contracting parties is that concluded between Venice and Ferrara, October 26, 1191. Two years later a treaty having the same purpose was concluded between Venice and Verona. A treaty between Florence and Siena, of 1245, minutely regulated the procedure to be followed in case of controversies over debts between Florentines and Siennese and established which magistrates were to have jurisdiction on these matters in the two states.

[18] See Woolf, *Bartolus of Sassoferrato*, pp. 198 ff. See also Elbe, "Evolution of the Concept of the Just War in International Law," 33 Am. Int. L. (1939) 670 ff., and Nys, *Le droit international*, I, 229 ff.

who, like the Greeks, had been detached from the ancient Roman Empire for centuries or, like the Tartars, had never been a part of it. Thus, although the contents of these rules of law, which were based on natural equity, remained unchanged in principle, the basis of their validity and their ambit of application came to be changed. In fact, they assumed the character of a law superior to the states and so came to be raised to the rank of true international law. Later they also came to be distinguished from the rules of municipal law existing within the different states by their contents, which tended to refer more clearly to relations among states. The international character of these rules and their binding force upon the states were early recognized by the Italian cities. It was generally agreed among these cities that there existed a law superior to them which prescribed the granting of some rights to foreigners and the recognition of the validity of foreign laws, acts, and judgments which did not contravene public policy. When the judge of an Italian city decided that the form of a will executed abroad was governed by the law of the place where the will had been executed, or when a *podestà* prescribed that a foreigner could not be deprived of his property or liberty without just motive, they so acted on the basis of provisions of municipal laws in force in their own cities. But it was the common opinion of the rulers, the legislators, and the judges of Italian cities that a higher law existed, superior to the municipal rules they enacted and applied, which imposed on the different states the duty of enacting laws such as to grant a given treatment to foreign citizens and foreign acts. The fact that when the empire fell part of the common law—that relative to the treatment of foreign persons and foreign acts—became international law has been until now frequently overlooked. Apparently this is due to the circumstance that a great part of the rules of international law which were so created disappeared in the following centuries.

The intensity of international relations of Italian states is the reason for the Italian origin of permanent legations.[19] During the Middle Ages frequent recourse was had to the dispatch of diplomatic missions to foreign countries. Consequently there were formed a number of rules relative to the treatment of foreign missions, which were precise enough and generally observed. Missions, however, were generally of a contingent character and were sent only for the fulfillment of a given transaction or group of transactions, since the relations between the peoples

---

[19] On the origin of permanent legations see Nys, "Les Commencements de la diplomatie et le droit d'ambassade jusqu'à Grotius," 15 Rev. dr. int. et lég. comp. (1883) 577 ff.; Krauske, "Die Entwicklung der ständigen Diplomatie vom fünfzehnten Jahrhundert bis zu den Beschlüssen von 1815," 5 Staats-und Sozialwissenschaftliche Forschungen (1885) No. 3; Schaube, "Zur Entstehungsgeschichte der ständigen Gesandtschaften," 10 *Mitteilungen der Institutes für oesterreichische Geschichtsforschung;* Mowat, *A History of European Diplomacy.* On Italian diplomacy of the Renaissance see Reumont, *Della diplomazia italiana dal secolo XIII°.*

were still occasional and somewhat intermittent. A notable contribution to the establishment of permanent legations at the end of the Middle Ages was given by the popes by dispatching legates to represent them permanently at the various national courts (*legati a latere*). The functions fulfilled by these legates were largely religious, but of necessity also political.[20] Venice, governed by an aristocracy which was particularly methodical and farseeing and which controlled vast commercial interests in several relatively distant countries, was perhaps the first modern state to make considerable effort toward the creation of an ordered diplomatic service and a system of permanent legations. The first permanent legations of Venice date as far back as the thirteenth century.[21] In the fourteenth century Venice had permanent ambassadors resident at the Papal court and in the most important Italian states. Venice also had regular diplomatic relations with the dukes of Burgundy. In 1478 a Morosini was Venetian ambassador to Maximilian of Austria. After 1479 a permanent ambassador was accredited to Paris. In 1497 a permanent Venetian ambassador was sent to the court of England. During the sixteenth century Venice had ambassadors at Vienna, Madrid, Paris, and Rome; residents at Naples, Turin, Milan, London, and the Swiss cantons; and an administrator (*baglivo*) at Constantinople, who was charged with the affairs of the Orient and upon whom the Venetian consuls in the East were dependent.[22] Venetian ambassadors were sent to Egypt and Persia. Likewise, Philippe of Commines (d. 1511), visiting Venice in 1494, found there representatives of all countries. The other Italian states quickly followed the example of Venice. The duke of Savoy in 1460 accredited an envoy to the Papal court, with instructions to remain there permanently and deal with spiritual as well as temporal matters. Under Cosimo de' Medici, Florence had a permanent ambassador at Milan. The duke of Milan, Francesco Sforza, had a permanent envoy stationed at the Republic of Genoa in 1455. Ferdinand of Naples was similarly represented in the larger states of Italy, in France, in Spain, in Hungary, in Tunis, and in Algiers.

Thus a certain number of practices relative to diplomatic procedure grew up which were largely of Italian origin. Some of the practices concerned matters of courtesy and etiquette, while others developed into actual rules of international law. Some of these rules concerned the manner of the accrediting and the legal position of diplomatic agents. The

---

[20] On the origin of permanent nuncios see Pieper, *Zur Entstehungsgeschichte der ständigen Nuntiaturen;* Nys, "Le droit international et la papauté," 10 Rev. dr. int. et lég. comp. (1878) 501–538; Nys, "La Papauté et le droit international," 37 Rev. dr. int. et lég. comp. (1905) 150–180.

[21] See Anzilotti, *Corso di diritto internazionale,* 3d ed., p. 239.

[22] See Cappello, "Les Consulats et les bailages de la République de Venise," 29 Rev. dr. int. et lég. comp. (1897) 152–187.

inviolability of ambassadors came generally to be recognized in Italy;[28] and thus trespassing on ambassadorial residence and molesting their personal possessions was forbidden.[24] On the other hand, any abuse of hospitality on the part of ambassadors was severely repressed. When in 1540 three Venetians who were enlisted as spies by the French ambassador at Venice took refuge in the legation to escape arrest, the Venetian authorities did not hesitate, in face of the ambassador's refusal to hand over the culprits, to place two cannons before the door of the embassy until they surrendered. The incident was finally closed to the satisfaction of Venice. For a long time it was customary in Italy to transport, lodge, and provide for ambassadors during their mission at the expense of the state to which they were accredited. Such treatment was accorded in 1288 at Naples by King Charles of Anjou to the ambassadors of the King of France; and in 1475 at Milan by Galeazzo Maria Sforza to the Venetian ambassadors. In the sixteenth century, the use of permanent legations having become more common, this system grew to be too costly and was superseded by the practice of offering presents to ambassadors on the occasion of their arrival and departure. At this time the first attempts were made to confer a rank upon ambassadors according to the importance of the countries they represented and the functions to be fulfilled. Frequent questions of precedence arose among Italian states, as a result of the punctilio of interested parties or as a manifestation of more profound reasons of conflict. They degenerated at times into political controversies of real gravity.

Precise rules regulated the duties and functions of the ambassadors in various Italian states. Venice had the most progressive legislation on the subject. As far back as 1263 a decree of the *Maggior Consiglio* (Greater Council) prohibited Venetian envoys at the Papal court from procuring a benefice for anyone, whoever he might be, without the order of the doge and of the *Minor Consiglio* (Lesser Council). In 1268 it was made mandatory for ambassadors to turn into the treasury the gifts which it was customary for them to receive. At about the same time provision was made for the ambassadors to submit a written report to

---

[28] After the Reformation the right of Protestant ambassadors to exercise the functions of their religion in the legation was recognized in Italy. At Venice in 1607, the papal nuncio having complained that there were held in the house of the English ambassador Protestant services which Venetian citizens attended, the doge replied that it would not be suitable to interfere with the affairs of the ministers of princes, since this would constitute a violation of *jus gentium*. On the practice of Venice in the matter of diplomatic immunities see Adair, *The Extraterritoriality of Ambassadors in the Sixteenth and Seventeenth Centuries*.

[24] However, as recalled by Walker, *A History of the Law of Nations*, p. 176: "Sforza, Duke of Milan, in 1533 tried and beheaded Merveille, the French envoy at his court, after decoying him into a duel in which the Frenchman killed his antagonist. The justification offered on behalf of the Duke, which was grounded upon the fact that Merveille was only a secret agent, was by subsequent generations deemed insufficient."

their superiors upon their return. It is to this provision that we owe those monuments of political wisdom which constitute the reports of the Venetian ambassadors.[25] Also in the thirteenth century there began to be issued a series of Venetian decrees which set the maximum duration of time for a diplomatic mission. At first a period of four months seemed quite a long time for any diplomatic mission. In the fifteenth century the rule was established that an ambassador should not remain in office at the same court for more than two years. Toward the end of the century this term was extended to three years. Other rules fixed the manner of appointing ambassadors and their salary.[26]

In the Italian states of the Renaissance the exercise of diplomacy rose to the dignity of an art. Consummate politicians, artists, and learned men were appointed for a diplomatic career. The reports of the Venetian ambassadors show the perspicacity, the ability, and the political sense of the Venetian republic's envoys. In the thirteenth and fourteenth centuries Florence counted among its envoys Brunetto Latini, Dante, Petrarca, and Boccaccio; later, Capponi, Guicciardini, and Machiavelli. The legations, however, proved to be more of a burden than an honor. Citizens engaged in lucrative business tried to avoid being nominated to diplomatic missions. Hence in many states a few conditions whereby it was permissible to refuse the nomination were expressly established. In the correspondence of Venetian and Florentine ambassadors there are to be found frequent complaints concerning the limited stipend which, according to the writers, did not permit them to meet the heavy expenses of their mission.

INTERCOURSE WITH COUNTRIES OVERSEAS

The Italian penetration in the north of Europe at the beginning of the Renaissance was chiefly carried on through the endeavor of single individuals and was exclusively limited to the business field. Italian emigrants to the north of Europe were for the most part merchants, bankers, and artisans who established themselves in foreign countries, where they set up industries, trading firms, and banks. Italian merchants regularly attended the fairs of Champagne, London, and Flanders. In this general movement no territorial ambitions were at stake.

On the contrary, the economic penetration of the Italians toward Asia, Africa, the Balkans, and the Mediterranean isles was organized almost exclusively on a corporative basis and was sustained by a more direct intervention of the Italian states, finally culminating in a series of territorial acquisitions. During their period of greater expansion the Italian

---

[25] For a collection of them see Alberi, ed., *Relazioni degli ambasciatori veneti al senato.*
[26] For a collection of Florentine regulations of the fifteenth century concerning the diplomatic service see Maulde de la Clavière, *La diplomatie au temps de Machiavel*, III, 411–436.

maritime cities endeavored to obtain a monopoly of trade with the Levant, promoted colonizing enterprises, and penetrated into the Orient by means of expeditions and caravans as far as the heart of Asia and Africa. Marco Polo, a Venetian, traveled as far as China, while the Genoese crossed the Sahara and the Sudan and in 1336 established a settlement in northern China. In order to protect their commercial interests the Italian cities had recourse, when necessary, to military enterprises.

From the beginning of the twelfth century a tight net of treaties bound the Italian maritime cities with the potentates of the Balkans, the Black Sea, the Sea of Azov, and the Asiatic and African shores of the Mediterranean.[27]

Very little is known of the treaties negotiated by Amalfi. More precise information is available covering the treaties concluded by Pisa. The trade of the latter city was developed in large part with the central and western Mediterranean areas. Especially developed was the commerce with Egypt to which Pisa was bound by a commercial treaty of 1154. In 1173 a treaty was concluded between the Sultan Saladin and Pisa. In 1175 Pisa concluded a treaty with the sultan of Babylon (Cairo). When Pisa was absorbed by Florence, new treaties were concluded between the latter and Egypt—among others that of the year 1423. There still remains the text of the Pisan treaties of 1230, 1264, and 1397 with Tunis. In 1133 Pisa concluded a treaty with Morocco. Also Pisa's commercial relations with Byzantium were very active, giving rise to a treaty of 1124 with the Emperor Alexius Comnenus. Pisan trade pushed on to the Black Sea. Having, however, been defeated in 1284 by the Genoese in the naval battle of Meloria, Pisa was forced to renounce its own trade in the Black Sea in favor of the victors.

Especially important was the expansion of Venice and Genoa. Commercial relations between Venice and Byzantium date from the very origin of Venice. At the end of the eleventh century Emperor Alexius Comnenus exempted Venetian trade from every duty and impost in Romania, the name then given to the European territory of the Byzantine Empire, and also exempted Venetians from local jurisdiction. A new treaty was concluded by Venice with Emperor Emmanuel Comnenus in 1174. The apogee of Venetian power in its relations with the Byzantine Empire was reached during the period of the fourth Crusade. The success of this enterprise was due in large measure to the Venetians, who furnished the bulk of the fleet. In 1204 the Crusaders stormed Constantinople and placed on the Byzantine throne a Latin dynasty. To Venice was as-

[27] On treaties between the Italian maritime cities and the countries of the East see Schaube, *Handelsgeschichte der lateinischen Völker des Mittelmeergebiets bis zum Ende der Kreuzzüge*; Depping, *Histoire du commerce entre le Levant et l'Europe*; Mas Latrie, *Traités de paix et de commerce et documents divers concernant les rélations des Chrétiens avec les Arabes*; Miltitz, *Manuel des consuls*; Heyd, *Histoire du commerce du Levant au moyen âge*.

signed a portion of land equal to three-eighths of the Byzantine Empire; as a consequence of this territorial acquisition the Doge of Venice assumed the title of Lord of a quarter and a half of the Empire. However, Venice did not get actual and direct possession of all the land assigned her. She occupied Durazzo in Albania, various ports and islands of the Aegean Sea and three-eighths of the city of Constantinople. In Constantinople Venice established the bailiff (*bali*), who was a kind of doge, assisted in the government, like the Doge of Venice, by a Lesser Council and a Greater Council, with judges for civil and criminal cases, chamberlains in charge of the finances, and officers to settle disputes with the fisc. The Patriarch at the head of the episcopal hierarchy of the Latins was likewise a Venetian. Part of the territories granted to Venice was ·assigned by her to Venetian patricians, who held it as dependents of the Venetian government. Latin sovereigns, moreover, granted special privileges to Venetians in other parts of the empire. Such privileges were, however, placed in grave jeopardy in 1261, when the Latin dynasty was dethroned and replaced by the Greek dynasty of the Paleologi. The success of the latter was due to the aid from the Genoese to whom exceptional favors were granted as recompense. Nevertheless, Venetian commerce throughout the Empire was important enough to induce the new sovereign Michael Palaeologus to restore to the Venetians in 1265 the greater part of their old privileges. These were renewed by their successors until the fall of the Eastern Empire in 1453. When the Turks took Constantinople, the Venetians were persecuted for having helped the Byzantines. The Venetian bailiff was put to death and five hundred Venetians were made prisoners. However, in the following year the treaty of Adrianople was concluded between Venice and Mahomet II. As a result of this treaty a new capitulation was granted to the Venetians, which, among other things, recognized the jurisdiction of the Venetian bailiff over Venetians in the countries ruled by the Sultan.[28] However, the Moslem invasion marked the beginning of Venetian decadence in the eastern Mediterranean. The new treaty of 1479 with the Turks was less favorable to the Venetians than the preceding one. In a subsequent treaty of 1539 Venice had to make certain territorial cessions and was forced to meet conditions highly prejudicial to her trade.

Venice concluded treaties with the Christian princes of Syria and Palestine in the years 1111, 1123, and 1139, with Beirut in 1221, and after the fall of the Latin princes, with the Moslem sovereigns of Syria in 1229, of Aleppo in 1229, and with the Emir of Jaffa. Venetians enjoyed free-trade privileges in the port of Jaffa, which was the center of debarkation for pilgrims to the Holy Land. Venice acquired special privileges by

[28] An English translation of the capitulation is published in Ravndal, *The Origin of the Capitulations and of the Consular Jurisdiction*, p. 92.

her treaties of 1306, 1328, and 1360 with the island of Cyprus, which ultimately fell under Venetian sovereignty in 1489 through cession by the last queen of the island, Catherine Cornaro. Treaties were also concluded by Venice with Trebizonde in 1303, with Little Armenia, which was governed by Latin princes, in the years 1201, 1245, 1307, 1321, and 1333, with the Tartars of Tauris in the fourteenth century and the Tartars of Tana on the Sea of Azov, 1333, 1347, and 1358, with the lord of Soldaia on the Black Sea, 1383; and with the Emperor of Zagora in Bulgaria, 1352. Venice concluded a series of treaties with Egypt, among which was the treaty of capitulation of 1238, renewed several times—in 1303, 1355, 1361, and 1388. The decadence of the influence of Venice over Egypt is revealed by the provisions of subsequent treaties which came to be progressively less advantageous for Venice. For example, the provisions of the treaty of 1512, compared with those of preceding treaties, were plainly humiliating for Venice. With Tunis, where Venetian commerce was particularly flourishing, Venice concluded treaties in 1251, 1271, 1305, 1317, and 1320. The last treaty guaranteed safety to Venetian caravans directed to the interior. In 1356 there was a Venetian treaty with Tripoli.

Genoa, the principal competitor of Venice in Mediterranean trade, also concluded various treaties with the Byzantine Emperors: with Johannes Comnenus in 1142, with Emmanuel Comnenus in 1155, and with Isaac Angelus in 1188 and 1192. In 1261 the Greek dynasty of the Palaeologi, having gained the throne with the help of the Genoese, rewarded the latter by conferring upon them a privileged position within the Empire. By treaty of 1261 Michael Paleologus, the first of the Greek Emperors, accorded to the Genoese a monopoly of trade in the Black Sea. Furthermore the whole quarter of Pera (or Galatea) in the City of Constantinople passed under the exclusive possession and control of the Genoese, who surrounded this area with a high wall and were able to maintain their dominion until the Moslem conquest, which marked the decline of Genoese power. Genoa also concluded several treaties with the Christian princes of Syria, with the Kingdom of Cyprus, 1218, 1232, 1233, and 1291, and with Candia (Crete), where, however, through the opposition of Venice, the Genoese succeeded in acquiring a consulate only. By means of the treaty of 1312 the Genoese obtained legal privileges at Trebizonde, which were increased toward the end of the century, and, by treaties of 1201, 1215, and 1288 in Armenia. Genoa concluded other treaties: with Bulgaria, 1387; with Egypt, 1290; with Tripoli, 1216; with Tunis, 1250, 1272, 1433; Bithynia, 1387; with Ceuta and Morocco. From the Christian kings of Spain the Genoese also won concessions, which, however, proved less important than those obtained in Asia and Africa. In the first half of the twelfth century Genoa received the town of Almeria, in Spain, which was given in fief to a Genoese family, and also came into possession of a third of the town of Tortosa, which was subsequently sold to the count of Barcelona. Later Catalan power arose in that part of the Mediterranean to rival the Genoese.

By agreements concluded with the Tartar princes the Genoese enjoyed a position of absolute priority in the Black Sea. A convention with the Khan of Crimea, in 1380, granted the greatest privileges to the city of Caffa, founded by Genoese in the Crimea in the thirteenth century. This city became the principal market and entrepôt of the Black Sea and the center of the most flourishing Genoese trade in that area. At Caffa resided the *Uffizio di Gazaria,* the office upon which depended the Genoese possessions in the Black Sea along the Crimean coast. These possessions comprised not only settlements but also vast neighboring lands which were veritable colonies. A special Genoese code, known as the *Statutes of Gazaria,* governed the Genoese colonies of the East. The fame of Genoese justice in this region was so renowned that the Tartars preferred to submit to the Genoese courts legal controversies among themselves. Thus a special magistracy was created at Caffa, the *"Ufficio della Campagna,"* for decision of disputes among Tartars. With the conquest of Caffa by Mahomet in 1475 Genoese dominion in those regions ended. Other treaties with the countries of the East were negotiated by Ancona and various towns of Sicily.

Treaties concluded by Italian states with oriental sovereigns present a precise and complete picture of the special rules of international law governing the Italian expansion in the East from its beginning to its decadence. This decadence occurred toward the fifteenth century by a concatenation of factors among which the more important were the rising competition of France and Spain, the deflecting of trade from the Mediterranean, and the Moslem invasions.

Since the aims of all those treaties were in substance similar, their provisions also were usually alike. They especially provided for:

a) Concession of economic and commercial privileges.—To the Italian cities was conceded the right to trade on the territory of the other contracting party. This right was sometimes given in the form of a monopoly, at other times in the form of a special privilege with respect to other foreigners, and, more rarely, on a footing of equality with them. In addition exemptions and reductions of taxes on persons, imports, and exports were often granted.

b) Reciprocal prohibition of piracy and aid to pirates.—Contrary to general belief, such prohibitions were established not only to protect Italians against Saracen pirates, but also to a large extent to protect Saracens from Italian pirates. The practice of piracy on Saracen coasts was in fact largely carried out by Italian sailors.

c) Suppression of the right of shipwreck.

d) Establishment of individual responsibility.—In case illegal acts were committed by the citizens of an Italian state, only the guilty party could be held responsible. Innocent citizens of such states could not be held liable for these acts. Such a provision was enacted for the purpose of preventing the taking of reprisals. To assure the continuity of trade, some treaties, such as that between Pisa and Tunis of March 25, 1264, stipulated that the ships of the contracting parties might not be detained for any reason. The principle of individual responsibility was abandoned only in a very few treaties, such as that concluded between Tunis and Pisa in 1397, when the power of the latter was already in decline. Article 26 of this treaty prescribed that the consul or consuls of Pisa be held responsible for damages inflicted by any Pisan upon any person in the lands of the Sultan.[29]

e) Territorial concessions.—In almost all the states of the East there were populous colonies of Italian subjects and of persons enjoying the protection of Italian states. For reasons of commerce and defense, and also because of the difference of the religion, language, and customs of the rest of the population, these peoples tended to live together in the same quarter. By means of a series of treaties Italian states sought to obtain special territorial concessions in favor of their subjects. Among other things these concessions included the granting of a tract of land on which could be built a church, the *fondaco* (an office and warehouse), and generally a fountain, a bakery, and a bathhouse, providing for the needs of a trading community. At times these concessions covered entire quarters, such as those given to the Venetians and Genoese at Constantinople, and even whole cities, such as Caffa. At the beginning of the thirteenth century the Genoese obtained from Baldwin a third of the cities of Arsul, Caesarea, and St. John of Acre. During the same period Pisans acquired a quarter at Jaffa. In 1123 Venetians obtained the property of a third of the city of Tyre in Syria. Although in theory subject to the local government, the Italian quarters were endowed with great autonomy. To all intents and purposes the inhabitants were almost exclusively subject to the jurisdiction of their own consuls, who enjoyed ample administrative and political powers within the quarter. These establishments of Italian cities in the East, or *fattorie,* as they were then called, constituted the direct forerunners of the "settlements," obtained by Western powers in the Orient during the nineteenth and twentieth centuries. In addition, Genoa and Venice exercised their own direct domination over vast regions in the Crimea and the Balkan peninsula, respectively. Since the political regime of these territories was one of ab-

---

[29] "Item quod nullus Pisanus in portubus terrarum dicti regis audeat vel presumat damnum inferre, quoniam tunc per omnibus consul sive consules Pisanorum puniretur sive punirentur."

solute political dependence upon the dominating Italian cities and since these territories were inhabited by a population ethnically diverse, their situation with respect to the Italian cities was similar to that of modern colonies with respect to their motherland.[30]

f) Personal privileges.—Practically all treaties recognized the exemption of subjects of Italian cities from the law of escheat. In case of death the estate was administered by local consuls or compatriots of the deceased. Moreover, exemption from local taxes and jurisdiction was often granted to subjects of Italian cities. In judicial matters they were subject almost exclusively to their own consuls.

g) Recognition and powers of consuls.—Almost all treaties provided for the establishment of consuls, to whom broad powers were entrusted. One of the greatest contributions to the progress of international law made by the Italian states during the Renaissance consists of the development of the consular institution.[31] The citizens of Italian states who settled abroad for reasons of trade were inclined to create in the countries to which they migrated institutions similar to those of the mother country. Thus Italians abroad united in professional guilds, at the head of which were elected chiefs, called *consules electi* (consuls elected), who among other things had the duty of administrating justice among guild members. Thus, consuls of Italian cities were established in the West, especially in France, England, and Spain. In the Levant, however, the consular institution became particularly important, for the interests of Italians here were stronger and the powers conceded to the consuls by local authorities were greater than in western countries. In the Levant the Italian consuls ceased to be elected by members of the local community, instead they were sent out from the mother country for the protection of their own subjects in foreign countries. These *consules missi* were organs of the state, and their legal characteristics were, therefore, similar to those of modern consuls. In addition to their administrative functions, consuls of Italian states in the Near East were also required to fulfill diplomatic and judicial activities. First Amalfi, then Pisa, Genoa, Venice, and other Italian maritime cities had consuls in almost all parts of the Near East.[32] These consuls were above all political agents charged

[30] Some Italian cities held protectorates. In 1447 Venice assumed the protectorate over the Dalmatian Republic of Pogglizza, which lasted until the end of the Republic of Venice in 1797. The same protectorate relationship existed between Venice and the Dalmatian Republic of Ragusa from 1571 to 1797.

[31] For the historical development of the consulates, beyond the works cited by Miltitz, Contuzzi, and Ferrara, see Genevois, *Histoire de la juridiction consulaire;* F. F. Martens, *Das Konsularwesen und die Konsularjurisdiction im Orient;* Salles, *L'Institution des consulats, son origine, son développement su moyen-âge, chez les différents peuples;* Ravndal, *The Origin of the Capitulations and of the Consular Jurisdiction.*

[32] Florence, Ancona, and many cities of Sicily had consuls. On Sicilian consuls see Besta and Fedozzi, "I consolati di Sicilia all' estero e i consolati esteri in Sicilia sino al secolo XIXº," 2 Zeitschrift für Völkerrecht (1908) 119–140.

not only with the protection of the persons and goods of their fellow citizens [33] but also with the maintenance of political contacts with the local authorities. For this purpose many treaties conferred upon the consul the right of visiting the local sovereign at determined intervals—a right which today is a prerogative limited only to diplomatic agents of the highest rank. In general the consuls were vested with exclusive jurisdiction of civil cases between fellow citizens. Their jurisdiction extended to litigations between fellow citizens and other foreigners and sometimes even applied to litigations between their subjects and those of the native state. At times these consuls exercised jurisdiction over their fellow citizens in penal matters, especially in cases of minor importance. The administration of the common treasury of the colony also belonged to the consul. These consuls, in addition, fulfilled functions which even today belong to this class of agents; that is, they acted as public notaries, administered decedents' estates, and lent assistance in cases of shipwreck. Minute provisions regulated the number and appointment of the consuls, their remuneration, and their right to collect fees and taxes and to appoint subordinates. There also existed among consuls a kind of hierarchy. For instance, the consuls of Genoa around the Black Sea east of the Crimea were dependent upon the consul general at Caffa, while those in the west of the Crimea were dependent upon the consul general at Pera. From the end of the fifteenth century consuls appointed by Venice to countries conquered by Moslems were dependent upon the Venetian bailiff at Constantinople.

Toward the end of the fifteenth century the importance of the consulates of Italian cities began to decline. This was due in part to the establishment of permanent legations, which assumed diplomatic functions hitherto exercised exclusively by consuls, but especially to the decline of Italian trade in the Near East, which brought with it the gradual disappearance of Italian *fattorie*. The loss of the prestige of Italian consuls is an eloquent indication of the diminishing power of Italian cities. When Constantinople was taken, the bailiff of Venice was put to death. In 1464 the Venetian consul at Alexandria was imprisoned as a measure of retaliation. In 1473 the Venetian consul at Damascus was condemned to the bastinade.

The weakness of state organization and the existence of powerful institutions intermediary between the individual and the state were the reasons why some peculiar institutions of international law developed in Italy at that time. The small Italian states were not always in a position directly to provide their own forces for the conquest of new territories

[33] Sometimes they also had the right to grant diplomatic protection to non-citizens whom the natives considered to be foreigners. For instance, Venetian consuls exerted protection over Jews in many countries of the Orient.

or for the preservation of those already conquered. Hence these states favored the initiative of private organizations formed by their own citizens for the achievement of those ends. At Venice such enterprises were generally promoted by families of the aristocracy, around whom were grouped merchants, professional soldiers, clients, friends, servants, and adventurers. In 1204 Venice acquired Candia (Crete) from the Marquis of Monferrato, but instead of governing it directly large franchises were granted to Venetians, who went there to live and who undertook to provide for its defense. A hundred families made up of patricians and the common people were settled in the island, constituting one of the first modern examples of demographic colonization.[34] After 1207 Venice, which was unable to secure the direct control of all the islands and ports of the Aegean belonging to her as booty from the time of the victorious fourth Crusade, granted to various Venetian patricians the right of settling in some of these islands and also conferred upon them certain sovereign powers. Marco Dandolo and Jacobo Viaro settled at Gallipoli; Marino Dandolo, at Andros; Marco Sanudo, at Naxos, Paros, Melos, and Lemnos. Thus were formed small aristocratic principalities which, though in some respects dependent upon Venice, enjoyed a large measure of autonomy. The legal status of these Venetian principalities is difficult to ascertain in view of the fact that at that time a distinction between subjects of international law and some entities which were parts of an independent state was not as clearly delineated as it is today. Due to the large measure of decentralization existing in the independent states of that period, some of their provinces practically enjoyed the same powers which belonged to subjects of international law. On the other hand, some international subjects were subordinated to others by bonds of allegiance that today would be considered incompatible with the status of subject of international law. However, it would seem to be more exact to classify many of these aristocratic Venetian principalities as subjects of international law, since they exercised many rights which today are the exclusive prerogatives of states, such as the conclusion of treaties, the issuance of their own currency and the maintenance of their own troops. Their dependence upon Venice could be compared to the vassalage existing in the nineteenth century between the Danubian principalities and the Ottoman Empire. Some of these Venetian principalities lasted until the end of the fifteenth century, when they were gradually submerged by the rising tide of Islam.

At Genoa these enterprises, often called *maone*, were constituted on a basis more distinctly commercial and corporative. Long before Holland, France, and England attempted to stimulate private initiative by form-

---

[34] Venice held colonies in Greece and Albania, which she administered directly. Pisa and Genoa had fiefs and vassals in Corsica.

ing commercial associations licensed for the economic development of colonial territories, Genoa had already created the first colonial companies.[35] Through the merger of various colonial enterprises there was constituted at Genoa in 1407 the Bank of St. George (*Banco di San Giorgio*), whose capital stock was divided into shares owned by private individuals. In payment of various debts to the bank, the Republic of Genoa ceded to it the administration of Caffa and other colonies on the Black Sea. Thus the *Banco* became one of the most powerful institutions of that period and the master of vast territories over which it exercised its own exclusive political power. The bank enacted laws for those territories, administered justice, appointed officials, and even exercised the right of war, to which it was more and more frequently compelled to resort against the Moslems, until finally its power was exhausted and its territory diminished.

In 1346 the island of Chios was conquered by a Genoese admiral. The expedition was financed by private citizens, but the Republic guaranteed interest on the sums invested. The island was ceded to the *Istituto dei maonesi*, set up by a committee of subscribers of the capital invested in the venture. In the agreement of cession it was stipulated that the Republic had the right to redeem Chios by making restitution of the principal. This right, however, was never exercised. The dominion of the island remained, therefore, under control of the *maona*, which also conquered Samos, Patmos, Icaria, Psara, and Tenedos, finally succumbing in 1516 to the assault of the Turks.

It is not always possible to distinguish piracy from legitimate military operations in this period, for sometimes associations of citizens were organized to undertake regular military expeditions overseas. The first *maona* was set up in Genoa in 1234 for the conquest of Ceuta, which was carried out with good results in 1236 with the intervention of approximately one hundred Genoese ships.

Trade with the East was one of the principal sources of wealth for Italian cities. This explains why this trade continued even after the Moslem invasions and in spite of the protests and the prohibitions of the popes, who repeatedly tried to prohibit any intercourse with Moslems or at least attempted to prevent supplies of war materials from reaching the Turks by means of this trade. The third Lateran Council, 1179, forbade trade with infidels in iron, nails, arms, tow, cables, lumber, and ships of any kind. The fourth Lateran Council, 1215, renewed this prohibition. In 1307 Clement V tried to prohibit all trade with infidels under pain of

[35] For the colonial companies see Heyd, *Le compagnie coloniali degli Italiani in Oriente nel Medio Evo;* Fedozzi, "Le compagnie coloniali e la politica coloniale italiana," 24 *Rivista Italiana per le scienze giuridiche* (1897) 1 ff.; Ebner, "Compagnie coloniali," in *Nuovo digesto italiano*, III, 411 ff.; Bonolis, *Sulle maone genovesi e una maona fiorentina.* For the Banco di San Giorgio see Marenco, Manfroni, and Pessagro, *Il Banco di San Giorgio.*

a fine equal to the value of the goods exported, to be paid to the Apostolic Chambers. Another attempt to forbid Italians from trading with infidels was made by Clement VIII as late as 1595. This constant repetition of ecclesiastical prohibitions was an indication of the laxity with which they were observed.[36] In reality relations between Italy and Moslem states until the middle of the fifteenth century were relatively friendly in spite of the Crusades. The numerous treaties concluded testify to this.

It must be especially stressed that Italian states attributed more or less the same legal value to agreements concluded with Mohammedan sovereigns as to those concluded with Christian states; thus the former were considered binding international acts. It is true that sometimes agreements with Moslems were violated. However, similar violations of agreements did then occur and still occur today between Christian states.

Concessions granted to Italian states in the Near East were generally grounded upon bilateral acts which from the point of view of form as well as of their contents possessed an international character. Sometimes concessions were apparently granted in the form of unilateral privileges conferred by oriental sovereigns by means of internal legal acts. These acts were usually divided into several sections (*capitula*), each section containing a request for concessions by the Italians and the granting of the same by the Oriental sovereigns, sometimes accompanied by well-defined amplifications or restrictions. Because of this formal character such agreements were known as "capitulations." Though apparently in the nature of acts of domestic legislation, these instruments were in substance international agreements, and they gradually became international in form as well. The capitulation concluded in 1238 between Venice and the Egyptian Sultan Adil III (Malek al Adel) and those which Mahomet II concluded with the Genoese in 1453 and with the Venetians in 1454 are in all respects international treaties. So the first capitulations having the characteristics of international agreements are of Italian origin.[37] The opinion held by many French authors that the capitulation of 1535 between Francis I of France and the Sultan Suleiman, was the first international agreement of this type does not seem to be grounded upon historical fact.

MARITIME INTERCOURSE

The prosperity of Italy during the Renaissance was to a notable extent due to the active participation of Italian cities in trade by sea. Profiting by their favorable geographic position, not only did these cities promote the development of maritime trade between Italy and other countries

---

[36] Jessup and Deák, *Neutrality; Its History, Economics and Law*, I, 7–8.
[37] Ravndal, *The Origin of the Capitulations and of the Consular Jurisdiction*, pp. 33–35.

washed by the Mediterranean, but they also tried to control direct trade between Mediterranean countries other than Italy. In order to impose their naval superiority, the Italian cities did not hesitate to dispatch military expeditions throughout the Mediterranean from Majorca to Constantinople and from the coasts of southern France to the shores of Barbary. At the beginning of the Renaissance, when the maritime activity of French and Spanish cities was in its infancy, Italian cities had sufficient economic and military power to realize at least in part their ambitious projects.

Obviously the Italian contribution to the development of international maritime law during this period was influenced by the general condition of Mediterranean navigation and by the ambitions of Italian cities. Freedom of navigation was then practically unknown in the Mediterranean. The chronic state of war existing in this sea, the impossibility of drawing a distinction between warships and merchantships, the widespread practice of piracy and privateering made navigation extremely unsafe. It is hardly too much to say that, in the absence of an express international agreement to the contrary, a foreign ship encountered on the sea could be treated as an enemy ship and if possible captured. With such a state of affairs, it was force alone which constituted the law of the sea. This was the reason why zones adjacent to the coasts, over which a state could exercise actual dominion, came to be considered part of its territory. The existence of territorial waters came then to be universally accepted in Italy, although there was no complete agreement as to their extent. For a long time following the teaching of Bartolus, the extent of Italian territorial waters was considered to be 100 miles.[38] However, some Italian states even tried to extend their jurisdiction over zones of the Mediterranean beyond the limit of territorial waters in the proper sense. Pisa, at the height of its power, claimed dominion over the Tyrrhenian Sea; Genoa, over the Gulf of Liguria; and Venice, over the Adriatic Sea. For centuries Venetians asserted that no foreign warship might penetrate the Adriatic and that foreign merchantships must pay toll. The doges of Venice are lords of the Adriatic as the king of England is king of the English sea, wrote an English monk, a pilgrim to the Holy Land in 1344. The exclusive dominion of Venice in this sea already recognized in the treaty between Emperor Otto IV and the doge of Venice, August 18,

[38] Sicily, through the influence of the Norman invaders, followed the Nordic criterion of limiting territorial waters to the range of vision. This criterion was followed as late as 1740 in the treaty between the Kingdom of the Two Sicilies and the Ottoman Empire of April 7, which provided that neither of the two contracting parties would permit the vessels of the other to be pursued or molested in the vicinity of their own coasts, if the ships were near enough to discern the coast. Similarly, in the proclamations of neutrality issued by Tuscany and Venice, 1778–1779, the range of vision marked the limit beyond which foreign vessels leaving a port were authorized to attack incoming ships, while the range of cannon shots marked the more general limit for ordinary hostilities.

1209, was reaffirmed in the treaty between Emperor Frederick II and the doge of Venice, September 20, 1220.[39] All Mediterranean Sea powers came to acknowledge more or less willingly the Adriatic dominion of Venice. As late as 1478 and 1479 Emperor Frederick III was compelled to ask the permission of the doge to transport grain from Apulia across the Gulf of Venice.

In the sixteenth century the duke of Savoy exacted the payment of a tax by foreign ships which passed less than one hundred miles from the city of Villefranche, near Nice. This toll was called *droit de Villefranche*, and its collection gave rise to frequent conflicts with foreign nations, especially with France.[40]

Claims of dominion over the sea and tolls did not fail to arouse the liveliest opposition. This opposition often originated in states which were not strong enough to impose their own exclusive dominion over certain maritime zones and therefore advocated the freedom of the seas for all. It was only after severe struggles with Bologna that Venice was at last able to force the former city to acknowledge its dominion over the Adriatic. In 1226 Venice blockaded Ancona for the purpose of compelling the latter to recognize this dominion. At other times the opposition emanated from the pope, who in his capacity of defender of all Christendom was opposed to the exclusive dominion by one people of any part of the sea. The pope did try to reaffirm the Roman principle that the sea is common to all men. October 11, 1169, Pope Alexander III wrote to the consuls of Genoa exhorting them to desist from interfering with the freedom of navigation of the citizens of Montpellier "quia non decet vos huius modi proprietatis in mari requirere, quam paganos etiam non legimus requisisse." [41] However, the opposition of the weaker cities and the pope proved ineffectual, until the larger Italian maritime cities were strong enough to enforce their privileges. The Holy See itself, during the pontificate of Julius II, was compelled to conclude a treaty with Venice in order to obtain free access to the Adriatic for the ships of his subjects.

[39] See Bonolis, *Il diritto medioevale marittimo dell'Adriatico*, p. 44; and Gidel, *Le Droit international public de la mer*, I, 131. On the origin of the maritime dominion of Venice on the Adriatic Sea see Lenel, *Die Entstehung der Vorherrschaftes Venedigs an der Adria*.

[40] According to Raestad, *La Mer territoriale*, p. 21, the right of Villefranche was abolished in the seventeenth century, following a Franco-Piedmontese agreement of 1633. It seems, however, that such a toll had been collected even later. Miltitz, *Manuel des consuls*, II, 2, 154, cites a treaty between France and Sardinia of December 15, 1753, providing for the suppression of such a right over French ships. Similar agreements were entered into by Sardinia—with Great Britain, October 17, 1754; with Denmark, January 30–February 4, 1785; and with Spain, August 6, 1791. In 1787 the exercise of the right of Villefranche gave rise to disputes between Sardinia and the Low Countries which do not seem to have been entirely settled during the eighteenth century. Cf. Martens, *Cours diplomatique*, III, 336.

[41] Valery, "La Pape Alexandre III et la liberté des mers," 14 Rev. gén. dr. int. pub. (1907) 240 ff.

Besides claiming exclusive dominion over a number of zones of the Mediterranean, the stronger Italian cities also tried to restrain the sea trade of the weaker ones. This was the policy followed by Genoa in the twelfth century against the maritime cities of southern France. By the treaty of 1143 Genoa secured from Montpellier the promise that the ships of the latter would not sail further east than Genoa. In 1174 Genoa obtained from Raymond V, count of Toulouse, the monopoly of sea trade from La Turbie and Narbonne. In 1175 a treaty of peace between Genoa and Pisa placed certain restrictions upon the sea trade of the latter with the southern French ports. In the twelfth century Arles and St. Gilles were bound to Genoa to limit their direct traffic with the Orient to ships carrying pilgrims. On the basis of a treaty of 1166 with Genoa, Narbonne was permitted to send each year only one ship of pilgrims to the Holy Land. The pilgrims were not permitted to take supplies except those necessary for their maintenance during the voyage.[42] It was only with the rise of Marseilles, due in part to the rivalry between Pisa and Genoa, that the monopoly of the latter over the sea trade of southern France was broken.[43] The policy of Venice was in no respect different from that of Genoa. In 1100 the Venetians, having defeated the Pisans at Rhodes, obtained from them the solemn pledge not to trade by sea with the Greek Empire. Contemporaneously Venice secured from the Greek emperor a number of privileges. Some of them were obtained by treaty; others were apparently acquired in the form of concessions unilaterally granted. They gave Venice important advantages in sea trade with the Byzantine Empire.[44]

In exchange for concessions granted to them the Italian cities secured to other contracting parties the benefit of protection at sea, which at that period was extremely desirable because of piracy, privateering, and the existence of chronic sea warfare. Thus, for instance, in exchange for a number of concessions obtained from Montpellier under a treaty of 1201, Genoa promised the citizens of that town protection and full security of person and goods on the seas, except when using enemy ships.

However, by the thirteenth century, with the development of the Spanish and French maritime cities, the sea monopoly of the Italian cities

[42] On the treaties between Genoa and Narbonne see Kohler, "Handelsverträge zwischen Genua und Narbonne im 12. und 13. Jahrhundert," in *Juristiche Gesellschaft, Festgabe für dr. R. Koch,* pp. 275 ff.

[43] For more detailed information on treaties of commerce and navigation of Genoa see Schaube, *Handelsgeschichte der lateinischen Völker des Mittelmeergebiets bis zum Ende der Kreuzzüge.*

[44] International treaties were sometimes concluded for the transportation of Crusaders, on which Italian cities realized huge profits. A treaty of 1189 between Philip Augustus of France and Genoa recites the obligation of Genoa to transport to the Holy Land the said sovereign with his squires, horses and provisions, against the payment of a certain sum. The king also guaranteed to the Genoese commercial exemptions and other advantages in all the lands to be conquered. St. Louis concluded a treaty with Venice in 1268 for the transportation of his army to the Holy Land.

began to decline. Ironically enough, in the sixteenth century, when the military power of the Italian states began to ebb while their sea trade was still flourishing, the positions were reversed. Italian merchants were granted by powers now grown stronger the exemptions and protection which until then the Italian states had granted to ships and merchants of other states. In 1510 England and France agreed that the merchants of Venice, Florence, and Genoa might freely trade in goods belonging to themselves or to others in ships of their own or of others without any impediment.[45] This indicates the interest of both states in the commerce still largely carried on by the Italian cities.

Although inspired only by economic motives of self-interest, the policy of the Italian maritime states exerted a beneficent influence over the development of international maritime law. The interest in the security of navigation which was common to all Italian cities explains why Italy was the country in which the movement for the suppression of the barbarous right of wreck originated. Depredation of the goods of ship-wrecked persons, which everywhere was held to be a right of the lordship or at least was a practice to be tolerated, was very soon considered in Italy to be a disreputable act, punishable by law.[46] The movement for its abolition, which dates back to a treaty between Siccardus, prince of Benevento, and the city of Naples, developed especially after the twelfth century. By statute of 1181 Venice provided for the abolition of the right of wreck on its own territory. By several international treaties, such as that with Ravenna of 1234, she obtained that this right should not be exercised against her citizens abroad. Between Rome and Pisa, the right of wreck was abolished by treaty in 1174. In almost all the treaties of Italian cities with oriental princes it was agreed that if ships were wrecked which belonged to citizens of the contracting parties, the local consul should take care of the shipwrecked persons, goods, and vessel. The prohibition of the right of wreck was established in the treaty of 1113 between Pisa and the Byzantine emperor, Alexius I Comnenus. The Genoese obtained similar treatment from the Byzantine emperor, Emmanuel I Comnenus, by a treaty concluded about 1170. In the treaty between Venice and the sultan of Iconium of 1229, safety was assured for the goods and persons of both states in case of shipwreck. The Church also contributed to the suppression of the right of shipwreck. In 1268 Clement IV wrote Charles of Anjou exhorting him to restore the possessions taken from a shipwrecked Venetian vessel.

The paramount interest of Italian cities in avoiding friction in maritime affairs with foreigners led to the establishment in several Italian cities of the *consoli del mare*. These consuls of the sea were a special class

---

[45] See Jessup and Deák, *Neutrality* I, 127; see also pp. 31, 59–60.
[46] See Catellani, *Il diritto internazionale privato e i suoi recenti progressi*, I, 297 ff.

of magistrates who contributed much to the regularity of trade and to the formation of uniform, precise, and equitable rules of international maritime law. As Van Vollenhoven points out:

To Pisa belongs the credit for this successful and promising innovation. In order to encourage overseas maritime trade and for the supervision of matters relating to the conditions under which it is carried on, not least for the purpose of protecting that trade against the local pirates, you have persons who occupy high positions in the trading community, organizing maritime guilds, "ordines maris," whose authority is delegated to a certain extent to "maritime consuls," i.e. persons enjoying a certain prestige, whose function it was to guarantee equitable treatment for foreign merchants and international trade. These consuls are partly protectors of trade to whom the merchant can take his trouble, and partly magistrates in the true sense of the term, competent to deliver judgment in any dispute covered by the customary maritime law, the title of "consul" at that time and in that part of the world simply meaning a local authority enjoying a certain repute.[47]

Besides the *consoli dell'arte del mare* at Pisa, there were at Florence the *consoli del commercio*, at Genoa the *consoli del mare*, and at Venice the *magistratura degli stranieri* (magistracy of the foreigners), exercising almost the same functions. Similar institutions existed in the maritime cities of southern Italy, such as Trani and Amalfi. The original jurisdiction of these magistrates over maritime matters gradually was broadened to comprise all matters in which foreigners were involved. It should be pointed out that these officials were not similar to modern consuls. The latter are officials appointed by a state to fulfill certain activities in a foreign country in accordance with international agreements between the state which appointed them and the state to which they have been dispatched. On the contrary, the maritime consuls of Italian cities were officials appointed by the local authorities to take care of matters affecting the interest of foreigners. They were appointed according to local laws, and not international rules; and they were not subject to international control.[48] Also different from modern consuls were the so-called *defensores et protectores*, sometimes called *consules hospites*, whose functions resembled those of the *proxenoi* of the classical period. They were influential citizens, who in some Italian cities, such as Pisa or Genoa, took under their protection the citizens of a given foreign city, such as Marseilles or Barcelona, helped them in their local matters, at times acted as their guarantors, and often granted them hospitality in their homes.[49]

[47] *The Law of Peace*, p. 7.
[48] Contuzzi, *Trattato teorico—pratico di diritto consolare e diplomatico*, I, 28; and *Ferrara, Manuale di diritto consolare*, p. 9.
[49] Schaube, "La Proxenie au moyen âge," 28 Rev. dr. int. et lég. comp. (1896) 524 ff.

The Italian cities made a worthy contribution to the formation of that compact system of international rules which controlled navigation in the Mediterranean at the beginning of the Renaissance. Toward the end of the Middle Ages there were compiled in many Italian cities collections of maritime laws. These codifications governed matters which up to that time had been controlled by custom derived in part from Roman tradition, with some infiltrations from medieval conceptions. Among these codifications the laws of Venice and of Genoa are well known, as are the *Breve curiae maris* of Pisa (1298 and 1305) from which the *Consolato del mare* is deemed to have originated, the *Breve portus Kallaritani* (Cagliari, 1318) the *Capitula* of Amalfi (end of the 13th century) the codes of Messina, Catania, Palermo, and the ordinances of Trani, Ancona, and Ragusa.[50] Such codifications were compilations of rules of national law, which were only valid in the country where they had been enacted. However, the sphere of application of many of such codifications extended beyond the limit of the states enacting them, either because such collections sometimes codified rules already observed over extensive zones of the Mediterranean or because these rules came to be accepted by other countries as a consequence of their intrinsic merit. Thus a uniform maritime law came into existence, applicable in all Mediterranean countries, or at least in those of Christian faith, and more or less similar at Barcelona, Marseilles, Genoa, Pisa, and Venice. The most worthy monument of this uniform maritime law of the Mediterranean is the *Consolato del mare*. It is believed that the oldest known redaction of this law was originally compiled in Catalan at Barcelona and that it was subsequently translated into other tongues. It matters little, however, where the oldest collection of the *Consolato* was originally published, since no doubt remains that the first compiler of the *Consolato* only collected a body of rules which was already in force in the Mediterranean and which was applied in the principal maritime cities by the maritime consuls, from whom the work derived its name. What is important to note is that the greatest part of the rules of the *Consolato del mare*, even its very name, are of Italian origin. These rules had been imposed upon the Mediterranean area by the Italian cities when they obtained the supremacy over maritime traffic in that sea.[51] In and by themselves the rules of the *Consolato del mare* are rules of municipal law: they are part of the domestic legislation enacted in

[50] On such compacts see Solmi, *Storia del diritto italiano*, p. 189.
[51] The Sardinian jurist Azuni, of whom more will be said further on, in his *Sistema universale dei principii del diritto marittimo dell'Europa* and *Origine et progrès du droit de la législation maritime*, attributed to Pisans the origin of the *Consolato del mare*. The thesis of Azuni has been accepted by Schaube, *Das Konsulat des Meeres in Pisa*. The most important Italian comment on the *Consolato del mare* is that of the celebrated expert on commercial law, G. M. Casaregis (1678–1737), reprinted by O. Sciolla, Turin, 1911.

different countries of the Mediterranean. In fact, the rules of the *Consolato del mare* governed the relations between private individuals such as shipowners, charterers, sailors, and merchants, not between states. These rules were applied by the municipal courts of the maritime cities, not by international tribunals. However, what has already been said apropos of the legislation of the Italian cities concerning the treatment of foreigners and the recognition of foreign laws and acts applies also to the *Consolato del mare* and to the other codes of Italian maritime cities of this period. Although the *Consolato* and the other codes were municipal law, the different states enacted and applied them because of the conviction that their enactment and respect for them were required by rules of international law. To use the expression of Triepel, such rules of maritime law were municipal law, the enactment of which was internationally imposed upon the state. Therefore, above the rules of the codes and of the *Consolato del mare* the Mediterranean states admitted the existence of certain principles and rules of international law to which they had to conform with regard to their maritime legislation. The rules of the *Consolato* were the application of these international rules and thus came to be applied directly in relations among states, especially in matters of contraband, prizes, and neutrality. A state, for example, was internationally entitled to apply to a subject of a neutral state or to a neutral ship which traded in enemy goods the rules of the *Consolato*. If such rules were applied, the state to which the subject or the ship belonged had no right to protest. On the contrary, he could have requested some reparation in the event that such rules had been violated. It is a fact that for centuries the rules of the *Consolato del Mare* were nearly always observed in the Mediterranean.[52] Hence the existence of a notable body of rules of international Mediterranean maritime law, the origin of which, it must be admitted, was largely Italian, came to be recognized.

[52] According to Nys, *Les Origines du droit international,* France was the first among Mediterranean powers systematically to infringe in the sixteenth century the rule of the *Consolato del Mare* providing that friendly goods on enemy ships could not be confiscated.

Chapter III: SETTLEMENT OF INTERNATIONAL DISPUTES AMONG ITALIAN STATES

THE subjection by Italian communes of the neighboring rural dis tricts and of the feudal lords, the rivalry between communes, the pitiless competition between maritime cities, and, finally, during the las period of the Renaissance, the struggles between the *signorie* and betweer Italian principalities to preserve the balance of power against attempt at hegemony—all these factors caused frequent wars among the Italiar states of the Renaissance. Their consequences were not limited to the Italian peninsula alone. For the struggles of the maritime cities were fought all over the Mediterranean and frequently involved their oversea possessions.

PEACEFUL SETTLEMENT

However, one should not exaggerate the scope and gravity of Italian continental wars. Although frequent and numerous, especially in the period of the communes, yet these wars were not very intensively fought. Sometimes they continued for years; they were, however, for the mosi part, limited to military skirmishes and forays. Far more men were made prisoners than were killed, and prisoners, as a rule, were soon ran somed. It was no less easy and quick to make peace than to make war. Reconciliation quickly followed discord, even when it was destined rapidly to give way to new discords and subsequently to new reconcilia tions.[1] The ideal of concord and peace constantly remained in the minds of the contenders, since there were no profound moral and ethical splits such as exist today among various peoples. The Italians of the Renais sance, although politically divided, formed a profound moral unity and already felt that they all belonged to a common country.[2]

Any conflict among Italian states also brought grave damage to many of the states of the peninsula which were not directly involved. In fact war was an impediment to trade and communications. Moreover, as a result of the frequent encroachments and intermingling of territories be longing to different states, hostilities were often carried over to terri-

[1] Guicciardini, "Ricordi politici e civili," in *Opere inedite*, p. 102: "Before 1494 wars were long, battles were not bloody and methods of conquering countries were slow and difficult; and although artillery was already used, it was manned with so little ability that the damage was not great; thus it was almost impossible for one who held a state to lose it."
[2] See Salvatorelli, *A Concise History of Italy*, p. 206.

tories belonging to noncombatant states. Finally, during the period of the *signorie* and principalities, the neutral states, no less than the losing side, were desirous to prevent that a crushing victory should upset in favor of the victors the balance of power. Hence the interest felt by Italian states in avoiding war or, once it had begun, in hastening its end. This interest was shared by the Holy See, not only for humanitarian reasons and in deference to the principle of equilibrium, but also because any conflict among Italian states constituted an obstacle to the formation of that coalition of Christian powers against the infidels which the popes were constantly attempting to promote during that epoch.

These factors explain the frequent intervention of other powers in conflicts among Italian states. This intervention came as a rule in the form of mediation, a procedure to which frequent recourse was had in Italy during the whole Renaissance period. In 1199 the city of Asti interposed its mediation between the cities of Chieri and Turin, thus bringing about peace in the following year. In 1270 the mediation of St. Louis, the king of France, brought a five-year truce between Genoa on one side and Venice and Pisa on the other, then allied. Again in July, 1381, peace was concluded between Venice and Genoa, through the mediation of the supreme pontiff, who delegated the task to the cardinal of Santa Croce. Peace was concluded April 14, 1428, between Venice and Florence and Milan. In 1454 the king of Sicily, through his representative Bishop Nicholas, acted as mediator between Milan and the marquis of Monferrato, in the dispute relative to the city of Alessandria; and in the same year the marquis of Este acted as mediator between Venice and the king of Aragon. There were no great differences between the procedure of mediation in the Renaissance and that employed today. In both cases the mediator performed a conciliatory activity, mainly through diplomatic channels. As today, it was often a personal and direct interest on the part of the mediator that induced him to offer his good services. For this reason the work of persuasion was sometimes accompanied by actual coercion over one or all contenders, so that in many cases doubt existed as to where good offices ended and where interference and political pressure on the part of the pretended mediator began. In some instances mediation degenerated into open intervention.[3]

Although exhaustive investigation into the rich material of the period is still to be made, the available documents show that international arbitration was very extensively resorted to, especially in northern Italy, from the beginning of the twelfth century to the end of the fifteenth

---

[3] This form of intervention by one or more states for the settlement of disputes among others has found recent application in the so-called "arbitrations" of Germany and Italy between Hungary and Czechoslovakia, October, 1938, and between Rumania and Hungary, August, 1940. Germany and Italy, in dictating a solution which the parties to the conflicts were forced to accept, were moved chiefly by their own personal interests.

century.[4] By "arbitration" we mean the solution of a dispute between two states by a decision binding the parties and issued by an international tribunal.[5]

Mediation and arbitration might be distinguished from other procedures for the prevention of, or for the pacific settlement of, international disputes which were in use in Italy during the Renaissance.

A procedure different from international arbitration was the intervention of the emperor in the controversies between powers subject to his sovereignty, such as dependent cities and feudal lords. In such cases the emperor did not intervene in his capacity as judge but as an overlord in order to preserve in his own interest peace among his subjects.

Nor was there arbitration, in the technical meaning of the expression, when for the solution of a dispute each party did not appoint a real arbitrator, bound to decide according to law, but instead named a representative who was charged exclusively with the protection of the interests of the party who had appointed him. To this category belonged those mixed commissions which were frequently set up to determine damages growing out of war, or from the arbitrary collection of taxes. A mixed commission was set up for such a purpose between Bologna and Ferrara in 1194. Such commissions were also appointed for the liquidation of questions arising out of the transfer of territory, for instance, the mixed commission between Milan and Savoy which was established in accordance with the treaty of August 30, 1454. These commissions had functions similar to the conciliatory commissions provided for by several contemporary treaties.

The character of arbitrators cannot be attributed to the *conservatori della pace* (conservators of the peace), who were appointed in some treaties, especially peace treaties, to see that there should be no violation of their provisions. Hence the functions of the *conservatori* were supervisory rather than judicial.[6]

---

[4] On international arbitration in northern Italy in the twelfth and thirteenth centuries see the work of Frey, *Das öffentliche Schiedsgericht in Oberitalien im 12. und 13. Jahrhundert*, based directly on the sources. It is to be hoped that this work will be continued to cover the succeeding centuries. For other Italian arbitrations of the Renaissance see the somewhat defective work of Novacovitch, *Les Compromis et les arbitrages internationales du XIIe au XVe siècle*, and for many more references to Italian practice see Contuzzi, "Arbitrati internazionali," in *Digesto italiano*, VII, 304–524. See also Lange, *Histoire de l'internationalisme*, pp. 123–130; Mérignhac, *Traité théorique et pratique de l'arbitrage international*; Ralston, *International Arbitration from Athens to Locarno*; Sereni, "Arbitrato internazionale," in *Nuovo digesto italiano*, I, 637 ff. For interesting conclusions on medieval arbitration in general see Anzilotti, *Corso di diritto internazionale*, III, 45–57; and Vollenhoven, *The Law of Peace*, pp. 43 ff.

[5] According to Article 37 of the Hague Convention of October 19, 1907, for the pacific settlement of international disputes, the object of arbitration is "the settlement of disputes between States by judges of their own choice, and on the basis of the respect of the law."

[6] The appointment of "conservators of the peace" was not common in Italian treaties of this period. However, their nomination was provided for in the treaty of peace of January 16, 1382, between Milan and Monferrato.

To assure the execution of treaties, provision was sometimes made for the appointment of guarantors, that is, third states who pledged themselves to act against the defaulting party. At other times mixed commissions and "conservators of the peace" were combined with the arbitration. The treaty of 1454 between Milan and the duke of Savoy provided that should the questions submitted to the mixed commission fail to be settled by it, they were to be decided by means of arbitration. In 1566 Emmanuel Philibert of Savoy was appointed to act as mediator in a controversy between Florence on one side and Lucca and Ferrara on the other, with the understanding that if it should prove impossible to reach an amicable agreement, he would render a decision in the capacity of arbitrator. After the disagreement of the parties the duke pronounced an arbitral award, which was laid down for him by Pierino Belli. In a treaty between Milan and Venice, concluded February 26, 1379, two "conservators of the peace" were named, with the understanding that in case of dispute concerning the interpretation of the treaty they would act as arbitrators.

Resort to arbitration was sometimes agreed upon for any controversy whatsoever between two states: for example, in the treaty between Venice and Genoa of 1235. However, arbitration was usually resorted to only for the solution of controversies covering particular matters of minor importance, such as the liquidation of war damages, controversies about tariff matters,[7] and feudal rights, or boundary disputes. But some arbitrations settled questions of notable political importance. The arbitrations of December 28, 1391, and January 26, 1392, between Milan, Mantua, Perugia, and Sienna on one side and the League of Florence, Bologna, Padua, Imola, and other cities on the other;[8] and the one mentioned above of Duke Emmanuel Philibert of Savoy, relative to the province of Garfagnana, decided the fate of vast territories. A decision of Emperor Charles V, in 1530, awarded full sovereignty over Ferrara, Modena, and Reggio to Alphonse of Este, who had formerly held these cities under the pope's suzerainty. Clauses providing for the settlement through arbitration of disputes arising from the interpretation of their provisions were included in many treaties; for example, the peace treaty of January 10, 1353, between Milan, Florence, and various other Italian cities; the peace treaty of July 7, 1377, between the duke of Milan and the marquis of Monferrato; the peace treaty between Milan and Venice, February 26, 1379; the peace treaty of August 30, 1454, between Milan and Savoy. A peculiar method for stipulating a compromissary clause was adopted by Venice, Florence, Genoa, and other Italian cities in 1443. The parties to the controversy, in the act of acceptance of an award

---

[7] Arbitration between Modena and Ferrara of November 14, 1179.
[8] See text in Dumont, *Supplément au Corps universel diplomatique du droit des gens*, II, 129 ff.

pronounced among them on November 20, 1443, declared themselves bound to submit to arbitration any future dispute upon the same subject.

In the controversies between communes the arbitrators were often other communes, who adjudicated the dispute through their own representatives. This was an application of the German principle of *judicium parium*, in accordance with which cities were appointed as arbitrators in disputes between cities, and in disputes between princes, princes were chosen. Sometimes the pope was elected arbitrator. Arbitrators were often individuals—professional jurists or whole legal faculties, such as those of Bologna, Perugia, and Padua. Sometimes the arbitrators named by the parties were empowered to name an umpire in case of disagreement between themselves; for example, in the treaty of 1426 for the cession of territories by the Swiss cantons of Lucerne, Uri, and Unterwalden to the duke of Milan. In the period of the *signorie* a prince was generally named as arbitrator. In the arbitration of January 20–26, 1392, already mentioned, between Milan and the Florentine League, the arbitrators were the doge of Genoa in person, the city of Genoa, represented by four councillors, and Richard Carozolo, papal nuncio.

Since the issues involved in the disputes submitted to arbitration mainly concerned facts, the arbitrators were generally empowered to decide *ex aequo et bono*. In the arbitral award pronounced April 26, 1453, by Nicholas of Este and Louis, marquis of Saluces, between Venice and Florence on one hand and Milan on the other, the arbitrators expressly declared "potius sequentes viam arbitratorum et amicabilium compositorum quam arbitrorum, inter dictas partes dicimus." But even in this case the distinction between arbitration and mediation was very clear.

Italian arbitral procedure differed from that followed in other countries during this same period in that it was of strictly legal character.[9] The progress of the legal theory and practice in Italy at that time had its favorable repercussion in the field of international relations. Arbitration was generally preceded by a detailed compromise which enunciated in detail the issues involved and set forth the procedural rules to be followed, with special reference to those concerning the appointment of the arbitrators, the presentation of documents and briefs, the examination of witnesses, the issuance of judgments, and the terms and guarantees of execution. Documents relating to the arbitration of December 28, 1391, and January 26, 1392, between Milan and the Florentine League, published by Dumont,[10] give a precise idea of the procedure followed. Generally arbitral awards could not be appealed from.

---

[9] See Novacovitch, *Les Compromis et les arbitrages internationales du XIIᵉ au XVᵉ siècle*, p. 87.

[10] *Supplément au Corps universel diplomatique du droit des gens*, II, 229 ff.

To guarantee execution of judgments, various devices were adopted; well-known citizens of the parties to the litigation swore rigid compliance with the award pronounced; hostages were exchanged; excommunication was threatened. Damages were assessed against the defaulting party. In 1318 the Ferrarese were excommunicated by the papal legate for having violated an award with Venice. Penalties were agreed upon against the defaulting party: for instance, in the compromises between Thomas of Savoy and Pignerole, 1236; between Bergamo and Cremona, 1263; between Verona and Mantua, 1276. In the arbitration of 1433 between Venice and Florence on one hand and Milan on the other, the parties set a penalty of one hundred thousand gold florins, an enormous sum for that time. There were, of course, not a few cases in which awards were not respected.[11] It is, furthermore, certain that in many cases in which judgments were respected this was due to the pressure that the arbitrator and the victorious party were able to exercise over the defeated litigant rather than to respect for the authority of *res judicata*.

Recourse to international arbitration in Italy during the Renaissance was due to a number of reasons. The satisfactory results obtained through arbitration as an institution of private law induced the Italian cities to extend this same institution to relations between states. Because of the interrelationship then existing between private law, public law, and international law, this transposition was not difficult. The patrimonial conception of the state then prevalent also favored the extension to relations among states of institutions of private law. An original theory explaining the frequent recourse to arbitration in northern Italy during the period of the communes has been recently advanced by the Swiss writer Frey. In his opinion the Italian communes resorted to private arbitrators chosen by the parties or to arbitration by another city, in order to bar any interference in their conflicts on the part of the emperor and thus affirm their own sovereignty and independence.[12] The correctness of Frey's thesis would seem to be confirmed by the fact that the emperors in general considered arbitration in Italy with disfavor.

Toward the end of the fifteenth century arbitration began to decline in Italy. It practically disappeared by the middle of the following century. This decline was in part due to the establishment of permanent legations and to the practice of settling disputes between states through diplomatic channels. In the event of failure of such methods, direct recourse was had to the use of force. However, the disappearance of arbitration in Italy, as in all other countries of Europe at that time, was especially due to the change which took place in the international relations at the end

[11] For numerous cases of violation of Italian arbitral decisions see Contuzzi, "Arbitrati internazionali," in *Digesto italiano*, VII, 304 ff.

[12] See Frey, *Des öffentliche Schiedsgericht in Oberitalien im 12. und 13. Jahrhundert*, pp. 19 ff.

of the Renaissance. In the seventeenth and eighteenth centuries the international community was completely disorganized by struggles for political and economic supremacy among the great European states. International relations then became mere relations of force. It is obvious that in such a type of society there was no place for the institution of arbitration.

REGULATION OF WARFARE

The subjection of the rural districts and the feudal lords which occurred in vast regions of Italy during the twelfth and the thirteenth centuries resulted everywhere except in Piedmont and in southern Italy in a sharp reduction in number of private wars. Beginning with the communal period Italian wars generally assumed the character of public wars, that is, of real conflicts between states, while private wars were still very frequent in the rest of Europe.[13] As we shall see later, the writers of that period who dealt with this problem agreed in attributing the character of public wars to the wars of the Italian communes.

The relative mildness of the wars fought by the Italian states was not due to the absence of military virtues in the Italian people. The Italians had demonstrated their valor against the Germans at Legnano, as well as against the infidels in expeditions overseas. But in case of war the whole territory of the Italian states, because of its small size, became the theater of hostilities, and their trade, based as it was upon international intercourse, suffered immense damage. Thus the evils of war were present with striking directness before the eyes of all Italians and acted as a powerful deterrent from military ventures against neighboring states. Moreover, the victors of today abstained from excessive exactions against the defeated party in contemplation of the possibility that tomorrow they might find themselves in the same situation. War, in brief, was throughout Italy considered an evil, never a fortunate opportunity for the acquisition of booty.[14] This also explains why in Italy from the beginning of the Renaissance there existed some kind of legal discipline governing the conduct of warfare and especially intended to lessen its evils. During the period of *signorie* and principalities, when wars became less

---

[13] Nevertheless A. Pertile, *Storia del diritto italiano*, I, 289, affirms that "also in Italy private war resisted the numerous prohibitions, still being met in the sixteenth and seventeenth centuries."

[14] On the comparatively mild character of the Italian wars of the Renaissance see Walker, *A History of the Law of Nations* pp. 130–131. Walker's assertion of the existence in Italy at that time of a "villainous practice," unknown elsewhere, of poisoning wells, does not seem to be historically founded. In quoting some writers of the Renaissance, Walker overlooks that many authors of that period gave free rein to fantasy when dealing with the subject of stratagems of war. Gentili himself, *De jure belli libri tres*, Book II, ch. 6, speaks with great seriousness of an absurd stratagem of war that the Spaniards, besieged in Naples, had used against the French, in order to spread the contagion of *morbus gallicus*.

frequent, an additional factor in the establishment of legal principles concerning warfare was represented by the creation of companies of mercenaries (*compagnie di ventura*). They subjected the conduct of military operations to fairly fixed legal rules, which, however, were more severe for noncombatants than the rules existing during the period of the communes.[15]

Beginning with the period of the communes the observance of truces, respect for the life of civilians, if not for their property, and a certain degree of humane treatment toward prisoners was generally practiced by Italian states.[16] In a treaty of 1213 between the cities of the March of Treviso-Verona, precise and humane rules with regard to the treatment of prisoners of war were included. Prisoners of war might not be killed or wounded or kept in prison or in unhealthful surroundings. It was provided that the clothing of prisoners should not be taken from them. The beheading by Charles of Anjou at Naples on October 29, 1268, of Conradin of Swabia, who had been taken prisoner after the defeat of Tagliacozzo, made a great impression throughout Italy. Whether it was legal to kill a prisoner of war was widely discussed, and this question was generally decided, at least in principle, in the negative, even by jurists who believed that there existed special reasons in this specific case to justify the conduct of Charles of Anjou. It was, perhaps, under the influence of Italian practice that the Third Lateran Council, 1179, enacted the famous provisions relative to the observance of truces and to the respect for noncombatant populations.

When the Italian principalities started to hire foreign mercenaries, the moral level of Italian wars was considerably lowered. No ties bound these soldiers to the country for which they were fighting, except lust of gain. Consequently these mercenaries had no respect for either civilians, whether enemies or friends, or their property, which they laid waste without mercy. On the contrary, as between the combatants themselves the use of mercenaries had a mitigating effect upon the horrors of war, for the emphasis was placed not so much upon the killing or wounding of the enemy as upon its capture for purpose of ransom.

REPRISALS

Italy is the country where the movement for the limitation and subsequently for the suppression of reprisals originated.[17] By "reprisals,"

---

[15] Cf. E. Nys, "Le Droit de la guerre et les condottieri," 43 Rev. dr. int. et lég. comp. (1911) 217–232.

[16] On the Italian origin of international rules providing for humane treatment of prisoners of war see Maulde de la Clavière, *La Diplomatie au temps de Machiavel* I, 208.

[17] Fundamental on reprisals in Italy is the work of A. del Vecchio and E. Casanova, *Le rappresaglie nei comuni medioevali e specialmente in Firenze.* On the subject, besides the various manuals of history of Italian law, see Muratori, *Antiquitates italicae Medii Aevi,*

or "letters of marque," [18] was meant the license that an authority granted to a subject to capture the persons or sequestrate the goods of subjects of a foreign state. This license was usually granted to a person who had suffered damages as a result of unlawful acts of citizens of the state against whose subjects reprisals were directed. Therefore reprisals were usually granted only for the amount necessary to make good for the losses suffered by the grantee. Reprisals could be practiced on land or on sea. They were distinguished from privateering, which was indulged in for the purpose of damaging enemy sea trade. Privateering presupposed the existence of a state of war, whereas reprisals were conceded only in peacetime.

Reprisals are not of Italian origin. This practice arose in the late Middle Ages and was based upon the Germanic principle of the joint liability by all the members of a social group for the wrong committed by one of its members against an outsider. The practice of reprisals, often arbitrarily granted and exercised, created a state of chronic war among certain countries. Thus Italian jurists were emphatic in deploring this institution, which, in addition, was so contrary to the principles of Roman law. Bartolus, who was moved by the desire to suppress reprisals, or at least to limit them, exaggerated their gravity and saw in them a consequence of the divine punishment, manifested in the fall of the Roman Empire, which was inflicted on the men for their sins.

Repraesaliarum materia nec frequens nec quotidiana erat tempore quo in statu debito Romanum vigebat Imperium . . . Post quam vero peccata nostra meruerunt quod Romanum Imperium prostratum iaceret per tempora multa, et reges et principes ac etiam civitates, maxime in Italia, saltem de facto in temporalibus dominum non agnoscerent, propter quod de iniustitia ad superiorem non potest

---

especially "Dissertatio quadragesima, de civitatum italicarum foederibus ac pacibus," IV, 337 ff., and "Dissertatio quinquagesimaquinta, de repressaliis," IV, 741 ff.; Catellani, *Il diritto internazionale privato ed i suoi recenti progressi*, I, 316 ff.; Mas Latrie, *Le Droit de marque ou droit de represailles au moyen âge*; Faccio, *Le rappresaglie*; Guarino, *Le rappresaglie in tempo di pace*. On the economic basis of reprisals see Arias, "La base delle rappresaglie nella costituzione economica del medioevo," 9 *Atti del Congresso di scienze storiche*, 347–367. On the procedural aspects of Italian reprisals see Wach, *Der Arrestprocess in seiner geschichtlichen Entwicklung.* Several monographs have been written on reprisals in various Italian cities, for instance, Degli Azzi Vitelleschi, "Le rappresaglie negli statuti perugini," 5 *Annali dell'Università di Perugia* (1895) 183 ff.; Bizzarri, "Le rappresaglie negli statuti e nei documenti del comune di Siena," in *Studii di storia del diritto italiano*, pp. 237 ff.; Landogna, "Le rappresaglie negli statuti e nelle carte lucchesi," 8 *Rivista di storia del diritto italiano* (1935) 68 ff.; Cassandro, *Le rappresaglie e il fallimento a Venezia nei secoli XIII°–XIV°.*

[18] In Italy, as in the rest of Europe, reprisals could also consist of the personal capture of foreigners. Cf. A. del Vecchio and E. Casanova, *La rappresaglie nei comuni medioevali e specialmente in Firenze*, p. 47, where they quote a Florentine charter of October 23, 1281: "Nos Mapheus Madiis, potestas Florentiae . . . damus et concedimus . . . licentiam et potestatem capiendi, detinendi, sequestrandi et inframittendi *personas, homines,* bona et res subditorum et fidelium . . . domini Frederici, comitis [of Paterno]." (Italics ours.)

haberi regressum, coeperunt repraesalia frequentari et sic effecta est frequens et quotidiana materia.

This was the picture that Bartolus traced in the preamble of his *Tractatus repraesaliarum*.[19] The truth is, however, that in Italy reprisals were less common than is generally believed; moreover, Italy was the first country where they were subjected to severe legal restrictions.[20] This was due to practical reasons rather than to motives of humanity. Reprisals were a threat to international trade, on which the prosperity of the Italian states depended.[21] Thus provisions tending to limit reprisals were inserted in statutes of almost all Italian cities. These provisions began by prohibiting anyone who claimed an injury to resort directly and immediately to reprisals for the reparation of damage suffered.[22] The exercise of reprisals was to be preceded by the authorization of competent authorities, who issued the so-called "letters," or charter, of authorization.[23] Only the higher magistrates were empowered to issue reprisals: that is, at Florence, the mayor, later the official of the merchants' guild, 1448, and finally the *priori*; at Venice, first the doges, then the Greater Council, later a special magistracy called the "College for Reprisals," and finally the Senate, 1456. Such magistracies granted reprisals only after the alleged offender had been regularly cited and after the demand of the injured party had been carefully considered.[24] Very often such demands were rejected, either because they were ill-founded or because the authorities feared the consequences of such a grave measure. Re-

[19] "Reprisals were neither a current nor an everyday matter at the time when the Roman Empire existed with proper authority. But after we deserved for our sins that the Roman Empire lay prostrated for a long while and that the kings, the princes, and even the cities, especially in Italy, did no longer recognize, at least in fact, a superior authority in secular matters so that in case of a wrong, there was not a superior power to which recourse might be had, reprisals gradually were resorted to with greater frequency and thus became a current and everyday matter." "Tractatus repraesaliarum," in *Consilia, quaestiones et tractatus*, Vol. X. Giovanni da Legnano expresses himself in the same manner in his *Tractatus de bello, de represaliis et de duello*, ch. 123: "Tempore praecedente Summorum Pontificum et Romanorum Imperatorum, cum omnes subiciebantur et de jure et de facto, non erat opus represaliis, cum per principes, juris ordine servato, justitiae complementum exhiberetur. Postquam autem Imperium paulisper coepit exinaniri, adeo per eos justitia negligitur, idcirco fuit opus subsidiario remedio, deficientibus ordinariis, quibus exstantibus, ad illud nullatenus recurrendum." Note that this author, a fervent defender of the papal authority, attributes the origin of reprisals to the decadence of the authority not only of the emperor but of the pope as well.

[20] Cf. Nys, *Les Origines du droit international*, p. 64, and Hindmarsch, *Force in Peace*, p. 49.

[21] For the same motive the Hanseatic cities also were hostile to reprisals. Cf. Nys, *Le Droit de la guerre et les precurseurs de Grotius*, p. 43.

[22] The *Costitutiones Siculae* of Emperor Frederick, Book I, sec. 8, state: "Ut nullus auctoritate propria de injuriis et excessibus factis vel faciendis in posterum se debeat vindicare nec Praesalias seu Repraesalias facere, vel guerram in Regno movere."

[23] On the Italian origin of these magistracies see Hindmarsch, *Force in Peace*, p. 49.

[24] For a detailed exposition of such proceeding see the work of Giovanni da Legnano, *Tractatus de bello, de represaliis et de duello*, pp. 153–156, which subsequently will be examined in greater detail.

prisals were generally granted only for certain offenses—murder, highway robbery, nonpayment of a debt, breach of guarantee, refusal to extradite fugitives, undue collection of duties—and only when the damage was such as to justify such an extraordinary remedy. In fact, as the statute of Lucca prescribed, *pro modico damno represalia non concedatur, sed pro magno et enormi*. An essential condition for the granting of reprisals was that the injured party should have applied for justice from the superior authority of him who had committed the injury and that this request should have been denied. The official granting reprisals determined the amount to be collected and could at any moment suspend or even revoke the license.

Contrary to generally accepted opinion, reprisals are evidence of the existence of an international community and were recognized as a means of avoiding the even more serious damages of war. That the practice of reprisals implied the existence of an international community was already observed by Bartolus in the passage cited above. In Italy, he observed, recourse is had to reprisals for the cities "de facto in temporalibus dominum non agnoscerent propter quod de injustitiis ad superiorem non potest haberi regressum." [25] In his opinion reprisals are, then, a consequence of the disappearance of the authority of the emperor over the cities. In case of an offense committed against a subject of an independent city by a subject of another independent city there was no remedy by way of recourse to an authority superior to both cities, whenever justice had been denied to the plaintiff by the authorities of the offender's city. In such cases the city to which the plaintiff belonged could secure redress from the other city only by making war or by granting reprisals. In other words, reprisals were a consequence of the equality and independence attained by the Italian cities which were no longer subject to a common superior power.[26] Reprisals were, then, a consequence of the Italian cities having become subjects of international law. In this respect another point is to be considered: that is, that reprisals were not a form of private war, but a relationship established between the city granting the reprisals and the city against the citizens of which they were granted and existing between them in their capacity as subjects of international law. What the authorizing state intended to punish was not so much the wrong committed by the foreign individual wrongdoer as the tortious act committed by the foreign state in refusing redress to the plaintiff through its own courts. The denial of justice suffered by the victim represented an international wrong against the state of which the victim was a citizen. Thus the gloss, in a passage reported by Bartolus in his *Trac-*

---

[25] "*De facto* they do not recognize any lord in secular matters, so that there is no superior authority to which recourse may be had in case of a wrong."
[26] See Figgis *The Divine Right of Kings*, 2d ed., p. 360.

tatus repraesaliarum, had early expressed the opinion that reprisal "non exigitur propter delictum illius privati sed propter delictum totius civitatis denegantis facere justitiam." [27] Reprisals were, then, an act of one state against another. In this respect they were the same as war. "Concedere represalias est indicere bellum," wrote Bartolus.[28] And Bartholomaeus of San Concordio (d. 1347) in his *Summa,* called the *Maestruzza,* which enjoyed great authority among his contemporaries, explains that by "reprisals" is meant, not that one individual is punished for another, but rather that the prince or the city is punished through his citizens for his own negligence.[29]

Finally, reprisals were an institution established for the purpose of avoiding the ills of war. It is often remarked that reprisals were based on the principle of "passive solidarity," by which the compatriots of the offender were held responsible for torts committed by single individuals. This is certainly true; it should not be overlooked, however, that reprisals tended to exclude the consequences of the principle of "active solidarity," by which the compatriots of the offender, or the state representing the whole community, would have been expected to co-operate with him in repairing the damage suffered. The exercise of active solidarity would have meant war between the state to whom the plaintiff belonged and that of the offender. On the contrary the state to whom the injured party belonged renounced, by the concession of letters of marque, the right to take unto its own hands the reparation of the wrong suffered by one of its citizens and left it to him to seek reparation at his own risk and peril without giving rise to a conflict between states. Moreover, this defense of their own rights by private individuals came to be subjected by the state granting reprisals to a careful procedure for ascertaining whether the complainant was entitled to the concession.

Even so, it is certain that reprisals represented an element of disorder in international relations. The danger of reprisals was for instance one cause of the high cost of insurance, which noticeably increased the price of goods and transportation. Limitations of reprisals were then introduced in Italian cities. These cities exempted from the exercise of the

[27] "(Reprisals) are not granted by reason of the wrongful act of the private person (who actually committed the wrong), but by reason of the wrong of the whole city in refusing to do justice."

[28] "To grant reprisals is like waging war." Nys, *Le Droit de la guerre et les precurseurs de Grotius,* does not clearly understand this passage and accuses Bartolus of considering the grant of reprisals the equivalent of a declaration of war. What Bartolus means, on the contrary, is that reprisals give rise, like war, to a relationship between one state and another, not to a relationship between the person to whom reprisals have been granted and the citizens of the offending state.

[29] On the basis of the same principles Jacopo da Belvisio (d. 1335) attempted to deny that reprisals might be directed against private individuals and maintained that only public officials responsible for having denied justice ought to suffer them. However, this is only a doctrinal opinion which had no following in practice.

reprisal certain persons, such as scholars, students, women, children, lunatics, and sometimes clergymen; certain goods, such as arms, supplies, and ships; and certain roads. Reprisals were suspended on special occasions, such as fairs and solemn religious ceremonies, and safe conducts were granted.[30] Political considerations often induced Italian states not to comply with requests for reprisal and to revoke or to suspend the privilege. A suspension occurred, for instance, between Venice and Bergamo for ten years, from 1287 to 1297. Some times, for the purpose of repairing damages, devices other than reprisals were resorted to. In 1218 Perugia and Florence, instead of granting letters of reprisal to satisfy reciprocal claims of their citizens, agreed to levy special duties on the merchandise of their merchants and to allot them to the payment of indemnities. A similar treaty was concluded in 1318 between Venice and Marseilles. Some times special duties were placed on the goods of the offender's compatriots, or the latter would be expelled. Venice often threatened to withdraw its own merchants from the cities, where they had experienced denials of justice, and such threats, which if put into effect would have paralyzed the commerce of those cities, were often sufficient to secure reparation.[31] Many cities pledged themselves by treaty to compel their own citizens to pay debts owing to those of the other contracting party: for example, Venice by treaties with Ferrara, October 26, 1191; with Verona, October 4, 1192; with Treviso, 1198; with Padua, 1209; with Cervia, 1224; and with Florence, 1227. For the ascertainment of the sums due, some of these treaties set up special arbitral tribunals—for instance, between Venice and Ferrara, Venice and Verona, Venice and Padua—and established special summary procedures.

Very often it was considered opportune to conclude treaties suppressing the concession of reprisals outright. This result was reached through an agreement between the contracting cities that the creditor could prosecute only his personal debtor, not the compatriots of the latter. As far back as the twelfth century dozens of these treaties were concluded in Italy. One of the first was that between Bologna and Modena, 1166. A little later the Lombard League adopted this principle in a resolution of the Diet of Lodi, May 3, 1168. Venice introduced provisions to this effect in several treaties: with Rimini, 1170; with Cesena, 1173; with Verona, 1175. Ferrara did likewise in her treaties with Brescia, 1195; with Modena, 1198; with Mantua, 1208. Bologna signed a similar treaty with Bergamo in 1203. Florence had such treaties: with Faenza, 1204; Prato, 1212; Bologna, 1216; Perugia, 1218; Orvieto, 1229; Città di Castello, 1232; Siena, 1237; and various other cities of northern Italy.

---

[30] See Mas Latrie, *Le Droit de marque ou droit de représailles au moyen âge*, p. 14.

[31] A curious device was established by a treaty between Venice and Como of June 11, 1328. To make good the damages suffered by certain Venetians, a few citizens of Como were obliged to enter into partnership with them,

In the fourteenth century the prevalence of a peaceful spirit in Italy and the need for stability and security in commercial relations made reprisals very rare. In the fifteenth century they were no longer granted at Venice and Florence, and the example of these cities was rapidly followed almost everywhere in the peninsula. Thus Italy, the first country in which reprisals were subject to legal limitations, was also the place where they first fell into desuetude.[32]

NEUTRALITY

The contribution of Italian states of the Renaissance to the development of neutrality is of little importance. It has already been emphasized that the geographical situation of Italian states, whose territories were frequently intermingled, caused frequent invasions of neutral territory in time of war. Moreover, the neutrality of many Italian states was jeopardized by their weakness, as a consequence of which in case of war between stronger states they were not able to oppose the demands of the belligerents. Furthermore, the political principle of the balance of power, on which was founded the policy of Italian states, was opposed to the very idea of neutrality. In fact the doctrine of the balance of power led to the intervention of a state in disputes between others whenever it was necessary to prevent one of them from gaining supremacy. Proof of the general validity of this statement is to be found in the history of the seventeenth and eighteenth centuries. The principle of the balance of power having then developed from an Italian into a European principle, the whole of Europe and the American colonies became involved in an interminable series of wars.

During the Renaissance a series of principles were developed in Italy which were the very opposite of neutrality. What is today considered the very basis of the rights and duties of neutrals was then not recognized. Not only were neutrals not forbidden to provide passage across their territory to the troops of belligerents, but rather it was debated whether a belligerent did not have a real right to cross the territory of neutrals, provided only that compensation for damage and costs should be assured. It is true that belligerents sometimes protested against the granting of passage to enemy troops by neutral states and that the neutral states justified themselves by alleging that they had had to yield to force. It is also true that sometimes neutral states denied passage to belligerents, for example, Venice denied passage to the troops of the Emperor Maximilian of Austria. But it is apparent that in these cases purely political consider-

[32] One of the last cases of reprisals in Italy was constituted by the granting of letters of marque against Florence in 1505 by the governor of Nice, which then was subject to the Duke of Savoy, in favor of one Rufino Belmondi of Villefranche. In France and Holland letters of reprisal were granted until the end of the eighteenth century. In England, they were granted in the seventeenth century. Provisions relative to reprisals were contained in the treaties of Ryswick, 1697, Art. 12, and Utrecht, 1713, Art. 3.

ations guided the parties and that it was never asserted that there existed a positive rule of international law restraining neutral states from granting passage to belligerent troops.

The current practice of Italian states, when neutral, was to give aid to belligerents even for wars outside Italy, in the form of troops, victuals, arms, and ships. Thus, Genoese mercenaries took part in the wars of the kings of France and the kings of England [33] and fought in the naval battle of Shuys (1340). Neutral princes favored such operations. Sometimes they placed themselves at the head of troops conscripted in their states by one of the belligerents. Prohibitions against such practices were sometimes enacted. In 1503 Venice, in order not to offend France, prohibited all her shipowners and sea captains from entering the service of Spain. In 1509 the pope issued a decree forbidding his subjects from lending military assistance to foreign governments. But these were contingent prohibitions, issued merely because of political opportunism and not based upon the belief that they constituted the fulfillment of international obligations. This is the fundamental difference between these provisions and the declarations of neutrality issued in the eighteenth century by some Italian states, which are examined below. Neutrality, in short, was not a legal institution, but a purely political expedient which was also considered somewhat inopportune. Expressing the opinion then prevalent in Italy, Guicciardini wrote:

Neutrality in the wars of others is good for him who is powerful enough to need fear nothing from the victor, no matter who he may turn out to be; for such a neutral can maintain himself without difficulty and can hope to take advantage of the disorders of others. Except for this case, neutrality is dangerous, for one remains the prey of the victor and of the vanquished. That kind of neutrality is the worst of all, which one observes not by reasoning, but through irresolution: namely, when by not deciding yourself whether to be neutral or not you act in a way which does not satisfy even the belligerent, who for the time being would be content that you should aid him by remaining neutral.[34]

[33] Walker, *A History of the Law of Nations*, pp. 135–136.
[34] "Ricordi politici e civili," in *Opere inedite* p. 103n. Accordingly, Machiavelli, *Il principe*, ch. 21: "A prince is well esteemed when he shows himself either a true friend or a real enemy; that is, when, regardless of consequences, he declares himself openly for or against another, which will always be more creditable for him than to remain neutral. If two of your neighbouring potentates should come to war among themselves, it will always be better for you to declare yourself openly and make fair war; for if you fail to do so, you will be very apt to fall a prey of the victor, to the delight and satisfaction of the defeated party, and you will have no claim for protection or assistance from either the one or the other. . . . And it will always be the case that he who is not your friend will request you to remain neutral, whilst your friend will ask your armed intervention in his favor. Irresolute princes, for the sake of avoiding immediate danger, adopt most frequently the course of neutrality and are ruined in consequence."

Botero (1533–1617), author of the treatise *Della ragion di stato e delle cause della grandezza delle città* (1589), published in 1598 some additions, "Aggiunte," to his treatise. One of them deals briefly with neutrality, which he considers from the political point of view.

Italian states sometimes concluded agreements especially dealing with neutrality, by means of which the parties bound themselves to refrain from aiding the enemies of the other contracting party and to remain neutral. Such agreements were sometimes concluded even with Moslem states. In a treaty of 1154 between Pisa and Egypt it was agreed that Pisa should not participate in attacks of the Franks of Syria or in expeditions against Egypt. Though concerning neutrality, such treaties must be classified in the same category as treaties of alliance and even of subsidy, inasmuch as they bound each contracting party to grant to the other special favors which, in the absence of such an express treaty, it would not have been required to grant at all. The very fact that these treaties were entered into is conclusive evidence that in their absence each of the contracting parties would have been internationally free to lend aid to the enemies of the other.

MARITIME WARFARE

Unlike war on land, wars on sea between Italian states were continual and ferocious. The most important commercial interests and the very existence of the adversaries were at stake, which explains the intensity with which these wars were fought. During the twelfth and thirteenth centuries Genoa and Pisa were almost constantly fighting maritime wars, until the naval battle of Meloria, 1284, marked the end of Pisan power.[35] Venetian and Genoese fleets met with alternating success throughout the Mediterranean: at Durazzo, 1264; Trapani, 1265; Acre, 1267; in the Black Sea, 1294; at Laiazzo, 1294; at Galata, 1296; at Curzola in the Adriatic, 1298. It was only in the fifteenth century, when the military power of the two republics began to decline, that hostilities between them became less frequent.

To the harmful consequences of the rivalries between Italian cities there must be added those which were derived from the rivalries between citizens of the same state. In 1323 a great number of Genoese Guelphs, exiled and proscribed by their Ghibelline opponents, fitted out ships for privateering and operated throughout the Mediterranean, seizing Genoese ships and those of other nations indiscriminately. They thus collected a booty of more than 300,000 florins. Encouraged by their successes and impelled by the spirit of vengeance, they then entered the Black Sea, where they committed every sort of excess against the Genoese colonies, until they were all massacred treacherously, for lust of booty, by the Turkish lord of Sinope, who had received and welcomed them.[36]

[35] It is reported that in the battle of Meloria ten thousand Pisan prisoners were taken, an enormous figure in proportion to the population of Pisa in that period. From the great number of Pisan prisoners the saying arose: "Who wishes to see Pisa should go to Genoa."
[36] Pardessus, *Collection de lois maritimes antérieures au XVIIIe siècle*, III, 85.

The provisions of the *Consolato del mare* confirm that the normal relationship between the Italian states on the sea was war, interrupted only when they concluded a truce. International maritime law of the Mediterranean in that period contained several rules relative to the distribution of prizes, the capture and recapture of ships,[37] and other related matters. The distinction between combatants and noncombatants, which was coming into existence in land warfare, was not recognized upon the sea. The reason was that it was difficult to distinguish armed ships of a state and privateers from merchantships, and privateers from pirate ships, which then constituted one of the worst scourges of the Mediterranean. Merchantships were armed not only for defense; in fact, when these ships met an enemy vessel, they did not hesitate to attack her if they felt that they could capture her.[38] The rules of the *Consolato del mare* which in anticipation of such cases provided for the disposition of the booty, are ample evidence that this was current practice.[39]

Piracy, against Christians, as well as against Saracens, was such a great source of gain that Italian cities could not take effective measures against their subjects who practiced it. If not legally admitted, the practice was in many cases tolerated. If this had not been the case, it would be hard to understand why so many treaties with Saracen princes required Italian cities to forbid their citizens from practicing piracy against the subjects of the other party and to deny asylum in their ports to pirate ships. For the purpose of waging war against pirates, private associations of merchants were created. This general license of cruising against pirates, called *la guerra del corso*, degenerated in course of time into something very much akin to the evil practices that it was intended to suppress. In fact these societies of cruising merchants, or *corsari*, were allowed to appropriate to themselves the property which they captured at sea without bringing in their prizes for adjudication before disposing of them. Thus, *corsaro* became and still is in Italy synonymous with "pirate" rather than with "privateer." It became necessary for the Italian republics to regulate in its turn this practice of cruising. The statutes of many Italian maritime cities contained provisions relative to it. In general the *corsari* had to take an oath not to attack the ships of friends and were obliged to set up a bond (statutes of Pisa, 1298, and of Genoa, 1313 and 1316). In such a state of affairs it is natural that the cities would arrange for their ships to sail together for protection against enemies, *corsari*, and pirates. Treaties between Italian cities provided for the navigation of their ships in convoy or, in the words of those treaties, *di conserva*. Moreover, associations of merchants were created for the pur-

---

[37] *Consolato del mare*, sec. 287, in the aforementioned edition of Casaregis.
[38] *Ibid.*, sec. 169.   [39] *Ibid.*, secs. 245, 285.

pose of furnishing their own navies to escort other ships. Independent sovereigns enlisted into their services the armed fleets of these voluntary associations when the occasion presented itself to attack an enemy by sea or when it became necessary to defend themselves against any attack by sea.[40] There was a mercantile association at Pisa, called *Gli Umili* (The Humbles), which was constituted like an independent state, waging war and making conquests with a military marine of its own. It lent powerful aid to the prince of Antioch in 1188 and obtained from him in return special privileges for the company.

Naturally maritime neutrality was little more than a myth. The ships and the merchandise belonged to friends or enemies. Enemies were all those with whom there had not been expressly concluded a treaty of friendship. Ships and goods of enemies were good prizes. The rule was so obvious that the *Consolato del mare* declares that when an armed vessel meets a merchant vessel, if the latter as well as her cargo, belongs to the enemy, it would be useless to speak of it because everyone knows well enough what ought to be done; to lay down any rule in this case would be superfluous.[41] Frequently any ship that traded with enemy ports was considered subject to capture, thus rendering superfluous any provisions concerning blockade and contraband.[42]

The rigor of such principles induced the Italian states to conclude treaties both with each other and with Saracen princes in order to protect their marine. The clauses of some of these treaties are very liberal. In the treaty between Pisa and Tunis of 1264 it was agreed that ships could not be detained for any reason. In the treaty of 1290 between Genoa and the sultan of Egypt it was provided that even in case of war persons and ships of the contracting parties should be respected. In other treaties a time limit was established for persons and ships, within which they could depart in case of war. At the end of the fourteenth century it was often arranged that ships should be immune from reprisals. The right of angary was sometimes resorted to.[43] It was held that an indemnity should be paid in case of the loss of a ship so requisitioned.[44]

The distinction between friends and enemies at sea served as a basis

[40] Twiss, *The Law of Nations*, II, 143.

[41] Sections 227 and 228 provide for the case of ransom from imminent danger of capture or from actual capture by the enemy. The merchants or owners of the cargo were held to contribute to the ransom proportionally with the owners of the vessel.

[42] From the end of the sixteenth century Italian states undertook to capture all ships that carried arms and in general contraband of war to Moslem countries, even in peace time. See the cases discussed by Gentili, *Hispanicae advocationis libri duo*, Book I, chs. xx, xxv.

[43] Venetians in 1617 forced some English ships to unload and serve in the war against the Duke of Ossuna.

[44] See Gentili, *Hispanicae advocationis libri duo*, Book I, ch. xxvi: A request for payment for an English ship subject to angary by the Tuscans, who used her for an expedition against the Turks, during which she was lost.

for rules from which the first principles of neutrality emerged. Italian states followed and perhaps introduced the principle accepted by the *Consolato del mare* (sec. 273) that goods of friends found on an enemy ship were safe and that enemy goods on a friendly ship were a good prize, but did not subject the ship to condemnation. Equitable provisions governed the payment of freight for enemy goods captured on a friendly ship. These rules of the *Consolato* were confirmed in several special treaties. A treaty of 1221 between Pisa and Arles provided that when a ship of one of the two cities had on board goods of the enemy of the other party, these goods might be confiscated. Similar provisions were contained in the treaty between Genoa and England, 1460, which also provided that the captor should pay for the freight of the enemy goods captured on the neutral ship.[45] Similar principles were applied to enemy persons: they could be taken prisoner on board friendly ships,[46] and their passage had to be paid by the captor.[47] By way of exception the above-mentioned treaty between Pisa and Arles provided that enemies on friendly ships could not be made prisoners. According to the *Consolato del mare*, if the captain of the friendly ship refused to carry the goods seized on his vessel to the port designated by the captor, his ship could be sunk without compensation. It was generally admitted that the goods and the ships sold by the captor could not be reclaimed by the former owner except by payment of the price for which, after condemnation, they had been sold. Apparently, however, the same principle was not applied to goods bought from pirates, even through acquisition in good faith; because acquisition by pirates did not defeat the right of the former owner (*pirata non mutat dominium*).[48]

Already in the twelfth century the right of visit and search was recognized both by Christian and Mohammedan powers as a right of the belligerent with regard to neutrals. In 1164 the Pisans, then at war with the Genoese, seized a cargo on a Saracen ship, on the ground that it belonged to Genoese merchants. The sultan of Egypt did not deny the right to visit neutral ships and to seize any enemy cargo on board, but he protested against the seizure on the ground that the merchandise belonged to his

---

[45] "Nec caricabunt nec portabunt in navigiis eorum supradictis bona, aut mercimonia alicuius inimici nostri, aut inimicorum nostrorum, et casu quo fecerint petiti et interrogati per nostros, dicti Januenses debent immediate et sine dilatione (mediante juramento suo, cui subditi nostri fidem dabunt) veritatem dicere, et fateri quae et qualia bona inimicorum nostrorum, vel inimici, ducunt in navibus suis, et illa sine qua difficultate tradere et deliberare capitaneis vel ducentibus navigia nostra pro custodia maris, vel aliis subditis nostris, quos obviare contingeret navibus dictorum Januensium ubioumque super mare, recipiendo pro rata nauli vel affretamenti huiusmodi mercium inimicorum."

[46] See the case discussed by Gentili, *Hispanicae advocationis libri duo* Book I, ch. xxvi.

[47] Walker, *A History of the Law of Nations*, p. 136, notes that "the Venetians and Genoese when at war searched the ships of neutral Greeks and made prisoners of the subjects of their opponents found hidden on board."

[48] See the cases discussed by Gentili, *Hispanicae advocationis libri duo*, Book I, chs. xii, xv.

subjects. The validity of the claim was recognized by the Pisans, who released the cargo.

Toward the end of the fifteenth century the naval practice of the Italian cities underwent a noticeable change. The decadence of military power of the Italian maritime cities and the sense of solidarity among the Christian powers in face of the rising flood of Islam, forced all the Christian maritime powers of the Mediterranean, especially the Italians, to a greater reciprocal tolerance. It was then that the use of the sea became truly common to all people. The principle was established that the goods and the ships of a nation with whom there was no state of war ought to be respected even in the absence of a special treaty. The distinction between a neutral and an enemy was clearly drawn, with all the ensuing consequences in the question of contraband. Navigation became more peaceful, but not secure; as late as in 1485 Venice had a prolonged controversy with France concerning the depredation by a French pirate of four Venetian galleys. This deed, however, occurred in the Atlantic.

It should be noted that with regard to persons even in maritime warfare a certain leniency always prevailed. In case of the capture of a Christian ship by another Christian vessel the life of the crew, if not its liberty, was almost always spared, unless, of course, the captured crew consisted of pirates.

Chapter IV: ITALIAN DOCTRINES ON THE
INTERNATIONAL COMMUNITY

THE revival of Roman law that occurred in Europe in the twelfth and thirteenth centuries is undoubtedly the most important legal factor in the early development of the doctrine of international law. Sir Henry Maine observes that "a great part of international law is Roman law spread over Europe by a process exceedingly like that which, a few centuries earlier, had caused other portions of Roman law to filter into the interstices of every European legal system." [1]

The reason for the influence of Roman law in the early development of international law is obvious. The international community as it first developed in Italy during the thirteenth and fourteenth centuries was the opposite of the feudal organization. Therefore its juridical organization could not possibly be based on the principles of feudal law, but had to deduce its rules from a different system of law that would contain principles in better agreement with the nascent conception of territorial sovereignty. Such principles were to be found in the system of Roman law. Because of its intrinsic merits and especially because of its comprehensiveness and its universally recognized conformity with principles of right and justice common to all peoples, Roman law was admirably adapted to govern relations between peoples with diverse civilizations and juridical traditions. The patrimonial conception of the state prevalent at the period in which the international community arose favored the application to international law of principles of private law.

In addition to the intrinsic excellence of its particular provisions, Roman law furnished a complete dogmatic elaboration of fundamental institutions, upon which it was possible to pattern the new institutions of international law. The conception of territorial sovereignty was largely deduced from the Roman rules on real property; rules concerning international treaties were derived from the Roman rules as to the con-

---

[1] *International Law*, p. 20. See also Triepel, *Völkerrecht und Landesrecht*, pp. 221 ff.; Pound, "Philosophical Theory and International Law," 1 Bibliotheca Visseriana, 77 ff.; Lauterpacht, *Private Law Sources and International Law*, pp. 66 ff., and the other works quoted by him; Finch, *The Sources of Modern International Law*, pp. 4, 23. The idea of an international law was foreign to the juridical mind of the Romans. The so-called *jus gentium* or *jus naturale* was for them a compound of juridical principles common to the people that lived within the bounds of the empire, i.e., a part of the municipal law of the Roman Empire, not international law. See Fiore, *Diritto internazionale pubblico*, 4th ed., I, 15, and Finch, *The Sources of Modern International Law*, p. 4.

clusion, validity and interpretation of contracts; and those concerning diplomatic agents, considered at that time as the personal representatives of the sovereign, from the rules concerning the mandate.

Nor should it be forgotten, in fine, that the first founders of the science of international law were followers of the doctrines of natural law and held that international law should be in harmony with certain abstract principles of reason and justice: now in that age Roman law was considered the *ratio scripta*, and therefore it was believed that even international relations should be regulated in conformity with its precepts. For all these reasons principles of Roman law constituted the juridical framework of the nascent international community; they were the basis of natural law, which was one of the first sources of international law; they were also the foundation of many rules concerning territorial sovereignty, treaties, diplomatic missions, and other fundamental institutions of the law of nations.[2]

The rebirth of Roman law is an Italian phenomenon. By reviving the study of Roman law, the Italian schools of glossators and post-glossators laid the foundation upon which were to be based the legal organization of the international community and the new doctrines of international law.

TRANSFORMATION OF THE HOLY ROMAN EMPIRE INTO AN INTERNATIONAL COMMUNITY: BARTOLUS AND THE CIVITATES SUPERIOREM NON RECOGNOSCENTES

The contribution of Italian jurists to the development of international law is not limited to this preparatory work of a general character.[3] To the Italian post-glossators, especially to Bartolus, also belongs the merit of having understood and decisively pointed out the radical change which took place in the thirteenth and fourteenth centuries in the structure of the Holy Roman Empire. This, from a unitary organism under the supreme power of the emperor, disintegrated into an international

---

[2] When for the first time an international community arose, international practice was too recent, rare, and uncertain to make possible the deduction of precise rules from it. It was therefore to a great extent necessary to resort to rules elaborated by scholars. So in the beginning the works of jurists were a veritable source of international law, whereas this is no longer true today. Thanks to the industry of writers, principles of Roman law became principles of international law. As late as 1777 Neyron, in his *Essai historique et politique sur les garanties*, wrote that "many principles of Roman law, salutary in themselves and independent of Roman constitutions, have been adopted by the European powers and retained by reason of their intrinsic value until today." It was only at a later period, when the nature of international relations came to be distinguished from that of private law, that many rules of international law acquired a content of their own independent of the principles of Roman law.

[3] For the Italian writings on international law of this period see, in addition to the works on the history of international law already mentioned, Ompteda, *Litteratur des gesamten sowohl natürlichen als positiven Völkerrechts*, and Rivier, *Notes sur la litterature du droit des gens avant la publication du Jus belli ac pacis de Grotius.*

community endowed with those fundamental characteristics which it retains to this day.

The idea of an international community composed of equal and autonomous entities not subject to a common authority was foreign to the minds of the early Italian lawyers of the Renaissance. To the glossators there could be no doubt that every secular power in Europe was subject in fact and in law to the supreme authority of the emperor, heir and successor to the *populus Romanus*. This principle, which implied the denial of the possible existence of an international community, composed of equal and independent states, was affirmed by them with relation to the conflicts between the emperor and the Italian cities. At the Diet of Roncaglia (1158) the "four doctors" of the University of Bologna, applying the doctrines of Roman law and the principles of feudal law, reaffirmed the rights of the Emperor Frederick Barbarossa over the Italian cities and declared them imprescriptible, thus incurring the ire of Placentinus, another Italian jurist of that time (1135–1192), who branded them as "Miserable Bolognese, traitors of Italian liberty." But when the authority of the emperor over the Italian cities, diminished by the defeat of Legnano (1176) and the provisions of the Peace of Constance (1183), within a little more than a century fell into desuetude, the Italian jurists were quick to grasp and to expound the legal principles that sprang from the new political situation in Italy.

The most authoritative representative of this new Italian doctrine of public law is Bartolus of Sassoferrato, whose importance in the field of legal thought during the Italian Renaissance can be equaled only by that of Dante, Marsilio of Padua, and Machiavelli in the field of political theory.[4] For Bartolus the supreme political and juridical authority is still legally, *de jure*, vested in the emperor, but his almost mystical reverence for the emperor did not prevent his understanding of the situation of the Italian cities of his time, already emancipated from the imperial authority. Thus he points out that whereas the emperor possesses *de jure* authority over the entire empire and *de facto* exercises this authority in Germany, no *de facto* authority is exercised by him over the Italian cities. "Imperator est modo in Alemannia et de jure est superior, tamen de facto in partibus istis ei non paretur." [5] In Perugia, where

---

[4] For the political and legal ideas of Bartolus see Hrabar, "L'Époque de Bartole (1314–1358) dans l'histoire du droit international," 7 Rev. gén. dr. int. publ. (1900) 732 ff.; Woolf, *Bartolus of Sassoferrato*; Figgis, "Bartolus and the Development of European Political Ideas," in *The Divine Right of Kings*; Carlyle, *A History of Medieval Political Thought in the West*, Vol. IV; Ercole, *Dal comune al principato* and *Da Bartolo all'Altusio*; Zancla, *La dottrina della sovranità dello stato e il problema dell'autorità internazionale in Bartolo*; Kamp, *Bartolo da Sassoferrato*.

[5] "The Emperor still is in Germany and *de jure* is superior, but *de facto* they do not obey him in these parts." *Tractatus represaliarum*, quaestio II, 5, sec. 12.

Bartolus taught for a long time, "the people is free." [6] Florence, where he certainly had the opportunity of sojourning, and the other cities of Tuscany had cast off the authority of the emperor.[7] Almost all the Italian cities, Bartolus observes, do not in fact recognize any authority over them, "non recognoscunt de facto superiorem." On the other hand, they exercise *de facto* full authority over their subjects.

This political situation gives rise to new principles of law: the independence and equality of the Italian cities. In solemn words Bartolus affirms that these cities are now independent.

"Cum quaelibet civitas Italiae . . . hodie dominum non recognoscat, in se habet liberum populum et habet merum imperium in ipsa et tantam potestatem habet in populo quantam imperator in universo." [8]

In other words, these Italian cities have now become autonomous powers, not subject to any other sovereignty than their own: "Ipsae sunt principes sibi ipsis." [9] In a famous passage Bartolus declares that there are "civitates quae principem non recognoscunt ut dominum et sic populus liber est . . . quia ipsamet civitas sibi princeps est." [10]

With a lively understanding, with an exact vision of the political reality of his age, Bartolus, under cover of theoretical deductions, builds up a legal order of *de facto* institutions based upon the actual existence of these independent Italian cities, "civitates superiorem non recognoscentes," [11] capable of establishing their own government and law.[12] For the very reason that they are *de facto* independent, the Italian cities have the right to wage war, the highest and most exclusive prerogative of sovereignty.[13] A war between Italian cities "superiorem non recognoscentes" is not a civil strife or a rebellion against the emperor, but a true example of public warfare.

---

[6] Ad Cod. tres libri, C, XI, 32, 3.   [7] Ad Dig. nov. II, D, XLVII, 22, 4, 20.

[8] "Some Italian cities . . . nowadays do no longer recognize a superior lord. They have within themselves free people, and have full *imperium* over themselves, and have as much power over their people as the Emperor has over the universe." Ad Dig. nov. II, XLVII, 1, 7.

[9] "They are the only princes over themselves." Ad Dig. nov. II, D, XLVIII, 19, 4.

[10] "Cities which do not recognize a prince as lord over them, so that their people are free . . . because the city itself is its own prince." Ad Dig. vet. I, D, IV, L, 3.

[11] Ercole, in "Le origini francesi di una nota formula bartoliana," 4 Archivio storico italiano (1915) 241 ff., and authors cited there have proved that the formula "civitates superiorem non recognoscentes" was in reality a formula of French origin, probably introduced into Italy by Italian jurisconsults, like Cino da Pistoia, Oldrado da Ponte, and Andrea d'Isernia, who taught in France. The formula had, however, its completest elaboration in Italy and owes its celebrity to Bartolus and Baldus. Baldus formulated it in the following terms, which have become proverbial: "Rex in regno suo est Imperator regni sui." He was considered its inventor even by French writers who later made use of the formula to lay claim to the independence of the king of France with regard to the emperor.

[12] Winogradoff, "Historical Types of International Law," 1 *Bibliotheca Visseriana* (1923) 44.

[13] Ad Dig. nov. II, D, XLVIII, 4, 3: "Nota quod ille qui preparat exercitum sine jussu superioris, incidit in legem Juliam majestatis. Sed hodie civitates Italiae possunt licite preparare exercitum contra subditos et inimicos suos, cum dominum non recognoscunt."

All the cities, however, all the states, are in Bartolus's mind co-ordinated within the empire. The emperor is the Lord of the world: to deny it would be heresy. "Et forte si quis diceret dominum Imperatorem non esse Dominum et Monarcham totius orbis, esset haereticus." [14] The apparent contradiction between the superiority of the empire and the independence of the Italian cities is resolved with the affirmation that the aims pursued by both powers are identical, since both are directed toward the welfare of mankind. As the aim of every *civitas* is the good of all its citizens, the aim of the empire, as the world's supreme temporal institution, is the good of all humanity and the conservation of Christian unity in the fight against infidels.[15] Thus the superiority of the empire over the cities is admitted on a purely ideal plane. Bartolus's elevation of the empire to the function of a spiritual institution amounts to a complete denial of its political authority, in accordance with the reality of the age. The empire is envisaged by Bartolus as the necessary universal society, in which all the powers of Christendom must co-operate. In Italy, Dante, Marsilio of Padua, Cino da Pistoia, and many other political thinkers, jurisconsults, and poets had invoked the authority of the empire on the same ideal plane. The empire was to have been the unifying force of the Christian world, to have appeased all discords, suppressed wars and reprisals, affirmed the reign of peace and justice on the earth. For Bartolus as well as for these other Italians the empire was then but a messianic dream, an ideal aspiration.

If we are to understand the superiority of the empire over the independent Italian cities in this ideal and limited sense, it becomes evident that, when Bartolus speaks of the juridical situation of the Italian cities, he enounces and applies those principles which still today are at the basis of the international community. The Italian cities, not subject to a superior authority, capable of negotiating treaties, of concluding peace, and of waging war, equal among themselves and supreme over their subjects, correspond to the modern states; the empire, understood as the organization co-ordinating the various independent cities, is the equivalent of the modern international community within which the independent states operate.[16] As the Italian society of the Renaissance is in fact the microcosm of the modern international society, so Bartolus, who realizes its characteristic aspects, is the first theorist of international law.[17]

[14] De captivis et postliminio reversis.   [15] Zancla, *La dottrina della sovranità*, p. 49.

[16] Balladore Pallieri, "Le dottrine di Hans Kelsen e il problema del rapporti tra diritto interno e diritto internazionale," 27 *Riv. dir. int.* (1935) 69: "When Dante and the other writers of the age asked for a restoration of imperial authority, so necessary for the peace of the states, they actually complained, to put it in modern words, of the sad circumstances of international law which was without the support of the emperor's authority, in exactly the same way in which people complain today of the lack of any superior authority in the international order able to control the states."

[17] Goebel, *Equality of States*, pp. 28–29.

In his admirable work on Bartolus, Cecil W. S. Woolf, in spite of his unbounded admiration for the great jurisconsult, observes that he is still far from the beginnings of international law for two reasons: in the first place, Bartolus still recognizes the existence of the empire, and not of an international community; secondly, Bartolus still thinks in terms of Roman law, not of international law.[18]

These two arguments, however, are not convincing. As to the first, it may be observed that from a historical point of view there is no real contrast between the Holy Roman Empire and the international community. The modern international society is but the same empire transformed and amplified, and Bartolus, who lived during the epoch in which this process of transformation was going on and in Italy, where the phenomenon was most striking, had more than anyone else the merit of calling attention to the legal aspects of this transformation. It is true that Bartolus still speaks of the "Holy Roman Empire" and does not expressly refer to an international community. Nevertheless, he is the first to enrich the concept of empire and to portray it as similar to the international community of today.

Bartolus not only transforms the juridical conception of the empire; in a few passages he goes so far as to deny even its actual universality. In his classification of the peoples of the earth Bartolus observes that there exist peoples who live outside the empire. These peoples are to be divided into several categories: those who are *foederati*, that is, allies of the empire in its struggle against the Turks—for example, the Greeks, who belong to the Christian community, but not to the empire; those, like the Tartars, who do not belong to the Christian community, and yet the empire is at peace with them and has international dealings with them; finally, those like the Saracens and later the Turks, with whom there is eternal warfare. With other peoples, the Indians, no international relations whatsoever exist, because with them, as Bartolus puts it in his uncouth Latin, "non habemus pacem nec guerram, nec aliquid facere." [19] This passage clearly affirms the existence of an international community including peoples not belonging to the Holy Roman Empire, such as the Greeks, the Tartars, and even the Turks, for strictly speaking the Turks, too, belong to the international community, even if rela-

---

[18] *Bartolus of Sassoferrato*, pp. 201 ff.

[19] Ad Dig. nov. De captivis et postliminio reversis et redemptis ab hostibus: "Quidam ex istis sunt nobis foederati ut erant Graeci nobis foederati contra Turchos. Quidam sunt cum quibus habemus pacem ut Tartari nam merchatores nostri vadunt ad illos et illi ad nostros. Quidam sunt cum quibus non habemus pacem nec guerram, nec aliquid facere. ut cum illis de Indis. Quidam sunt cum quibus habemus guerram indictam ut cum Saracenis et hodie cum Turchis."

This opinion by Bartolus, which perhaps is derived from some earlier writer, was generally accepted by those that succeeded him. In fact, we find it reproduced almost literally by Giovanni da Legnano, *Tractatus de bello de represaliis et de duello*, and by Angelo da Perugia, brother of Baldus (In L. Summa, Dig. XXXIX, 3).

tions with them, according to this passage, are restricted to war. Vice versa, the Indians do not belong to the international community, since with them there is no international intercourse, neither of peace nor of war.

The second criticism, that Bartolus still thinks in terms of Roman rather than international law, is founded largely on a misunderstanding. To be sure, Bartolus did refer almost constantly to principles of Roman law in solving problems which today would be considered as pertaining to the sphere of international law; but this does not imply the absence in Bartolus of a clear understanding that he was dealing with matters not within the realm of private law. The truth is rather, as has already been said, that the international law of that age was in the main Roman law. It was only later that international law acquired distinct content and autonomous characteristics of its own.[20] Nor should it be overlooked that although Bartolus strenuously endeavored to attach his theories of public law on principles of Roman law, in reality he came to establish new rules of international law. To deny the originality of Bartolus's theories simply because he appealed to principles of Roman law would be tantamount to denying the originality of great artists of the Renaissance, such as Bramante, Mantegna, and Michelangelo because they built, painted, and modeled with their eyes turned intently toward the models of classical antiquity.

The harshness of his antiquated formulas; his very celebrity in the field of private law, which darkened his fame as a publicist; and the impression that can arise from a hasty reading of his works that he was a defender of the temporal power of the emperor against the independence of the states cast a shadow over Bartolus's fame in the field of international law.[21] With his peculiar absence of all historical sense, Grotius was incapable of understanding Bartolus's problems. The Dutch jurist held that Bartolus was a champion of the one and only empire, ruled by an emperor to whom the world owed obedience [22] and that therefore he

[20] Vollenhoven, *The Law of Peace*, p. 36, remarks that "Medieval law is built on the solid foundation of recognition of a common law applying equally to kings and to their subjects, to international no less than to domestic relations." But the fact, that international law and internal law were governed by the same principles does not justify the author's statement, *ibid.*, p. 34, that "there was just no separation between the spheres of international and national law."

[21] The strangest accusations were flung at Bartolus and his school. According to Alciatus, the Bartolists were *blaterones, insipientes, improbi, avari*. The Latin of Bartolus, according to Rabelais, was a "latin de cuisinier et marmiteux, non de jurisconsulte."

[22] *De jure belli ac pacis*, Book II, ch. xxii, 13: "I should hardly trouble to add that the title which certain persons give to the Roman Emperor is absurd, as if he had the right of ruling over even the most distant and hitherto unknown peoples, were it not that Bartolus, long considered first among jurists, had dared to pronounce him a heretic who denies to the Emperor this title."

was opposed to the establishment of independent states. On the contrary, Bartolus merely affirmed the need for a general organization superior to the states, but not incompatible with their independence.[23] To a generation that is experiencing today the grave evils arising from the lack of any authority superior to the states and from the want of a solid organization of the international community, the ideas of Bartolus acquire a flavor of modernity which emphasizes even more strongly the loftiness of his conception.

Bartolus's ideas were at the basis of those treaties, mainly Spanish, of the sixteenth century, affirming the idea of a universal community not limited to the Holy Roman Empire and to the *Respublica Christiana*.[24] As Walker observes:

Combining with the denial of the universal sovereignty of the Emperor and the more daring of the universal temporal Lordship of the Pope, the acceptance of those conceptions of Nature and Universal Law with which ancient Roman and medieval civilians had made the world familiar, the Spanish divines represented Christendom as a society of independent princes and free commonwealths with rights *inter se*, defined by *Jus naturale et gentium*, and so advanced a new theory of international law.[25]

Francisco de Victoria (1483–1546), a student of Bartolus, in his famous *Relectiones, De Indis noviter inventis*, and *De jure belli*, prepared in 1532 and published for the first time in 1557, affirmed that the law of nations should also apply to relations between Spaniards and Indians, even if the latter were not Christians. Under natural law the Indians had full ownership, "privatim et publice," of their country; this could not be denied, because even infidel nations, whether they were Saracens or Jews, had a right of ownership over the territories where they lived. The Spaniards therefore had no right to resort to the excuse that the Indians were not Christians in order to wage war on them and take possession of their country.

Another Spaniard, on whom Bartolus also had influence, Covarruvias (1517–1577),[26] definitively solved in the negative the theoretical

[23] Figgis, "Bartolus and the Development of European Political Ideas," in his *The Divine Right of Kings*, p. 343: "Grotius and Gentili and Bodin not merely quote Bartolus, but are what they are largely because of him."

[24] *Ibid.*, p. 359. The influence of the Italian theological and juridical doctrines on Spanish scholars and especially theologians can be no cause for surprise if we consider the frequent visits of Spanish ecclesiastics to Rome, particularly under the Pontificates of Calixtus III (1435–1458) and Alexander VI (1492–1503), both of the Spanish family of the Borgias. There was a continuous flow of Spanish students to the University of Bologna, where the Spanish College, that still exists, had been founded to receive them, under the will of the celebrated Cardinal Albornoz.

[25] *A History of the Law of Nations*, pp. 213–214. For the Spanish school of international law see Scott, *The Spanish Origin of International Law*.

[26] *Opera omnia*.

question, so often debated in that age, whether the emperor was the sovereign of the entire world.[27]

The ideas of Victoria, Covarruvias, Soto (1494–1560),[28] and the other Spanish theologians of the age in their turn profoundly influenced Alberico Gentili (1552–1608),[29] whose work shall be considered in greater detail further on. Gentili resorted to arguments already used by Covarruvias to deny the universal sovereignty of the emperor, to whom in particular he denied the right to lay claim to the provinces, which at one time belonged to the Roman Empire but in the age of Gentili no longer belonged to it.[30] According to Gentili, the secular power of the pope, too, was considerably reduced, and his spiritual authority was confined to those who still recognized his rule. While he restricts the power of the pope and the emperor, Gentili affirms the existence of an international community. All the peoples on the earth, even those yet unknown, are united in the *societas humana*, or *societas gentium*, governed by the *jus gentium*, or international law.[31] The *societas gentium* comprises on a footing of absolute equality the heretics and the infidels.[32] Gentili denies, to be sure, the lawfulness of a treaty of alliance with the infidels, but on the other hand he admits the lawfulness of the other forms of international intercourse with them, for example, the validity of commercial treaties. A law superior to the single nations, which can be only international law, governs the relations between Christians and infidels.

The idea of an international community with a law of its own regulating the relations between all the peoples underwent, then, from Bartolus to Gentili a continuous evolution, influenced by political changes.

[27] On the influence of Spanish writers of that period over international law see Barcia Trelles, "Francisco Suarez (1548–1617); Les Théologiens espagnols du xviᵉ siècle et l'école moderne du droit international," 43 Rec. des cours (1933) 385 ff.; Hentschel, "Franciscus de Victoria und seine Stellung zum Völkerrecht," 17 Zeitschrift für öffentliches Recht (1937) 388 ff.; Von der Heidte, "Franciscus de Victoria und seine Völkerrecht," 13 Zeitschrift für öffentliches Recht (1933) 239 ff.; Scott, *The Catholic Conception of International Law* and *The Spanish Origin of International Law*; Verdross, *Die Verfassung der Völkerrechtsgemeinschaft*, pp. 23 ff.; Wright, *Catholic Founders of Modern International Law* and *Francisci de Victoria De jure belli relectio*.

[28] Soto, *Libri decem de justitia et jure*.

[29] Molen, *Alberico Gentili and the Development of International Law*, pp. 109–110, 114–115. This author remarks that Gentili cannot have felt the influence of Suarez, because the work of the latter on international law, the *Tractatus de legibus ac Deo legislatore*, did not appear before 1612. after the death of Gentili. The plan of this book renders it advisable for us to postpone discussion of Gentili's life and the general aspects of his work until a later section.

[30] *De jure belli*, Book I, ch. 22. p. 178, and ch. 23, pp. 180–185. The quotations refer to the edition of the *De jure belli* of 1612, reprinted in the "Classics of International Law." The English translation, published in the same edition, gives in the margin the pagination of the Latin edition.

[31] *De iure belli*, pp. 2. 9. 107. 119. 121. 202, 475.

[32] Molen. *Alberico Gentili and the Development of International Law*, p. 242: "The *societas gentium*, round which Gentili builds up his international law, includes the whole world, also beyond the pale of Christianity. It is worth mentioning that he also includes the Turks among others in the community of international law, as completely equal partners."

Bartolus still conceives the Holy Roman Empire as a living reality or at least as a moral value; yet, at the same time, he takes the first steps toward its transformation into an international society of equal and independent members and toward the transformation of the law of the empire into international law. Moreover, in a few passages of Bartolus's work the concept is already discernible that the human community, governed by the law of nations, is not limited to the peoples belonging to the empire. The Spanish jurisconsults, who taught in an age when the empire has become a mere fiction were confronted with the problem of the relations with the native population of the Americas, which never belonged to the empire, and to the *Respublica Christiana*. So they denied the universal authority of the empire and posited the existence of a universal community embracing all the peoples without distinction of religion. It was also the Spanish theologians who affirmed the existence of a body of rules derived from the precepts of natural justice and destined to regulate the relations between all the peoples belonging to this universal community.

Gentili, with the ability of a political expert and with the rigor of a lawyer, once more took up the problem. As a public man, living in England in the sixteenth century, he understood the essence of the modern states, which were then coming into being. As a lawyer he laid down the basis of a system no longer solely moral, but rigorously juridical, that was to regulate the relations between these states. In this way the philosophico-theological speculations of the Spanish were by him transformed into a body of juridical rules suited to the needs of the international society of his age. Such rules, although formulated with the aid of Roman law, constituted a system distinct from this and based upon the principles of natural justice. In this way from Bartolus to Gentili the cycle was completed and the foundations were laid for an international law.[33]

The Italian school of glossators and post-glossators must also be credited with having contributed to a notable degree to the development of the theory and practice of private international law and of the conflict of law. Italians and Frenchmen, educated in the school of the glossators and the post-glossators, expounded in Italy the statutory theory, the first doctrine of private international law.[34] This doctrine spread in the six-

[33] As late as the end of the sixteenth century there were still Italian jurisconsults who endeavored to maintain the supremacy and the universality of the authority of the pope and the emperor. Let us mention Ristoro Castaldi of Perugia, who lived toward the middle of the sixteenth century, author of a treatise *Tractatus de imperatore*, and Francesco Giovannetti of Bologna (d. 1586) author of a treatise *De Romano imperio ac eius jurisdictione*. The two treatises were reprinted in Vol. XVI of Ziletti, *Tractatus*.

[34] The most noteworthy representatives of the Italian statutory school, besides Baldus and Bartolus, were Cino da Pistoia (Cinus de Pistorio, 1270–1336), Alberico da Rosate (Albericus de Rosciate, d. 1354), Bartolomeo da Saliceto (Bartholomaeus de Saliceto, d. 1441), Paolo di

teenth century to France and subsequently to Holland; from there it passed to England and the United States.

In northern Italy, every city, as it attained its independence, had also acquired the power of enacting its own municipal laws, called statutes: besides, they were all governed by the common law of Italy, that is, of the empire. Hence numerous questions relating to the co-ordination of the statutes with the common law and to the respective spheres of application of one statute with regard to another. It was these questions that the doctrine of the statutes was called upon to solve. Obviously the problems considered by the theory of the statutes were not in themselves problems of international law. In fact, private international law and conflict of laws are a part of municipal, not of international, law. For this reason the doctrine of the statutes is not taken into consideration in this work. However, in considering the problems of private international law, the followers of the statutory theory had frequent occasions to affirm that the rules relating to conflicts between laws issued by the various cities had to conform to certain superior principles of justice, which each state was expected to follow. These superior rules were dictated by the *jus gentium*. The *jus gentium* imposed on every state the obligation of recognizing a minimum of rights for all foreigners and to recognize, within certain limits, the authority of foreign laws, judgments, and acts. In cases of conflict of laws, statutes should be disregarded which contained provisions contrary to these precepts of the *jus gentium*. Bartolus also referred to the *jus gentium* in order to determine what was the law governing a will executed by a diplomatic agent abroad.[35] For the post-glossators the *jus gentium* was not, as it was for the Romans, a part of the municipal law of the empire, dealing with relations between persons belonging to various peoples. On the contrary, it was a superior and universal law, to which the law of every country had to be subordinated. Therefore the authority of the *jus gentium* was not confined within the empire, but was applied even outside Christendom. Baldus, in a consultation relating to the validity of a will executed by a merchant of Ancona in Babylon (Cairo), in the land of infidels, invokes the *jus*

Castro (Paulus de Castro or Castrensis, d. 1441), Alessandro Tartagni (Alexander Tartagnus, o de Tartagnis, d. 1477). Of the Frenchmen we may recall Guillaume Durant (Durantis, d. 1296), Jacques de Révigny (Jacobus de Ravena, d. 1296), Pierre de Belleperche (Petrus a Bellapertica d. 1308), Barthélemy Chasseneux (Bartholomaeus a Chassaneo, 1480–1541), and, last of all, the two famous jurisconsults André Tiraqueau (Tiraquellus, 1480–1558) and Charles Dumoulin (Molinaeus, 1500–1560). For the Italian period of the theory of the Statutes, Lainé, *Introduction au droit international privé*; Catellani, *Il diritto internazionale privato*; Beale, *Bartolus and the Conflict of Law*; Gutzwiller, "Le Développement historique du droit international privé," 29 *Rec. des Cours* (1929) 287 ff.; and *Der Einfluss Savignys auf die Entwicklung des Internationalprivatrechts*. See also the works already quoted of Anzilotti, Bonolis, Kohler, Meili, and Neumeyer.

[35] Bartolus, in Dig. quia a latronibus, D. 28, 1, 13.

gentium, not the law of the empire: "nam istud jus gentium est bonum et equum, ergo servandum . . . sed jus imperatoris non viget ubique locorum." [36]

Since this *jus gentium* operates everywhere as a limitation to the sovereignty of the states, it should be identified with international law. That the post-glossators recognized the existence of a body of rules of international law concerning the conflict of laws, is clearly pointed out by Meijers. The Dutch scholar writes: "We found among the post-glossators as the basis of private international law the same principles which today are still expounded: the sovereignty of the states over persons and things, an international law which sets limits to sovereignty, and the principle of the autonomy of parties." [37]

By affirming the existence of rules of international law with which the states were bound to comply in matters of private international law, the "statutists" attributed to international law a sphere of application much more extensive than it has today. Their conception, as has been seen, coincided with the positive law of their age, whereas today it would be difficult to maintain that a state is bound to recognize foreign laws, judgments, and acts in the absence of specific treaty obligations to that effect.

Many of the rules affirmed by the statutists were general principles of justice, desumed from Roman law, the maxims of which they generalized.[38] The rules originally enunciated by the scholars developed into rules of positive law, since the doctrine at that period was a real source of international law.

SOVEREIGNTY OVER LAND AND SEA

The influence of Roman law extended to almost all the theories of international law expounded by the Italian jurisconsults of the Renaissance. The doctrine of the sovereignty of the states, which exerted such a notable influence on the development of international law, was inspired by Roman conceptions. When the empire declined, the Italian cities,

---

[36] Baldus, in Cod. 6, 32, 2.

[37] Meijers, "L'Histoire des principes fondamentaux du droit international privé à partir du moyen âge," 49 Rec. des Cours (1934) III, 635.

[38] It would be beyond the scope of the present study to consider all the consequences deduced by the statutists from the existence of rules of international law relating to the treatment of foreigners and to the recognition of foreign acts and laws. They extended to all the fields of private law. Problems that are usually thought to be of recent origin, such for instance as that of double taxation, were discussed by Bartolus, Baldus and Oldrado da Ponte (Cf. Seligman, "La Double imposition et la coopération fiscale internationale," 20 Rec. des Cours (1927), 790). The existence of rules of international law concerning the jurisdiction on crimes committed abroad and the recognition of foreign judgments in penal matters was recognized in Italy, in addition to Bartolus by Gandinus (d. circa 1300) and Clarus (d. 1575). See Kohler, "Beiträge zum internationalen Strafrecht," 5 Zeitschrift für internationales Recht (1895) 232 ff., and *Internationales Strafrecht.*

which in the meantime had consolidated their independence and extended their own domination over the neighboring territories, strove to
affirm their own absolute authority to the exclusion of any other power
whatsoever over the subjected territories.

The new conception thus arose of territorial sovereignty, a typical
product of the Renaissance.[39] The new doctrine could not be based upon
principles of feudal law, because the latter accepted the opposing conception of the possible co-existence on the same territory of a hierarchy
of property rights, which limited and completed each other. On the contrary, it was natural to have recourse to the principles of Roman law,
which viewed the right of the owner over his land as the absolute and
exclusive dominion over the *res*. The reference to the principles of Roman law on property was also favored, as we have already remarked,
by the development then beginning of the patrimonial conception of
sovereignty.

The Roman concept of the *res extra commercium* was invoked in order to give a legal basis to certain anomalous situations in international
law. To explain the exercise on the part of one state of jurisdiction over
the territory of another, Baldus refers to the Roman conception of pre-
dial servitudes, observing that such jurisdiction was "quasi servitudinis
sive ac similitudinis servitudinum." [40] The conception of international
servitudes in this way began to be formed.

The Roman concept of the *res extra commercium* was invoked in order to establish the principle of the freedom of the seas. It would not seem
that the Romans admitted this principle. To them the Mediterranean was
the *mare nostrum*, over which they exerted their sway not only in order
to free it from pirates, but also to exclude from it their own competitors
—first the Carthaginians and later any people that was not federated
with the Romans. Roman jurisconsults, such as Paulus, Ulpian, and Mar-
cianus had taught that the sea was a *res extra commercium*; by that they
had meant to affirm merely that the sea could not be the object of private
property.[41]

The distinction in Roman law between *res in commercio*, which are
susceptible to appropriation, and *res extra commercium*, which are not,
was transposed by the Italian jurisconsults of the Renaissance from the
sphere of private to that of international relations, in order to affirm that
there were parts of the earth's surface which could not be subjected
by any state to its exclusive dominion. Among these were the high seas.
We have here a typical example of the procedure frequently followed

[39] The development in Italy of the concept of territorial sovereignity was also aided by the
geographical nature of the country which, as we have mentioned, permitted the laying down
of exact boundaries between the states along the natural frontiers.

[40] Cf. Crusen, "Les Servitudes internationales," 22 Rec. des Cours (1928), 15.

[41] Gidel, *Le Droit international public de la mer*, III, 35.

by the Italian jurists of the Renaissance, consisting of the creation of entirely new principles by means of an arbitrary interpretation of Roman
texts.

When they taught that the high seas are free, the Italian lawyers of
the Renaissance meant to affirm only that no state could prevent the
other peoples from using them freely for navigation and fishing. This
did not signify that the high seas were not subject to the empire of any
law; had that been true, no magistrate could have punished piracy and
other crimes committed on the high seas, with great detriment to the
security of navigation. What they intended to say was that the *dominium*,
that is, full sovereignty over the high seas, could not be acquired by any
state; whereas *jurisdictio*, that is, that aggregate of powers required for
punishing wrongs and repressing piracy could be acquired by every
state.

The principle of the freedom of the high seas and the distinction between *dominium* and *jurisdictio* originated at the beginning of the
Renaissance and were maintained throughout this period. These legal
concepts underwent, however, an evolution, corresponding to the changes
in Europe's political situation; this may be noted especially with regard
to the *jurisdictio*. To the glossators, who lived in the age of the full
splendor of the imperial idea, it was only natural that the jurisdiction
over the high seas should belong exclusively to the emperor: "Mare est
commune, quo ad usus: sed proprietas est nullius: sicut aer est com-
munis usu: proprietas tamen est nullius . . . sed jurisdictio est
Caesaris." That is what the gloss taught.[42] But this conception gradually
changed as the authority of the empire declined and the rise of the great
independent maritime powers made itself felt.

The transformation undergone by the doctrine is especially evident
in Alberico Gentili, who lived in the epoch in which the states had
achieved their full independence and taught in England when she was
becoming a great maritime power. Although a follower of the traditional
doctrine, Gentili modified it considerably. To Gentili the law governing the high seas is no longer the law of the empire, but international
law; in accordance with the precepts of natural law, the rules of the *jus
gentium* guarantee the freedom of the high seas. These are not susceptible
of *dominium*, but *jurisdictio* over them may be exerted by every sovereign state [43] in order to punish crimes committed at sea and to repress

---

[42] Glossa ad Dig. 1, 8, 2. Fenn, "Origins of the Theory of Territorial Waters," 20 Am. J. Int.
L. (1926) 466, observes that it seems impossible that any modern idea of sovereignty could
have entered in the doctrine of the glossators concerning the jurisdiction of the Roman people
or of Caesar over the seas.

[43] Gentili, *De Jure belli libri tres*, chs. 4, 19. In the *Hispanicae advocationis libri duo*, Book
I, ch. 8, Gentili reasserted the distinction between *dominium et jurisdictio* with reference to a
case he encountered during his practice of law. The Dutch had captured, on the high seas,

piracy. This jurisdiction, however, should not degenerate into abuse; that sovereign who refuses the sea to others will bring war upon himself, and whoever is refused this privilege of nature may lawfully wage war against him.[44]

That those ideas were vital and useful from a practical point of view is demonstrated by the fact that today they are still followed substantially in international practice. The freedom of the high seas, now universally admitted, does not exclude the right on the part of every state to exercise a large measure of jurisdiction over events that may have occurred on them. The principle was declared by the Permanent Court of International Justice in the case of the "Lotus." Particularly the principle by which every state has the right to repress piracy on the high seas continues to belong to positive international law.

The conception of a territorial sea, on the contrary, developed outside Roman sources. The Romans, who considered that the entire sea was subject to their sway, had no reason for setting up a distinction between the high seas and the sea adjoining the coast. It was only during the early Renaissance, when the Italian maritime cities started to advance claims upon the neighboring waters, that the doctrine of territorial waters commenced to be developed in the Mediterranean through the ingenuity of Italian jurisconsults.[45]

The impossibility of connecting the new doctrine to principles of Roman law explains how the jurists who first expounded it were canon lawyers rather than civil lawyers. Inasmuch as it was held that the Roman texts affirmed the principle of the freedom of the seas,[46] the doctrine

---

a ship belonging to their Spanish enemy, but they were surprised, still on the high seas, by the English, who brought the captors and the prize to an English harbor, where the Spaniards were freed and got their property back. The Dutch demanded the restitution of the prize, alleging that the action of the English had been unlawful, since there was no war between the Dutch and the English and the latter had acted on the high seas. Gentili, who defended the Spaniards, maintained the lawfulness of the action of the English, alleging that it had taken place during the exercise of the *jurisdictio* of the King of England on the high seas, directed at ending a conflict in which the Spaniards, with whom he was on friendly terms, were involved. The argument in all truth seems a specious one. Potter, in *The Freedom of the Seas in History, Law and Politics*, p. 53, affirms that with regard to the question of the freedom of the seas that "Gentilis did attain a more balanced position than any writer, with perhaps one exception (Stypmann, 1652) was to attain for over a century. . . . Needless to say, Gentili's was a voice crying in a wilderness of confusion and contention."

[44] *De jure belli libri tres*, Book *1*, ch. 19; see also Molen, *Alberico Gentili and the Development of International Law: His Life, Work and Times*, p. 165.

[45] The concept of territorial waters, spread throughout the Mediterranean by the efforts of Italian jurisconsults, was developed in a thoroughly independent fashion in the countries bordering on the North Sea, which as early as the thirteenth and fourteenth centuries considered their territorial waters part of their territory. See Fedozzi, *Trattato di diritto internazionale; introduzione e parte generale*, p. 381.

[46] For the difficulties encountered by the jurisconsults of the seventeenth century in their attempt to reconcile the principle of the freedom of the seas, which they believed had been affirmed by the Roman jurists, with the principle of the sovereignty of the coastal state over its territorial waters see Cansacchi, *L'occupazione dei mari costieri*, pp. 75–78.

of territorial waters was developed by utilizing to a notable extent principles of feudal law.[47] Short references to the concept of territorial waters are to be found in the Commentary to the Sixth Book of the Decretals of Boniface VIII by Domenico di San Gimignano, celebrated Tuscan canonist of the fourteenth century.[48] But the first passages capable of being developed into a complete legal theory of territorial waters are to be found in the works of the glossators. Azo (d. 1230) affirmed that dominion could be acquired even on the sea "per privilegium vel per longam consuetudinem." Thus the principle of the freedom of the seas underwent a first limitation, and it is interesting to note that of the two modes of acquiring the dominion of the seas indicated by Azo, one, the *privilegium*, that is, the investiture by the emperor, is of a feudal nature; the other, the *longa consuetudo*, that is, acquisitive prescription, is of Roman origin. From the time of the glossators the Roman and the feudal theories both contributed to the formation of the doctrine of territorial waters.

It is with Bartolus that the concept of territorial waters takes a more precise shape. "Mare sub cuius territorio comprehenditur." "Mare dicitur illius domini sub cuius territorio comprehenditur," he writes. Contrary to the common opinion, this does not mean that Bartolus considered adjacent waters part of the territory and therefore included in the terrestrial dominion. In the classical Roman texts the word *territorium*, which derives from the verb *terrere*, not from *terra*, indicates that space over which a power can exert its own authority. *Jus terrendi* is used in the Roman texts as synonymous with *jus imperii*. The Italian jurists of the Renaissance continued to use the word *territorium* with the technical meaning it had in classical Roman law. Therefore, when Bartolus affirmed that the neighboring waters belonged to the *territorium*, he merely meant that they were susceptible of forming the object of jurisdiction [49] on the part of the coastal sovereigns. However, his powers should not be identified with full sovereignty. In fact, to Bartolus the sovereign powers over the adjacent sea are limited to the exercise of repressive jurisdiction.

The concept of the adjacent sea was further utilized by Bartolus for the purpose of determining who holds sovereignty over islands. Those islands which lie within the adjacent sea belong to the coastal sovereign, because to him alone belongs the jurisdiction over this part of the earth's

[47] See Gidel, *Le Droit international public de la mer*, III, 26; Domenico di San Gimignano in his *Lectura prima super sexto libro Decretalium*, expresses himself as follows: "Appellatione territorii alicuius civitatis comprehenditur mare districtum per illam civitatem."
[48] See Fenn, "Origins of the Theory of Territorial Waters," 20 Am. J. Int. L. (1926) 465 ff., which contains an ample analysis of the theories of the glossators and the post-glossators. Not less important on the same subject is the book by Fenn, *The Origin of the Right of Fishery in Territorial Waters*.
[49] Baldoni, *Il mare territoriale nel diritto internazionale comune*, p. 8.

surface. In view of the fact that the adjacent sea marks the limit for the exercise of sovereignty, Bartolus limits its extension to that maritime zone over which the coastal sovereign can actually exercise his authority. Consistently with this criterion Bartolus fixes the extension of the territorial waters at a hundred Italian miles [50] which was about the distance that a ship at that time could normally cover in two days' sailing. Since this measure is established on the basis of a functional criterion, it has not an absolute character. An island distant more than one hundred miles from the coast is subject to the sovereignty of the coastal sovereign, provided that it be distant less than one hundred miles from another island belonging to the same sovereign, and lying within his territorial waters. Thus, according to Bartolus, Sardinia belongs to the sovereign of Italy, although it lies outside the limits of the Italian territorial waters, because it is near Corsica, which lies within Italy's territorial waters.[51] This doctrine of the *vis attractiva* of the islands is in my opinion one of the most characteristic aspects of Bartolus's theory.

It is clear that the modern notion of the territorial sea was foreign to Bartolus's mind. He certainly did not mean to assimilate the powers over the territorial sea belonging to the coastal sovereign with those which he exercised over the land.[52] Yet Bartolus, by asserting the existence of maritime zones over which certain powers of the coastal sovereign might be exercised in an exclusive way and by determining the extension of this zone, certainly contributed to the formation of the modern conception of territorial waters.[53]

The right of the coastal sovereign to exercise certain exclusive powers over the adjacent waters was reaffirmed by Baldus, who taught that *territorium et in aquis se extendit*. According to him the coastal sovereign is not vested with the absolute sovereignty over the adjacent waters, but only with the rights of ownership, of use, and of jurisdiction, coupled with the obligation of protecting ships sailing throughout them against pirates. For this reason in another passage Baldus affirmed that the sea is not a *territorium*, but only a *districtus*.[54] The limit of the waters over

---

[50] Bartolo da Sassoferrato, "De insula," in *Consilia, quaestiones et tractatus*, X, 137. The criterion developed in northern countries, according to which territorial waters were limited to the range of vision, was introduced into Sicily by the Normans, and advocated, in harmony with local practice, by Guglielmo di Perno, a jurisconsult of Syracuse of the fifteenth century (see Freccia, *De subfeudis baronum et investituris feudorum*, p. 119).

[51] Tyberiadis. *Tractatus de fluminibus*.

[52] Angelo de Ubaldis of Perugia, a brother of Baldus, and himself a well-known jurisconsult, extended the powers of the coastal state over the territorial waters by asserting that it had jurisdiction over contracts concluded on them. For this jurist the limit of the territorial waters was the median line between the two opposite shores (*Super prima ff. veteris*, Mediolani, 1477).

[53] Raestad, *La Mer territoriale* p. 15n., and Baldoni, *Il mare territoriale*, p. 54.

[54] Baldo degli Ubaldi, *Usus feudorum commentaria*, p. 85, secs. 1, 2: "Porro territorium non

which such rights and powers might be exercised was, according to Baldus, sixty miles, the distance that a ship might cover in a day. The conception of territorial waters accepted by Baldus is still different from the modern one. The merit of Baldus is that he was the first who attempted to build a complete body of rules relative to the territorial waters, mainly based upon principles of feudal law.[55]

The distinction between territorial waters and the high seas is presented more clearly by Alberico Gentili. In his view, the territory, that is, that part of the earth's surface over which a state can exercise its power, includes both the land and the sea: "territorium et de terris dici et de aquis." [56] Following Bartolus's measure, Gentili limits the extension of the territorial sea to one hundred miles, a distance which can be augmented if the proximity of another state does not interfere: "vel etiam ultra si non propinquant alteri provinciae."

Differing from Bartolus and Baldus, Gentili goes so far as to assimilate the territorial waters and the land for all that concerns the powers that the coastal sovereign can exert over them.[57] Against the exercise of sovereignty of the coastal state Gentili sets up, however, a few limitations, which today are in part accepted by international practice. A state cannot bar foreign ships from free passage through its territorial waters. "Et iter marinum non est liberrimum?" he asks himself.[58] The Venetians who deny the ships of other nations free passage through the waters over which they claim exclusive dominion act against natural law.[59] Moreover, Gentili also affirms that the free use of harbors cannot be refused to foreign ships, [60] thereby anticipating a rule which positive international law adopted only at the beginning of this century.[61]

The doctrine of the territorial sea put forth by the glossators thus finds in Gentili the first writer who enounces it in modern terms. After assimilating, in principle, the territorial sea to the land in so far as concerns the powers of the prince, he sets such limitations to this assimilation as are imposed by the necessities of navigation and by natural equity.

The dominion which Pisa, Genoa, and Venice claimed over vast zones of the Tyrrhenian and the Adriatic included, in the opinion of these cities, far broader rights over their adjacent waters than the Italian jurisconsults normally accredited to coastal states. Pisa, Genoa, and Venice

---

est aliud quod terrae spatium munitum et armatum jurisdictione. In mari autem non dicitur territorium . . . sed dicitur districtus, id est, aquae spatium, seu latitudo munita jurisdictione et imperio."

[55] Fenn, "Origins of the Theory of Territorial Waters," 20 Am. J. Int. L. (1926) 465 ff.

[56] *Hispanicae advocationis,* Book I, ch. 8, p. 32: The quotations refer to the Latin edition of 1661, reprinted in the "Classics of International Law." The English translation, published in the same edition, bears in the margin the pagination of the Latin edition.

[57] *Hispanicae advocationis,* Book I, ch. 8, p. 36.   [58] *Ibid.,* ch. 6, p. 21.

[59] *De jure belli,* Book I, ch. 19, p. 148.   [60] *Ibid.,* Book III, ch. 11, p. 565.

[61] Baldoni, *Il mare territoriale nel diritto internazionale,* p. 98.

claimed the right to prohibit foreign ships free passage through their maritime dominion. For warships the prohibition was absolute; for mercantile ships the passage was subject to the rendering of homage or to payment of a tribute. In addition, as we have already seen, these cities asserted that their own exclusive dominion embraced maritime zones which far exceeded the normal extent of territorial waters.

The existence of exceptional rules, which only could justify these claims, was asserted by numerous jurisconsults, who endeavored to champion the pretensions of Genoa and Venice.[62] In support of Venice's claims over the exclusive domination of the Adriatic, in 1442 Raffaele Fulgosio and Raffaele de Curris composed the *Consilium per quod declarant Gulphum esse dominium Venetum.* Venice's claims were also supported by Angelo Matteacci (Mattheacius) in *De jure Venetorum et jurisdictione maris Adriatici* (1617); Giulio Paci (Julius Pacius, 1550–1635) in *Disceptatio de dominio maris Adriatici* (1619); by Marco Antonio Pellegrino, Paduan jurisconsult, who was the opponent of Gentili in a case in England; by Cornelio Frangipane, *Allegazione in jure per la vittoria contro Federico l'Imperatore e atto del papa Alessandro III° per il dominio della republica veneta nel suo golfo contro alcune scritture napoletane* (1618); and Paolo Sarpi (1552–1623), author of the work *Del dominio del mare Adriatico,* printed in 1676.[63]

The most noted defender of the Genoese claims was Pietro Battista Borgo, author of the work *De dominio Serenissimae Genuensis Reipublicae in mari Ligustico* (1641).

The arguments adopted by these writers to support their thesis are derived both from Roman and from feudal law. Relying upon the principles of Roman law, they maintained that exclusive dominion was based on acquisitive prescription and on a long-established custom; it had in fact been exercised for centuries with the acquiescence and consequent recognition of the other countries. On the basis of feudal law they claimed, with questionable historical accuracy, that this dominion was derived from the investiture conferred upon the cities by the emperor or the pope. For Venice this investiture was considered to be confirmed by the ceremony of the wedding with the sea, celebrated every year by the doge. They added that the dominion was justified by the cities' naval

---

[62] The claims of the Venetians were resisted by the Neapolitans who referred to the ancient possession exercised over the Adriatic by the Normans, whose successors they claimed to be. The claims of the Neapolitans were supported by various writers recalled by Giannone (1676–1748) in his *Istoria civile del Regno di Napoli* (English translation by T. Ogilie, 2 vols., London, 1729–1731) Book 13, ch. 1, secs. 1–2.

[63] Under the pseudonym Franciscus de Ingenuis, Sarpi published in 1619 the *Epistula de jurisdictione Venetae reipublicae in Mare adriaticum.* For a detailed résumé of the book *Del dominio del Mare adriatico* see Pierantoni, *Storia degli studi del diritto internazionale,* 2d ed., pp. 646–672, where the names of medieval Italian jurisconsults are also mentioned, who held that the sea might be subjected to the sovereignty of the states.

victories and by the power actually exercised over those waters to the exclusion of any other state whatsoever; moreover, that it constituted a reward for the protection against pirates guaranteed by them in these zones.

The works of these writers, crammed with learning and legal subtleties, did not however have more than a mere academic value. As long as they were able actually to exercise their rule, Venice and Genoa had no need to recur to legal arguments to obtain recognition of it. Bartolomaeus Cepolla, who lived in the fifteenth century, when the power of Venice in the Adriatic Sea had not yet been shaken, would not admit that one could even question the authority of the Venetian doges over the Adriatic "quia tantam jurisdictionem habent in mari, quantam in civitate Venetiarum." It was only toward the end of the sixteenth century, when the military power of Genoa and Venice was declining, that these cities were obliged to have recourse to legal defenses of their pretended rights. But no matter how rich they were in ingenious contrivances and erudition, the works of these writers were unable to maintain claims which could be upheld by force alone and, moreover, were contrary to the spirit of the new times, directed toward the principles of the absolute liberty of the high seas and the liberty of passage through the territorial waters.

INTERNATIONAL TREATIES

The Italian jurisconsults of the Renaissance also examined several relationships and institutions connected with intercourse between subjects of international law. The first juridical works on international treaties date from this time. During the course of the Renaissance the legal concept of an international treaty continually gained in clearness and was gradually purified of all canon-law influence. At the same time international treaties acquired characteristics quite distinct from those of private law contracts.

The first Italian works on international treaties are of very little value. The oldest one that has come down to us is perhaps the treatise *De confederatione, pace et conventionibus principum,* by Martino Garati of Lodi (Martinus Garatus Laudensis),[64] a jurisconsult of the first half of the fifteenth century, who taught in Pavia in 1438 and at Sienna in 1448. The word "treatise" scarcely fits this collection of maxims. In sixty-three propositions (*quaestiones*) Martino axiomatically states certain fragmentary and disconnected rules relating to treaties, with special emphasis on treaties of alliance (*confederationes*), of peace, and of truce. The author indicates what subjects may conclude peace and alliances

---

[64] The treatise is published in Ziletti, *Tractatus,* Vol. XVI.

(among whom he includes the independent Italian cities) and what conditions are required for the validity of treaties. Among other things the author teaches that the pope and the emperor are entrusted with the preservation of peace and truces; that treaties between princes are bona fide contracts; that a prince cannot be released from a treaty without just cause; that a treaty by which a city or a nation subject themselves to a prince other than their own lord is void; that an alliance against the pope or the emperor is not lawful; that the allies of our enemies are our enemies; that it is not permissible to violate a truce even when the enemy has been the first to violate it.

Martino does not clearly distinguish between an alliance and a truce; in fact he teaches that: "Foederatus populus dicitur qui habet treugam cum alio populo vel principe" (quaestion 24). This definition denotes a situation very frequent at a time when the legal conception of neutrality had not yet arisen. Treaties were often concluded providing that one of the contracting parties was to remain neutral if the other was belligerent. This situation certainly bore some aspects of an alliance, and others of a truce.[65]

This brief pamphlet, of little importance, is historically interesting, because it shows how the internationalist doctrine was still dominated at that time by religious conceptions. To Martino the binding force of treaties still depended on the utterance of an oath; the pope had the power to compel the recalcitrant party to respect his given word. The violation of a treaty constituted a canonical offense, with all the ensuing disadvantages (questions 12 and 19). Another consequence of this theory was that the pope was entitled to release the parties from their oath.

Another writer on alliances between princes was Giovanni Lupo (Lopez or Lupus), a canon of Segovia. This Spaniard spent many years in Rome, where he came to disculpate himself from an accusation of heresy; he died there in 1496. In the brief treatise *De confederatione, pace et conventionibus principum* [66] he discusses, in the form of a dialogue, when confederations (alliances) are permissible, who it is that may enter upon them and whether it is permissible for Christians to ally themselves with infidels. The book has very little value.

In other writers it is the civilistic side of the treaties that receives particular attention. For Baldus, for instance, agreements between sover-

[65] Martino is also the author of the treatise *De principibus*, which is a collection of 559 questions dealing with princes. The work would be classified today among the treatises of constitutional law, inasmuch as it deals especially with the relationship between princes and their subjects, between the emperor, the pope, and the princes, and between superior and inferior princes. The treatise also enunciates a few rules of international law: for example, in question 85 Martino lays down the principle that a prince cannot expel foreigners from his territory without a just cause; he can, however, prohibit their entrance *ab initio*.
[66] The treatise is published in Ziletti, *Tractatus*, Vol. XVI.

eigns are contracts which must be interpreted *stricti juris*, that is, in accordance with the rules of civil law.

Alberico Gentili was the first to free the concept of an international treaty from the shackles of canon and civil law. With remarkable modernity of view Gentili affirmed that the kingdoms do not exist for the sovereigns, but the sovereigns for the kingdoms: "non regna esse propter reges, sed reges propter regna factos esse." [67] Hence certain limitations to the content of the treaties that a prince may stipulate: he may not, for instance, alienate by treaty his own kingdom, because a king may not dispose of his own subjects as though they were cattle.[68] From the public nature of treaties it follows that the sovereigns and the peoples are bound by the legitimate treaties of peace, friendship, and alliance concluded by preceding sovereigns on behalf of the state. If negotiated by the sovereign, the treaty is valid as soon as it has been signed; if by a representative, after the ratification. Treaties can be annulled if they are vitiated by fraud or error; treaties of peace are valid even if they are concluded under the coercion of the victor, because such coercion is inseparable from war. Pacts must be respected, but in every treatise is implicit the clause *rebus sic stantibus*. The difference between an international treaty and a contract also influences the interpretation of the former. In opposition to Baldus, Gentili holds that treaties are not contracts *stricti juris*, but in good faith, *ex bono et aequo*. Consequently, in interpreting them it is necessary to refer to the intention of the contracting parties rather than to the words used. This is especially true for military conventions, which are concluded between simple men at arms, not lawyers; from their interpretation every quibble (*capeduncula*) must be banned.[69] Before there can be violation of a treaty, it is necessary, according to Gentili, that one of the contracting parties, not only one of its subjects, commit a breach of its provisions.

The influence exerted by religious doctrines over questions of international law gave rise to the problem concerning the permissibility of treaties with infidels. Considering the imposing number of treaties concluded between Italian cities and the Saracens, a general prohibition of all agreements with them could hardly be maintained. The question, then, was principally whether one might conclude treaties of alliance with infidels. According to Martino [70] it was not permissible for a Christian prince to avail himself of the aid of infidels except when he was unable to defend himself otherwise.

The question became a vital one toward the beginning of the sixteenth

[67] *De jure belli*, Book III, ch. 22, p. 676.   [68] *Ibid.*, ch. 15, p. 609.
[69] For the doctrines of Gentili concerning the interpretation of treaties see Ehrlich, "L'interpretation des traités," 24 Rec. des Cours (1928), 1929.
[70] *De bello*, quest. 3.

century, after the conclusion of the alliance between Francis I of France
with Suleiman II in 1535 and especially when the Turkish fleet joined
the French fleet in 1543 during the siege of Nice. Italian scholars altogether denied that such alliances were permissible. Pierino Belli, who
shall be considered in greater detail further on, in his capacity as ad-
viser to Emmanuel Philibert of Savoia in 1564 fiercely opposed a pro-
jected alliance between that prince and the Turks, who offered as a
compensation the island of Cyprus. Belli's opinion prevailed. This jurisconsult maintained the same thesis years later in the work *De re militari,*
in which he affirmed that an alliance with a people of unbelievers is
permissible only if directed against other infidels, but not against a
Christian nation.[71] The same thesis was maintained by Ottaviano Cacherano da Osasco, another Piedmontese, in his book *Disputatio an principi
christiano fas sit foedus inire cum infidelibus,* published at Turin in 1569.

Even the broadminded writer Gentili felt it necessary to devote the
entire Chapter XIX of the third book of his *De jure belli* to a discussion
of the question "Si foedus recte contrahitur cum diversae religionis
hominibus." Gentili begins by stating that the question is posed only with
regard to Christians and infidels, because an alliance between Protes-
tants and Catholics is certainly valid. Commercial treaties can certainly
be concluded with infidels, and similarly unequal agreements are legitimate, such as those whereby infidels bind themselves to pay a tribute.
But positively no alliance can be admitted, and therefore Gentili ex-
plicitly condemns the action of Francis I. Although Gentili was hostile to
the influence of religious doctrines in deciding questions of international
law, yet in this particular case he did not depart from the teaching of
theologians. He points out that the solution of this question depends not
only on civil but also on canon law. It is worth observing that the conclusions reached by Gentili were later accepted by Grotius too.

DIPLOMATIC AGENTS

The ever-more-frequent use of missions for the exercise of international relations attracted the attention of writers. The canonists were
perhaps the first to assert the inviolability of the ambassadors in their
capacity of men of peace. In the writings of the glossators and the post-
glossators diplomatic agents are mentioned, but generally only with reference to questions of civil law that might arise with regard to them: for
example, validity of a will executed by a diplomatic agent in foreign
countries and the obligation of the sovereign to pay the stipend of the
deceased legate to his heirs.

The first Italian juridical work devoted exclusively to legates is a
pamphlet by Martino of Lodi, *Tractatus de legatis, maxime principum.*[72]

[71] *De re militari et bello tractatus,* Book II, ch. 18, secs. 4–7.
[72] The treatise is published in Ziletti, *Tractatus,* Vol. XVI.

This author was especially qualified to deal with the subject, since he had opportunities personally to execute diplomatic missions. Notwithstanding the pretentious denomination "treatise," the book in reality consists solely of a collection of 39 propositions (*quaestiones*) relating to legations and extracted from the works of the glossators and the postglossators. Not all the questions examined appertain to international law; some of them can indeed hardly be classified as juridical at all.

According to Martino the right of legation belongs in Italy exclusively to the free cities; the others have to request the authorization of the prince upon whom they depend, and the diplomatic agents are furnished with credentials from the latter (quest. 25). The diplomatic agent cannot refuse his nomination by alleging that someone else is better fitted than he (quest. 17). He is excused from all public office (quests. 29 and 30) and from guardianship (quest. 32); he must revoke the power of attorney to his agent if the mission is to last for a considerable time (quest. 28); he acquires the legal status of an absentee (quest. 30). Missions have a temporary character (quest. 24) and give origin to rights and duties of the legates both in the state from which they have been sent as well as in that to which they are dispatched (quest. 4). With regard to the relationship between the prince who sends him and his own legate, Martino observes that this relationship is not one of private agency inasmuch as it occurs between public personages. Therefore, in this case there can be no *actio mandati* (quest. 20). The diplomatic agent is entitled to salary (quest. 3), to be reimbursed for his expenses in case of illness (quest. 1), and to be compensated for damages suffered on his journey without fault on his part (quest. 16); he may keep the gifts received during his mission (quest. 22). With regard to the legate's status in the country to which he has been dispatched, Martino observes that the diplomatic agent is sacred and whoever offends him is guilty of sacrilege (quest. 38); he is inviolable (quest. 5), even in an enemy country (quest. 18); he is not subject to reprisals (quest. 31); he is exempt from duties (quest. 16); if poor he must be supported by the state to which he is dispatched (quest. 9). Martino teaches that a person of lower condition than the diplomatic agent may be put out of an inn in order to make room for the former (quest. 2). The diplomatic agents of the greater princes have precedence over those of the minor ones (quest. 26). Other questions concern the law governing the succession of a diplomatic agent (quests. 7–8) and the heir's right to his unpaid salary (quest. 37). The mission terminates with the legate's return to the territory of the prince who had accredited him (quest. 34)—in case of the pontifical legate, when he re-enters Rome (quest. 33); the legate who delays his return without justification loses his privileges (quest. 11).

The work of Martino of Lodi, although devoid of any doctrinal importance whatsoever, is significant from the historical viewpoint, because with all likelihood it exactly reproduces the rules followed by Italian practice during the period in which it was written.

The Italian writers of the Renaissance posterior to Martino that dealt with missions, as a rule considered them from a general point of view. Emphasis was especially laid on the political aspects of the ambassadorial functions, and advice was given as to the best way of successfully carrying out a mission. Legal problems concerning diplomatic agents were as a rule considered as secondary: no clear distinction was made between the rules of international law governing the status of ambassadors and the rules of municipal law governing both the relationship between the ambassador and his sovereign and the private law relationships which might originate from the exercise of the diplomatic mission. Works on the subject, which deserve little more than passing mention, are the treatise *De Officio legati* (fifteenth century), by Hermolaus Barbarus, the *Tractatus de oratoribus seu legatis principum et de eorum fide et officio*, by Giulio Ferretti (1480–1547),[73] published in 1562, which is devoted above all to the functions of legates in times of war, and the treatise *De legato* (1566) by Ottaviano Maggi (d. 1586).[74] A certain popularity fell to the work on legations by an Italian, Pier Andrea Cannonieri (Canonherius), published in 1615 in Antwerp, where he practiced law with success. Pontifical legates were dealt with by Andrea Barbazza (Andrea de Barbatia) of Messina (1400–1479), professor at Bologna, who wrote the *Tractatus de cardinalibus legatis a latere*; by Pier Andrea Gambaro (1480–1528), auditor of the Apostolic Palace under Clement VII, who wrote the *Tractatus de officio atque auctoritate de legato a latere*; by Enea de Falconi, author of the *Tractatus de legato a latere*, and by Raffaele Cyllenius Angeli, author of the treatise *De legato pontificis*, published at Venice in 1588.[75]

The first Italian work on legations of any real juridical importance is *De legationibus*, by Alberico Gentili.[76] In 1584, four years after his arrival in England, Gentili was consulted in the well-known case of Don Bernardino Mendoza, Spanish ambassador to England, whose complicity

---

[73] For Ferretti and the other writers mentioned below see the article of Nys, "Les Commencements de la diplomatie et le droit d'ambassade jusqu'à Grotius," 15 Rev. dr. int. et lég. comp. (1883) 577 ff.

[74] For Ottaviano Maggi see Catellani, "Ottaviano Maggi," 16 Rev. dr. int. et lég. comp. (1884) 410 ff.

[75] Several rules concerning legates may be found in the *Repertorium juris*, a dictionary of law published by the Italian jurisconsult Johannes Bertachinus. Excerpts from works of Italian Renaissance authors (Martino, Hermolaus Barbarus, Andrea Barbazza, Johannes Bertachinus, Giulio Ferretti, Raphael Cyllenius, Ottaviano Maggi) dealing with ambassadors are published by Hrabar, *De legatis et legationibus tractatus varii*.

[76] Gentili, *De legationibus libri tres*, with an introduction by E. Nys in the "Classics of International Law," 2 vols. The pages are quoted with reference to the Latin edition of 1594, which is that reprinted in the "Classics of International Law." The English translation, published in the same edition, bears in the margin the pagination of the Latin edition.

in a conspiracy to liberate Mary Queen of Scots and dethrone Elizabeth had recently been discovered. Although the queen and public opinion demanded Mendoza's severe punishment, it was considered advisable, before proceeding against him, to obtain the opinion of two foreign jurisconsults. Gentili and Jean Hotman, son of the famous François Hotman, were consulted. Both were of the opinion that the case fell under the provisions of international law granting penal immunity to ambassadors. Their opinion was followed, and Mendoza was not tried, but merely compelled to leave England. In the same year Gentili had another opportunity to revert to the subject, in a speech delivered at Oxford.[77] A year later he compiled an exhaustive treatise on the subject in his *De legationibus*.

Following the system of his predecessors, he did not limit himself to the consideration of the diplomatic agent from a purely legal point of view. Of the three books that form the work, the first concerns the history of legations and questions of ceremonial, and the third deals with the qualities and the behavior of the perfect ambassador. The second book, on the other hand, as Gentili observes on various occasions, is not intended to be a historical description, but an effort to define the juridical principles of ambassadorial law. "Nec ego hoc libro de factis, verum de legitimis sententiis disputo." Gentili's definition of the ambassador is as follows: "Legatus est, qui non modo publice, sed publico etiam nomine et publica indutus persona missus est." [78] The distinction is thus expounded between the legate and the secret agent, and emphasis is laid upon the public nature of an organ of the state, which is peculiar to the former. It is to Gentili's credit that he stressed the fact that the status of the legate is regulated by international law.[79] His contracts [80] and his debts [81] are governed by international law. Another merit of Gentili's is that he advocated truly liberal principles and freed discussion of the subject from all religious influences. He asserts, for instance, that even infidels and heretics may have diplomatic agents, since "in quocumque religionis discrimine manent jura legationum." [82] The *jus legationis*, on the other hand, cannot be invoked by rebels or brigands, because they possess no public character, or, in modern terms, they are not subjects of international law. According to Gentili a sovereign has the right to refuse an ambassador only if there are justifiable motives for doing so, because the eternal rules of the law of nations cannot be violated by anyone without a reason. In case an ambassador has been accepted, he must be granted certain immunities and privileges.

---

[77] The speech was published in the first months of 1585 under the title *Legalium comitiorium Oxoniensium actio* (Molen, *Alberico Gentili*, p. 50).
[78] *De legationibus*, Book I, ch. 2, p. 6. [79] *Ibid.*, ch. 14, p. 39.
[80] *Ibid.*, Book II, ch. 13, p. 105. [81] *Ibid.*, ch. 16, p. 115. [82] *Ibid.*, ch. 14, p. 109.

The greater part of the second book is dedicated to an analysis of the legal status of the diplomatic agent. In dealing with this subject Gentili attempts to establish a just balance between diplomatic inviolability and immunity, on one hand, and the necessary protection of the state to which the diplomatic agent is accredited against any abuses on his part. Although Gentili often refers to principles of Roman law, this part of his book proves that he clearly realizes the distinction between international and Roman law; for example, he points out, that the principle of Roman law embodied in the *Lex Julia majestatis,* by which whoever is guilty of conspiracy against the state is punishable with the death penalty, even if the crime has not been consummated, is contrary to the natural law, and that for this reason the *Lex Julia* cannot be applied in case of conspiracy on the part of an ambassador.

Gentili lays special emphasis upon the inviolability of the ambassador. This principle, however, is not derived from the nature of the mission fulfilled by the diplomatic agent so much as from his status as the sovereign's personal representative. The diplomatic agent is not subject to the criminal jurisdiction of the state in which he exercises his mission; if he plots a crime, the sole measure that can be taken against him is expulsion. If, however, he has actually committed a crime against the sovereign or even against any other person, he may be punished. The concept of the absolute penal immunity of the diplomatic agent was foreign to Gentili's mind as to that of the other writers of his age.[83] Even the absolute exemption of ambassadors from civil jurisdiction is in the main denied by Gentili, who affirms, however, that the personal property of the ambassador, indispensable for his support, cannot be subjected to a lien or seized in payment of his debts either by order of the judges or by that of the king. With regards to taxation, Gentili is of the opinion that the property indispensable to the ambassador should not be subject to it. He does not, however, consider it unjust that the legate should pay certain taxes. The ambassador's residence is inviolable. The staff of the legation enjoys the same immunities as the ambassador and must be tried in accordance with the *jus gentium.* It is not clear what Gentili means when he asserts that the staff of the legation is subject to the ambassador's jurisdiction. In case of war the ambassador's immunities do not cease, and he must therefore be granted safe conduct so that he may freely leave the country. The ambassador's inviolability and immunity begin only at the moment when he is accredited and exist only in the states to which he is accredited. This, in the main, is the substance of that part of the book that deals with the rules of international law concerning ambassadors.

[83] See Molen, *Alberico Gentili,* p. 80.

. The *De legationibus* has given rise to contradictory judgments.[84] The opinion of Sir Travers Twiss that "this treatise alone would have been sufficient to obtain for Gentili a place in the front rank among the jurists of his age," [85] is perhaps somewhat exaggerated. The greatness of Gentili does not lie so much in the particular results he achieves in this or that of his writings as in the spirit of modernity that pervades all his works, in the clear understanding of the needs felt by his times, and in his constant effort to find a juridical solution for problems which previously had been considered only from an ethical or religious point of view. These general qualities compensate for the defects which may be found in each of his works. On the other hand, not all the criticism addressed to *De legationibus* seems justified: for example, it does not seem exact to affirm that this work "presents perhaps less a development of principles of the law relating to ambassadors than a historical account of legations." [86] The principal merit of the book is precisely that it is the first organic work on diplomatic agents in which are considered from the viewpoint of international law.[87] In the *De legationibus* are encountered many of the elements upon which Gentili's greatness is founded: coherence of treatment; emphasis on the autonomy of international law, which Gentili conceives as a system of rules based upon reason and the natural understanding; the frequent recourse to concepts of Roman law, which does not, however, imply the identification of Roman law with international law. On the other hand, an examination of the single propositions announced by Gentili reveals uncertainty and contradictions: the chapter devoted to the ambassador's exemption from civil jurisdiction is somehow vague and seems to be vitiated by inconsistencies. Similarly, it is not easy to understand what Gentili means when he maintains that the contracts and the crimes of legates are governed by international law. Possibly he intended to lay down the principle that the rules of international law impose on the states the obligation to refrain from applying the general rules of municipal law to acts concerning ambassadors or committed by them and to grant them certain extraordinary immunities and privileges. But since at that time the distinction between substantive and adjective law was not clearly defined, it is also possible that Gentili was here

[84] The book was certainly esteemed by contemporaries: it was twice reprinted during the author's lifetime: in 1594 and in 1607.
[85] Twiss, "Albericus Gentilis on the Law of War," *The Law Magazine and Review* (1878) 149–150.
[86] Coleman Philipson in his article on "Alberico Gentili," in Macdonell and Manson, eds., *Great Jurists of the World*, p. 113; see also H. Nézard in his monograph on "Alberico Gentili," in *Les Fondateurs du droit international*, pp. 69 ff.
[87] Cf. Thamm, *Albericus Gentilis und seine Bedeutung für das Völkerrecht, insbesondere seine Lehre um Gesandtschaftswesen*, p. 33; Nys, *Les Commencements de la diplomatie* p. 44; Molen, *Alberico Gentili*, p. 71.

stating a problem of adjective law in terms of substantive law; what he actually intended to assert was that, within the state, jurisdiction over ambassadors' contracts and crimes was not vested in the courts of ordinary jurisdiction, but solely in an organ endowed with international functions—that is, in the sovereign.[88] In another passage of his work Gentili affirms, in fact, that according to the law of nations the magistrate whose function it is to judge ambassadors is the sovereign.

These uncertainties in Gentili's ideas are justified if we consider that, in the age when he was writing, the subject matter he was dealing with was still in a fluid state and that his attempt to gather juridical principles from practice encountered a serious obstacle because of the inconsistencies of the latter. It is easier to appreciate the virtues of Gentili's book if we compare it with the works on diplomatic agents that preceded it, which are immensely inferior. Gentili has the merit of considering from a legal point of view and at the same time with a keen sense of reality a series of problems which, given the development of legations in that period, were then arousing great practical interest.[89] Certainly many of Gentili's ideas influenced the evolution of positive law, and no less remarkable was his influence over the writers of the succeeding age. It would be hazardous to affirm that Grotius' pages on legates are superior to those by Gentili; for indeed Grotius, by introducing the fiction of extraterritoriality and weighing down his treatise with the heavy impedimenta of classical examples, lost that direct contact with the reality of his age which is, on the contrary, the principal merit of Gentili's work.

[88] *De legationibus*, Book II, ch. 17, pp. 118–119.
[89] Molen, *Alberico Gentili*, p. 74, correctly remarks that it is strange how little consideration Gentili conceded to the permanent legations, which in his days were already very widely spread.

Chapter V: THE DOCTRINES OF THE JUST WAR

IN DEALING with the laws of warfare the Italian jurisconsults of the early Renaissance were especially influenced by the religious theories of the day. Almost until Gentili, attempts to consider the problems raised by war from an exclusively, or at least a prevalently, juridical viewpoint, disregarding the political, moral and religious aspects of the question, were extremely rare in Italy.

EVOLUTION OF THE DOCTRINE OF THE JUST WAR FROM BARTOLUS TO BELLI

The first Christian writers posed the problem whether war as such is lawful; that is, whether it is permissible for Christians to fight. May blood be shed by him whom the law of Christ forbids to revenge the offenses? Writers were not lacking who like Tertullian solved the question in the negative by condemning the use of violence for any reason.[1] But the ideas of medieval Catholicism had been rather inclined to follow the teachings of St. Augustine, who had declared war permissible provided it were just. A war was just, in St. Augustine's opinion, that had not been undertaken from *libido dominandi*,[2] *nocendi cupiditas, ulciscendi crudelitas, implacatus atque implacabilis animus, feritas rebellandi.*[3] Thanks to Gregory of Tours and Isidore of Seville, these ideas had passed into the lexica and glossaries that were current in the Middle Ages; they were encouraged by the French publicists (Alcuin, Regino of the monastery of Prum, and Yvon, bishop of Chartres); they formed the basis of various papal decisions; were codified in the Decree of Gratian[4] and in the Decretals;[5] were developed by Thomas Aquinas, and in fine "became the nucleus round which the glossators, especially Pope Innocent IV, Hostiensis, Johannes Andreae, Guido the Archdeacon of Bologna and Dominicus de Sancto Geminiano spun a web of fine distinctions, which at last amounted to a considerable body of doctrine."[6]

Thus the problem of the *bellum justum*, of the just war, came to be the fundamental problem of the doctrine of warfare. The medieval concept of the *bellum justum* had nothing in common with the *bellum justum* of the Romans. To the latter, *bellum justum* did mean merely a war, preceded by certain formalities and by certain religious rites, among which

---

[1] Tertullian, *De corona militari*, XIX. [2] Augustinus, *De civitate dei*, III, 14.
[3] Augustinus, *Contra Faustum*, XXII, 74. [4] *Causa* 23. [5] *De homicidio.*
[6] Holland, "The Early Literature of the Law of War," in *Studies in International Law*, p. 44.

was the intervention of the Fetiales, who pronounced the words "bellum justum piumque." [7] To the theologians of the Middle Ages, on the other hand, a war was just or unjust according to the motive that had determined it, and this conception inspired almost all the Italian jurisconsults of the Renaissance until the period of humanism. The solution of the problem could be only religious, or at best ethico-political, only. This explains how all discussions of the subject, even when contained in the works of jurisconsults, were void of all legal value.

Connected to the problem of the just war and yet distinct from it, was the problem of determining who was entitled to wage war. In the mind of the glossators the idea of warfare was associated with that of an emperor lord of the entire Christian world. The glossators held that war should conform with public law. And since according to them this law set up the authority of the emperor over that of all the princes, the emperor alone had the right to declare war. Azo did not hesitate to declare that legitimate enemies (*hostes*), entitled to such treatment, were only those upon whom the emperor and the Roman people declared war; the others were *praedones vel latrones*, who therefore could have no claim to be treated as legitimate combatants.[8] Thus, a struggle conducted by a Christian people against the emperor could not be a just war, but was merely a rebellion; in the same way a conflict between two Christian princes was not a war but an intestine struggle. The inevitable conclusion of the theory was that only wars against infidels, who were outside the bounds of the *Respublica Christiana*, could be just wars.

At the bottom of this theory there was undoubtedly, a lofty moral conception: that between the peoples of the *Respublica Christiana* war could not be permitted and that all their controversies had to be solved by pacific means, that is, through the decision of the emperor, their common secular sovereign, or of the pope, the supreme spiritual authority. This theory, however, was manifestly in contrast with practice, which saw frequent wars and rare arbitrations. Moreover, at least in Italy, the latter were generally directed against the imperial authority. Yet the cult of the imperial idea was so strong in jurisconsults educated in the Roman tradition that Baldus himself, who lived when the Italian cities had finally

---

[7] Giuseppe Salvioli, *La Concept de la guerre juste d'après les écrivains anterieurs à Grotius* (trans. by G. Hervo), 2d ed., pp. 13 ff. See also Nys, *Les Origines du droit international* and *Le Droit de la guerre et les précurseurs de Grotius*; Vanderpol, *Le Droit de guerre d'après les théologiens et les canonistes du moyen-âge*, and *La Doctrine scolastique du droit de guerre*; Focherini, *La dottrina canonica del diritto della guerra da S. Agostino a Balthasar d'Ayala*; Beaufort, *La Guerre comme instrument de secours ou de punition*; Brière, "Les Droits de la juste victoire selon la tradition des théologiens catholiques," 32 Rev. gén. dr. int. publ. (1925) 366 ff., and "Les Étapes de la tradition théologique concernant le droit de juste guerre," 44 Rev. gén. dr. int. publ. (1937) 129 ff.; Régout, *La Doctrine de la guerre juste de Saint Augustin à nos jours*; J. Epsstein, *The Catholic Tradition of the Law of Nations*; Elbe, "Evolution of the Concept of the Just War in International Law," 33 Am. J. Int. L. (1939) 665 ff.

[8] Azzo, *Summa Codicis*, L. VIII, *de postliminio*, p. 972.

achieved their independence, did not hesitate to affirm these principles, so opposed to the facts, and to fling himself against the French jurisconsults, whom he called *asini ultramontani,* because they did not accept this doctrine and rejected the theory that the emperor had supreme authority over the king of France. Baldus asserted that "the sole judge and arbiter of disputes between the peoples is the emperor, who alone can punish cities unfaithful to treaties and violators of the peace; the cities have no authority either to wage war or to have recourse to arms in order to obtain justice."

The conception of Bartolus was much more realistic; as we have already mentioned, he taught that whoever *de facto* recognizes no superior has the right to wage war; the Italian cities *superiorem non recognoscentes* therefore possess the right of waging war; the wars fought by them are true and proper public wars.

In this way Bartolus laid down a first exception to the ancient principle of the exclusive right of the emperor to wage war and exploded the doctrine of the just war. Other exceptions were recognized later, especially through the influence of French writers who affirmed the right of the king of France to wage a war as a manifestation of his independence of the emperor. Among Italian jurisconsults, Albericus of Rosate taught that the wars of the kings of France, England, and Aragon were quite as legitimate as those of the emperor, because these sovereigns had by prescription acquired sovereignty and did not recognize any superior.[9] This same jurisconsult reached the conclusion that all sovereigns have the right to wage war.[10] The canonists, too, were opposed to the theory that the emperors had exclusive right to wage war; by the impact of their doctrines, the same right was also recognized to the pope.

To the Italian jurisconsults, however, the principal question was still whether the Italian cities had the right of waging war. This right was first of all recognized as belonging to Venice, although for varying motives, by various writers, such as Bartolus, Baldus, Albericus of Rosate, and Paolo di Castro.[11] In spite of the authority of Bartolus, the reluctance was great to extend this right to the other Italian cities, even when they had been exercising it *de facto* for a considerable time. At the beginning of the fifteenth century, however, the turn of events had prevailed over the dogmas of the jurisconsults. The teachings of Bartolus finally triumphed, and it was generally admitted that any power whatsoever endowed with *imperium* might wage war.

[9] Albericus a Rosate, In l. imperium, Cod. III, 13.
[10] Albericus a Rosate, In l. imperatorem, Dig. III, 3.
[11] The motive adduced by Paolo di Castro (Cons. CCCCXXIV) is interesting. "Notorium est civitatem Venetiarum sive de jure, sive de facto non cognoscere superiorem: posse ergo jure belli sibi satisfacere, *quia quando cessant qui possunt compellere, redimus ad jus naturale vel gentium.*" The right of Venice to wage war was recognized by these jurists on various grounds; see Giuseppe Salvioli, *Le Concept de la guerre juste,* 2d ed., pp. 54–56.

The problem then arose concerning the circumstances under which it was legitimate to wage war, and the distinction of wars as just and unjust with reference to the motive that had caused them again resurged. The importance of the problem was evidenced by the consequences that were attributed to it. It was believed that only the party that waged a just war had the right to make slaves of the enemy and to take as booty the property of the defeated; that only in the case of a just war were vassals bound to follow their sovereign; that, in fine, whoever had started an unjust war was bound to make good the damage inflicted.[12] But drawing the distinction between a just and an unjust war was considered to be the task of theologians and philosophers rather than of lawyers. This explains why the works considered to be the first Italian legal treatises on the rights of warfare largely deal with the subject from an ethico-religious point of view. Moreover, the jurisconsults who dealt with war intended to consider the problem from all viewpoints. Hence the peculiar content of their works, mere compilations in which legal questions are set forth without any systematic order, confused with problems of theology, of the art of war, and even of astrology. Furthermore, in many works the discussion of warfare was joined to that of the ordeal, since both were considered judicial procedures for ascertaining the rights and wrongs of the parties by resort to arms. By will of divinity, the result was necessarily in favor of the contendent that was in the right.

The *De bello, de represaliis et de duello,* by Giovanni da Legnano, is generally considered the first Italian treatise devoted to the law of warfare.[13] The author was born in Milan, of a noble family; he studied the liberal arts and philosophy and also devoted some attention to medicine and astrology.[14] In 1351 he became a teacher of canon law in the University of Bologna. Until his death, in 1383, he held numerous public offices in matters connected with the relations between Bologna and the pope, who in 1377 appointed him vicar of Bologna. His public activities did not hamper his studies. Numerous works of his survive, dealing with astrology, theology, moral and political philosophy, civil and canon law, and the history of Bologna, which won him the admiration of his contemporaries.[15]

The treatise *De bello* was composed or completed in 1360, when Bologna was threatened by an assault by the army of Barnabo Visconti, lord of Milan. "Its contents are highly characteristic of the age, and imply a conception of the subject, which was substantially that of all the writers

[12] Martino, *Tractatus de bello,* quest. 2.   [13] Giovanni da Legnano, *Tractatus de bello.*
[14] For the life and works of Giovanni da Legnano, besides the works already mentioned and the introduction by Holland, see Rossi, *Degli scritti inediti giuridico-politici di Giovanni da Legnano;* Bosdari, *Giovanni da Legnano;* Breyne, *Le Droit de guerre selon Giovanni da Legnano.*
[15] See the complete list in the Preface by Holland, pp. xxi–xxvii.

of the period now under consideration." [16] The book consists of a fore-word, containing the dedication and a few words on the history of Bologna, and of three "main treatises." The first and second very briefly deal with the definition of war and distinguish between the various kinds of warfare—celestial spiritual war; human spiritual war; universal corporeal war; private corporeal war in self-defense; private corporeal war in defense of the state (that is, reprisals), and private corporeal war to defend the character of a person (that is, the duel). This classification is based upon concepts borrowed from theology and astrology, a science much cultivated by the author. The third "main treatise" deals *in extenso* with these baroque categories of war. By "war" the author means every kind of armed conflict: that is, not only a public war, a civil war, or a rebellion, but also reprisals, an armed conflict between lords and their vassals, and even duels. What today would be considered questions of international law occupy only a very few parts of the book, in the third section of the third treatise (chs. 9–77). Here the author deals with just wars; those who can wage war and those against whom war can be waged; the elements of war; the rights and duties of the troops; booty; stratagems; prisoners; and the various types of war. War is a "contentio exorta propter aliquid dissonum appetitui humanum propositum ad dissonantiam excludendam tendens," that is, a contest arisen from the conflict between certain facts and the human desire and tending to eliminate this disaccord. In conformity with the teachings of St. Augustine and the Pandects, the author opines that war in itself is not prohibited: indeed, a just war *tendit in bonum*, because it serves to eradicate evils. It must however be inspired by just motives: thus a war because of religion is not legitimate against Jews, inasmuch as they do not persecute Christians (ch. 70).[17] The criterion to be used in order to distinguish between just

---

[16] Holland, "Early Litterature," in his *Studies in International Law*, p. 45.

[17] Whether it was lawful to wage war against heretics or infidels for the sole reason that they were not Christians was one of the questions most frequently discussed by theologians and jurisconsults during the Middle Ages and the Renaissance, until the Reformation. Among Italian theologians, Enrico di Susa, Hostiensis (d. 1271), approved of war against heretics and infidels, which he defines as "bellum romanum," since Rome was the capital of the faith and the mother of religion. Cardinal Sinibaldo de' Fieschi (d. 1254), noted jurisconsult who became Pope Innocent IV, rejected this theory. St. Thomas distinguishes the heretics from infidels: the latter cannot be obliged to believe and they may not be attacked, unless they persecute Christians. Most Italian jurisconsults were in favor of a holy war for recapturing Jerusalem. Bartolus, Petrus de Ancharanis, Oldrinus, and Franciscus Aretinus declared lawful wars against the Saracens who occupied the Holy Land, a territory belonging to the emperor which had been stolen from him. Paolo di Castro justifies the holy war because the end is a good one. Bartolus distinguishes between the Jews and the Pagans, on one side, and the Saracens, on the other: no violence may be inflicted upon the former; on the contrary violence against the latter is lawful, for they seized the Holy Sepulcher. Baldus denies the right to attack Jews or Saracens without provocation, but in one passage he writes that it is lawful to despoil and pillage the enemies of the Church. Concerning this question see Nys, *Les Origines du droit international*, p. 7.

and unjust wars tends, however, to shift from the motives that caused them to the quality of the belligerents. The prince alone may declare war by his own authority, for he has no superior to whom he may resort to obtain justice. Peoples who do not recognize any actual superior, "populi non recognoscentes superiorem de facto" may declare war (ch. 14). The author is a strenuous champion of the rights of the Church. The emperor cannot declare war against the pope (Ch. 15), whereas the pope may declare war against an emperor who is either a schismatic or a heretic or usurps the rights and liberties of the Church. In such a case all the faithfuls are bound to help the pope, and even vassals of the emperor may be absolved from the oath that binds them or may be declared to be not bound (ch. 16).

A few references to the positive law of war are to be found in the chapter devoted to booty and prisoners ("De spoliis et captivis"), perhaps the most interesting chapter for the modern reader. The author asserts the obligation to show mercy toward prisoners captured in a lawful war (ch. 69) and of sparing those who do not take part in the war, even if they belong to the hostile army (ch. 71). Many of the questions dealt with in this part of the book have nothing to do with law in general and still less with the laws of war: for example, the question whether the priest who is attacked while celebrating mass shall continue the sacred rite or turn against the enemy. Long discussions concerning courage and virtue in general, philosophical distinctions between the various kinds of wars, and other ethico-theological or technical military topics reduce considerably the juridical interest of this part of the book.

To the modern reader, who experiences difficulty in entering into the spirit of that age and who is insensible to many of the theological problems then so urgent, the book of Giovanni da Legnano seems tedious and at times incomprehensible. Many of the questions he discusses strike us as otiose and abstruse. Yet it is certain that many of the problems he considers must have had a real importance in his day—for example, the problem of the just war was important in determining the vassal's duty toward the lord in case of war (chs. 32–35). According to Legnano the vassal may refuse military service in case of an unjust war started by his feudal overlord. The book also contains an interesting attempt, the first of its time, at a juridical analysis of the institution of mercenaries, aimed at ascertaining whether they have any right under certain circumstances to be paid (chs. 53, 58). This subject was of great importance in practical life at that time, when the introduction of companies of mercenaries has given rise to new rules of warfare.[18] To the modern reader the value of Giovanni da Legnano's book is essentially historical; it is the first co-

---

[18] Solmi, "Alberico Gentili e il nuovo diritto internazionale," in De Francisci, P., and others, *Alberico Gentili, Scritti e discorsi*, p. 17.

herent attempt to deal with the laws of war. Therefore, as Holland observes, it "marks the *terminus a quo* from which the literature of the subject had to start, in order to arrive at the *terminus ad quem*, which has so far been reached." [19]

Toward 1455 Martino da Lodi, of whom we have already spoken, wrote the treatise *De bello*, dealing with the laws of war. In reality the work consists simply of fifty-three disjointed propositions void of all organic unity. Some of the questions do not deal with the legal aspect of war; for instance, Martinus teaches that those who die in a just war for the defense of the Church and the faith will enter the kingdom of heaven (quest. 45).[20] A few of the questions debated concern the effects of war on private law relations: whether tithes are payable on a vineyard destroyed in a just war (quest. 46) and whether the *redemptus ab hostibus* may conclude certain contracts (quest. 6). The major part of the questions, however, concerns problems which today would be considered as pertaining to international law. Martino accepts the distinction between just and unjust wars. War is lawful if it is waged by someone who has been unable to enforce his rights in any other way and after due warning, "Ubi aliter mediante justitia non potest consequi debitum, licitum est bellum praemissa diffidatione" (ch. 9). The princes and the Italian cities, who do not recognize any superior, may wage war against their own citizens and enemies (ch. 2), since there is no authority superior to them. Whoever brings an army into the field without an order from a superior commits the crime of *lesae majestatis*. Whoever declares an unjust war must be held responsible for all the damage done (chs. 1, 14) and must return all booty (ch. 11), whereas whoever wages a just war may keep the booty and does not commit any sin (ch. 32). His friends may help him, even if not summoned. The war should be preceded by a declaration (ch. 37). Minors under eighteen years of age are not eligible to fight (ch. 12), neither may prelates fight (ch. 20) unless invited by the pope. Wounded soldiers may not quit the army (ch. 47), under penalty of losing their pay (ch. 49). In just wars stratagems are lawful in order to obtain victory, but the given word may not be broken (ch. 44). There may be no fighting from Thursday through Sunday. The requisitioning of oxen and other cattle belonging to subjects is permitted (ch. 23). Chattels taken from the enemy belong to the captor, whereas real property and the cities conquered belong to the prince or to the cities who have conquered them. The use of arbalests is not tolerated (ch. 30). The commanding officer may grant safe conducts (ch. 51) and conclude truces (ch. 8). At the

[19] Introduction to *Tractatus de bello, de represaliis et de duello*, p. ix. In the *De bello* there is no mention of the problems of maritime war. This topic, however, it would seem, was treated later by Giovanni da Legnano in a work *De multiplici genere monarchiae*. L. Rossi, *Degli scritti inediti giuridico-politici di Giovanni da Legnano*, p. 59.

[20] Question 10 concerns ordeals: they are lawful when permitted by the prince.

end of the truce a new war does not begin; but the old one continues (ch. 29). Whoever ransoms prisoners may not demand of the prisoner a sum superior to that paid by himself (ch. 23). The conquered cities are not enslaved, but become subjects, and their citizens do not lose their civil rights (ch. 21).

The work proves that in that age a situation intermediate between peace and war and yet different from the modern status of neutrality might exist in case of a conflict. According to Martino a prince should allow transit through his territory to the troops of a friend, but "armigeri debent transire per viam rectam non dando per viam damnum, alias impune possunt aggredi et offendi" (quest. 28). Martino recognizes the right of the vassal to refuse military service to his overlord in case of a war against the king, since the latter is superior: "et quod debent obedire regi tamquam maximo tribunali" (ch. 40). Other questions treated by Martino which to a modern reader may seem void of any legal value were certainly not devoid of juridical consequences on that age: the definitions of army (quest. 33), of *castrensiarii* (quest. 34), and of *cominarchae* (quest. 35) are probably aimed at distinguishing military bodies, whose components are entitled to be treated as legitimate combatants, by bands of marauders and unemployed mercenaries who in that age infested Italy. A product of the time in which it was written, the work of Martino, like that of Giovanni da Legnano, certainly does not deserve the contemptuous treatment given it by Grotius.[21]

Paride del Pozzo (Paris de Puteo, 1413?–1493) wrote a verbose work, *De re militari* (ca. 1471), which deals, however, mainly with questions of military art and with duels [22] Del Pozzo touches on the law of war only

[21] *De jure belli ac pacis*, Prolegomena, p. 37: "I have seen also special books on the law of war, some by theologians, as Francisco de Victoria, Henry of Gorkum, William Matthaei; others by doctors of laws, as John Lupus, Franciscus Arias, Giovanni da Legnano, Martinus Laudensis. All of these, however, have said next to nothing upon a most fertile subject; most of them have done their work without system, and in such a way as to intermingle and utterly confuse what belongs to the law of nature, to divine law, to the law of nations, to civil law, and to the body of law which is found in the canons." No express reference to Martino da Lodi is to be found in the *De jure belli* by Gentili; as for Giovanni da Legnano, Gentili limits himself to mention the boredom excited by reading his work (*De jure belli*, Book I, ch. 1).

[22] The treatise is published in Ziletti, *Tractatus*, Vol. XVI. Another work of little importance, dealing with military art rather than with the law of war, is the treatise *De re et disciplina militari aureus tractatus*, by Ferretti, which is also published in the same volume of Ziletti's *Tractatus*. Italian doctrines concerning war exercised a certain influence on Christine de Pisan, who was born at Venice in 1363 of Italian parents and was educated in France, where she died in 1431. She wrote, about 1405–1407, the *Livre des faits d'armes et de chevalerie*, which enjoyed great celebrity in its day in France, and where some questions are discussed relating to the laws of war. The book derives directly from the *Arbre des Batailles*, by Honoré Bonnet, which in its turn contains numerous passages translated *verbatim* from Italian authors, especially from Giovanni da Legnano. For Christine de Pisan see Nys, "Honoré Bonnet et Christine de Pisan," in *Etudes du droit international et de droit politique*, Vol. 1.

incidentally, and therefore his book is of very slight importance for international law.

Various questions relative to war are examined in the short treatise *De bello et bellatoribus*, by Giovanni Lupo (Lupus or Lopez),[23] who draws his inspiration from the teachings of St. Thomas. He discusses, in the form of a dialogue between a master and his disciple, the various kinds of war; who has the right to wage it; the formalities of declaration of war and certain questions relative to booty. Lupo, who agrees with the theories of Martino, affirms, however that the subject should always presume the legitimacy of a war waged by his superior. Theological considerations concerning the causes and the justice of war are to be found in almost all the *Summae* published in Italy during the fourteenth, fifteenth and sixteenth centuries and in the other work of theologians.[24] The problem of a just war is considered in the *Summa theologiae* and *Summula* published respectively in 1517 and in 1524 by Tomaso da Vio (1469–1534), better known under the name Cardinal Cajetanus.[25] The ideas of Cajetanus are extremely severe; to him war is a judicial procedure and is directed toward the punishment of the guilty party. For this reason it may not be arrested until the chastisement has been meted out. It is lawful for the prince to order the sack of a city by way of punishment: indeed in such a case the prince is not even bound to distinguish between the guilty and the innocent, because all the subjects of the enemy should be presumed to be hostile and guilty. The prince who wages an unjust war must yield all that he has unjustly conquered and make compensation for the expenses and the damages suffered by his opponent during the campaign.[26]

Mention should also be made of the treatise *De eversione singularis certaminis*, by Antonio de Bernardi of Mirandola (1503–1565), whom Gentili eulogizes.[27] The work is devoted mainly to ordeals, yet it contains remarks concerning war.

The distinction between just and unjust wars is also at the basis of the *Tractatus de re militari et bello,* by Pierino Belli (1502–1575), of Alba in Piedmont. After perfecting himself in law in the University of Perugia, Belli was at the age of thirty-three named auditor of war in the

[23] The treatise is published in the sixteenth volume of Ziletti's *Tractatus.* Another Spaniard, who lived in Italy and wrote on the law of war is Francisco Arias de Valderas, author of a short treatise *De belli justitia injustitiave tractatus,* 1533, reprinted in Vol. XVI of Ziletti's *Tractatus.*

[24] For a list of Italian *Summae* of this epoch see Nys, *Les origines du droit international,* pp. 118–119.

[25] On Cajetanus see the Introduction by J. Marega in Thomas da Vio, *Scripta philosophica.*

[26] In *De jure belli,* Book III, ch. 26, p. 413, Gentili reveals a knowledge of the writings of Cajetanus.

[27] For Antonio de Bernardi see Nys, "Antoine Bernardi, évêque de Caserte," 16 Rev. dr. int. et lég. comp. (1884) 283 ff., and Fusinato, "Antoine Bernardi," 16 Rev. dr. int. et lég. comp. (1884) 599 ff.

armies of Charles V. In the fulfillment of his functions he displayed notable skill, as a result of which he was promoted counsellor of war by Philip II, to whom he dedicated *De re militari et bello*.[28] In 1561 Emmanuel Philibert, of Savoy, who by the Peace of Château-Cambrésis had regained possession of his states, appointed Belli counsellor of state. On behalf of the duke of Savoy he carried out various missions of a politicojuridical character, also acting more than once as arbitrator. The ability manifested in the execution of the various missions entrusted to him, his rectitude, and his independent judgment won for Belli the gratitude of the prince and the esteem of his contemporaries.

De re militari et bello was probably composed in 1558. In writing it Belli took advantage of the experience he had gained during his long years of service with the Spanish armies; in fact there are frequent references to cases which the author had had the opportunity of examining as arbitrator or in the exercise of his function with the armies.

Some passages in the dedication of the book suggest that Belli had the intention of writing a treatise on the international law of war based upon principles of natural law. In fact, however, he mingled with the subject of the law of war certain problems of an entirely different nature, which concerned the public administration and military affairs.[29] In reality the book, as Efisio Mulas, a modern biographer of Belli's, observes, examines and decides all the questions that an auditor of war ought to be acquainted with, allowing ample space to public law in so far as it affects and modifies private relations between citizens. Moreover, Belli does not content himself with expounding doctrine, but adds the lessons of his practical experience and gives an account of all the cases upon which he had been called to pass judgment during his years as an auditor. He considers each case with reference to Roman law and to the opinions of the doctors, so that his book may be considered a veritable handbook of theory and practice combined, of great usefulness to all who aspired to the office of auditor, then greatly sought after and extremely difficult to discharge.[30] This is the reason for the book's immediate success, but it is also in part the cause of some of its principal defects—such as the prolixity of the treatment and the continuous confusion of heterogeneous matters referring to military discipline and combatant forces.

Belli's treatise is divided into eleven parts, these in turn being subdivided into chapters, of which there are 69, containing 1079 numbered cases or questions. The eleven parts deal respectively with the origin and kinds of war, the power to declare it, and the persons who may be per-

---

[28] Pierino Belli, *De re militari et bello tractatus*, 2 vols., with an introduction by A. Cavaglieri and an English translation. For Pierino Belli, besides Cavaglieri's Introduction, see Randolino, *Pierino Belli*; Mulas, *Pierino Belli da Alba precursore di Grozio*; Chialvo, *Pierino Belli*.

[29] *De re militari et bello tractatus*, pp. 63 ff.   [30] Mulas *Pierino Belli*, p. 56.

mitted to take part in a war; with the principles that ought to be followed in initiating and terminating a war, the causes that render it just, and the extent of the duty of obedience to superiors; with *postliminium;* with the relations between prisoners and their captors; with truces; with various secondary questions that may arise from the state of war; with the organization of armies; with crimes committed by soldiers and their punishment; with safe conducts; with peace, its conclusion, and the consequences that may derive from it; and, in the last part, with hostages. It clearly appears that the treatment does not follow a logical order; yet Belli's constant fidelity to some fundamental principles produces a certain coherence between the parts of the book that deal with questions of international law.

Like his Italian precedessors and his Spanish contemporaries, Belli bases his reasoning on premises of a religious character. Wars are divided into just and unjust: a war is unjust if it is not waged for defense, for securing restitution, or from necessity. It is not merely permissible, but a matter of duty to take up arms for the defense of one's country, of liberty, of public order, and of one's own sovereign. In an unjust war, however, it is not lawful to serve: a vassal may not serve his lord, and all combatants are answerable for losses inflicted upon the enemy.

In order to be just a war must be waged not only for a just motive (*justitia causae*) but also by one, who has the power to declare it (*justitia potestatis*). This prerogative is an inherent attribute of sovereignty. Therefore "any people or nation living under its own laws and its own charges, and any king or other ruler who is fully independent, may declare war at will and when occasion arises." [31]

A declaration should precede war, unless it is waged (*a*) against pirates, (*b*) against those whom the emperor and the pope have declared public enemies, and (*c*) against the vassals, confederates, or allies of those against whom war is waged, whenever they lend effective aid to the latter.[32]

War must be just not only in its origin but also in all the activities that take place during its course. This leads Belli to examine the conduct of warfare.

He condemns stratagems of a perfidious nature and deplores the use of mercenaries who combat solely from a desire for booty. Prisoners of war should be treated with moderation, and all cruelty should be avoided.[33] Noncombatants and enemy legates must be respected. The inhabitants of occupied territories should not be considered enemies, provided, however, that they abstain from hostile acts and respect the au-

[31] *De re militari et bello tractatus,* p. 7.
[32] Cavaglieri, Introduction to Belli, *De re militari et bello tractatus,* p. 15a.
[33] Belli, however, justifies the death sentence of Conradin of Hohenstaufen on the basis of the supreme interest of the state.

thority set up in the country by the occupant power. Private property should be respected as much as possible. Neither pillage nor the destruction of property should be permitted, nor should the levying of contributions of any kind be allowed; indeed payment must be made for everything which has to be appropriated for the needs of the army.[34]

The right to enemy spoils is recognized by the law of nations. Every consequence of the war ends with peace, which must cause a veritable *restitutio in integrum*. The occupied territories must be restored, unless otherwise expressly stipulated. The treaties must be interpreted in good faith, and the same applies to the truces. *Neque decet*, Belli remarks, *cavillari pactiones et foedera*.

It is to Belli's credit that he advocated certain principles relating to neutrality, of which he stressed the territorial character. He asserts that it is not lawful to imprison or molest any enemy found on neutral territory, that foreigners on the territory of belligerent states must not suffer any harm from the latter, and that neutral territory must not be violated for any purpose incidental to warfare. Not even the transportation of prisoners across neutral territory may be admitted; should such transportation be proved, the prisoner must be held to have regained his liberty at the moment when he entered the neutral territory.

Belli is strongly in favor of arbitration. If one of the contending parties declares in favor of submitting the matter to arbitration, the other party is obliged to lay down his arms and submit to the decision of arbitrators. The war is unjust on the part of that combatant who refuses to submit to arbitration.[35]

Opinions concerning Belli's work vary greatly. Among foreigners, Nys in his work of the origins of international law devotes only a few sentences to Belli, and Holland's opinion is unfavorable.[36] The recent reprint of his work in the "Classics of International Law" is a proof of the renewed interest in this author. Among Italians, with the exception of Tiraboschi, no authoritative scholar took any interest in Belli's work previous to Mancini.[37] At the end of the nineteenth century, when the Italian writers rediscovered Gentili, especially after Holland had once more attracted the attention of scholars to him, they by reflex brought Belli into the lime-

---

[34] Cavaglieri, Introduction to Belli, *De re militari et bello tractus*, p. 16a.

[35] Belli's book lacks a discussion of the juridical problems arising from maritime warfare.

[36] *Studies in International Law* p. 50, "Belli lived just too early to think of placing his science upon another foundation than that of the Church, nor had he such a grasp of his subject as would have enabled him to abstract it from topics with which it had no further connection than that they, like it, are brought under notice of a President of Courts-Martials."

[37] Mancini, *Diritto internazionale* pp. 13–15, considers the *De re militari et bello tractatus* the first treatise on the law of Nations and gives particular credit to Belli for having solved "some of the grave and controversial questions propounded in the course of his book with a courageous liberality of principles, which, considering the official position he held, cannot but be marveled at, affording as it does a splendid contrast to the timorous servility of many celebrated writers of the following centuries."

light. Unfortunately the interest of the Italian writers of that period was focused especially on establishing the comparative merits of these two writers, and their judgments were often influenced by regional jealousies. In reality the question had been badly posed, because a comparison is barely conceivable between two writers who lived in different countries and dissimilar environments. Belli remains in the rank of the Catholic thinkers of Spain and Italy; Gentili, a Protestant who lived in England, therefore enjoys greater liberty of thought. Among the more authoritative of the recent Italian writers, Solmi holds that "Belli, whom some writers would like to define as a forerunner of Grotius, is merely a continuator of the old Italian school of thought, aimed at considering legal problems concerning fighting troops" [38] rather than the laws of war.

Much more favorable is the judgment given by Cavaglieri in his excellent introduction to the edition of the *De re militari et bello*, published in the "Classics of International Law." Cavaglieri observes, and one cannot but agree with the statement, that in spite of Belli's defects he is certainly one of the most authoritative and direct forerunners of Gentili and Grotius, for both of them were undoubtedly influenced by his writings. The criticisms that have been made of Belli's work, as regards lack of logical order, deficiency of style, confusion in treatment brought about by the injection of extraneous questions, lack of unity and insufficient critical spirit, cannot easily be answered. Belli's book gives the impression of a patient work of erudition unsupported by a solid and accurate foundation of general principles. This accounts for the fragmentary impression aroused by the whole work. The weakness of the contribution given by it to the formation of general doctrines of international law is also due to the fact that Belli, as a devout Catholic, never succeeds in freeing himself from religious influences and inhibitions with regard to certain problems of international law. In particular he is still very far from conceiving international law as a system of juridical rules distinct from religious precepts. In this sense he is the last great writer of the Italian theologico-religious tradition, to which Giovanni da Legnano and Martino of Lodi also belong, whereas Alberico Gentili is the first among the great Italian scholars of international law to break with this tradition.

Yet Belli's defects are in great part justifiable. As regards the flaws of his method, it should be noted that Belli was unable to profit by the writings of previous writers: he was in fact the first to write a book really deserving to be called a treatise on international law of war. If we compare it with the works of Giovanni da Legnano or Martino of Lodi, the *De re militari et bello* is a masterpiece of methodical skill, order, proficiency, and clarity. As for the excess of erudition, it is worthy to note that the

[38] Solmi, "Alberico Gentili e il nuovo diritto internazionale," in De Francisci, P., and others, *Alberico Gentili, Scritti e discorsi*, p. 17.

works of Gentili and especially of Grotius are also not free from that defect.

As for Belli's lack of originality—apart from the fact that one does not look for originality in a jurisconsult—this defect is due at least in part to the purpose of his book which did not aim at creating a new system of laws of war or at championing new ideas, but mainly at commenting on the juridical norms relating to war commonly accepted, with which an auditor of war was supposed to be familiar for the fulfillment of his functions. Nor should we forget that Belli, unlike almost all the other jurisconsults considered in this book, was exclusively a practitioner, not a theoretician of the law.

These defects of Belli's are counterbalanced by noteworthy merits. Although Belli shows his reverence for certain religious premises, he still tries to reconcile them with the new historical and political situation, which he thoroughly grasped. For instance, he accepts the theological distinction between just and unjust wars, but at the same time he widens the concept of just war to such a degree that almost every war could be considered just, and in this way he ends by annulling a distinction that no longer existed in practice. In the same way he professes the deepest respect for the pope and the emperor, but also expresses the opinion that every sovereign nation has the right to wage war. He thus recognizes the existence of the sovereign states that were taking shape in those years. On this point it is easy to see that Belli is a direct forerunner of Gentili and Grotius. But on the other hand he is far from asserting the full internal sovereignty of the state or the obligation of unquestioning obedience to it on the part of citizens. Various chapters of the second part of his book are in fact devoted to an examination of cases in which a citizen, a soldier, or a vassal may refuse to take part in an unjust war.

A still greater merit of Belli's lies in the fact that he raises the whole discussion to a lofty and human level, especially in all that concerns the treatment to be allotted to the wounded, to prisoners, and to noncombatants, and the respect for private property. In his treatment of these objects he reveals a breadth of ideas truly exceptional for his times, which we are obliged to appreciate all the more if we recall how many years of his life Belli spent in the staff of combatant armies. It is in this part of Belli's work that his religious ideas exercise a singularly beneficent influence.

These merits of a moral character must not lead us to overlook the fact that the *De re militari et bello* also has merits of a juridical nature. From this point of view, in my opinion, Belli's work is especially valuable in its details, where he discusses the solution of particular questions that came up during the course of his career. Apart from the fact that such questions provide a lively picture of the juridical problems arising from military activity in those days, it is in the solution of such problems that Belli drops all moralizing and religious prejudices and becomes realistic, rapid, orderly and precise in his arguments. From the way he handles these particular cases we realize that Belli must have been an exceptionally able practitioner, and this explains why he was entrusted with the solution of delicate problems and how he managed them with credit to himself. It is in his rare attempts to achieve the construction of a juridical system that Belli proves in his book his great inferiority to Gentili and Grotius.

Belli's influence on later writers was far from insignificant. It is certain, as Mulas has exhaustively demonstrated, that Gentili's and even Grotius's works on the law of war in many points are too much like Belli's for the resemblance to be simply accidental. For this reason the fact that Gentili never even mentions Belli in his *De jure belli* is, to say the least, strange; for he certainly must have been familiar with it, and indeed he quotes Belli in support of certain opinions expressed in his *Advocatio Hispanica.*[39]

OPPOSITION OF THE ITALIAN JURISTS TO REPRISALS

Belli's *De re militari et bello* does not contain even passing mention of the usage of reprisals. The omission is all the more significant, inasmuch as the book gives a precise picture of military practice of the author's times. Gentili's *De jure belli,* too, which frequently alludes to Italian practice of the day, mentions reprisals only incidentally. This silence is due to the fact that in the sixteenth century reprisals no longer had any practical importance in Italy. During the precedent centuries, when reprisals were common in Italy, scholars paid much attention to them. Writers such as Bartolus and Martino of Lodi devoted entire works to reprisals; others, such as Giovanni da Legnano, dealt with them copiously in works devoted to war or even to questions of private law. The exercise of reprisals, in fact, also gave rise to private law questions, such as the right of the individual against whom the reprisals had been exercised to seek reparation against the one for whose wrongdoing reprisals had been granted.

The attitude of Italian scholars toward reprisals was one of contempt and hostility. It is but in passing, and often with scorn and commiseration, that they are mentioned by Odofredo (d. 1265), Nicola Malombra (d. 1285), Guido da Suzzara (d. ca. 1292), Iacopo de Arena (d. 1296), Lambertino dei Ramponi (d. 1304) Andrea d'Isernia (d. ca. 1316), Oldrado da Ponte (d. 1335), and Jacopo da Belvisio (d. 1335).[40] Cino da Pistoia (1270–1337) went even so far as to affirm that reprisals "regulariter per iura nostra prohibitae sunt." Bartolus opines that reprisals are

[39] Mulas, *Pierino Belli*, p. 17.   [40] A. del Vecchio and Casanova, *Le rappresaglie*, pp. xii ff.

an odious and exceptional remedy. This attitude of scholars is easily explained. From the practical point of view reprisals constituted a notable obstacle to the security and regularity of international trade, upon which the prosperity of the Italian cities was based, and the Italian juriconsults, who took an active part in the life of their age, realized it perfectly. From the theoretical point of view reprisals clashed with the idea of imperial authority for which the Italian lawyers professed such profound reverence. For the emperor's privilege to grant justice whenever a wrong has been committed led to the conclusion that he alone ought to provide for reparation, not the offended person himself. It is not surprising, therefore, that several writers followed Cino's teaching that reprisals were not in conformity with the law of the empire and that some, like Bartolus, asserted that the foundation for reprisals was not to be found in the *jus commune*. Giovanni da Legnano, following the ordinarily accepted opinion of earlier writers, declares that reprisals are an extraordinary remedy based on the *jus gentium*: "istud remedium extraordinarium ortum habuit ex jure gentium."[41]

Reprisals could only be justified on the theory that all the members of a political organization must be considered jointly responsible for the wrong committed by any member of the group, a principle extremely unpalatable for Italian jurisconsults educated in the principles of Roman law, according to which everyone is responsible for his own wrongs and for them alone. When the revival of Roman law occurred, Italian writers denied the lawfulness of reprisals and attempted to limit them by referring to its principles. In this way they seconded with the authority of scholarship the movement first toward the limitation and then toward the suppression of reprisals, to which we have already alluded. Triepel observed:

It was especially the Romanistic reaction against the exaggeration of the principle of collective responsibility, inherent in the old practice of reprisals, which succeeded, if not in abolishing at least in considerably mitigating and transforming them. The fact that the movement tending to restrain this unlimited responsibility began in Italy whence it spread throughout Western Europe, is a sure sign of the influence of Roman law.[42]

Although scholars deplored the use of reprisals, it was yet not possible for them to remain utterly indifferent toward a practice which was widely followed. *Ex facto oritur jus.* Bartolus, who of all Italian jurisconsults of that age considered the recent juridical developments with the greatest realism, was the first Italian to write a treatise devoted exclusively to reprisals: the *Tractatus represaliarum*. This subject was again discussed with much method and juridical precision by Giovanni da Le-

[41] Giovanni da Legnano, *Tractatus de bello, de represaliis et de duello*, ch. 123.
[42] *Völkerrecht und Landesrecht*, pp. 215–216.

gnano in his *Tractatus de bello, de represaliis et de duello,* in the fifth part of the third treatise. On reprisals we also have a short treatise by Martino of Lodi,[43] and another by Giovanni Iacopo de' Cani (d. 1430),[44] which in the main repeat the teachings of Bartolus. Short references to reprisals are to be found in writers not much later than Bartolus, such as Alberico da Rosate and Baldus. Later the discussion of the subject disappeared from Italian law books.

It is interesting to note that as a rule when Italian writers examine reprisals they expound the same principles—frequently use even the same words. This is probably due to the fact, that virtually they expound well-established rules which had gradually arisen from practice. The first problem that confronts scholars is to find a legal justification for the new practice of reprisals, conflicting so strongly with the idea of the emperor's sovereignty. As has been said, their justification could not be based on the *jus commune;* it was based on the *jus gentium,* which alone was held to satisfy the imperious demands of justice and the new legal problems springing from changes in the organization of the empire. As Bartolus made perfectly clear, the juridical and practical basis of re-prisals is to be sought in the circumstance that the emperor has *de facto* lost his authority over the entire community of Christian nations, whereby, in case a wrong is committed, it may so happen that there exists no authority superior to both the offender and the offended and capable of repairing the tort. The doctrine endeavors to reduce reprisals to a strictly judicial procedure. It does so by distinguishing between reprisals and individual self-defense. Bartolus remarks that it is not lawful for anyone to take the law into his own hands: "non licet alicui sua auctoritate jus sibi dicere." [45] Italian scholars firmly lay down the principle that reprisals, to be lawful, must be allowed by a superior—more precisely, by an authority endowed with sovereignty. Thus, the Italian cities may allow reprisals, because they are superior to their own citizens and, on the other hand, recognize no superiors; that is, they are sovereign. Cor-relatively, he against whom reprisals are granted must not be *de facto* amenable to the *superioris copia.* This is at the root of the whole treat-ment of the question by Bartolus. The *superioris copia* is wanting.[46] Moreover, for the purpose of transforming reprisals into a judicial pro-cedure Italian writers tend to put reprisals on the same legal footing as war, which, we have remarked above, was at that time conceived as a judicial procedure. "Concedere represalias est indicere bellum," Bar-tolus explains. Giovanni da Legnano teaches that the remedy of reprisals, inasmuch as it is permitted by the *jus gentium,* "est quaedam species

---

[43] Martino of Lodi, "Tractatus de represaliis," in Ziletti, *Tractatus,* Vol. XII.
[44] Giovanni Jacopo de' Cani, "Tractatus de represaliis," in Ziletti, *Tractatus,* Vol. XII.
[45] Introduction to *Tractatus represaliarum.*   [46] Woolf, *Bartolus of Sassoferrato,* p. 204.

belli liciti." [47] From the almost complete identification between war and reprisals scholars deduce that reprisals too, like war, are admissible only when they are just. Reprisals are just only if granted in cases in which a war would be just. This principle is destined to limit the possibility of granting and applying reprisals.

In the discussion of reprisals jurisconsults constantly refer to conceptions taken from civil law and therefore from Roman law. Bartolus declares expressly that he discussed reprisals "cum speculationibus ad jus civile spectantibus." Resort to Roman law, which ignored reprisals, was intended to limit their usage: for instance, scholars refer to the Roman law conception of *res extra commercium* in order to teach that against them reprisals may not be exerted. Once the principle had been admitted that some kinds of property were not subject to reprisals, their number began to grow continuously. From the *jus civile* the rule of construction was also derived that since reprisals are a hateful act the rules regulating them had to be strictly construed against the person who exercises them.

Reprisals, according to scholars, may be accorded for one motive only: denial of justice. Reprisals cannot be granted if the petitioner has not had proper recourse to the authorities of the defender to obtain damages and if justice has not been refused to him. With some rare exceptions reprisals can only be granted to citizens or residents of the conceding state or to merchants damaged in the execution of business deals connected with the conceding state: for example, to merchants robbed on their way to a fair in the territory of the conceding state. The reprisals may as a rule be conceded only against citizens and residents of the offender's state. Scholars tended gradually to enlarge the sphere of persons against whom reprisals might not be conceded or who were immune from their exercise.

Although the disappearance of reprisals in Italy was chiefly due to economic reasons, yet we must recognize that scholars had the merit of having constantly advocated in their teachings first the limitation and then the disappearance of this odious practice.

DISAPPEARANCE OF THE DISTINCTION BETWEEN JUST AND UNJUST WARS: ALBERICO GENTILI

The distinction between just and unjust wars had already lost its importance in Europe at the time when Belli wrote his *De re militari et de bello*. Writers were by this time not so much interested in establishing this distinction as in ascertaining to whom the right to wage war belonged. Against the empire, the Church, and the feudal lords the national states —Spain, France, England—were asserting themselves, and with the national state the idea of sovereignty was coming into being everywhere.

[47] *Tractatus de bello, de represaliis et de duello*, ch. 123.

War was considered an attribute of sovereignty; whoever was a sovereign had the right to wage a war. Every war is just which is waged by a party vested with sovereignty. The principle is not even debated by Machiavelli (1492–1550),[48] is enunciated without hesitation by Alciatus (1492–1550),[49] and it is clearly expressed by Bodin (1530–1596).[50] Machiavelli and others replace the conception of a just war with that of the raison d'état.[51] In the sixth chapter of the Prince Machiavelli recognizes as legitimate property that which the prince obtains by force of arms; Machiavelli does not even mention just wars, because for him "that war is just which is necessary." [52] The same principle was taken up in France by Bodin, who declared "bellum justum quia necessarium"; it was generally followed in Italy, where it was in fact proclaimed even by writers such as Francesco Guicciardini (1482–1540) and Giovanni Botero (1540–1617), who professed political ideas entirely different from Machiavelli's. The same principles were accepted in Italy by jurists proper, such as Calderini [53] and Castiglioni,[54] who occasionally touched on the problem of war. These principles, moreover, were in harmony with the political events of that era. In the continual struggles which were then being fought to maintain a European balance of power, it would have been impossible to determine which side was in the right and which in the wrong, no matter what criterion one had followed. Moreover, the distinction was opposed by the modern state then arising, which asserted the principle that it was not lawful for citizens to question, on the basis of their religious and ethical principles, the legitimacy of the wars waged by their sovereigns.

The change that had occurred in principles and in the political situation was felt even by the theologians and canonists, who more than any one else had attempted to keep alive the distinction between just and unjust wars based on theologico-moral theories. In a serious attempt to grapple with the difficulties which arose out of controversies between princes in which there was equality of right between the conflicting parties or serious doubt as to the relative merits of their competing claims, theologians such as Vasquez (1551–1604) expounded the theory of probabilism.[55] They maintained that either by "invincible ignorance"

---

[48] Il principe, ch. 3. [49] "Paradoxa," Book 2, in Opera Omnia, Vol. I.
[50] De republica libri sex, Book 3, p. 338.
[51] For the influence of Machiavelli's ideas on international law see Benoist, "L'Influence des idées de Machiavel," in 9 Rec. des cours (1925) 233 ff. For the history of the idea of the raison d'état in Italy see Ferrari, Histoire de l'idée de la raison d'état and Corso sugli scrittori politici italiani; Meinecke, Die Idee der Staatsraison in der neueren Geschichte.
[52] Il principe, ch. 26: "qui è giustizia grande, perchè quella guerra è giusta che è necessaria." (Italics ours.)
[53] Consilia, ch. 94. [54] Consilia, ch. 12.
[55] Butler and Maccoby, The Development of International Law, p. 111. Vasquez' theories on the subject matter are expounded in his Controversiarum illustrium aliarumque usu frequentium libri tres.

or by "inexcusable ignorance" it might happen that a prince waged an unjust war with the conviction that it was a just one. In this case the war was just on both sides. Similar principles were expounded by Victoria and even more definitely by the famous theologian Molina (1535–1600). In this way the foundations were laid for the later attitude toward war—that the average class of hostilities is not without justification or either side.[56] The distinction between just and unjust wars, about to disappear in the Catholic countries, was denied even more vigorously in Protestant countries, where it was considered as dependent upon the idea of the papal supremacy. In fact its initiators had from the outset maintained that since the distinctions between just and unjust wars was of a theological character, it should be the pope's prerogative, as supreme spiritual authority, to pass judgment on the justice or injustice of a war. Thus, in Catholic countries, as well as in Protestant countries, the ground was prepared for dropping the old conception.

There is almost a symbolic significance in the circumstance that the final rejection of the doctrine of just war was due to Alberico Gentili, a writer born in Italy and brought up in the juridical tradition of the Italian post-glossators and in the study of the Italian and Spanish Catholic canonists, who, however, was a Protestant and lived and taught in Protestant Elizabethan England. Alberico Gentili was the first among writers on international law firmly to grasp the new historico-political situation arising from the disappearance of the universal authority of the empire and from the rise of the great independent national monarchies. In harmony with the new situation, he abandoned the traditional distinction between just and unjust wars, based on theological criteria and on ideas of civil and canon equity, and set up on a strictly secular basis a system of autonomous juridical norms, a law of nations, destined to regulate the relations between states in case of war. This task Gentili performed in the *De jure belli*, his principal work, in which he deals with the laws of war. In reality the book examines all the fundamental problems of the law of nations and therefore has a content and an importance that transcend its title and have won for Gentili an eminent place in the history of international law. Starting with the *De jure belli*, we shall make an attempt to give a general picture of Gentili's conception of international law and its historical value.[57]

[56] *Ibid.*, p. 113. Molina's theories are expounded in his *De justitia et jure tomi sex.*
[57] For a complete list of the writings of Gentili and writings about him see G. del Vecchio, "Saggio di bibliografia Gentiliana," in De Francisci and others, *Alberico Gentili, scritti e discorsi.* For numerous biographical notes on Gentili see the excellent book, already cited, by Molen, *Alberico Gentili.* As we have already stated, it is the merit of the Carnegie Endowment of International Law to have published in the "Classics of International Law" the *De Legationibus*, the *De jure belli* and the *Hispanicae Advocationis*, with English translations and introductions by E. Nys, C. Philipson, and F. Abbot, respectively.

Alberico Gentili was born in 1552 of a noble family of San Ginesio, in the March of Ancona. He studied law in the neighboring University of Perugia, where Bartolo had taught and Belli had studied.[58] After having received the degree of doctor in jurisprudence in 1572, he held several public offices in Ascoli and San Ginesio, respectively. This was the period during which the ideas of the Reformation were having their greatest successes in Italy, and the reaction of the Roman Catholic Church was most violent.[59] Persecuted by the Inquisition for his Protestant ideas, Gentili was obliged to abandon his fatherland a few years after receiving his degree, and thus he began the succession of Italian international lawyers, continued by Mancini and others, who from love of liberty had to take the road of exile. After a brief sojourn in Laibach, in Kaernten, and in a few cities of Germany, Alberico toward the middle of 1580 reached England. By the following year he taught law at Oxford. Until his death in 1608 he resided almost uninterruptedly in England, teaching at Oxford, holding public offices, and practicing law in London. Educated in the school of the Italian post-glossators, Gentili was a fervent admirer of Bartolus and of the Italian juridical method, the *mos italicus*, the defense of which he undertook against Cujas, Zasius, Budaeus and the other champions of the *mos gallicus*.[60]

Gentili's greatness was fostered both by his juridical formation in Italy and by his life in England. To the full and certain possession of Italian juridical science Gentili owed the aptitude for the systematic, logical, and rational treatment of juridical questions, which permitted him, in the *De jure belli*, to plan an international community based on solid principles of law. Proud Protestant sixteenth-century England, freed from all subordination to the emperor and the pope, furnished him

[58] This was mentioned by Gentili in his work *Laudes academiae Perusinae et Oxoniensis*.
[59] During the whole Middle Ages and the Renaissance Italy was upset by religious movements of a heretical character, which often gravely endangered the supremacy of the Catholic Church. See Volpe, *Movimenti religiosi e sette ereticali nella società medioevale italiana*. The ideas of the Reformation were much more widely spread in Italy than is generally supposed. On this point see Brown, *Italy and the Reformation to 1550*, and Rodocanachi, *La Réforme en Italie*. It was only by means of bloody persecutions and at the cost of the suppression of all intellectual liberty that the Counter-Reformation succeeded in arresting the spread of Protestantism in Italy. It is by this time recognized even in Italy that the Counter-Reformation was one of the principal causes of the decadence of the country in the 16th century. Even recently several Italian writers, such as Missiroli, *La monarchia socialista*, have attributed the political immaturity of large classes of the population of Italy to the lack of a religious reformation in Italy.
[60] Gentili's first book written in England, the *De legibus interpretibus dialogi sex*, is devoted to the defense of the *mos italicus* in the study of jurisprudence against the French method, the so-called *mos gallicus*, which tends to examine legal texts from an historical point of view rather than from that of pure juridical exegesis. The *mos gallicus* also is partly of Italian origin: this method in a large measure originated from the teaching of Giasone del Maino and, above all, of his great disciple Andrea Alciatus, who was the teacher of Cujas. Zasius too felt the influence of Giasone del Maino, for he was a disciple of Cittadini, who had been educated in the school of Giasone. Cf. Stinzing, *Ulrich Zasius*, p. 57.

a typical example of the independent modern state. Moreover, the vision of the growing civil, mercantile, and political greatness of the country, based on its maritime power and on international intercourse and steeled by continuous violent struggles with other nations, gave Gentili a lively understanding of the reality and importance of international relations. The spectacle of continuous, intense relations between states convinced Gentili of the necessity that these relations should be governed by actual rules of law, not by the vague abstractions of theology and by the uncertain dogmas of empiricism. Gentili understood that if the states wished to achieve stability in international relations they must subordinate their intercourse, not to the fluid rules of a confused and uncertain practice, but to fixed juridical principles derived from a law of nature superior to the nations. These were the principles that inspired the *De jure belli*.

Like Gentili's other works, this book was suggested by a political question of a contingent nature that faced English citizens of the Catholic faith after the expedition of the Spanish Armada: may a Catholic subject of Queen Elizabeth lawfully combat against a monarch professing the Catholic religion? [61] This question led Gentili to consider the more general one to which the *De jure belli* proposes to find an answer: under what circumstances is a war lawfully begun, conducted and terminated? To answer this question, Gentili had to consider in his book almost all the principal problems of international law.

In the edition of 1598 the work is divided into three books.[62] The first treats of war in general—who can wage war and what motives or causes justify it. The second treats of the lawful manner of conducting operations of war; declarations of war; acts permitted and prohibited after the hostilities have begun; the use of spies, of poison, and of stratagems; the treatment of enemy persons and of the noncombatant population during the campaign; prisoners and hostages; the conclusion of pacts and truces, and so forth. The third book examines the conclusion of the war: the rights of military occupation, the rights of the conqueror with regard to the persons and the property conquered, and the conclusion of the peace.[63] The work is strictly juridical and departs from the tradition of Italian writers, who confused the subject of the international law of war with that of military science or of military regulations of single states.

As Gentili indicates at the outset of the *De jure belli*, the book is intended "to give an account of the laws which we have in common with

---

61 Cf. Molen, *Alberico Gentili*, p. 51.
62 In 1588, the year of the Spanish Armada, Gentili published the first part of the work *Prima commentatio de jure belli*. The second and third parts appeared in the following year. The *De jure belli libri tres* appeared in 1598 and is practically a new work, five times larger than the work mentioned above.
63 C. Philipson, Introduction to *De jure belli*, pp. 16a, 17a.

our enemies and with foreigners." [64] These laws must not be confused with the laws of the single peoples; they are in fact a law superior to them, which disciplines "that great community formed by the entire world and the whole human race." [65] Under this law enemies are placed on an equal footing. Gentili observes that from the very etymology of the word *hostis* it appears that to be enemies signifies to be equal.[66] The law of war is a subdivision of the *jus gentium*, and this leads Gentili to consider what the *jus gentium* is. In the *De jure belli* the old and ambiguous expression *jus gentium* has acquired the meaning of international law—that is, of a law regulating the intercourse between states. Later Gentili had occasion to give a precise definition of the *jus gentium* in his book *De nuptiis*, published in 1601: "Jus gentium dicitur quod naturalis ratio inter omnes gentes constituit, quod hominibus inter se commune est." This *jus gentium*, a gift of God to men, is and ought to be recognized by all present and future peoples, inasmuch as it is based upon the *naturalis ratio*.[67] With Gentili there thus begins the naturalistic conception of international law,[68] later accepted by Grotius. Although in general this conception has today been supplanted, it marked progress and constituted a necessary basis of procedure for the epoch in which it arose. It marked progress because it affirmed the existence of an autonomous system of rules of law distinct from the precepts of religion and ethics and directed at regulating international relations according to abstract principles of justice. It thus claimed for law what previously had been the domain of ethics and theology. It was a necessity, because amid the frequent uncertainties and oscillations of the practice of those times, juridical rules could only be created by the enunciation on the part of scholars of fixed general principles intended to govern the actions of men in a way analogous to that in which general physical laws govern human life. In harmony with the doctrine of natural law, Gentili did not try to desume the principles he enounced from practice, but insisted, on the contrary, that practice must be guided by certain abstract principles of justice "nam facta nos non quaerimus, aut ex factis jus constituimus; sed ex jure examinamus facta, et faciendis praejudicamus." [69]

Gentili considers international law distinct not only from history and theology but also from the other branches of law. He criticizes, in fact, just as much the earlier interpreters, "who have gone astray in introducing into this subject a bald and inappropriate discussion of civil law,"

---

[64] *De jure belli*, pp. 1–2. [65] *Ibid.*, p. 2. [66] *Ibid.*, Book I, ch. 1, p. 1.
[67] Already in the *De legationibus*, Book II, ch. 18, p. 121, Gentili had taught that "international law is based on natural principles, which have been implanted in all by nature and are so well known that they need neither argument nor art to establish them."
[68] Kaltenborn und Stachau, *Die Vorlaeufern des Hugo Grotius auf dem Gebiete des jus naturae et gentium*, pp. 228–231.
[69] *De jure belli*, Book I, ch. 20, p. 151.

as the modern French writers such as Bodin and Petrus Faber, who handle international questions from a prevalently historical viewpoint. He criticizes the theologians, too, who pretend to solve problems of the law of war by means of theological arguments. Speaking of the lawfulness of war, he inveighs against them: "silete theologi in munere alieno." [70] What the characteristics of the international community are, according to Gentili, has already been outlined.

After premising these ideas about law and the international community Gentili goes on to define war. "Bellum est publicorum armorum justa contentio." War is a just and public contest of arms. The definition, which even today seems acceptable, felicitously stresses the public character of war, because of which it may only be waged between states, and its juridical nature, by which it is not beyond the law but regulated by juridical rules. [71]

The purpose of the book is to determine when a war is just. For a war to be just, Gentili predicates it must be perfect in every part, that is, it is not enough for it to have been begun lawfully, it must also be carried on lawfully. For a war to have been begun lawfully (*jus ad bellum*) there are three requisites: (1) recourse must be had to arms; (2) the war must be fought between sovereigns; and (3) it must be waged for a just cause.

The first requisite distinguishes war from pacific ways of settling international disputes. In connection with this distinction Gentili emphasizes the desirability of solving disputes whenever possible by pacific means, such as arbitration.

The second requisite is extremely important. When Gentili proclaims that war can be waged only between sovereigns, he intends to call attention to the fact that war can take place only between subjects of international law. For this reason it is not possible to qualify as a war a conflict between private individuals or a duel. The enemy must be a state. In order to determine who can be an enemy Gentili strays from his subject proper, the law of war, to the general problem of the law of nations: which organisms are subjects of international law. Gentili invokes Cicero in order to declare: "He is an enemy who has a state, a senate, a treasury, united and harmonious citizens, and some basis for a treaty of peace, should matters so shape themselves." [72] Sovereign is thus defined: one who recognizes no superior and therefore is independent. The necessity for a war derives from the fact that as between two sovereigns there is no authority having jurisdiction to settle their disputes. "Non est principi in terris judex aut ille princeps non est, supra quem capit alius locum pri-

---

[70] *Ibid.*, Book I, ch. 12, p. 92.
[71] C. Philipson, Introduction to *De jure belli*, p. 32a: "Gentili's definition is the briefest and—regard being paid to its brevity—the most precise that has ever been enunciated."
[72] *De jure belli*, Book I, ch. 4, p. 40.

mum. Necessarium itaque judicium armorum inter hos fuerit." [73] On
the basis of these criteria Gentili proceeds to an examination of the question: which political entities of his age have the right to wage war? He
conducts this analysis with a strict juridical method not unaccompanied
by a lively historical sense. Gentili reaches the conclusion that not only
the great monarchies but also the Italian and German principalities possess the right to wage war; since only sovereigns have this prerogative,
it is clear that neither operations to suppress piracy nor civil wars are
veritable wars. Sovereigns at war with one another are on a footing of
equality; this means that the same laws of war are applied to each side.
This principle was at that time far from being as obvious as it is today.
Gentili's admission of it is a denial of what many earlier writers affirmed,
that whoever fought against the pope and the emperor might be subjected
to a far severer treatment than other belligerents.

The third requisite for a lawful war is that it must have been resorted to
for a lawful reason. According to Gentili wars may be defensive or aggressive. All defensive wars are lawful, but Gentili admits that some
offensive ones can also be lawful. In addition, certain wars can be lawful for both sides—not only subjectively, that is, in the opinion of those
who wage them, but also objectively, that is, from an extrinsic point of
view—if both sides are convinced of the righteousness of their cause.
The deeper Gentili proceeds into this subject, the closer he gets to Machiavelli's opinion that every war based on necessity is justified. Gentili
asserts, in fact, that in case of necessity a state may intervene in an armed
conflict between a foreign state and the subjects of the latter, also that
a war waged to defend the balance of power in Europe against the hege-
monic attempts of Spain is a lawful war.[74] And since according to Gentili the decision, concerning the lawfulness of a war is on the whole left to
each belligerent, it becomes obvious that the distinction between lawful
and unlawful wars has for him come to lose all meaning whatsoever. In
consequence of his rejection of all theological influence on the subject,
Gentili denies that a war may be waged for religious motives.[75] As to the
relations with the Turks, Gentili insists that a war waged for purely religious reasons is unlawful; yet he is forced to admit that there exists a
permanent state of war with the Turks.

The principle that in order to be just a war must also be fought legitimately leads Gentili to the exposition, in his second book, of the rules

---

[73] *Ibid.*, Book I, ch. 3, p. 23.
[74] It should be noted that for Gentili the principle of the balance of power has an exclusively political value, whereas a few later writers, such as Heffter, *Das Europäische
Völkerrecht*, p. 8, committed the error of attributing to it the character of a principle of
positive international law.
[75] It may be observed that a question of such urgent interest for that epoch was prudently
omitted by Grotius in his *De jure belli*.

relative to the conduct of war (*jus in bello*). He declares that "there is no phase of war which can be devoid of justice." [76] This means that the conduct of hostilities is also governed by rules of the law of nations, which every state is bound to respect. Without going into detail, it will suffice to observe with regard to this part of the book that Gentili on the whole sets forth with objectivity and precision the rules of positive international law and the norms regulating the practice of war in his days. If he sometimes strays from this course, it is only in order to advocate milder principles than were currently practiced; these milder principles, he affirms, ought to be deduced from natural law. In Gentili's opinion war should be preceded by a declaration; and an interval ought to be allowed to lapse between the declaration and the beginning of hostilities. Stratagems of war may be tolerated, but not unlawful ruses. The use of poison and the treacherous slaying of an enemy is not permitted. Truces should be concluded and continued in good faith. Those who surrender must be spared, and in no case may prisoners be killed. Gentili states that the law of nations warrants reducing prisoners to slavery, but he discourages this barbarous usage. The noncombatants, or innocents, as he calls them, should be respected, and their property might not be seized.

From the conduct of the war Gentili passes to the discussion of the problem of neutrality. He begins by positing two fundamental principles: first, that war normally involves only the belligerents and their subjects, and, secondly, that war has a territorial character and is therefore exclusively limited to the territory of the belligerents. These principles imply some very important consequences for the *non hostes*, as Gentili calls neutrals: in case of war aliens sojourning on enemy territory may not be considered enemies unless they have become enemy citizens, and their property may not be seized. The *non hostis* becomes, however, a belligerent if he renders assistance to one of the parties to the war. Military operations may not be carried out on neutral territory, and for this reason the property of enemies captured on neutral territory must, upon his request, be restored to the neutral sovereign. Nor may prisoners be taken there, and a prisoner who has taken refuge in neutral territory is automatically freed.

Since the object of every war is the restoration of peace, Gentili, in his third book, discusses the rules relating to the conclusion of peace. This part of his work is of utmost importance. Gentili, to be sure, expounds the juridical principles relative to the end of the war and to the consequences of the peace with a precision exceptional for those times. Yet with sound political intuition he exhorts the winner not to lay claim to the integral application of such principles as might hamper the con-

[76] *De jure belli*, Book II, ch. 1, p. 209.

clusion of a lasting peace.[77] Every peace treaty, he maintains, should in fact aim at establishing a lasting peace. Consistently with these principles Gentili holds that by the letter of the law the victor may lay claim not only to that part of the enemy's territory his army occupied at the moment when hostilities ceased but also to the entire territory of the vanquished. The victor may change the form of government of the territory he has annexed. If the victor absorbs the totality of the conquered state he must also take its obligations upon himself. But Gentili counsels treating the vanquished with leniency and leaving him a certain amount of liberty, especially in religious matters. For if the peace conditions are not founded on justice, the peace cannot be a lasting one. The termination of the war is reached with the treaty of peace, which contains the conditions actually agreed upon by the contracting parties and is valid even if concluded as a result of coercion brought to bear by the victor on the vanquished. A kindred problem is the question of treaties of friendship and alliance; Gentili's principles on this subject have been examined elsewhere.[78] In the same connection Gentili also goes into the question of the validity of treaties concluded with infidels.[79] The book ends with a stirring invocation to the Divinity that an end may be made of all war.

The originality of the *De jure belli* lies in its treatment of the problem of just wars, entirely different from the method followed by Gentili's predecessors. Before Gentili the problem of just wars had consisted especially of determining what the causes were that authorized the waging of war. Although Gentili apparently asked himself the same question, yet the way he discusses the subject is completely new. The motive for which a war is waged is, according to Gentili, entirely irrelevant in the eyes of the law. War is a prerogative of all sovereign states which they may exercise whenever they think fit. In addition, Gentili observes, war is a necessary consequence of the equality and independence of states. Since there is no power superior to the states which may settle their controversies in case of a conflict "necessarium atque judicium armorum inter hos fuerit." By the hackneyed assertion that war should be just Gentili means to express a new conception: that war is not outside the law, but on the contrary is a juridical procedure. As such, it is subject to certain juridical rules; they determine who may wage a war; they distinguish war from civil war and from the repression of piracy; they bind the belligerents to respect certain rules of conduct during the hostilities.

---

[77] Philipson, Introduction to *De jure belli*, p. 40a: "On the whole of this subject the teaching of Gentili is distinctly progressive, though he takes up a position between that of the idealists and that of the uncompromising partisans of *Realpolitik*, who say that 'necessity knows no law,' that 'war is war' and relaxations are out of place in it and incompatible with its purpose and precision."

[78] See supra, p. 77.   [79] See supra, p. 78.

The task of the jurisconsult is to study these rules and to free this subject from the shackles of theology. Gentili's conception corresponds to the historic reality of his age, when the great independent monarchies were constituted; and even today it is still juridically correct.

In 1605 Gentili was appointed to defend the Spanish interests at the English Court of Admiralty, and he continued to hold this office until his death. At that time Spain was in open conflict with Holland, and the English courts were frequently called upon to decide questions rising from the maritime war between the two nations. It was this practical and professional activity that gave rise to Gentili's book *Hispanicae advocationis libri duo,* also known as *Advocatio Hispanica,* which is in fact a collection of pleas in support of Spanish claims, law opinions, and letters dealing with the author's practice at the bar. The material collected in the book has not undergone a complete re-elaboration: a few of the documents are little more than scarcely developed notes; in addition, the book is fragmentary rather than organic, since no attempt was made to give any strict unity to the arguments discussed in the various chapters. These defects and the obscurity of certain portions of the book are probably due to the fact that Gentili died before he terminated it and the book was published posthumously in 1613 by his brother Scipione, who gathered together the material, notes, and documents which death had prevented the author from completing. Nonetheless the value of the work is considerable for three reasons. First, because more than any other book of Gentili's it bears the imprint of the author's personal character in the directness of its style and in the rapidity of its reasoning. Secondly, because it gives an exact idea how cases were handled at that period. Lastly and especially, because many of the questions dealt with offer notable interest for international law. The second book is without this particular interest, inasmuch as it concerns only questions of civil law and of procedure, but the first book deals with various fundamental questions of international maritime law, postliminy, and neutrality. Gentili was well aware of the book's importance; although he gave orders for all manuscripts left unfinished at his death to be burnt, he instructed his brother Scipione to publish the *Advocatio Hispanica.*

As a lawyer Gentili was sometimes obliged to plead contradictory theses in the various cases he had to defend. This accounts for certain contradictions in the *Advocatio Hispanica.*[80]

The ideas set forth by Gentili in the *Advocatio Hispanica* on the liberty of the sea, on the jurisdiction of the states over the sea, and on territorial waters have already been detailed.[81] In this work Gentili reasserts the

---

[80] A few of the contradictions are pointed out by Molen, *Alberico Gentili,* pp. 170–174.
[81] See supra, pp. 69–70, 73.

territorial nature of sovereignty and the rights of neutrals, which he takes into consideration with special reference to maritime warfare. The book, given its special nature, does not contain the enunciation of general principles on the subject, but these may be deduced from their practical application to particular questions made by Gentili. The author maintains that the Tuscans, who carry out warlike operations against the Turks without even being at war with them, have no right to attack an English ship directed to Turkey, since England is not at war with Tuscany and the ship and its cargo are not destined to give the Turks military aid against Tuscany.[82] English mercenaries hired to fight with the Spaniards against the Dutch cannot legitimately be killed by the latter, who have captured them on their way, because until the moment in which they begin to serve they are neutrals, not enemies.[83] As regards the duties of neutrals, Gentili asserts that a neutral ship that takes part in an attack made by a belligerent on an enemy ship must be considered a pirate ship.

From the principle of the extraterritoriality of sovereignty Gentili concludes that an enemy ship cannot be attacked or blockaded in the territorial waters of a neutral power;[84] that prizes brought into neutral territory are lost by the captor and revert to the former owner;[85] that enemies may not be captured in the territorial waters of a neutral power;[86] and that prisoners transported through the territorial waters of a neutral and landed in a neutral harbor automatically gain their freedom.[87] It is doubtful whether these principles defended by Gentili were practiced in his times.

Gentili is in agreement, however, with the rules enforced in his days when he asserts that prizes are lawful when captured by an enemy ship, not by a pirate, and that contraband may be captured on neutral ships.[88] This forces Gentili, though reluctantly, to admit the legitimacy of the right of search, which however, he believes, can be exercised only off the coast of the power that practices it.[89] The captor must pay the freight for the goods and passengers captured on board a neutral ship.[90] Gentili, in fine, maintains that prizes do not belong to the captor until he has brought them inside his fortified lines, no matter how long he may have had possession of them.[91]

In harmony with the opinion defended in the *De jure belli* Gentili denies to pirates any right whatsoever. They are the common enemies of humanity; merchandise appropriated by them does not change ownership; the buyer of such goods or the person who receives them from the pirates for the purpose of selling them must give them back to the owner, without any right to reimbursement even if they have acted in good

---

[82] *Hispanicae advocationis*, Book I, ch. 25.   [83] *Ibid.*, ch. 9.
[84] *Ibid.*, ch. 14.   [85] *Ibid.*, chs. 6, 8.   [86] *Ibid.*, ch. 5.   [87] *Ibid.*, chs. 2, 11.
[88] *Ibid.*, ch. 20.   [89] *Ibid.*, ch. 27.   [90] *Ibid.*, ch. 28.   [91] *Ibid.*, ch. 12.

faith.[92] As a result of its very character, the book does not contain a definition of "pirate." Indeed, it would not have been easy to draw a distinction between a pirate and a lawful combatant in the days of Sir Francis Drake and the "beggars of the sea." As has been seen, there is one particular case in which Gentili holds that a ship could be considered a pirate ship: when her crew is chiefly composed of neutrals and she joins another ship of a different nationality in order to attack a third ship belonging to a power at war with the latter.

As for privateering, Gentili admits that such practice is recognized by the law of his age, yet he deplores it resolutely. Letters of marque granted to privateers are "latrocinium verius quam bellum"; [93] they give rise to "a predatory warfare waged in accordance with no discipline or custom of war, a war against noncombatants and harmless merchants and others situated far from the battle lines, although it is only what takes place at the front that really seems to be done in war." [94]

This brief account is sufficient to prove how important the *Advocatio Hispanica* still is today for students of international maritime law.[95]

The outline of Gentili's books dealing with international law, given in the course of the present work, permits us to attempt a general appreciation of this author. Gentili's merit is obvious if we compare his work with that of the previous writers who had considered the topics dealt with by him. His first merit lies in having cleared the field of international law from the dogmas of a particular religion and of having distinguished the juridical from the ethical and political aspects of the problems debated. This certainly does not mean that Gentili was insensible to religious and moral problems. On the contrary, all his work is imbued with principles of lofty moral significance. This is clear in his condemnation of wars waged for purely religious motives. His invitation to princes to exhaust pacific means and above all arbitration before resorting to war is equally inspired by moral scruples. So are his constant effort to mitigate the harsh laws of war by recommending leniency toward noncombatants,

---

[92] However, Gentili supports the opposite opinion in the case of certain Venetians who, having been despoiled of their merchandise by English pirates, demanded them back from English merchants, to whom they had been sold by the Treasury of Tunis. *Ibid.*, chs. 11–12.

[93] *Ibid.*, ch. 11.

[94] *Ibid.*, ch. 8, p. 35. The same idea is expressed by Gentili in an unpublished opinion on the right of prize, quoted by Nys, *Les Origines du droit international*, p. 77: "dico esse odiosissimum hoc jus literarum markae quod merito divinissimus rex noster abominatur: per quod geritur latrocinium verius quam bellum: contra inermes et innoxios mercatores et alios aciebus longe positos."

[95] Apart from the *Hispanicae advocationis*, no noteworthy contribution was made to international maritime law by Italian authors of this period. Giulio Ferretti, whose work on diplomatic agents has already been mentioned, wrote a short treatise *De belli aquatici praeceptis*, which deals with the strategy rather than with the international law of naval warfare. Ferretti is also the author of a treatise on the law of land warfare, *De re et disciplina militari aureus tractatus*. This book, too, is of little importance.

prisoners, and the defeated and his condemnation of privateering and of abuses committed by belligerents against neutrals. Gentili's historical sense is not less admirable. He disposes of the old theories of the supremacy of the pope and the emperor and recognizes the existence of independent states, whose equality he proclaims; he affirms that all peoples, including the infidels, belong to the international community; he stresses the territorial and exclusive character of sovereignty. Perfectly conscious of the needs of his age, Gentili derives from these fundamental principles further consequences of extreme importance. He outlines the principle of a balance of power between the states and asserts the principle of the freedom of the seas, tempered, to be sure, by the principle that each state has exclusive jurisdiction over its own territorial waters. Gentili's historical sense leads him also to reject the ancient theories of a just war and guides him to an understanding of the importance that the idea of neutrality had gradually been acquiring with relation both to land and to maritime warfare.

The importance of the principles expounded by Gentili is equaled by the excellence of his method, characterized by strict reasoning and precision of concepts. He is the first to set forth in a complete and organic fashion the body of general principles that form the framework of the international community. Without a doubt certain aspects of Gentili's system reveal the influence of the Roman conceptions and of the scholastic methods of teaching prevalent during his age in Italy. Yet we have seen that Gentili did not confuse international law with Roman law and was able in a large measure to protect himself against the defects of the Italian school, by his time in full decadence. Gentili rose from the rules of Roman law to the elaboration of the principles of natural law, which were destined to exert a wholesome influence on the development of international law.

Obviously Gentili owes a good deal to his predecessors. He owes his method to Italian jurisconsults; his lofty sense of humanity to Spanish theologians; the political substratum of his system to Machiavelli, to Bodin, and to Sir Thomas More.[96] The novel element of his theories is in part an inevitable product of the changes that took place at that period in the structure of the international community. But if Gentili had not possessed remarkable personal qualities, these factors would not in themselves have been sufficient to establish his superiority over his predecessors.

The conviction that Gentili owes so much to previous writers saves us from repeating the error, for so long a commonplace, of comparing Gentili and Grotius in order to determine which of the two deserves to be

---

[96] For the relations between Belli, Victoria, and Gentili, see now Scott, *Law, the State and the International Community*, Vol. I, pp. 387 ff.

called the father of international law. The problem is wrongly posed, because both had forerunners who laid down the bases without which neither of them would have been able to produce his works. It has been already demonstrated by other writers that "there was little novel in the legal system of Grotius and there was equally but little original in the arrangement of the matter of his work." [97] The fame of Grotius' *De jure belli et pacis* is due after all rather to the timeliness of his work than to his originality of ideas or method. Considered now at a distance of centuries, the works of Gentili and Grotius both appear as the offspring of the same epoch, theories, and historical problems. Their general characteristics are very similar. In the opinion of the present writer, Gentili is from a purely juridical point of view the superior, because he is more accurate. A good instance of this is his definition of war, which so effectively stresses both its public and its juridical character and is therefore much superior to that of Grotius, who conceives war merely as a violent conflict and fails therefore to distinguish between private and public wars. Gentili's superiority is also shown by his strictly legal discussion of the immunity of ambassadors, of rights and duties of noncombatant enemies and of neutrals, whereas Grotius reveals himself as far less just and less precise.[98]

But which is superior, Gentili or Grotius, is after all nothing more than a question of personal likes and dislikes. The criticism Voltaire flung at Grotius, that he was a tedious writer, is far less superficial than it appears, and it goes to the root of the Dutch writer's shortcomings. In fact his entire work is burdened by the weight of cumbersome scholarship and by the abuse of quotations and examples from classical writers, from the Bible, and from religious authorities. It is sometimes not very easy to grasp the connections of this material with the subject discussed. This hampers Grotius's line of thought and diminishes its directness and effectiveness. To this may be added Grotius's habit of quoting almost exclusively cases taken from the classics, not from contemporary practice, which lends to his work an air of existing in a vacuum. In short, Grotius's mode of reasoning lacks vigor and juridical precision. These shortcomings cannot be imputed to Gentili.[99] It is certain that in the works of the latter there is far less display of erudition. Gentili's style is harsh and

---

[97] Walker, *A History of the Law of Nations*, p. 333. This author also remarks, "Again and again, the reader of the pages of Grotius who shall have made the acquaintance of the lights of moral and legal learning of the sixteenth century, will catch the echo of their opinions and of their very phrases." More recently Clark, *The Seventeenth Century*, p. 126, speaking of Gentili's work, remarks, that "there is no need to argue against the mistaken statement still current in some works of reference that the science of international law was founded by a still later writer: Hugo Grotius."

[98] G. del Vecchio, "Ricordando Alberico Gentili," in De Francisci, and others, *Alberico Gentili, Scritti e discorsi*, pp. 56–57.

[99] Yet it is undeniable that Gentili's concise style sometimes harms the clarity of his reasoning.

knotty and far from the perfection of Grotius's writings. But Gentili is closer to the reality of his age, he continually refers to examples drawn from contemporary practice; he realizes what were the urgent problems of his times and tries to solve them; he is concise, direct, and aggressive in his reasoning.[100] Through the pages of Gentili's books the man appears as he must have been: realistic and passionate. Therefore, if Grotius is more philosophic and impartial by temperament, and so more adapted to the elaboration of a system of doctrines capable of serving as a guide to later writers, Gentili strikes us as more realistic and as a better jurisconsult. He is a great lawyer in the complete sense of the word.

[100] Clark, *The Seventeenth Century*, p. 125: "His books are typical of the way in which international law was built by the union of academic study with the experience of practice in the courts."

IMPORTANCE OF ITALY'S CONTRIBUTION TO THE PRACTICE OF
INTERNATIONAL LAW

THE examination of the Italian practice of the Renaissance has shown that beginning with the twelfth century the Italian states maintained diplomatic relations, concluded treaties concerning frontiers, communications by land, by river, and by sea, the protection of the rights and the property of subjects abroad, extradition, and the recognition of civil and penal judgments. These states established protectorates, settlements, and colonies; founded colonial companies; appointed consuls; and laid claim to territorial waters. Even in the absence of treaties they recognized the existence of a law superior to the states which imposed the obligation on the latter to grant certain rights to aliens; to recognize, within certain limits, the validity of foreign laws, acts, and judgments and to follow certain uniform rules in the field of maritime law and of the conflict of laws. So far as concerns the settlement of international disputes, they often resorted to peaceful means, such as mediation and arbitration; they subjected reprisals to a legal discipline and in the end suppressed them; they introduced into war on land certain rules of leniency; they accepted a few principles relating to war on the sea; they concluded truces, capitulations, and peace treaties; they developed a few principles on neutrality. Some international institutions that still exist, such as legations, consulates, extradition, and international settlements, are related to institutions which originated or at least reached their full development in Renaissance Italy. If we consider these multiform aspects of the relations between the Italian states of the Renaissance, the assertions of Van Vollenhoven that international law of medieval times, regulating international relations was as slight as it was rare, and that in point of fact, it comprised only a number of rules for the transaction of commerce and some rules of conduct for the case of war would not seem to be quite justified—at least, not so far as Italy is concerned. On the contrary, the conclusion would seem more justified that among the Italian states an entire juridical system had gradually come into being, a complete and organic system which can be considered only as international law.

The most widespread opinion differs from the one expressed in the present work. It is believed that during the Renaissance no international community in the veritable sense of the word existed in Europe. European society of the Middle Ages and the Renaissance are supposed to have consisted of an agglomerate of political groups with limited autonomy—often depending upon one another in manifold relationships, feudal by origin and by nature—and all subjected to the supreme authority of the Germanic emperor and the pope. The Germanic emperor, by the will of Providence heir to and continuator of the Roman emperors, was considered the political leader of this republic of Christian nations, and the pope its spiritual sovereign.[1] This society, constituted, as it were, like a pyramid of powers, was believed to have been framed in a fashion diametrically opposed to the structure of the modern international community. The latter was believed to have arisen at the time of the Peace of Westphalia, 1648, having the characteristics, which it still preserves, of a society formed of equal and independent entities, for the greater part states not subjected to any superior common power. The treaties of Münster and Osnabrück, in this conception, distinctly separate the modern epoch from the preceding one, in which no international community and no international law existed, at least none with characteristics similar to such as exist today.[2] For this reason several histories of international law begin (Westlake's) or end (Walker's) with the Peace of Westphalia.

As a matter of fact, the contrast between the international society of the Renaissance and that of the era following upon the Peace of Westphalia seems to be artificial and contrary to the reality of history. The modern international community was not suddenly born at the time of the treaties of Münster and Osnabrück with the characteristics that it still displays, but was slowly formed during a continuous process of growth that goes back for many centuries. The international community of today is nothing but the ancient *civitas Christiana*, which united all the peoples of Europe in one organism under the supreme authority of the emperor and the pope.[3] At first this organism was certainly not an international

---

[1] Romano, *Corso di diritto internazionale*, 4th ed., p. 15, and Anzilotti, *Corso di diritto internazionale*, 3d ed., p. 4.

[2] On the significance of the Peace of Westphalia from the point of view of international law see the fundamental work by Rapisardi Mirabelli, "Le Congrès de Westphalie," 8 Bibliotheca Visseriana (1929) 5–102.

[3] Cf. Balladore Pallieri, "Le dottrine di Hans Kelsen e il problema dei rapporti tra diritto interno e diritto internazionale," 27 Riv. dir. int. (1935) pp. 68–69, "The disappearance of the imperial and papal authority did not break the unity of the Christian world and did not destroy the general juridical order that centered in these powers; even after claiming and obtaining their internal and external independence, the states continued to cultivate among one another relations still based on the same rules as existed when the pope and the emperor were authorities superordinated over the other powers. It is not true that the states, after the destruction of the imperial authority, found themselves isolated in dealing with one another and absolved of all juridical bonds until, at a much later date, after the Peace of Westphalia, they constituted *ex novo* an international order superior to themselves. On the contrary,

community, but it became such when the various countries of which it was made cast off *de facto* the authority of the pope [4] and the emperor, refused to recognize any *de facto* superior, and after establishing complete independence negotiated with one another and with the emperor on a footing of equality. This transformation of the republic of the Christian nations into an international society began to take place as early as the twelfth century. There then were formed areas in Europe comprising countries between whom relations were established similar in kind to those now existing between the independent modern states: that is, relations governed by international law.[5] The first of these areas was formed in Italy. The relations between the Italian states of the Renaissance, especially in the epoch of the *signorie* and the principalities, were international relations.

It is not merely a coincidence that the crisis of the medieval republic of Christian peoples—which led to the transformation of this organization into the modern international community—had its origin in Italy. Nor is it surprising that the Italian states were the first to adopt in their external relations a position similar to that of the modern independent states. The modern international society, with the peculiar qualities and rules which it still preserves, is a typical product of the mercantile capitalist society that rose in Europe toward the end of the seventeenth century. This mercantile and capitalist society, however, had already taken shape in Italy at the beginning of the Renaissance.[6] The mercantile bourgeoisie, impatient of all limitations to its free economic and political activity, was the ruling class in the Italian cities. It was a capitalistic impulse that led the bourgeoisie of the Italian communes to subdue the feudal aristocracy, which thus lost in Italy that political function it kept centuries longer in other countries. This same capitalistic impulse also led the Italian communes to claim their autonomy in relations with the pope and the emperor. By destroying within themselves the feudal system and by annulling the authority of the emperor over them, the Italian communes and later on the *signorie* and principalities, who followed the

---

the sense of unity, of many common interests, and of manifold bonds that held the state together never failed, and legal rules regulating their relations still continued to exist and to be enforced. The legal order of the international community is therefore still the legal order of the ancient Holy Roman Empire, limited in its jurisdiction solely to international matters because of the formation of the modern states, and radically modified in its constitution because of the reluctance of the modern states to admit in any field whatsoever a power superior to them."

[4] The Bull "Unam Sanctam" issued in 1302 by Pope Boniface VIII was the pope's last attempt to assert his own universal authority in the temporal field. As everyone knows, that attempt was not crowned with success.

[5] Before the Peace of Westphalia the same phenomenon took place in other zones of Europe too. For Central Europe see Zimmermann, *La Crise de l'organisation internationale à la fin du moyen âge*, 44 Rec. des cours (1933) 315 ff.

[6] For a thorough demonstration of this point see Sombart, *Der moderne Kapitalismus*.

same trend, wiped out the hierarchical system upon which the society of
the Middle Ages had been founded. Although the Italian states kept alive
a few frail bonds with the emperor, in practice they went as far as completely to deny any power superior to the state; this is the primary canon
of modern international law. The struggle for the balance of power between the Italian states gave rise to the principle of the equality of the
states, which is another of the canons of international law. The uninterrupted international relations between the Italian states caused the formation of numerous rules of international law. In the limited society of the
Italian states there thus arose principles and rules of international law
which were later extended to the whole of Europe. Nys justly observes
that "cette Italie . . . était organisée dès lors en petit comme l'Europe
le fut plus tard en grand." [7] Rapisardi Mirabelli observes strikingly that
the Italian society of the Renaissance was the microcosm that constituted
the archetype of the future international society of Europe.[8]

It should also be noted that the society centered in the Italian states
was not exclusively Christian and European, because the Italian states,
as has been seen, also had frequent and active relations with Mohammedan states. The treaties concluded with the latter did not differ either in
form or in binding value from those concluded among Christian states.
The international society that revolved about the Italian states already
comprised, therefore, Christian and non-Christian states on a footing of
equality.

The denial of the existence of such an international society will not be
justified by noting that the rules of international law were often violated
in those days. Would anyone dare to say that this is truly a feature capable of distinguishing the society of that time from our own? On the contrary, in those days violations of international law had far less serious
or far-reaching consequences than today. This was due to the fact that
the states were not omnipotent, as they are today, within their own frontiers and were not supported by nationalistic ideologies. There were on
the other hand powerful organisms intermediate between the individual
and the state, whose activity extended even beyond the territory of a single state; there was at least within the sphere of the Christian society a
communion of religion, of culture, and of ideals which it was difficult to
break. Today it is far otherwise. The unity of the world is shattered; the
state is all powerful within its sphere. The most brutal violations of law
are committed with totalitarian technique, and moreover they are not
checked by moral or religious forces capable of contending with them.

The point that should rather be stressed is this: that while the Italian
states had actually attained independence and equality, there was on
their part no formal expression of such principles. Writers like Bartolus

---

[7] *Les Origines du droit international*, p. 168.   [8] *Storia dei trattati*, p. 133.

asserted that the cities were *de facto* independent of the emperor, but he did not deny the superiority of the latter *de jure*, even if the deductions he drew therefrom were exclusively moral rather than juridical and political. At first a clear assertion of their own independence was not forthcoming even from the communes themselves.[9] In this respect the Italian society of the Renaissance differs from the modern type of international community, of which Gentili was the first theorist, based on the principle of the juridical equality of the states. We must, however, recognize that in modern times it is precisely the opposite phenomenon that is to be observed. Whereas the juridical equality of the states is generally recognized in principle, there is no *de facto* equality and some of them are not even politically independent. Moreover, in the present struggle for world hegemony, totalitarian states have attempted to form constellations of states based on the supremacy of one of them over the other members of the group, not only *de facto* but *de jure* as well.

LIMITED IMPORTANCE OF ITALY'S CONTRIBUTION TO THE THEORY OF INTERNATIONAL LAW

Although Italy's contribution to international law during the Renaissance was eminently practical, her doctrinal contribution ought not to be neglected either. First, there was an indirect contribution, which consisted of the revival accomplished by Italian jurisconsults of Roman law; from its principles are derived the principles of natural law that for centuries functioned as the source of international law. The direct contribution is not less important. This consisted of the elaboration of several theories of international law. It is the principle of the *civitates superiores non recognoscentes*, affirmed by Bartolus, that opens the path before the modern doctrine of international law. The Italian jurisconsults were well aware of the existence of an international community and contributed effectively to the development of its fundamental principles: first they transformed the conception of the empire into that of an international society; then they extended the sphere of this to embrace even the peoples outside the empire and the infidels themselves. The universal character of the international commonwealth is unequivocally asserted by Gentili. For this reason it is very largely due to Italian jurisconsults that the *jus gentium* really became a *jus inter gentes*. Another merit of the Italian jurisconsults is their constant effort to extend the authority of international law. They maintained the existence of principles of the law of nations binding the states to grant a minimum standard of rights to aliens; to recognize foreign laws, acts, and judgments, and to follow certain rules in questions of maritime and international private law. As far as particular doctrines are concerned, it is they who are specially respon-

[9] Salvatorelli, *A Concise History of Italy*, p. 204.

sible for the creation of the doctrine of territorial waters and for the limitation and the outlawry of reprisals. In Gentili, Italian scholarship made a decisive contribution to the development of diplomatic and international maritime law. Naturally it would be a mistake to read more between the lines of these old writers than they themselves ever meant to say or to attribute to them principles which were not enunciated until later and which in that age would indeed have been quite inconceivable. It has sometimes been stated that the only portion of the doctrine of international law to which both the Middle Ages and the Renaissance made an appreciable contribution was the law of war. As far as Italian jurisconsults are concerned, it cannot be denied that on the whole this is the weakest part of their work, vitiated as it is by theological premises and by its confusion with questions of an entirely different nature.

Let it clearly be understood that during this period no Italian school of thought existed which was capable of creating or even of developing with any pretense of uniformity an original and coherent body of doctrines in the field of international law. Only single jurisconsults in their writings studied particular questions relating to international law. Some of these men were important enough to exercise considerable influence on other lawyers in Italy and elsewhere. For this reason an attempt at synthesis can with difficulty be made, and in many parts of this chapter it has been difficult to go beyond an analysis of the individual doctrines of the most important thinkers. An Italian school of international law, endowed with its own characteristic doctrines, was not to arise until the *Risorgimento.*

The Italian contribution to international law during the Renaissance was for some time underrated. This is partly due to insufficient knowledge of the materials, which even today are available only to a limited extent. But to a great degree it is due to ideological reasons. The political and juridical thinkers of the seventeenth century and even more those of the eighteenth and the nineteenth centuries considered the Peace of Westphalia the close of a period dominated by the empire and the papacy and the opening of an era in which the independence and the equality of the states were first recognized. The importance of the Peace of Westphalia was also stressed by Protestant writers, for whom it represented the beginning of a period during which the supremacy of the Church began to be counteracted by the sovereignty of the states, no longer subject to any religious control.[10] French historians, too, were inclined to lay

[10] Westlake, *Collected Papers on Public International Law,* p. 43: "Through the labor of Grotius, . . . a fairly complete body of international law was produced at the moment when the international society for which it was to serve was assuming the form which a little later was consecrated by the Peace of Westphalia. The coincidence was not casual. Then for the first time, through the decay of the Emperor and of the coercive power of the Catholic Church, it could be seen that the society would be a purely secular one and would be com-

much emphasis on the Peace of Westphalia, inasmuch as it opened the era of France's political supremacy in Europe.[11] All these currents contributed to the creation of the widespread opinion that there was no practice of international law during the epoch that preceded the Peace of Westphalia. Similarly, the assertion was frequently made that Grotius was the father of the science of international law, simply because he was the first famous author on the subject after the Peace of Westphalia. Out of the oblivion that covered the authors before Grotius the only one to emerge, and indeed he was revealed only in part and not until quite recently, was Gentili, perhaps because in his writings he was one of the bitterest adversaries of the supremacy of pope and emperor. The truth is that this overvaluation of the Peace of Westphalia is repugnant to the historical sense of our generation. Without in any way wishing to diminish the fundamental importance of the Peace of Westphalia, it is only fair to recognize that it represented a single step in the slow and continuous evolution of international law and that it would, be wrong to ignore all that it owes to the practice and the theory of the preceding ages.

---

posed of such a crowd of practically independent states that only general considerations could be applied to their actual relations. Then too, as the volume of history was being finally closed on mediaeval Europe, the jealousy of Roman law also finally disappeared."

[11] For instance, Mably, *Le Droit public de l'Europe fondé sur les traités*, who took the Peace of Westphalia as the point of departure for his treatment of the international law of Europe, called attention, in his Preface, to the fact that there was almost no act anterior to said Peace still in force in the relations between states at the time he was writing.

PART TWO

The Period of Foreign Ascendancy

ALBERICO GENTILI, constrained by religious intolerance to leave his
country for a foreign land just entering upon a period of greatness,
where his genius and his learning were to be justly appreciated, is token
of Italy's decline in the sixteenth century and of the displacement of the
center of the intellectual, economic and political life of Europe from
Italy to other regions.

THE END OF THE ITALIAN INDEPENDENCE

A few years before Gentili quitted Italy the Peace of Château-Cambrésis, 1559, had allotted to Spain the Duchy of Milan, the Kingdom of
the Two Sicilies, Sardinia, and the *Stato dei Presidii* in Tuscany and had
opened the period of foreign ascendancy in the peninsula. Italy had
ceased to be a factor in European politics. Even those Italian states that
continued to remain independent—that is, Venice, the Duchy of Savoy,
the Duchy of Parma and Piacenza, and the Papal States—had sunk to
comparative insignificance in international politics and even in the general destiny of the Italian peninsula itself. The whole of Italy was subject to the direct rule or the preponderant influence of Spain, only in part
counteracted by France's anti-Spanish policy. In addition, this period of
Italian history was characterized by absolute governments and the ecclesiastical regime of the Counter Reformation.

The germs of this profound decadence of Italy had their remotest
origin in the period of the very splendor of the Renaissance. The cult of
the individual, though it had made of the Renaissance Italian, singly considered, one of the most robust examples of humanity, had been an obstacle to the political unification of the country. Individualism had degenerated into egoism and indifference toward the public interests and had
hampered the formation of a civil consciousness in the citizens. The Renaissance Italian, completely absorbed in his own affairs and his own hu-
manistic studies, was above all, to borrow a phrase from Guicciardini,
"intent on his particular business," and he neglected his public duties.
Military discipline in particular had fallen into disuse, with the resulting
decadence of citizen militias, which were replaced by companies of mercenaries, one of the worst scourges of Italy. Individualism, restive to all
political and moral discipline, also resulted in the factious character of

the Italians, which provoked rivalries between one Italian state and another and petty jealousies between the various cities within each state.

The period between the Peace of Lodi, 1454, and the invasion of Charles VIII, 1494, is generally thought of as an era of peace and stability for Italy, during which the peninsula, free from all foreign ascendancy, attained a notable degree of national unity through the formation of five great states: Milan, Florence, Venice, the Papal States, and Naples. According to the current opinion they formed a sort of confederacy which decided the destinies of the peninsula and meanwhile perfected their own internal consolidation. The reality was very different. Besides the five major states there also existed a great number of minor states, which at times encroached upon their territory. Some of them were of considerable importance: independent republics,[1] minor principalities,[2] smaller independent *signorie*,[3] small fiefs of the empire,[4] and the very small fiefs.[5] There were, besides, diminutive vassals of the greater, especially in the Papal States.[6] The consolidation of the larger states was also subject to restrictions. Notwithstanding certain measures of absolutistic centralization, they had to a great extent the character of a conglomerate of divers cities and territories, which was no longer a civic government and had not yet become a united territorial state of the modern type.[7] Nor did this disintegration of Italy come to an end with foreign ascendancy: besides the Spanish dominions and the formally independent principal states, there still subsisted in Italy a bevy of little states. Their gradual disappearance, a process which continued until the French Revolution, was a prominent factor in the unification of Italy.[8]

The principle of a balance of power, extolled as a monument of political wisdom, had helped to hinder the unification of Italy by perpetuating the division of the peninsula into small states which were jealous of one another. It had even favored foreign ascendancy, because the states that feared to be placed in a position of inferiority did not hesitate to invoke foreign intervention. The foreign invasions of Italy, such as that of the French in 1454 and later that of the imperial troops, culminating in the Sack of Rome, in 1527, had demonstrated the country's political disruption and inflicted extremely serious economic damage. Moreover, when

[1] For instance, Genoa, Siena and Lucca.   [2] For instance, the duchy of Savoy.
[3] For instance, the *signoria* of Piombino in Tuscany.
[4] For instance, those of the Marquis Malaspina at Massa and Carrara, and of Del Carretto at Finale Ligure.
[5] For instance, those in the "Langhe," in Piedmont, and in Lunigiana, in Tuscany.
[6] For instance the Montefeltro at Urbino and numerous other *signorie* in the Marches, in Romagna, and in Latium.
[7] Salvatorelli, *A Concise History of Italy*, pp. 337–338.
[8] *Ibid.*, p. 416: "To afford an idea of the small dominions still existing in Italy, we may cite the case of Lunigiana, where Pontremoli belonged to Milan, Sarzana to Genoa, and other parts to the Duke of Florence and to the Cybo; but there were also twenty-four feudal lordships, eight under the protection of Spain, and eight directly dependent upon the Empire."

the principle of an Italian balance of power later became a European principle, it marked the end of Italian independence. In the struggles for a European balance of power between the great monarchies that were taking shape at that time, the Italian states, too small to exert an active political function, had sunk to the role of inert pawns in the hands of the Great Powers, when they did not serve as battlefields for their wars.

Neither in the military nor in the economic sphere were the small Italian states able to compete with the great European monarchies. Not in the military sphere, because they lacked the financial resources that permitted the great states to recruit numerous and well-equipped standing armies of mercenaries. Not in the economic sphere, because the great states, by means of a rigid policy of protectionism, shut the Italians out from the markets existing on their own territory. In addition, the great states competed with the Italians in the foreign markets that were still open. England, the Netherlands, France, and Spain were now able to get together fleets superior to those of Venice, Genoa, and Florence. As early as the fifteenth century the Florentine and Milanese wool industries had lost their paramount position in Europe because of the competition of English wools, inferior in quality, but cheaper. Silk and mirrors industries were still flourishing in the fifteenth century; later they felt the effects of French competition. In the sphere of mechanical industries, too, Italy in the fifteenth century betrayed the first symptoms of decline, in striking contrast with the rapid rise of Germany. Financial leadership also passed into German and French hands. The decline of Italy was also largely fostered by the great geographical discoveries which opened new paths toward the fabled markets of the Orient and new continents for colonization, to which the Italians had no access. The center of European traffic was displaced from the coasts of the Mediterranean to the Atlantic, cutting off Italy, who lost the commercial supremacy which she had enjoyed hitherto. Even in the Mediterranean area Italy lost ground, because of the competiton of the Great Powers and the increasing intolerance of the Turks, with whom commercial relations continued to grow more and more difficult. Nor should the military pressure exerted by the Turks be forgotten: toward the end of the fifteenth century they attempted the invasion of Italy—both the North and the South.[9] The death of Mahomet II (1481) saved Italy from the danger of direct invasion, but could not prevent the loss of the greater part of the overseas possessions of Genoa and Venice. To these evils were joined that of piracy, carried on with great energy by the Barbary pirates of North Africa, who infested the Mediterranean until the first half of the nineteenth century.

[9] In 1473 and 1477 the Turks made raids into Friuli. In 1480 Mahomet II occupied Otranto in Apulia, which was recaptured with much difficulty by the king of Naples in the following year.

This political, military, and economic decadence was accompanied by a cultural decline largely due to the Reformation, which took out from the papacy, and consequently withdrew from Italian intellectual influence, large zones of Europe. But above all the decline was due to the Counter Reformation promoted by the Roman Catholic Church after the Council of Trent (1546–1563) and to the resulting introduction into Italy of the Inquisition. After Giordano Bruno (1548–1600), burned by the Inquisition as a heretic, Tomaso Campanella (1568–1639), secluded for thirty years in prison because of his political ideas, and Galileo Galilei (1564–1642), condemned in 1633 for his scientific ideas, all free scientific or philosophical research came to an end in Italy.

The accumulation of wealth during the previous centuries had been so great that the factors of economic decline operated in Italy with extreme slowness. Moreover, seventeenth-century Italy was still, from the agricultural point of view, one of the most flourishing countries in Europe. With a total population of thirteen millions of inhabitants, it was the most populous country in Europe except France and represented a very tempting bait for invaders who wanted money and men.[10] Many Italians, unable because of the general conditions of the peninsula to hope for prominence at home, entered the service of foreign powers: Columbus, Vespucci, Cabots, and Verazzano discovered new lands and new maritime routes for Spain, England, and France; Leonardo and Alciatus emigrated to France; Mazarin and Alberoni [11] contributed their political genius to increasing the greatness of France and Spain; Farnese, Montecuccoli, and Prince Eugene of Savoy led the armies of Spain and Austria; young enthusiasts of military life enlisted in the infantry of the duke of Alba. But the brilliant personal success of a few individuals only emphasized the sad general situation of Italy, which, in the heartfelt words of Machiavelli, was "more enslaved than the Hebrews, more servile than the Persians, more dispersed than the Athenians, without a head, without order, beaten, despoiled, ravaged, overrun, and enduring every kind of ruin." [12]

However, as early as the eighteenth century some symptoms of improvement might be noted. The treaties of Utrecht (1713) and of Rastatt (1714), which ended the War of the Spanish Succession, also marked the end of Spanish rule in Italy. This does not mean that the peninsula was freed from foreign control: Spanish rule was replaced by Aus-

[10] Clark, *The Seventeenth Century*, p. 9.
[11] Cardinal Giulio Alberoni (1664–1752) is classified among the champions of international pacifism because of his "Scheme for Reducing the Turkish Empire to the Obedience of Christian Princes, together with a Scheme of Perpetual Diet for Establishing the Public Tranquillity." It is published in English in 7 Am. J. Int. L. (1913) 82–107, as an annex to the article by Vesnitch, "Cardinal Alberoni, an Italian Precursor of Pacifism and International Arbitration." On Alberoni see also Fitzgibbon, "Alberoni and International Organization," 17 *Social Science* (1942) 375 ff.
[12] *Il principe*, ch. 26.

trian, better from the administrative point of view, but more robust and therefore more difficult to eradicate. Although it was restricted solely to Lombardy and Mantua, yet it exerted, especially after the treaty of Aix-la-Chapelle (1748), preponderant influence over all the affairs of the peninsula. The struggle for Italian independence during the succeeding century was therefore above all a struggle against Austria. The eighteenth century saw the progress of Italian political unification: many of the smaller fiefs, principalities, and vassal states which existed in 1559 were gradually absorbed by the bigger states. Among the latter Piedmont, soon to become the Kingdom of Sardinia, began to emerge. It was its destiny to assume the leadership in achieving the unity of Italy, while Venice and the Papal States declined and the Kingdom of the Two Sicilies tended to isolate itself.

During the second half of the eighteenth century the spiritual and economic life of Italy awoke. Under the influence of Voltaire and the Encyclopaedists, culture was renewed. Economists such as Antonio Genovesi, the Abbé Galiani, and Pietro Verri defended the ideas of the physiocrats. In the field of jurisprudence Gaetano Filangieri (1752–1788) and Cesare Beccaria (1738–1794) were distinguished for their liberal theories.

An original thinker was Giambattista Vico (1668–1744), of whom more will be said further on. A convinced believer in natural law, Vico, in his main work, the *Scienza nova* (1725–1744), developed theories concerning the history of juridical institutions. A fervent admirer of Grotius, he intended to annotate his work, but was too scrupulous to proceed with his commentary, thinking it unseemly that a Catholic should annotate a Protestant author.[13]

Many Italian states, such as Milan, Tuscany, and for a certain space of time the Two Sicilies and Sardinia, took part in the general European movement of the age and accomplished useful reforms in the field of economics and sometimes even of legislation; their chief effort was to emancipate themselves from ecclesiastical interference. During this period Italy also witnessed, especially in Milan and the Two Sicilies, the development of liberal tendencies which were revived by the influence of the French Revolution and finally found their outlet in the Italian liberal movement of the Risorgimento.

DECADENCE OF THE SOVEREIGN POWER OF THE ITALIAN STATES

In considering the Italian practice of international law during this period it should be pointed out that this was a critical phase for international law throughout Europe. The seventeenth and eighteenth centuries

[13] For G. B. Vico see Croce, *The Philosophy of Giambattista Vico*, tr. by R. G. Collingwood, London, and the monograph *"Vico"* by Rufferty, in Macdonell and Manson, *The Great Jurists of the World*, pp. 345–389.

were, in the history of international relations, centuries of strife for political and economical preponderance. Each state strove to impose its own hegemony and regarded the increase of its own power as the final goal of its international intercourse. This gave rise to the individualist character of the international relations of that era, in the sense that the affirmation of the personality of each state prevailed over every idea of co-operation with others toward common ends. This is the reason for the incoherent aspect of international relations. They were characterized by the coexistence of opposed political groups; occasional coalitions; continual wars, and, as a remedy to them, the application of the principle of the balance of power (*justum potentiae equilibrium*, according to the phrase of the treaty of Utrecht), which was intended to insure peace, but in reality almost always furnished the occasions and pretexts for wars.[14]

However, the development of international law was not interrupted during the seventeenth and eighteenth centuries. For during that epoch were stipulated numerous treaties on questions then of interest to the states. Treaty law was thus developed to an unprecedented extent. The provisions of the treaties had at times a contradictory content. Many of them however contained uniform clauses from which were to arise many of the principles still in force today concerning diplomatic law, the treatment of enemy property, the laws of land and sea warfare, and neutrality. The preponderance of provisions enacted by treaties over those established by custom was the main reason for the development of the new contractual theory of international law which was to supersede the natural-law doctrines.

The favorite subjects of international law were those that most intimately responded to the needs of the times: relations between the courts, titles,[15] and ceremonial; in addition, diplomatic law, especially after the establishment by all the states of permanent legations, certain branches of the law of war, especially of sea-warfare, and neutrality. But in consequence of the weakness of the Italian states and the prevalently passive character of their international policy, Italy, which until then had been a leader in the development of international law, contributed little to the development of the new principles.[16]

In the sphere of diplomatic law, whatever specific activity of the Italian states there may have been consisted of the attempt to combat interference in their own internal affairs and the excessive pretensions of the ambassadors of the great powers. Nor were such attempts always crowned

[14] Anzilotti, *Corso di diritto internazionale*, 3d ed., p. 9.
[15] For the importance attributed by Italian sovereigns to titles see Butler and Maccoby, *The Development of International Law*, pp. 32–33.
[16] For ample information on the international relations of the Italian states during this period, with particular reference to the principal treaties concluded by them, see G. F. von Martens, *Cours diplomatique*.

with success. Venice, however, was strong enough to expel the Spanish ambassador, Bedmar, who had tried to provoke a revolution in the Republic (1648).

When the political power of the Italian states began to decline, foreign states demanded as a diplomatic right increasingly extensive immunities and privileges for their ambassadors: for example, the *diritto di quartiere* (right of quarter) claimed at Rome by the ambassadors of various countries. This right consisted of two privileges: the right to prevent the arrest of persons living in the quarter of the city in which the legation was situated and the exemption from any tax of supplies brought into this quarter nominally for the use of the embassy. Whole zones of the city were thus exempted from the criminal jurisdiction of the local authorities. The arrogance with which the French abused this privilege led to a serious incident in 1660 between Pope Alexander VII and Louis XIV,[17] which was followed by another still more grave in 1662, almost resulting in a war between France and the Holy See.[18] This was settled in 1664 by the treaty of Pisa in a manner which proved humiliating for the Holy See. Pope Innocent XI obtained the renunciation of this right from Spain in 1683; from Poland in 1680; from England in 1686; and also from the Republic of Venice. It was only in 1693 that the king of France at last consented to renounce this privilege.

The contribution of Italy was particularly insignificant in the development of the international law of war on land; in the shaping of this part of international law the active role fell to the great military powers, not to the Italian states, who were rather the victims of the wars waged by others. On the contrary the frequent occupation by foreign armies of territories belonging to Italian states, which often was prolonged, ended by clouding the conception of territorial sovereignty which had developed in Italy earlier than in other countries. The distinction between the rights of the legitimate sovereign and the more limited and provisory rights of the military occupant was not always scrupulously observed in the frequent occupations of territories. Direct research has shown that throughout the seventeenth century in large sections of Italy it was considered that military occupation made the invaded territory an integral part of the invading state without further formalities. The line reached by the invader in the territory of another state constituted the limit up to which the occupant's full sovereignty extended. This was the practice followed by France in certain zones of Piedmont, and in the counties of Nice and Savoy.[19]

---

[17] See Satow, *A Guide to Diplomatic Practice*, 3d ed., p. 208.

[18] See K. von Martens, *Nouvelles causes célèbres du droit des gens*, II, 546–554.

[19] In this regard see the important studies by Lambert, *Théorie et pratique de la conquête dans l'ancien droit* and *Les Occupations militaires en Italie pendant les guerres de Louis XIV* and *Les Déplacements de souveraineté en Italie pendant les guerres du XVII° siècle.*

It is obvious that this state of affairs was not favorable either to the practice or to the theory of land neutrality in Italy. However, some earlier Italian writers influenced the doctrines of neutrality that were being developed in other countries. Neumayr von Ramla, who is generally considered the first writer to have dealt extensively with neutrality from the point of view of international law, was deeply influenced by the ideas of Machiavelli and Guicciardini.[20]

If we consider the numerous foreign invasions of Italy, the repeated violations of the neutrality of the Italian states, and the continual occupations and frequent changes of sovereignty of territories, it is surprising to note how carefully the Italian states provided for determining and maintaining their frontiers during that period. Almost all the Italian states had special magistracies *ad hoc.* In Venice, the *Maggior Consiglio* instituted as early as 1554 the *Provveditori ai Confini* (supervisors of the boundaries). Mixed commission for biennial inspections of the frontiers were established between Venice and Austria, and their procedure was regulated by agreements made in 1753 and 1756. Analogous inspections were agreed upon between Venice and Mantua in 1754. Milan established the *Magistrato ai Confini* in 1749. Analogous magistracies were instituted in the domains of the House of Savoy during the first half and in the duchy of Parma and Piacenza in the second half of the eighteenth century. In 1637 the *Congregazione dei Confini* (Congregation of the boundaries) was created in Rome; inspections of the frontiers, to take place every five years, were agreed upon between Tuscany and the Papal States. A magistrate for the boundaries existed at Lucca in the sixteenth century.[21]

THE PROCLAMATIONS OF NEUTRALITY OF 1778–1779

Notwithstanding the rapid decline of their mercantile and military fleets, the Italian states took a certain part in the formation of the rules of international maritime law that were established during the sixteenth and the seventeenth centuries.[22] The Italian states contributed especially to the formation of a body of uniform rules concerning maritime war and neutrality that was being laid down at that time in the Mediterranean. These rules were enunciated with considerable precision by Giuseppe Lorenzo Maria Casaregis (1678–1737), one of the greatest authorities

[20] Waldkirch, "Neutralitätsrecht," in *Handbuch des Völkerrechts*, VI (Part 5), 20.
[21] For detailed accounts see the writings by Adami, *I confini di stato nella legislazione internazionale; I magistrati ai confini della Republica veneta;* "La magistratura dei confini nello Stato di Milano," 40 *Archivio storico lombardo* (1913) 211 ff.; "La magistratura dei confini negli antichi dominii di Casa Savoia," 16 *Miscellanea di storia italiana* (1916) 24 ff.
[22] Some of the problems of international law arising from the change in economic conditions and in international communications did not affect the Italian states: for instance, the problems arising from the slave trade. Italian states did not import slaves, for they had no colonies and took no part in the trade.

of his time on maritime law, in his *Discursus legales de commercio* (1719).[23] The distinction between the high seas, which were free, and the territorial waters, subject to the jurisdiction of the coastal sovereign, was clearly established; the right of prize against enemy ships was admitted; friendly merchandise on enemy ships was immune from capture; twenty-four hours had to pass for the acquisition of the seized ship and its cargo; the right of search was admitted; privateering without letters of marque was prohibited. It is to be noted that Casaregis recognized the right of pursuit of an enemy ship in neutral waters and reasserted the absolute prohibition of trade in arms, iron, warships, or war material with the Turks.

During the second half of the eighteenth century, when there was a re-awakening of the international relations of Italian states, their weakness did not permit them to take any energetic stand. Yet they sought to save at least their own citizens and their merchandise and ships from the deleterious consequences of the wars then being waged between other states, especially by sea. This explains why Italy's greatest interest and her principal contribution to international law was in the sphere of the practice and the theory of neutrality, especially at sea.

The proclamations of neutrality enacted during the American Revolution by Tuscany (August 1, 1778), Naples (September 19, 1778), the Papal States (March 4, 1779), Genoa (July 1, 1779), and Venice (September 9, 1779) are generally considered the most progressive and complete among the early laws on the subject of maritime neutrality.[24] The striking resemblance between the provisions of these acts shows that by the end of the eighteenth century the Italian states already admitted more or less identical principles on the subject of maritime neutrality.

With regard to the duties of belligerents toward the neutral states, all the proclamations contained the prohibition to belligerents against accomplishing acts of hostility within cannon range from the land or the harbors. The proclamations also contain a few provisions for insuring respect for such prohibitions and abstention from military activity on the part of belligerent ships inside the waters subject to the jurisdiction of neutrals. Thus, for instance, the Tuscan regulations prescribed that twenty-four hours must pass between the departure of a ship belonging to one belligerent and the departure from the same harbor of an enemy ship, unless the commander of the warship gave his word of honor not to molest enemy ships in sight or any which had left port during the

[23] The English-speaking reader will find a summary of the rules of maritime war expounded by Casaregis in Reddie, *Researches, Historical and Critical, in Maritime International Law*, I, 224–226.

[24] The proclamations were published by Lampredi in the second volume of his work *Del commercio dei popoli neutrali in tempo di guerra* and were printed by G. F. von Martens, 3 *Recueil des traités*, 24–74. The principal Italian maritime laws until the eighteenth century may be consulted in Pardessus, *Collection des lois maritimes antérieures au XVIIIᵉ siècle*.

preceding twenty-four hours. All captures of prizes in violation of such rules were to be null and void.

With regard to the duties of neutrals toward belligerents, the Italian proclamations of neutrality enjoined citizens and other subjects from building or fitting out privateers in the harbors of the state [25] and from owning any interest in such ships outside the state; it was, on the other hand, lawful to carry out the repair of warships and also the building, sale, and outfitting of merchant ships for the belligerent states. The enlisting of sailors (and, Venice added, even of soldiers) among citizens and residents was prohibited; foreign ships arriving in harbor might reinforce their crews, but only with foreign sailors and on condition that they were not forcibly seized.[26] It was prohibited to ships belonging to citizens to accept as passengers or in any other capacity sailors or soldiers of powers at war or destined to them. The Tuscan proclamation expressly and that of Genoa by implication permitted the sale of arms and ammunition to belligerents; only Venice prohibited it. Naples, the Papal States, and Venice even prohibited their own citizens and the ships flying their flag to transport contraband of war, by which was meant arms and ammunition. All the states allowed the unrestricted admission of prizes to their ports, as well as their sale. The proclamations provided that the local authorities were competent to decide questions regarding the nullity of prizes captured in violation of their provisions. The Neapolitan proclamation extended the jurisdiction of local courts to "all controversies with the neutral powers that might arise as to the quality and the property of the merchandise, the legitimacy of prizes, and similar cases, over which our courts have jurisdiction, in accordance with common practice deriving from existing treaties between the various nations of Europe."

Not infrequently the courts of neutral Italian states into which a captured ship had been taken were called upon to decide whether or not a seizure was lawful, either as a result of an agreement between the captor and the captured or because it had been alleged that the capture implied a violation of the jurisdiction of the neutral state.[27] On the other hand,

---

[25] The Genoese proclamation prohibited the fitting out, but not the building of ships.

[26] The Tuscan proclamation prohibited the surrender of deserters who were on the territory of the state, unless they had deserted in Tuscan ports.

[27] For various examples see Azuni, Le Droit maritime de l'Europe, II, 318n. The treaty of commerce between Denmark and Genoa of July 30, 1789 (G. F. von Martens, Recueil des traités, IV, 438), provides, art. 13, that: "Si l'une des deux parties contractantes vient à avoir la guerre avec une puissance tierce, l'autre partie contractante, qui est restée neutre, sera la maîtresse, en vertu de l'art. 4, d'admettre ou de refuser dans ses ports, de juger dans ses tribunaux d'Admirauté ou de ne pas juger des prises qui se feraient respectivement par les puissances belligérantes." The object of art. 4 is not to enlarge the rights of a belligerent party, but to secure the recognition on its part of the rights of the neutral party. It seems reasonable to construe art. 13 as intended to provide that the courts of the neutral power might take cognizance of captures which involved a violation of its sovereignty, if the captor and its prize should have been found within its jurisdiction. Twiss, The Law of Nations, II, 373.

the belligerents were not allowed to set up prize courts in the harbors of the Italian neutral states. England had officers in the harbor of Leghorn who carried out preliminary inquiries as to the prizes brought by English ships to that harbor, collected evidence, and examined cargoes and papers. This activity was tolerated by the Grand-Duchy of Tuscany inasmuch as the English officers in Leghorn did not pronounce judgment as to the validity of the prizes and therefore did not condemn the ships; their activity was limited to the preparatory acts aimed at expediting the cases, and often resulted in the release of the ship without further legal procedure.[28]

In comparison with the earlier European practice the Italian regulations of 1778–1779 reveal some undeniable progress. They are remarkable for the precision, thoroughness, and equity of their provisions, and they are certainly more advanced than other neutrality regulations of the same period and than the provisions of the Armed Neutrality of 1780. The Italian decrees were codifications of a practice already followed in Italy and confirmed by many treaties concluded by the Italian states. Under the government of the House of Medici, Tuscany had already adopted the custom of calling together the consuls of the belligerent powers whenever a war broke out in order to come to an agreement as to the conditions under which the harbors of Tuscany were to remain neutral. When Francis of Lorraine succeeded to the Medicis he followed the same custom, and during the war that broke out in 1734 he published a manifesto in the month of December. In 1757, however, when he had become emperor, he did not call the consuls together; but on February 15 of the same year he published of his own accord a manifesto of neutrality which contains in fieri the principles of that of 1778. Some of the principles contained in the manifestoes of 1778 and 1779 had already been consecrated by the treaties between Genoa and Denmark of 1756, between Tuscany and Morocco of 1778, between the Two Sicilies and Turkey, 1740, Sweden, 1742, Denmark, 1748, and the Netherlands, 1753.[29] In 1740 and in 1756 the Two Sicilies denied access to their ports to the privateers of all the belligerents. The same practice was followed by the Kingdom of Sardinia during the American Revolution. It should also be remembered that in 1738 Clement XII, in his capacity as spiritual sovereign, had proclaimed the principle that neutral merchandise on an enemy mercantile ship was not subject to capture and had declared lawful the capture of the merchandise of Greek Christians only if discovered

---

[28] Butler and Maccoby, *The Development of International Law*, pp. 244–245, recalls that when Catherine of Russia dispatched the famous expedition of Orloff from the Baltic ports to the Mediterranean in 1778, she instructed the admiral that, as long as a regular prize court had not been constituted, he was to bring the prizes before the Russian plenipotentiaries at Venice and Naples, if the governments of these states did not raise objections.

[29] Lucchesi Palli, *Principes du droit public maritime*, pp. 47–48.

on board Turkish warships or privateers, not on merchant ships belonging to the infidels.[30]

In 1793, not many years after the publication of the above-mentioned Italian regulations, the first American law on neutrality was issued, which is worthy of high praise for the high standard of its provisions relating to maritime neutrality. Some American writers have held that although the principles of the American law are more or less the same as those contained in the Italian edicts of 1778–1779 its importance is much greater because the Italian edicts were only of a temporary character and were not even actually applied.[31] It seems inaccurate to maintain that the Italian edicts were only temporary. In fact, they represented only the confirmation, with a few improvements, of a practice the Italian states had already followed for a considerable time and consecrated in previous edicts and treaties. Furthermore, the provision of the edicts of 1778–1779 were repeatedly confirmed after their proclamation. Thus, in edicts of April 28, 1792, and March 1, 1795, the Grand-Duchy of Tuscany confirmed the edict of 1778; and similarly the treaty of friendship, navigation, and commerce between Russia and the Two Sicilies of January 6–17, 1787, expressly refers to and confirms the provisions of the edict of the Two Sicilies of 1779, which prohibited the building of ships on behalf of a belligerent power.[32] Nor does it appear that these edicts were frequently or openly violated. It is probable, rather, that the authors of the American law of 1793 were acquainted with the edicts of the Italian states. Before the revolution the American colonies had already, in fact, developed a noteworthy trade with Mediterranean harbors.[33]

The point is that there is absolutely no reason for a discussion as to

[30] Bull. XXIV, 390.

[31] On this question see a few important remarks in Hyneman, *The First American Neutrality,* p. 178, who writes that "without at all denying that the neutral policy of the United States is worthy of high praise, one may still question that it deserves to be recognised as the first neutrality to maintain so high a standard. Such a conclusion can be established only by proof that the neutrality edicts which were enforced from 1778 to 1779 by the Italian states were not enforced. If those codes were carried out in such manner as their language promised, there seems but little choice but to conclude that the first American neutrality possessed few features not anticipated in those countries."

[32] The treaty enunciates a few important principles concerning maritime warfare and neutrality. It expressly recalls (Article 17) the Two Sicilies' acceptance of armed neutrality, which took place on February 10, 1783; it reconsecrates and repeats the principles of armed neutrality (Article 18); it binds each one of the contracting parties, when engaged in a war, to respect the maritime neutrality of the other (Article 19); it recognizes the right of search, but provides that ships escorted by warships will not be subject to search, as long as the officer commanding the latter declares, on his word of honor, that the escorted ships do not transport contraband (Article 20); it prohibits the practice of angary (Article 12) and in case of war allows a year's time to the subjects of each of the contracting parties to leave the territory of the other with their own property.

[33] Borchard, "The United States as a Factor in The Development of International Relations," in Walsh, *The History and Nature of International Relations,* p. 276.

priority. On the whole the Italian edicts and the first American neutrality law did nothing but codify principles that were known at least partially to the practice and had been proclaimed in various treaties. The Italian edicts and the American neutrality law were the products of the same epoch and of the same needs. At that time neither the Italian states nor the United States had imperialistic ambitions: the former because they were too weak, the latter because it was too young. Italian states and the United States of America were above all interested in the protection of their own trade and of the rights of neutrals during the wars of others. The identity of interests explains their identical attitude toward the problem of maritime neutrality. It should rather be noted that the principles accepted by the Italian and the American states, although they were considerably widespread in that epoch, were yet not universally accepted. At the same time, in fact, governments continued to conclude treaties of subsidy and benevolent assistance, whereby one of the contracting parties bound itself, when not at war, to supply the other with men and materials and to allow the passage and recruiting of troops on its own territory, as well as the supplying of ships.[34] In those times the principle of neutrality conflicted with that of discrimination in favor of friendly states on the part of states not actively engaged in a war. Some states followed the former principle; others, the second principle. The strongest states, especially, when engaged in a war, attempted to subordinate the rights of neutrals to the needs of belligerents.

DOCTRINES OF MARITIME NEUTRALITY

The problems of maritime neutrality were also examined at that time by Italian scholars. In 1782 was published in Naples a work on the *Doveri dei principi neutrali verso i principi guerreggianti e di questi verso i neutrali* (Duties of neutral sovereigns toward sovereigns at war and of the latter toward the neutrals), by the Abbé Fernando Galiani (1728–1787).[35] He was a typical representative of eighteenth-century culture, an encyclopedist, brilliant though sometimes superficial. His treatise *Della moneta* (1751) and even to a greater degree the *Dialogues sur le commerce des blés,* published in 1770 in Paris, where he had been secretary to the Neapolitan embassy from 1759 to 1769, had procured him an extraordinary reputation as an economist. Endowed with a versatile mind of an extreme vivacity, he also composed literary, historical, and philosophical works and is remembered for his witticisms, some of which are still repeated in Italy. Galiani wrote the book on the rights and

---

[34] See on such treaties Nys, "Traités de subside et troupes auxiliaires dans l'ancien droit. Politique des subsides," 45 Rev. dr. int. et lég. comp. (1913) 173–196. See also Jessup and Deák, *Neutrality,* I, 24–39.

[35] For Galiani, see Nicolini, *Il pensiero giuridico dell'abate Galiani,*

duties of neutrals, as he himself recalls in a passage of it, "by irresistible command." It is still an open question whether by this phrase he meant to allude to financial want, which obliged him to write for remuneration, or to instructions received from the Neapolitan government to write a book defending the principles of the First Armed Neutrality which the government of the Two Sicilies accepted the following year (February 10, 1783).[36] One thing is certain, that the book is a vivacious and skillful defense of the rights of neutrals in the face of restrictions imposed by the belligerents upon their commerce. Galiani begins with a series of definitions and a few general principles concerning the obligations of men and of states to supply one another with whatever is required for their subsistence. He then proceeds to point out that in case of a war between other rulers a sovereign may remain neutral unless he has bound himself by treaty to assist one of them; the fact that a state remains neutral does not entitle others to wage war against it. After a brief discussion of the admissibility of neutrality treaties, the author goes on to examine the rights and duties of neutrals in general. Galiani especially insists upon the obligation of the belligerents to respect the territorial sovereignty of neutrals and upon the obligation of neutrals not to furnish troops to the belligerents; the neutrals may, however, authorize the belligerents to recruit troops on their territory. The principal part of the book is devoted to neutral trade with the belligerents. The first duty of neutrals, according to Galiani, is impartiality in their dealings with the belligerents. The belligerent's natural right to defense imposes certain limitations on the neutral's freedom of trade, which Galiani examines in detail, attempting as a rule to give them a strict interpretation. He admits that neutral ships may not sail to the harbors of a belligerent if these are blockaded, but he correctly stresses that the blockade must be effective. He asserts the obligation of neutrals not to transport contraband and goes so far as to declare, in opposition to positive law, that neutrals may not even on their own territory sell contraband goods to belligerents. Galiani makes a serious effort to limit the concept of contraband of war. In his opinion contraband of war consists only of things that can be exclusively of use for military purposes. Things that can be used also, but not exclusively, for war purposes may be captured, but the captor should pay for them. Galiani denies that the belligerents may on neutral ships capture enemy merchandise that is not contraband. The author tries to demonstrate that the rule by which the enemy merchandise may be captured on a neutral ship was not in the beginning generally observed, but was merely imposed by a few stronger states on weaker ones and then, regrettably, ac-

---

[36] See Nys, "Les Droits et les devoirs des neutres par Galiani," 21 Rev. dr. int. et lég. comp. (1899) 382 ff. The act of accession of the Two Sicilies to the First Armed Neutrality is published by G. F. von Martens, *Recueil de traités depuis 1761 jusqu'á present*, III, 274.

cepted by the *Consolato del mare*. The premises thus expounded lead Galiani to admit the right of search, but only in so far as it is aimed at ascertaining whether a ship is hostile, has false papers, is attempting to run the blockade, or is transporting contraband of war. Within these limits the search is lawful, according to Galiani, because it is not an act of superiority on the part of the belligerent toward the neutral, but an act of defense. The search is not lawful, on the contrary, if aimed at ascertaining whether a neutral ship is carrying enemy merchandise which is not contraband. The right of search gives rise to the right of prize. Contrary to practice, Galiani asserts that the belligerent has no jurisdiction in matter of prizes on neutral ships. The adjudication of neutral ships should be the prerogative of the power whose flag they fly: this, according to Galiani, would offer greater guarantees of impartiality. Finally Galiani deals with privateers, the refuge allowed by neutrals to belligerent warships and privateers, the right of asylum, embargoes, and related matters. For this last section Galiani on the whole follows the positive law of his age.

This brief account shows that Galiani discusses all the principal problems concerning the laws of maritime neutrality that interested the world in those days. The book is praiseworthy for the strict legal order with which it is conducted and for the clarity of its exposition.[37] Although Galiani felt the influence of previous writers, such as Hübner, he is on the whole original, and he is superior to them from the doctrinal point of view. In fact, he drops the confusing fiction of Hübner's that the neutral ship is part of the territory of the neutral sovereign, nor does he pretend to affirm, like Hübner and Martens, that simply because certain principles were accepted in a few treaties between the principal powers, they have become general principles of international law, which all states must respect, even when they did not accept them by special agreement. With much greater accuracy of method Galiani goes back to the idea of neutrality and to its aims in order to desume from them the rules which he thinks ought to be followed. True, Galiani sometimes is in complete disagreement with practice and must base his thesis on alleged principles of natural law. This attitude, however, is not due to a scanty knowledge on his part of positive law, but to his anxiety to defend the rights of neutrality even beyond the standards commonly accepted by the practice of his time. This led to his sometimes being accused of going too far in the defense of the rights of neutrals.[38] The changes of practice advocated by Galiani were never actuated. His book is interesting nonethe-

[37] Recently Cohn, *Neo-neutrality*, p. 18, after considering Galiani's ideas, remarks that "he was the first to expound the traditional concept of neutrality in complete clarity and consistency."

[38] See in this sense the criticisms of Galiani's ideas by Hautefeille, *Des Droits et des devoirs des nations neutrales en temps de guerre*, 2d ed., Vol. I.

less, because it shows what the aspirations of neutrals in those days were. In addition, from the doctrinal point of view it is perhaps superior to all the preceding works on maritime neutrality for its completeness, its strict logic, and its attempt to formulate general principles on the subject.

A few remarks in Galiani's book about the ideas of Lampredi induced the latter to retort with an essay *"Del commercio dei popoli neutrali in tempo di guerra"* [39] (Neutral Trade in Wartime), 1788. Giovanni Maria Lampredi (1732–1793) was a professor of public law at the University of Pisa. In 1776–1778 he published a work *Juris publici naturalis sive juris naturae et gentium theoremata,* in which the foundations of international law were considered in accordance with the theories of natural law.[40] The city of Leghorn, only a few miles from Pisa, had at that time become, thanks to the solicitude of the grand-dukes of Tuscany, who had made it a *porto franco,* one of the principal trade centers of the Mediterranean, frequented not only by merchant ships of every flag but also by warships that put in there for supplies, repairs, and in order to dispose of their prizes. Lampredi was therefore enabled directly to follow the practice of maritime law and neutrality and to obtain a personal impression of the conflicts to which it gave rise. This helps to explain the genesis and the merits of Lampredi's book, which joins a profound knowledge of doctrine with wide experience and an accurate study of the practice of his time. Lampredi states the problem of neutrality in strictly juridical terms, influenced naturally by the naturalistic conception which he follows. In his opinion natural reason is the basis of the law of nations. Among the rules that constitute international law two groups, he teaches, are particularly important: *primary international law,* which is immutable natural law, binding the states independently of their consent, and *secondary international law,* created by agreements accepted by all the states, which is therefore conventional law and subject to change. It is a fundamental principle of the primary law that all the states at peace with one another have the right to trade; therefore, even in wartime the neutral states do not lose the right to trade, provided that they comply with the obligation to remain impartial in their relations with the two parties at war. Opposed to this right of the neutral nations is the not less absolute right that primary law grants to each belligerent to take the necessary steps to diminish the adversary's strength, such as those taken by a belligerent to prevent the trade of neutral powers with the enemy. There is, accordingly, in the opinion of Lampredi, a collision between two rights equally natural and perfect: that of the neutrals to trade with

[39] Lampredi's book was translated into French by J. Penches, *Du Commerce des neutres en temps de guerre.*
[40] A few years before Lampredi had written a short monograph, *De licentia in hostem.* This work follows the doctrines of natural law; it is aimed to ascertain the cases in which resort to war is lawful and the limits within which violence between belligerents is lawful.

the belligerents and that of each belligerent to prevent the trade of neutrals with the enemy. It is Lampredi's merit to have stressed what even today is still the crux of the problem of neutrality. Lampredi observes that this contradiction of principles prevents the establishment of any rules of primary law relative to relations between belligerents and neutrals. It was precisely in order to remedy the lack of general standards in this matter that the states concluded particular treaties establishing the rights and duties of neutrals. But these treaties, Lampredi observes, cannot be considered as evidence of uniform and well-established rules on the subject of neutrality. In fact, as Lampredi in a very accurate analysis proves, the principles laid down by the treaties with reference to neutral rights and duties are basically different and at times even contradictory. Yet according to Lampredi it is possible to heal the apparently irreconcilable conflict between the above-mentioned principles of international law. To this end the two problems should be carefully distinguished: (1) What are the rights of neutrals with regard to trade with the belligerents? (2) What are the rights of the belligerents with regard to the trade of neutrals with the enemy?

Neutrals have the right to carry on, first of all, any trade whatsoever on their own territory, as long as they respect the obligation to remain impartial. Lampredi contradicts Galiani and demonstrates that by a generally accepted rule neutrals may on their own territory trade in contraband articles unless they are bound by a special treaty to refrain from doing so. The neutral right to trade also implies that neutrals may even outside neutral territory freely trade with the belligerents. From the premise that there are no general principles of law relating to neutrality Lampredi reaches the conclusion, unlike Galiani, that nothing prevents neutrals, unless they are bound by special treaties, from transporting contraband on their own ships. In support of this conclusion Lampredi adduces that no belligerent has ever protested against neutrals because their ships transported contraband. However, this does not mean that the right of the belligerent to his own defense need be sacrificed; in fact he may capture the contraband carried on neutral ships, if he can. In short, the neutral may transport contraband, but the belligerent may capture it. Contraband goods, Lampredi observes, can therefore only be goods destined to the enemy and found outside the territory of the neutral. He points out that there is no perfect agreement with regard to the categories of goods that constitute contraband; however, by repeated agreements of the states, a few rules on the matter have taken shape, which he expounds. The same principles that are stated as affecting contraband are also applied to enemy merchandise: the neutral may transport it, but the adversary may capture it. Lampredi then proceeds to examine the principle that a ship must be considered as forming part of the territory of the state whose flag she flies. This fiction was invoked by Hübner to justify the exemption of enemy merchandise on a neutral ship and the capture of neutral merchandise on an enemy ship. The Italian author denunciates this fiction as a fallacy and asserts the impossibility of drawing further the conclusions that Hübner advocates. It is the ownership of the goods that must determine whether they can be seized or not. Thus, from the point of view of logic and equity the rules should be adopted that the neutral flag does not cover the enemy merchandise and that neutral merchandise on an enemy ship is not subject to capture; he recognizes, however, that practice in this regard is contradictory. In the case of enemy merchandise on a neutral ship, how is it possible to reconcile the right of the neutral to liberty of trade with that of the belligerent to his own defense? Of these two rights the one should be preferred the violation of which would cause the greater harm. In transporting the enemy merchandise the neutral is only seeking profit, whereas in capturing it the belligerent is fighting for his own life against the danger of an enemy victory; it is the belligerent's right therefore that should be preferred. It is on the basis of the same principle that in case of condemnation of property for public use the legitimate rights of the individual are sacrificed. But this in no wise implies that the neutral must suffer a loss. The belligerent is bound to pay the neutral the freight of the merchandise captured. If there is to be complete reparation, the belligerent also ought to reimburse the damages for the delay caused by the capture, and in fact Lampredi advocates such a measure; but at the same time he is forced to admit that in practice payment of damages for the delay is not allowed. In consequence of all this, the belligerent must have the right to search. This right must, however, be carried out with the formalities requisite for protecting the neutral ship against the danger of being attacked by a pirate disguised as a belligerent. The right of prize may be exercised against a neutral ship only in certain cases specifically indicated and must be preceded by a prize judgment. In contrast with Galiani, and by means of a careful and detailed examination of the practice, Lampredi proves the existence of a universally recognized rule providing that jurisdiction over prizes belong to the courts of the state to which the captor belongs, even if the prize has been taken to a neutral port; that prize courts are not usually set up by the belligerents on neutral territory; and that Galiani's proposal to entrust the judgment on neutral prizes to the power to whom the captured ship belongs, does not seem reasonable. Yet if the captor takes the ship to a neutral port, there are two cases in which the local authorities can have jurisdiction as to the validity of the prize: (1) if the captor is accused of violating neutrality; (2) if he is accused of not being a belligerent ship, but a pirate or a privateer without letters of marque. Such are the principal conclusions reached by Lampredi.

Even from this rapid summary it appears that Lampredi's work is remarkable for its rigorously methodical and strictly juridical examination of the problem of neutrality. It is Lampredi's great merit to have called attention to the juridical problems that come into consideration and sometimes lead to conflicts concerning questions of neutrality. In discussing them Lampredi limited himself to positive law, of which he proved his extraordinary grasp and avoided proclaiming as principles of positive law what merely constituted individual aspiration. He established the juridical foundation of the principles exposed, and thus rose to the formulation of general juridical principles concerning neutrality on the basis of which he believed it would be possible also to solve the questions concerning neutrality which at that time were still subjects of controversy. If a defect is to be noted in Lampredi's work, it consists in his constant and excessive desire to find a rational foundation for every rule accepted by practice. Since these rules often arose from the clash of conflicting interests and without any preconceived plan, his attempt could not always lead to satisfactory results. He was, moreover, hampered by the constant effort to reconcile the principles of neutrality with the rules of natural law of which he was an advocate. But this did not lead him to forget the rules of positive law. Galiani is the brilliant writer, intent above all on defending with vivacious dialectic the rights of neutrals, even beyond the limit of positive law. Lampredi is the great jurisconsult, poised, lucid, and faithful to reality, who tries not to distort the rules of practice, but to overcome their apparent contradictions by means of the formulation of a coherent and harmonious system of general principles relating to neutrality.

The last of the leading Italian writers on the problem of neutrality was the Sardinian Domenico Alberto Azuni (1749–1827). Having been for many years in Napoleon's service, he was nominated senator and president of the Court of Nice. Azuni shared the admiration of the nascent progressive bourgeoisie of Italy for Napoleon, held to be the man capable of uniting Italy as one nation, under the rule of a liberal government, independent of foreign rule and of ecclesiastical oppression. The liberal bourgeoisie, to which Azuni belongs, given over as it was to industry and commerce, had experienced grave harm from the blockade England had inflicted on Europe during the Napoleonic wars. This and Azuni's admiration for Napoleon explain the profound anti-British sentiment that runs through all Azuni's work. Great Britain is constantly pictured as the principal opponent of neutrals' rights and combated as such. Azuni's principal book is the *Sistema universale dei principii del diritto ma-*

rittimo dell' Europa, 1795, amplified and translated into French in 1798 under the title *Droit maritime de l'Europe.*[41] We discuss Azuni together with Galiani and Lampredi, although chronologically he belongs to a later period, because he is more or less a continuator of the latter, to whom he owed much. The first volume of Azuni's *Droit maritime,* is devoted to the sea and to the rights that can be exerted over it, and has an almost exclusively historical character. The author narrates the history of the maritime power of the chief states; considers the various theories relating to the extension of territorial waters; examines what rights can be exerted over them and over fisheries, straits, bays, gulfs and anchorages, and briefly passes in review the maritime laws of the principal states of his time. In the second book, which deals with the maritime law of Europe in wartime, he deals especially with relations between belligerents and neutrals. Neutrality is "the exact continuation of the pacific state of a power which at the outburst of a war between two or more other powers absolutely refrains from taking any side whatsoever in their quarrels." In contradiction to Galiani, he shows that neutrality is founded not only on particular treaties between the neutrals and the belligerents but also on the very nature of international relations. The sole obligation incumbent on neutrals is to remain impartial. In all other things they have the right to continue as before their relations with the belligerents, except that they may not trade with actually blockaded ports. For the remainder of his discussion he more or less faithfully follows Lampredi's plan and also frequently adopts his arguments in order to polemicize with Hübner and Galiani. His book, although less accurate and strict than Lampredi's, is useful for its numerous references to practice and to the treaties of the age. On the basis of such material Azuni tries to prove that in his times a rule had definitely come into being by which enemy merchandise, with the exception of contraband, was exempted from capture on a neutral ship. On this point, as well as in the part of his treatise dealing with prize adjudication, Azuni dissociates himself from Lampredi. In addition to the cases listed by Lampredi, Azuni extends the jurisdiction of neutral courts on prizes taken to them and in cases of litigation as to the neutral or enemy quality of goods and ships, especially if the goods and ships are claimed by subjects of the local sovereign. The last part of the book deals briefly with the right of asylum, with reprisals in time of peace, with privateers and pirates.

Azuni's work is certainly less brilliant and less original than Galiani's or Lampredi's.[42] It suffers from prolixity and a display of learning which

[41] Azuni's book was translated into English by W. Johnson, *The Maritime Law of Europe.*
[42] Azuni was accused of plagiarizing, in one part of his book, a project of maritime code for the Two Sicilies, the "Codice Ferdinandeo," the author of which was a Neapolitan lawyer, Michele Di Jorio. The latter is also the author of a remarkable book, *La giurisprudenza del commercio,* which deals with various questions concerning maritime law. The accusation of

is largely secondhand. Yet the author reveals his familiarity, because of direct experience, with the subject discussed.

The proclamations of neutrality of 1778–1779 and the works of Galiani, Lampredi, and Azuni are the first symptoms of the revival of international law which was to take place in Italy in the next century.[43]

NEGLIGIBLE VALUE OF ITALY'S CONTRIBUTION TO INTERNATIONAL LAW DURING THE PERIOD OF FOREIGN ASCENDANCY

The negligible value of the Italian contribution to the theory and practice of international law from the middle of the sixteenth century to the end of the eighteenth is a consequence of the general decadence of Italy during this period. Many of the principles applied in international relations at this time originated in Italy in the Renaissance: for example, the principle of the independence and the territorial sovereignty of the states; the system of the balance of power; the end of the distinction between just and unjust wars; the concept that war is not an unlawful means of augmenting the national wealth.[44] Ironically enough, when these principles were adopted by the great European monarchies, their impact on the little Italian principalities resulted in their decline.

Italy was thus relegated to a merely passive function, at a moment particularly decisive for the development of the theory and practice of international law. As we have already observed, an international community and international law already existed before the Peace of Westphalia; and the period following the Peace of Westphalia, until the end of the eighteenth century, is among those in which violations of international law were most frequent. However, it is true that after the Peace of Westphalia international relations were extended and intensified as never before. Hence the rise of a very considerable set of rules of international law, many of which are still in force, and the contemporaneous development of an extensive doctrinal movement. In this intense renewal of international law Italy took almost no part whatsoever.

In the field of practice Italy made no outstanding contribution. The proclamations of neutrality of 1778–1779, which are probably the most notable examples of Italian practice during this period, are appreciable for the equity, the completeness, and the precision of their provisions,

---

plagiarism, maintained by Pardessus, was recently confuted by Era, *Storia dell'accusa di plagio mossa a Domenico Azuni.*

[43] For a comparative judgment on the works of Galiani, Lampredi, and Azuni see Vidari, "Galiani, Lampredi e Azuni," in 1 Arch. Giur. (1868) 210 ff.

[44] Butler and Maccoby, *The Development of International Law*, p. 116, remarks that "the wars of this period, largely commercial, colonial and naval in aim, were fought almost avowedly on the old pagan basis that war was not an illegitimate way of increasing colonial possessions, national wealth and trade and national well-being of every kind. It was one of the results of the Renaissance thought, particularly in Italy, that amongst other notions of the ancient world, it had given renewed life to this."

but they contain no new principles. It is, however, only fair to remark that this lack of originality in Italian practice, due, indeed, principally to the poverty of the international relations of the Italian states, is also in part due to the tendency peculiar to that epoch, toward the formation of uniform rules of international law.

In the field of theory the only Italian authors worthy of note were Galiani, Lampredi, and Azuni. These authors, in spite of the excellence of their method and the juridical precision of their writings, cannot be compared to Zouche, Rachel, Pufendorf, Bynkoershoek, Wolff, Vattel, Moser, and G. F. de Martens for originality of views or scope of the problems dealt with. Obviously it is impossible to speak of an Italian school of international law at this period. The doctrines of Galiani, Lampredi, and Azuni are not the expression of juridical and philosophical theories characteristic of Italy; nor are they directed at defending interests and aims peculiar to Italian governments or political classes. The works of Galiani and Lampredi belong to a period during which, notwithstanding its violent political upheavals there still existed in Europe a uniformity of culture and ideas especially apparent in studies on international law. Azuni is a defender of the Napoleonic policy rather than of Italian interests.

Not until the nineteenth century, with the development of nationalistic doctrines, will there arise the first Italian school of international law possessing characteristics of its own, the "school of nationalities."

PART THREE

The Risorgimento

Chapter VIII: THE UNIFICATION OF ITALY

D URING the last decade of the eighteenth century, when the progressive currents were about to be submerged almost throughout the peninsula by the antiliberal tendencies of the majority of the rulers, the consequences of the French Revolution upset the whole of Italy. The years of the French Revolution and the Napoleonic epic were for Italy, as for many other countries of Europe, years of passion and hope, of dreams and disillusionment. The rising progressive bourgeoisie, a tiny but active minority of the Italian population, had hoped that with the Napoleonic eagles liberty, too, would make its advance: liberty, political, economic, and spiritual, from foreign domination, absolutism of the local sovereigns, political disintegration, spiritual oppression by the Church and all the other obstacles which had prevented the free development of the Italians. Their disappointment was great when it became clear that Napoleon had set the interests of France above the aspirations of the Italians. In order to satisfy the interests of the former, he did not hesitate to follow, with regard to Italy, the traditional legitimist policy of the absolute rulers. Territories were bartered, separated, and reunited without consulting the population; a series of state satellites of France, governed by relatives of Napoleon, was more or less arbitrarily created with the principal aim of establishing a defensive barrier in the interests of France. The Republic of Venice, after undergoing the devastating passage of various belligerent armies with full disregard for its neutrality, was first compelled by a treaty of 1796 to consent to the passage of French troops, and then, without even being consulted, was ceded by Napoleon to Austria by the treaty of Campoformio of 1797. Austrian hegemony in Italy was thus strengthened. If to these political disappointments we add the pillage and other acts of brutality committed by the French in Italy and the resentment for the loss of tens of thousands of Italians fallen fighting in Napoleon's armies in Spain and Russia, for a cause which was not theirs, it is easy to understand how the return to the *status quo ante* in Italy, aimed at by the Congress of Vienna, of 1815, did not excite extreme dissatisfaction in the peninsula.

INFLUENCE OF THE FRENCH REVOLUTION AND OF THE NAPOLEONIC GOVERNMENT ON ITALY'S POLITICAL DEVELOPMENT

Great, however, were the benefits Italy received from the Napoleonic domination: the introduction of modern laws; the abolition of the surviv-

ing fiefs in the Neapolitan; the impulse given to public works, and th
assistance given to the development of a progressive and active bou
geoisie. Even the participation of Italians in the Napoleonic wars wa
not altogether useless. For it revived the military spirit of the Italian
gave them a desire for glory, and united in the ranks of the Napoleoni
armies soldiers from all over Italy, and so contributed to wipe out re
gional barriers. The placid languid Italy of the late eighteenth centur
came out of the Napoleonic epic toughened by harsh contacts with realit
and spiritually and economically inclined toward the ideas of unity an
political liberty—in those classes, at least, which formed public opinio
In the conscience of these classes, if not among the whole of the Italia
people, three ideas began to penetrate: the idea of the rights of the in
dividual; the idea that the state relies upon the consent of the people
which must therefore have the means to influence the direction of publi
affairs; and, in fine, the idea of the right of every nation to determine it
own destinies. These ideas had indeed contributed powerfully to the anti
Napoleonic movement, by awaking a violent reaction against Napoleon'
despotism and his policy of conquest. They had been used as ideologica
weapons against him in Italy by the victorious coalition. In February
1814, when the Austrian generals Bellegarde and Nugent started a reso
lute effort against Napoleon in Italy, joining political to military pres
sure, they asserted in their proclamations that they were coming to fre
Italy from the foreign yoke and to enable her to decide her own future
Similarly, Lord Bentinck, when he landed in Leghorn in March of the
same year to operate in co-ordination with the Austrians, exhorted the
Italians to join the English in order to regain their national independence.
On the other hand Joachim Murat, in his famous Rimini proclamation of
May 30, 1815, urged the Italians to close their ranks about him in un-
broken union for the independence of Italy. The seed of the new ideas had
been sown; the decisions of the princes could not prevent their spreading

From the Congress of Vienna, Italy emerged divided into the follow-
ing states: (1) the Kingdom of Sardinia; (2) the Lombardo-Venetia, a
kingdom united with the Austrian Empire; (3) the Duchy of Parma and
Piacenza; (4) the Duchy of Modena and Reggio; (5) the Duchy of
Massa and Carrara; (6) the Duchy of Lucca; (7) the Grand-Duchy of
Tuscany; (8) the Papal States, and (9) the Kingdom of the Two Sicilies.

There were, in addition, the independent republic of San Marino,
the principality of Monaco, which until 1859 remained under the protection of the king of Sardinia, and a few territories belonging to foreign
states.

In the process of the political unification of the Italian peninsula, the
Congress of Vienna, even though it was inspired by reactionary principles
and aimed at restoring the ancient order, represented a step forward. A

few of the states restored by the congress were intended to have a brief existence. The Grand-Duchy of Lucca was annexed to Tuscany in 1847, and the Duchy of Massa and Carrara to Modena at the death of Marie-Louise of Bourbon, to whom it had been assigned by the Congress of Vienna. Moreover, in the surviving states the composite character they had preserved since the Renaissance yielded to forms of a centralized and unified administration. The benefits that the union between the various populations within each state produced for all its inhabitants revealed the even greater advantages that would come to them from the union of all Italians. On the other hand Austria, with the acquisition of the Lombardo-Venetia and the right to maintain garrisons in the Papal States, at Comacchio and Ferrara, asserted even more strongly her own control of Italy.

After the Congress of Vienna the three fundamental problems of Italy: unity, political liberty, and independence from foreign powers were visibly connected. And in fact Austria, the foreign power against whom the struggle for independence was directed, was also the most interested in maintaining absolutist and legitimist principles. This interdependence of the problem of internal and international policy explains why the internal political events in Italy had immediate international repercussions and vice versa. In particular, the struggle for political liberty was also a struggle against the foreign rule, and the political revolutions in the Italian states often provoked foreign intervention.

The political problems already pointed out were further complicated by the peculiar situation of the papacy. This, besides being a spiritual authority, also was a temporal dominion. Not only did the popes not intend to surrender it; on the contrary, for its defense they did not hesitate to exert religious pressure on the Italians. It was therefore necessary to find a solution which would make it possible to realize political unity without affecting the profound religious faith of the majority of Italians. In order to overcome this difficulty, which seemed unsurmountable, some advocated the constitution of a federation of Italian states under the presidency of the pope. But far-seeing Italians, such as Mazzini and Cavour, succeeded in assuring the triumph of the only logical solution: that is, the unity of all Italians in one state and the suppression of the political power of the pope.

ITALY'S PROCESS OF UNIFICATION

From 1815 to 1870 the history of Italy is the history of insurrections and foreign interventions, of conspiracies and wars for liberty, unity, and independence. Six years after the Congress of Vienna the first insurrections broke out in the Kingdom of the Two Sicilies and in Piedmont, but they soon came to nought because of the inexperience of their chiefs, the lack of preparation of the masses, and the intervention of Austria. In 1831 Central Italy revolted; Austria again intervened. In 1848 all Italy insurged: the Austro-Sardinian war of 1848–1849 ended with the defeat of Novara, and Austrian, French, even Spanish intervention in the Italian states. Sardinia became liberal and seized the leadership of the movement for independence. By merit of Cavour it also gained insight into European affairs not limited to the affairs of the Italian peninsula. In 1855 it took part in the Crimean war. In 1859 France and Sardinia defeated Austria, and Lombardy was annexed to the Kingdom of Sardinia. Central Italy once more arose and in a series of plebiscites demanded and obtained to be united to Sardinia under the constitutional rule of the House of Savoy. Garibaldi's expedition and an internal revolution, followed by the intervention of Sardinia, led to the annexation of the Kingdom of the Two Sicilies. On March 17, 1861, was constituted the Kingdom of Italy, and in 1865 the capital was moved to Florence. In 1866 the war against Austria led to the annexation of Venezia; in 1870 the last remnant of the Papal States was annexed, and Rome was declared the capital.

With the Napoleonic epoch also began the spiritual and cultural revival of Italy. The center of Italian life, which during the Napoleonic period had been Milan, then the capital of the *Regno Italico*, after 1848 shifted to Turin, then the seat of the most liberal government in Italy, which encouraged the influx of exiles from all over the country. Piedmont thus became the center of the cultural as well as the political rebirth of Italy.

The formation of Italian unity through wars, plebiscites and interventions, the disappearance of numerous states, and the creation of the Kingdom of Italy gave rise, as will easily be understood, to a flourishing practice of international law. Especially important, however, is the body of doctrines of international law developed in Italy during this period, which are generally referred to as the "doctrine of nationalities." It may be affirmed that the practice offers original aspects only in so far as it constituted the application of the new doctrines expounded by the Italian school in international relations. The doctrine being more important than the practice, it will be advisable to have the analysis of the theory precede the analysis of the practice in this section of the book.

Chapter IX: THE DOCTRINE OF NATIONALITIES

LIKE all movements that tend to achieve any universal validity and a permanent character, the Restoration which took control of Europe with the Peace of Vienna, attempted to fortify itself with a body of philosophical and political doctrines. The fundamental political and moral idea of the Restoration was the principle of legitimacy. Sovereigns sprung from legitimate dynasties instituted by God were alone entitled to guide the destinies of mankind. The princes were entrusted with a divine mission; they were the instruments of Providence, called upon to watch over the welfare of the peoples and to restore peace, which had been so gravely troubled by the Napoleonic adventure. Thus the mystical, medieval idea of the divine right of kings, which had been at the basis of the Holy Roman Empire, was reborn in a new form, through the substitution for the single emperor of a "directory" of legitimate sovereigns joined in a sacred union, which found its juridical consecration in the treaty of the Holy Alliance concluded on September 26, 1815. The two mystical systems had in common a religious tendency: just as the empire's aim had been the defense of religion in the temporal field, the powers of the Holy Alliance proclaimed: "de ne vouloir prendre pour règle de leur conduite que les préceptes de cette réligion sainte, préceptes de justice, de réligion et de paix." [1]

REACTION AGAINST THE DOCTRINE OF THE HOLY ALLIANCE: MAZZINI

The legitimist theory had far-reaching consequences in the field of both international and constitutional law. In the former, from the premise that sovereigns were vested with their authority by Providence, to whom alone they were responsible for their acts, the corollary was derived that sovereignty might not be taken away from legitimate sovereigns without their consent. In consequence, conquest alone could never confer a valid title to sovereignty. No crown and no territory could be declared in abeyance if the legitimate sovereign had not formally abdicated; every state and every government established in opposition to the will of the legitimate sovereign of the territory might not be internationally recognized. It also ensued from the providential mission of sovereigns that it was their right, or, as they assumed, their duty, to eliminate any motives which might result in a disturbance of human peace in any state what-

[1] Redslob, *Histoire des grands principes du droit des gens*, p. 364.

soever. Thus organized in a sort of international senate or Areopagus, the Great Powers of the Holy Alliance decided complaints brought by princes, adjudicated disputes, did not hesitate to interfere even in the internal affairs of other states in order to maintain peace and order. Faithful to the theory of the balance of power, which the Treaty of Vienna had confirmed once more as a canon of international law,[2] the members of the Holy Alliance thought it lawful and even imperative to repress every attempt likely to disturb the principles upon which they based their conduct in the sphere of international law. The legitimist theory emphasized that it behoved sovereigns alone to guide the destinies of the people; the latter were incapable of understanding their own interests or of providing for them directly. De Gentz, who was one of the ablest diplomats of the period, observed that it was the aim of legitimism to preserve the principle of authority from shipwreck and to save the peoples from the ill consequences of their own errors. The liberal doctrine, which asserted the right of every people to decide its own destiny, was the chief error to be combated. The circular dispatches sent out at the close of the Conference of Laibach (1821) reiterated that "the three sovereigns [of Austria, Prussia, and Russia] regarded themselves and all other sovereigns and legitimate powers as more than ever called upon to watch over the peace of Europe and to protect it not only against the errors and passions which might compromise it in the relations between states, but even more against those fatal attempts which delivered the civilized world to the horrors of a universal anarchy." This closing phrase was an allusion to the uprisings in Piedmont and Naples. It was understood that in order to defend the principles and the interests of the legitimate sovereigns against the revolutions attempted by their peoples, the powers of the Holy Alliance were to interfere wherever a liberal movement might develop.

This doctrine ought not to appear surprising if we reflect that even today there are some chiefs of state and of government in Europe and in Asia who claim to be called upon to carry out a divine mission, which they invoke as justification for the most revolting excesses. Nor should the fact be overlooked that at the moment in which the principles of the Holy Alliance were being proclaimed, the nations, exhausted by the Napoleonic wars, were principally anxious to obtain peace and order. Moreover, in the religious revival that made itself felt throughout Europe at the beginning of the Restoration, more than one religious mind was attracted by the mysticism emanating from the theories of the Holy Alliance. Thus was there no lack, especially in Germany, of those who endeavored to justify such doctrines from the theoretical and rationalist

---

[2] See Dupuis, *Le Principe de l'équilibre et le concert européen,* and Donnedieu de Vabres, *Essai sur la théorie de l'équilibre.*

point of view.[3] But in Italy, where the absolutist reaction of the governments after the French Revolution was even more violent than in other countries and the doctrines of the Holy Alliance were merely a convenient pretext for justifying tyrannical regimes and foreign oppression, the struggle for unity, liberty, and independence was in the intellectual field a struggle against the theories of the Holy Alliance.

It was then felt necessary to counterpoise the legitimist principle with a doctrine justifying the novel aspiration of the Italians, which might be equally applied in the political, moral, and juridical field. Moreover, if the new doctrine was to arouse sympathy, support, and co-operation in all countries, it also had to have a universal significance; it had to be applicable not only in Italy but also in all the countries of Europe, so that the struggle for Italian independence would become the symbol of and the prelude to a vaster movement appealing to all free men throughout Europe. It was to satisfy these needs that was born the Italian "doctrine of nationalities." [4]

This doctrine arose toward the middle of the nineteenth century and quickly conquered the whole of Italy. In every part of the peninsula and among the Italian exiles abroad, statesmen, philosophers, and lawyers supported the new doctrine with striking unanimity. It became an act of faith for the majority of the Italian intellectuals of that age.

In the political sphere the most authoritative, convinced and resolute champion of the new doctrine was Giuseppe Mazzini (1805–1872). Though during the Risorgimento, Mazzini's importance was great as the principal upholder of the republican form of government, even more decisive was his influence as apostle of Italian unity. Having grown up at Genoa in a republican environment with little enthusiasm for the House of Savoy, Mazzini, in 1821, when still a boy, had been profoundly struck by the spectacle of the Piedmontese exiles who had been obliged to sail for foreign countries after the failure of the recent uprising. Ten years later he himself was an exile at Marseilles, after undergoing imprisonment the previous year in Piedmont for his liberal ideas. Since that time Mazzini began to mature his political program, which he pursued unwearyingly until his death. The core of his doctrine was the prin-

[3] For a defense of the principle of legitimacy see Brockhaus, *Das Legitimitätsprinzip.* For an objective evaluation of the principle see Nippold. "Le Développement historique du droit international," 2 Rec. des cours (1924) 26–32.

[4] The principal juridical works by Italian authors belonging to the school of nationalities will be recalled further on. For the theory of nationalities in general, the most important Italian works are: Battaglia, "Nazione," in *Enciclopedia italiana,* XXIV, 470; B. Donati, "Lineamenti per una teoria giuridica della nazione, 79 Arch. Giur. (1907); Di Carlo, *Una polemica tra Gioberti e Padre L. Taparelli intorno alla nazionalità;* Panunzio, *Principio e diritto di nazionalità;* Pisanelli, *Lo stato e la nazione.* Other Italian works on the subject will be mentioned in the course of this book. On the principle of nationalities there exists a vast literature in other languages as well.

ciple of nationality. At the outset of his political life he enunciated this principle in the *"Introduzione per gli affratellati alla Giovine Italia"* (1831), which contained the declaration of the aims of this patriotic society, and at the eve of his death he again reasserted it in *"Nazionalismo e nazionalità"* (1871). Realizing that the excessive individualism of the Italians was one of their worst defects and one of the gravest obstacles to political unification, Mazzini was naturally inclined to oppose it. The defects of excessive individualism were demonstrated by the experience of the French Revolution, which, in Mazzini's words, "having begun with a Declaration of the Rights of Man, could end only with a man, Napoleon." Mazzini's theory, on the contrary, centered in the principle that at the basis of every human society there must be, not the individual, but the nation. The nation is the "association of all men who by language, geographical conditions, or the role designed to them by history form one group, recognize one principle, and direct their action under the protection of one law toward the actuation of one end." The institutions and instruments of Providence are, not the sovereigns, but on the contrary the nations. "By the courses of the great rivers, by the lines of the high mountains and other geographical features God has marked the natural boundaries of the nation."

From the fact that the nations are natural and perfect organizations three principal consequences are derived: (1) that every nation should be set up as a unit; thus the Italians ought to form one political unit; (2) that every nation should govern itself and therefore be independent of foreign domination; (3) that the government of every nation should be based on the consent of the nation itself and therefore on free democratic institutions, not on the caprice of sovereigns.

The originality of Mazzini's ideas and of the other Italian thinkers of his school consists of this: that their doctrines were not intended to be applied to one people only, but were destined to have value for all the nations on earth. The French Revolution had in the beginning been more individualistic than national, and when later it proclaimed the rights of the nation, it was nationalistic rather than national, because it had in mind the French nation alone. Mazzini, on the contrary, asserted the right of all nations to liberty and independence. In his opinion it is not conceivable that one nation be superior to the others. Just as men are equal, so are the nations equal; thus Mazzini defines nations as the individuals of humanity. Each nation has a special mission assigned to it by God for the good of all humanity, and toward this end all of them ought to collaborate. Nationality is the role that God has assigned to each people for the fulfillment of a common task, the mission which each people must accomplish on the earth. Among the nations, therefore, there ought not to be and there could not be conflicts, but rather collaboration. Conflicts between peoples are due solely to the ambitions and the personal interests of absolute sovereigns; once all the nations have been re-established within their natural boundaries and on a footing of equality, no reason for a conflict will survive. Against the Holy Alliance of sovereigns Mazzini proclaimed the Holy Alliance of peoples consecrated to liberty. It was Italy's task to initiate the movement toward redemption of the nations from the absolute sovereigns; Italy's cause thus became the cause of humanity itself and acquired a universal value.

Mazzini did not fail to divine the revolutionary bearing of his apostolate: "the countries of the nations will arise, awakened by the voice of the free, upon the ruins of the countries of the kings and the privileged classes. Between the nations there will be humanity and brotherhood." For the practical actuation of his ideas in Italy, Mazzini founded in 1831 at Marseilles the *Giovine Italia*. In 1834 he founded at Berne the *Giovine Europa* destined to spread the same program throughout the rest of Europe.

Because of its affinity to the aspirations of the best Italians, the new doctrine made an enormous impression in Italy. It was spread by secret societies, advocated by political leaders, and divulged by writers. Thousands perished on the Austrian gallows, in the prisons, and on the battlefields for this lofty ideal. It was for the nineteenth century the political gospel of the Italians. Cavour, a realistic statesman whom political events more than once placed in harsh opposition to Mazzini, was a resolute champion of the principle of nationality. He affirmed that "nature has decided that the nations should preserve their special autonomies, that they should respect one another's boundaries, usages, and language, that each should live by itself, and that they should not be violently flung against one another or enslaved." Among philosophers, Vincenzo Gioberti (1801–1852) [5] and Bertrando Spaventa (1817–1882); [6] among the constitutional lawyers, Giandomenico Romagnosi (1761–1835),[7]

[5] *Del primato morale e civile degli Italiani.*
[6] *Della nazionalità nella filosofia.* Spaventa understood national and political unity as a requirement necessary for permitting the individual to express in the best and most complete way his own personality. In *La filosofia italiana nelle sue relazioni con la filosofia europea*, he wrote: "The Italian nation is no longer for us, indeed it never was, a mere geographical expression, as the Austrian statesman [Metternich] remarked. It is more than the mere unity of custom or even of language, of art, of literature, of sentiment, and of intuition throughout the peninsula. We have had this nationality for a long time and it was not enough for us. Nationality is for us political unification, a living, liberal, powerful unity as one state. And why do we desire to be united as a free state? *Because solely in the unity of a free state can all the capacities of our life be truly developed;* solely therein can we be and know ourselves truly great." (Italics ours.)
[7] Gian Domenico Romagnosi was one of the greatest Italian jurisconsults of the beginning of the nineteenth century. He held public offices during the *Regno Italico* and was persecuted after the return of the Austrians because of his liberal ideas. His fundamental work is *La scienza delle costituzioni.* Romagnosi held that every well-governed state should be based on a nation. "A true and independent nation, ruling upon its entire territory, and living

Pellegrino Rossi (1787–1848),[8] and Diodato Lioy (1830–1912);[9] among politico-military writers, Giacomo Durando (1817–1894)[10] affirmed the new principle, although they sometimes reached it by divers paths.

MANCINI'S THEORIES OF PUBLIC AND PRIVATE INTERNATIONAL LAW

The theory of nationalities exerted a decisive influence on the Italian doctrines of international law of the nineteenth century.[11] The great majority of Italian writers on international law accepted *in toto* and unconditionally the new doctrine, so that in 1870 Von Holtzendorff was able to write that a history of the literature of international law in Italy is at the same time a history of the conceptions of the principle of nationality.[12]

---

under a sole temperate government; there you have the ultimate state desired by nature and by reason in order to establish internal and external peace and prosperity."

[8] In 1820 Pellegrino Rossi became a Swiss citizen and professor at the University of Geneva. He was then invited to the chair of political economy at the University of Paris, and in 1839 he became a member of the French Parliament. In 1848 he returned to Italy, became a minister in Pius IX's liberal cabinet, and was assassinated by extremist elements. Rossi was one of the most brilliant minds of his age and contributed powerfully to the science of international law. In his *Cours de droit constitutionnel* he dedicates the tenth chapter to an examination of the principles that preside over the formation of a state, among which he places the existence of a nation.

[9] *Del principio di nazionalità dal lato della storia e del diritto pubblico.*

[10] Giacomo Durando quitted Piedmont in 1831 for political reasons. In 1844 he returned home and proceeded to examine "the variations arisen since 1831, as well as the political and social conditions" of Italy. The result of this study was his book *Della nazionalità italiana; saggio politico e militare*, in which he intended to demonstrate that "in Italy there existed the elements for elevating the people to a puissant and lasting degree of nationality." He understood "by nationality the political union of various populations, naturally associated by geographical situation and artificially united by language, customs, traditions, legislation, material and moral interests." Durando particularly stressed the importance of strategy in the formation of nationality (see pp. 405–446, "Principles of Geostrategy Applied to the Genesis of Nationality"). Durando is a forerunner of *Geopolitik*. During the wars for Italian independence he was a courageous general.

[11] Besides the writings that will be considered separately, the following Italian works are devoted to the principle of nationalities: Agnetta Gentile, *Del principio di nazionalità*; Buzzati, *Appunti di diritto internazionale*; Carnazza Amari, *Trattato sul diritto internazionale pubblico di pace*; Carutti, *Principii di libero governo*; Celli, *Sistema di diritto internazionale*; F. P. Contuzzi, *Diritto internazionale pubblico*; Del Bon, *Istituzioni di diritto pubblico internazionale*; Esperson, *Il principio di nazionalità applicato alle relazioni civili internazionali*; Ferrero Gola, *Corso di diritto internazionale pubblico, privato e marittimo*; L. Palma, *Del principio di nazionalità nella moderna società civile europea*; Pertile, *Elementi di diritto internazionale moderno*; Pierantoni, *Trattato di diritto internazionale*; Sandonà, *Trattato di diritto internazionale moderno*; Turcotti, *Introduzione ad un nuovo codice del diritto delle genti.*

[12] The juridical concept of nation and the relations between nation and state in the field of international law had already been studied by L. Casanova (1799–1853) who had been called in 1848 to fill the chair of international law in the University of Genoa. Yet Casanova cannot be called a champion of the doctrine of nationalities in the strict sense of the word. Moreover, his lessons exerted no wide influence for the reason that they were only published posthumously (3d ed. Florence, 1876, with excellent introduction and notes by B. Brusa).

The leading exponent of the new tendency was the distinguished jurist and statesman Pasquale Stanislao Mancini (1817–1889).[13] Born at Castelbaronia, in the Kingdom of the Two Sicilies, he participated in the revolutionary movement of 1848 and was obliged to take refuge in Turin, where he devoted himself to the practice of law. He was several times a cabinet minister of the Kingdom of Italy and was elected president of the *Institut du droit international*. In 1851 Mancini was appointed to the chair of international law newly founded at the University of Turin. On this occasion he pronounced the famous inaugural lecture *Della nazionalità come fondamento del diritto delle genti* (Nationality as the foundation of the law of nations), which remains the fundamental document of the Italian juridical school of nationalities.[14] It has been pointed out that Mazzini and Mancini never mention one another in their writings. Almost certainly they reached the same conclusions independently of one another. The striking analogies between the doctrines of these two thinkers are due probably to the fact that the ideas they advocated were widely spread through Italy. These ideas were in fact but the expression of the spontaneous desire for unity, liberty, and independence then shared by all the best Italians. Besides, as Francesco Ruffini justly remarks,[15] the origin of the theories, both of Mazzini and Mancini, must probably be traced to all that conglomerate of propagandist literature of the secret societies, that were numerous, especially in the south of Italy, toward the beginning of the nineteenth century. In these writings the first elements of a doctrine of nationalities may be discerned. Such writings and doctrines were probably familiar to Mazzini, who had many dealings with the secret societies, and to Mancini, who was born and who spent the earlier part of his life in southern Italy. These propagandist writings in their turn took up an ideological theme expressed in the writings of Giambattista Vico, who, although having led a solitary life, had nevertheless exerted considerable influence on southern thinkers of the early nineteenth century.[16] According to Vico, the world was "the great city of the nations, founded and governed by God," who "making use of the very customs of men, rules and leads them." For the progress and preservation of humanity Providence has divided men into diverse nations, which constitute the basis upon which the states are to be established. In his imaginative and intricate style Vico wrote that "at the moment when these republics [nations] come into existence, the materials likely to receive

[13] Holtzendorff, "Le Principe des nationalités et la littérature italienne du droit des gens," 2 Rev. dr. int. et lég. comp. (1870) 93.
[14] The principal lectures by Mancini, together with an essay of his on Machiavelli, were collected in the volume *Diritto internazionale*, ed. by Pierantoni.
[15] Ruffini, "Il principio di nazionalità in G. Mazzini e in P. S. Mancini," in *L'insegnamento di Mazzini*, pp. 17–58.
[16] On Vico's conception of the nation see Bösch, *Beitrag zu den Grundlagen des internationalen Rechts; Recht und Nation bei Giambattista Vico*.

the form had been prepared and were all ready, and the result was the organization of the republics, composed of mind and body." The materials prepared were "different religions, different languages, different lands, different marriage rites, different names and races and houses and arms and therefore different governments, different courts, and in fine different laws; and inasmuch as they were different, therefore they were also independent in every respect from each other and constituting veritable republics [nations]."

Vico had made a serious effort to prove that in the whole course of history the states which had passed from splendor to decadence had been regenerated only when they had had as a foundation the cohesion and the moral energies of a nation. He had taught, moreover, that only nations organized with their own institutions could be considered as such according to natural law. "A people or a nation that has not inside itself a sovereign civilized government endowed with all the aforesaid characteristics is not truly a people or a nation, nor can it enter into relations with other peoples based on the natural law of nations." Vico had therefore expressed, even if confusedly, the conception that humanity is divided into different nations; that every state must be based upon a nation; and that every nation tends to establish itself as a state.

This conception, which lies at the basis of the doctrine of nationalities, inspired Mancini with his own conception of international law. In his inaugural lecture, mentioned above, Mancini points out that international law, like every other branch of law, is never the product of human will alone. It must be founded on rational and moral premises. The moral and rational basis of the law of nations is the principle of nationality. The nation is an aggregate of men, united by certain common characteristics which constitute what Mancini calls the "factors of nationality." These factors are: the territory upon which they reside, race, language, custom, a common past, laws, and religion. These are the material factors of nationality, which Mancini divides into natural factors, such as geographical factors, and historical factors, such as religion. Yet for the creation of a nation not all these factors are either necessary or sufficient. They are not all necessary, because even if some of them are lacking a nation can still exist. There are in fact nations whose inhabitants differ from one another in race, language, and religion. They are not sufficient, because to create a nation there must be also another and a binding element, the "consciousness of nationality" (*coscienza della nazionalità*). This consists of the conviction that a nation acquires of its own existence, which gives it the ability to organize itself in the interior and to manifest itself exteriorly.[17] In other words, a population forms a nation only in so far as it possesses, in addition to certain common characteristics, the consciousness that it constitutes one unity and the will to live politically

17 *Diritto internazionale*, p. 35.

united. Mancini quite consistently defines nationality as "a natural society of men whom unity of territory, origin, customs, and language molds into a community of living and of national consciousness." [18] International law is the law of these nations. According to Mancini, international relations should not be based upon the states, mere arbitrary products of human artifice, but upon the nations, natural and divine creations. These are the sole entities capable of becoming political societies, that is, states in the favorable sense of the word, and of establishing through their co-operation the only real society of civilized humanity.[19] Individualism, nationality, and humanitarianism are not conflicting but correlated concepts. Like individuals, nations too must be free. They must both contribute to the common welfare of humanity. The principle of nationalities is the very liberty of the individual extended to the aggregate of the individuals that composes the nation; nationality is merely the collective manifestation of human liberty, and therefore it is as holy and divine a thing as liberty itself. Thus the liberty of each nation cannot be restricted save in so far as limitation is required in order to protect the same liberty which must be respected in all the other nations.[20] "Just as individuals should be organized as nations, so all humanity must be organized in an international society, based upon the coexistence and reciprocal independence of all the nations under the universal rule of justice." [21]

From these general principles Mancini derived the following consequences:

a) Every nation should constitute one state and one alone.

b) Every nation should be left free to organize itself as an independent state (principle of the self-determination of the peoples). [22]

c) Nations, and therefore states consisting of them, should all be equal.

d) Nations and states consisting of them should be independent; hence the absolute prohibition of any intervention by any one state in the internal affairs of any other.

e) Treaties contrary to the principles of nationality, of equality, and of independence should be revised.

f) All nations should be united in a juridical organization capable of settling disputes between them and of eliminating injustice by means of amicable procedures. From this premise Mancini deduces that the states

[18] *Ibid.*, p. 37.   [19] *Ibid.*, p. 79.   [20] *Ibid.*, p. 38.   [21] *Ibid.*, p. 194.

[22] Mancini maintained that plebiscites might be resorted to as an expedient means for determining the nationality of the inhabitants in regions where the sentiment of the population were doubtful and especially in frontier districts. He expressed, however, some mistrust for the plebiscite system. He feared that a population might be induced by passing and contingent considerations to deny, by means of a plebiscite, its own nationality. Mancini probably had in mind the case of Savoy and Nice which by the plebiscite of 1860 voted for their own annexation to France, in spite of the fact that they had Italian traditions. In an inaugural lecture of 1872 Mancini wrote that a plebiscite cannot destroy the fact of nationality.

should be obliged to have recourse to international arbitration, and other Italian publicists of the same school derive the necessity for organizing a league of nations.

g) The pope, not being the ruler of a nation, cannot be a territorial sovereign, indeed not even a subject of international law. From this Mancini concludes the inadmissibility of concordats, understood as being international treaties between a state and the Catholic Church. This, however, would not leave the religious faith of individuals unprotected, since every state should respect religions as manifestations of personal liberty.

It is easy to observe that Mancini's theory was diametrically opposed to the principles of the Holy Alliance and offered a juridical justification of the political program of Italian liberals.

The doctrine of nationalities was also an attempt to provide a new basis for the solution of the fundamental problems of private international law (conflict of laws). From the sixteenth century to the middle of the nineteenth century Italy's contribution to the progress of private international law has been neither remarkable nor original. As in other countries, the doctrine of the statutes had prevailed during that period; although there had been some resistance, due in part to the persisting influence of earlier doctrines and in part to the strong tradition of Roman law.[23] An important treatise on private international law was published in 1838 by Nicola Rocco (1811–1877), a magistrate of Naples.[24] Rocco, who followed the statutory theory, advocated that in case of conflict of laws, the law of domicile should be preferred.

The basic ideas of the Italian school of nationalities in the field of private international law were expounded by Mancini in a report submitted in 1874 to the session of the *Institut de droit international*.[25] It excited much attention at the time. The doctrine is based on the principle

[23] Thus, for instance, whereas almost everywhere the well-known principle regulating succession prevailed: *quot territoria tot haereditates* (which was also accepted by Italian jurisconsults such as Cardinal de Luca [1614–1683]) the Italian courts sometimes applied the Roman principle of the unity and universality of a succession. This was determined by the law of domicile of the deceased without any regard for the place in which the property was situated, Anzilotti, *Corso di diritto internazionale privato*, 1925, p. 34.

[24] *Uso e autorità delle leggi del Regno delle Due Sicilie considerate nelle relazioni con le persone e con il territorio degli stranieri.*

[25] The report is published in 1 Journal du droit international privé (1874). Mancini's theories had already in part been advanced by Pescatore (1810–1879), in *La logica del diritto*, Part II, especially ch. xvii. For a complete exposition of the theories of the Italian school of international private law see the book by Catellani, *Il diritto internazionale privato*, which centers the entire historical exposition of private international law in the Italian doctrine. Among the writers that agreed with the theories of Mancini in the field of private law are, besides those whom we may mention further on, Esperson, *Il Principio di nazionalità applicato alle relazioni civili internazionali* (1868), and "Le Droit international privé dans la législation italienne," 7 Journal du droit international privé (1880) 245 ff.; Contuzzi, *Diritto internazionale privato*; Ferrero Gola, *Corso di diritto internazionale publico*; Fiore, *Diritto internazionale privato*, 3d ed., and *Elementi di diritto internazionale privato*, 3d ed.; Lomonaco, *Trattato di diritto civile internazionale*.

of the community of law, derived in part from Savigny. According to this doctrine, just as the modern state respects and safeguards the liberty and the interests of private citizens in so far as they do not interfere with the requirements of sovereignty, so nothing prevents the recognition of foreign laws in so far as they do not conflict with the provisions of municipal laws safeguarding the interests of the state. With reference to their recognition abroad, the private laws of a state can be divided, according to Mancini, into "necessary private law" and "voluntary private law." Necessary private law comprises, roughly speaking, the laws governing the status and the capacity of persons, domestic relations, and successions, a topic strictly linked with the family. Mancini holds that these same natural factors which form the national character of the inhabitants of the state do also mold the particular content of the rules of the necessary private law of that state. For instance, if the law of a state provides that its citizens attain majority at the age of twenty-one, this is due to the fact that individuals belonging to the nation composing such a state attain their intellectual maturity at that age. In other words, the rules of necessary private law constitute the expression of the particular characteristics of the nation composing the state in which they are enacted. The principle of nationalities thus becomes the principle that binds together public and private international law. For the nation constitutes the legitimate basis of every subject of international law; moreover, the nation impresses upon a part of the municipal law of every state some particular characteristics which are especially relevant in the field of private international law (conflict of laws). Since the necessary private law of every state corresponds to the particular characteristics and needs of its citizens, every other state ought to apply on its own territory to the citizens of the foreign states the provisions of the necessary private law of the foreign state to which they belong. According to Mancini, therefore, the questions within the resort of necessary private law should be determined in every country by the provisions of the national law of the individual concerned, that is, by the provisions of the law of the state of which he is a citizen. This conclusion is to be deduced from the principles of nationalities and of the community of nations.

Unlike necessary private law, voluntary private law governs those matters in which the particular characteristics of a nation are not involved and with regard to which the principle of nationalities need not be taken into consideration: for example, contracts. Since voluntary private law affects only private interests and no public interest whatsoever, in dealing with the matters governed by this part of the law the largest discretion should be left to individuals. Thus every state should leave the contracting parties at liberty to elect which law should govern their relationships belonging to the sphere of voluntary private law. The law chosen may be either the national law of all the contracting parties, if they are all citizens of the same state, or the law of the place in which the transaction was concluded or even any other law the parties may have decided to accept as the law governing their relationship.

The recognition of foreign laws as well as of foreign acts and judgments is not, however, unconditional. From the very concept of sovereignty it derives the right of every state to deny validity on its own territory to foreign laws, acts, and judgments contrary to public policy, to the *ordine publico*. By *ordine publico* Mancini understands that body of fundamental principles of a social, moral, and legal character that are at the root of the entire constitution of a state. A principle of public policy is, for instance, that which in all civilized states prohibits polygamy.

Nationality, sovereignty, and liberty are thus the principles upon which the Italian school builds an entire system of private international law, which Anzilotti thus tersely summarizes:

In all matters concerning the status and the capacity of persons, domestic relations, and successions, the state recognizes and applies on its own territory the foreigner's private law, in conformity with the principle of nationalities. In other matters, especially in all that concerns contracts, in conformity with the principle of liberty, it applies the law expressly or tacitly referred to by the interested parties; it rejects, however, all foreign laws conflicting with its own sovereignty.[26]

CRITICISM OF THE DOCTRINE OF NATIONALITIES

The doctrine of nationalities, largely because of its political implications, at once received enthusiastic support in Italy. At the same time, criticisms were not scarce. At first, these were voiced chiefly abroad. They then extended to Italy too, especially after the unification of the country had been effected. Perhaps many Italian writers felt then free to criticize a doctrine which previously they had considered themselves bound to accept by reason of the ideological support it gave to the national movement.

As for the accuracy of the doctrine of nationality in the field of public international law, there were a few who criticized the doctrine, appealing against it to the old legitimist principles. As a mere historical curiosity, it may be recalled that among these critics were F. Cavazzoni Pederzini [27] and Father Luigi Taparelli d'Azeglio (1793–1862), brother of the patriot and liberal statesman Massimo Taparelli d'Azeglio.[28] Father Taparelli set the principle of the self-determination of the peoples beneath that of obedience to legitimate sovereigns, who alone were competent to

[26] *Corso di diritto internazionale privato*, 1925, p. 38.
[27] *Studii sopra le nazioni e sopra l'Italia.*
[28] *Della nazionalità*; see also his *Sintesi del diritto naturale.*

determine within what limits the principle of nationalities ought to be followed.

More serious criticisms were expressed by others, especially foreigners, who questioned the accuracy of the principle of nationalities in the form given to it by the Italian school, pointed out the dangers implied in the doctrine, and demonstrated its absolute lack of juridical foundation.

As far as the first point is concerned, they stressed the fact that the concept "nation," advanced by the Italian school, was at best confused, vague, and arbitrary. The very followers of the doctrine could not agree in establishing the factors of nationality.[29] When they attempted to apply the school's principles, they had to admit that populations existed which with regard to certain factors (for example, language) belonged to a given nationality, and with regard to others (for example, religion or customs) to an utterly different one. For this reason the Italian writers, after strenuous efforts to determine which were the factors that constituted nationality, were constrained to come to the conclusion that not one of them was necessary and adequate.[30] In consequence, the only determinant of nationality was in the last resort the so-called "consciousness of nationality," which the Italian school considered the essential ingredient in a nationality. But in reality the consciousness of nationality is at best a vague, imponderable, and artificial concept. The pretense at ascertaining the national consciousness of a given population seemed at least in many cases a ludicrous undertaking. In many populations the sentiment of nationality was divided; in others it did not exist at all.

It was also observed that the principle according to which every nation ought to set itself up as a state and every state ought to be made up of one nation was often unrealizable and fraught with grave consequences. For two reasons it was feasible in Italy. First, because the Italian people possessed all those prerequisites: unity of language, customs, culture, religion, national consciousness, and so forth, demanded by the Italian doctrine in order to form a nation. So no matter what criterion was adopted to appraise it, there could be no doubt that all the Italians constituted and intended to constitute one nation. Secondly, because the Italian nation seemed to occupy, to the total exclusion of all others, a

---

[29] The Italian jurist Padelletti, in "L'Alsace et la Lorraine et le droit des gens," 3 Rev. dr. int. et lég. comp. (1871) 464 ff., remarked (p. 477): "la théorie de nos publicistes sur ces points, sans compter qu'elle est bien loin d'être unanime et uniforme, est presque partout vague, inexacte, incertaine dans ses développements et jamais pratique dans ses conclusions extrêmes." For very discerning criticisms see also Holtzendorff, "Le Principe des nationalités et la littérature italienne du droit des gens," 2 Rev. dr. int. et lég. comp. (1870) 93 ff., and Mohl, "Die Nationalitätenfrage," in Staatsrecht, Völkerrecht und Politik, III, 333–372.

[30] Cf. for this point the acute analysis of the principle of nationalities of E. Brusa in his "Introduction," previously quoted, to Casanova's Lezioni (pp. ccci–ccclxxviii). Brusa carefully examines all the factors considered by various Italian writers as the component elements of nationality and points out their inconsistencies.

territory whose natural boundaries were clearly established by the Alps and the sea. But there were many regions inhabited by populations whose nationality it was very difficult to determine by means of the criteria enunciated by the Italian school. Besides, even where it had been possible to determine the inhabitant's nationality, it could only have been found that they were divided into several nationalities, so commingled that it would have been impossible to create on those territories exclusively national states. The attempt to apply everywhere the principle of nationalities with absolute strictness would have led in many regions to violence and injustice. Von Bulmerincq was not far from right when he declared that the principle of nationalities was one that led to war, not to peace.[31]

The political and sociological criticism against the principle of nationalities were complemented by criticisms of a more strictly juridical character. It was submitted that the doctrine of nationalities was beyond the sphere of international law. In affirming what was to be the social and ethnical foundation of a state, namely, one nation and one alone, the doctrine considered a problem that was not juridical in the strict sense of the word. In fact this problem, in so far as it referred to the way the states were formed or ought to be formed, belonged to the sphere of sociology, not of international law, which does not consider the historical or sociological process of the formation of states, but only the states themselves inasmuch as they are subjects of international law. In addition it was pointed out that the assertion made by various Italian writers belonging to this school, that is, that nations, not states, are the subjects of international law,[32] was contrary to one of the fundamental and most firmly established rules of international law according to which the states are the addressees of the provisions of general international law, without any consideration for the ethnical composition of their populations or for their internal constitution.

On the other hand, if the writers of the school of nationalities did not mean to affirm that the nations were the subjects of international law, but only that they ought to be, then they were not expressing a problem of positive law, *de jure condito*, but a problem *de jure condendo*, that is, they were expressing a merely ideal aspiration concerning what the law should have been. Understood in this sense, the doctrine of nationalities

[31] Bulmerincq, *Praxis, Theorie und Codification des Völkerrechts*, I, 64. For similar criticisms, see also F. F. Martens, *Traité de droit international*, I, 197 (French translation by A. Leo); and more recently Fauchille, *Traité de droit international public*, 8th ed., I, 15.

[32] The emphatic assertion that nations, not states, are the subjects of international law is to be found, for instance, in the work by Fiore, *Nuovo diritto internazionale pubblico secondo i bisogni della civiltà moderna*. In this regard note the remarks of Bluntschli, *Das moderne Völkerrecht der civilisirten Staaten als Rechtsbuch dargestellt* in his comment to section 25: "Würde das Völkerrecht wirklich auf die flüssige Nationalität, nicht nur auf das feste Staatswesen gegründet, so würde es allen Halt verlieren und unfähig werden, sich Anerkennung und Geltung zu verschaffen."

simply gave a new content to the old theories of natural law. It admitted an eternal, absolute law, above and often in conflict with positive law and emanating directly from Providence, on the basis of which the nations ought to have been organized as free and independent states. The mere enunciation of these principles was sufficient to underline their inexactitude and even dangers. With the peremptory affirmation that the nations were divine or natural creations and that it should be the mission of international law to reorganize humanity into juridical entities on a national basis, the new doctrine fell practically into the same errors as the old legitimist theory. Just as the latter held that sovereigns were sent to earth to execute the plans of Providence and that for this reason they were entitled to claim absolute obedience from their subjects and to dispose arbitrarily of their destinies, just so, according to the new conception, did the same function and the same prerogatives belong to the nations. They thus became a sort of *Deus ex machina:* the purpose of international law was only to protect them; to them alone was absolute obedience due; and in their name the extremest acts of tyranny might be committed and justified. The new doctrine thus came to introduce into international law that providential element which must be banned from all juridical conception. What was worse, it created a new form of juridical idolatry—idolatry of the nation, which might degenerate into oppression. Brusa quite correctly wrote that "the so-called 'principle of nationalities' has all the original flaws of the theocratical state." [33] In his turn Von Holtzendorff remarked that "the Italian school had erected nationality, with the associated democratic principle of universal suffrage, into a sort of radical legitimism." [34]

The doctrine of the Italian school was not less seriously criticized for its results in the field of private international law. It should be noted that the conclusions reached by the doctrine in the field of private international law did not meet among Italian writers that unanimity of opinions that had greeted the doctrine of nationalities in the field of public international law. This was partly due, perhaps, to the fact that there was no patriotic reason in favor of the acceptance of this part of the doctrine. The conception of the school of nationality in the sphere of private international law was criticized in Italy by Gabba,[35] Saredo,[36] and Brusa,[37] who rather tended to favor Savigny's system; by Bianchi,[38] Sandonà,[39] and a few others, who still clung to the statutory theories; by independent

---

[33] *Introduzione*, p. ccclxvi.   [34] *Handbuch des Völkerrechts*, p. 41.
[35] "Introduzione al diritto civile internazionale," in *Atti della R. Accademia dei Lincei* (1906–1908), and even earlier in *Rivista di legislazione e giurisprudenza* (1867), Part 3, pp. 1–12.
[36] *Saggio sulla storia del diritto internazionale privato.*
[37] "Note" to the *Lezioni* of Casanova, Vol. II.
[38] *Corso elementare di diritto civile*, I, 115–120.
[39] *Trattato di diritto internazionale moderno.*

writers, such as Laghi [40] and in fine by others such as Fiore [41] and Fusi-. nato, [42] who while concluding to accept the chief implications of the Italian doctrine, did not fail at the same time to reject some parts of the system. To these national critics must also be added a few prominent foreign scholars, such as Brocher, [43] Strisower, [44] and Von Bar. [45]

Part of these criticisms concerned some particular concepts expounded by the doctrine: for example, its concept of *ordine pubblico* and the theory of the autonomy of the will of the contracting parties to choose the law that is to determine their contract. Others went further to the core of the doctrine. First of all, it was pointed out that the Italian school considered the problems of international law *de jure condendo* rather than *de juro condito*. In consequence, although it supplied some useful materials to be utilized in the enactment of new norms of private international law, it contributed nothing to a solution of the problems of conflict of laws rising from rules already in existence. In short, the school considered problems dealing with legislative policy rather than with positive law.

But even from the point of view of the legislative policy the excellence of the principles advocated by the school was questioned. The concept "national law," from which the Italian school set out, was ambiguous and incorrect. If national law meant the law of a nation, that is, a specific ethnical grouping, it was easy to retort that jurisprudence knows no laws of nations, but only laws of states. And since a state is not necessarily identified with a nation, the link created by the school between nationality and private international law collapsed completely. In addition, as Strisower remarked, the laws of a state rarely manifest what according to the Italian school constitutes the national characteristics of the ethnical group composing the state. It will suffice to observe that although northern peoples are physically less precocious than those of the South yet according to many northern systems of law the age for entering upon a marriage is much lower than in the countries of the South. And even if it were true that the laws of a state reflect the characteristics of a nation in its entirety, that fact would not suffice to prove that they also reflect the personal characteristics of that given individual with regard to whom the actual problem of conflict of laws is posed and that their application to that given individual would in consequence be advisable. Similar logic

---

[40] *Il diritto internazionale privato nei suoi rapporti con le leggi territoriali.*
[41] *Trattato di diritto internazionale,* 2d ed.
[42] "Il principio della scuola italiana nel diritto privato internazionale," in *Scritti giuridici,* I, 539 ff.
[43] *Nouveau traité de droit international privé,* Genève, 1876, and "Etude sur le traité de droit civil international publié par M. Laurent," 13 Rev. dr. int. et lég. comp. (1881) 531 ff.
[44] *Die italienische Schule des internationalen Privatrechts.*
[45] *Theorie und Praxis des internationalen Privatrechts,* 2d ed.

might be employed to advocate the application to this individual of the law of domicile instead of his national law. If, in fact, a person has set up his domicile in a foreign country, this should mean that he has found the adopted country and its laws better adapted to his temperament and to his needs. It was also pointed out how arbitrary it is to distinguish between a necessary and a voluntary law with no criteria other than those furnished by the matters regulated by these laws: for example, wills, contracts and so forth. There are some provisions which may opportunely be in the nature of permissive rules in spite of the fact that they govern matters which according to the Italian school are within the sphere of necessary law; others should not be permissive rules, although according to the Italian school they ought to be classed with voluntary law. In fine, the conception of sovereignty and *ordine publico* invoked by the Italian doctrine as a possible limitation to the recognition of foreign laws and judgments was no doubt correctly conceived, even though not original. It failed, however, to solve the real problem, which was to decide which criteria should determine whether foreign law should be granted or refused recognition.

We must admit that not all the criticisms against the Italian doctrine of nationality were merited. The accusation that it confused the ethnico-political concept of "nation" with the formal-juridical concept of "state" is only partly correct. Mancini, for instance, recognized that at the moment when he was writing states were not identified with nations. What he maintained was that by an inevitable historical process nations would become the basis of states and that the scholar ought not to close his eyes to this trend, which Mancini considered to be characteristic of the international law of the age. A clear-cut distinction between "state" and "nation" can be found in the work of Terenzio Mamiani (1798–1885), who was undoubtedly one of the most brilliant and accomplished thinkers of the Italian school in its first period.[46] In his work, of a historical, philosophical and juridical character, *Di un nuovo diritto pubblico europeo*,[47] Mamiani, after examining the characteristic aspects of law and international politics since the beginning of the century, reaches the conclusion that (1) the states are perfect moral and juridical entities; (2) every state should be independent of every other state; (3) the existence of a state is compatible even with a population of diverse nationalities. From

[46] Terenzio Mamiani was a publicist, man of letters, philosopher, and political leader. An exile in Paris from 1831 to 1846, he was a minister of Pius IX's in 1848, deputy of Genoa to the Sardinian Parliament in 1856, minister of public instruction in 1860–1861. From 1855 on he taught philosophy in the University of Turin, and in 1864 was appointed senator of the Kingdom of Italy.

[47] The book was published for the first time in Turin, in 1860, and brought as an appendix another writing of Mamiani's of 1856, *Dell'ottima congregazione umana e del principio di nazionalità*. The book was published in an English translation by R. Acton, London, 1860, without any addition.

these he draws other conclusions. A few are of a juridical nature: for example, that a state is not to be identified with its sovereign and that under no circumstances can intervention be permitted. Others are political: it is to the peoples that the right of self-determination belongs; the inhabitants must be consulted in case of transfer of territory from one state to another; it is not desirable that any prince be vested with more than one crown; all the states should be invited to be parties to the more important treaties; the Church, which is not based on a nation, should not have any temporal power. Mamiani also notes that although the states, not the nations, are the subjects of international law the nations tended to set themselves up as independent states, and the states tend to be composed of only one nation. "The nations are a favored creation of God. In course of time and with the maturity of civilization, it appears that nations alone are to constitute the true and right individual members of the great human family."

Pasquale Fiore (1837–1914), too, who in 1865 had declared that nations, not states, are the subjects of international law,[48] ended by admitting in 1879 that the subjects of international law are states, not nations.[49] He reaffirmed this principle in his *Diritto internazionale codificato*, a project for a code of international law which was of questionable value, in which rules of positive international law and politico-social suggestions are jumbled together.[50] Yet he remained a strenuous champion of the principle that every state ought to be set up on national foundations, and in one of the sections of the project he declared that "international law should protect the formation of national states, safeguard the rights of people of the same nationality, and see that the national aspirations, spontaneous and constantly asserted, are not repressed by deception or force. In order to strengthen the legal organization of international society and to eliminate several causes of internal struggle, it is especially advisable to favor the formation of national states" (sec. 94). This led Fiore to give in his project a legal definition of the people (sec. 84) and of the nation (sec. 85).

REVISION BY MANCINI'S FOLLOWERS

A serious attempt to revise the doctrine of nationalities so as to overcome the various criticisms against it was made toward the end of the nineteenth century by Guido Fusinato (1860–1913).[51] Fusinato draws

[48] Fiore, *Nuovo diritto internazionale pubblico secondo i bisogni della civiltà moderna*; French translation by Pradier Fodéré, Paris, 1868, 2 vols.
[49] *Trattato di diritto internazionale pubblico*, 2nd ed., 2 vols. Torino, 1879.
[50] *Il diritto internazionale codificato e la sua sanzione giuridica*; English translation by Borchard.
[51] Guido Fusinato was one of the greatest Italian jurists because of his juridical precision, accompanied by a profound culture and great practical sense. It was a grave detriment to

a clear distinction between state and nation. Subjects of international law are states, not nations. "The concept of state is a formal one, in the sense that it does not depend upon the quality of its population or upon the characteristics of its internal juridical or political organization." [52] The existence of a state as a subject of international law depends upon its recognition, while the ethnical constitution of the state is entirely irrelevant. Yet, Fusinato remarks, the nations are relevant for international law, because "it is a historical fact that although the state, and the state alone, always remains the subject of law, every state, however, tends gradually to become national; so that when every state will be a nation, and every nation will form a state, it will be possible to say that it is truly the nations that are subjects of international law, but never as nations, always and only as states." [53] Furthermore, as regards the concept of nation, Fusinato makes the following remarks:

1. In determining whether a nation exists or not, it is not possible to rely on natural or historical factors, such as language, religion, customs, but only on the spiritual factor, the *consciousness of nationality*, that is, the desire of a group of persons to live together in the bond of political unity. The national consciousness is therefore not one of the factors concurring to constitute nationality, but it is the exclusive factor of nationality.

2. Nationality, therefore, is a concept based exclusively on moral and spiritual values.

3. "If it is true that the nation exists purely because there is a consciousness of nationality, it is not equally true that every nation has the right to constitute a political independent unity." [54] A nation can aspire to become a state only when it has attained its political maturity and when the national sentiment is shared by all its components, not only by one class.

4. The modifications of national sentiment can lead to the disappearance of existing nationalities, to their disintegration, and to the formation of new nationalities.

By admitting that the states, not the nations, are the subjects of international law, Fusinato practically excludes the doctrine of nationalities from the field of international law and recognizes that its value is purely political. But even on the grounds of politics he diminishes the importance of the principle of nationalities. According to Fusinato the nations are not natural and immutable entities. On the contrary, the formation

---

science that his manifold activity in public life drew him away from teaching. A collection of his legal writings, almost all devoted to international law, was published at Turin, 1921. The writings to which we refer here are: "Il principio della scuola italiana del diritto internazionale pubblico," in his *Scritti giuridici*, I, 213–249 and "La teoria delle nazionalità nel sistema del diritto pubblico internazionale," in his *Scritti giuridici*, II, 333–340.

[52] *Ibid.*, II, 335.　　　[53] *Ibid.*, I, 245.　　　[54] *Ibid.*, I, 240.

of the nations and of the national states is simply a historical phenomenon. Nations are considered to be changeable entities; as they arise, so can they also change and disappear.

In Fusinato the doctrine of nationalities has completed its cycle. Having sprung up in the heroic years of the Risorgimento, the doctrine was enthusiastically and unconditionally welcomed because of the aid it gave to the national cause. It wore itself out toward the end of the century when the Risorgimento was well-nigh accomplished. Even the adherents of the doctrine in Italy recognized then that it was quite void of value from the point of view of positive law. It expressed only an aspiration and a political program: that humanity ought to be organized in national states. The doctrine was therefore only political, not juridical, and even from the political point of view the doctrine was of questionable accuracy.

The doctrine of nationalities, in spite of the fact that its supporters meant it to have universal character and importance, was actually a doctrine created by Italians for the clear purpose of justifying the political striving of their country toward national unity and with an eye fixed on the peculiar situation in Italy. In fact the doctrine amounted to the assertion that a country endowed with the requisites to be found in Italy: that is, community of language, religion, customs, culture, traditions, and national sentiment in all the inhabitants, ought to be constituted as an independent state. But there is still another political motive of the doctrine which in my opinion has been overlooked. At the beginning of the Risorgimento the unity, liberty, and independence of the country were the ideals of the better part of the population, but this was a mere minority. Centuries of political divisions and enslavement had made many Italians more sensible to the regional divisions and local jealousies than to the lofty ideals of national unification. In spite of the unity of tradition, culture, usages, religion, and language, many divisions had been created among Italians. Many of them were far from feeling themselves linked in national unity with the other inhabitants of the peninsula. By affirming that inasmuch as Italians had certain common characteristics they formed one nation and ought therefore to form one state, the doctrine of nationalities in reality was not so much aimed at recognizing an already existing national unity as at removing any doubts which the Italians might still maintain as to their forming a nation. In other words, the doctrine was intended to stimulate, and in fact did stimulate, the formation of the national unity of all Italians. The doctrine of nationalities thus became the doctrine of the Risorgimento and acquired the value of a "myth" in the sense Georges Sorel gave to the word, that is, an ideology which, although logically inaccurate, was however capable of impelling a certain political action.[55] The politico-revolutionary implications of the doctrine were perceptible not only to the partisans, such as Mazzini, but to opponents as well. In 1851 the Austrian ambassador in Turin took steps to obtain the interruption of Mancini's lectures, but the Piedmontese prime minister, Massimo d'Azeglio, opposed a dignified refusal. The Neapolitan government seized Mancini's property situated in its territory.

The essentially political nature of the doctrine of nationalities explains its fortunes abroad. In France, where at the time of the French Revolution the doctrine of natural boundaries prevailed, on the basis of which it was claimed that the boundaries of the republic ought to be carried to the Rhine, the doctrine of nationalities was at first criticized by conservatives. In the 1867 session of the legislative body Thiers declared: "Pour vouloir qu'une pareille doctrine fût applicable il faudrait se rapporter à mille ans en arrière." The doctrine was, on the contrary, advocated by Napoleon III as an expedient for acquiring a personal ascendancy over the liberal opinion throughout Europe and for giving France the leadership in the movement for the emancipation of nationalities, which was at that time agitating the whole of Europe, especially to the detriment of Austria and Russia. Emile Ollivier, the author of *L'Empire liberal,* saw in this doctrine the significant manifestation of the period.[56] But in the main the doctrine was unpopular in France. Only in 1871 was it invoked to oppose the annexation of Alsace-Lorraine by Germany, and not many years later it inspired a celebrated page of Renan's.[57] In other countries of Europe the doctrine exerted considerable influence, especially in the political field, and it contributed to the movement of national emancipation of many populations, which won for the last century the name "century of nationalities." Before and during the first World War the doctrine was revived in order to support various nationalist internal movements, especially in Austria.[58]

The revolutionary value of the doctrine was recognized during the first World War by the Entente, which proclaimed, among its other war aims, the right of self-determination of the peoples and the reconstruction of Europe on national bases.[59] But when the doctrine had to face situations other than that for which it had been created in Italy, it revealed how inconsistent, inaccurate, and unfeasible it was. To draw a map of Europe

[55] For this peculiar characteristic of the Italian school of nationalities see Rashofer, "Volk und Staat in der italienischen Rechtstheorie des 19. Jahrhunderts," 6 Zeitschrift für ausländisches öffentliches Recht und Völkerrecht (1936) 538–550.
[56] *L'Empire liberal,* Vol. I.   [57] *Qu'est-ce qu'une nation?*
[58] See, for instance, Renner, *Das Selbstbestimmungsrecht der Nationen in besonderer Anwendung auf Oesterreich.*
[59] In March, 1941, President Roosevelt, after signing the Lend-Lease Bill, declared: "We believe that any nationality, no matter how small, has the inherent right to its own nationhood."

exclusively based on the principle of nationality was an impossible task and might lead to grave injustice. The doctrine exasperated the problem of nationalities without being able to solve it. The consequence was that although it was not possible to set up states on an exclusively national basis the national sentiment of the various nationalities of which their populations were composed had been excited, resulting in violent conflicts between majorities and minorities. The doctrine thus contributed to the development of the problem of minorities, which is certainly one of the gravest inheritances from the first World War.

No matter how inacceptable the Italian doctrine of nationalities may have been from the juridical and even within certain limits from the political point of view, it must be appreciated for the nobility of the principles that inspired it. When it affirmed that the fundamental factor in the formation of a nation is the consciousness of its nationality, the doctrine posited that the concept "nation" is essentially a spiritual and moral one. Hence, two important consequences, which suffice to distinguish this doctrine from the barbarous racist theories, followed in Germany.[60] First, according to the Italian doctrine the fact of belonging to a given nationality is determined by a spiritual factor—the will of a population to live as one—not by alleged natural factors, such as blood or race. Nothing is more opposed to the Italian doctrine than the assertions frequently repeated by the modern German theories, that is, that American-born citizens of Germanic descent remain Germans from generation to generation and owe allegiance to Germany by reason of their ancestors. Secondly, the Italian doctrine makes the decision whether people belong or do not belong to a given nationality purely voluntary, and therefore no one can be constrained to belong to a given nationality against his own will. Nothing is more opposed to the Italian doctrine than the German doctrine of "unconscious nationality," put forward when Alsace-Lorraine was annexed, according to which the Alsatians had to be annexed because they were Germans by race even if they did not know it or wish to become German subjects. Another lofty principle advocated by the Italian doctrine is equality of nationalities. According to the Italian doctrine men are equal so nations must be too. To speak of superior and inferior nations was an absurdity to Mancini. From this point of view the contrast is again striking between the Italian doctrine and the modern racial theories of German origin, according to which the German nation claims superiority over the others. The doctrine of nationalities, which

[60] It is not worth while to waste any time in outlining the distinction between the Italian doctrine of nationalities and the racist theories recently advanced in Italy by Fascists. They were a vain attempt to justify the recent anti-Semitic persecution, to which the majority of the Italian people were opposed. The new fascist racist theories constituted a supine acceptance of absurd German theories, accomplished in a spirit of servility toward Germany. Quite obviously, they have not had any effect on the Italian doctrine of international law.

for the Italian school was a doctrine of liberty, became for the Germans an instrument of oppression.

According to the Italian school the organization of humanity into nations was to be the first step toward the organization of international society based on the principle of the co-operation of all the peoples. From this society war was to be entirely banned, and its place was to be taken by arbitration.

In the field of private international law many of the original defects of the theory were corrected in the process of its evolution. It was Fusinato's merit that he modified the theory in such a way as to base it on considerations which even today are still acceptable. In his study *Il principio della scuola italiana del diritto internazionale privato* (The Principle of the Italian School in the Field of International Private Law) he recognized that adoption of the national law as the law determining the relations concerning the status, the capacity of persons, successions, and domestic relations could not be based on the motives adduced by the Italian school. "Perhaps the alleged national character of laws was true once, but now it is in flagrant contrast with reality." Fusinato remarks, however, that there are other motives that render advisable in these matters reference to the national law rather than to the law of domicile. First of all, domicile in a certain country is an unstable and occasional criterion. Besides, the legal concept of domicile is vague and uncertain and differs from one state to another; furthermore, various states provide that a person may have several domiciles. Last of all, choice of domicile is a voluntary act, depending exclusively on the will of the person, without any intervention on the part of the state of which the individual is a citizen or of that in which he sets up his residence. Nationality, on the other hand, is a simple criterion, precise and well settled, or at least it was in Fusinato's days, when conflicts of citizenship were rare and cases of statelessness exceptional. Fusinato also remarks that relationships concerning personal status, family, and inheritance are linked to the very basis of the organization of the state. It is therefore reasonable for the state of which an individual is citizen to have the privilege of regulating such relationships on the basis of its own laws and for every other state to recognize the validity of such a law. In favoring, on the contrary, the principle of the autonomy of the parties in contract matters Fusinato remarks that contracts do not concern the organization of the state and that it is therefore desirable to let the parties choose which law is to govern their transactions. As for the recognition of foreign law in matters concerning foreigners, Fusinato remarks that a state which admits to its own territory an individual whom it recognizes as a citizen of another state must also recognize the law of that state as applicable to this individual in certain matters. On the other hand, every state has the right to deny validity on its own territory to such foreign laws and acts as are contrary to public policy, that is, to the fundamental principles of the state itself.

These reasons were certainly plausible and may explain the success met by the Italian doctrine of private international law even abroad, where it was accepted by writers such as François Laurent [61] and André Weiss.[62] The Italian doctrines found application in the Italian civil code of 1865 and in the laws of various other states (Japan, Germany, Poland). The acceptance of the principle of nationalities in the Italian legislative system was due above all to a motive foreign to the mind of the first exponents of the doctrine. After the formation of Italian unity the migratory movement of Italians to foreign countries assumed huge proportions and by far exceeded the immigration into Italy. Italy adopted the principle of the application to the individual of his own national law because it helped to keep alive the links between the individual and his mother country.

To the influence of the theory of nationalities are due the particular characteristics of the works on public international law that were published in Italy during the nineteenth century. Most of these works dealing with the general principles of international law are of scant doctrinal value and frequently consist merely of a more or less emphatic enunciation of the principle of nationalities. The part dedicated to an examination of the practice relating to particular topics possesses, however, greater importance, because the treatment takes on a strictly juridical character and reveals the gifts of precision, clarity, and juridical rigor which are so frequent in Italian jurisconsults. In the solution of questions of a particular character the theory of nationalities exercised a negligible influence. A few writers attempted to apply it to the problems of the binding force of treaties and of intervention. As regards treaties, a few maintained that a state is not bound to respect treaties contrary to the principle of nationalities, or, in general, contrary to what is right and just.[63] As for intervention, it was asserted that although it is normally unlawful it is, however, permissible when intended to free a nation from a foreign yoke or from a tyrannical government.[64] Such opinions, however, found few adherents.

Among the treatises on international law of a general nature we should recall those, already mentioned, by Casanova, Ferrero Gola, Sandonà, Celli, Carnazza Amari, Pertile, and Pierantoni. A bigger reputation was enjoyed, not only in Italy but also abroad, by the bulky works of Fiore.

---

[61] *Droit civil international.*

[62] *Manuel du droit international privé,* and *Traité théorique et pratique de droit international privé.*

[63] Mamiani, *Di un nuovo diritto pubblico europeo,* p. 345.

[64] Carnazza Amari, "Nouvel Exposé du principe de non-intervention," 5 Rev. dr. int. et lég. comp. (1873) 352–389, 531–565.

Although this author deserves appreciation for his tremendous learning, it is perhaps not too easy to express a favorable judgment of the method he followed and of his juridical accuracy. His works amount to little more than a hodgepodge of facts. It may seem peculiar that when foreigners want to mention an Italian work even today they quote the books of Fiore, which almost nobody in Italy reads now. Later works on international law of a general nature were written by Contuzzi, Olivi,[65] Lomonaco,[66] Grasso,[67] Catellani,[68] and Diena.[69] The last two are greatly superior to their predecessors.

Among studies on special subjects we must recall the works by Laghi on treaties,[70] by Fusinato on territorial annexations and changes,[71] by Focherini on state succession,[72] by Catellani [73] and Pierantoni [74] on international rivers, and by Esperson,[75] Fiore,[76] and Contuzzi [77] on diplomatic and consular law. Diena's book on the bankruptcy of states is still an authority.[78] On international arbitration, besides the books by Contuzzi already cited, there is a work by Pierantoni.[79] Among writings on the law of warfare and neutrality there might be recalled those by Pierantoni on the declarations of war,[80] by Corsi on military occupation,[81] by Vidari on private property in time of war.[82] The problems of maritime warfare and neutrality, which later Italian scholars neglected, then received considerable attention. Besides Lucchesi-Palli's general work on international maritime law [83] there were the books by De Gioannis Gianquinto on contraband of war,[84] by Schiattarella on maritime neutrality,[85] by Carnazza Amari on the blockade,[86] by Romagnosi [87] and Carnazza Amari [88] on prizes, and by Diena on prize courts.[89] Several articles on subjects of international law are published in the legal encyclopaedia *Digesto italiano*, by Buzzati, Contuzzi, Fusinato, Gemma, and others.

[65] *Diritto internazionale pubblico e privato.* [66] *Trattato di diritto internazionale pubblico.*
[67] *Principii di diritto internazionale pubblico e privato.* [68] *Diritto internazionale.*
[69] *Principii di diritto internazionale pubblico e privato.* [70] *Teoria dei trattati internazionali.*
[71] *Le mutazioni territoriali e il loro fondamento giuridico*, 1885, and *Effetti giuridici delle annessioni*, 1890, reprinted in *Scritti giuridici*, I, 455–528 and II, 341–429.
[72] *La successione degli stati.*
[73] *La navigazione fluviale e la questione del Danubio secondo il diritto delle genti.*
[74] *I fiumi e la convenzione internazionale di Mannheim.*
[75] *Diritto diplomatico e giurisdizione consolare marittima.* [76] *Degli agenti diplomatici.*
[77] *La istituzione dei consoli e il diritto internazionale europeo nella sua applicazione in Oriente*, and *Trattato teorico-pratico di diritto consolare e diplomatico.*
[78] *Il fallimento degli stati e il diritto internazionale.*
[79] With regard to the Cerrutti case see Pierantoni, "La nullité d'un arbitrage international," 30 Rev. dr. int. et lég. comp. (1898) 445 ff. [80] *Le dichiarazioni di guerra nella storia.*
[81] *L'occupazione militare in tempo di guerra e le relazioni internazionali che ne derivano.*
[82] *Del rispetto della proprietà privata in tempo di guerra.* [83] *Diritto pubblico marittimo.*
[84] *Della confisca per contrabando di guerra.*
[85] *Il diritto della neutralità nelle guerre marittime.*
[86] *Del blocco marittimo.* [87] *Delle prede marittime.* .
[88] *Del rispetto della proprietà privata nelle guerre marittime.*
[89] *I tribunali delle prede belliche e il loro avvenire.*

Nor was there any lack of works on the history of international law. Worthy of note are the books of Schiattarella [90] and Pierantoni,[91] to which must be added those of Saredo [92] and Catellani [93] for the history of private international law. In Catellani the Italian school of nationalities found its historian.[94] That period also witnessed attempts to codify international law: for example, the *Diritto internazionale codificato*, by Fiore, and the far more worthless works by Paroldo [95] and Turcotti.[96] Another attempt at codification, which fortunately was not brought to a conclusion, was announced by Farnese.[97] Various foreign works on international law were translated into Italian, among which, to limit ourselves to the Americans, the *Elements of International Law* and the *History of the Law of Nations*, by Wheaton, and the *Draft Outlines of an International Law*, by Dudley Field. Sandonà published as an appendix to his *Trattato di diritto internazionale moderno* Dr. Lieber's *Instructions for the Government of Armies in the Field*.[98]

As for private international law and the conflict of laws, besides the works already cited by Fiore, Ferrero Gola, Gabba, Grasso, Olivi, and Diena and the fundamental monographs, mentioned above, by Brusa and Fusinato, we should mention the treatises of a general nature by Lomonaco,[99] Contuzzi,[100] and Esperson; [101] the essays by Laghi [102] and Catellani [103] on the nature of private international law; works by Buzzati on renvoi [104] and family law,[105] by Gianzana,[106] Esperson,[107] and Pieran-

[90] *Organismo e storia del diritto internazionale*, and *Propedeutica al diritto internazionale*.
[91] Besides the *Storia degli studii del diritto internazionale in Italia*, 2d ed., see the 1st ed., Modena, 1869, partly different.
[92] *Saggio sulla storia del diritto internazionale privato*.
[93] *Il diritto internazionale privato e i suoi recenti progressi*.
[94] "Les Maîtres de l'école italienne du droit international du XIXe siècle," Rec. des cours (1933) 709–826. Same in Italian, *La dottrina italiana del diritto internazionale nel secolo XIXo*.
[95] *Saggio di codice del diritto internazionale*.
[96] *Introduzione ad un nuovo codice del diritto delle genti*. On this work see Meulen, *Der Gedanke der internationalen Organization in seiner Entwicklung*, II, 113–118.
[97] *Proposta di un codice di diritto internazionale*.
[98] Italy, too, witnessed at that time the first efforts tending to promote the conclusion of treaties relative to the treatment of the wounded. In 1861 Ferdinando Palasciano, a Neapolitan physician, in two addresses to the Accademia Pontaniana on the "Neutrality of the wounded in wartime," invoked the conclusion of conventions exempting the wounded from all hostile acts.
[99] *Trattato di diritto civile internazionale*.
[100] *Il codice civile nei rapporti col diritto internazionale privato*, and *Diritto internazionale privato*.
[101] *Il principio di nazionalità applicato alle relazioni civili internazionali*, and "Le Droit international privé dans la législation italienne," 7 Journal de droit international privé (1880) 245 ff.
[102] *Il diritto internazionale privato nei suoi rapporti con le leggi territoriali*.
[103] *Dei conflitti tra le norme di diritto internazionale privato*.
[104] *Il rinvio nel diritto internazionale privato*.
[105] *Trattato di diritto internazionale privato secondo le Convenzioni dell'Aja*.
[106] *Le straniero nel diritto civile italiano*. [107] *La capacità giuridica dello straniero in Italia*.

toni [108] on the legal status of foreigners and on foreign juridical persons, by Diena on real property,[109] by Contuzzi on successions,[110] and by Buzzati on the form of acts.[111] On conflict of laws in commercial matters, besides the basic treatise by Diena [112] we should mention the studies by Fiore [113] on bankruptcy, by Esperson on negotiable instruments [114] and on industrial property and copyright,[115] and by Fusinato on stock-exchange contracts.[116] In the field of admiralty there is an interesting work by Buzzati on collisions between ships at sea.[117] On conflict of tax laws we have a work by Esperson.[118] As has been observed, the influence of the Italian doctrine of nationalities in the field of private international law was far less important than in that of public international law. This produced happy consequences for the science of the conflict of laws. In dealing with this subject the authors were almost exempt from the influence of political considerations. As a result, their works have a more strictly juridical content, and for this reason some of them can today still be usefully consulted.

[108] *La capacità delle persone giuridiche straniere in Italia.*
[109] *I diritti reali considerati nel diritto internazionale privato.*
[110] *Il diritto ereditario internazionale.*
[111] *L'autorità delle leggi straniere relative alla forma degli atti.*
[112] *Trattato di diritto commerciale internazionale.*
[113] *Del fallimento secondo il diritto internazionale privato.*
[114] *Diritto cambiario internazionale.*
[115] *La proprietà industriale nei rapporti internazionali,* and *Dei diritti d'autore sopra le opere dell'ingegno nel diritto internazionale.*
[116] *Dell'esecuzione in Italia dei contratti di borsa stipulati all'estero.*
[117] *L'urto di navi in mare.*
[118] "La Législation fiscale italienne dans ses rapports avec le droit international," 25 Rev. dr. int. et lég. comp. (1893) 286–312.

Chapter X: INTERNATIONAL RELATIONS IN ITALY
DURING THE RISORGIMENTO

DURING the French Revolution and the Napoleonic period international relations were considerably disturbed in Italy as well as in the rest of Europe. The smaller Italian states, at the mercy of their powerful neighbors beyond the Alps, had to suffer a good deal from the numerous wars of those times: their territory was crossed by the armies of both sides; the plains of northern Italy were favorite battlefields in the struggles between France and Austria; even the British and the Russians undertook military operations in the Italian peninsula. When at last the peace was concluded, the great states disposed of the Italian regions without much consideration for the aspirations of the inhabitants or for the previous rights of the local sovereigns.

ATTEMPTS AT THE PRESERVATION OF THE *STATUS QUO*

After 1815 the efforts made by almost all the Italian sovereigns, supported by Austria, were especially directed at the consolidation of the political and territorial system fixed by the Congress of Vienna. Normal relations were resumed between the Italian states; they concluded among one another and with the other states a great number of those treaties that states are used to make in times of peace. In general these treaties do not present special features. It should, however, be noted that the Congress of Vienna extended to Italy, too, the attempt to organize Europe on an international basis: for example, Article 96 of the Treaty of Vienna of June 9, 1815, provided that the general principles adopted by the congress with regard to the navigation of international rivers were also to apply to the Po. Commissaries were to be nominated by the riparian states, who were to regulate all that concerned the navigation of said river. For the enforcement of these provisions agreements were concluded among the riparian states, dealing with duties on navigation (agreements Austria-Parma of October 16, 1821, and September 3, 1825); with the suppression of contraband (agreements Austria-Sardinia of December 4, 1834, and November 22, 1851) and with the delimitation of the boundaries (treaty between Austria and Modena of August 8, 1849; treaty of peace between Austria and Sardinia of August 6, 1849, Secs. 3–4; and Sec. 4 of the separate articles; treaty of peace of Zurich with Austria, France, and Sardinia of November 10, 1859, Secs. 1, 3, 18; protocol of

Zurich of November 21, 1859; acts of Peschiera of June 16, 1859, which adopted the *thalweg* boundary). In the treaty of July 3, 1849, between Austria, Modena, and Parma, navigation on the Po was declared free along all the territory of the signatory states from the confluence with the Ticino as far as the Adriatic and exempt from any financial burden save for the expenditures required for maintenance works. The Papal States accepted the treaty by the act of February 12, 1850. Freedom of navigation on the Po and its affluents in conformity with already existing treaties was recognized by Sardinia in the Treaty of Zurich of November 10, 1859. The Po ceased to be an international river as a result of the Treaty of Vienna of October 3, 1866.[1] It may be worth while to recall as a curiosity and because it would not appear that the attention of scholars has hitherto been called to the subject, a series of treaties between Austria and the Duchy of Parma, of July 25, 1831, of July 11, 1834, and of July 3, 1849 (this last distinct from the treaty of the same date mentioned above) which laid down the rules to be followed in determining sovereignty over the islands in the Po in case of variation in the river's course. These treaties provided for the cases that an island belonging to one state should be attached to the mainland of the other; that it should form a new island; and that two islands belonging to different states should unite permanently.[2]

The most characteristic aspects of international relations in Italy during the Risorgimento are those resulting from the conservative tendencies of various Italian states, backed by Austria, and the attempts, generally furthered by Piedmont or in Piedmont, towards the unification and independence of Italy. According to the spirit of the Treaty of Vienna it was Austria's privilege to watch over events in Italy and to safeguard the maintenance of the *status quo* in this part of Europe. The exercise on the part of Austria of this power of supervision is of interest to international law from various points of view. Treaties of assistance and alliance bound various Italian states to Austria. Under an agreement of 1815 the Kingdom of Naples was bound to supply to Austria in case of need 60,000 men fully equipped, on the Po. On December 24, 1847, Austria concluded two separate treaties of offensive and defensive alliance with the duchies of Modena and Parma. Attempts were made by Austria to establish on a permanent juridical basis its own supervision over the Italian states. At the Congress of Verona in 1822 Austria proposed the constitution of a "committee of inquiry" with its seat at Piacenza, aimed at the repression of liberal movements in the peninsula. The proposal, thanks to the energetic opposition of the Papal Legate, came to naught. Aus-

---

[1] Fiore, *Diritto internazionale pubblico*, 4th ed., p. 64.
[2] A list of the international agreements relating to Italian rivers will be found in Ogilvie, *International Waterways*.

trian interference was above all directed against the unification of the peninsula. It extended to all the activities of the Italian states both domestic and international. In 1847 Austria succeeded in provoking the failure of a plan for a customs union between Sardinia, Tuscany, and the Papal States, which was to have constituted the first step toward a federation of Italian states. An attempt to carry the plan into practice was made by a treaty of customs union of November 3, 1847, between the three states. The execution of the treaty was subordinated to the adhesion of Naples and Modena, which because of the pressure brought to bear by Austria did not take place.

Austria also interfered in Italian affairs in order to suffocate all manifestations of liberalism. In 1847 Austria exerted diplomatic pressure on the Grand-Duke of Tuscany in order to induce him to modify the system of university education in an antiliberal sense; soon afterward she made a new *demarche* against the convocation of a congress of Italian scientists in Pisa. We have already mentioned the step taken by Austria in Turin to induce the Sardinian government to interrupt Mancini's lectures.

Especially serious were the military interventions, whether of a preventive or repressive character, undertaken by Austria in various Italian states in order to suppress any liberal movement. As a consequence of the liberal uprising in 1821 in Piedmont and in the Two Sicilies, the Austrian troops intervened in both states in the following year. The Austrians remained in the state of Sardinia until Oct. 1, 1823, and in the Kingdom of Naples until 1824. In 1831 a new Austrian intervention took place in the duchies of Modena and Parma and in the Papal States, at Bologna. In 1832 Austria occupied the Legations, and in 1847 Ferrara, which both belonged to the pope. In 1849 the Austrians intervened in Tuscany, where they remained until 1855. Some of these occupations acquired a semipermanent character. Piacenza was for many years occupied by Austrian troops.

The Austrians were not the only ones to intervene in Italy. Either because intervention was the fashion of the period, or because she wished to counterbalance the influence of Austria, France occupied from 1832–1838 Ancona in the Papal States; in 1849 the French intervened once more in the Papal States against the Roman Republic; from 1867 to 1870 there was a French garrison in Rome; from 1870 to 1874 a French ship, the "Orénoque" was stationed before Civitavecchia, the nearest harbor to Rome, in contemplation of the possibility that the pope might wish to leave Italy. In 1849 even the Spaniards intervened in the Papal States coming from the Two Sicilies. Sometimes, however, the intervention of states other than Austria was directed to induce the absolutist regimes of Italy to behave with moderation. In May, 1855, England and France protested to the government of Naples because of the reign of terror it had created. The failure of this step led to the breach of relations between France and England on one side and the Two Sicilies on the other. Equally fruitless were the remonstrances to the Papal government made at about the same time by these two powers.

On the other hand, the movement for Italian unification and independence often led to military expeditions, sometimes carried out with the acquiescence and the support of the state from which they went out. In 1834 General Ramorino coming from Switzerland, with a group of Mazzini's followers, attempted to invade Savoy, in order to set up a Republican government in Piedmont. The attempt failed. In 1844 an expedition led by two brothers Attilio and Emilio Bandiera set out from Corfu to raise a revolt in the Kingdom of the Two Sicilies. The group was scattered almost as soon as it landed in Calabria, and the two brothers were shot. In 1853 Pier Fortunato Calvi, with a group of patriots, attempted to invade Venetia and was killed by the Austrians. In 1857 Carlo Pisacane set out from Genoa to foment an uprising in the Kingdom of the Two Sicilies; he was killed near Salerno. In 1860 Garibaldi, with the "Thousand," sailed from Genoa and landed in Marsala in Sicily; from there he began the victorious conquest of the Kingdom of Naples that was completed by the Sardinian troops. The latter intervened only after the success of the expedition had become apparent. In October, 1867, a military expedition set out from Terni, in the Kingdom of Italy, to start an uprising in the Papal States; this ended with the death of the brothers Enrico and Giovanni Cairoli at Villa Glori near Rome. A few days later another expedition lead by Garibaldi was defeated at Mentana, near Rome, by the papal and French troops.

THE FORMATION OF THE KINGDOM OF ITALY

The theory of nationalities exercised a practical influence on the method followed in the formation of the Kingdom of Italy. In accordance with the principle of the self-determination of peoples, the various enlargements of Piedmont and the annexations to the Kingdom of Italy that were achieved during this period were preceded by plebiscites aimed at ascertaining the will of the population. During the unsuccessful uprisings of 1848, Lombardy, Venice, Modena, Parma, Piacenza, and Reggio had voted by plebiscite for annexation to Sardinia. In 1860 the annexation of Tuscany, Enilia, the Marches, Umbria, Naples, and Sicily was in each case preceded by plebiscites with which the citizens almost unanimously voted for their incorporation into the Kingdom of Italy, one and indivisible, under Victor Emmanuel as constitutional monarch and his legitimate descendants.[3] The cession of Venetia to Italy in 1866 was accomplished "sous réserve du consentement des populations, dûment consultées." A plebiscite was held and the Venetian population by an immense majority declared itself Italian. The plebiscite of October 2, 1870, consecrated the union of Rome to Italy. It was also desired to justify by means of plebiscite the annexation of Nice and Savoy to France.[4] Many affirmed at the time that, unlike the plebiscites previously listed, the result of this one was obtained by means of pressure and abuses. Cases were pointed out like that of the town of Levanzo, which with only 407 registered voters counted 481 votes in favor of France; these figures appear in the official report.[5] But on the whole it seems that these two plebiscites expressed the real feelings of the voters.

The way in which the Kingdom of Italy was formed, by means of the fusion of various pre-existing states which were now completely extinguished, gave rise to the question whether the Kingdom of Italy was a new state or the continuation of the Kingdom of Sardinia. Although the first opinion was advocated by Anzilotti with his usual skill,[6] the more correct one seems to be that defended by Romano[7] and Perassi,[8] who by means of an accurate analysis of the constitutional procedure followed during the annexations proved that the Kingdom of Italy is the ancient Kingdom of Sardinia, with a changed name and altered dimensions, because of the annexation of much vaster territories and a much larger population than before. In its practice the Italian state followed the theory that it was the continuation of the Kingdom of Sardinia. The treaties concluded by the Kingdom of Sardinia were regarded as remaining valid unless they were incompatible with the new situation, and they were extended to the new territories.[9] The Franco-Sardinian agreement of 1760 for the recognition of judgments in civil questions remained valid until only a few years ago. The treaties concluded by foreign governments with the annexed states were considered as no longer valid.

[3] A fundamental work on the history and the legal consequences of the Italian plebiscites from the point of view of constitutional and international law is Fusinato, "Le mutazioni territoriali e il loro fondamento giuridico," in *Scritti giuridici*, I, 423–534, especially pp. 481–527. See also Arangio Ruiz, *Storia costituzionale del Regno d'Italia* (1848–1898); Marchi, *La fondazione storico-giuridica dello stato italiano;* Wambaugh, *A Monograph on Plebiscites*, which contains the principal documents relating to the Italian plebiscites of the Risorgimento.
[4] During the French Revolution, Savoy and Nice were annexed to France. The annexation had been preceded by plebiscites in 1792 and 1793, respectively.
[5] Published in "Senato Subalpino, Atti," 1860, p. 33.
[6] "La formazione del Regno d'Italia nei riguardi del diritto internazionale," 6 Riv. dir. int. (1912) 1 ff.
[7] "I caratteri giuridici della formazione del Regno d'Italia," 6 Riv. dir. int. (1912) 345 ff.
[8] *Lezioni di diritto internazionale*, 69 ff. See also Orlando, "Regno d'Italia (Formazione del)" in *Nuovo digesto italiano*, XI, 312 ff.
[9] See the Italian "Circolare ministeriale" of March 14, 1862, and the opinion of the Italian "Consiglio del Contenzioso diplomatico" in Fusinato, *Scritti giuridici*, II, 358.

Strangely enough, the United States did not regard its treaties concluded with the Two Sicilies in 1855 as terminated in consequence of the annexation of the two Sicilies to Sardinia in 1860, and even after the establishment of the Kingdom of Italy, it regarded these treaties as in force with respect to the territories with reference to which they had been concluded. Likewise the United States deemed its treaty with Sardinia of 1838 to be in force with respect to Sardinia, after the establishment of the Kingdom of Italy.[10]

The Italian courts also often decided that the Kingdom of Italy was the continuation of Sardinia.[11]

The Kingdom of Italy was soon recognized by almost all the other states. Great Britain recognized the Kingdom of Italy before Francis II of Naples was entirely dispossessed. Prussia, however, held up recognition until July, 1862, Russia until August of the same year, and Austria still longer.[12] Recognition by foreign governments was not in truth recognition of a new state or of a new government, but acknowledgment of the new situation that had arisen from the growth of the Sardinian state, by means of the total or partial absorption of other states, and implied acceptance of the procedure followed and of the legal consequences of these events.

The annexation by Piedmont of territories belonging to states that, with the exception of Austria, had then totally ceased to exist gave rise to various questions of state succession.[13] When Lombardy and Venetia were annexed, it was expressly provided by the peace treaties that the annexing state should be answerable for the financial obligations of the ceding state regarding the ceded territory (Treaty of Zurich, November 10, 1859, Sec. 8, and Treaty of Vienna, October 3, 1866, Sec. 8). The assumption by France of the financial obligations and of the contracts of the Sardinian state in the provinces of Nice and Savoy were provided for in the Treaty of March 24, 1860, and by the Convention of August 23, 1860, Sec. 5, between France and Piedmont.[14] Because of the way in which they took place, the annexations of Tuscany, of the duchies of Modena and Parma, of the Kingdom of the Two Sicilies, and of the Papal States did not give rise to the conclusion of international acts providing for the obligation of the annexing state to assure the obligations of the annexed state. After the first hesitation had been overcome, the principle

[10] Hyde, "The Termination of the Treaties of a State in Consequence of Its Absorption by Another," 26 Am. J. Int. L. (1932) 133.

[11] To the same effect see Cassazione Civile, Dec. 3, 1927, 22 Riv. Dir. Int. (1930) 102 ff.

[12] When after the formation of the Kingdom of Italy certain German states persisted in refusing to recognize it, Count Cavour withdrew the exequaturs from their consuls. Recognition was then accorded.

[13] For a detailed analysis of the questions connected with state succession, arising from the Italian annexations see Fusinato, "Effetti giuridici delle annessioni," in *Scritti giuridici*, II 341–459.

[14] On this topic see Brunet, *Consequences juridiques de l'annexion de la Savoie et de Nice à la France*.

was generally accepted by scholars, administrative authorities and the courts, that the annexing state assumed all the financial obligations of the annexed states; that is, debts, contracts, franchises, indemnities, damages, and so forth. Besides a sincere spirit of justice, considerations of a political nature guided the conduct of the Italian state in this regard. The annexations had been carried out on the theory that the annexing state was, not a conqueror, but a liberator of the annexed territories. It would therefore have been contrary to the ideal reasons upon which the annexation was based, not to say extremely impolitic, if the annexing state had disaffirmed the obligations of the annexed state with regard to its citizens. As for foreigners, they benefited by a no-less favorable treatment, for in carrying out annexations for which the recognition of other states was desired, it was not admissible to use any discriminations detrimental to their citizens.

It may be of interest to recall that Italy's annexation of Venetia, in 1866, created a little-known case of international servitude with regard to fisheries. When Venetia and Dalmatia were part of the Austrian Empire, the fishermen of Chioggia, a little town near Venice, used to go fishing off the Dalmatian coast in Austrian territorial waters. The practice continued after the separation of Venetia from the Austrian Empire and was sanctioned, either by tacit agreement or by custom, until in 1884 an Italo-Austrian agreement concluded at Gorizia formally recognized this practice and established rules regulating it.

The disappearance of the Papal States affected the international status of the Holy See. In September, 1870, when the Italians occupied Rome, the project was formulated for the survival of an independent pontifical state under the pope's sovereignty to be constituted by the Leonine City, a small section of the City of Rome close to the Vatican. But the Romans wanted the whole city of Rome to be annexed to Italy, and consequently the pope's temporal power came to an end.

In a circular dated October 18, 1870, and directed to all Italian diplomatic agents abroad, the Italian Foreign Secretary announced the annexation of Rome to the Kingdom of Italy and declared that Italy formally bound itself to maintain the personal position appertaining to the pope as a sovereign, with all his immunities and exemptions; to ensure liberty of communication and of diplomatic intercourse between the pope and foreign states; to ensure and put into practice the principle of the separation of Church from State. This unilateral promise of Italy to foreign states was fulfilled with the law May 13, 1871, called Law of Guarantees (*Legge delle guarentigie*) [15] because it guaranteed to the

[15] The note of Oct. 18, the answer of the Belgian and the Spanish governments, and the text of the Law of Guarantees are published in Fiore, *Diritto internazionale pubblico*, 4th ed., I, 556–567. For the law of guarantees see the article by Jemolo, "Guarentigie pontificie," in *Nuovo digesto italiano*, VI, 526–529.

Supreme Pontifex absolute independence in the execution of his spiritual mission (Secs. 8 and 10). The same privileged position and protection enjoyed by the king of Italy were granted to the pope. His person and the places where he lived or where a conclave or an oecumenical council was held were granted immunity of jurisdiction. The Vatican and a villa at Castel Gandolfo, near Rome, were left in the pope's ownership, and he was allowed an annuity called *lista civile*. Freedom of diplomatic communications and of intercourse with foreign courts were guaranteed to the pope. The Law of Guarantees was a municipal law of the Italian state, not an international act. It did not constitute the fulfillment of an obligation toward the Holy See, which stubbornly refused to recognize it. It rather constituted the means chosen by Italy to fulfill the promise made to the other states with the circular of October 18, 1870. The law was a monument of political wisdom, because it shut the pope off from all interference in the internal affairs of Italy, yet at the same time it respected his dignity and protected his liberty in the performance of his religious mission. The Lateran Treaty of February 11, 1929, which together with the concordat of the same date put an end to the conflict between Italy and the Holy See, provided (Sec. 26) for the abrogation of the Law of Guarantees. Execution in Italy was given to the Lateran Treaty by the law of May 27, 1929, No. 810. Several provisions of the law were embodied in the Lateran Treaty.

Inasmuch as the Pontifical State ended in 1870, the State of Vatican City, established in 1929, is not the continuation of it, but an entirely new state. The prevailing opinion among Italian writers is that the Catholic Church—or the Holy See, which constitutes its supreme organ—continued to be vested with international personality even after the extinction of the Papal States. This personality was held to manifest itself in the exercise of the right of active and passive legation and in the conclusion of concordats, to which these writers recognize the character of international agreements.[16]

In normal diplomatic intercourse the Italian state proved that it wished to respect general international law and to enjoy the rights and privileges which it derived therefrom. In 1885 Italy informed the United States that in consequence of certain public utterances at a public meeting in 1871, Mr. Keiley would not be *persona grata* as United States Minister to Italy, and Mr. Keiley returned his commission to the President.[17] Numerous treaties of all kinds were concluded by the Kingdom of Italy with almost all the other states.

In the field of municipal law it is of interest to point out two aspects connected with international law: the attempts that were made to apply

[16] Anzilotti, *Corso di diritto internazionale*, 3d ed., pp. 128–140, and the authors cited there.
[17] U.S., *Foreign Relations*, 1885, p. 550.

the doctrine of nationalities and the favorable treatment granted to foreigners. Applications of the doctrine of nationalities were to be found in the Preliminary Provisions of the Civil Code, issued in 1865. They provided that: the personal status and the capacity and successions were determined by the national law of the person; real property by the *lex rei sitae;* contracts by the law chosen by the parties, or if no choice had been made by the *lex loci contractus* if the parties were of different citizenships, or by their national law if they had the same citizenship. Recognition of foreign laws, judgments, and acts contrary to public policy was prohibited. In accordance with the principle of nationalities, foreign citizens who were of Italian descent—the so-called Italians *non regnicoli,* for example, the Italians of Trieste—were granted special facilities for obtaining Italian citizenship. With notable liberality, Article 3 of the Civil Code provided that foreigners were considered as the equals of citizens in the enjoyment of civil rights. This equality of treatment was not subject to any condition of reciprocity. The provision was also held to apply to foreign juridical persons. In questions of civil procedure, too, foreigners were assimilated to citizens and were not subjected to give security for costs. As a result of Mancini's personal efforts the Italian doctrines of private international law exercised a notable influence on the conferences of private international law held at the Hague.

Another application of the principles of the school of nationalities is seen in the fact that international arbitration enjoyed great favor in Italy at that time. As early as 1856 Sardinia concluded a treaty of arbitration with Chile. After the proclamation of the Kingdom of Italy, treaties of arbitration were concluded with Venezuela (1861), Chile (1862), Costa Rica (1863), Hawaii (1863), Siam (1868), and Birmania (1873). In 1873 the Chamber of Deputies, acting on a proposal of Mancini, unanimously approved a resolution in favor of international arbitration. According to Bluntschli, Italy was the first state to introduce the compromissory clause into treaties of commerce and navigation. The Italo-Argentine treaty of arbitration of 1898, never ratified, is considered one of the most comprehensive and unconditional on the subject.[18] It acted as a model for many other analogous treaties concluded by Italy with various Latin-American states and was taken as a model by the first Hague Peace Conference.[19]

There were also several international adjudications. Before the proclamation of the Kingdom of Italy an arbitral solution was found for a dispute between the Two Sicilies and England, caused by the pretension of the Neapolitan government to introduce a monopoly of Sicilian sulphur that threatened to affect the rights acquired by certain British mer-

[18] Mérignhac, *Traité de droit public international,* II, 473.
[19] Nippold, *Le Développement historique du droit international,* 1 Rec. des cours (1924) 73.

chants. Through the mediation of the king of France a mixed commission was set up which by an award of December 24, 1841, allowed £.st.21,307 to the claimants.[20] Czar Nicholas of Russia also acted as mediator in a dispute between Austria and Sardinia concerning the salt trade, which, however, dragged on for another two years.[21] In 1869 Italy and Turkey requested the Minister of Sweden at Constantinople to decide whether Italy was entitled to compensation for the stopping of an Italian steamship, the "Principe di Carignano," which during the blockade of Crete had been stopped by a Turkish cruiser outside the lines of blockade. In a decision of May 4, 1873, the arbitrator decided in favor of Turkey.[22] On December 31, 1873, an arbitral solution was reached for a boundary dispute between Switzerland and Italy regarding possession of the Alp of Cravairola, which was attributed to Italy.[23]

Among disputes not settled by means of arbitration the one between England and Modena in 1841 is worth mentioning. Instigated by Duke Francis IV, who hated everything liberal, the press of Modena, which was strictly controlled by the government, printed insults of all kinds concerning the British government and British parliamentary institutions. The duke denied any responsibility and alleged that the press campaign had been purely "spontaneous." But Lord Seymour, British minister resident at Florence, brought home to the duke that a government may not be held responsible for what is printed if it admits the liberty of the press, but on the contrary must be held responsible where a preliminary government censorship exists. The duke had to write a letter of apology to Lord Palmerston. The incident is worth remembering, because it constitutes a precedent as to the proper way of dealing with the "spontaneous" press campaigns of totalitarian countries. Greater weight should be attached to the dispute between Sardinia and Austria relative to Austria's seizure of properties situated in the Lombardo-Veneto, belonging to the Lombard and Venetian political refugees who had settled in Piedmont and acquired Sardinian citizenship. The dispute led to the recall of the Sardinian diplomatic representative in Vienna, on February 13, 1853.

THE WARS OF THE RISORGIMENTO

The numerous wars waged during the Risorgimento do not offer particular interest for international law. In many cases they were preceded

---

[20] Darby, *International Tribunals*, p. 779. In order to force the Neapolitan government to settle the dispute, on April 17, 1839, the British fleet began to capture Neapolitan vessels in the vicinity of Naples. An embargo was at the same time laid in the ports of Malta and England against the Neapolitan vessels. Naples, on the other hand, laid an embargo on all British vessels in Neapolitan and Sicilian ports. After the settlement of the dispute the vessels seized by the British fleet were restored to their Neapolitan owners.

[21] *Ibid.*, p. 780.   [22] Lapradelle and Politis, *Recueil des arbitrages internationaux*, II, 618.

[23] Moore, *A Digest of International Law*, p. 2028.

by treaties of alliance. The participation of Sardinia in the war of the Crimea against Russia was preceded by an act of accession (January 26, 1855) of Sardinia to the Franco-British Alliance of April 10, 1854. On the same day, this adhesion was accepted by France and Great Britain in two separate acts. These were followed by the military Convention of Turin, which determined the extent of Sardinia's military contribution. A supplementary convention between Sardinia and Great Britain provided for a loan and the free transportation by Great Britain of Sardinian troops to Crimea. As for the relations with the Turkish government, which was also at war with Russia, the Convention of Constantinople of March 15, 1855, provided for the adherence of Sardinia to the alliance of April 12, 1854, between the Porte, Great Britain, and France. Sardinia took part in the acts signed at Paris on March 30, 1855, on the conclusion of the peace. The French-Sardinian war of 1859 against Austria was preceded by the verbal agreement of Plombières of July 20, 1858, which almost immediately afterward was consecrated in a secret agreement. Peace was restored with the Treaty of Zurich of November 10, 1859, which consists of three separate acts: one between Sardinia and Austria, one between France and Sardinia and a third between France, Austria and Sardinia.[24] Lombardy was ceded by Austria to France who transferred it to Sardinia. The cession of Savoy and Nice to France was provided for in the Treaty of Turin of March 23, 1860.

The war of 1866 against Austria was preceded by the Italo-Prussian Treaty of alliance of April 8, 1866. Hostilities with Austria terminated with the Treaties of peace of August 23 and October 3, 1866. Venetia was ceded to France, who transferred it to Italy.[25] In these treaties as well as in those of Zurich, special provisions protected the rights of private individuals, assured the faculty to change citizenship, and determined the allocation of pecuniary obligations, public debts, and so forth, relative to the territories ceded.

Numerous armistices and capitulations were concluded during the wars of the Risorgimento. During the Austro-Sardinian war of 1848–1849 Sardinia was constrained to ask for an armistice in August, 1848 (the so-called Salasco Armistice). When at the end of the armistice hostilities were resumed, Sardinia was obliged to ask for a new armistice

---

[24] For an English translation of the Treaty of Zurich see Oakes and Mowat, *The Great European Treaties of the Nineteenth Century*, pp. 226 ff.

[25] Article 2 of the Treaty of Prague of August 23, 1866 (the peace between Austria and Prussia), recited that the Emperor of the French had officially declared through his ambassador at Berlin "that insofar as regards the Government of the Emperor, Venetia is secured to Italy, to be made over to her at the peace; and consequently that the Emperor of Austria acceded on his part to that declaration, and gave his consent to the union of Venetia with the Kingdom of Italy." For an English translation of the Treaty of Vienna, October 3, 1866, see Oakes and Mowat, *The Great European Treaties of the Nineteenth Century*, pp. 233 ff.

(Novara, March 26, 1849), which was followed by the Peace of Milan. We must also mention, during this war, the capitulation of the Austrian fortress of Peschiera (May 30, 1848) and of the city of Venice, which after setting up an independent government and offering heroic resistance to a severe siege was constrained to capitulate to the Austrians on August 28, 1849. On July 3, 1849, the Roman Republic had to surrender to the French. In the War of 1859 an armistice was agreed upon on July 8. It was followed after three days by the verbal preliminaries of peace, which were put into writing the following day. The occupation of Rome by the Italian troops gave rise on September 20, 1870, to the capitulation of the papal troops (the so-called Kanzler capitulation).[26]

As far as maritime warfare is concerned, we should note the general mildness of the Italian wars of the Risorgimento. During the war of 1859 the embargo laid by Sardinia on Austrian ships at the commencement of hostilities brought after it no condemnations and had only the effect of a temporary measure.[27] Article 3 of the treaty of Zurich of 1859 between Austria and Sardinia provided that in order to mitigate the evils of war and in derogation to general rules the Austrian ships already captured and not condemned by the prize court would be fully restored.[28] In the war of 1866 the two parties at war provided for the exemption from capture of merchant ships.

Provisions concerning neutrality were issued by Tuscany and the Two Sicilies on the occasion of the Crimean War and by the Kingdom of Italy in 1864 on the occasion of the American Civil War and of the Dano-Prussian War. The Kingdom of Italy and the Papal States announced their neutrality during the Franco-Prussian War of 1870; the former once more during the Russo-Turkish War of 1877.[29]

An alleged case of piracy occurred in 1857 and aroused great excitement. The "Cagliari," a Sardinian merchant ship plying between Genoa and Tunis, left Genoa on June 25, 1857, on one of its regular trips.[30]

[26] The capitulation is published by Fiore, *Diritto internazionale pubblico*, 4th ed., I, 556.
[27] Katchenowsky, *Prize Law* (English translation by F. T. Pratt), p. 167.
[28] The treaty of commerce between the United States and Italy of February 26, 1871, provided, Article 13: "Les hautes parties contractantes conviennent que, si par malheur la guerre éclatait entre elles, la propriété privée de leurs citoyens et sujets respectifs, à l'exception de la contrebande de guerre, soit dans la haute mer, soit dans tout autre lieu, soit exempte de capture ou de confiscation de la part de navires armées ou des forces militaires des deux parties; toutefois cette exemption ne s'étendra pas aux navires et aux cargaisons que l'on tentera d'introduire dans un port bloqué par les forces navales de l'une ou de l'autre partie."
[29] The texts of these acts are published in Jessup and Deák, *Neutrality Laws, Regulations and Treaties*, I, 711–735.
[30] Wheaton, *Elements of International Law*, 6th English ed., I, 279–280, and Martens, *Causes célèbres du droit des gens*, V, 600–605. The judgment of the Neapolitan prize court is published as an appendix to the Italian translation of Wheaton, *History of the Law of Nations in Europe and America*.

The crew was overpowered by the members of the Pisacane expedition,[31] who had gone on board disguised as passengers. They obliged the captain to change his course and to land them on Neapolitan territory. After the expedition had landed and the ship had been given back to the crew, which resumed their normal course, the steamship was captured by a Neapolitan cruiser. The ship was condemned by the Neapolitan prize court. The jurisdiction of the court and the legitimacy of the ship's condemnation were widely questioned. Great Britain intervened in the dispute on behalf of two British machinists on board the ship and obtained their liberation and the payment of an indemnity of £3,000 for their compensation. On the other hand, no compensation was given to the Sardinian government, although the steamer was later on given back to its owners.

AN APPRAISAL OF THE ITALIAN CONTRIBUTION TO INTERNATIONAL LAW DURING THE RISORGIMENTO

The doctrine of nationalities represents the most important contribution made by Italians during the Risorgimento to the theory of international law. It also gave rise to the first Italian school of international law; in fact the writers belonging to this school expounded a body of doctrines substantially uniform, which may be called Italian not only because they were advocated by Italian scholars but also and especially because they were connected with the political situation of Italy and aimed at resolving the principal problems that faced Italy at the period during which the doctrine of nationalities was developed.

The doctrine was mainly political, since it aimed at furthering the unification of Italy in a national and liberal state, which was then in progress. To the accomplishment of this program the doctrine was a powerful aid, and therefore its results from the political point of view were certainly satisfactory. From the moral point of view as well the doctrine is worthy of esteem for the loftiness of its ideals. Because of the nobility of their conceptions the juridical theories of the Italian school of nationalities constitute a worthy complement of the political theories of Mazzini.

The influence on the Italian people of the juridical doctrines of the school of nationalities is profounder than even the Italians themselves realize. The principle of nationalities became part and parcel of the spiritual heritage of the Italian people. Even today the spontaneous sympathies of the vast majority of Italians go out to the peoples fighting for their liberties and independence. The doctrines of violence, cynicism, and pseudo-realism preached by the Fascists have been unable sensibly to modify in this regard the profound convictions of the Italian people. No dialectic effort and no political consideration will succeed in justify-

[3] See above, p. 185.

ing in the eyes of the Italians the oppression of the Poles and the Czechs at the hands of Germany. Mazzini and Mancini are today more alive than ever.

Less favorable is the judgment that must be passed on the doctrine of nationalities from a strictly juridical point of view. As we have seen, the doctrine will not bear serious juridical analysis: it prevented a clear vision of the basic distinction between law on one side and politics and ethics on the other, which lies at the root of any jurisprudential treatment of all branches of the law; it merely gave a new content to the old conception of natural law, that is, to the form of thought traditional in the science of international law, thus contributing to maintain alive its influence over Italian writers. In addition, the doctrine assumed in Italy a position of absolute and unquestioned monopoly in the field of international law, thus for a long while preventing international lawyers in Italy from absorbing the influence of other doctrines and so shutting out all fruitful clashes of ideas. Italian science of international law thus came to be spiritually isolated from the broad currents of European juridical thought and had no part in the renewal of methods and ideas that took place in that period in other countries. It must not be forgotten that at the time in which the school of nationalities flourished in Italy there were, to limit ourselves solely to England and America, writers such as Wheaton, Phillimore, Halleck, Twiss, Hall, Lorimer, and Wharton and that at the same time Germany beheld an extraordinary development of new juridical doctrines which profoundly influenced the theory of international law as well.

To these particular defects of the Italian juridical school must be attributed a few characteristics of the development of the theory of international law in Italy. First, several important Italian writers, like Brusa, assumed a critical attitude toward the doctrine; others, like Fusinato and Catellani, subjected the doctrine to a radical revision that practically led to the elimination of its principal characteristics; some, like Diena, developed their scientific activity at a time in which the doctrine had been superseded and so hardly felt its influence at all. Another consequence is that the followers of the doctrine of nationalities reached the most satisfactory results in the field of private international law, for it is in this field that the political aspect of the doctrine exerted least influence, and the problems treated were dealt with by the majority of writers from a strictly juridical viewpoint. Moreover, in the field of private international law the doctrine had merit in that it grasped the ever-growing ascendancy of the criterion of citizenship over that of domicile in matters of conflict of laws. Last of all, the subordination of the doctrine of nationalities to political doctrines and to natural law led to a reaction on the part of later Italian writers. This found its expression in the so-called "positive conception" of international law, supported in Italy by Anzilotti and Donati, which aimed at liberating international law from the influence of politics, ethics, and natural law. We thus have a clear break between the Italian doctrine of nationalities and the theories later asserted in Italy, which are rather derived from foreign juridical doctrines.

The practice of international law in Italy during the Risorgimento does not offer particular characteristics. The diplomatic and military interventions of Austria in the Italian states are manifestations of a practice largely followed in that century. The formation of the Kingdom of Italy went on by means of procedures not unknown to international law. Nor did the Kingdom of Italy introduce any new practice in international relations. This is the natural consequence of two factors. First, the international problems facing the new kingdom had already been encountered by other states, so that it was able to make use of and to follow their experience. Second, the Kingdom of Italy, situated as it was in its beginnings in diplomatic difficulties, because of the manifold hostility and suspicion that in many countries accompanied its creation, was especially intent on proving that it meant and was able to assume and respect international engagements just as scrupulously as the older states. The new kingdom therefore was punctilious in following, in its international relations, a policy of strict respect for law. In fact, the young Kingdom of Italy cannot be accused of any serious violation of international law during the first decades of its existence. Arisen in the name of justice and liberty, the Kingdom of Italy in the beginning followed essentially liberal principles in its international relations: it justified its territorial annexations by plebiscites; it favored international arbitration; it took upon itself the financial obligations of the states to which it succeeded; it granted generous treatment to foreigners, to whom it recognized almost complete equality of rights with Italian citizens in questions concerning private law.

In this chapter we have considered the Italian contribution to international law during the formation and the first period of existence of the Kingdom of Italy. At the end of the nineteenth century the new kingdom may be said to have come of age: its political growth profoundly affected both Italian theory and practice of international law. An analysis of this theory and practice in contemporary Italy will form the subject of the next chapters.

PART FOUR

The Contemporary Period

Chapter XI: ITALY COMES OF AGE

IN 1871, having established Rome as its capital, Italy inaugurated a new historical era. Aspirations long pursued had finally been realized: unity, independence, and liberty had been achieved. As the exhilaration of success and the enthusiasm of the Risorgimento subsided, it became evident to the Italian people that these feats, though memorable, were not sufficient to make Italy a great nation. This required the solution of numerous and serious political, economic, and cultural problems. Some of them arose from three centuries of despotic government and foreign domination, which had impoverished and disorganized the country and lowered the political, moral, and cultural level of the Italian people; others, from the poverty of the soil, lacking in minerals and cultivable only in part, exhausted and laid waste by centuries of excessive and negligent exploitation; others, finally, from the unification itself, which had resulted in some maladjustment and in deep resentment in large groups of the population.

THE ORGANIZATION OF THE KINGDOM OF ITALY

To solve these problems the romantic fervor of that heroic minority which was mainly responsible for the success of the Risorgimento was not sufficient. Crude realism, tenacious effort, and assiduous co-operation on the part of all Italians was now required. In a speech from the throne the king himself warned the nation that the heroic period of young Italy was over. The time had come for constant and strenuous work. Prose, he said, was to succeed poetry.

If we reflect on the magnitude of the problems that confronted the Italians in the first fifty years of their life together, we must admit they accomplished a great deal. Important public works were completed throughout Italy; entire regions were reclaimed; deforestation was reduced; streets, canals, railroads, harbors, and aqueducts were constructed. Agriculture was enriched and revived by the introduction of modern methods of cultivation, the breaking down of large estates (*latifundia*), and the better use of the land taken from the Church. Industry was developed mainly in northern Italy, and commerce was revived with other countries as well as between the various regions of Italy. Banks and insurance companies rose to international importance. The nation was endowed with a modern navy and merchant marine. In all large cities major developments took place. Rome became a modern, spacious capital; Naples and other centers were cleared of slums, and notable improvements were achieved in public health and morality.

The structure of the state, too, became rapidly consolidated. The administrative organization of the new kingdom was patterned largely on that of France as it had been established by Napoleon. A strong central government controlled the provinces through the prefects, who were officials of the administration entrusted with ample powers of supervision and control. The administrative body consisted mainly of scrupulous, though sometimes incompetent, functionaries. Legislation was unified and improved. There was on the whole better distribution of taxation. Certain very unpopular taxes, such as that on the milling of wheat (*imposta sul macinato*), were suppressed. Great care was given to the army, which, unlike that of France, Spain, and Portugal, never participated in political activities. Compulsory service brought into the ranks of the army young men from all parts of Italy, thus contributing greatly to national unification.

The results of this general progress were evident in the rapid growth of the population, which rose from 21 million in 1861 to 32 million in 1901 and to 40 million thirty years later, despite the heavy emigration; the considerable increase in the national wealth; the noticeable decrease in the number of illiterates, who still comprised 78 percent of the population in 1861; and finally the disappearance of certain social diseases that ravaged entire regions, such as pellagra, due to the poor diet of the peasants, and malaria, caused by polluted swamp lands.

Naturally this powerful movement of national expansion also created some dissatisfaction, disorder, and often very serious upheavals. Too violent a strain had been put on the fragile structure of the young regime. Too many interests and prejudices deeply entrenched in many social classes had been affected. The Risorgimento itself had left a trail of rancor and diffidence; animosity of Republicans toward the monarchy; refusal of many Catholics to collaborate with a regime which was at odds with the Vatican and had deprived the Church of great part of its property and political power; hostility on the part of former ruling classes which had lost traditional privileges; diffidence on the part of the ignorant and superstitious masses of peasants, who resented all attempts to modify their traditional customs, even for the better. Jealousies existed among the various regions. Moreover, the new parliamentary regime, styled too closely on that of England, did not suit the tendencies and political traditions of the nation. All this, during the second half of the last century, resulted in economic crises, financial scandals (for example, that of the Banca Romana in 1893, which involved many political figures), the furthering of emigration among the less prosperous classes,[1] social agitation, and the development of extremist political movements. These brought about frequent insurrections (Sicily, 1893; Tuscany, 1894; Milan, 1898), cruel suppressions, and finally, almost logically, the assassination of King Humbert (1900). Despite these disturbances, which might be called the growing pains of a young nation, the country progressed steadily.

THE FUNCTION OF THE STATE IN THE ITALIAN SOCIETY

Scarcity of available capital and the lack of an enterprising bourgeoisie made it necessary that the public works and the reclamation of land be accomplished mainly through the initiative or financial assistance of the state. Many of the young industries, such as iron works, shipyards, and the shipping companies were able to withstand foreign competition only with the help of state subsidies. Economic enterprises, such as railroads and telegraph, which had been created and operated in other countries by private enterprise, were in Italy the property of the state. The attitude of the state toward business was imitated by the municipalities. In many cities of Italy they operated the principal public utilities, they held co-operative stores, and they even owned cemeteries. Therefore there was greater and more active intervention by the state in the economic life of Italy than in other countries. This policy was fostered also by the labor movement as a step toward collectivism. At the end of the nineteenth century the proletarian movement had undergone a noticeable evolution. Organized political struggle had substituted former anarchistic tactics. It was especially through the pressure of the labor movement organized into the Socialist Party that the Parliament was induced to pass legislation protecting the working classes from the exploitation of great landowners and the growing industrial bourgeoisie. Compulsory social insurance against professional diseases, accidents, and unemployment was established; working conditions for women and children were improved; wages and hours of labor were fixed; and compensation was provided for in case of dismissal.

The intervention of the state in the economic life of the nation was

[1] Foerster, in *The Italian Emigration of Our Times*, remarks that "so embracing has been this emigration that a chronicle of its development must constitute an indispensable chapter in the history of the Italian people"; Italian emigration became considerable after Italy's unification. Italian emigrants were: in the period 1876–1880, an average of 108.797 per year; in the period 1891–1895, an average of 256.511 per year; in the period 1906–1910, an average of 651.287 per year; and in the year 1913 they were 872.598. During the last century most Italian emigration was temporary; now most of it is permanent. During the World War, Italian emigration decreased considerably; it took a sudden upturn in the years 1919 to 1925 and has become almost negligible in the recent years as a consequence of the obstacles raised both by the Italian and the foreign governments. Foerster (pp. 506 and 524) has words of praise for Italian emigration.

coupled with the exaltation of its moral, philosophical, and political function on the part of philosophers and jurists. The majority of the men who had achieved the Risorgimento were from northern and central Italy. They realized fully that the citizen owes many duties to the state and that a nation is strong only if the state is well-organized, respected, and endowed with the necessary power over its subjects. However, they were interested especially in the political aspects of these problems, being little inclined by temperament and education to indulge in abstract speculation. Legal and philosophical problems concerning the nature and final purpose of the state had not attracted much attention. Once the unification had been accomplished, these problems began to arouse the interest of scholars in all Italy chiefly because of the growing influence of scholars from southern Italy.

The philosophical tradition of the South was glorious and of a remote origin. Aquinas, Bruno, Campanella, Vico, and most of the greatest philosophers of the Risorgimento (Tari, Fiorentino, Spaventa) were from southern Italy. One of the subjects that had especially attracted the attention of southern scholars was the doctrine of the state. In the nineteenth century the doctrines of Hegel enjoyed greater vogue in Naples than in any other part of Europe with the exception of Germany. By a strange paradox in Germany and the Two Sicilies, the countries on the continent where the state was weakest, the doctrine of the state was studied most profoundly in the middle of the nineteenth century and the function of the state was most exalted by philosophers and jurists. For many southern scholars the state was supreme in human organizations and represented the most elevated spiritual entity. The highest ideal of the individual should consist in contributing to the welfare of the state. In the final analysis the individual would have to identify himself with the state, the highest expression of mankind. The doctrine of the nation, which had been the philosophy of the Risorgimento, was now superseded by the doctrine of the state.

Many factors contributed to the triumph of this conception in Italy. Above all, it was felt necessary to give the state a lofty spiritual value. For centuries it had in most parts of Italy enjoyed little prestige and had been a symbol of foreign oppression and bad government, an enemy of its subjects instead of their representative. It was necessary to strengthen with the support of a philosophical doctrine the new Italian state, which was young and fragile and confronted with powerful opposition, both internal and external. It was considered particularly important to oppose the universal ideal of the Church, with which the Italian state was then in bitter conflict, with that of the national state, equally elevated and common to all Italians. To the diffusion of the new doctrine of the state, contributed also the profound juridical spirit of the Italian people, who, living under a system of codified law, recognized in the state the fountain of all law and therefore the supreme authority in every civil organization. Socialist doctrines also contributed to glorify the state. At the beginning of the twentieth century they were subjects of profound study in Italy, chiefly through the work of Antonio Labriola and Benedetto Croce. Many socialists considered the state the only authority capable of seizing all the powers which until then had been monopolized by the capitalist classes and to exercise them in the interest of all the citizens.

So from the end of the nineteenth century the state had already begun to acquire a dominant position in the economic and spiritual life of the nation and had paved the way for that glorification of its function which was later to find an exaggerated manifestation in fascism.

ITALY'S FOREIGN POLICY

In the first decades of its existence the Italian state did not develop a vigorous international policy. The process of internal consolidation absorbed almost all the energy of the nation. Besides, any Italian attempt at expansion was checked by the declared hostility of Austria, which had not even subsided with the Triple Alliance in 1881, and by France's strong jealousy, which at times manifested itself in violent crises, such as the lynching of Italians in France and tariff wars ruinous for Italy. At the end of the nineteenth century the seizure of African colonies and the political hegemony in the Balkans, where Turkish power was rapidly declining, were at stake. Italy, politically isolated and in full process of internal development, was not in a position to take active part in the imperialistic struggle between the leading European powers. Territories in which Italy had claims of long standing, such as Tunisia, colonized pre-eminently by Italians, and Egypt, tied to Italy by strong economic and cultural bonds, fell under the control of France and England, respectively. Albania, strategically situated so as to control the entire Adriatic, was the object of Austrian aspirations, which seemed to preannounce military occupation. Colonial expansion by Italy was practically non-existent, confined as it was to the Eritrean colony and to a few colonial protectorates along the Somaliland coast of the Indian Ocean. This state of affairs provoked disappointment, resentment, and accusations of political inability against the government, which made themselves felt especially after the disastrous ending of the Italian protectorate over Abyssinia and Italy's renunciation of the Tigre territory in 1896. But despite hesitation, weaknesses, and mistakes, progress on the part of Italy could be noted in the international field. It became particularly evident in the beginning of the twentieth century.

This was due in part to the rapid internal development of the country, which increased its prestige also in international relations, and in part to the establishment of better relations with France (1900–1905). Italy was enabled to counter the influence of France and England on the one hand by that of Austria and Germany on the other, so exercising an independent and fairly active policy.

The new policy had its most important manifestation in the war with Turkey (1911–1912) which resulted in the annexation of Tripolitania, Cirenaica, and the occupation of the Dodecanese. In foreign countries the war was described as a cynical act of capitalist imperialism, the first attempted by the young kingdom. In Italy, on the contrary, the war was very popular even among the lower classes. The peasants, especially in the South, saw in Libya the promised land, open to the overflowing population. For the Catholics the war was a crusade against the infidels. To many Socialists it appeared a struggle for social justice, designed to benefit the working classes. Moreover, they believed that martial spirit and military experience resulting from the war would arouse in the masses that revolutionary enthusiasm upon which the final triumph of the Socialist movement depended. This myth of a proletarian war waged by Italy for motives of social justice found its lyrical expression in the poems of Giovanni Pascoli. He was the greatest Italian poet of this era, and his poetry was often inspired by socialist motives. Italy, "the great proletarian, has arisen," he wrote, exalting the Libyan campaign. That characteristic type of imperialism which was later to become one of the fundamental motives of Italian policy then began to manifest itself. It was not the capitalist imperialism of the financiers and industrialists, but the proletarian imperialism of the poorer people who had been raised in an impoverished land. They did not want conquest, they only sought to establish themselves in a new country, where they might live and work without being exploited by foreigners and without having to relinquish their national characteristics. This imperialism, in which patriotism, proletarian emancipation, and social justice were blended, was in large measure equalitarian and democratic.

It was in the same spirit that a few years later (1915) Italy entered the World War. In the opinion of the vast majority of Italians it was a war of liberation, not only of their oppressed compatriots of Trento and Trieste but also of all the peoples subjugated by the tyrannical Hapsburgs: a democratic war against the autocratic monarchies of central Europe. For this reason the war was popular among the Socialists, the Republicans, and all democratic groups in general.

As a result of the victory Italy obtained Trento, Trieste, Istria, the city of Zara, and a few years later (1924) the city of Fiume and absolute sovereignty of the Dodecanese Islands. A few colonial possessions of minor importance were granted to Italy by France (1919 and 1935) and England (1924, 1925, and 1934). These concessions were a good deal less than had been promised in the London Treaty of April 26, 1915, which established the conditions of Italian participation in the World War.

FASCISM

The history of Italy after the first World War is too well known to necessitate a reminder here, even of the aspects essential to international law. It is characterized above all by the conquest of power by fascism and by the misuse that it made thereof. The tremendous strain exerted by the war on the young nation; the disillusion of many Italians who saw the promises made at the time of Italy's entrance into the war forgotten; the impression disseminated among Italians that their country had been deprived of its rightful share of the spoils of war by stronger and more cynical nations; economic and social crises; old imperialistic motives; youth's misguided patriotism and spirit of adventure; personal ambition; egoism and cowardice on the part of the Italian bourgeoisie; the unpreparedness of the working classes—these were only some of the factors responsible for the situation which gave rise to fascism.

It is unnecessary to repeat the condemnation of this movement which obtains in every civilized country. What is important is to dispel several misconceptions regarding modern Italy. Because of the number and virtues of her population, her geographical position, and her traditions, Italy, when free again, is destined to play an important part in Europe. Contrary to what is currently believed, Italy is in a period of ascendancy. It dates back to the beginning of the nineteenth century and first manifested itself in the national unification achieved by the Risorgimento. Italy's progress continued during the past twenty years in spite of fascism. However great are the errors and wrongs committed by this regime, the everlasting vitality of the Italian people could not be destroyed by it. For this reason a note of hope and a promise of better days remains alive in the hearts of those who continue to love Italy in spite of the insults endured and the pain suffered. May Italy rise to greater dignity and by one of those miracles so frequent in her history become once more the land of saints and heroes, of poets and idealists, the land we love, Italy of Giuseppe Mazzini.

Chapter XII: THE POSITIVIST DOCTRINE

THE legislative reforms which followed national unification gave new impetus to the study of law in Italy. In the beginning the interest of Italian scholars centered chiefly in the interpretation of the new statutes, especially of the five codes.[1] Ponderous commentaries were then written along the lines of the French commentaries on the *Code Napoleon:* for example, those of Bianchi and Pacifici Mazzoni on the Civil Code; of Vidari on the Code of Commerce, and of Mattirolo on the Code of Civil Procedure. From the analysis of the particular sections of fhe codes and of the other statutes, which was obviously fragmentary and narrow in scope, Italian jurists evolved at the end of the nineteenth century toward a most comprehensive interpretation of the law. The systematic study of the main institutions of Italian law, both public and private, was then undertaken by Fadda, Coviello, and Gianturco for the civil law, Bolaffio, Sraffa, and Vivante for the law merchant, Mortara, Chiovenda, and Carnelutti for the civil procedure, Ferri and Garofalo for penal law, Orlando, Romano, and Ranelletti for constitutional and administrative law, Scaduto and Ruffini for ecclesiastical law. Their research was carried on along strictly juristic lines and in a spirit of strict adherence to the provisions of existing law. It was never disassociated, however, from a clear understanding of the social factors underlying legal institutions.[2] This realistic approach was greatly helped by the teaching of historians of law such as Scialoia, Bonfante, and Riccobono for Roman law, and Pertile, Schupfer, and Brandileone for Italian law. They exhorted the jurists to seek out the origin and the historical development of the existing institutions as means toward the understanding of their present value.

Legal studies also benefited from the keen interest of jurists in the philosophical studies which were at that time in full progress, especially through the work of Benedetto Croce. Influence of philosophical theory is

---

[1] Civil Code, Code of Commerce, Penal Code, Code of Civil Procedure, and Code of Criminal Procedure.

[2] Carnelutti, *Scuola italiana del diritto*, p. 12, remarks: "The movement whereby politics and law are not confused but the influence of political factors in the formation of legal concepts is duly appraised, represents . . . one of the most interesting characteristics of the Italian legal school." On contemporary Italian legal doctrines see also Battino, *Les Doctrines juridiques contemporaines en Italie.*

largely responsible for the development of the dogmatic and theoretical tendencies in Italian jurisprudence, which was in no way harmful, since it did not degenerate, as in Germany, into pure abstraction.

The approach of Italian scholars to legal problems was obviously connected to the particular characteristics of Italian law. These depended upon its Roman origin and its peculiar evolution. They do not differ much, however, from those of other continental systems of law. From the point of view of the present work, the most important are the following.

1. Italian law is codified. Law in force in Italy is chiefly written law. Resort to written law is necessary and sufficient for the solution of any legal problem. As a rule custom has no legal force; it cannot repeal or modify statutory provisions.[3] Nor are the decisions of the courts a source of legislative rules; for their authority does not extend beyond the particular case decided. Judicial precedent is not binding. The rule *stare decisis* is not recognized.

2. All law is created through enactments by the state or by delegated agencies of the state. The state is therefore the only direct or indirect source of legal provisions in Italy.

3. Italian law is a highly typified legal system. It tends to classify any possible legal act or transaction within categories which are established a priori. Legal provisions embodied in statutes are reduced to short and comprehensive statements which express general principles and rules. Under each of them a large number of particular questions may be comprehended. Sections defining the general features and purposes of the various legal institutions can be frequently found in the codes and in the other Italian statutes.[4]

As a result of the above-mentioned characteristics of their legal system Italian jurists, as a rule, adopt the following concepts of general jurisprudence:

1. Since in the Italian legal system written laws are sufficient to solve any legal problem, Italian jurists are inclined to deny any legal validity to principles and rules which are not expressly consecrated by statutory provisions. Hence their legal positivism. In no system of law would an Italian jurist admit the binding force of principles of metaphysical justice and of alleged rules of natural law.

2. Since in the Italian legal system the state is the only source of law, Italian jurists are inclined to identify the law with the state. The state is

[3] Article 3 of the Preliminary Provisions of the Civil Code of 1865.
[4] Those characteristics of the Italian law result from its derivation from Roman law and the process of codification which it underwent. Roman law is the classical model of a highly typified legal system which expresses with perfect appropriateness the fundamental interests and relationships which can arise from the social activities of men. Codification results in the condensation of a whole legal system into a comparatively small number of general rules.

the law. The provisions of any legal system must find their source in the will of one or more states.

3. Since legal rules are expressed in the Italian statutes in a general and comprehensive form, so that the solution of any particular legal problem is usually found by bringing that particular case under the provisions of a general rule, Italian jurists, as a rule, admit that in any legal system there is a group of general principles or rules governing any possible legal case. Hence their inclination toward a deductive rather than an inductive method in the solution of legal problems.[5]

By an almost unconscious process of generalization many Italian jurists have sometimes applied these methods and principles in the field of international law, thus disregarding the basic diversity of domestic and international law.

THE POSITIVIST DOCTRINE AS A REACTION AGAINST NATURAL LAW

The complete renewal of the doctrines of international law is one of the most important manifestations of the maturity reached by the Italian legal studies. Until the end of the nineteenth century the doctrine of nationalities had been accepted almost unanimously by Italian scholars. Since it was devoid of any scientific basis, it rapidly lost ground at the end of the Risorgimento, when its historical and political functions came to an end. Any attempt to give it new content could only fail. The Italian doctrines of international law of the last fifty years are inspired by entirely different principles. In order to proceed to their analysis, they must be divided into three groups: (a) the positivist conception; (b) the reaction against it; and (c) the fascist conception.

The tendency toward the positivist method in the study of international law developed in many European countries toward the end of the nineteenth century. In Italy it acquired some peculiar characteristics, thus giving rise to the Italian positivist school of international law. Its origin and development are closely connected with the teaching of Dionisio Anzilotti.[6] Equally great are the merits of Donato Donati, another positivist scholar who explored all branches of public law and to whom I wish to express here my deep admiration and gratitude.[7] Because of his

[5] This tendency is also furthered by the method of legal education adopted in Italy, as well as in other European countries. Lectures consist of a statement by the teacher of legal rules which are later explained by way of exemplification. Legal principles are not established by a process of generalization of the principles expounded by particular cases analyzed. The case method and case books are wholly ignored in Italy.

[6] Dionisio Anzilotti was born in 1869. He taught public and private international law and related subjects in various Italian universities, finally at the University of Rome, until his retirement in 1939. He is a judge at the Permanent Court of International Justice and a member of the Academy of Italy.

[7] Donato Donati was born in 1880. He taught international law and related subjects in various Italian universities, finally at the University of Padova. He was dismissed in 1938 after the racial laws were enacted.

more active participation in academic life and his personal contact with many of the younger students of public law, to whom he was an affectionate teacher and a shining example of dignity and generosity, Donati exercised a wider and more direct influence than did Anzilotti in the field of legal studies. Anzilotti, however, is identified more closely and exclusively with international law,[8] to which he devoted all his activities as teacher, writer, attorney, judge, and for a time president of the Permanent Court of International Justice. For logical and chronological reasons the analysis of the Italian positivist conception must start with Dionisio Anzilotti. The development and revision of the doctrine through the work of Anzilotti himself and of other writers, such as Donati, Gemma,[9] Cavaglieri,[10] and Perassi,[11] will then be examined. To the further development of the doctrine younger students, such as Ghirardini,[12] Marinoni,[13] Ottolenghi,[14] Baldassarri,[15] Udina,[16] Morelli,[17] Bosco,[18] Baldoni,[19] Ago,[20] and the present writer [21] contributed.[22]

[8] The contribution to the study of private international law of Anzilotti is also extremely important.

[9] Scipione Gemma was born in 1867. He taught public and private international law and related subjects in various Italian universities, finally at the University of Bologna, until he retired in 1937.

[10] Arrigo Cavaglieri (1880–1936) taught public and private international law in various Italian universities, finally at the University of Naples, until his death.

[11] Tomaso Perassi succeeded Anzilotti as professor of international law at the University of Rome.

[12] Carlo Ghirardini (1882–1920) taught international law in various Italian universities, finally at the University of Pisa, until his death.

[13] Mario Marinoni (1886–1922) taught international law in various Italian universities, most recently at the Institute of Social Sciences in Firenze, until his death.

[14] Giuseppe Ottolenghi (b. 1876) taught international law at the University of Torino. He was dismissed following racial laws.

[15] Aldo Baldassarri (b. 1885) teaches international law at the University of Bari.

[16] Manlio Udina (b. 1902) teaches international law at the University of Trieste.

[17] Gaetano Morelli (b. 1900) teaches international law at the University of Naples.

[18] Giacinto Bosco (b. 1905) teaches international law at the University of Firenze.

[19] Claudio Baldoni (1904–1939) taught international law in various Italian universities, finally at the University of Bologna, until the time of his death.

[20] Roberto Ago (b. 1907) teaches international law at the University of Milano.

[21] Angelo Piero Sereni (b. 1908) taught international law and related subjects at the University of Ferrara. He has been living in the United States since 1939.

[22] The reader who wishes to get acquainted with the most significant works of the Italian positivists may consult the following: Anzilotti, *Teoria generale della responsabilità dello stato nel diritto internazionale*; Anzilotti, *Il diritto internazionale nei giudizii interni*; Anzilotti, *Corso di diritto internazionale*, 1914–1915; Anzilotti, *Corso di diritto internazionale*, 3d ed., 1928; Donati, *I trattati internazionali nel diritto costituzionale*; Same, *Stato e territorio*; Cavaglieri, "La Conception positive de la société internationale," 18 Rev. gén. dr. int. pub. (1911) 259 ff.; Cavaglieri, "Concetto e caratteri del diritto internazionale generale," 14 Riv. dir. int. (1922) 289 ff.; Cavaglieri, "I soggetti del diritto internazionale," 17 Riv. dir. int. (1925) 18 ff.; Cavaglieri, *Lezioni di diritto internazionale*; Perassi, "Teoria dommatica delle fonti di norme giuridiche in diritto internazionale," 11 Riv. dir. int. (1917) 195 ff.; Perassi, *Lezioni di diritto internazionale*, 1922, and *Lezioni di diritto internazionale*, 1937–1938.

For a comparison between the theories of Anzilotti and those of Romano see C. Vitta,

Complete differentiation between positive law and metaphysical justice is the point of departure of Anzilotti's doctrine. Positive law consists
of the legal provisions which are created in a given social organization
through the processes which it has established for the enactment of legal
rules. Metaphysical justice comprises those ideal principles and exigencies which according to a given jurist or social group should be translated
into positive law.[23] The positivist school asserts that jurisprudence is primarily interested in the study of positive law, that is, law as it is (*jus
conditum*), not law as it should be (*jus condendum*). In the field of international law the main function of jurisprudence is to "organize and explain scientifically the legal system of relations between states. In conducting this analysis any premise other than those of positive law should
be excluded." [24] Thus international law must be distinguished from the
precepts of natural law. Anzilotti remarks that the entire doctrine of international law, almost to the present day, developed within the framework of natural law conceptions.

From its very origin, international law was combined with the concept of the law
of nature. This was understood to be a law pre-existing any empirical reality,
flowing from the invariable essence of human nature, and therefore absolute and
eternal. It existed before and irrespective of its recognition by laws and custom.[25]

As a result of the great legal codifications in Continental Europe
and Latin America and of the enactment of statutory law in the Anglo-
American countries, natural law has almost entirely lost its influence over
domestic legislation. To quote Jellinek, "It continued, however, to cele-
brate its orgies in the systems of international law." [26] Even the progressive schools, such as the Italian school of nationalities, only gave new content to this traditional form of thought. The main purpose of the positivist
school is to eliminate from the field of international law the natural-law
doctrines, which are only traditional residues, not law actually in existence between states.

Rigorous distinction between legal and ethico-political problems of
international relations is also necessary. Political and ethical problems
must be studied on the basis of principles and methods of their own which
differ from those employed by jurisprudence. Thus, the positivist school
reacts against the doctrines of writers such as Fiore, in Italy, who identify
their ideals of justice with positive rules of international law. The posi-

---

"Divergenze nella dottrina italiana sui principii fondamentali del diritto internazionale
pubblico," 21 Riv. dir. int. (1929) 501 ff. A thorough analysis of the positivist doctrine may
be found in the works of Lauterpacht.

[23] Anzilotti, *Corso di diritto internazionale*, 1914, I, 12.

[24] Anzilotti, "Trattati generali di diritto internazionale," 1 Riv. dir. int. (1906) 37.

[25] *Corso di diritto internazionale*, 3d ed., p. 16.

[26] *System der subjectiven öffentlichen Rechte*, p. 297.

tivist school opposes also doctrines, such as the Italian doctrine of nationalities, which base the solution of problems of international law upon political, not legal, considerations.[27]

This strictly legalistic attitude toward international problems does not mean that the Italian positivist school is merely formalistic and agnostic. The Italian positivists do not deny the influence of political, economic, and sociological factors in the development of international law. The knowledge of the historical background of the law is an indispensable element for its interpretation. Positivist writers also point out that international law is not a static system of rules, but a dynamic and changeable one that modifies itself continually in connection with the new needs of the international community and of human life in general. To the revision of the existing rules of international law which no longer correspond to ideals of justice and to practical needs, the jurist must also contribute. But the problems concerning the possible changes and improvements of the law should not be confused with those concerning the ascertainment and the application of the existing law. A positive rule of international law does not become void only because it has been historically superseded. Nor can the existence of an international rule be denied on the ground that it is opposed to ethical principles or to political interests.[28] Any legal rule remains in force unless it has been duly modified through the processes established by international law for the modification of its own rules. In ascertaining existing law the jurist must accept a rule as it is. To quote Anzilotti, the program and the method of the positivist school can therefore be summed up in the following words:

It must distinguish law actually in force from the mere aspirations of social conscience and of the doctrine. It must build positive international law into a logical order so that all classes of its rules might be co-ordinated into a unified system which will permit their complete understanding. It must point out the legal aspects of each relationship by severing them from its ethical and political aspects. It must distinguish carefully between the interpretation of the positive law and any critical appraisal or proposal of change in it. Interpretation is only intended to ascertain the real meaning of the existing rules. On the contrary, in evaluating these rules with a view to their change, jurisprudence obviously must refer to criteria other than those embodied in the law in force.[29]

[27] International law in Italy is considered a strictly legal subject absolutely disassociated from international relations; it is compulsory study for law students. The teaching of international law is associated with that of international private law (conflict of laws).

[28] Anzilotti, *Corso di diritto internazionale*, p. 17, explains, however, that the "legitimacy of a research intended to explain and coördinate the ideal principles of justice governing human relations is not contested thereby; it is only stressed that it is necessary to keep these principles absolutely separate from positive legal rules. Since their source and validity are different, any mingling and confusion would lead to the attribution to some factors of a value which belongs to others."

[29] *Corso di diritto internazionale*, 3d ed., p. 18.

A systematic conception of international law must be based, according to the positivist school, on the legal rules which are actually observed by the states in their relations. No theory can be deemed correct unless its conclusions, with respect to any particular question, are consistent with the international practice. Precise knowledge of this practice is therefore a prerequisite to the formulation of any theory of international law. But the analysis of particular rules cannot be assumed as the point of departure for a complete and systematic study of international law. It is necessary, on the contrary to start with the basic principles of international law and to ascertain the nature and fundamental characteristics of this legal system. A comprehensive vision of the entire system is a prerequisite to the understanding of the various rules and to the solution of the specific problems. Only by placing the scattered rules of international law under the appropriate general principles from which they are derived is it possible to grasp their meaning and implications, to reconcile their apparent contradictions, and to find a solution for cases of first impression.

In carrying on their research along these lines the jurists should bear in mind that the international community differs in structure and characteristics from the human societies organized into states. Hence, there is considerable difference between the system of international law and those of national law. Any attempt to apply principles and methods of one law to the other law would result in grave errors.[30] Because of this theoretical and dogmatic approach to international problems, Italian students have paid more attention than the English and the Americans to questions of system, method, and legal philosophy.[31]

The revision of international law, inspired by these principles, requires the re-examination of nearly all the fundamental problems of legal theory. Previous Italian studies of international law were of no avail for this purpose, for they either disregarded these problems or followed the doctrine of nationalities. In the study of the fundamental problems of international law French writers of this period were inspired by a vague naturalism. The same was true, with a few notable exceptions, also of the English and Americans, although they followed international practice more closely in the analysis of particular problems.[32] Thus, in the beginning Italian positivists were especially interested in the works of the German and Austrian writers who had undertaken a critical revision of the fundamental concepts of public law and the theory of the

---

[30] It will be demonstrated, however, that the positivists did not always keep faith with these premises.

[31] Lauterpacht, "The So-called Anglo-American and Continental Schools of Thought in International Law," 12 British Year Book of International Law (1931) 61. With the exception of Focherini, *Problemi di diritto internazionale pubblico*, no collections of problems of international law have been published in Italy.

[32] Lauterpacht, *Private Law Sources and International Law*, p. 27n.

state which affected also the traditional theories of international law. The works of the first Italian positivists reveal a careful study of the theories of Jellinek, Laband, Binding, Bierling, O. Mayer, Bergbohm, Heilborn, Kaufmann, Nippold, and Triepel.

ANZILOTTI'S BASIC THEORIES OF INTERNATIONAL LAW

The above-mentioned program and methods of the positivist school remained unchanged from its inception until now. On the other hand, many fundamental theories underwent radical changes. The original theories of the positive school, as outlined by Anzilotti, and the subsequent changes brought about by Anzilotti himself and by other writers will be considered separately.

The peculiar characteristics of the international community are first considered by the Italian positivist school. It points out that the natural development of human aggregations brings about the formation of groups permanently established on a certain territory and subjected to the authority of a unified power. These organizations are called states. Solidarity of certain interests and community of civilization keep these groups from remaining isolated. Relationships arising among them create the "society of states" or "international community." [33] The existence of an international community composed mainly of states is an historical fact which can be proved through observation. [34]

The characteristics of the international community are a result of the manner in which it came into existence. The positivist school accepts the traditional concept that the present-day international community arose or assumed its actual characteristics in the sixteenth and seventeenth centuries. Feudalism then disappeared within the states, while the authority of the Church and the empire over them collapsed. Each state set itself up as an exclusive power over its subjects and an independent power in relation to other states. In place of the Holy Roman Empire, an international community was then created between states. The relationship between them became one of co ordination between equal and independent entities. Even today this is the characteristic trait of the international community. [35]

The existence of an international community is possible only in so far as its members do not act arbitrarily but conform to certain rules limiting their freedom and governing their mutual relationships. Experience proves the existence of a system regulating the society of states. It is composed of two main elements: governing forces, such as public opinion, and rules of conduct, which determine the limits and the forms of the

---

[33] Anzilotti, *Corso di diritto internazionale*, 3d ed., p. 41.
[34] Perassi, *Lezioni di diritto internazionale*, 1937, p. 1.
[35] Anzilotti, *Corso di diritto internazionale*, 3d ed., p. 5.

activities of the members of the international community in their mutual relationships. A special category of rules of conduct, the most important, is the one to which the states attribute juridical value. A body of legal rules which co-ordinates and controls the activities of the members of the international community does exist. This legal order constitutes international law.[36]

The international order differs from the legal orders of the single states because the international community is different from statal organizations. The main differences are: (a) the international community is composed only of abstract entities, chiefly states, while in each national society members are mainly individuals; (b) the international community is constituted of equal and independent entities. All its members are on an equal footing, no superior power existing above them. In every national organization, on the contrary, above the single individuals which compose the community there exists the state, which is endowed with jurisdiction over its subjects. International organization is based upon the co-ordination of its members, while each state is a hierarchy based upon the respective pre-eminence and subordination of its components.

At the time Anzilotti first expounded his theory (1900), the peculiar structure of the international society was invoked as an argument to deny that an international law could exist. Austin's conception of the law as a "command by a political superior to a political inferior" was then almost generally accepted. Since the international organization lacked a power superior to its members with authority to create, ascertain, and enforce legal rules, the conclusion was drawn that there could not be a system of international law.

To refute this contention Anzilotti points out that each juridical system reflects the characteristics of the society whose legal order it constitutes. No doubt in national organizations law is a command by the state to the subject. It is, however, wrong to assume, as Austin does, that the law must present in every legal system the characteristics which it acquired within the states. A precept does not need to consist of a command by a superior to an inferior in order to be law. The essential requirement of law, according to Anzilotti, consists of its coercive power. In other words, a rule has legal validity whenever it authorizes coercion to secure compliance with its provisions. How this coercion is exercised is immaterial. In the national systems of law it is exercised by the states, the superior powers. Coercion by the state replaces any different form of coercion, and for this reason the individual is usually forbidden from taking the law into his own hands and self-defense is permitted only in a few cases. In the international community also there are precepts which authorize coercion in order to secure compliance with their provisions. Hence, these precepts

[36] Anzilotti, *Corso di diritto internazionale*, 1914, I, 28 ff.

are law. But since there is no superior power to enforce the law, it is the state whose right has been violated that must exert direct and personal coercion in order to obtain redress. Thus, self-defense, which is the exception in state organizations, is the rule in the society of states.[37] This detracts nothing from the legal validity of international law. It must be admitted, however, that because of the lack of a power superior to the states international law appears to be more primitive and rudimentary than national legal systems. It is more fragile, but also more flexible.

It is hardly an exaggeration to say that when Anzilotti first formulated his theory he was obsessed by the idea of rejecting any influence of natural law on international law. This constant preoccupation is especially evident in his theory on the sources of international law and accounts for its somewhat artificial character. Anzilotti distinguishes between "material" and "formal" sources of law. "Material" or indirect sources are the exigencies and needs which provoke the creation of legal rules. The analysis of the motives behind the formation of legal rules is within the scope of sociology, history, and economics, not of jurisprudence. The latter is only interested in the direct or "formal" sources of the law. The formal sources of international law are for Anzilotti all facts which create legal rules in the international community.

Every legal system determines its own sources. The rules establishing the sources of the law are called by the positive school *norms on the legal production* (*norme sulla produzione giuridica*). One of the essential points of Anzilotti's theory is that in each legal order every rule of positive law can find its source only in an act of will of one or more subjects of that order. All law is voluntary. In national systems the will which creates the law is that of the state, which is the personification of the juridical order itself. For this reason, within the states the creation of law generally takes place in the form of a command issued by a superior (the state) to an inferior (the subject). In the international order the source of the legal rule cannot consist in an act of will addressed to its members (the states) by a superior power, because no such power exists. The only will which can be the source of legal rules is therefor the will of the states themselves. "According to a strictly positivist conception, the source of international law can only be found in the very will of the states." [38] The problem consists in ascertaining which are the acts of will of the states which may create international law.

The state cannot by its own act of will alone create international rules binding it to other states. "If the subordination of a state to a rule of international law were based only on an act of will of the state itself, no

[37] *Ibid.*

[38] Anzilotti, "Trattati generali di diritto internazionale," 1 Riv. dir. int. (1906) 41; and *Teoria generale della responsabilità dello stato nel diritto internazionale,* p. 37; Cavaglieri, "La Conception positive de la société internationale," 18 Rev. gén. dr. int. publ. (1911), 260.

dialectic effort could demonstrate that the same state could not by another act of will, free itself from its obligation." [39] The theory of self-limitation on the part of the state, which had met with great success among German jurists, especially of the nineteenth century, is therefore exploded.

Since no superior power exists which is endowed with authority to create international law, the source of an international rule can only be found, according to Anzilotti, in the agreement (*accordo*) of two or more states. Every international agreement gives origin to legal rules creating rights and duties between the contracting parties. These rules are in the form of mutual promises which are binding upon the states. By concluding a treaty, the parties agree to fulfill these promises. International law is a voluntary law in the sense that a state is only bound by the rules that were created with its consent through its agreements with other states. Each state is free to conclude or not the international agreements from which its obligations derive. But once its consent is given and the agreement has been reached, the norms resulting from it cannot be modified by any one of the parties to it with a unilateral act of will, because by the agreement the individual wills of the parties to the agreement merge into the common will which henceforth constitutes a binding rule of law. This common will of the states cannot be changed by a single state. Thus, although the will of the state is essential for the creation of the common will resulting from the agreement, it is the common will, not the will of the single states, which is the source of international obligations.

The basis of all international law is the rule that the agreements must be respected (*pacta sunt servanda*).[40] The rule itself is based upon the common consent of the states. "States are bound because, and so far as, they wish to be bound. Even the obligatory force of the rule *pacta sunt servanda* is derived from nothing other than the collective will of the states." [41]

Agreement is the primary source of international rules, because all members of the international community recognize that they are bound by the rules created through their mutual promises.[42] It is also the only

[39] Anzilotti, *Corso di diritto internazionale*, 3d ed., p. 43.
[40] Cavaglieri, "Concetto e caratteri del diritto internazionale generale," 14 Riv. dir. int. (1921–1922) 483: "The principle *pacta sunt servanda* is accepted by the positive doctrine, which finds its corroboration in solemn declarations and in the constant practice of the states."
[41] Anzilotti, *Note* in Riv. dir. int., 7 (1913) 64.
[42] In the first formulation of his theory Anzilotti affirmed that law can only be conceived as a "command" directed to the person who must comply with its precepts. In order to explain how the will of single parties to an international agreement may originate a rule of objective law which binds their wills, he then resorted to the distinction of the treaties into "contracts" (*trattati-contratti; Verträge*) and "agreements" (*trattati normativi; Verein-barungen*) which had already been expounded by Bergbohm and Triepel. By a treaty-contract the parties exchange different considerations; for example, state A cedes a part of its territory to state B which pays an indemnity. By a treaty-agreement the parties express an

general source of international law. The principle is tersely formulated by Perassi.

The only general norm on the legal production existing in the international order can be formulated as follows: agreement is the act through which rules of international law are created, modified, or repealed between the states which contributed to its formation with their will.[43]

Since international rules are created by their consent, the states are at the same time the legislators and the subjects of the international order.

All the most important consequences of Anzilotti's theory are derived from the principle that agreement is the only source of international rules.

1. *Pacta sunt servanda* constitutes the criterion defining and unifying into a legal system the rules of international law. International law is a system of rules whose binding force is derived from the principle *pacta sunt servanda*. It comprises the rules resulting from the promises that the states make to each other in their capacity of independent and equal entities, not subject to any common power.

2. Since international rules are created only through state agreements, the following are not general rules of international law:

a) Natural law, abstract reason, and exigencies of justice.

b) Needs arising from social life.

c) *Comitas gentium*, that is, the rules which the states observe in their intercourse, without, however, attributing them binding force, such as many rules concerning courtesy, ceremonial, etiquette, and treatment of heads of states and governments and of diplomatic agents.[44]

d) "General principles of law recognized by civilized nations," mentioned in Section 38 of the Statute of the Permanent Court of International Justice. Their binding force is limited to those states which consent to recognize them, and therefore they are sources of international

---

identical will and aim to achieve the same result—for instance, in a treaty whereby all parties agree to suppress the slave trade. International rules are created by treaty-agreements. These result in the formation of a collective will different from the will of the states which are parties to the agreement and therefore binding upon them. "The treaty-agreement being a fact aimed at the creation of the law, precedes it and therefore is beyond its scope. Such a treaty is not a juridical, but a prejuridical fact." (*Corso di diritto internazionale*, 1912–1914, p. 48.)

This artificial and unconvincing conception was later repudiated by Anzilotti himself (*Corso di diritto internazionale*, 3d ed., p. 43). The positive school now rejects the distinction between treaty-contracts and treaty-agreements. Every treaty is conceived as a set of promises which the parties to it are bound to respect by force of the rule *pacta sunt servanda* (Cavaglieri, "Concetto e caratteri del diritto internazionale generale," 14 Riv. dir. int. (1922) 489; and *Lezioni di diritto internazionale*, 48 ff.)

[43] *Lezioni di diritto internazionale*, 1937, I, 5.

[44] On the rules of ceremonial followed by Italy see Toscani, *Norme e consuetudini di cerimoniale*. On diplomatic procedure see A. Bettanini, *Lo stile diplomatico*.

law only as a consequence of a special agreement and within its limits.[45]

e) Decisions of the international courts. A judgment, as a rule, does not create, but only declares the law governing the case decided.[46]

f) Acts performed by a state within its national jurisdiction. A law or a judgment of a domestic court can never be a source of international law.[47]

g) Works of the jurists.

3. International law admits, however, that facts other than state agreements may give rise to international rules. Article 26 of the Covenant of the League of Nations provides that amendments to the Covenant will bind all the members of the League, when approved by the Council and the majority of the members of the Assembly. A member of the League can then be bound by new rules which are not created through an agreement to which it consented, but through resolutions of organs of the League. Article 38 of the Statute of the Permanent Court of International Justice gives the Court the power to decide cases *ex aequo et bono.* In so deciding, the Court does not declare the existing law, but creates new law,[48] and therefore the states which are parties to the case are bound by international rules which do not result from their agreement but by an act of an independent body, the Court.

[45] Anzilotti, *Corso di diritto internazionale,* 3d ed., p. 106 ff., remarks that in applying the general principles of law recognized by the civilized nations the Permanent Court of International Justice does not fulfill the normal task of a judicial body, which consists in declaring the law. By consent of the parties to the litigation it creates, by analogy to those principles, new law which will govern these particular cases. In agreement with Anzilotti are Morelli, *La sentenza internazionale,* pp. 265 ff., 288 ff., and Cavaglieri, *Lezioni di diritto internazionale,* p. 82.

The compulsory force of the general principles of law recognized by the civilized nations is based, not upon the consent of the states, but upon a fundamental principle of international law, according to Scerni, *I principii generali di diritto riconosciuti dalle nazioni civili nella giurisprudenza della Corte permanente di giustizia internazionale,* and to the other opponents of Anzilotti.

[46] Under the influence of domestic legal conceptions, Italian doctrine and practice attributes to the decisions of international courts, and even to the practice of the states, less importance than Anglo-Americans do. Italians hold that an international judgment usually ascertains, but does not create, law and that the precedent is not binding. Besides, neither decisions nor practice constitute conclusive evidence of the existence and of the meaning of a legal rule, because they may be the result of a mistake of law or, in the case of the practice, of the violation of a legal rule.

[47] For this reason Italian doctrine and practice refer to domestic laws and judgments less frequently than Anglo-American doctrine and practice for the purpose of establishing the existence of international rules. However, domestic laws and decisions may be referred to as authoritative indications of the opinion of the states from which are issued as to the content of the rules of international law. In fact, these laws and decisions constitute acts of the states, and until the contrary is proved every state is presumed to act in compliance with international law.

[48] That an international court, in deciding a case *ex aequo et bono,* does not ascertain the existing law but creates new law is now generally recognized. See Habicht, "Le Pouvoir du juge international de statuer *ex aequo et bono,*" 49 Rec. des cours (1934) 277 ff.

Rules which provide for processes other than the agreement for the creation of international law have been defined by Perassi as "secondary norms on the legal production" (*norme secondarie sulla produzione giuridica*). Their existence is not inconsistent with the principle that the agreement is the only primary source of international law. In fact, all these secondary rules are based upon special agreements between the states, which are bound by them. The procedure established by Article 26 of the Covenant of the League is based upon the agreement of the states who ratified this instrument; the power of the Permanent Court of International Justice to decide *ex aequo et bono*, is based on the agreement of the states who ratified its Statute. "At the basis of the binding force of the rules created by a fact envisaged by a secondary rule on the legal production, there is always the consent of the states bound by them." [49]

4. Agreements creating international rules are divided into treaties and custom. Treaties are express declarations, generally in writing, of the common intention of two or more states to follow certain rules. The expression "treaty" comprises conventions, exchanges of notes, protocols, and all other written instruments whereby two or more states consent to follow certain international rules. International custom is a tacit agreement. It develops when the conduct of one state coincides with that of one or more other states. The existence of an international custom whereby a bay is recognized to be within the jurisdiction of the state enclosing it results from the fact that the state claims such power over it and that the other states recognize its claim.

Rules arising from treaties and custom have the same legal nature and therefore the same binding force. Hence, the ancient and frequent definition of "custom" as a tacit agreement (*pactum tacitum*). Considerable difference exists between the process which gives origin to a custom in national law and that which is responsible for its creation in international law. Custom in national law arises from the constant and uniform repetition of a certain conduct on the part of a group of persons, coupled with their conviction that they are bound to that conduct. This slowly creates legal rules. In national law the elements of custom are two; *opinio juris*, that is, the conviction of the obligatory character of certain conduct, and the *diuturnitas*, that is, the repetition of this conduct for a certain period of time. International custom being a tacit agreement, the only requirement for its existence is the consent of the parties, resulting from their uniform conduct (*opinio juris*). [50] The tacit agreement manifests itself in "acts of the states in the field of international relations from which their

[49] Perassi, *Lezioni di diritto internazionale*, 1937, pp. 6 ff.
[50] Perassi, "Teoria dommatica delle fonti di norme giuridiche in diritto internazionale," 11 Riv. dir. int. (1917) 210 ff.; and *Lezioni di diritto internazionale* (1922) 40 ff.

will appears to conduct themselves reciprocally and compulsorily in a certain manner." [51] *Diuturnitas* is not an element in the formation of an international custom, but only evidence of its existence. Therefore there is no conceptual difference between custom and treaty.

5. The scope of international rules depends chiefly on the fact that they are created through agreements.[52]

Scope with regard to their addressees.—International rules are binding only upon the parties to the agreement creating them. Agreement as to a certain conduct may be reached by all the members of the international community, or by a certain number, or by only two of them. Thus, some rules are binding upon all the states while others are in force within a more or less limited group of states. The former constitute "common" or "general" international law; the latter, "special" or "particular" law (or better, "particular laws").

Since general international law is the result of agreements, it has nothing to do with the alleged universal law, whose existence is assumed by the doctrine of natural law. This would bind all the states, irrespective of their consent, by force. For the positivists general international law consists only of customary rules created through tacit agreements. No treaty exists to which all members of the international society are parties.[53] General law is substantially the result of long historical evolution. It started in Europe and gradually extended to other parts of the world where states of a European type arose, as in America, or states having a different civilization accepted the European principles of international intercourse, as in the Orient. General international law is of fundamental importance, because it determines the structure and the peculiar characteristics of the international order. Its rules, however, are few and often somewhat vague, because they have to adapt themselves to the needs of groups having different social conditions and civilizations. Among the general rules of international law Anzilotti classifies, during the first period of his teaching, the rule *pacta sunt servanda;* the rule providing for the freedom of the high seas; some rules concerning diplomatic immunities; and the rule whereby a state, not bound by particular obligations to the contrary, is entitled to resort to war for the protection of its interests.

International law is mainly constituted by particular law; almost all its rules derive from treaties or special custom binding only a limited number of states. With regard to a state who is not a party to it, an in-

---

[51] Anzilotti, *Corso di diritto internazionale,* 3d ed., p. 43. On international custom see also Cavaglieri, *La consuetudine giuridica internazionale.*

[52] Besides the authors already mentioned see also Rapisardi Mirabelli, *I limiti di efficacia delle norme internazionali.*

[53] Obviously the rules embodied in the Covenant of the League of Nations bind only its members, not all the subjects of the international community.

ternational agreement is *res inter alios acta*. Third states do not derive therefrom either rights or duties. The principle is especially important with respect to treaties.[54] A treaty between two states may be actually prejudicial to a third state, but it cannot impose legal obligations on it.[55] It may happen that state *C* recognizes a treaty between states *A* and *B* (for example, a treaty establishing *A*'s protectorate over *B*). In this case the recognition is in reality a new agreement between state *C* and states *A* and *B*, whereby the former assumes some obligations toward the latter.[56] A state may also derive actual benefits from a treaty between other states (for example, a treaty between *A* and *B* whereby they agree to respect the territorial integrity of state *C* is in fact beneficial to the latter, but *C* does not acquire any right from that treaty. In contrast to the United States law, international law does not recognize the third party beneficiary principle.[57] State *C* has not the right to claim the performance of the provisions in its favor existing in the treaty between *A* and *B*. A further agreement may, however, intervene between *C* on one side and *A* and *B* on the other whereby *A* and *B* obligate themselves to perform toward *C* the duties under their treaty.

Scope with regard to duration.—Every rule of international law becomes effective when the agreement creating it is concluded, or at the specific moment provided by it. Because of the process of the formation of custom it is difficult to establish when it becomes a legal rule. Usually it is possible to ascertain the existence of a custom, but not when it first arose. However, it is often possible to establish when a pre-existing custom extended to other members of the international community, because their consent is usually manifested in well-defined acts or facts. Treaties generally indicate the time when they are to become effective. In the absence of a provision to that effect, determining when it becomes effec-

---

[54] See Anzilotti, *Corso di diritto internazionale*, 3d ed., pp. 80 ff., 369 ff.; Cavaglieri, *Lezioni di diritto internazionale*, pp. 92 ff., 482 ff.; Perassi, *Lezioni di diritto internazionale* (1922), pp. 44 ff. See also Gabriele Salvioli "I terzi stati nel diritto internazionale," 12 Riv. dr. int. (1918) 229 ff.

[55] Anzilotti, *Corso di diritto internazionale*, 3d ed., p. 370, recalls in this respect the repeated declarations of the American government that it did not consider itself legally bound by the "old rule" of the Ottoman Empire whereby the Bosphorus and the Dardanelles were closed to warships, inasmuch as that rule was established by the treaties of London, 1841, of Paris, 1856, and of London, 1871, to which the United States was not a party.

[56] The protectorate relationship creates rights and duties only between the protecting and the protected state. If it provides for the compulsory representation of the protected state by the protecting one, a third state is not bound to deal only with the latter in matters concerning the protected state. But the recognition of the protectorate on the part of the third state implies its acquiescence to the relationship and therefore its obligation to deal only with the protecting state in those matters. Sereni, *La rappresentanza nel diritto internazionale*, pp. 137 ff.

[57] Anzilotti, *Corso di diritto internazionale*, 3d ed., p. 379, demonstrates that the Hay-Pauncefote Treaty, November 18, 1901, between the United States and Great Britain concerning the Panama Canal did not create rights of third states.

tive depends upon the interpretation of the will of the contracting parties. The presumption is that the treaty is intended to become effective as soon as concluded.[58]

As international rules are created by agreement, so are they only terminated or modified by agreement. In this respect treaties and custom are similar, since they are only different forms of agreement. Therefore customary rules terminate (a) by desuetude or the formation of a contrary custom or (b) by a treaty expressly repealing the custom or creating rules inconsistent with it. Rules created by treaties become ineffective (a) as a consequence of a new treaty expressly repealing or creating rules inconsistent with them or (b) by desuetude or the formation of a contrary custom.[59] Consistent with the principle that international rules can only be created through agreements, Anzilotti denies that international right or duties may arise by prescription. Mere lapse of time not accompanied by the consent of the states cannot create or terminate legal rules. Silence of a state in case of violation of its rights may, however, be construed under certain circumstances as acquiescence and therefore as a tacit approval of the conduct of the delinquent state.[60]

Anzilotti considers whether there exists a rule of international law whereby a treaty would become ineffective in consequence of a substantial change in the conditions motivating its conclusion (doctrine of *rebus sic stantibus*).[61] From a careful examination of international practice he reaches the conclusion that the states do not deny the admissibility of the doctrine *rebus sic stantibus* notwithstanding many general statements which may seem incompatible with it. What they did really oppose was its applicability in some of the specific instances in which recourse to it had been attempted. Anzilotti believes that there does not exist a general principle of international law whereby the clause *rebus sic stantibus* is a condition tacitly implied in every agreement. But the parties to a specific treaty may have tacitly agreed that certain facts constituted the premise for the obligations resulting from them. In this case a change in the situa-

---

[58] The positive school believes that treaties in general acquire binding force at the moment of the ratification.

[59] The provisions of some Capitulations with Oriental states have been modified or abrogated by desuetude.

[60] Anzilotti, *Corso di diritto internazionale*, 3d ed.; Cavaglieri, "Alcune osservazioni sul concetto di rinunzia nel diritto internazionale," 12 Riv. dir. int. (1918) 3 ff. and "Il decorso del tempo e i suoi effetti sui rapporti giuridici internazionali," 18 Riv. dir. int. (1926) 169 ff. Cavaglieri believes that a tacit agreement between all states created an international rule whereby prescription is recognized in international law.

[61] See Anzilotti, *Corso di diritto internazionale*, 3d ed., pp. 406 ff.; Cavaglieri, *Lezioni di diritto internazionale*, pp. 497 ff., and "La funzione della clausola rebus sic stantibus nei rapporti internazionali," 70 Archivio giuridico (1903) 106 ff. The existence of the clause *rebus six stantibus* is denied by Gabriele Salvioli, "Sulla clausola rebus sic stantibus nei trattati internazionali," 8 Riv. dir. int. (1914) 264 ff., and by U. Borsi, "Ragione di guerra e stato di necessità nel diritto internazionale," 10 Riv. dir. int. (1916) 175 ff. On the problem of the revision of treaties see Zancla, *La revisione dei trattati*, and Cereti, *La revisione dei trattati*.

tion would provoke the termination of such obligations. Therefore, the problem of *rebus sic stantibus* depends upon the interpretation of the will of the parties to each single treaty—whether the parties agreed that the provisions of that treaty should continue to be in force in any case or only as long as a certain situation remains unchanged. A party to a treaty cannot claim unilaterally that the provision *rebus sic stantibus* was agreed to by the parties and that the change in the situation contemplated by it has taken place. Whether or not these contentions are sound is a matter of interpretation of the treaty and any interpretation of a treaty is binding upon all parties to it only if it was reached through procedures to which they have agreed. If the parties consented to submit to arbitration their disputes concerning the interpretation of the treaty, the question whether *rebus sic stantibus* applies will be the object of a judicial decision. The doctrine *rebus sic stantibus*, so understood, is not inconsistent with the principle that an agreement can only be modified by consent of the parties to it.[62]

Whether an international rule is retroactive or refers only to facts subsequent to its enactment also depends upon interpretation of the will of the contracting parties.[63]

In the absence of a special provision to the contrary, all rules of international law can only be modified or repealed by agreement of all parties to them. A change in a multilateral treaty does not affect the parties which did not consent to it.

6. Co-ordination, interpretation, and application of international rules is also affected by their contractual nature.

Co-ordination.—International rules created by treaties have the same validity and legal effects as those created by custom. Thus they have the same capacity to modify pre-existing rules of either class. The principle that subsequent rules may change preceding ones applies to all international rules, whatever their source may be. *Lex posterior derogat priori.* In relations between general international law and special international law, the rule applies that the latter prevails over the former. *In toto jure genus per speciem derogatur.* This rule, however, is not absolute; some general rules may not be changed by special agreement. There are also some cases in which subsequent general rules do not change preceding special rules. *Lex posterior generalis non derogat priori speciali.*[64]

[62] On the effects of war on treaties see Anzilotti, *Corso di diritto internazionale*, 3d ed., pp. 400 ff.; Ghiron, "Gli effetti della guerra odierna sulla convenzioni per la tutela dei diritti industriali," 10 Riv. dir. int. (1916) 355 ff., and (1917) 53 ff.

[63] On the mandatory and permissive rules of international law see Morelli, *Norme dispositive di diritto internazionale.*

[64] Anzilotti, *Corso di diritto internazionale*, 3d ed., pp. 94 ff. For instance, the procedures for the amiable settlement of international disputes established by the Covenant of the League of Nations do not supersede the special agreements for the same purpose already in existence between members of the League.

Interpretation.—Since international rules can only be created through agreements and their interpretation is binding upon all the contracting parties only if it is established through their agreement, formal agreements concerning the interpretation of pre-existing international rules are sometimes concluded by the states.

By common consent of the parties to an agreement its interpretation may be submitted to the decision of a third state or of a judicial body (judicial interpretation). Their judgment is binding on the parties only because they consented to it. Jurisdiction of international tribunals is voluntarily accepted by the states.

There are no rules governing the process of interpretation. It is therefore merely a rational process, governed by rules of logic and by the extremely general criteria which may be derived by the nature and characteristics of the international order. Recourse to the technical rules of the doctrine and domestic legislation on the subject can only be made to the extent to which they are rules of logic and good sense.[65] Special principles and rules of interpretation can be established between two or more states by their particular agreement.

Application.—According to Anzilotti, through the correct interpretation of international rules the conclusion may be reached that a given case does not fall under any of them. The existence of gaps (*lacunae*) in the international order must be recognized. However, it is always possible for a judge to decide a dispute among states. In fact, whenever it cannot be proved that there exists a rule supporting the plaintiff's demand, the court must decide in favor of the defendant. This is consistent with the spirit of the international order. Every state is free in its international relations. It may limit its freedom by international agreements, whereby it consents to refrain from certain activities. Apart from the obligation which it has accepted, the state is free, and any attempt to further limit its freedom should be rejected.[66]

Since the international order is self-sufficient, notwithstanding the existence of gaps,[67] there is no need for the creation of rules through processes other than the agreements. Recourse to analogy is therefore not

[65] *Ibid.*, pp. 101 ff., Anzilotti remarks that difficulties in matters of interpretation often arise from the fact that members of arbitral tribunals are inclined to apply to international rules, the rules of construction and of evidence adopted by their national systems of law. An English judge will have the tendency to disregard preparatory work, while French and Italian jurists will resort to it. As a judge at the Permanent Court of International Justice, Anzilotti had the opportunity of applying his principles on interpretation to actual cases. See Hyde, "Judge Anzilotti and the Interpretation of Treaties," 27 Am. J. Int. L. (1933) 502 ff.

[66] Anzilotti, *Corso di diritto internazionale*, 3d ed.; Cavaglieri, "Lo stato di necessità nel diritto internazionale," 60 *Rivista italiana per le scienze giuridiche* (1917) 367 ff.; Morelli, *La sentenza internazionale*, pp. 254 ff. The existence of gaps in the international order is denied by Donati, *Stato e territorio*, p. 4n.

[67] Lauterpacht, *Private Law Sources and International Law*, p. 7. "The chief postulate of the positivist school can be expressed in one word: self-sufficiency. It rejects the taking over of rules and precepts from sources other than international custom or treaty."

permitted in international law. Analogy (*analogia legis*) is the process through which rules governing situations not expressly contemplated by the law are derived by way of generalization from rules governing similar situations. It consists in a process through which new rules are created by reference to pre-existing rules. In order to admit recourse to analogy, the existence of a rule of international law which recognizes analogy as a source of international rules should be proved. This is not possible. On the contrary, the very nature of international law is against the extension of the obligations of states beyond the particular cases with regard to which they have been expressly undertaken.[68]

Most subjects of international law are states. Each of them has its own legislative, judicial, and administrative organization. Hence the problem of the relationship between international law and the national law of the various states. Through Donati [69] and Anzilotti [70] the Italian school accepted and developed the dualist theory expounded by Triepel in his fundamental work, *Völkerrecht und Landsrecht* (1899). International order and national orders are absolutely separate.[71] The same clear-cut distinction which separates the legal systems of two different states [72] separates international from national law. The distinction between international law and national law is apparent in (1) the sources; (2) the subjects; and (3) the scope of their rules.

1. The sources of international law can only create international law; the sources of national law (statutes, and so forth) can only create national law. Hence, a rule of international law created by the agreement of two or more states can never be in itself, in a technical sense, part of the law of the land; even more important, the sources of national law, such as a statute or a judgment of a national court, can never give rise to rules of international law. A law or a judgment, however, can constitute an authoritative indication of what are in the opinion of the states from which they proceed the existing rules of international law. In fact, statutes and judgments are acts of the state, and until there is proof to the contrary it is to be assumed that every state is acting in accordance with, not in such a way as to violate, its international obligations.

2. International law and national law are separate with regard to

[68] Anzilotti, *Corso di diritto internazionale*, 3d ed., p. 105.

[69] *I trattati internazionali nel diritto costituzionale*.

[70] *Il diritto internazionale nei giudizii interni* and *Corso di diritto internazionale*, 3d ed.

[71] For a vigorous and in our opinion final criticism of the monist theory based on the primacy of international law see Perassi, *Lezioni di diritto internazionale*, 1937, II, 23.

[72] The separation which exists between international law and national law exists also between international law and the legal orders which exist within international persons other than states. Scerni, *Saggio sulla natura giuridica delle norme emanate da organi creati con atti internazionali*; Monaco, "I regolamenti interni degli enti internazionali," 1 Jus gentium (1938) 52 ff., and for a special instance, Sereni, "Problemi nuovi del diritto internazionale delle minoranze," 23 Riv. dir. int. (1931) 216 ff. On the Italian doctrine concerning the relationship between legal orders see Pilotti, "Plurality and Unity of Juridical Orders," 19 Iowa Law Review (1934) 244 ff.

the subjects which are the addressees of their rules. In the relations between subjects of the international community, international law only
can be applied; for example, a military alliance between two states can
only be governed by international law. On the other hand, in the relations
between entities which are not all subjects of international law, this law
can never apply. The rules concerning a dispute between a state and an
individual subject of another state can never be rules of international law,
because an individual is not a subject of international law. The distinction between the two classes of relations and rules is not always easily
ascertainable, because the same entity may sometimes act as a subject of
international law and in other cases act as a subject of national law. A
loan from state A to state B can be granted through an international agreement, and such a loan would be governed by international law; it can also
happen that in concluding the loan the two states are not acting in their
capacity of subjects of international law, but as two subjects under the
national law of one of them or even of a third state, C. In this case the loan
shall be governed by the law of A, of B, or of C. In what capacity a state
has acted can be determined with reference to its intention. If it has acted
on a basis of legal equality with the other states and without considering
itself submitted to any superior power, it has acted under international
law; otherwise it has acted under the law of the state to whose jurisdiction
it wants to submit itself.

3. International law and national law differ also with regard to the
field in which they have validity and authority. In the international community, international law is the only one applied. International tribunals
apply only international law in deciding the cases submitted to them.
Another consequence of this principle is that a state can never justify the
breach of a rule of international law on the ground that its national legislation does not enable it to perform that international obligation. On the
other hand, within a state the only law to be applied by its own national
tribunals (including the prize courts) [73] is its municipal law,[74] even if
the application would produce a violation of the international obligations
of the state. If the laws of a state do not exempt foreign diplomats from
jurisdiction, its national courts will have to entertain jurisdiction in a
lawsuit against a foreign diplomatic agent, although this would consti-

[73] According to the positivist school, prize courts are organs of the state by which they are
created. They apply its national law. This, however, is generally consistent with the international
law concerning the matters decided. On the project of an international prize court see
Cavaglieri, "La natura giuridica della Corte internazionale delle prede," 7 Riv. dir. int. (1913)
121 ff.

[74] Anzilotti explains that national courts apply their own national law even when they affirm
that their decisions are based on international law. The so-called reception of international
law within the domestic system of law of the state consists in reality of the creation of rules of
domestic law which are consistent with the international obligations of the state. *Corso di
diritto internazionale*, 3d ed., p. 58.

tute a breach of international law, giving rise to an international responsibility on the part of the state. The diplomatic agent cannot claim exemption from the jurisdiction of the national court on the grounds that the law denying it is in opposition to the international obligations of the state, because this would not invalidate the authority of the law within the jurisdiction of the state which enacted it. Nor could the diplomatic agent claim an individual right to immunity, because such right is denied to him by the law of the state, which is the only one applicable. But the state which accredited the diplomatic agent has an international right of its own toward the other state, whereby the latter must grant the agent exemption from jurisdiction. The denial of it would constitute an international wrong toward the state represented by the agent. In this case the state would be entitled to redress.

International law is not superior to national law and vice versa. The two systems function in different spheres. Strictly speaking, conflicts between their rules are not possible, since they originate from different sources and apply to different subjects for different matters. But the two systems are not mutually indifferent. For international law presupposes the existence of the national law. One of the requirements upon which depends the quality of subject of international law is for a state to be endowed with a legal organization of its own.[75] Moreover, the obligations imposed by international law upon the states constitute a limit to its internal activities including legislation. There might be legislative acts prohibited by international law. The treaty for the protection of minorities between the principal Allied Powers and Poland of June 28, 1919, prohibited the enactment by the latter of laws discriminating against minorities of race, language, and religion.[76] International law may in the same way impose upon a state the obligation to enact certain laws. There might be therefore legislative acts prescribed by international law. The largest portion of the legislation of a state is, however, internationally irrelevant. But "like every other activity of the state, it is protected by international law. The latter prohibits states which have no special title to it from limiting its free exercise." [77]

This classification of the domestic activities of a state is only of importance from the point of view of international law. Within the sphere of domestic jurisdiction of the state the rules of its national law must always be applied, even if contrary to international law. In general, how-

---

[75] Perassi, *Lezioni di diritto internazionale*, 1937, I, 26.

[76] Anzilotti, *Corso di diritto internazionale*, 3d ed., p. 56.

[77] Anzilotti, in *ibid.*, pp. 54–55. He also remarks that "since international rules constitute a limit to the activity of the state as a whole, and therefore also of the state as a legislator, its legislative activity is taken into consideration by international law, not as such, but as a behavior of the state which is internationally relevant. See the decision of the Perm. Ct. Int. Jus., A. 7, p. 19. See also Monaco, *L'ordinamento internazionale in rapporto all'ordinamento statuale.*

ever, each state takes the necessary steps to insure that its legislation shall not be in conflict with its international duties.

The nature of private international law must also be determined by the preceding criteria.[78] In almost all the European countries private international law comprises the body of rules and provisions governing matters which are somehow connected with foreign law: for example, treatment of foreigners and conflict of laws. The source of the rules of private international law is to be found in acts of domestic legislation of the states. For this reason each state has its own system of private international law. Nevertheless, at the beginning of the present century the opinion was still widespread in Europe that private international law, although enacted by each state within its own jurisdiction, was to some extent international law. This concept was a residue of the situation which existed in Europe centuries ago. At that time there was not a clear distinction between international law and national law. A considerable body of rules of international law governing the status of persons and the conflict of laws were in existence. Since the legislation of the various states conformed with them, it was believed that the international rules would apply directly to the individuals.[79] The disappearance of the common law of the empire, the loss of influence of natural law, and the increasing individualism of the states brought about the almost complete disappearance of these international rules. Each state became almost entirely independent in regulating the aforementioned matters. Moreover, the separation between international law and national law became more apparent. There should be no doubt now that private international law is exclusively a part of national law.[80] It should not be overlooked, however, that some matters regulated by private international law are also the object of rules of international law. International law, for instance,

[78] The most extensive Italian work on the general theory of private international law is Ago, *Teoria del diritto internazionale privato.* Exhaustive biographical information on the Italian works on private international law can be found in it. Of the same author see also "Règles générales des conflits des lois," 58 Rec. des cours (1937) 243 ff.

[79] See *supra,* p. 14 ff. As a result of this conception international law is often called in Italy "public international law," and conflict of laws, "private international law." For the same reason the two subjects are taught in Italian law schools by the same instructor and in the same course.

[80] For important remarks on this matter see Perassi, *Lezioni di diritto internazionale,* II, 1937, 45 ff. He explains that the rules of private international law are neither international nor private law. Since they are part of the domestic law, they are not international law; since they designate the substantive law applicable to a given relationship, they are rules concerning the sources of the law and they belong to public law. The Permanent Court of International Justice held that international private law is a part of domestic law. Judg. no. 14, July 12, 1929 (*Case of the Serbian loans*) p. 41: "The rules thereof may be common to several states and may even be established by international conventions or customs and in the latter case may possess the character of true international law governing the relations between States. But apart from this, it has to be considered that these rules form part of municipal law."

provides that every state must grant a minimum standard of treatment to foreigners. Besides, an ever-increasing number of international agreements is concluded, which provide for the enactment by the contracting parties of special legislation on matters concerning private international law. But the two classes of rules are distinct. The international rules concerning questions of private international law create rights and obligations of the states among themselves in their capacity of subjects of international law. They may impose the duty on the state to enact certain legislation concerning private international law. They do not grant any right to individuals. The rules of private international law, on the other hand, are in force within the legal system of the state which enacted them and bind all and only the subjects of that legal system with regard to their mutual relationships. Because of the difference in scope of the two classes of rules, this situation may arise: state A may enter into a treaty with state B providing that the former shall grant to the citizens of the latter the right to own real property. If, however, state A by law denies to the foreigners the right to own real property, the citizens of B cannot claim this right, because no provision of A's national law grants them this right, and within the jurisdiction of state A, its own legislation, not international law, finds application. There is no duty of state A toward the citizens of other states to grant them the right to own real property. However, this is the duty of state A toward state B under their international agreement. In denying to B's citizens the right to own real property A violates its international obligations toward state B. The latter is entitled to redress from state A. It is apparent, therefore, that when a state exercises the right of diplomatic protection of its citizens in such cases, it is enforcing, not their right, but its own. Any indemnity which may be granted belongs to the state, not to its citizens.

To be a person in a legal order means to be the addressee of its rules, that is, an entity to which these rules grant rights or duties, powers or burdens. "Personification (*personalità*) expresses only a relationship between an entity and a given legal order. There are no persons by nature. Persons exist only within a given legal order and by virtue of it." [81] Each legal order establishes by its own rules who its "persons" are. In the rules designating the subjects of international law the peculiar structure of this system is reflected. In international law rights and duties, powers and burdens may only result from agreements between its subjects, deriving their binding force from the fundamental rule *pacta sunt servanda*. International persons (or international subjects) are, therefore, all the entities, and only those, which enter into agreements governed by that rule. This conception of a subject of international law is merely a formal one. It does not depend upon the internal structure of

[81] Anzilotti, *Corso di diritto internazionale*, 3d ed., p. 112.

the entity endowed with such quality. Besides the states, the British Dominions,[82] the Holy See, the insurgents, and some unions of states (for example, the League of Nations) are subjects of international law, inasmuch as they are addressees of its rules.

According to Anzilotti, nations, barbarian populations, colonies, individuals, and the organs of the states are not persons in international law, because they are neither parties to international agreements nor addressees of international rules. They may be, however, the *object* of international rules binding the states to grant them a certain treatment (for example, rules concerning the protection of minorities, the privileges and immunities of foreign ambassadors and heads of states, and the suppression of slave trade).[83] These rules create only rights and duties for the states which are parties to them, not for the entities protected.

Anzilotti and the positivist school only affirm that individuals are *not today* persons in international law. They do not believe, however, that it is impossible for an individual to enter into an international agreement and thus acquire international personality.

International unions are persons only if vested with international rights and duties separate from those of the states which are their members.[84] The theory that recognition may exceptionally vest entities other than states with international personality was especially developed in Italy by Cavaglieri.[85] Baldoni believes that while the states acquire international personality by reason of a fundamental rule of international law and without need for recognition, international unions are persons in international law only if recognized as such and only with regard to the subjects which recognize them.[86]

The question whether the Holy See is an international person was for obvious reasons the object of particular analysis by Italian writers. Since the creation of Vatican City a very large number of works on the subject

[82] That British Dominions are international persons is affirmed by Anzilotti, *ibid.*, pp. 197 ff.; Perassi, *Lezioni di diritto internazionale*, 1937, I, 66 ff.; Mazzoleni, *L'odierno impero britannico*; Gemma, *L'impero britannico*; and Sereni, *La rappresentanza nel diritto internazionale*.
[83] With special reference to minorities see Sereni, "Il diritto internazionale delle minoranze," 21 Riv. dir. int. (1929) 461 ff.
[84] Anzilotti, *Corso di diritto internazionale*, 3d ed., pp. 140 ff.; Ottolenghi, "Sulla personalità internazionale delle unioni di stati," 17 Riv. dir. int. (1925) 313 ff.; Rapisardi Mirabelli, "Théorie générale des unions internationales," 7 Rec. des cours (1925) 347 ff., and *Gli stadii dell'organizzazione internazionale*; Pilotti, "Les Unions d'Etats," 24 Rec. des cours (1928) 447 ff.; Baldoni, "Le unioni di stati," N. S. 6 Rivista italiana per le scienze giuridiche (1931) 475 ff.; and "Gli organi e gli istituti nelle unioni internazionali," 23 Riv. dir. int. (1931) 352 ff. On the League of Nations see Breschi, *La Società delle Nazioni*; Del Vecchio, "La Société des Nations au point de vue de la philosophie du droit international," 38 Rec. des cours (1931) 545 ff.; Baldoni, *La Società delle Nazioni*. On the Pan-American Union see Cereti, *Panamericanismo e diritto internazionale*. On European regional ententes see Sereni, "Piccola Intesa, Intesa balcanica e Unione baltica," 28 Riv. dir. int. (1936) 172 ff.
[85] Cavaglieri, "I soggetti del diritto internazionale," 17 Riv. dir. int. (1925) 18 ff.
[86] Baldoni, *La Società delle Nazioni*.

has been published in Italy. The prevalent opinion is that the Holy See and the Vatican state are both international persons.[87]

Anzilotti objects to the current opinion that states are the only subjects of international law. This principle was expounded by the early positivist doctrine in order to oppose the influence of natural law according to which some international rights belonged to entities such as individuals, nationalities, and so forth. But the principle is wrong if it is meant to affirm that only states can be subjects of international law. Moreover, the concept of the state in international law is not necessarily equivalent to that accepted in other branches of the law (for example, public law).

The expression "states" may be used in international law. It certainly has some advantages, among others, that of simplicity. It should be clear, however, that the word "state" does not mean the same in international law as it does in sociology, history, and domestic public law. "State" in international law means addressee of its rules, subject of the legal order, whether or not this concept coincides with that of other disciplines.[88]

A state of the United States or one of the states composing Brazil is not a subject of international law, because it is not the addressee of international rules, although it might be defined a "state" under the constitutional law of those countries. A British Dominion is a state, or at least a subject of international law, because it is the addressee of international rules, although it is not a state in the constitutional law of the British Commonwealth.

International law determines the moment at which a state becomes its subject. To be a subject of international law means to be the addressee of the rules of international law. An entity becomes therefore an international subject the moment it becomes an addressee of international rules. All international rules are created by agreement. An entity becomes an international subject when it first becomes a party to an international agreement.

Against the prevailing opinion and consistent with his contractual theory, Anzilotti thinks that the recognition is a bilateral transaction, an agreement between the new and the recognizing state, whereby they consent to treat each other as subjects of international law. Recognition is the act creating international personality.[89] It is a voluntary act, since it is left to the discretion of the parties to it.

[87] See Anzilotti, *Corso di diritto internazionale*, 3d ed., pp. 127 ff.; Perassi, *Lezioni di diritto internazionale*, 1937, I, 66 ff.; Romano, *Corso di diritto internazionale*, 4th ed., pp. 65 ff.; D. Donati, *La Città del Vaticano nella teoria generale dello stato*; and D'Avack, *Chiesa, Santa Sede e Città del Vaticano*, where additional bibliographic information may be found. On ecclesiastic international law see Balladore Pallieri, *Diritto internazionale ecclesiastico*; and Jemolo, "Norme di diritto ecclesiastico nei cinque trattati di pace," 13 *Rivista di diritto pubblico* (1921) 65 ff.

[88] Anzilotti, *Corso di diritto internazionale*, 3d ed., p. 115.   [89] *Ibid.*, p. 146.

Each subject of international law is bound only by the rules which it consented to respect and only toward those states to whom the promise was made. Therefore the new state would not be bound to respect the general rules of international law, but usually the new state and the recognizing state reciprocally assume this obligation by the agreement of recognition. General international law is therefore binding on the new state only because of its consent and within the limits of it.

Anzilotti thinks that the correctness of his theory is proved by the international practice according to which (a) recognition depends entirely upon the will of the states, the new state having no right to be recognized, and the other states no obligation to recognize it; and (b) there are no legal relations with an unrecognized state.

Anzilotti does not deny that the contrary opinion, whereby personification of a new state would be derived from the very fact of its material existence, still prevails. Recognition would be a unilateral act on the part of the former state, ascertaining not creating, the quality of an international subject in the new state. This theory, Anzilotti observes, is based on the natural-law concept that certain entities have innate rights.[90] It does not correspond, however, to international practice, according to which recognition is a matter of discretion. Moreover, Anzilotti observes, if there were an international rule providing that every state is a subject of international law by virtue of its existence, this rule should indicate what requisites qualify an entity as a state. On the contrary, there is no definition of "state" on the part of international law.

Anzilotti's conception of recognition leads to the following conclusions,

1. The act of recognition produces legal consequences only between the recognizing and the recognized states. The new state then acquires the status of an international subject, which is the legal consequence of recognition, only with respect to the recognizing state, not *erga omnes*. A state may acquire the status of an international subject at different times

---

[90] A follower of Anzilotti's theory of recognition is Gemma, *Appunti di diritto internazionale pubblico*, pp. 57 ff. Anzilotti, in "Trattati generali di diritto internazionale," 1 Riv. dir. int. (1906) 34 ff., affirms (3 Riv. dir. int. 1908, p. 167) that the theory whereby a state would be an international person by reason of its inherent qualities is the result of natural-law misconceptions. When Anzilotti advanced his theory of recognition, the existence of a customary rule granting to each state international personality merely because of its existence had been expounded in Italy by Diena in *Principii di diritto internazionale pubblico e privato*. See also Diena, *Il riconoscimento e i diritti fondamentali degli stati*, and "Ancora qualche osservazione in tema di riconoscimento di stati," 24 Riv. dir. int. (1932) 405 ff.

On recognition see also Miceli, "Il problema del riconoscimento in diritto internazionale," 19 Riv. dir. int. (1927) 169 ff.; Fedozzi, *Trattato di diritto internazionale; introduzione e parte generale*, pp. 90 ff.; Ottolenghi, "Il principio del'effettività e la sua funzione nell'ordinamento internazionale," 28 Riv. dir. int. (1938) 3 ff. On international problems arising from the formation of new states see Biscaretti di Ruffia, *Contributo alla teoria giuridica della formazione degli stati*, and Biscottini, "Sulla formazione dello stato," 31 Riv. dir. int. (1939) 378 ff.

with regard to the various states, and sometimes it may be a subject with relation to some states and not to others.

2. Recognition is not conditioned by the process through which the new state came into existence. It does not depend upon its legality. There are not legal and illegal states. The legality of a state is in its very existence.[91]

3. Recognition is not subject to any special form. It might be express or tacit, individual or collective. The distinction between *de facto* and *de jure* recognition has a political rather than a legal connotation. The question is only whether a recognition agreement has been entered into; if so, it does not matter whether more or less solemn relations follow.

4. Recognition carries whatever obligations the parties to it may agree upon. Poland's recognition in 1919 was subject to the acceptance on her part of some obligations concerning her minorities.[92]

5. Recognition, being an agreement, cannot be revoked unilaterally by the recognizing state.

6. The unrecognized state, not being a subject, has no international rights or obligations. Other states are not bound to grant it the treatment due to international subjects.[93]

7. Recognition of a new state creates its personality and therefore differs entirely from the recognition of a new government. Personality of a state and its international rights and duties continue even in the case of changes in its constitution. Recognition of a new government is only intended to ascertain for international purposes who has the power to act for the state in its external relations. If a change has actually taken place and the new regime appears to be stabilized, the other states cannot refuse it recognition.[94]

The natural-law doctrine of international law affirms the existence of

[91] Anzilotti, *Corso di diritto internazionale*, 3d ed., p. 154, "Considerations of the timeliness of recognition, developed with particular care by English and Anglo-American writers, seem to be political rather than legal." By special agreements states may bind themselves to recognize or not to recognize certain entities as states.

[92] This, however, was not a condition proper whose breach would have determined the revocation of Poland's recognition. See Sereni, "Il diritto internazionale delle minoranze," 21 Riv. dir. int. (1929) 464.

[93] Cavaglieri, "La situazione giuridica dello stato non riconosciuto," 24 Riv. dir. int. (1932) 305 ff.

[94] Anzilotti, *Corso di diritto internazionale*, 3d ed., p. 164, remarks that "a refusal [of recognition of a new government] based upon the alleged unlawfulness of the change would imply a judgment that no state is allowed to pass. It would constitute an illegitimate intervention in the internal affairs of a state. Every state, however, is free to evaluate the effectiveness and stability of the change, and it can be easily understood that there are ample possibilities here for political considerations which may induce a state to favor or to oppose the new order of things." Obviously recognition may be denied if the new government acts in violation of international law and particularly if it disregards the obligations assumed by the preceding government. On *de facto* governments see Gemma, "Les Gouvernements de fait," 4 Rec. des cours (1924) 297 ff.

some fundamental rights of the states. They arise from nature and correspond to the innate rights of the individuals. Much attention is devoted to these rights even in recent treatises. Authors, however, disagree as to their number and classification. The positivist school denies the existence of fundamental rights of states. The belief in their existence is based on the erroneous assumption that each activity of the state is the object of a distinct right toward the other members of the international community (a right to conclude treaties, to wage war, and so forth). This is not true. The state has no special right to conclude treaties, to participate in international relations, to wage war, to act in self-defense, or to choose its own constitutional regime. What international law grants in principle to each state is absolute freedom of action. It is inherent in its legal personality. This freedom is limited only by international agreements with other states, whereby the state consents to refrain from certain activities and only within the limit of the agreements. The inherent error of the theory of fundamental rights is proved by the lack of any consent of international lawyers as to what these rights are.[95]

The "international community," as conceived by the positivist school, is an organization of equal entities, whose mutual duties are confined exclusively to the obligations which they have voluntarily assumed.[96] Its peculiar characteristic, in contrast to national communities, is the greater individualism and the broader autonomy of its members. What is not expressly forbidden is permitted. Since no state can limit the autonomy of the other without special title, intervention in the internal affairs of another state, as a rule, is not permitted. Intervention is only lawful when based upon a special title established with the consent of the state against which it is exercised, or when it is intended to obtain reparation for a tort committed against the intervening state.[97] Self-preservation does not justify intervention.[98]

The concept of "state sovereignty" has no place in the positivist conception. The word "sovereignty" cannot be found in the works of major

[95] Anzilotti, "Trattati generali di diritto internazionale," 1 Riv. dir. int. (1906) 178 ff. Anzilotti's conclusions are accepted and developed by Cavaglieri in *I diritti fondamentali degli stati nella società internazionale.*

[96] Since the international activity of the states is limited only by the obligations that they assume, there is no place in international law for the concept of abuse of right. Scerni, *L'abuso di diritto nei rapporti internazionali.*

[97] This conclusion is reached by Cavaglieri, *Nuovi studii sull'intervento.* In his earlier work, *L'intervento nella sua definizione giuridica,* he held that a collective intervention was admissible for the protection of not only rights but also mere interests of the intervening powers. On intervention see also Ghirardini, "A proposito d'intervento," 7 Riv. dir. int. (1913) 89 ff., and Cereti, *La tutela giuridica degli interessi internazionali.*

[98] This is the opinion of Borsi, "Ragione di guerra e stato di necessità," 10 Riv. dir. int. (1916) 175 ff., and of Cavaglieri, "Lo stato di necessità nel diritto internazionale," 60 Rivista italiana per le scienze giuridiche (1917) 367 ff.

Italian positivists. For them international law establishes only rights and duties among subjects. Among the duties is that of each state to respect the acts which other states perform within their internal legal order. In the absence of special provisions to the contrary, international law does not impose any limitation upon the powers of the state over its subjects and territory,[99] but by special agreement states may assume any duty concerning their activity. They may limit their powers over their subjects or territory; a state may even consent to the termination of its own existence.[100] Positivists point out that "sovereignty" is a misleading and unnecessary expression. Sometimes it is used to signify international personality. At other times international subjects are qualified as sovereigns in order to indicate that they are equal. Equality among its subjects is one of the essentials of the international order. However, as Cavaglieri observes, "the rule establishing legal equality of states, means only that one of them cannot claim from the others any concession or any restriction in their activities which does not have its formal base in their free will, consecrated by international agreement." [101]

Legal equality does not imply political equality. The relationship between a strong and a weak state is similar to that between a rich and a poor man within the state. Although they enjoy the same civil rights, they are in a position of actual inequality in bargaining.

International persons cannot be affected by legal disabilities in a technical sense. In the systems of domestic law, where all the rights are granted by the state, a superior power, there are some general rules denying certain rights or the possibility of exercising them to some classes of persons (for instance, lunatics, infants, and foreigners). In international law all subjects are legally equal. Personality and legal capacity are identified. Since international law relies only on the will of its subjects, there are no general rules prohibiting the enjoyment of certain rights to some of them. The alleged disabilities of some states are only limitations of their freedom of action (for example, the neutralized state is bound not to wage

[99] Rules limiting the normal powers of the state over its subjects and territory are for instance the rules of the treaties for the protection of minorities which bind the states to grant a certain treatment to some of their own subjects and the rules which prohibit the state from exercising jurisdiction on foreign legations. Extraterritoriality does not mean that a portion of the territory of the state is not part of it, only that the state must refrain from certain activities in it. On the relationship between the state and its subjects from the view point of international law see Quadri, *La sudditanza nel diritto internazionale.* On the relationship between the state and its territory see D. Donati, *Stato e territorio.*
[100] Cavaglieri, "Concetto e caratteri del diritto internazionale generale," 14 Riv. dir. int. (1922) 502. "One of the peculiarities of the legal society of states is that it accepts to its fullest extent the principle that any right may be waived by the state. A state may even lawfully consent to the termination of its own existence." This happened to the Free State of Congo. Anzilotti, "L'annessione del Congo," 4 Riv. dir. int. (1909) 237 ff.
[101] Cavaglieri, *Corso di diritto internazionale,* p. 7.

offensive warfare).[102] But these disabilities are established with the consent of the state affected by them and are therefore far from being disabilities in a technical sense; they are manifestations of the capacity of these subjects to assume international obligations. The practical consequence of the distinction is that acts performed in violation of these obligations are unlawful, but not necessarily void. The neutralized state, which is bound not to wage offensive wars, and the protected state, which is bound not to directly take part in diplomatic intercourse, are usually considered instances of states affected by legal disabilities. Anzilotti points out that no state can be neutralized or protected without its express or implied consent. The particular status of these states arises, therefore, from obligations freely assumed. Moreover, a neutralized state which wages an offensive war performs a wrongful act, since it violates its obligation to remain neutral. But this act, however, is not void; it gives rise to a relationship which international law qualifies as a real war. Nor is a protected state unable to enter into direct diplomatic relations with a third state, but in so doing it would violate its duty toward the protecting state.

The problem of state succession is solved negatively by Cavaglieri, who devoted more attention to it [103] than any other positivist. This author observes that much confusion exists on the matter, because not enough attention has been paid to the fact that the expression "state succession" applies to various problems which arise in different legal orders.

A distinction must be made, first of all, between partial succession and total succession. The former takes place when only a part of the territory or population of a state is annexed by one or more states or when it becomes independent; the latter, when a state is extinguished and all its territory and population become part of one or more other states. A distinction must also be made between legal problems to which state succession gives rise. In case of total succession legal problems arise in the international order and in the national order of the successor state or states. In cases of partial succession legal problems arise also in the legal order of the reduced state.

International agreements governing succession are usually concluded between old and new sovereigns in case of partial succession. In cases of

---

[102] Perassi, *Lezioni di diritto internazionale* (1937) I, 76, 83; Anzilotti, *Corso di diritto internazionale*, 3d ed., pp. 186 ff., 242 ff., and especially Sereni, *La rappresentanza nel diritto internazionale*, pp. 27 ff. International persons may be affected by legal disabilities according to D. Donati, *I trattati internazionali nel diritto costituzionale*, pp. 4 ff.

[103] *Lezioni di diritto internazionale*, pp. 243 ff.; same author, *La dottrina della successione di stati e il suo valore giuridico*, and "Note in materia di successione da stato a stato," 16 Riv. dir. int. (1924) 26 ff. On this matter see also Anzilotti, *Corso di diritto internazionale*, 1914, I, 278 ff.; Udina, "La Succession des états quant aux obligations internationales, autres que les dettes publiques," 44 Rec. des cours (1933) 665 ff.; Biscottini, "L'annessione e la fusione di stati e i loro riflessi sul fenomeno successorio," 32 Riv. dir. int. (1940) 133 ff.

total succession the processes (for example, *debellatio*) which give rise to it usually prevent the conclusion of such agreements. Reference must then be made to the general rules of international law. Cavaglieri is mainly interested in the problems arising from total succession in international law. The more important is whether by reason of the succession the new state is bound to take over all or part of the obligations of the old state.

International obligations, Cavaglieri observes, are generally connected with the particular status of the state assuming them. Because of their personal character they terminate if the obliged state comes to an end. Even so-called "international servitudes" (for example, obligation not to fortify a certain territory) are usually entered into in contemplation of the particular situation of the obliged state. Thus they are extinguished when the sovereignty of the territory to which they refer is changed. They continue to exist only if it was expressly so agreed when they were established.[104] To the general principle that the new state does not assume the obligations of the old state there is only one exception. By general custom the new state is bound toward the other states to take over the financial obligations toward foreigners contracted by the old state within its domestic order.[105]

The problem of state responsibility for international delinquencies has been thoroughly considered by the positivist doctrine.[106] International responsibility can only arise from a wrongful international act, that is, from the violation of an obligation imposed on a state by international law. Since an international obligation consists of the duty in one state to maintain a certain conduct toward another subject, a wrongful act consists of conduct other than that which should be followed. The elements of a wrongful act are three: (1) that the performance of the act is imputable to a state; (2) that the act is contrary to an obligation of a state; (3) that both the author and the victim of the wrongful act are subjects of international law.

1. A state, being an abstract entity, is not capable of personal activity. Acts of the state are in reality acts of individuals which interna-

[104] *Lezioni di diritto internazionale*, p. 250. Cavaglieri here assumes that an agreement concluded between two states may bind a third state which was not a party to it, although this result is inadmissible according to the positivist conception. On international servitudes see Anzilotti, "La formazione del Regno d'Italia nei riguardi del diritto internazionale," 6 Riv. dir. int. (1912) 1 ff., and Mazzoleni, "Servitù internazionali," *Nuovo digesto italiano*, XII, 209 ff.

[105] The new state is not internationally bound to respect the obligations that the old state assumed toward its own subjects because there is no international person toward which such obligation exists.

[106] On this problem see Anzilotti, *Teoria generale della responsabilità dello stato nel diritto internazionale*, and "L'azione individuale contraria al diritto internazionale," 5 Rivista di diritto internazionale e legislazione comparata (1902) 8 ff., and *Corso di diritto internazionale*, 3d ed., pp. 416 ff.; Marinoni, *La responsabilità degli stati per gli atti dei loro rappresentanti*.

tional law imputes to the former. The problem, then, consists in establishing which acts of individuals constitute an international activity of the state. A well-established rule of international law attributes to the state the acts of its organs and agencies. A state is responsible for an act of its organ even when the latter acted beyond its powers and even when in so acting it violated the duties of its office. On the other hand, acts of an individual person who is not an organ of the state cannot be imputed to the state. If a private citizen of state A throws a bomb at the head of state B, who is visiting state A, the act of the citizen can never be considered an act of state A. Responsibility of a state can only arise from an act or omission which is imputable to it. In the example given, the responsibility of state A does not arise from the act of its citizen. It may arise from the fact that the state did not take the necessary measures to protect the visitor from state B. State responsibility would be due in this case to its failure to exercise due care, that is, from an omission.[107] Liability may arise in other instances from the commission by the state of an act contrary to international obligations. Practice of the states proves that a vicarious responsibility of a state for the wrongful act of another cannot exist in international law. Each state is responsible only for its own tort.[108]

2. Violations of international duty on the part of a state may consist of the commission of an act (for example, unjustified arrest of a foreign subject) or of an omission (for example, denial of justice). International liability arises from the mere fact that there has been a violation of a duty. Whether or not the violation was willfully committed is immaterial. Anzilotti stresses the point that it is not fault (*culpa*), but a fact contrary to international law which creates responsibility. To create international liability, lack of diligence or malicious intent are not essential. This is a consequence of the peculiar structure of international law. Since international obligations are based only upon the will of the state, the mere breach of the obligation makes a state responsible, irrespective of its state of mind. Besides, the ordinary conception of fault could hardly apply to acts of state organs.

3. An international tort arises from the violation of an international rule. It presupposes the quality of addressee of international rules: that is, international personality, both in the delinquent and in the victim. An individual cannot commit an international wrong—but only the international person to which the individual act can be imputed.[109] If X, official

107 On the denial of justice see Ago, "La regola del previo esaurimento dei ricorsi interni in tema di responsabilità internazionale," 3 Archivio di diritto pubblico (1938) 180 ff.
108 For a demonstration of this point see Ago, "La responsabilità indiretta nel diritto internazionale," 1 Archivio di diritto pubblico (1936) 12 ff.; Sereni, *La rappresentanza nel diritto internazionale*, pp. 417 ff., and "Agency in international law," 34 Am. J. Int. L. (1940) 683 ff.
109 Anzilotti, "L'azione individuale contraria al diritto internazionale," 5 Rivista di diritto

of state A, searches the legation of state B, thus violating the right of state B to exemption from jurisdiction, X incurs no international liability, but state A does. As already mentioned, the state is responsible for unauthorized acts of its officials which are contrary to international law.[110] International liability cannot exist toward an entity which is not an international person. If state A condemns without compensation the property of a subject of state B, the former has no international responsibility toward the individual offended but only toward state B. The international right violated is that of state B to indemnification of its citizens when their property has been condemned.

General rules establishing what redress may be claimed by the state offended do not exist. Usually international practice derives two possible consequences from a fact contrary to international law: (a) the duty to grant satisfaction (for example, an apology); and (b) the duty to grant redress. This may consist either in *restitutio in pristinum*, when possible, or in compensation for damages.

These two forms of redress may be granted separately or together. In international relations matters of prestige play a much greater role than among individuals. Redress is therefore claimed even where economic damage is negligible or nonexistent (for example, offenses to the flag). For the same reason, forms of redress have often a merely symbolic character (for example, apologies and salute to the flag).

Procedures for the amicable settlement of international disputes and arbitration especially have been carefully examined by the Italian positivists.[111] Two reasons prompt their interest in this institution: first, that arbitration is a field in which international law has greatly progressed in the last years and in which Italy has been more actively interested, and second, that it is one of the most characteristic institutions of international law. Its existence and peculiarities are closely connected with the particular structure of the international order.

---

internazionale e legislazione comparata (1902) 8 ff.; Monaco, "La responsabilità indiretta dello stato per fatti degli individui," 31 Riv. dir. int. (1939) 3 ff.

[110] Since the international and the domestic order are separate, the act of the functionary giving rise to the international responsibility of the state may be lawful under the domestic law. Moreover, a state may be internationally liable for an act of its officer even when it has no power according to its own domestic law to prevent the act of the functionary from which the international responsibility arises. As will appear later, this situation arose in Italy when Italian courts refused to recognize the immunity from civil jurisdiction to foreign diplomatic agents. Foreign governments took the position that the Italian government was guilty of a violation of international law, although it had no power to limit the discretion of the courts in deciding the issue.

[111] Anzilotti, *Corso di diritto internazionale*, III, 39–131; Cavaglieri, *Lezioni di diritto internazionale*, pp. 560 ff.; Perassi, *Lezioni di diritto internazionale*, 1937, I, 13 ff.; Morelli, *La sentenza internazionale*, and "La Théorie générale du procès international," 61 Rec. des cours (1937) 253 ff.; Bosco, *Rapporti e conflitti tra giurisdizioni internazionali*. For a comprehensive analysis of the problems connected with arbitration and for further bibliographic references see Sereni, "Arbitrato internazionale," in *Nuovo digesto italiano*, I, 637 ff.

Italian positivists point out that jurisdiction of international tribunals depends entirely upon the consent of the states and exists only within the limit of their agreement.[112] This is a consequence of the peculiar structure of the international community, which lacks a general instrumentality for the judicial settlement of disputes between its members. Consequently no state can be compelled to submit a difference to judicial settlement without its consent. Consent may be given either before a dispute arises, through compromissory clauses and treaties of arbitration, or later, through a *compromis*.

Anzilotti remarks that although it is always possible to decide an international dispute according to the law, states could hardly consent to submit all their controversies to arbitration. Experience has shown that differences submitted to arbitration are in general of minor importance and do not affect the vital interests of the parties to them. Acceptance on the part of the states of general compulsory arbitration finds an obstacle in the circumstance that many controversies do not consist of conflicts in the interpretation of the law in force; they arise from the desire of one of the parties to modify existing international law which is contrary to its interests.

Arbitration can be also resorted to in order to change existing law. Judgments *ex aequo et bono* serve this purpose. They do not ascertain law in existence, but create new provisions regulating the matter in dispute, which in the opinion of the court are more consistent with justice. Changes in international law through arbitration meet, however, with two obstacles: first, that resort to arbitration is conditioned by the consent of the parties, and it is improbable that a state in whose favor the existing law stands, will agree to a judicial change to its own detriment; and second, that in cases where vital interests of the states are at stake the parties do not dare entrust with settlement of their dispute the small group of men constituting the tribunal, no matter how able and honest they may be. In order to reach a favorable conclusion states prefer in these cases to employ all resources at their disposal, including force.

Positivist doctrine examines problems of arbitration from a strictly legal point of view. While indicating the deep structural difference between international and national arbitration, it utilizes doctrines and principles expounded by scholars of civil procedure insofar as they are compatible with international law. Apart from the infrequent cases in which a third state is appointed arbitrator, an arbitral tribunal is not an international person. According to Anzilotti international tribunals are organs common to the states which are parties to the controversy. Their acts, therefore, are imputed to the parties. According to Morelli and Perassi, they are special instrumentalities devoid of legal personality

[112] Perassi, *Lezioni di diritto internazionale*, 1937, I, 13.

existing in the international community, and their acts cannot be imputed to the parties to the dispute. Since an international tribunal is not a person, its decisions are not international acts, but mere facts. They are binding upon the parties to the controversy because this was consented to in the agreement granting jurisdiction to the court. These theoretical questions, to which Italian authors have devoted much attention, are of little practical value; [113] but from the general principles on arbitration Italian positivists derive the solution of many important practical questions (that is, problems relating to evidence, jurisdiction, *res judicata*, revision of judgments). Many Italian works are devoted to the analysis of the principal arbitral conventions, of the rules governing international tribunals and their procedure, and to the relationship between arbitration and other methods for the amicable settlement of international disputes.[114]

The legal problem of war is connected with that of the structure of the international community.[115] It was always hard for students of the law of nations to reconcile the principle that international rules should be respected with the other rule, certainly existent in the international community, whereby in the absence of special obligations to the contrary a

[113] For a detailed analysis of the various Italian theories on international arbitration see Bosco, "La natura giuridica dell'arbitrato internazionale nella dottrina italiana," 23 Riv. dir. int. (1931) 490 ff.

[114] On international arbitration see, in addition to the works mentioned above, Cavaglieri, "La natura giuridica della Corte internazionale delle prede," 7 Riv. dir. int. (1913) 121 ff.; Perassi, "Il trattato di arbitrato e di conciliazione tra la Germania e la Svizzera," 14 Riv. dir. int. (1921) 155 ff.; Diena, "Le Traité de conciliation et de règlement judiciaire entre l'Italie et la Suisse," 52 Rev. dr. int. et lég. comp. (1925) 1 ff.; La Terza, "Il trattato di conciliazione e di regolamento giudiziario tra l'Italia e la Svizzera," 17 Riv. dir. int. (1925) 257 ff.; Gabriele Salvioli, "La Corte permanente di giustizia internazionale," 15 Riv. dir. int. (1924) 11 ff.; Baldoni, "La Corte permanente di giustizia internazionale e gli Stati Uniti d'America," 19 Riv. dir. int. (1927) 17 ff., and Gli Stati Uniti e la Corte di giustizia internazionale, 21 Riv. dir. int. (1929) 237 ff.; Meriggi, "Le funzioni consultive della Corte permanente di giustizia internazionale," 22 Riv. dir. int. (1930) 62 ff.; Gabriele Salvioli, "La Jurisprudence de la Cour permanente de justice internationale," 12 Rec. des cours (1926) 1 ff.; Scerni, "Cenni sul diritto processuale della Corte permanente di giustizia internazionale," 3 Riv. dir. int. (1937), and "Di una speciale figura di intervento nella procedura della Corte permanente di giustizia internazionale," in Studi in onore di Santi Romano, III, 213 ff.; Borsi "Il nuovo procedimento conciliativo nelle controversie internazionali," 16 Riv. dir. int. (1924) 1 ff., and "Le clausole eccettuative di controversie nei trattati italiani di arbitrato obbligatorio, 7 Riv. dir. int. (1913) 153 ff.; Anzilotti, "La riconvenzione nella procedura internazionale," 21 Riv. dir. int. (1929) 309 ff.; Gabriele Salvioli, "Le prove nella procedura internazionale," in Studii in onore di Santi Romano, III, 67 ff., and "Motivi di nullità delle sentenze internazionali," 29 Riv. dir. int. (1937) 305 ff.; Venturini, "Le misure cautelari nel diritto internazionale," 111 Archivio giuridico (1938) 318 ff.

[115] Anzilotti, Corso di diritto internazionale, III, 1915, 179 ff.; Perassi, Lezioni di diritto internazionale, 1937, I, 14 ff.; Gemma, Il rapporto di belligeranza studiato nei suoi caratteri differenziali; Rapisardi Mirabelli, Il significato della guerra nel diritto internazionale; Marinoni, L'efficacia del diritto internazionale; Breschi, La dottrina della guerra nel diritto internazionale; Enriques, "Considerazioni sulla teoria della guerra nel diritto internazionale," 20 Riv. dir. int. (1928) 27 ff.

state may resort to war, not only to enforce existing law, but also in order to change it to its own advantages. The phenomenon of war is especially hard to fit into the positivist conception, which bases international law only upon agreements. To overcome this difficulty Anzilotti, in the first phase of his teaching, affirmed that war is lawful because the states, in binding themselves to respect the rules created through their agreements, excepted the duty of complying with them in case they intended to wage war. After he repudiated this artificial and unconvincing theory, he was compelled to base the lawfulness of war in the international order on an alleged general agreement whereby the states recognized it as a procedure for the enforcement or change of the existing rules. These premises have been the target of great criticism. They hardly can be reconciled with the realities of international life. The positivist doctrine reaches a more convincing conclusion when it affirms that the legitimacy of recourse to war for the purpose of enforcing or changing the existing law is a consequence of the peculiar structure of international community, which lacks general organs for the fulfillment of the judicial and legislative functions. In their absence states must act personally in enforcing or changing the law. A state waging war for the protection of its rights violated by the other belligerent is performing a judicial activity. In this case war is a form of self-defense which is perfectly legitimate. Self-defense, which is the exception in national law, is the rule in international relations. A state which wages war for the purpose of bringing about a change in international rules which are contrary to its interests is performing a legislative activity. This is also a legitimate activity, since there is no other general procedure for the change of international law. However states may by special agreement limit their right to wage war. Violation of such duty on their part would be unlawful.

Several consequences are derived from these premises:

1. War is a legal phenomenon. In the early period of his teaching Anzilotti thought that war was a legal phenomenon only when waged to protect a positive right of a state, that is, when it was intended to obtain redress. A war waged for the protection of a mere interest, that is, to modify existing law, was an act beyond the law. This opinion was consistent with the early theory of Anzilotti that any act creating legal rules (whether an agreement or a war) was, not a juridical, but a prejuridical act. This concept Anzilotti later repudiated. Every war is a legal phenomenon because it is contemplated and regulated by international law. A general rule of international law considers war as a procedure either for the enforcement or the change of existing law.

2. General international law does not distinguish between lawful and unlawful wars on the ground of their motive. Old theories distinguishing between just and unjust wars on the ground of their motivating reasons

(wars of aggression, of defense) are exploded. Rules of special international law may limit or entirely suppress the right of the state to resort to war for the protection of either its rights or its interests (Kellogg-Briand pact, Covenant of the League of Nations, treaties of nonaggression and neutrality). It is with respect to these particular rules that war may be lawful or unlawful; but even though unlawful, it still remains a real war. International rules concerning warfare (treatment of civilians, prisoners, and so forth) apply to it. A state may not have the right to wage war, but it always has the power.

3. General international law grants each state the power to change the structure and the law of the international community by waging war. These changes, however, may result only from a real war, not from mere use of force. In the absence of any special obligation to the contrary, it is lawful for state A to annex part of the territory, kill the citizens, and capture the ships of state B, even when the latter has not violated any right of the former. There must be, however, a war between A and B. There is an apparent contradiction in the fact that international law tolerates such grave violations of the normal peacetime rules as any war implies, while it does not permit minor breaches of the law by a state which is not at war. The reason is that any state which resorts to war, assumes great risks, very grave burdens, and special duties toward the opponent and other states. If it decides to resort to force, it must wage a regular war with all its inherent dangers. Resort to force will then be limited to cases of extreme gravity.

4. Since war is not beyond, but within the rules of international law, it is not unrestrained violence, but a relationship which the law governs in each aspect. A state has power to give rise by its own will to a state of war. Once war exists, operation of peacetime international laws is largely suspended. Other rules are substituted for them, the so-called "international law of war." Special relationships are established between the states at war (belligerency) and between each of them and the other states (neutrality); rights and duties arise from them.

5. War is based upon the intent of the state which performs the hostilities. Mere hostile acts without intent to wage war (for example, Italian occupation of Corfu in 1923) do not give rise to a war. The attitude of the state against which war is waged is immaterial. Its refusal to fight would not prevent the existence of a state of war.

The positivist school bases on these general concepts its analysis of the various rules concerning war and neutrality.[116] The contribution of the

---

[116] On neutrality see Ottolenghi, *Il rapporto di neutralità*, and "Il diritto dei neutri secondo la 5a e la 12a Convenzione dell'Aja," 4 Riv dir. int. (1909) 205 ff.; Gemma, *Il moderno concetto di neutralità*; Cavaglieri, "Belligeranza, neutralità e situazioni giuridiche intermedie," 13 Riv. dir. int. (1919–1920) 66 ff.

Italian positivist doctrine to their study is less important than that given to international law of peace.

EVOLUTION OF THE POSITIVIST DOCTRINE

Anzilotti's effort to eradicate any influence of natural law from the doctrine of international law, had gone too far. Anzilotti based the whole body of the law of nations upon the will of the states and conceived international order as a system of promises constituted exclusively through agreements based on the rule *pacta sunt servanda*. This rule itself rested upon the consent of the states which agreed to accept it as the basis of international relations.

This doctrine was obviously untenable. If one admits that the rule *pacta sunt servanda* binds the states because they consented to it by an agreement, the existence of a previous and superior norm which would bind the states to respect their agreement establishing the rule *pacta sunt servanda* should also be admitted. One would have to continue in this way *ad infinitum*.

The conclusion is inescapable that all international law cannot be conceived as a voluntary law based only upon promises of the states, particularly the rule *pacta sunt servanda* cannot be founded upon agreement.

It is the merit of Perassi that he placed the problem of the sources of the international law on a different plane. His "dogmatic theory of the sources of legal rules in international law" (*teoria dommatica delle fonti di norme giuridiche in diritto internazionale*) [117] is to a certain extent influenced by Kelsen's ideas. Perassi points out that the legal validity of a juridical order, considered as a whole, cannot be demonstrated from the point of view of the order itself. For every legal order its juridical validity (*giuridicita'*) can only be assumed as a postulate.[118] As to single rules of every legal order, the validity of each of them is based generally upon superior norms. In national law the provisions of a contract are binding because a rule of law provides that the parties to a contract must comply with its clauses. This rule in turn, is binding because a superior rule (for example, the constitution) so provides. But in the hierarchy of the rules of every legal order there is necessarily at the top a rule or a group of rules having a binding force which does not depend upon a superior norm; for instance, in the national systems of law the binding force of the highest rule which imposes obedience to the constitution or to the orders of the head of the state or of the parliament cannot be demonstrated from the point of view of the legal order which is based upon

[117] 11 Riv. dir. int. (1917) 195 ff.
[118] Triepel had already remarked that in every legal system one always arrives at a point where a legal explanation of the binding force of a legal precept becomes impossible. The foundation of the validity of a legal system is outside that system of law.

that rule. Every legal system must be considered a pyramid which is topped by a supreme rule (*norma base* or *Grundnorm*). The binding force of all the other rules of the system depends on this supreme rule, which does not depend on any other rule. The supreme rule of the international order is the rule *pacta sunt servanda*.

Anzilotti himself has now accepted these concepts. In the most recent edition of his *Corso di diritto internazionale* (1928) he observes that the logical processes followed by every science, be it mathematics or law, always start from an initial hypothesis the validity of which cannot be demonstrated from the point of view of the science based upon it. With regard to the science which is based upon it, the initial hypothesis must be considered a postulate. The rule *pacta sunt servanda* constitutes the initial hypothesis in international law.[119]

This principle, because it is the basis of the rules of international law, cannot be demonstrated from the point of view of the rules themselves. It must be assumed to have absolute, objective value or as an original hypothesis which cannot be demonstrated. The whole body of international law is necessarily based upon it.[120]

The existence of the rule *pacta sunt servanda* can be proved by the point of view of history, politics, and sociology. In the light of these sciences it is possible to prove that the states usually respect treaties and also to determine why the rule *pacta sunt servanda* arose. "But the demonstration of these principles from the points of view of ethics, politics, is irrelevant with regard to the discipline (international law) which originates from that rule."[121]

The positive school still maintains that all international rules other than *pacta sunt servanda* are based upon the consent of the states. The principal general conclusions which Anzilotti derived from this principle are still accepted. This is also true of its conception of the relationship between international and national law.

In the evolution of the positivist doctrine the concept of recognition underwent important changes. Anzilotti has conceived recognition as an agreement between the recognizing and the recognized state in a desperate attempt to be consistent with his premise that international law is only constituted of rules arising from mutual promises between states. The premise and the conclusion stand or fall together. Once the artificial character of Anzilotti's theory of recognition has been proved, the fallacy of its premise is also demonstrated. Contrary to Anzilotti's opinion, international practice disproves his doctrine of recognition. True, states already in existence do not feel bound to recognize a new state, nor do they enter into relations with it prior to recognition. But as will be seen

---

[119] Anzilotti, *Corso di diritto internazionale*, 3d ed., p. 42.
[120] *Ibid.*, p. 43.　　　　　　　　　　　[121] *Ibid.*, p. 43.

later, it cannot be inferred therefrom either that a state is not existent before recognition or that recognition is a bilateral agreement. While in the last edition of his *Corso* (1928), Anzilotti still maintains his conception of recognition,[122] other positivists sought more convincing solutions. Cavaglieri observes that the process by which the state is materially formed precedes the law and therefore is not subject to it. Law governs only the procedure by which the new state, once formed, becomes a legal entity and acquires the quality of a subject of international law. This, according to Cavaglieri, can only be the consequence of an act of will,[123] because international law, he maintains, in agreement with Anzilotti, is exclusively a voluntary law. Recognition is the declaration of will which grants international personality to the new state. Recognition cannot be an agreement, because an agreement, being a legal act, presupposes the legal personality of the parties to it, while before the new state has been recognized it is an entity devoid of international personality and therefore does not have legal capacity to enter into an international agreement. Recognition can only be the unilateral act of the pre-existing states. Through it they grant personality to the new state. Recognition thus does not ascertain, but creates, the existence of the new state. It is a discretionary act, because there is no obligation to recognize. As to the states already in existence, their personality would have arisen through the mutual recognition which took place when the international community was first established. The effect of the recognizing a new state would consist in granting it the right to the sphere of exclusive jurisdiction which belongs to each member of the international community. Moreover, the recognized state is enabled to take part in international relations. The newly recognized state accepts the pre-existing general rule of international law, which then become binding in its relations with the recognizing states.

Perassi's conception of the recognition is more convincing and is still compatible with the positivist doctrine.[124] First of all, he repudiates the theory according to which every state is the subject of international law by the mere fact of its material existence. This theory disregards the fact that membership in a legal order can be granted only by the rules of that order. Material formation of a state is an historical-political phenomenon. Its international personality can only be the result of rules of international law. Anzilotti's theory is also refuted by Perassi on the familiar grounds that it is impossible to conceive of an agreement between a sub-

---

[122] *Ibid.*, pp. 147 ff.

[123] Cavaglieri, "La Conception positive de la société internationale," 18 Rev. gén. dr. int. publ. (1911) 251 ff., remarks "comme il n'existe au-dessus des Etats aucune autorité qui puisse leur conférer la personnalité de droit, eux mêmes par leurs rapports mutuels, se la reconnaissent réciproquement, les uns à l'égard des autres, comme doués de certaines prérogatives et comme soumis à certains devoirs."

[124] *Lezioni di diritto internazionale*, 1937, I, 32 ff.

ject and a nonsubject. Anzilotti attempted to overcome this difficulty by construing the international agreement as a prejuridical act. An entity which has not yet become a subject of international law could then become a part to an agreement. It is submitted by Perassi that an agreement is a legal phenomenon which can only take place between legal subjects, as proved by recent studies of legal theory. To conceive recognition as the act constituting the personality of a new state and at the same time as an agreement is therefore an obvious contradiction. The same criticism as that against Anzilotti applies to Cavaglieri's theory. That a state by its own declaration of will may grant international personality to a new state seems contrary to the practice of the states. Moreover, this theory is contrary to legal principles. Every legal act, even if unilateral, presupposes two subjects—the one from which it originates and the one to which it is addressed. Even if we conceive recognition as a unilateral act, we cannot maintain that the legal personality of the entity to which it is addressed is first created by it.

Perassi reaches the conclusion that recognition, be it construed as an agreement or as a unilateral act, cannot constitute the act creating a new subject of international law. The rules concerning acquisition of international personality, Perassi observes, are inherent in the principle that all rules of international law are created through agreements governed by the basic principle *pacta sunt servanda*. This principle presupposes the existence of subjects among which treaties may be concluded. To say "treaties should be respected" is only a shorter way of stating that "they must be respected by those who are parties to them." The correct and complete formulation of the rule is *pacta inter gentes sunt servanda*. The rule itself must determine which entities may be the subjects of the *pacta*, the agreements. Moreover, the rule *pacta sunt servanda* itself is a precept which presupposes some subjects to which it is addressed. There must be some means of designating these subjects. The rule *pacta sunt servanda* presupposes, therefore, the existence of a group of fundamental principles of international law determining the subjects among which the rule is in force. The conclusion is thus reached by Perassi that there must be general rules of international law which establish the requisites for international personality. "These requisites consist in having the character of a state: that is, the entity must be capable of functioning continuously and of establishing regular relations with the other members of the international community." [125] In the light of Perassi's theory, recog-

[125] *Ibid.*, p. 41. Perassi admits, therefore, that international law has its own rules for determining which entities have the quality of states. According to Cavaglieri, "Règles générales du droit de la paix," 26 Rec. des cours (1929) 321, international law accepts the definition of the state given by public law. He therefore attributes to the international concept of the state an objective character. This can be hardly reconciled with his conception that the international personality of a state can derive only from recognition which would depend, in turn, on the discretion of the pre-existing states.

nition has a meaning different from that attributed to it by Anzilotti and Cavaglieri. Recognition presupposes the existence of a state. It consists of

. . . the declaration whereby a state ascertains the existence of a new state as a subject of international law. This declaration also constitutes an acknowledgment by the recognizing state that its rights or interests are not violated by the formation of the new state, taking into consideration the regime of the latter and the territory over which it has jurisdiction.[126]

Recognition is not a bilateral act, since it consists only of a declaration by the recognizing state that it does not raise any objection to the situation arising from the creation of the new state. Recognition does not ascertain the existence of the new state; it presupposes that the new state is already an international subject. It is only the starting point for regular relations with it. For this reason it is a discretionary act. Perassi believes that the practice of the states demonstrates that these are the characteristics and the function of recognition.

Perassi realizes that his conception of recognition is inconsistent with the doctrine that international law is only based upon agreements. Not only the rule *pacta sunt servanda* but also the rules determining the international subjects are not based upon the consent of the states. He is compelled to admit that, in addition to the rules resulting from agreements, international law

comprises a group, though extremely small, of fundamental rules. Their formation is only historically explicable, and their legal validity (*giuridicita'*) in the international order is a postulate. Because of the existence of these primary rules a new state becomes an international person, inasmuch as such norms refer to it directly. This happens whenever a state is endowed with the requisites that these norms presuppose in their addressee.[127]

The consequences of this admission are far-reaching. They subvert the very essence of the positivist conception of the international organization. For Anzilotti the international community is voluntary, since it is left to each state to enter it by the agreement of recognition. Theoretically, if a state does not desire to take part in the international community it may remain out of it, thereby acquiring neither international rights nor duties. International law is a voluntary law based upon the consent of its subjects. Perassi, instead, affirms that the international community is necessary. Certain entities, the states, could not refuse membership in it. They become members of it and are subjected to some of its rules because of the mere fact of their existence. Nor is international law voluntary; for the entities which are necessarily members of the international community cannot refuse to be bound by international law, which is the legal order of such an organization.

The logical process followed by Perassi to deduct from *pacta sunt servanda* the existence of other international rules, not based upon agreement, lends itself to further development. Ottolenghi observes that *pacta sunt servanda*, by providing that *pacta* should be respected, implies that international law contains the definition of *pacta*. A whole body of nonvoluntary international rules must then exist, not only defining the characteristics of the international agreements but also regulating their negotiation, validity, effects, interpretation, and termination.[128]

Perassi had attempted to limit the nonvoluntary international law to the rule *pacta sunt servanda*. The very force of his logic compels him to admit the existence of other rules, not derived from agreements. The breach so created in the positive doctrine is widened again and again by subsequent writers. Scerni, one of the younger Italian writers, observes that there is no reason why at the top of the hierarchy of the rules of international law there should be only one fundamental norm not resulting from agreement. In addition to the rule *pacta sunt servanda*, he asserts that there are other fundamental rules. Among them he places that whereby the general principles of law recognized by the civilized nations are principles of international law binding the state without need of their consent.[129]

The positivist theory is shattered by its own followers. In fact, it had been shaken the very moment when the rule *pacta sunt servanda* was conceived as a postulate. It is evident that the existence of the rule *pacta sunt servanda* is mere legal fiction. By itself this principle would be meaningless. It posits the co-existence of a whole group of principles and rules of international law governing the structure of the international community in all its fundamental aspects.[130] Anzilotti's incidental reference to certain structural rules of international law [131] and that of Perassi to certain primary rules not based upon agreement are evident admissions on the part of the most authoritative positivists that not all international law is voluntary.

[128] "Sulla personalità internazionale delle unioni di stati," 17 Riv. dir. int. (1925) 335.

[129] *I principii generali di diritto riconosciuti dalle nazioni civili nella giurisprudenza della Corte permanente di giustizia internazionale*, p. 35.

[130] Balladore Pallieri, *Diritto internazionale pubblico*, 2d ed.

[131] Anzilotti, *Corso di diritto internazionale*, 3d ed., p. 64, "In saying that international rules are created only by agreements, we do not intend in the least to affirm that only the rules written in the treaties or resulting from a certain custom constitute the international legal order. The necessary logical premises and logical consequences of the rules so established are equally a part of it. This is true because the will to observe a rule or a body of rules implies the will to respect also those rules in the absence of which the former would be meaningless or which are logically comprised in them. Such rules may be called constructive rules (*regole costruttive*). They are a juridical element of every legal order including ours." Cavaglieri, *Lezioni di diritto internazionale*, p. 84, denies the existence of these constructive rules.

So the cycle of the positivist school is completed. The doctrine intended to proceed to a strictly legal analysis of international law as a reaction to natural law and political and moral infiltrations. Its point of departure was that all international law is voluntary, but this principle was gradually abandoned. Some rules of international law may have a foundation other than the will of the states. The problem is to ascertain which these rules really are and to reject from the field of positive law the principles and rules not based on the will of the states whose existence had been arbitrarily affirmed by the doctrine of natural law.

Chapter XIII: THE REACTION AGAINST THE POSITIVIST DOCTRINE

AT THE beginning of the twentieth century the majority of Italian scholars accepted the doctrine of the positivist school as advocated by Anzilotti. Still, some authors followed more or less faithfully the doctrines of natural law. The most influential of these is Giorgio del Vecchio.[1] Although his principal interest is legal philosophy, he has also considered the problems of international law. While he affirms that natural law is superior to the state, Del Vecchio is reluctant to accept the existence of an international law endowed with the characteristics of a real legal system.

More or less valid criticism of Anzilotti's theories has also been advanced by Giuseppe Salvioli.[2] His doctrines are inspired by conceptions of natural law probably in consequence of his deep Catholic faith. Salvioli's activity has been devoted almost entirely to international law. While his general conception of the international community shows the deep influence of natural law,[3] Salvioli follows a strictly positive method in the study of particular problems.[4]

ROMANO AND BALLADORE PALLIERI

Del Vecchio and Salvioli are the last representatives of a school of thought which has been almost entirely superseded in Italy. Whatever the merits of their doctrines may be, they did not exert much influence on the Italian studies of international law.

Of much greater interest from the point of view of the development of the Italian doctrines of international law are the writers who reject the old-fashioned theories of international law but at the same time are not satisfied with some of the results reached by the positivist doctrine. The criticism of these authors against the positivist theory has been so strong and successful that the former does no longer hold the incontestable mastery of the Italian studies of international law. The present chapter is

---

[1] Giorgio del Vecchio (b. 1878) taught philosophy of law in various universities of Italy and finally at the University of Rome. In 1938 he was dismissed because of racial laws.

[2] Gabriele Salvioli (b. 1891) teaches international law at the University of Padua.

[3] "Studii sui caratteri dell'ordinamento giuridico internazionale," 14 Riv. dir. int. (1922) 30 ff.; "Principii generali di diritto internazionale," 20 Riv. dir. int. (1928) 571 ff.

[4] "La Jurisprudence de la Cour permanente de justice internationale," 12 Rec. des cours (1926) 2, and "La responsabilité des états et la fixation des dommages-intérêts par les tribunaux internationaux," 28 Rec. des cours (1929) 235 ff.

devoted to the analysis of the most important reactions against the positivist theory.

Positivist doctrine is based upon a general conception of the law from which it derives with impeccable logic a whole series of closely linked deductions. Criticism of the doctrine limited to only some of its aspects and conclusions would not be sufficient. In order to accomplish a satisfactory revision of it, one must re-examine its very foundation and substitute for its basic principles others from which different conclusions will be derived as to the various particular problems. Hence, the adversaries of positivism have been compelled to follow the positivist method of starting legal research from general premises. This approach to problems of international law has become a common characteristic of all Italian scholars. It also accounts for the fact that the most significant reaction against the positivist doctrine was inaugurated, not by a specialist in international law, but by a scholar who is mostly interested in the general theory of law. His name is Santi Romano.[5] Before devoting his attention to the problems of international law, this author had already expounded his own conception of law and legal order. Its analysis of the fundamentals of international law is primarily intended to test the correctness of his general theories by applying them to international relations. Aside from Santi Romano, the most authoritative critics of the positivists are Prospero Fedozzi [6] and Giorgio Balladore Pallieri.[7] The latter is a typical representative of the younger generation of Italian scholars, and the one whose works are most numerous.[8] The doctrines of these three, although not identical, have many traits in common, and therefore they can be considered together.

Romano and the other critics of the positivist conception of international law do not fail to recognize its merits. They acknowledge that this doctrine has overcome old natural law concepts; it has distinguished legal from moral and political problems of international relations and has treated the topics considered in a strictly legal manner.[9] The posi-

---

[5] Santi Romano (b. 1875) taught international law and related subjects for many years in various universities of Italy—most recently at the University of Rome. He is now president of the Council of State, the highest Italian administrative jurisdiction.

[6] Prospero Fedozzi (1872–1934) taught international law in various Italian universities. He was teaching at the University of Genoa at the time of his death.

[7] Giorgio Balladore Pallieri (b. 1905) teaches international law at the Catholic University of Milan.

[8] Among Italian students who took an independent position toward Anzilotti's theories, one should remember Andrea Rapisardi Mirabelli (b. 1883) who teaches international law at the University of Siena.

[9] On the conflict between Anzilotti's and Romano's conceptions see the remarkable article of Vitta, "Divergenze nella dottrina italiana sui principii fondamentali del diritto internazionale pubblico," 21 Riv. dir. int. (1929) 501 ff. For an effective criticism of the positivist doctrine see Balladore Pallieri, *La concezione positiva del diritto internazionale*; Siotto Pintor, "Posi-

tivist method meets their unconditional approval. Romano observes that "notwithstanding some reaction, especially accentuated by the post-war idealistic doctrines, it seems that the positivist method can be now considered a definite conquest by our discipline, which was raised by merit of it to the same level of other branches of law." [10]

The positivist doctrine is not rejected as a whole; only some premises and conclusions are opposed. The present analysis will consider the main points of dissent between the two schools of thought; aside from them, there are but few discrepancies.

Romano's and Balladore Pallieri's chief criticism is aimed at Anzilotti's conception of the international community as a voluntary organization whose rules are created exclusively by the consent of its members. This conception, they assert, merely constitutes an attempt to introduce into the legal system of international relations, theories which developed in other branches of the law and are inconsistent with the structure of the international community. The positivists overlooked the fact that the meaning of these theories would be entirely changed if they were applied to the international order. Balladore Pallieri observes that the positivists may be correct in asserting that the will of the state is the source of all law when they apply this principle to the power of the state within its own jurisdiction. The same principle, however, would assume a different meaning and would be no longer correct if transferred to international relations. In fact the positivist doctrine has affirmed that law within a nation is created by the state, not by single individuals, in order to establish the principle that law is not the result of the individual will of the single members of a human group, but the expression of the social organization as a whole, which finds its personification in the state. Positivist doctrine grew in opposition to the naturalistic and individualistic doctrine of Rousseau, who conceived law to be the result of a social contract concluded at a given moment between single individuals. By maintaining that law in the international community is created only through agreements between its members, the states, Anzilotti falls into the very error of the contractual doctrines of the natural law which are opposed by the positivists in the field of domestic law. If the positivists want to be consistent with the principles advocated by them in the field of national law, they must admit that international law is not only created through

tivisme juridique et droit international," Al Guanom vai iqtisad (Cairo, 1936–1937) 67 ff.; and Gabriele Salvioli, "Principii generali di diritto internazionale," 20 Riv. dir. int. (1928) 571 ff. Balladore Pallieri has also criticized Kelsen's doctrines in "Le dottrine di Hans Kelsen e il problema dei rapporti tra diritto interno e diritto internazionale," 27 Riv. dir. int. (1935) 24 ff. In answer to this article see Kunz, "La Doctrine dualiste chez Balladore Pallieri," 11 Revue internationale de la théorie du droit (1937) 12 ff.

[10] Corso di diritto internazionale, 4th ed., p. 26.

agreements between international persons, but is to a large extent the necessary consequence of the existence of an international community, a necessary and spontaneous product of this society, which in turn is the necessary result of the coexistence of several states.[11]

Romano applies to the international order his concept of law which he first expounded in his book *L'ordinamento giuridico* (*The legal order*) (1918). Law is but the internal organization assumed by any society in order to subsist. Every form of society requires some legal organization. Existence of a given society, or institution, to use his words, and of a legal system governing its life and organization are for him synonymous. Law exists not only in a society organized into a state but also in every particular institution whether it be intended to function under the jurisdiction of the state (as a stock corporation) or beyond (as the Catholic Church) or even against it (as a group criminal). Experience shows that there is a society of states. International law is but the necessary consequence of the existence of this international community; it constitutes the legal machinery of the entire international society.[12] Since he conceives the existence of international law as a natural phenomenon, Romano rejects all theories which derive its binding force from the collective will or self-limitation of states or, as Anzilotti does, from the basic norm *pacta sunt servanda.*

Romano and Balladore Pallieri agree with Anzilotti that the international community is an organization lacking power superior to its members. The relationship between international persons is one of coordination rather than subordination. In their opinion, however, equality among its members is not an essential characteristic of the international community. Legal equality means legal possibility of performing the same activity. It can exist among entities of the same nature only. Structural differences exist among certain international subjects (for example, the states and the Holy See) whereby there cannot be equality among them. Moreover, even international persons belonging to the same class may differ in legal status. Some of the states, for instance, may be affected by legal disabilities whereby they are in a position of inferiority (protected, neutralized states) with respect to other members of the same class.

The most significant features of the international order are that it is original and that it is necessary. It is original because "it does not depend upon other legal orders, such as the legal orders constituting the internal organization of the different members of the international community.

---

[11] *Diritto internazionale pubblico,* 2d ed., p. 25.
[12] Vitta, "Divergenze nella dottrina italiana sui principii fondamentali del diritto internazionale pubblico," 21 Riv. dir. int. (1929) 501 ff.; Orlando, "Recenti indirizzi circa i rapporti tra diritto e stato," 18 Rivista di diritto pubblico (1926) 273 ff.

It exists and modifies itself by its own power. Its validity is inherent and does not derive from external factors."[13]

International order is absolutely separate and independent from the national law of the states which are members of the international community. International order is necessary because all entities endowed with certain qualifications (the states) are subject to it irrespective of their consent. Anzilotti's conception of a voluntary international community whose membership would depend on the consent of the state is rejected as inconsistent with the structure of the international community and with the opinion of its members. In fact the practice of the states shows that they always admit that they are bound by certain international rules irrespective of their consent.

The historical development of the international community confirms its necessary character according to Balladore Pallieri. Many still believe that the international community arose in the seventeenth century, at the time of the Peace of Westphalia, through relations and agreements then entered into for the first time by the states, emancipated at that time by the pope and the emperor. According to Balladore Pallieri the present international community did not originate at that time and is not the result of agreements between the states. The present international community is the same republic of Christian people (*civitas gentium Christianarum*) which took shape around the twelfth century. Some centuries later, independent states were formed within it. They freed themselves from the superior authority of the Church and the empire, but they never intended, however, to abandon the international community. It would have been inconceivable for them to secede from it. Many international rules (for example, on diplomatic agents and maritime warfare) already in existence and dating back to the very inception of the republic of the Christian people continued in force after the creation of independent states. Even at the present time states refer to medieval rules and treaties, thus proving their conviction that the international community dates back to the period preceding the Peace of Westphalia. Present-day international law is therefore the result of a complex historical procedure, not of formal agreements between its members.

The sources of international law are three, according to Romano: (1) fundamental principles; (2) custom; (3) treaties.

1. Fundamental or constitutional principles are those which are inherent in the peculiar structure of the international community.[14] These

---

[13] Romano, *Corso di diritto internazionale*, 4th ed., p. 20. Romano and Balladore Pallieri classify the legal orders as original and derivative. The state is an original order, because the validity of its laws is not derived from the rules of another legal order. The legal organizations of a municipality or of a stock corporation are derivative orders, because the validity of their provisions depends upon the laws of the state by which they have been incorporated.
[14] *Ibid.*, p. 32: "These principles are few, as fundamental and basic principles always are,

principles are not voluntary law, since they do not depend upon the consent of the states. They are not customary law, since they did not arise from the constant repetition of certain practices. Many of them arose at the very moment when the international community first came into existence: for instance, the principle which permits war among states in the absence of special provisions to the contrary. Since other general procedures for the enforcement and change of international law do not exist, the principle which permits recourse to war for achieving those results is a legal principle inherent in the structure of the international community. Such a principle is not the result of custom because it arose contemporaneously with the international community, or of agreements, because these only limit war, thus assuming its pre-existence and lawfulness as an international institution. The following are also fundamental principles: (*a*) that states, with few exceptions, are equal; (*b*) that they may create legal rules through agreement (treaties); [15] (*c*) that each state may acquire territory *nullius* by original occupation.

According to Balladore Pallieri it is also a fundamental principle of international law that the general principles of law recognized by the civilized nations are an autonomous source of international law.[16]

2. Custom is an autonomous source of international law. In opposition to Anzilotti, Romano affirms that customary rules are not to be confused with tacit agreements. The latter are based on the consent of the states, while the former are binding upon them without their consent. In international law, as in any other legal system, *opinio juris* and *diuturnitas* are necessary requisites for the formation of legal rules through custom. Customs are general or special in so far as they bind all or some of the members of the international community.[17]

3. Treaties are sources of international law by virtue of the principle *pacta sunt servanda*. This is one of the fundamental principles inherent in the structure of the international community. Since this society lacks a superior authority endowed with power to create law, voluntary law can only be produced by agreements of its members. General international law, however, was not created through tacit agreements among the states

---

but their existence cannot be denied without impairing the solution of many problems. These principles should not be confused with the abstract or national principles invoked by the natural lawyers: in contrast with the latter they are institutional elements of the international community. They were transfused into its organization and they help to give it its present shape by establishing its external, formal, and objective aspect."

[15] *Ibid.*, p. 26, "The principle *pacta sunt servanda* cannot be accepted as a postulate which is not susceptible to legal demonstration. If it is a legal principle, its legal validity must be proved; otherwise it cannot be assumed as the foundation of a legal order."

[16] Balladore Pallieri, *I principii generali di diritto riconosciuti delle nazioni civili*, observes, however, that these principles are applicable only in so far as they are not in conflict with the peculiar structure of international community.

[17] On international custom see Balladore Pallieri, "La forza obbligatoria della consuetudine internazionale," 16 Riv. dir. int. (1928) 338.

as is maintained by the positivists; it consists of general principles and customary rules. In the present phase of international law, particular law alone has been created by treaties.

In addition to the above-mentioned sources of international law, there are various secondary sources creating law between smaller groups of states: for instance, between the members of the League of Nations.[18] Moreover, Balladore Pallieri believes that the opinion of the jurists and the decisions of international tribunals, though not technical sources, are subsidiary elements in the creation of international law. By constant practice states recognize in them the function to define the meaning of international rules.[19] In view of the plurality of the sources of international law, the aforementioned positivist definition of international law as the system of rules created through agreements governed by the rule *pacta sunt servanda* is unsatisfactory. International law can only be defined as the system of legal principles and rules governing the international community.

The scope of the rules of international law depends on their source. Fundamental principles and general customs bind all the members of the international community thereby constituting its common or general law. Because of the necessary nature of international law, each state from the beginning is bound by its general precepts. Anzilotti's unrealistic theory, according to which new states would be bound by pre-existing general law only because they consented to it by the agreement of recognition, is thus confuted. Fundamental principles and custom are not immutable. They change in connection with varying exigencies of the international community. For instance, the rule permitting each state to repress slave trade on the high seas is of fairly recent origin. Whether a particular custom applies to a new state is a question to be decided on the merits of each particular case. A custom which is binding all the states of a continent because of their geographical situation would extend to any new state created on the same continent. Treaties are binding only on the parties to them.

In opposition to Anzilotti, Balladore Pallieri affirms that *rebus sic stantibus* is a general principle of international law. Even in the absence of a previous agreement between the parties to a treaty, its provisions become ineffective if there is a basic change of conditions. Whenever a procedure has not been established to ascertain whether such change actually took place, the state invoking the clause may refuse compliance with the treaty until a settlement is reached. "Its conduct would be justified by the general rule that a state may act according to its rights." [20]

Lapse of time alone cannot terminate international rights. Although

---

[18] See above, p. 219.   [19] *Diritto internazionale pubblico,* 2d ed., pp. 146 ff.
[20] *Ibid.,* p. 133.

extinctive prescription is a general principle of law recognized by civilized nations, the practice of states shows that it never did apply to international relations. On the contrary, immemorial or acquisitive prescription of real rights is admitted.[21]

Plurality of sources raises questions concerning the co-ordination of
legal rules. Romano and Balladore Pallieri agree with Anzilotti concerning the existence in the international order of the rules *lex posterior
derogat priori* and *in toto iure genus per speciem derogatur*. There are,
however, some exceptions to these rules. Some fundamental principles
and rules are mandatory. Two states could not by special agreement
modify general rules prohibiting slave trade or assuring freedom of the
high seas. Others are permissive and can be limited, for example, that
which makes resort to war lawful. The question whether a fundamental
principle is mandatory or permissive must be decided as each case arises.
A treaty may be modified by a new agreement between the parties to it
or by the subsequent formation of a custom or fundamental principle
contrary to it.

Romano and Balladore Pallieri agree almost completely with Anzilotti
on the nature and function of interpretation. They admit, however, the
existence of a general principle of international law whereby gaps may
be filled by resorting to analogy (*analogia legis*).[22] Cases not expressly
regulated by international rules may be decided by applying general principles of law recognized by the civilized nations.

Anzilotti's theory concerning the relationship between international
law and national law is fully endorsed by Romano and to a great extent
by Balladore Pallieri. The latter is especially interested in refuting the
monistic conception in both its aspects; supremacy of national law or of
international law. That conception in its first aspect is contradicted by
the actual existence of an international community which is certainly
independent from the legal systems of the various states. In its second
aspect the monistic doctrine is erroneous, because it presupposes a system
of relations between national and international law which has long since
been superseded. As has already been seen, Balladore Pallieri affirms
that contrary to current opinion the international community, not the
state, was the first to come into existence. In fact, the present international
community is the continuation of the ancient republic of the Christian
people. States were originally derived from and dependent upon the
international community. For this reason states at first invoked legal titles
based on rules of the international community (for example, grants, tacit

---

[21] *Ibid.*, p. 173.

[22] Balladore Pallieri, *ibid.*, p. 142, believes that the rule permitting the states to acquire possession of territories which are *res nullius* extended by analogy to the bed of the sea. Many rules
concerning state jurisdiction over the territory and territorial waters extended by analogy to
the air space above them.

recognition by the emperor, acquisitive prescription, or custom) in order
to justify their independence from the emperor. The supremacy of the
international community personified by the emperor over the states was
thereby recognized. But from the thirteenth century the modern state refused to justify its own existence by invoking legal titles based on rules of
international law. Each state found its justification in its very existence,
thus claiming to be an original order. Since then, the international order
and the national orders of the various states are separate and independent.[23]

The distinction between international and national law cannot be based
upon the diversity of the relations governed by their rules. Matters usually governed by national rules (for example, treatment of foreign individuals) are sometimes controlled by international law. Individual
rights and duties concerning navigation of rivers are usually within the
jurisdiction of national law; however, individual rights concerning the
navigation of the lower Danube are directly regulated by international
rules. According to Balladore Pallieri, then, the individual may sometimes be the addressee of international rules.

Anzilotti's doctrine of recognition is the object of severe criticism by
his opposers. Salvioli affirms that the new state is entitled to a minimum
standard of rights even before official recognition. Other states could not
proceed to the wholesale slaughter of its population without violating
international law. International practice shows that states have recognized some rights of other states before the latter were accepted as members of the international community and that in so acting they were convinced that they were complying with a legal obligation, not with moral
considerations alone.[24]

A complete criticism of Anzilotti's theory of recognition is developed
by Romano. He agrees with Perassi that recognition cannot be construed
as an agreement, since there can be no agreement with a state which is
not yet a subject. To this criticism he adds two others. Since every legal
order is composed only of the subjects which mutually recognized each
other as persons, Anzilotti, by asserting that the new state exists only with
respect to the states which recognize it, splits the society of states into
many separate communities, each composed only of the subjects among
which recognition took place. This would negate the unity and therefore
the very existence of the international community. Besides, if it were
true that recognition is an agreement whose conclusion is left to the discretion of the parties, a new state might refuse to enter into it and so
would not become a member of the international society and would not

---

[23] *Ibid.*, p. 44. The first part of the present work proves that Balladore's theory is correct, at
least as far as the Italian states are concerned.
[24] "Il riconoscimento degli stati," 18 Riv. dir. int. (1926) 336.

be bound to respect any international rule. This was never thought possible by any state. In reality recognition is neither an agreement nor an
act constituting international personality. Some states may acquire international personality without it; others (for example, one of the states of
the United States) could not even if recognized, because they have not
the requisites necessary to be international persons.

According to Romano recognition consists of a declaration whereby
former members of the international community, each on its own account, expressly declare their intention of entering into international
relations with a new state. This intention is motivated by the belief that
the new state is willing to respect and capable of respecting international
law. Thus recognition neither creates nor declares international personality. It is related, not to the existence of the new subject, but to the establishment of international relations with it. Denial or withdrawal of recognition cannot affect the international personality, but only diplomatic
intercourse. Romano denies any substantial difference in nature and
effects between the recognition of a new state and a new government.[25]
Both express only the intention of establishing diplomatic relations and
are granted in view of the constitutional stability of the new state or government and of the guaranties which it offers to abide by international
law. In both cases it is a regime that is recognized. In view of its purposes,
recognition is in both cases left to the discretion of the state which
granted it. There can be no claim to recognition on the part of the new
state or government.[26] Even when requested by the new state or government, recognition is a unilateral act. It is never a mutual act, since old
states or governments never request recognition of new states or governments.

International law does not contain rules designating the requisites
necessary for a state to become a subject. In complete opposition to Anzilotti, Romano affirms:

International law does not contain its own definition of the state, and therefore
in the interpretation of its rules only those entities to which common usage
grants the name "state" must be deemed such: that is, territorial entities having
original organization. To broaden the concept of the state so that it would comprise other entities is not only arbitrary but also in open opposition to the lan-

[25] Although recognition has the same effects in both instances, the creation of a new state
and of a new government are absolutely different. The new state is not bound by many
international obligations of the old, while a change of government does not impair the
international obligations of the state. When there are at the same time a change of regime
and territorial changes, it is hard to ascertain whether there was a change of regime or a
state succession or both; for example, in the case of the destruction of the Austro-Hungarian
Empire and of the proclamation of the Austrian Republic.

[26] Anzilotti, on the contrary, holds that a new government has a legitimate claim to recognition if it has actual and stable control of the state.

guage of international rules. . . . From the point of view of positive law, the problem consists in ascertaining which states are actual, not merely prospective, members of international law.[27]

Whether a new state has international personality is a matter left to the decision of the old ones. Each case is decided on its particular merits. Romano's theory that a state becomes an international person as soon as it has been endowed with certain requisites has met with the objection that it does not indicate what these requisites are. Balladore Pallieri, who substantially agrees with Romano, feels the need of indicating these requisites. He believes that according to international practice they may be indicated as follows: "(1) that there actually exist an organization or entity; (2) that this organization intends to exercise jurisdiction for the fulfillment of its purposes and so actually does; (3) that this jurisdiction be territorial. These are the three elements which, in fact, constitute the state according to the common doctrine." [28]

Each entity endowed with these three requisites is necessarily an international subject. Balladore Pallieri's conclusions as to recognition do not differ much from Perassi's. Although starting from different premises and reasoning along different lines, positivist doctrine and opposing doctrines reach the same result.

The natural-law conception of the inborn rights of the state is rejected by Romano. He admits, however, that positive law grants some particular powers and rights to each state. Powers consist of a general capacity of the state to perform certain acts, while rights in a technical sense arise only from a specific transaction with other subjects. The complete enumeration of the powers and the rights of states would cover the entire field on international law. Romano only proceeds to classify them.

The classes of fundamental powers are three: (1) the so-called *jus contrahendi*, that is, the power of creating international rules through agreements with other states; (2) the powers of creating legal relationships through unilateral transactions (recognition, renunciation) or through material facts (occupation of land *nullius*); (3) the power of self-defense which comprises a series of particular powers (for example,

---

[27] In agreement with Anzilotti, Romano denies international personality to nomadic tribes, nationalities, colonies, colonial companies, international courts, state organs, and organs of international unions. He believes that some international unions, the British Dominions, the insurgents, and the Holy See are international persons. Balladore Pallieri agrees substantially with Romano. He believes, however, that individuals have sometimes acquired international rights by agreements between states. In the present phase of international law individuals are subjects, not of any general rule, but of some particular rules of international law. Balladore Pallieri attributes also international personality to the Order of Malta. On this question see Cansacchi, *La personalità internazionale del S.M. Ordine Gerosolimitano di Malta*, and Tacchino, *I rapporti diplomatici tra la Serenissima Repubblica di San Marino e il Sovrano Militare Ordine di Malta*.

[28] *Diritto internazionale pubblico*, 2d ed., p. 185.

to wage war, to exercise reprisals). Self-defense may be exercised to inforce or to change international law in favor of the state.

Among the fundamental rights, Romano lists the so-called "rights of personality," which he divides into four groups: (1) right to a particular status, to which a state may be entitled in international relations (for example, right to neutralization); (2) right to distinctions of state personality (name, title, emblem); (3) right to liberty and independence, whereby the lawful activity of a subject cannot be interfered with by other states (these rights protect both the internal [rights to elect the form of government and to enact the laws it prefers] and external [right to associate with other states]activities of a state); [29] (4) rights on its own territory.

On this point the theories of Anzilotti and of Romano, which Balladore Pallieri substantially follows, do not differ much. In fact Romano acknowledges that the fundamental powers and rights are only various positions taken by the state in its international activity. Anzilotti believes them to be aspects of the state's international personality.

Although international persons are usually equal, Romano observes that some inequality may exist among those belonging to different classes. Besides, even among subjects belonging to the same class (for example, the states) some are affected by general limitations to their activity in consequence of obligations freely entered into. Since these limitations affect the very personality as in the case of protected, neutralized, or vassal states, they constitute legal disabilities.[30]

States which have international personality may or may not be sovereign. A state legally subordinated to another (for example, a protected state), is a non-sovereign state. It is affected by a legal disability which reflects on all its international activities. Some acts performed by a non-sovereign state may be void.

State succession is dealt with by Romano consistently with his general premises.[31] When one state annexes another in whole or in part it ac-

[29] Both Romano, *Corso di diritto internazionale*, 4th ed., p. 148, and Balladore Pallieri, *Diritto internazionale pubblico*, 2d ed., pp. 337 ff., deny that a state may intervene in the internal affairs of another state except when a right of the intervening state has been violated (and, according to Romano, in case of the violation of the right of an associated state). Representations or analogous forms of political and diplomatic pressure do not constitute intervention. Concerning this matter see especially Balladore Pallieri, *L'intervento come istituto giuridico internazionale*. Romano, *Corso di diritto internazionale*, 4th ed., p. 148, observes that there is no inconsistency in the fact that international law grants to every state the broad power of waging war against another state but not the more limited one of intervening in its internal affairs. The reason is that war being a more serious undertaking, is surrounded by greater legal guarantees. Moreover, it involves such risks for the belligerents that states will resort to it only in extreme cases and after careful consideration.

[30] *Ibid.*, pp. 104 ff., 115 ff. Balladore Pallieri *Diritto internazionale pubblico*, 2d ed., pp. 248 ff.

[31] Romano, *Corso di diritto internazionale*, 4th ed., p. 129, and "Di una particolare figura di successione di stati. A proposito dell'annessione di Fiume," 17 Riv. dir. int. (1925) 304 ff.; Balladore Pallieri, *L'estinzione di fatto degli stati*.

quires not only its territory and population but also that part of its organization, including rights and duties referring to them. It is upon this phenomenon that the duty of the successor state to take over the obligations of the former is based.[32] Transfer of international obligations to the successor does not entail any substantial change in their substance. International law binds the annexing state to take over the obligations of the original state in cases of both total and partial succession. Personal obligations (for example, treaties of alliance) only are not transferable, with the exception of those relating to the territory (international servitudes), which are transferred in every case. In case of total extinction of a state, the new state takes over all transferable rights and duties of the former. In case of partial transfer of territory, the successor takes over only rights and duties referring to the portion of territory transferred. Romano admits that in case of partial succession obligations affecting the ceding state as a whole are not taken over unless the contrary be expressly provided. In the absence of special provision to the contrary, an international loan of state A for which no security relating to the ceded territory has been granted remains entirely the charge of state A, even if part of its territory is ceded to state B.

Balladore Pallieri reaches less extreme conclusions. As a rule, international obligations are not transferred by succession. In the absence of special agreements to the contrary, the only obligations of the successor consists in fulfilling the engagements taken by its predecessor within its legal order toward foreign subjects.[33] So-called international servitudes bind the state which takes over the territory subjected to them. This is not, however, an application of the doctrine of state succession. It derives from the character of any servitude, which is a grant of a real interest in the territory in favor of the state for whose benefit the servitude was created. Since this interest already existed, a change in the sovereignty over the territory cannot wipe it out.[34]

As to state responsibility, Anzilotti's theory is accepted by Romano and with a few changes by Balladore Pallieri too. The latter agrees with Anzilotti that when a state exercises diplomatic protection in favor of its citizens it acts to enforce its own right to a certain treatment of its citizens abroad. He believes, however, that the state which exercises diplomatic protection has no right to reparations for itself, but is entitled to adequate compensation for its citizens. A sum granted to a state as a reparation is not intended to compensate the damage suffered by the state but the one suffered by the citizen. Therefore, the state should turn it over to the latter. If, however, the state does not grant the sum to its citizen, it cannot

[32] The remarks of Romano, *Corso di diritto internazionale*, 4th ed., pp. 135–136, are very important and give a clear idea of his whole theory of persons in international law.
[33] *Diritto internazionale pubblico*, 2d ed., pp. 298 ff.
[34] *Ibid.*, pp. 459 ff.

incur an international liability, because the relationship between a state and its subjects is an internal one, which is not governed by international law.[35] Balladore Pallieri admits that a state may have an international responsibility arising from the act of another international personal (vicarious responsibility). In contrast with Anzilotti, he affirms that there cannot be international responsibility without fault. The doctrine that international responsibility presupposes the fault of the state has recently found another supporter in Italy—Ago.[36]

Positivist conceptions of arbitration and of the nature of international adjudications have been sharply criticized by Balladore. He believes that international tribunals, although usually not endowed with international personality, may be vested with some international rights. For instance, the exchange of notes of May 22, 1928, between the Dutch ministry of foreign affairs and the president of the Permanent Court of International Justice would have granted to the Court the international right to demand that certain rights and immunities be granted to its judges in Netherlands.[37] Balladore Pallieri also remarks that arbitral decisions are legal acts, not mere facts, although they do not emanate from an international person. For this reason the rules concerning validity and interpretation of international acts apply to international judgments. The deep differences of opinion among Italian writers concerning the legal nature of international judgments are of little practical importance.[38]

The legal phenomenon of war could hardly be explained by the positivist scholars. To base its legitimacy on an international agreement is obviously artificial. A legal explanation of the war is more consistent with the theory of Romano and Balladore Pallieri, who admit the existence of fundamental principles of international law, not derived by state agreement, but inherent in the international order.[39] Among them is the principle that any state may provoke a state of war by its own will manifested in appropriate acts. Apart from this difference in the fundamentals, Romano and Balladore agree with the positivist school as to the legal principles concerning war.

Balladore Pallieri is the only modern Italian writer who has written a complete work on the law of war and neutrality. The general part of this work is devoted to the analysis of the phenomenon of war in the

[35] *Ibid.*, p. 535, and "Gli effetti dell'atto illecito internazionale," 23 Rivista di diritto pubblico (1931) 64 ff.

[36] Ago, "La colpa nell'illecito internazionale," in *Studii in onore di Santi Romano*, III, 210, and "Illecito commissivo e illecito omissivo nel diritto internazionale," 2 Diritto internazionale (1938) 9 ff.

[37] *Diritto internazionale pubblico*, 2d ed., p. 272.

[38] Balladore Pallieri, "La natura giuridica dell'arbitrato internazionale," 21 Riv. dir. int. (1929) 328 ff., and "Due recenti teorie sulla natura giuridica della sentenza internazionale," 5 Annali R. Università di Messina (1930–1931) 186 ff.

[39] *La guerra*, Padova, 1935.

international community. It is, perhaps, the completest treatment of the problem from the point of view of the law of nations in modern literature. The second part of the work is devoted to the analysis of the special provisions on war and neutrality, and it does not reach the excellent standards of his other works. While the Italian doctrine has contributed to clarify the general problems of the theory of war, it lacks a satisfactory treatment of the subject [40] from a practical point of view.

The complete system of international doctrines expounded by Romano and Balladore Pallieri presents an adequate answer to all the fundamental problems of international law. It is not within the scope of the present work to analyze the solution given by these authors to many particular questions which are of considerable importance in the practice of international relations. It is sufficient to remark that the picture of the international community given by Romano and Balladore Pallieri is rich and realistic. In the opinion of these authors the very existence of several states gives rise to the formation of law. A complete group of fundamental principles has thus been created, to which several customary rules were later added. A large body of international rules is in existence which binds all international persons, thus assuring the unity of the international community. Its whole life is governed by these rules, which continuously evolve in accordance with its changing exigencies. Within the international community a multitude of entities belonging to different classes (states, unions of states, insurgents, the Holy See, and so forth) live and operate. To the general rules, others, more numerous, are to be added. These are created by agreement between various international persons. Because of their special agreements the members of the various classes or international persons tend to further diversify among themselves. Some acquire a position of supremacy; others, of subordination which results in legal disabilities. International community is therefore more varied and articulate than in the positivist conception. It is also more solid and coherent, because membership in it does not depend upon the consent of the subjects. The individualism of its components is moderated by a considerable body of rules which do not result from their consent. Compliance with the rules is compulsory. Many of them cannot be waived or changed by special agreement.

POINTS OF CONFLICT AND RAPPROCHEMENT BETWEEN THE
POSITIVIST DOCTRINE AND THE THEORIES OF ITS OPPOSERS

The preceding analysis shows the similarity and the points of conflict between the positivist doctrine and the theories of Romano and Balladore Pallieri. Both schools of thought are vigorously opposed to any influence

---

[40] The principal Italian works of a theoretical nature on war and neutrality have already been cited. Sandiford, *Diritto aereonautico di guerra*, and *Diritto marittimo di guerra*, contain a great deal of factual information.

of natural law in the theory of international law and intend to build the international organization on a purely legal foundation. There is, however, sharp conflict between them, which finds its deepest root in two different conceptions of the law that clash in every branch of jurisprudence.[41]

Anzilotti's conception finds its remotest origin in the theories of Jellinek and Laband, who reduce all law to the state. Jellinek affirmed that the process of creation of a state is a mere fact. Legal justification of the state cannot be found in a preceding principle or in the authority of a superior power; it consists in the mere fact of its existence. Once the state is created, it becomes a legal order;[42] it has an inborn power of control over its subjects. Since the state is the only agency for the creation and enforcement of the law, there cannot be any law which has not been recognized by the state.

This theory exerted a powerful appeal on Italian jurists. They belonged to a country in which the material influence of the state was very marked and its function had been extolled by philosophers and political thinkers. Perhaps unconsciously, Anzilotti, too, felt the influence of the environment. According to his original conception international law is based only on the will of the states. He still believes that all the rules of international law except *pacta sunt servanda* depend on their agreement. The very existence of the international subjects is based on their consent manifested in the agreement of recognition. Although there are some international persons (for example, the Holy See and the League of Nations) which are not states, yet the states are the most powerful and conspicuous international subjects.

The conception of the state as the only source of law did not remain unchallenged, especially in the field of public law. Among the continental jurists with whom Italian scholars are most familiar, Savigny's school of historical jurisprudence showed the first reaction against the conception of Jellinek and Laband.[43] This reaction later developed in the works of Gierke and Preuss. They asserted the existence of entities other than states, with power to create law. In consequence of the states' overwhelming power, the law created by other social groups may remain latent and ineffective, but it still maintains the intimate ethical strength which law always has. This conception regained influence in recent times in France, where the persistence of strong naturalistic currents favored its adoption. The French jurists Duguit and Hauriou exercised particular influence on Italian writers. Duguit affirms that law arises with social conscience and

[41] Vitta, "Divergenze nella dottrina italiana sui principii fondamentali del diritto internazionale pubblico," 21 Riv. dir. int. (1929) 516.

[42] *Allgemeine Staatslehre*, 2d ed., pp. 259 ff.

[43] Vitta, "Divergenze nella dottrina italiana sui principii fondamentali del diritto internazionale pubblico," 21 Riv. Dir. int. (1929) 517.

is connected with the very fact of life in common.[44] He denies, therefore, the identity between state and law and asserts that law may exist even outside the state and may impose its authority upon the state itself (or better, on its rulers) as well as on private individuals. Hauriou builds his system on the concept of "institution," which he modified throughout his works. An institution is in substance any social group in which there are a permanent organization and organs endowed with power of command for fulfilling the needs of the group. An institution carries in itself the right to be recognized and is therefore an original source of law. About the institution Hauriou affirms what others said about the state, that its legal character cannot be proved because it is a postulate.[45] The state is but one of the existing institutions.

Romano's derivation from Duguit and Hauriou, and to a lesser extent that of Balladore Pallieri, is obvious. In affirming that international law is the necessary result of the existence of an international community, not the result of the mere will of the state, they obviously apply the theories of the French writers to international relations.

The conflict between the positivist conception and its opposers has gradually disappeared. Anzilotti took an uncompromising attitude and expounded some theories (for example, that of state recognition) which were hardly consistent with the real relations among states, in order to remove any influence of natural law from the law of nations. Once this result was reached, Anzilotti's extreme position was gradually abandoned by his followers (for example, Scerni [46] and Quadri).[47] They admitted that the positivist doctrine had too often indulged in mere fictions and abstractions. It had therefore deviated from its original program, which was to have been an objective and realistic analysis of the international relationships.[48] Younger Italian followers of the positivist doctrine, including the present writer, are now willing to concede that international law is not exclusively a contractual one.

On the other hand, the doctrines of Romano and Balladore Pallieri do not represent a revival of the old natural-law theories based on theological and rationalistic considerations. These authors accept the positivist method. They criticize Anzilotti's contractual theory on the ground that it is inconsistent with positive international law. The international practice shows the conviction of the states themselves that international law is not entirely voluntary. The difference between the positivist doctrines

[44] *Traité de droit constitutionnel*, 2d ed., I, 33.
[45] *Principes de droit public*, 2d ed., *Précis de droit constitutionnel*, Paris, 1923, pp. 75 ff.; and *La Théorie de l'institution*.
[46] Mario Scerni (b. 1907) teaches international law at the University of Genoa.
[47] Rolando Quadri (b. 1907) teaches international law at the University of Padua.
[48] Quadri, "Stato," Nuovo digesto italiano, XII (part 1), 818; see also Lauterpacht, *The Function of the Law in the International Community*, p. 433,

and those of Romano and Balladore Pallieri therefore is actually one of degree rather than substance. There is agreement concerning the existence of a group of international rules which are not based on the consent of the states; the disagreement concerns only their number and content.

Chapter XIV: THE FASCIST CONCEPTION OF
INTERNATIONAL LAW

IN ORDER to understand the relationship between the Italian doctrine of international law and fascism, a few preliminary observations on the development of this movement are necessary.

FASCISM A PRAGMATIC MOVEMENT

Fascists asserted that their action was initiated according to a well-defined program, which was firmly and coherently developed after they gained control of Italy in October, 1922. This claim is absolutely unjustified.[1] In a few years fascism changed from republican to monarchistic —from ultrademocratic to totalitarian. From anticlericalism it shifted to bigotry, retaining, nevertheless, a definite antireligious inclination. Nor were the changes in its economic doctrines less radical. When asked what his program consisted of, Mussolini did not hesitate to declare: "To continue in power is our program" (*Il nostro programma e' durare*). The original lack of a body of doctrine with which to confront political opposition and to deal with problems of government was one of the principal weaknesses of fascism. Because it lacked a constructive program fascism was unable to find convincing arguments to refute mounting criticism aroused by its political and economic measures. It had no alternative but to suppress every opposition, which was accomplished by increasing the restrictions of the civil and political liberties of citizens, increasing state control over the whole nation's life, and concentrating all power in the hands of Mussolini. Imbued, as it was, with a pragmatic and empirical spirit, immediately after it took control of Italy it became antidemocratic —not because of its own program, but as a defense against the opposition it could not otherwise overcome and against difficulties it could not otherwise solve.[2] For the same reason it developed later into a totalitarian regime.

Only after completing its political, economic, and legislative reforms did fascism elaborate a set of political doctrines destined to give ideological content to the work it had already accomplished. The fascist doctrine,

---

[1] For a demonstration of this point see Sereni, *Italian Private Law Enacted in Contemplation of War*.

[2] It is not necessary to recall that the powers of the modern dictator are much greater than those of ancient absolute sovereigns, because the state, through which they are exercised, has much wider authority and is much stronger than in the past.

with which, we assume, the reader is familiar, can be summed up in three principles: first, the supreme interest of all human society is the welfare of the nation, personified by the state. The individual is only an element of the state, and therefore all his activities must be directed toward the satisfaction of the permanent interest of that state. All rights belong to the state. The state is all; the individual is nothing. That accounts for the totalitarianism of the fascist state. Second, the state confers civil and political rights on its subjects in proportion to their contribution to national life. This accounts for the principle of inequality among citizens. Third, power is derived from above, not from below; all officials are appointed rather than elected. This accounts for the antidemocratic character of fascism.

As long as fascism was in power all the organization of the state revolved around Mussolini. This was not only fact but also law. In the fascist legislative system of Italy he was the fountain of all power, whether as head of the government or as Duce of fascism.

The international relations of fascism were deeply affected by its pragmatic and empirical character. At first fascism did not advocate any original political doctrine in this field. It asserted Italy's right to the possession of regions which were considered Italian for historical or ethnical reasons: Dalmatia, Nice, Savoy, Corsica, and Malta. It also maintained the need of new colonies as an outlet for an overflowing Italian population. These territorial aspirations were not new in Italy; nor were they manifestations of an original fascist conception of international relations.

In fact, fascism at first asserted that it was a purely domestic phenomenon, which did not intend to make any changes either in international relations or in the internal organization of other states. This attitude was due to the fact that at the beginning the Fascists concentrated chiefly on international problems and also to the desire of dispelling the diffidence which the aggressiveness of fascism had created in other countries. Furthermore, Mussolini desired to acquire an honorable reputation in the eyes of the democratic governments from which he hoped to obtain financial help and territorial adjustments. They would bolster the prestige of the regime without struggle or risks. For this purpose the difference between bolshevism and fascism was carefully pointed out. It was alleged that the first, after having established itself in Russia, had proclaimed its universal character and its program for international expansion. Instead, fascism would limit itself to Italy. To quote Mussolini, "It was not a product to be exported."

The successive changes in fascism's international policy and ideologies only reflected the evolution which took place in its foreign policy. Italy's transformation into a totalitarian regime, which took place after

1934, influenced her international policy for economic and ideological reasons. For economic reasons, because all totalitarian economy is essentially war economy. This is particularly true if it is adopted by a poor country like Italy and is directed toward self-sufficiency. Totalitarian economy dictated an imperialist policy as an outlet for mounting economic difficulties. Ideological reasons existed also. Territorial expansion was the mirage fascism placed before Italians as a recompense for economic restrictions and the limitation of liberty.

In order to justify this new tendency in Italy's international policy, ideologies were devised for international relations. According to the fascists the world is divided into satisfied and dissatisfied nations: the first are decadent; the second, ascending. Italy, a dissatisfied nation, must obtain its place in the sun.

Resorting to a theme which had been popular in Italy from the beginning of the twentieth century and had a certain foundation of truth, fascism tried to shift the principle of struggle between classes from internal to international relations. Nations were divided into two groups, capitalist and proletarian. The first were the nations of the past; the second, those of the future. Italy was pictured as the typical proletarian nation, fighting for an equitable share of the world's riches.

The distinction between "haves" and "have-nots," capitalistic and proletarian nations, initially had nothing to do with the internal political regime of the various nations. According to circumstances, Russia was classified sometimes with capitalistic and sometimes with proletarian nations. This shows how lightly the fascists treated a doctrine which had some element of truth. Nor can it be overlooked that the doctrine of capitalistic and proletarian nations is logical only if the struggle for equality and liberty of nations is designed to bring equality and liberty to the men within those nations. This principle the fascists denied.

Only after the establishment of close ties between Italy and Germany (1936–1937) was an attempt made to determine a necessary connection between the international policy of the states and their internal regime. The international political struggle of the after-war period came to be depicted as a struggle between two diverse philosophies of life, the fascist and the democratic. Fascism was no longer considered the regime suitable for Italy alone. It acquired universal importance in opposition to the democratic concept. Fascism was proclaimed the form of government for all progressive nations, while democracy, whether in the capitalistic form, such as England, France, and the United States, or in the socialist form, such as Russia, were considered as forming the government of decadent nations. Democratic nations and fascist nations were said to form two opposing groups, whose co-existence was impossible because of the antagonism of the principles which inspired each. Conflict was inevitable, and victory was certain, according to the fascists, for the antidemocratic powers, which were younger, more vigorous, and inspired by more sound principles. Peace and prosperity would be re-established when the fascist nations would have imposed their principles throughout the world.

We do not need to waste time in refuting the accuracy of this doctrine. It is enough to point out that Axis powers advocated it because it had the advantage of being compatible with political tendencies prevalent in Italy, Germany, and Japan, and could be, if convenient, so adapted as to include Russia.

The decade begun in 1931 has been one of uninterrupted international successes for Germany, Japan, and Italy. Vast territories have been conquered. Entire nations have been subjugated, others have been militarily defeated or occupied and rendered subservient. Almost all continental Europe and large regions of Asia and Africa came under the direct or indirect control of the Axis powers. Now only the change of tide is beginning, and Italian Fascism has been the first Axis power to fall. But even during the decade 1931–1941 the weakness of the Axis lay in the fact that its successes had been almost exclusively military. Defeated nations have been kept subdued only by force of arms. Other revolutionary movements, such as the French Revolution, also succeeded by force of arms; but their principles had a universal character which made them acceptable to large masses of men even in the opposing countries. The French Revolution awakened enthusiasm and hope and won support and help among the best elements in all European countries. Hence, its everlasting success. This powerful idealistic motive has been lacking in the action of the Axis powers. Their expansion has been only the manifestation of brutal imperialism based upon the oppression and degradation of the conquered people.

The Axis powers themselves realized that they were unable to express an ideology generally acceptable because of its universal value. For this drawback the recently inaugurated conception of the "new order" did not bring any remedy. It found its legal expression in the Tripartite Agreement of September 27, 1940, between Germany, Italy, and Japan.[3] Adhesion to it is the mark of submission by which Axis powers brand their vassals and puppet states. The basis of this agreement is the above-mentioned ideology that only fascist powers are destined to rule the world. This has to be divided into spheres of influence or regions. In each region an Axis power will take leadership in establishing the "new order"— Japan in the greater East Asia, Germany and Italy in Europe. The new order will embrace all nations living in those sectors. The leading Axis power will extend over the entire sphere of its influence the principles adopted in its internal organization. Since the Axis powers are totali-

[3] English translation in 27 Am. J. Int. L. (1941) 34.

tarian, every region will be organized by co-ordinating the economy of the various nations into a totalitarian system under the control and for the benefit of the leading Axis power. Each of the nations living in a given region will be in a different legal position. There will be a hierarchy of countries—from the dominating Axis power at the head, down to the nations of pariahs, which will suffer the treatment now inflicted on the Polish people.

The conception of the "new order" does not require any further mention. Knowledge of the principles against which we are fighting is assumed. Only a few critical remarks will be necessary: first, the new order represents an international ideology to the elaboration of which Fascists, Germans, and Japanese have all contributed. It constitutes an attempt to create an ideology compatible with the internal regime and the imperialistic policy of each of the three countries. Second, it represents a compromise between the extreme consequences of any totalitarian doctrine and the need for coalition among imperialist states. Each fascist state tends to assume the same supreme and exclusive power in international relations, that it has assumed toward its own subjects. Hegemony over other states is inherent in the concept of the fascist state. The new order attempts to reconcile this concept with that of the co-existence of several fascist states on equal footing by establishing that each fascist state will exercise its leadership in a separate region. Third, the conception of the new order is evidently provisory. If the new order were established, it would logically lead to conflict among the Axis nations, since each of them inherently aspires to supremacy. There is no need to point out that the new order will never be universally accepted. It could be approved by the Axis powers so far as they were successful, but not by the defeated nations for which it resulted in persecution.

The entire doctrine of the new order is only an attempt to cover with a layer of ideology a military alliance among imperialist powers. Mention has been made of the doctrine only because of its official character in fascist Italy.

NONEXISTENCE OF A FASCIST THEORY OF INTERNATIONAL LAW

In Russia, Germany, and Japan the political doctrines of the regimes in power exerted some influence on the doctrines of international law. A Soviet as well as a Nazi and Japanese conception of international law exists today. Fascism, as seen above, has made some attempts at a philosophical political conception of international relations. It was unable, however, to express any conception of its own of international law. Fascism did not exert the slightest influence on the Italian doctrine of international law. To prove this it is sufficient to recall that Anzilotti's doctrine was completely revised and that of Balladore Pallieri was expounded when fascism was already in power. Neither of them felt the influence of fascism in any way. The word fascism could hardly be found in the works of Anzilotti, Perassi, Cavaglieri, Romano, Balladore Pallieri, Morelli, Fedozzi, Salvioli, and other contemporary international lawyers in Italy. The works of these authors could have been written by declared anti-fascist scholars and published in democratic countries.

On the other hand, fascism took no stand against these doctrines. As far as the studies of international law in Italy are concerned, we cannot agree with Morgenthau's observation that:

Totalitarianism has ostracized positivist jurisprudence as a manifestation of liberalistic decadence in Germany and Italy, where the domination of juridic thought by positivism has been at times almost undisputed and positivism has exerted its most far-reaching and fertile influence on the development of the legal science.[4]

This attitude of fascism toward the Italian doctrine of international law can be easily explained. First of all, fascism thought little of cultural problems and was not interested in the conclusions reached by technical doctrines such as the Italian theories of international law.[5] At any rate, the positivist doctrine of Anzilotti and Balladore Pallieri's theories were acceptable to fascism in so far as they constituted a criticism of the principles of natural law. Natural-law doctrines were sharply opposed by fascism, because they had generally advocated liberal principles. The so-called "immortal principles" of the French Revolution, which the fascists especially loathed, are typical natural-law conceptions. Even in the field of international law the influence of natural-law doctrines tended toward the creation of positive rules inspired by democratic and humanitarian principles. For instance, natural-law writers affirmed the existence of international rules binding every state to respect certain fundamental rights of humanity with regard to both foreigners and their own citizens. Some authors went so far as to assert that states have the right to intervene in the internal affairs of another state which is violating certain innate rights of its subjects to life, liberty, freedom of religion, and so forth. Fascism was obviously opposed to the influence of these liberal and humanitarian doctrines in the field of international law. The Italian doctrine of international law met with the approval of fascism in so far as it excluded principles of natural justice from positive law; it affirmed the prevailing function of the state in the creation of international law; it limited the duties of the states to those established by posi-

---

[4] "Positivism, Functionalism, and International Law," 34 Am. J. Int. L. (1940) at p. 263.

[5] Fascism, however, has greatly impaired the study of international law through racial persecution. Such teachers as Donati, Ottolenghi, C. Vitta, E. Vitta, F. Cammeo, G. Del Vecchio, Bassano, and Moscato have been removed by Italian universities. To them and to other Jews, now deceased, such as Catellani, Diena, Senigallia, Cavaglieri, Norsa and Enriques, Italian doctrine of international law owes much.

tive law; it denied the existence of fundamental rights of the citizens protected by international law; it admitted that each state, in the absence of special obligations to the contrary, can resort to war as an instrument of international policy and is not bound to submit its controversies to arbitration.

There is no actual similarity or connection, however, between the fascist doctrines and some conclusions of the Italian school. Italian scholars have made no attempt to please fascism. In denying that some humanitarian principles constitute positive rules, they never intended to deny their intrinsic justice, as did fascism. Italian scholars do not deny, therefore, that these principles should become part of positive international law. On the other hand, the Italian school impliedly condemns fascist practices by insisting on the duty of the states to comply with their international obligations. Moreover, the Italian doctrine condemns natural law. Fascism, on the contrary, while criticizing the former natural-law doctrines because of their liberal and humanitarian flavor, evolved its own form of naturalism by advocating a new international order based upon fascist principles, which were in conflict with positive international law.

Fascism was unable to influence Italian legal doctrines on positive international law. It was not even able to suggest any possible future development of international law along the lines of the fascist doctrine.

So far as the present writer knows, the only attempt to develop a fascist doctrine which could start a new trend in international law was made in 1938, when an Italo-German meeting for the study of legal problems was held in Rome.[6] It was purported to show that the political and military alliance had also developed similar legal trends [7] and that fascism and nazism had performed creative and constructive work in the legal field. One of the topics discussed was "New trends in public international law." The German delegation presented a report by Freiherr Freytag Loringhoven; the Italian presented one by Professor Costamagna.[8] If any guiding principle exists in the hodgepodge of phrases making up Costamagna's report, it is as follows. After the disintegration of the Holy Roman Empire,

---

[6] Comitato giuridico italo-germanico, *Atti del primo convegno.*
[7] The contention that Italy and Germany have unity of purpose in the legal field is contradicted by authoritative statements in both countries. Italians constantly extol the Roman spirit of their law, while for the Germans, Roman law is a symbol of degeneration. Article 19 of the Program of the National Socialist party reads: "We request that the Roman law ruling the materialistic world be replaced by German law." After the Italo-German *rapprochement* the Germans went through a great deal of trouble in attempting to appease Italian susceptibility without disclaiming this principle. See the speech of the former German Minister of Justice, Hans Frank, delivered in Rome, April 3, 1936, *Il nuovo indirizzo del diritto germanico,* and his speech of June 21, 1938, to the congress of Italo-German legal studies, *Comitato giuridico italo-germanico, Atti del primo convegno,* pp. 58 ff.
[8] Comitato giuridico italo-germanico, *Atti del primo convegno,* pp. 95 ff.

co-existence of the various states was based on the rule *pacta sunt ser-vanda*. This system of international law

satisfied the claim of the state to absolute equality of treatment and complete independence from any external power. It implied, however, the denial of any unity of Europe in relation to other world civilizations. . . .[9] Moreover, the rule *pacta sunt servanda* cannot determine the complete aims of a society of men or states. It only indicates the processes through which the international legal order can be created. . . .[10] The new conscience expressed by the popular and national revolutions (fascism and nazism) rejects the contention that the rule *pacta sunt servanda* indicates the purposes of the international community. . . .[11] The new teleogical rule advanced by the two revolutions seems to be that of autarchy, that is, recognition of the right of each nation to the possession of the necessary means for the achievement of its own purposes. . . .[12] This concept of autarchy has a dynamic meaning, and therefore it cannot be organized under the rule *pacta sunt servanda*.[13]

The Congress, after having heard such a brilliant report, approved the following conclusions on the subject:

The Committee of German and Italian jurists acknowledges the grave crisis of international law.

Maintains that it is owing to the prevailing formalistic conception of the international agreement and to the possibility that collective coercion be exercised against the will of the states.

Affirms that a new principle, recognizing the right of each state to satisfy its cultural and economic needs in its historical evolution, must be accepted.

Maintains that recognition of the right of the states to autarchy within the above-mentioned terms is the foundation of international order. A nation which cannot live, work, and defend itself independently is not sovereign.

Attributes great moral value to the proclamation of this concept as the expression of two great nations. It expresses the hope that compliance with treaties be co-ordinated with regard for autarchy in international relations.

In defense of Italian science it must be observed that the report and the conclusions emanate from a person who has no knowledge of international law and that no attention has been paid to these documents by Italian scholars. We would not consider them if they were not the only semiofficial manifestations of an alleged fascist conception of international law. Costamagna obviously fights against windmills when he affirms that the rule *pacta sunt servanda* does not express the aims of international community. Such is not the function of this rule, which is only intended to give legal foundation to the binding force of international treaties. By opposing the principle of autarchy to the rule *pacta sunt ser-*

[9] Page 96.   [10] Page 99.   [11] Page 100.
[12] The expression was used by Fascists to indicate the self-sufficiency of a nation, especially in the economic field.
[13] Page 101.

vanda Costamagna places in opposition two principles which have different purposes and are not therefore comparable.

Moreover, the alleged principle of autarchy is the denial of international law. Autarchy of a nation would mean, according to Costamagna, its right to "affirm its personality through its future evolution." In plain words, the right to expansion. It is Costamagna's opinion, confirmed by the adopted resolution, that each nation is entitled to decide how far and by what means it should expand. To this expansion the rule *pacta sunt servanda* should not constitute a limitation. In other words, the expansion of a nation should not be impeded by respect for treaties. Every state should be free to do whatever may be convenient without regard for any obligation, even if obligations have been freely accepted. The resolution adds that other states should not exert collective coercion against the will of one state. This only shows the fear of the totalitarian countries that international law may be made stronger. It is unnecessary to devote more space to the ideas of Costamagna. The absurdity of a doctrine of international law which denies the very existence of this law is obvious.

ANTAGONISM BETWEEN THE FASCIST DOCTRINE AND INTERNATIONAL LAW

Once the conclusion has been reached that no fascist doctrine of international law exists, it is worth while to examine the reasons for the inability of the fascist movement to exert any influence on the theories of international law. One important reason is the strict adherence of the Italian jurists to the positive method; since they consider law as it is, not as it should be, they do not deem it their task to express any political judgment on the existing law or to suggest such changes in positive law as would make it consistent with a given political theory. The Italian science of law is separate from politics. This legalistic trend in the study of the law somewhat divorced the doctrine from practical life. It had the advantage, however, to protect this branch of Italian life more than any other from the pressure of the political power. Until the German influence made itself felt in Italy the study of law in Italian universities did not suffer political compulsion to any noticeable extent. This was not because of fascist generosity, but because law in Italy is taught as a science. By limiting their lectures to strictly technical matters many law teachers could avoid manifestations of servility to fascism which were contrary to their feelings.

In the field of international law the tendency on the part of Italian scholars to concentrate on theoretical problems has been especially marked recently. Practical problems, the examination of which might involve a judgment on the legitimacy of fascist international practices, have been somewhat disregarded recently. It would be interesting to ascertain whether this trend, which extends more or less to every field of legal teaching in Italy, was not a form of mute protest against fascism, the only one possible in a totalitarian regime.

Another cogent reason is that the formulation of a fascist doctrine of international law would be a legal impossibility. Fascism claimed to be a revolution aimed at the destruction of the present international organization, for which it would substitute a different and better one. The concept of "revolution" is not compatible with that of an existing "legal order," which is the postulate of any legal science. In fact, every revolution denies the legal order against which it fights. On the other hand, while the revolution is in the making the new legal order which it advocates does not yet exist and cannot be the object of legal analysis.

Apart from this, the very idea of an international order understood as a permanent system of interstate relations is incompatible with fascism. The latter tends to establish the hegemony of one state over all the others, thus denying the independence of states, which is the basis of international law. The new order itself would be inconsistent with the normal conception of international law. The structure of each region into which the world would be divided would recall that of the Holy Roman Empire before the establishment of *civitates superiorem non recognoscentes*. In each section entities with limited jurisdiction would depend on one another through multiple relationships of quasi-feudal character, and all would be submitted to the supreme authority of the leading Axis country. Relationships similar to those now existing among international subjects could not exist among entities belonging to the same section but only among the leading Axis powers. Besides, these relations would be provisory, as shown above. There is no place in international law for these fascist delusions.

Fascism lacked also the moral basis for a new doctrine of international law. The doctrine of nationalities, although legally wrong and politically insufficient, enjoyed considerable success because it was pervaded by a deep spirit of justice. Since it was based on the principles of equality and liberty for all, it could be accepted by every nation and every man. Fascism represented inequality and oppression. It could never become a universal doctrine.

Chapter XV: INTERNATIONAL STATUS OF ITALY

NAME

In her capacity as an international person Italy has a name, an emblem, and a flag.[1] It is doubtful whether her international name is "Italy" or "Kingdom of Italy." The first seems to be the real one. The Kingdom of Italy comprises only the metropolitan territory. The name "Kingdom of Italy" is used in some treaties to indicate the constitutional organization of the subject. There is no need to point out that an Italian "empire" does not exist. The title "Emperor of Ethiopia" (not of Italy), which Victor Emmanuel III assumed in 1936 for himself and his successors is merely honorific. Since 1936 Ethiopia has been, not an empire, but an Italian colony devoid of international personality.

STATUS OF A GREAT POWER

Since 1870 Italy has augmented her metropolitan territory and has acquired colonies and possessions. Her population has almost doubled. Her political, economic, and military importance have greatly increased. As a result thereof she enjoys now the status of "Great Power," to which some authors attribute special legal consequences.

TERRITORIAL COMPOSITION

Italy is composed of metropolitan territory, colonies, and possessions. She administers a settlement in China. Some portions of the sea and of the atmospheric space are subjected to her sovereign powers.

METROPOLITAN TERRITORY

After its creation (1861) the Kingdom of Italy added to its territory Venetia (1866), Latium (1870),[2] and the territories acquired by her victory in the first World War.[3]

The peace Treaty of St. Germain-en-Laye, concluded with Austria on

---

[1] On this matter see Rapisardi Mirabelli, "Lo status dell'Italia nella documentazione dei suoi atti costitutivi," 43 Studi senesi (1929) 59 ff.

[2] See *supra*, p. 154.

[3] For further details and for abundant bibliographical information on the Italian annexations which followed the first World War see Udina, *L'estinzione dell'impero austro-ungarico nel diritto internazionale*, 2d ed., and, "Fiume (Città di)" in *Nuovo digesto italiano*, VI, 27 ff. On the problems of domestic legislation which resulted from the annexations see Menestrina, "Nuove provincie" in *Nuovo digesto italiano*, VIII, 1179 ff. The principal judgments in matters connected with the annexations are published in the law review *Il foro delle nuove provincie*, 1922–1929, later called *Il foro delle Venezie*.

September 10, 1919, granted Italy: Trentino; Venezia Giulia, including Istria; and the city of Zara, with a small interland which constitutes an Italian enclave in Yugoslavian Dalmatia. The demarcation of the boundaries established by the treaty was designated by a mixed commission. Boundaries with Yugoslavia were established by the Treaty of Rapallo of November 12, 1920.[4] From the point of view of the domestic Italian law Trentino was annexed by law September 26, 1920, No. 1322, Venezia Giulia and Zara, by law December 19, 1920, No. 1778.

In 1924 Italy acquired the city of Fiume. Before the first World War this important Adriatic port belonged to Hungary. A national council, having vested itself with full powers over the city, declared its annexation to Italy on October 30, 1918. This declaration resulted in internal disorder, Italian occupation, and then inter-Allied occupation. On September 19, 1919, Gabriele d'Annunzio entered the city with a corps of Italian volunteers. On September 8, 1920, D'Annunzio proclaimed the "Reggenza Italiana del Carnaro," thus making the city an international subject. An armed conflict ensued between the Reggenza and the Italian government (December 24–28, 1920). It terminated by the Pact of Abbazia, December 31, 1920. D'Annunzio left the city, and a new government was established. The city remained an independent entity until the Italo-Yugoslavian treaty of January 27, 1924, granted Fiume to Italy and the suburb of Porto Baros to Yugoslavia. From the point of view of domestic Italian law, the annexation of Fiume was effected by the decree-law of February 22, 1924, No. 211. The Treaty of Rome and the Italo-Yugoslavian agreements of Nettuno of June 20, 1925, contain provisions for the protection of the Yugoslavian minority in Fiume. From the point of view of Italian legislation, Trentino, Venezia Giulia, Zara, and Fiume are in the same legal situation as the other territories of the nation.

POSSESSIONS

Italian islands of the Aegean sea.—In 1911, during the Italian-Turkish war, Italy occupied Rhodes and the other islands of the Dodecanese, with the exception of Castelrosso.[5] By the peace Treaty of Ouchy, October 18, 1912, their occupation on the part of Italy continued as a pledge for complete evacuation of Tripolitania and Cirenaica by Turkey. Italian occupation still continued when the first World War broke out. It was extended on March 1, 1921, to Castelrosso, which was to remain under

---

[4] In 1941 Italy annexed the province of Lubiana and the most important tracts of the Dalmatian coast which belonged to Yugoslavia. See Sereni "The Status of Croatia under International Law," 35 American Political Science Review (1940) 1144 ff.

[5] On the legal status of the Italian islands of the Aegean Sea see Alhadeff, *L'ordinamento giuridico di Rodi e delle altre isole italiane dell'Egeo*; Udina, *La posizione giuridica attuale delle isole egee nell'ordinamento giuridico italiano*, and "Isole italiane dell'Egeo," in *Nuovo digesto italiano*, VII, 217 ff.

occupation by the Allied Powers under the armistice convention with Turkey.[6] In consequence of Turkey's renunciation stipulated in the peace Treaty of Lausanne of July 24, 1923, Italy acquired full sovereignty on the islands of the Dodecanese.[7] Their official name in Italian law is *Isole italiane dell'Egeo*. From the point of view of international law, the Italian islands of the Aegean sea are part of Italy; from that of Italian law, their situation is doubtful. The Dodecanese is not part of the metropolitan territory and has a special legal organization. Its inhabitants enjoy the same civil rights of Italian citizens but not the political ones and they are not subject to military service. Through compliance with certain requirements they may acquire full Italian citizenship. The legal situation of the Dodecanese is half-way in between that of the metropolitan territories and that of the colonies. Hence, the denomination of *possessions* is given to the Aegean Islands to distinguish them from the colonies.

Saseno, a small island near the Albanian coast, has a purely strategic importance.[8] It controls the Valona Bay. No civilians live on it, the only population consisting of an Italian naval garrison. Greece advanced claims on the island and occupied it on December 1, 1912, thus provoking a joint Italo-Austrian diplomatic step on December 6. In 1913 the Conference of the Ambassadors declared that the island belonged to Albania. In 1914 Greek occupation terminated. On October 30 of the same year Italian marines were landed on Saseno. The present legal status of the island is a juridical enigma. Italy's occupation is based upon an agreement of August 3, 1920, with a provisory Albanian government of that time. Since the terms of the agreement have not been made public, it is not known whether Italy was granted administration or full sovereignty. The meager Italian legislation referring to the island seems to indicate that Italy considers herself its full sovereign. From the point of view of Italian law Saseno's status is neither that of a metropolitan territory nor of a colony. If under full Italian sovereignty, Saseno must be qualified as a possession.

COLONIES

Italian East Africa.—Eritrea. By agreement of March 10, 1882, approved by the Law July 5, 1882, No. 857, the Italian company Rubattino transferred the territories surrounding the Assab Bay in the Red Sea, which it had acquired from native chieftains, to the Italian government.

---

[6] The island had been occupied during the World War by the French fleet on behalf of the Allies.

[7] They are Rhodes, Stampalia, Calchi, Leros, Scarpanto, Caso, Piscopi, Nisiro, Calino, Patmo, Lisso, Simi, Coo, and Castelrosso. To these a considerable number of small reefs, some of which are inhabited, must be added.

[8] On the legal status of Saseno see Cicchitti, "Saseno nella legislazione italiana," in Terzo congresso di studii coloniali, *Atti*, III, 316 ff.

On February 5, 1885, Italy occupied Massawa, then under the nominal sovereignty of Egypt. Some surrounding territories were acquired through conventions with local tribes. By Royal Decree of January 1, 1890, No. 6592, all those territories were consolidated in one colony called Eritrea.[9] Its boundaries with Anglo-Egyptian Sudan were established by agreements of December 25, 1897, December 7, 1898, January 1, 1899, April 16, 1901, and December 22, 1901. Boundaries with Ethiopia were agreed upon in principle by the peace Treaty of Addis Ababa, on October 26, 1896, and in greater detail by the convention of Addis Ababa of July 10, 1900. They were definitely established by the agreement of May 15, 1902, which fixed the boundaries between Sudan, Eritrea, and Ethiopia. Additional frontier agreements were concluded on February 18, 1903, and May 16, 1908. Boundaries with French Somaliland were established by the agreement of January 24, 1900, and the Protocol of July 10, 1901. They were slightly modified in favor of Italy by one of the Italo-French agreements concluded in Rome on January 7, 1935.[10] Eritrea never had an international personality. It was a colony vested with legal personality in Italian law until the creation of Italian East Africa (decree law of June 1, 1936, No. 1019, afterward law of January 11, 1937, No. 2185), of which Eritrea became a part.

Italian Somaliland was in part a possession of the Sultanate of Zanzibar acquired through agreements with it and Great Britain; in part it was, according to international law, *res nullius* and was acquired by Italy by the establishment of colonial protectorates over local tribes. By the agreements of February 8, and April 7, 1889, Italy established a colonial protectorate over the sultanates of Obbia and Mijertini. On March 8–14, 1891, Italy occupied the coastal tract between the two sultanates. By the so-called *compromis* of November 18, 1889, the English colonial company Imperial East Africa Company ceded the establishments of Benadir, of which it had obtained administration from the sultan of Zanzibar, to Italy. In 1890 Zanzibar became an English protectorate and shortly thereafter Italy obtained direct administration of Benadir through the agreements with Zanzibar and England of August 12, 1892, and May 15, 1893, respectively. By Protocol of May 5, 1894, Italy and England established their respective spheres of influence in the Gulf of Aden. The Italian colonial protectorate was extended to the territory of Lugh by the agreements of 1893 and 1895. The treaty of January 13, 1905, granted Italy full sovereignty over Benadir. Boundaries

---

[9] On the legal history of Eritrea see Mondaini, "Eritrea," in *Nuovo digesto italiano*, V, 459 ff.

[10] Italy, after having obtained the territorial advantages stipulated by said agreements, maintained that they were not in force. See letter dated, December 17, 1938, of the Italian minister of foreign affairs to the French ambassador in Rome and the latter's answer, dated December 25, 1938, 46 Rev. gén. dr. int. publ. (1939) 360 ff.

between the Italian possessions on the Indian Ocean and Ethiopia were established on paper by the Italo-Ethiopian convention of May 16, 1908, but demarcation on ground never took place. By law of April 5, 1908, No. 161, all the Italian possessions of the Indian Ocean were consolidated in the *Colonia Italiana della Somalia Italiana* (or Benadir) and in the *Protettorati Italiani della Somalia Meridionale*. In 1905 Italy acquired the territory of Nogal. By agreement of July 15, 1924, Great Britain transferred to Italy, Jubaland. All these Italian possessions were consolidated in 1925 in the *Colonia della Somalia Italiana*. It never was an international subject. Italian law granted legal personality to Somalia (law of July 6, 1933, No. 999, on the organization of Eritrea and Somalia) until the creation of Italian East Africa, of which it became a part.

Ethiopia was the victim of military operations commenced by Italy in October, 1935. At that time attempts were made by Italy to dispute the legal personality of Ethiopia. This country was described as a mere conglomeration of barbaric tribes not subject to a central power.[11] Italy could hardly deny that Ethiopia was an international person at the beginning of the conflict. She had recognized Ethiopia's international personality by entering into several international agreements with her (among which the Treaty of Conciliation and Arbitration of August 2, 1928), by sponsoring her admission into the League of Nations,[12] which was approved by the Assembly of the League on September 23, 1923, and, finally, by consenting to submit to international arbitration the Wal-Wal incident of December 5–6, 1939, which was the pretext for the Italo-Ethiopian conflict. Since Italy and Ethiopia were both international subjects, their military conflict was a real war.

On October 14, 1935, a few days after the beginning of the war, Italy annexed the Ethiopian provinces of Tigre and Agame. The illegality of this measure, taken when the conflict was in its inception and its outcome uncertain, is obvious. In the course of a few months Italy's military action destroyed the Ethiopian Empire. Addis Ababa, the capital, was occupied by Italian troops on May 5, 1936. Organized military resistance ceased almost immediately. The Negus fled the country, and the whole state structure collapsed. The extinction of Ethiopia took place in the first ten days of May, 1936. By Royal Decree Law of May 9, 1936, No. 754, Italy declared the annexation of the territory and the population of the Ethiopian Empire, and the king of Italy assumed the title of "Emperor of Ethiopia."

[11] This was the contention of the *Memoriale Italiano sulla situazione dell'Etiopia*, presented to the League of Nations in 1935.
[12] On Ethiopia's admission to the League of Nations see A. Giannini, *L'Etiopia nella Società delle Nazioni*.

The legitimacy of Italy's aggression of Ethiopia can hardly be sustained. But Ethiopia's annexation was nevertheless effective, even if the consequence of unlawful acts. For general international law provides that annexation as a consequence of *debellatio* is effective whenever the annexing state has actually destroyed the adversary and taken full control of its territory and population. The annexation of Ethiopia has been recognized by almost every state, either through formal declarations or through acts implying recognition: for example, request to the Italian authorities of the *exequatur* for the appointment of consuls in Ethiopia; conclusion of agreements with Italy concerning the Ethiopian territory; signature of treaties in which the king of Italy was designated "Emperor of Ethiopia"; exchange of diplomatic agents whose letters and credentials were signed by or addressed to the "King of Italy, Emperor of Ethiopia." But no act which might be construed as recognition of the annexation was performed by the United States.

By Royal Decree Law of June 1, 1936, No. 1019 (afterward Law of January 11, 1937, No. 2185) Ethiopia, Eritrea, and Italian Somaliland were consolidated into Italian East Africa (*Africa Orientale Italiana*). This colony has no legal personality. In Italian law it is a legal person under a general governor who has the title of "Viceroy of Ethiopia." Italian East Africa is divided into five governments: Amhara, Galla-Sidamo, Eritrea, and Somaliland, and the *Governatorato* of Addis Ababa, which comprehends the capital and its immediate surroundings.[18]

Libya was invaded by Italian troops immediately after Italy declared war on Turkey, on September 29, 1911. Her vital cities and points on the Libyan coast were occupied. By Decree Law of November 5, 1911, No. 1247 afterward Law of February 25, 1912, No. 83), Italy proclaimed her "full and entire sovereignty" over Tripolitania and Cirenaica. Since the war was not yet terminated, the annexation was certainly premature and internationally void. Italy obtained sovereignty over Libya by the peace treaty signed at Ouchy on October 18, 1912. In order to appease Turkish susceptibilities the sultan formally granted autonomy to the Libyan population the day preceding the signature of the treaty, so that Italy apparently took title over territory which had become *res nullius* by dereliction. This was a mere legal fiction; in reality there was a transfer of territory from Turkey to Italy. By the Treaty of Ouchy the sultan retained some powers over Libya in his capacity of religious head of Islam. Article 22 of the Lausanne peace treaty of July 24, 1923, between Turkey and the Allied and Associated Powers provides for the "abolition of all rights and privileges of any nature enjoyed by Turkey in Libya by virtue of the treaty of Ouchy and the acts relating to it."

---

[18] On the legal organization of Italian East Africa see Ambrosini, "Africa orientale italiana," in *Nuovo digesto italiano*, VI, 737 ff.; Borsi, *Diritto coloniale italiano*.

In consequence of the promise of colonial compensations made to Italy in the Pact of London, April 26, 1915, France consented to some rectifications of the boundaries between her colonies and Libya (agreements of Paris, September 12, 1919, and of Rome, January 7, 1935).[14] The frontier between Egypt and Libya was fixed by agreements of December 6, 1925, and July 20, 1934.

Libya never had international personality. According to Italian law it was originally divided into the colonies of Tripolitania and Cirenaica. By Decree Law, January 24, 1929, No. 99, they were consolidated into the colony of Libya, which was endowed with legal personality. Recently there has been a marked tendency toward the assimilation of certain parts of Libyan territory and of certain classes of Libyan subjects with metropolitan territory and citizens, respectively.

Tien-Tsin.—In 1901 Italy, who had taken part the year before in the repression of the Boxer Rebellion, occupied an area near Tien-Tsin in China.[15] By convention of June 7, 1902, the zone was ceded by the Chinese government to Italy in perpetual lease upon payment of a small annual rent. Tien-Tsin is under the nominal sovereignty of China. Its inhabitants are Chinese citizens. Italy has full administration, which is exercised according to a charter approved by the Italian Ministry of Foreign Affairs, on January 3, 1923, after agreement with the Chinese government. The charter was modified in 1929. Tien-Tsin is not a colony, but a settlement. It has no international personality,[16] though it is a legal person according to Italian law.[17]

Territorial waters.—Italy accepts the distinction between the high seas, which are free, and territorial waters, upon which certain powers are granted by international law to the coastal state. Freedom of the high seas was advocated in the official Italian project of the League of Nations (1918). Among the fundamental rules of conduct to be followed by the states as stated in the preamble, No. 4 proclaimed that "navigation is free to the merchant ships of every flag. Sovereign rights on territorial waters should not be exercised so as to substantially impair such freedom." [18]

As to territorial waters, Italy maintains that there are no precise rules of international law determining their extent. In principle each state is free to establish the limits of its territorial waters. Italy has consistently refused to recognize the three-mile limit.[19] It is doubtful whether there

[14] See p. 282n.
[15] On the legal status of Tien-Tsin see Cicchitti, "Tien Tsin nella legislazione italiana," in Terzo congresso di studii coloniali, *Atti*, III, 309 ff.
[16] C. A. (Court of Appeals) Ancona, July 1, 1925, in *Foro it.* (1926), I, 193.
[17] Consular Tribunal Tien-Tsin, April 23, 1923, in *Foro it.* (1923), I, 434.
[18] The project is published by Baldoni, *La Società delle Nazioni*, pp. 201 ff.
[19] While some liquor treaties concluded by the United States in 1924 affirm (Article 1)

exists a provision of Italian law determining the extent of Italian waters for every purpose. The provisions which determine the waters in which Italy can exercise her various powers on the sea establish different areas for each power.[20] Article 14 of the Service Regulations for the Royal Corps of the Finance Guard (*Regolamento di servizio per il corpo della Regia Guardia di Finanza*) approved by Royal Decree, January 17, 1909, No. 125, provides that "territorial waters comprise the zone of sea which starts from the littoral and extends toward the high sea for a length of ten kilometers."

This provision does not define territorial waters for the sole purpose of the statute in which it is contained. It is deemed to indicate the extension of Italian territorial waters for all purposes unless otherwise provided in special statutes.[21] It was so decided by the *Corte di Cassazione* of Turin by judgment of June 17, 1879, with reference to an identical provision contained in an earlier statute.[22]

"la ferme intention des Hautes Parties contractantes de maintenir le principe que trois milles marines constituent les justes (or réelles) limites des eaux territoriales," the one with Italy (June 3, 1924) declares (Article 1) that "les Hautes Parties contractantes conservent respectivement leurs droits et prétentions, sans dérogation à induire de la présente convention, en ce qui concerne l'étendue de leur juridiction territoriale." In 1922, at the meeting of the Hague Commission of Jurists to Consider and Report upon the Revision of the Rules of Warfare, the Italian delegation advocated a ten-mile territorial air belt. The delegation was of the opinion that international law, as generally accepted, contains no rule prohibiting a state from extending its territorial waters to a distance of ten sea miles from its coast (*General Reports of the Commission*, 1924 N.W.C., 96, 153). The prevailing opinion among Italian authors is that there is no positive rule of international law establishing the maximum extent of the territorial waters. See Anzilotti, "Nota," 11 *Riv. dir. int.* (1917) 110 ff.; Fedozzi, "La condition juridique des navires de commerce," 10 *Rec. des cours* (1925) 5 ff., and *Trattato di diritto internazionale*, p. 317. Baldoni, *Il mare territoriale nel diritto internazionale comune*, expounds the theory that a state can extend its territorial waters as far as they are an accessory of the land.

[20] Italy is a party to the convention concerning the Suez Canal which adopted the three-mile limit. However, she established a different distance with regard to her territorial waters in several statutes: twelve miles, in the royal decrees of February 4, 1913, and March 14, 1932, concerning the organization of the Lybian custom; ten miles, in the Law, June 16, 1912, No. 612, concerning the transit and sojourn of merchant ships in proximity of coastal fortifications; ten kilometers, in Article 66 of the customs law approved by royal decree of January 26, 1896, and in the royal decree of August 12, 1911, No. 1030, concerning the organization of Somaliland custom; three miles, in the royal decree of March 27, 1913, No. 312, containing fishing regulations for Tripolitania and Cirenaica. By the treaty of friendship, commerce, and navigation with Mexico, April 15, 1890, Italy agrees to recognize as Mexican territorial waters a zone of sea extending twenty kilometers from the shore. The three-mile limit was adopted in the Italo-Turkish convention of January 4, 1932, delimiting the territorial waters of Castelrosso. The Italian legislative acts and regulations delimiting the territorial sea are collected in Italy, *Ministero della Marina, Norme e disposizioni sul mare territoriale*.

[21] See Sandiford, "Il mare territoriale secondo il diritto positivo italiano," 60 *Rivista marittima* (1927) 122 ff.; Fedozzi, *Trattato di diritto internazionale*, p. 372; Scialoja, "Mare," in *Nuovo digesto italiano*, VIII, 155 ff.; Ago, "Sui limiti del mare territoriale," 3 *Rivista del diritto della navigazione* (1937) 370 ff.

[22] Fedozzi, *Trattato di diritto internazionale*, p. 373. This author recalls that the Court of

Italy's claim to territorial waters beyond the three-mile limit has not clashed with the interests of other nations and therefore has not aroused a marked opposition. However, at the beginning of the first World War, when Italy declared her neutrality and fixed the limit of her territorial waters to six maritime miles for the purpose of maritime neutrality (Royal Decree, August 6, 1914, No. 398), the United States declared, November 2, 1914, that they could not recognize Italian claims beyond three miles.[23]

In answer to a questionnaire sent to the various governments by the League of Nations Committee for the Codification of International Law, Italy declared that international law should establish the extent of territorial waters to six miles with special rights of the coastal states over six additional miles. The territorial waters should be measured from: "(a) along the coast, the line of low tide following the sinuosities of the coast; (b) in front of bays, a breadth of 20 miles; (c) in front of ports, six miles beyond the line to be fixed." [24]

Through international conventions Italy granted and received, respectively, fishing rights in her own and foreign territorial waters.[25] Treaties concluded with neighboring countries determined for certain purposes the limit of territorial waters of the contracting parties; for example, the treaty with France, January 18, 1908, limiting the fishing zone between Sardinia and Corsica; the treaty with Yugoslavia of September 14, 1921, which later was incorporated in the agreements concluded between the two powers in Rome, October 23, 1922, and was extended to the waters of Fiume and Susak on July 20, 1925. Fishing rights were expressly granted by Tunisia (Convention, September 28, 1896); Egypt (Convention, July 14, 1906); Albania (Treaty, January 20, 1924); Greece (Convention, November 24, 1926); and under certain conditions by France for the Algerian waters (Italo-French Convention, November 3, 1881). By convention, February 3, 1938, Albania granted a fishing monopoly in her territorial waters to an Italian company. Italian fishermen enjoy fishing rights in territorial waters of other countries con-

---

Cassation of Naples, in a judgment of November 10, 1892, established the limit of ten miles without any satisfactory reasons. The three-mile limit was adopted by the Tribunal of Sarzana, November 18, 1898, in the "Ortigia" case. In favor of the limit of the range of cannon are: C. A. Trani, December 20, 1884; C. A. Genoa, November 10, 1894; Tr. Naples, June 5, 1899; Tr. Grosseto, March 27, 1924; Pr. Venice, July 10, 1936.

[23] For. Rel. 1914, Suppl., p. 66, Washington, 1928. The State Department, however, brought the Italian decree to the attention of the Navy Department so that appropriate orders may be issued to avoid any possible "incident." (MS records, Department of State.)

[24] League of Nations, Conference for the Codification of International Law, *Bases of discussion; Territorial waters*, Geneva, 1929. The Italian answer is by letter dated November 19, 1928.

[25] For further details see Daggett, "The Regulation of Maritime Fisheries by Treaty," 28 Am. J. Int. L. (1934) 692, and Longhena, "Regime giuridico per la pesca," *Nuovo digesto italiano*, XI, 103 ff.

sequent to the "most favored nation" clause continued in most Italian commerce treaties. Italy and Switzerland concluded agreements regarding fishing in the Maggiore and Lugano lakes and in the neighboring rivers (Conventions, November 8, 1882; July 8, 1898; June 13, 1906, and February 8, 1911).

Aerial space.—Italy follows the principles announced by the Aeronautic Convention October 13, 1919, that state sovereignty extends to the aerial space above territories and territorial waters.[26] The Royal Decree Law, August 20, 1923, No. 2207, regulating aerial navigation provides (Article 1) that:

The Italian state exercises full and absolute sovereignty over the aerial space above her territory including territorial waters. Unless otherwise provided in international conventions, state territory, with respect to sovereignty includes national territory, both metropolitan and colonial, that of the protectorates and of the countries entrusted to the Italian state by mandate or any other title.

Several international conventions regulate transit of foreign aircraft above Italian territory.

Boundaries.—Frontiers of the metropolitan and colonial territories are established entirely by international agreements or arbitrations. There does not seem to be any pending dispute as to the Italian boundaries. The Italian-Swiss difference concerning sovereignty over the Alps of Cravairola was settled in favor of Italy by arbitral award of September 23, 1874.[27] Boundary differences between Italian Somaliland and English colonies were settled by arbitration on April 16, 1901.[28] By special agreement, on May 30, 1929, Italy and Turkey were to submit to the decision of the Permanent Court of International Justice the dispute concerning the delimitation of territorial waters between Castelrosso and Anatolia. The question was settled out of court by the above-mentioned agreement of January 4, 1932. During the Wal-Wal arbitration the Ethiopian government raised the question of the ownership of territory where Wal-Wal was situated. The interlocutory question was settled by the League Council, which decided that the two governments had not agreed in the *compromis* that the arbitral commission should examine frontier questions. The arbitral award of September 3, 1935, did not decide to whom Wal-Wal belonged.

The Italian government does not seem to have a particular theory of its own concerning the determination of boundaries. Where boundaries are established by treaties, Italy has consistently taken the position that they must be actually traced with regard to the real intention of the con-

[26] Enriques, *Lo spazio atmosferico nel diritto internazionale;* Giannini, *Le convenzioni internazionali di diritto aeronautico.*
[27] Moore, *History and Digest of the International Arbitrations,* p. 2027.
[28] Darby, *International Tribunals,* p. 907.

tracting parties. In order to ascertain it, resort to extrinsic interpretation may be made. This principle was maintained by Italy and accepted by Great Britain in the case of the Juba River. A Protocol of March 24, 1891, provided that the center of the channel constituted the dividing line between the colonial possessions of the two countries. An alteration having occurred in the course of the river, England maintained that the boundary should continue to follow the center of the original channel of the river, while Italy contended that it should be constituted by the middle of the new stream. Italy invoked the letter and spirit of the Protocol, according to which the boundary between the two colonies was to follow the actual center of the stream, not what had been the center of it at a given moment only. Italy's viewpoint was accepted by the exchange of notes of July 8–15, 1911. It also provided that "in case of any subsequent change in the river bed, the bank on the left or the river mouth and the territory contiguous to it will belong to Italy, and the bank on the right with the territory contiguous to it, will belong to Great Britain." [29]

An agreement between Great Britain and Italy designating the 49th parallel as the dividing line between Italian Somaliland and the British Dominions, on the assumption that the village of Bender Ziadeh would thereby be situated on Italian territory, was modified by the convention of March 17, 1907, when a survey showed that the line of demarcation following the 49th parallel would have placed Bender Ziadeh on English territory. [30]

Several international agreements regulate the use of boundary streams and of those which run through both Italian and foreign territories: for example, convention of December 17, 1914, between Italy and France which prohibits the exploitation of the water power of the Roja River and its tributaries to such an extent as to considerably affect their flow; [31] the convention of 1901 with England concerning the Gash River, which flows from Eritrea to the Anglo-Egyptian Sudan; the agreements with Great Britain of 1915 concerning the African River Juba; [32] and the exchange of notes between Italy and Yugoslavia whereby the latter promises not to bring about any changes in the sources and the flow of the torrent Recina which might affect Fiume's water supply. [33] By the Lateran Treaty of February 11, 1929 (Art. 6), Italy is bound to secure ownership of an

[29] The exchange of notes is published in 8 Riv. dir. int. (1914) 110. On this question see the official publication *La foce del Giuba*, Roma, 1912, in which the opinions of several eminent Italian jurists are published.
[30] Meriggi, "Trattati e convenzioni internazionali," *Nuovo digesto italiano*, II, 394.
[31] Text in 9 Riv. dir. int. (1915) 261, with important note of Anzilotti. For a judicial interpretation of the convention see Court of Cassation, Sezioni unite, February 13, 1939, in *Foro it.* (1939), I, 1036, with note of Bassano.
[32] Text in 10 Riv. dir. int. (1916) 310.
[33] The Italo-Yugoslavian agreement of October 23, 1922, provides for the affluence of a sufficient amount of water from the Yugoslavian territory to the city of Zara.

adequate supply of water to the Vatican City. A declaration embodied in the agreements between Great Britain and Italy, signed in Rome on April 16, 1938, provides that Italy shall not modify the *status quo* of the waters of Lake Tana, which is situated in Italian East Africa, so as to impair irrigation of Anglo-Egyptian Sudan.[34]

SPECIAL RELATIONS BETWEEN ITALY AND OTHER INTERNATIONAL SUBJECTS

San Marino.—This is one of the smallest states in the world. It is situated in Central Italy and is surrounded by Italian territory. This ancient republic is undoubtedly a state; it is endowed with a complete political, administrative, legislative, and judicial organization. It is also an international subject and participates independently in international relations. It exchanges diplomatic and consular agents with several states; it concludes international treaties [35] and participates in wars. Perhaps as a consequence of its proximity to Italy, San Marino has become increasingly belligerent. During the first World War it sided with the Entente, and since it was not included among the signatories of the treaties of peace, it remained at war longer than any other state. Recently San Marino made peace with Germany in order to declare war on England.

In 1862 Italy concluded a Convention of Friendship and of Good Neighbor's Relation with San Marino; others followed on March 27, 1872; April 13, 1892; June 28, 1897; and March 31, 1939. Postal, telegraphic, telephonic, scholastic, and transit conventions were also concluded. The Convention of March 31, 1939, regulates also judicial and administrative assistance.[36] The parties may exchange diplomatic representatives (Art. 2). In the states in which there are no representatives of San Marino, its citizens may request the assistance of Italian consular authorities (Art. 3).

The question has been raised whether San Marino is an Italian protectorate. Article 1 of the Treaty of 1939 repeats the formula contained in all the preceding treaties of friendship and good neighbors relation, that "the Republic of San Marino, inasmuch as it is certain that it will never be deprived of the protective friendship of His Majesty the King of Italy for the preservation of its 'most ancient liberty and independence,' declares that it will never accept that of any other power."

Neither in law nor in fact does the Italian state interfere with the internal and international affairs of San Marino. The above-mentioned article reaffirms the "most ancient liberty and independence" of the republic. The relationship between the two states is one of protection only,[37]

---

[34] Text in 2 Diritto internazionale (1938) 403.

[35] Treaties of extradition with Great Britain, October 10, 1899; Netherlands, November 7, 1902; Belgium, June 15, 1903; and the United States, February 19, 1906, and June 19, 1908.

[36] The convention is published in 32 Riv. dir. int. (1940) 291, with note of L. Marmo.

[37] Kunz, *Die Staatenverbindungen*, p. 289.

not of protectorate. Italy is bound to protect San Marino's liberty and independence; the latter cannot accept similar protection from any other state.

Albania.—The Pact of London, April 26, 1915, concerning Italy's participation in the first World War, provided for the creation after the war of an Albanian state under Italian protectorate. At the peace conference the suggestion of an Italian mandate on Albania failed. Since 1926 Albania fell under complete political, economical, and military control and was considered a *de facto* protectorate of Italy. In April, 1939, Italy intervened militarily forcing King Zog to flee the country. A new regime was established.[38] Victor Emmanuel III was proclaimed King of Albania and accepted the office for himself and his successors. He exercises his powers in Albania through a Lieutenant General, an Italian citizen who is an organ of the Italian state and at the same time of the Albanian state. A new constitution was issued on June 3, 1939. Albania is now a fascist state with a totalitarian organization. Only one party is permitted, the Albanian Fascist Party, which controls the entire political life of the country and depends in turn on the Italian Fascist Party. The Albanian army has been incorporated in Italy's. Immediately after the *coup d'état* several agreements were concluded between Italy and Albania. An economic currency and tariff union has been established (Conventions of April 20 and May 28, 1939); the management of the diplomatic and consular services of the two countries has been unified in the Italian Ministry of Foreign Affairs (Treaty June 3, 1939); Italians in Albania and Albanians in Italy enjoy all political and civil rights granted to them in their respective territories (Agreement April 20, 1939). An Undersecretariate for Albanian Affairs has been created in the Italian Ministry of Foreign Affairs. In Italy many Albanians have been appointed members of the Senate, of the Foreign Service, of the Academy of Italy, army officers, and university professors. Italian advisers control all Albanian ministries. Albania withdrew from the League of Nations and has entered the present war on the Italian side. Albania's status during the present war is not considered.

These measures are intended to give the impression that Albania is still a subject of international law. This was probably done in order to appease Albanians. In reality, however, Albania's international personality is a legal fiction. The country participates in international relations only through the compulsory agency of Italy. Its international and internal activities are under complete Italian control. If we assume that Albania is still an international subject, then its relationship with Italy is one of "real union," similar to the relationship which existed between

[38] Sereni, "The Legal Status of Albania," 35 American Political Science Review (1940) 311 ff.; Rizzo, "La unione dell'Albania con l'Italia e lo statuto del Regno d'Albania," 31 Rivista di diritto pubblico (1939) 42 ff.; Cansacchi, "L'unione dell'Italia con l'Albania," 37 Riv. dir. int. (1940) 113 ff.

Sweden and Norway, Denmark and Iceland. In fact, there is a prearranged community of the head of the state, since it is understood that the crown of Albania will always be vested in the head of the Italian state. There is, moreover, a unified organization for the satisfaction of common interests in the field of economics, tariffs, and currency affairs, of international relations and external defense. Formally the union is based on the legal equality of the partners; in fact, on Italy's hegemony. A characteristic of this union is the fact that the parties have not only a common organization but also an identical regime, inasmuch as Albania has accepted the Fascist principles. Because of the incorporation of the Albanian army in that of Italy, the relationship between the two states has some aspects of the suzerainty relationship. In its final period Turkey's suzerainty of Egypt was based chiefly upon the incorporation of the Egyptian forces into the Turkish army.[39]

Vatican State.—On February 11, 1929, Italy and the Holy See concluded a treaty and a concordat in the Lateran palace, thus putting an end to the Roman question, that is, the conflict between the two powers which arose from the occupation of Rome by Italy in 1870.[40] Article 3 of the treaty provides:

Italy recognizes full possession and exclusive and absolute power and sovereign jurisdiction of the Holy See over the Vatican, as at present constituted, with all its appurtenances and endowments. Thus the Vatican City is established for the special purposes and with the provisions laid down in the present treaty . . .

As a consequence of this treaty a new international subject arose, the Vatican City, the smallest state of the world. Its territory is limited to the Vatican palaces, the basilica and the piazza of St. Peter, and a few near-by buildings. The new state is completely surrounded by Italian territory, but provisions of the treaty guarantee freedom of communication with the rest of the world. Foreign diplomats at the Holy See may reside in Italy, where they will enjoy the same prerogatives, immunities, and exemptions granted to the diplomatic agents of the king of Italy (Article 12). Foreign diplomatic agents to the Holy See will have access to the Vatican City through Italy, even if their countries are at war with Italy (Article 19). Regular diplomatic relations are established between Italy and the Holy See. Because of the small size of the Vatican City the paradoxical situation exists that the Italian embassy to the Holy See is situated on Italian territory.

Vatican City is undoubtedly a state. It is endowed with its own ad-

[39] Since the present work does not deal with the Italian practice during the present war, we do not analyse the relationship between Italy and the new Kingdom of Croatia. For detailed information on it see Sereni, "The Status of Croatia under International Law," 35 American Political Science Review (1940) 1144 ff.
[40] Article 26 of the Treaty so expressly provides.

ministrative, legislative, and judicial organization, its own flag, army, and monetary system. It is also an international subject, which came into being in 1929, on territory formally belonging to the Italian state.[41] Its particular characteristics result from its relationship with the Holy See. As stated in the preamble of the Lateran Treaty, Vatican City is a state created "to secure absolute and visible independence to the Holy See and to guarantee its indisputable sovereignty in international relations." While the normal aim of a state is the welfare of the state itself and of its citizens, Vatican City has not an autonomous purpose. It is only intended to support a religious entity, the Holy See. For this reason Vatican City, like the medieval state and unlike the modern state, is an example of patrimonial sovereignty. It is owned entirely by its sovereign, the Holy See. The preamble of the Lateran Treaty declares that the Holy See has "complete ownership, exclusive and absolute power, and sovereign jurisdiction" over Vatican City. This formula is repeated in Article 3. The functional character of Vatican City is also evident in its autocratic constitution, whereby all power is concentrated in the Holy See, and in the composition of its population, composed only of persons connected with the Holy See (Article 9 of the Treaty). If we accept the opinion that the Catholic Church is an international person, we must reach the conclusion that the Catholic Church and Vatican City are two distinct international persons united by a relationship similar to that of "real union." The two subjects have the same head, the Holy See: and the Vatican City exists only for the realization of the aims of the Catholic Church.

This particular characteristic of the Vatican City affects its relationship with Italy.[42] In view of its peculiar function Vatican City

will always and in every case be considered neutral and inviolable territory (Article 24).

In conformity with the regulations of international law, aircraft of any kind are prohibited from flying over the territory of the Vatican (Articles 7, 2).

The Holy See declares that it wishes to remain and will remain extraneous to all temporal disputes between nations and to international conferences invoked for the settlement of such disputes, unless the contending parties make a joint appeal to its mission of peace; nevertheless it reserves the right in every case to exercise its moral and spiritual power (Article 24).

As a consequence thereof, neither the Holy See nor Vatican City could become members of the League of Nations or intervene in a peace con-

[41] Vatican City is a new state, not the continuation of the Papal State which ended by *debellatio* by Italy in 1870.
[42] Article 1 of the Treaty provides: "Italy recognizes and reaffirms the principle set forth in Art. 1 of the Constitution of the Kingdom of Italy of March 4, 1848, whereby the Roman Catholic and Apostolic Religion is the sole religion of the state." Italy is therefore bound by an international treaty, not only by concordate, to be a confessional state. The far-reaching consequences of this obligation can be easily realized.

ference without Italy's consent. In view of the essentially spiritual aims of Vatican City, some material activities on its behalf are performed by Italy. The Piazza of St. Peter, which is part of Vatican City shall be normally open to the public and subject to the police power of the Italian state (Article 3). Upon request by delegation of the Holy See, Italy will punish crimes committed within Vatican City; but if the author of the crime has taken refuge in Italian territory, Italy shall proceed against him in her own right and according to her own laws (Article 22). Many agreements subsequent to those of February 11, 1929, have been concluded by Italy with Vatican City for the regulation of various questions (financial problems, recognition of judgments) which arise from the existence of the new state.

League of Nations.—Italy was one of the original members of the League of Nations and was granted from the very beginning a permanent seat in the Council. Italy was also a member of the International Labour Organization. Until 1935 Italy's participation in the League was inconspicuous, although some Italian delegates, such as Scialoia, enjoyed considerable prestige.[43] Italy granted the League the necessary means for the creation in Rome of the International Institute for the Unification of Private Law, which was established in 1926, and of the International Institute for Educational Cinematography which was established in 1928. An Italian-Greek dispute caused by the assassination of a member of an Italian military mission on August 27, 1923, resulted in Italian occupation of Corfu. Finally it was satisfactorily settled through the intervention of the League. The Italo-Ethiopian incident of Wal-Wal, of December 5, 1934, was also submitted to the League. As a consequence of the failure of every conciliatory effort economic sanctions against Italy were approved in November, 1935. The failure of the sanction procedure largely accounts for the subsequent crisis of the League. On December 11 and 14, 1937, Italy announced her withdrawal from the League and the International Labour Organization. By letters dated December 27, 1937, the Italian Minister of Foreign Affairs denounced the obligations assumed by Italy for the creation and the maintenance of the International Institute for the Unification of Private Law and the International Institute for Educational Cinematography.

The conflict between Italy and the League existed in a latent form long before 1935. Fascism accused the League of being only an instrumentality created by France and Great Britain for the preservation of the international status quo against any attempt at revision. The International

[43] The speeches, reports, and communications of the Italian delegates at the League of Nations have been collected by Bruccoleri, L'opera dei delegati italiani alla Società delle Nazioni.
    A similar work concerning the Italian contribution to the activities of the International Labour Office is De Michelis, L'Italia nell'organizzazione internazionale del lavoro.

Labour Office was criticized on the grounds that it opposed the Fascist conception of the relationship between capital and labor. Italy showed much greater deference to the Permanent Court of International Justice. On only one occasion did the Court decide a controversy between Italy alone and another state. This was the case of the *Moroccan Phosphates,* decided in favor of France on June 14, 1938.[44]

Axis powers.—Italy is a signatory of the so-called Tripartite Pact with Germany and Japan of September 27, 1940. Other states, more or less openly controlled by the original signatories, have subsequently adhered to the pact. The philosophy underlying it has been already considered. The agreement is in substance a military and political understanding whereby the parties promise each other reciprocal aid and agree upon respective spheres of influence. The Fascist press hailed the pact as an act changing the entire structure of the international community. In reality it does not effect any general or permanent change in the legal status of Italy, important as its political repercussions may be.

[44] The decision is published in Perm. Ct. Int. Jus., June 14, 1938, Publ. Ser. A/B, No. 74.

Chapter XVI: INTERNATIONAL RELATIONS OF THE KINGDOM OF ITALY

THE Italian practice of international law during the last fifty years is of much less importance than its theory. It did not attain much originality even after fascism came to power. Some fascist practices during recent years are not the expression of new tendencies, but plain violations of international law; others are indications of a change in international relations to which democratic and totalitarian states have both contributed.

The present analysis is not intended to examine the Italian practice of international law as a whole. Only those aspects which present some special interest will be examined.

The analysis goes only to Italy's entrance into the present World War (June 10, 1940).

TREATIES OF PARTICULAR INTEREST

Italy is a party to most of the important multilateral treaties concluded in the last fifty years. Until it withdrew from the League of Nations and the International Labour Organization it ratified most of the agreements stipulated under the auspices of these organizations. The analysis of these instruments, however, is not of particular interest here. Attention will be given to some agreements (generally bilateral) which Italy has concluded by reason of her particular political and economic status.[1]

Treaties of judicial and administrative assistance.—Italian policy concerning the conclusion of international conventions has been deeply affected by the excess of population in the country. Until a few years ago it found an outlet in emigration. At first a large part of Italian emigration, especially to other European countries, was temporary. After the first World War most Italian emigrants settled permanently abroad, but they did not break all ties with their mother country. There ensued an intense legal intercourse, which prompted Italy to conclude conventions concerning judicial assistance with almost all foreign countries.[2] Italian

---

[1] For statistical data on the languages used in the Italian treaties see Hudson, "Languages Used in Treaties," 26 Am. J. Int. L. (1932) 371.

[2] For further information on these treaties see Sereni, *La rappresentanza nel diritto internazionale*, pp. 249 ff.; Italy, Ministero degli Esteri, *L'Italiano all'estero e la sua condizione giuridica*; Cucinotta, *L'assistenza giudiziaria nei rapporti internazionali*, and *Attività pubbliche dello stato esercitate da organi di uno stato straniero*; Morelli, *Il diritto processuale civile internazionale*.

conventions on judicial assistance relate both to civil and criminal proceedings. With regard to civil matters, they provide for the service of documents, the execution of letters rogatory, the obtaining of information with regard to proceedings concerning minors, lunatics, and bankruptcies, and the execution of measures concerning the status of persons. Provisions concerning the co-operation in these matters between Italian and foreign authorities are enclosed in most of the Italian consular treaties. Many treaties dealing especially with the exchange of documents and the execution of letters rogatory have also been concluded.[3] Italy entered into treaties with many states for the recognition of foreign judgments and other acts, both judicial and nonjudicial. Some of the most recent conventions on these matters (for example, that with France of July 3, 1930; Switzerland, January 3, 1933; Netherlands, June 7, 1935; and Germany, January 3, 1936) have reached a considerable technical perfection and have been taken as a model by several other states.[4] These conventions generally establish the principle that a foreign judgment or any other judicial act which answers to the requisites indicated in the convention will be recognized in Italy without need of any further proceeding. Acts of execution based on a foreign judgment, however, can only be performed after its recognition. This requires a special proceeding (*giudizio di delibazione*), in which the merits of the case are not re-examined.[5] Several Italian treaties on judicial assistance provide that each contracting party shall excuse citizens of the other from the duty of giving security for costs (*cautio judicatum solvi*) when parties to a law suit and shall allow them to prosecute or defend as poor persons.

Judicial assistance in penal matters deals especially with the execution of letters rogatory and extradition. Article 13 of the Italian penal code provides that "extradition is governed by the Italian penal law, conventions and international usages." The same article provides that Italy may grant extradition of her own citizens only when so provided by international conventions. Extradition may be granted for political crimes. It does not appear, however, that Italy in her more recent conventions consented to the extradition of nationals or of persons indicted

[3] Italy adhered to the Hague conventions of 1902 and 1905 on private international law, to the Geneva protocol of September 24, 1923, concerning the arbitration clauses, and to the Geneva Convention, September 26, 1927, concerning the recognition and the execution of foreign arbitral awards. See Sereni, "La convenzione di Ginevra per l'esecuzione delle sentenze arbitrali straniere," 23 Riv. dir. int. (1931) 595. Italy recently concluded conventions for judicial assistance with Hungary, Austria, Yugoslavia, Czechoslovakia (all signed April 6, 1922), Turkey, August 10, 1926, Great Britain, December 17, 1930, and the Vatican City.

[4] For a detailed analysis of these conventions see Morelli, *Il diritto processuale civile internazionale*, pp. 401 ff.

[5] In the absence of international conventions the conditions for the recognition in Italy of foreign judgments are indicated by Article 941, Code Civil Procedure, modified by Royal Decree Law, July 20, 1919, No. 1272 (later, Law, May 28, 1925, No. 283).

or convicted of political crimes.[6] Assistance on administrative matters deals especially with the transmission of acts concerning vital statistics (birth, marriage, and death certificates) and of information concerning the status of persons.

Agreements for administrative assistance in tax matters have been concluded by Italy, especially in connection with agreements against double taxation. The financial administrations of the contracting parties shall co-operate in the assessment and the collection of taxes and by the exchange of information on the matters (Italo-German Convention of June 9, 1938, Italo-Rumanian Convention of December 3, 1938).

Treaties for the assistance of Italians abroad.—Italy concluded several agreements of the usual type concerning gratuitous assistance and repatriation of indigent and diseased citizens.[7] Some of these agreements deal especially with sailors. Of peculiar interest are some agreements concluded by Italy to prevent the exploitation of Italian emigrants. Some of them are intended to provide equitable treatment and hygienic facilities during the journey (Agreement, November 25, 1925, between Italy and Spain concerning the co-operation of their respective emigration services for the protection and assistance of emigrants during the journey). Others are intended to secure equitable labor conditions in the countries of immigration.[8] They usually provide that wages of the Italian workers shall not be lower than those of the nationals of the other contracting party and that the Italians shall enjoy the same benefits with regard to social assistance, working conditions, insurances, and compensations for accidents, diseases, disabilities, old age, and unemploy-

[6] A list of Italian treaties of extradition concluded until 1934 is published by Aloisi, "Estradizione," *Nuovo digesto italiano,* V, 687. See also Cucinotta, *L'assistenza giudiziaria nei rapporti internazionali,* p. 250. Recently Italy concluded treaties of extradition with Latvia, July 13, 1935; Estonia, August 30, 1935, and Brazil, November 5, 1936 (additional protocol to the treaty of extradition of November 28, 1931). The treaty of extradition between Italy and Brazil of November 28, 1931, which is one of the most progressive among those concluded by Italy, contained a provision whereby each contracting party consented to surrender his own citizens in the cases contemplated by the treaty. Article 1 of the additional protocol of 1936 provides that the parties are not bound to surrender their own citizens unless they acquired citizenship by naturalization after the commission of the crime for which extradition is requested. Analogous provisions are contained in the treaties of Italy with Panama (August 7, 1930, Article 7) and Estonia (August 30, 1935, Article 6). Italy has concluded a treaty of extradition with the United States, March 23, 1868, complemented by the additional acts of July 19, 1868, and June 11, 1884. Italy is not an original signatory of the Geneva convention of November 16, 1937, for the prevention and repression of terrorism. It has been reported that Italy recently ratified this convention and that under its terms she successfully requested the surrender by France, after the armistice of 1940, of many Italian political refugees who had migrated to France before the second World War.

[7] Italy waived her privileges under Capitulations in almost all foreign countries: lately she signed treaties ending the capitulation regime in Siam, May 9, 1926; Persia, June 25, 1927; China, November 27, 1928, and Egypt, May 8, 1937.

[8] For further information concerning these conventions see Gemma, *Il diritto internazionale del lavoro.*

ment. Some of these treaties provide for a minimum standard of treatment to be granted the Italian workers, irrespective of the treatment which may be accorded to local workers.

Italy's first labor treaty was concluded with France on April 15, 1904. It dealt mostly with general principles, which found concrete application in the treaty of June 9, 1906, later modified by another on September 30, 1919. Labor treaties were also concluded with Luxembourg, November 11, 1920, Brazil, October 8, 1921, and Belgium, September 29, 1938. Some of these treaties contain provisions for the compensation of workmen's accidents. Bilateral conventions on workmen's insurances, pensions, and compensation for accidents were concluded with Hungary (September 19, 1909, and November 12, 1932), Germany (July 31, 1912), the United States (February 21, 1913), the Argentine (March 26, 1920), Sweden (July 12–August 28, 1920), Switzerland (March 4, 11, 15, 16, 1921, and March 3, 1929), France (May 22, 1924, June 4, 1924, August 13, 1932, and January 31, 1933), Belgium (September 29, 1938), and Yugoslavia (July 20, 1925). Since part of the Italian immigration is temporary, some of these conventions provide that in case the workers return to Italy the contributions paid by them for social security shall be credited in their favor with Italian insurance companies.[9]

Italian immigration raised many problems of double nationality. Individuals born in countries other than Italy of parents who are Italian citizens are considered Italians by the Italian law, which follows the criterion *jus sanguinis*, whereas they are considered citizens of the country where they were born by that country if its legislation follows the criterion *jus soli*. This happens especially in American countries. Several Italian treaties of establishment contain provisions intended to eliminate conflicts arising from double nationality. One of the consequences of double nationality is that it renders the individual liable to military service in both countries. To avoid this particular inconvenience Italy has concluded an agreement with Argentine on August 8, 1938.[10]

Economic agreements.—Italy's economic structure has changed considerably in the last ten years. Freedom of international transactions has been practically suppressed. Economic relations with foreign countries are submitted to the control of governmental agencies, which determine what products may be imported or exported, at what prices, and in what quantity. Foreign exchange is supplied by state-controlled banks upon governmental authorization. Most of the international payments are effected through clearings supervised by the state or by the *Banca d'Italia,*

[9] Very important is the monograph on this subject by Perassi, "Le assicurazioni sociali nel diritto internazionale," 4 Atti dell'Istituto Nazionale delle Assicurazioni (1932) 56 ff.
[10] 32 Riv. dir. int. (1940) 104.

the bank of issue which acts as an agent for the state. This system is intended to prevent the creation of financial liabilities for Italy and to prevent those financial transactions which are not considered strictly necessary to the national economy.

In order to enforce this economic system, Italy has concluded clearing agreements with almost all foreign countries, whereby payments to or from Italian residents take place through the Bank of Italy or other government-controlled institutions. The agreements determine also the rate of exchange between the Italian currency and that of the other contracting party and very often the type, amount, and price of goods which will be exchanged. Due to the instability of economic relations between nations, these agreements are concluded for very short periods of time and are frequently modified. It is unnecessary, therefore, to give a list of them here.[11]

Ideological agreements.—On November 25, 1936, Germany and Japan signed an agreement generally known as Anti-Comintern Pact against the Communist International. The pact includes two articles:

(1) The parties will inform each other concerning the activities of the Communist International and consult concerning measures to combat it.

(2) The parties will invite third parties whose domestic peace is endangered "to embark upon measures for warding these off in accordance with the spirit of this agreement or to join in it."

By protocol of November 6, 1937, Italy adhered to the pact, and Germany and Japan agreed "that Italy shall be considered an original signatory of it." Apparently the agreement has an ideological content; it is aimed to fight communism, a political movement which is not identified with any particular state. In the opinion of the contracting parties, as expressed in the preamble, communism "not only endangers the internal peace and the social well-being of the contracting parties, but threatens the general peace of the world." Thus, the pact may be linked with the agreements concluded by the Holy Alliance powers to fight the liberal movements. In reality the ideological aspect is merely a fiction intended to appease the other states. The Anti-Comintern Pact was only the prelude of the military alliance between Germany, Japan, and Italy which materialized in the Tripartite Agreement of September 27, 1940. In view of the close ties between the Russian government and the Comintern, the agreement was in reality aimed against the former. Italy's adhesion to it was only a step in the formation of the Axis. Contrary to the claims of the Axis writers, the Anti-Comintern Pact is not an instrument of

[11] For further information on these treaties see Renzi, *Tecnica degli scambi con l'estero,* 2d ed.

unique character, but a political understanding camouflaged under the appearance of an ideological entente.

Cultural agreements.—Cultural agreements concluded by Italy with Austria (January 4, 1935), Hungary (April 10, 1935), Germany (November 23, 1938), Japan (April 23, 1939), and Bulgaria (June 5, 1939) are substantially of a political nature. Their apparent aim is to strengthen cultural relations between the contracting parties through the diffusion of the culture and the language of each of them by the opening of schools and the exchange of teachers and students. In totalitarian countries culture is under the influence of the political power and cultural expansion is considered a means of political penetration. Thus, through the cultural agreements each party seeks in reality to establish on the territory of the other centers for the diffusion of its own ideologies and at the same time seeks to prevent conflicting ideologies. This purpose is evident in many provisions of these treaties. The Italian-German agreement for instance, provides:

Art. 21: the High Contracting Parties will take care that the content of the school texts shall correspond to the truth and the spirit of the Italian-German entente.
Art. 26: the High Contracting Parties will hinder the translation and diffusion of works containing falsification of the truth, aimed against the other party, its regime and institutions, and also of biased works of emigres of the other party.

These agreements have not a cultural, but a political or even an inquisitorial purpose. Through them totalitarian regimes seek to extend abroad those limitations on freedom of thought which they have imposed upon their own subjects.[12]

Agreements for the transfer of populations.—In 1939 Italy and Germany entered into agreements aimed at the elimination of the German minority in the Italian provinces of Alto Adige (Southern Tyrol) so that the territorial and ethnical boundaries of the two countries would coincide. These agreements, the full text has not been published, provide for a period of a few months within which Italian citizens of German ancestry residing in Alto Adige must elect whether they intend to remain in Italy or to migrate to Germany. If they elect to remain in Italy, they must migrate within a short period of time to Italian provinces remote from the German boundaries, where they will be easily assimilated. If they elect to migrate to Germany, they must leave within a short period of time; they lose Italian citizenship and immediately acquire German citizenship. Real property in Alto Adige belonging to the emigrants becomes the property of Italian landowning institutions, which distribute it among Italian colonists. Payment for the land is made to the German

[12] By provisional agreement of December 26, 1921, Italy and Russia undertook to refrain from direct or indirect propaganda within their territories against each other.

authorities, which will take care of the claims of the emigrants. This cruel procedure, by which entire populations are eradicated from lands upon which they lived for centuries and are shipped like cattle to different regions or to a foreign country, shows what limited rights the citizen enjoys in totalitarian countries. In 1939 the Italian press announced the negotiation of analogous agreements with Yugoslavia for the repatriation of Italian families from that country.

Military agreements.—It is presumable that Italy is bound by secret military agreements. Among the public ones, the military treaty with Germany on May 22, 1939, is particularly important, especially in the light of subsequent events. Article 3 provides that:

If contrary to the wishes and hopes of the contracting parties it should happen that either of them becomes involved in military entanglements with another power or with other powers, the other contracting party will immediately rally to his side with all his military resources on land, at sea, and in the air.

The article obviously provides that each country must assist the other contracting party, even in case the latter should be the aggressor. Nevertheless, Italy did not rally to Germany's side on August 29 when she attacked Poland or when England and France declared war against her. Whether Italy acted in compliance with secret clauses of the treaty or with subsequent understanding, with Germany, or whether she acted in plain violation of her obligation, we have not sufficient information yet to decide.

PEACEFUL INTERCOURSE DURING THE PRE-FASCIST PERIOD

The international intercourse of Italy during this period lacks particular characteristics. She followed the traditional principles governing international intercourse, thus continuing the policy of substantial compliance with international law which she had practiced from the beginning of the Kingdom of Italy. There were, indeed, violations of international law on the part of Italy, but they were of minor importance; for example, the violation of the immunity of the archives of the French consulate in Florence in 1888 upon the order of an Italian magistrate, which brought an apology for the act by the Italian government, the punishment of the magistrate, and the conclusion of the France-Italy Convention of December 8, 1888, concerning consular archives.[13] The premature annexation of Tripolitania and Cirenaica in 1911, during the Italian-Turkish war was also unlawful. German propaganda maintained that in 1914–1915 Italy violated its obligations toward Germany and Austria arising from the Treaty of Triple Alliance concluded in 1881

[13] Concerning the incident see Gabba, "L'incident consulaire franco-italien à Florence," 20 Rév. dr. int. et lég. comp. (1888) 229 ff. The convention concerning the archives is published by Ferrara, *Manuale di diritto consolare*, p. 116.

and renewed finally with modifications on December 5, 1912. The violation would have consisted, first, in the Italian declaration of neutrality and, second, in her intervention in the war on the side of the Entente. The German claim is wholly unjustified. Italy was bound to intervene on the side of Austria or Germany only in case one of them should be attacked without provocation (Article 3). It was Austria, backed by Germany, who provoked and started the war. The treaty was violated by Austria, who started her military action in the Balkans without previous consultation with Italy, contrary to what had been expressly provided (Article 7). Italy's subsequent conduct was fully justified.[14]

In the interpretation and application of treaties Italy followed the principle that the real intent of the parties should be considered; the alleged clear meaning of the text can never be a bar to extrinsic interpretation. In fact, no expression of a treaty has clear meaning in itself; for it is only possible to ascertain whether the text clearly expresses the intention of the parties after it has been established what they really intended to say.[15] Italy has consistently maintained that parties are not bound by technical rules in the interpretation of the treaties. This conception is obviously influenced by the repugnancy of civil law for technical rules of evidence and construction.

Italy was frequently involved in differences concerning reparation of damages suffered by its citizens abroad in consequence of wars, revolutions, and mob violence. Especially frequent are those with Latin American states: Chile, 1882; Colombia (Cerruti case), 1886 and 1899; Brazil, 1895 and 1896; Guatemala, 1898 and 1902; Equador, 1898; Peru, 1899; Venezuela, 1903; Peru (Canevaro Case), 1912; Venezuela (Martini Case), 1920; and Mexico, 1927. In these differences Italy has usually insisted upon the traditional principles concerning the treatment of foreigners: that there is a minimum standard of treatment to which they are entitled, even where a lower one is granted to the nationals; that the denial of justice to foreigners gives rise to international responsibility; and that a state is responsible for wrongful acts of insurgents toward foreigners. On occasion of the lynching of Italians in Louisiana in 1891, Italy contended that the United States was responsible for the wrongful acts committed against foreigners by the authorities of one of the states, even though the acts were within the exclusive power of the state and could not have been prevented by the Federal government. The Italian thesis has found some support even in this country.[16] Italy, on her part,

---

[14] Sereni, "Casus foederis," in *Nuovo digesto italiano*, II, 1118.   [15] See *supra*, pp. 288 ff.
[16] E. G. Wilson, *International Law*, 9th ed., p. 82; see also the draft of the convention on "Responsibility of States for Damage Done in Their Territory to the Person or Property of Foreigners" prepared by the Harvard Law School, Research on International Law (Article 3): "A state is not relieved of responsibility because an injury to an alien is attributable to one of its political subdivisions, regardless of the extent to which the national government, according to its constitution, has control of the subdivision."

has been accused of violating international rules concerning treatment of foreign property by the establishment of a form of limited state monopoly on life insurance (law of April 4, 1912). It was contended that said measure represented an expropriation without compensation of private insurance companies, which by reason of the sudden cessation of that branch of the activity were deprived of the good will attached to it. These measures, in so far as insurance companies were affected, would violate the principle of international law that foreign property cannot be expropriated without compensation.[17] However, no official protest was apparently lodged with the Italian government.

It is probably because violations of international law on the part of Italy were neither greater nor more numerous than those of other countries that her international intercourse during this period does not have any particular characteristics. Typical treaties concluded by Italy have been already considered. Her practice as a neutral and a belligerent and her domestic acts concerning international law shall be considered later.

PEACEFUL INTERCOURSE DURING THE FASCIST PERIOD

It has been already pointed out that the international ideologies of fascism were largely the consequence of developments in Italy's domestic policy. It is equally true that the international intercourse of fascism has been deeply affected by the changes in the internal structure of the Fascist state.

Italy, a constitutional monarchy based on democratic and liberal principles, was changed by the Fascists, first into an authoritarian and antidemocratic regime and later into a totalitarian state. The phases of this evolution and the Fascist organization of the Italian state can be briefly summarized as follows. Within a few years after they came to power (1922) the Fascists took full political control of the country by regimenting the Italian masses in the Fascist Party and its accessory organizations. The Fascist Party was the only party allowed. Membership in it was an indispensable requisite for the appointment to any public office. The Italian state was governed by Fascists. Since the organization of the Fascist Party was regulated by legislative acts of the Italian state, state and party tended toward legal as well as political identification. If not an organ in the organization of the Italian state, the Fascist Party was certainly an element. The political control of Italians was followed by that of culture, education, recreation, and the diffusion of information (press, radio, and movies). All these manifestations of the national life were controlled by the state and by the Fascist Party, either directly or indirectly through special agencies expressly created for this purpose.

[17] Clunet and others, *Consultation pour les sociétés étrangères d'assurances sur la vie établies en Italie.*

Economic control then followed. Its first phase consisted in the organization of labor. All classes of employers and employees were organized in unions depending upon the Fascist Party. They were under the control of the Corporations (*corporazioni*), which are organs of the state supervised by a special Ministry of Corporations. Strikes and lockouts were punished. Arbitration of labor conflicts was made compulsory.

Control of business organizations followed, especially after 1933. The state took control of the most important commercial and economic enterprises, such as great utilities companies. It is their principal financer and in many cases their majority stockholder. A state-controlled institute *Istituto per la Ricostruzione Industriale* (I.R.I.), has been created for this purpose. The state became the principal client of the great industrial concerns which are working almost exclusively for national defense and public works. Financial investments in private business have been discouraged in every way. Most of the savings of private citizens are collected by the state, which utilizes them for financing the enterprises and transactions which it considers convenient for its own purposes. In such a system the banks have lost almost all reason for existence. There are fewer of them, and their capital stock has been purchased by the state. Although apparently acting as private institutions, the banks are only an emanation of the state, which dictates the criteria that they must follow in doing business.

As already stated, economic relations with foreign countries are under the strictest state control, which is exercised through a special Ministry for Exchange and Currency. The state has the monopoly of foreign financial transactions, for all import or export of its currency is subject to its approval. Italians residing in Italy cannot own foreign exchange in Italy or abroad. Currency for foreign payments can only be obtained with the authorization of the *Istituto Italiano per i Cambi coll'estero*, a state-controlled agency. Whoever receives foreign currency from abroad must hand it over to this *Istituto* and obtain Italian currency at the rate of exchange dictated by the state.

The strain imposed upon Italian economy by the Ethiopian and Spanish wars has resulted in an even stricter state control. The state decides which new plants may be built. It distributes raw materials and decrees which goods may be manufactured, which may be used for internal consumption, and which may be exported. The state fixes all prices, salaries, and rents. Even domestic relations are under state control. Marriage between an Italian and a foreigner is subject to state authorization. Marriage between a state employee and a foreigner is forbidden. State interference with private activities, which already existed in Italy, has been carried to an extreme by the Fascists.

One point, however, should be stressed. While in some totalitarian countries, such as Russia, state control has materialized in collectivist economy, the Italian system differs both from the collectivist economy and from capitalist economy based on free competition and private initiative. In Italy a great many activities are still carried on in the legal and economic forms which in other countries are typical of private business, but they are supervised by the state and exercised in its paramount interest. It is difficult to ascertain whether the Italian system has undergone radical changes after the fall of Fascism.

This radical transformation of Italy took place slowly but surely over a period of about fifteen years (1923–1938). International intercourse of Italy during this period is the reflection of the internal changes of Italy.

Italy's transformation into an antidemocratic and authoritarian regime (1923–1926) had little influence on her international relations. Nor did the Italian regime commit open violations of international law during this period. Peaceful coexistence of democratic nations and a Fascist state, all equally subservient to the traditional rules of international law, seemed to justify the conception that no internal regime of a state is incompatible, as a rule, with the traditional structure of international law and that consequently international law is not interested in the form of government of the states.

Italy's evolution into a totalitarian regime has deeply affected her international relations. In totalitarian Italy all relations with foreign countries and all the activities of Italians who resided abroad and maintained their allegiance to Italy were more or less under the control of the Fascist government.[18] This was true in the political field as well as in the cultural and economic fields.

In the political field Italy's control was exercised chiefly, but not exclusively, through the Fascist Party, which had created a special organization for this purpose, called *Fasci Italiani all'Estero*. Its aim was to guide the sentiments of Italians abroad; to establish contacts and co-operation with foreign groups with Fascist tendencies. The *Fasci Italiani all'Estero* worked in close co-operation with the Italian diplomatic and consular agents. In view of the ties existing between the Italian state and the Fascist Party, Fascist activities abroad were imputable to the Italian government.

The diffusion of culture and information was considered an element of Fascist propaganda. It was directed by a special Ministry for Popular Culture (formerly Ministry for Press and Propaganda). Officials in charge of propaganda in foreign countries were on the staff of each Italian legation. The official name was *Addetti Stampa* (Press Attachés) and *Ad-*

---

[18] Before the present war functionaries of the Italian secret political police (Ovra) were attached at the Italian consulates in New York, Paris, and Marseilles.

detti Culturali (Cultural Attachés). The Royal Decree Law, January 17, 1938, No. 48, created the *Istituto Italiano per le Relazioni Internazionali coll' Estero*, under the supervision of the Ministry of Foreign Affairs. The *Istituto* was in charge of cultural propaganda abroad. It saw to it that Italian teachers and students abroad would act as agents for Fascist propaganda. It printed material for this purpose. Italian schools abroad were under the control of the state and the Fascist Party, and they were financed by the Italian government. Special organizations exist for the preservation of national feelings among Italians abroad, for example, *Società Dante Alighieri*. This corporation already existed before fascism as a private organization; now it is under state control, its president being selected by the head of the government and appointed by royal decree. A state-controlled agency, the *Ente Italiano Audizioni Radiofoniche* (EIAR) broadcasts propaganda abroad. A state-controlled motion picture corporation (*Istituto Nazionale Luce*) produces motion pictures for foreign propaganda.

Economic control in international transactions has already been examined. It is sufficient to recall that many business transactions are performed by the state itself, either directly or through special agencies such as the *Azienda Generale Industria Petrolii* (AGIP), which is in charge of the purchase of oil.

The type of state created by the Fascists in Italy differs greatly from that presupposed by the majority of international rules. In the centuries when international law took shape the distinction between state activities and individual activities was well established. The former was limited to relatively few and well-defined functions of an essentially political nature—the so-called public functions—while all other national activities (industry, commerce, banking, shipping, diffusion of culture and information) were considered within the sphere of private activity. The state might supervise them within certain limits but would not take them over.

The distinction between public and private activities continued for centuries, notwithstanding the changes which took place in the state organization. It has been accepted by the states, irrespective of their political regime. Many international rules still presuppose it. Immunities and privileges are granted to foreign states and diplomatic agents on the assumption that their activities are confined to those necessary for state intercourse. Rules on international responsibility are based on the distinction between acts of the state and those of private individuals for which the government cannot be held responsible. Rules concerning neutrality are based on the assumption that certain acts (supply and transportation of contraband and violations of blockade) cannot be lawfully performed by states, but that no state responsibility would be involved if they were performed by private individuals. Matters such as the diffusion of information and propaganda abroad are the object of only a few vague international rules, since they were seldom the object of state activity.

While international rules crystallized on the assumption that the distinction was still in force, in some countries the function of the state broadened to such an extent as to absorb most of the private activities.[19] In democratic countries the phenomenon is chiefly limited to wartime. In totalitarian regimes it represents the normal peacetime situation.

The totalitarian regimes, such as Italy and Germany, which did not establish a full-fledged collectivistic organization, derive considerable advantage from the fact that international rules still presuppose a distinction between public and private activities. These states, being in control of all national activities, can elect to carry on these activities in either a public or a private form, whichever is most convenient from the point of view of international law. For instance, the Italian state exercises in public form certain activities which traditionally were private. It buys abroad raw materials for industries; it manufactures armaments for foreign countries; it owns and operates merchant ships. On the other hand, organizations which are allegedly private, for example, the *Società Dante Alighieri*, perform activities of the state and for the state. Italian banks abroad perform foreign transactions along political lines, not business lines, in the interest and upon the orders of the state.

Obvious advantages result therefrom for the Italian government. Diplomatic agents of the Italian state and of the state itself enjoy privileges and immunities in the performance of private activities. Upon governmental instructions, allegedly private organizations perform activities in foreign countries, which the Italian state could not perform without incurring international responsibility. If a Fascist agent were to violate the hospitality of a foreign country, or if the Italian press and radio were to offend foreign states or governments, the Italian government would disclaim responsibility on the ground that they were private individuals.[20]

[19] On this problem see Lauterpacht, "Revolutionary Propaganda by Governments," 13 Grotius Society, Transactions (1938) 143 ff.; Preuss, "Some Effects of Governmental Control on Neutral Duties," 31 American Society of International Law, Proceedings (1937) 108 ff.; Friedman, "The Growth of the State Control over the Individual and Its Effects upon the Rules of State Responsibility," 19 British Year Book of International Law (1938) 118 ff.; and Kunz, "Neutrality and the European War 1939–1940," 39 Michigan Law Review (1940) 719 ff.

[20] At the beginning of 1936 Italy notified Great Britain that she had no authority to prohibit the Italian broadcasting station of Bari from broadcasting anti-British propaganda in Arabic to the Near East. However such propaganda came suddenly at an end when the two governments signed the Rome declaration concerning propaganda, annexed to their agreement of April 16, 1936. It provided that "any attempt by either of them to employ the methods of publicity or propaganda at its disposal in order to injure the interests of the other would be

By exploiting the distinction between public and private activities for obtaining advantages that international rules were not intended to grant, totalitarian states are certainly violating the essence of international law. Mere technical compliance with international rules results in a fraud against the law of the type that French students of administrative law have defined as "detournement de pouvoir."

The exceptional advantages which the present structure of international law granted to fascism explain why it never attempted to introduce new rules concerning international intercourse. When accused of violating international law, the Fascist government did not advance new principles in justification, but maintained that it was complying with traditional rules. Thus the bombing and occupation of Corfu were justified as reprisals for the assassination of a member of an Italian military mission (August 27, 1923). Military action against Ethiopia was declared an act of self-defense intended to prevent Ethiopian invasion of Italian colonies. Sanctions by the League were opposed on a strictly legalistic ground. As to intervention in Spain, at first Fascists denied having sent troops,[21] later they admitted it, but contended that it was justified by preceding acts of intervention on the part of other states; finally they asserted that General Franco's was the only legitimate government in Spain and that therefore he was entitled to foreign support, whereas the Loyalist government would have fallen into the hands of irresponsible elements and would no longer have been representative of the Spanish people. According to the Fascists, intervention in Albania was requested by the majority of the Albanians, who favored a union with Italy. Another official justification was that King Zog was trying to provoke military hostilities between Italy and Yugoslavia.

Pseudo legal justification cannot mitigate the fact that in the last ten years Italy has acted in a manner contrary to international law. Refusal to continue to recognize the legitimate Spanish government and the recognition of Franco's regime as the only Spanish government on November 18, 1936, when civil war was still undecided, was certainly unlawful interference in Spanish internal affairs. International law was further violated when entire divisions of the Italian army, labeled as volunteers, were sent to the aid of Franco. No legal justification can be found for

inconsistent with their good relations." There is no need to point out that Italy did not sign the international convention of September 23, 1936 concerning the use of broadcasting in the cause of peace.

[21] In apparent compliance with her duty of non-intervention Italy issued the Royal Decree Law February 15, 1937 No. 102 and the Ministerial Decree February 19, 1937 prohibiting the enlistment of volunteers for Spain. The fiction of the Italian *volunteers* has been completely exploded in 1939 when Italy presented to Spain a bill of 7 billion lire for expenses incurred in sending troops and materials to Franco. An agreement concerning the settlement of Spain's financial obligations toward Italy was announced on February 5, 1942. It seems however that new difficulties concerning payments have recently arisen.

Italy's intervention in Albania. The contention that Albania is still an international subject is a case of fraud against the law. It is aimed at granting Italy an additional vote in international congresses and unions to which she and Albania are parties; if convenient, to keep Albania neutral in conflicts to which Italy is a party, and possibly to disclaim Italy's responsibility for torts committed by Albania. The truth is that the Albanian state has no autonomous life, but exists only in the interest of Italy. Italy's annexation of part of the Yugoslavian territory and the creation of a puppet state in Croatia in 1941 were certainly unlawful acts, since they took place while Yugoslavia was still in existence.

Until Italy's entry into the present war, June 10, 1940, Italy expressly denied that she was neutral and claimed for herself the status of "nonbelligerency." This was her only attempt to establish a new practice of international law. It resulted in complete failure. Italy never was able to give a legal definition of "nonbelligerency" and to determine the special rights and duties which would derive therefrom. The reason is that there is no such status as "nonbelligerency" in positive international law.

The concept of "nonbelligerency" is not a legal one if it is intended to mean that even before Italy's intervention on the side of one of the belligerents she hoped for its victory. International law is not interested in the hopes and desires of one government. If the term means that Italy was only temporarily neutral and reserved her right to enter the war later, as she did, "nonbelligerency" again has no legal significance. As Kunz remarks, "the rules of neutrality apply only, if and when and as long as a state is neutral, but contain no duty, except by treaty, either to be neutral or to remain neutral." [22] Nonbelligerency would have a legal significance if it consisted of a position intermediary between neutrality and belligerency, granting special exemptions and rights: for example, exemption from the duty of absolute neutrality which binds a neutral and the correlative right to lend some material support to a belligerent without becoming thereby involved in the war. Italy, however, never claimed these rights. Whenever her claims were to be defined in legal terms, she took the position that she was a neutral. In the protest lodged on March 4, 1940, against the British export blockade of German merchandise,[23] Italy invoked her rights as a neutral. The Allies treated Italy as neutral, submitting Italian ships to the British blockade. Nor did Italy admit that other states could be "nonbelligerent." After her entry into the war she demanded absolute neutrality, even neutrality of the press, from Switzerland, Greece, and Yugoslavia. As Kunz properly puts it, "nonbelligerent

[22] Borchard, "The Attorney General's Opinion on the Exchange of Destroyers for Naval Bases," 34 Am. J. Int. L. (1940) 697: "The concept of 'non-belligerency' like that of 'measures short of war' has no legal status. It is apparently designed to justify breaches of neutrality or acts of war, perhaps with the hope that they will not result in a state of war."
[23] New York *Times*, March 5, 1940.

Italy was in law a neutral, having no other rights but the rights of a neutral state, and any action by her incompatible with neutrality constituted a violation of neutrality." [24] Very probably Italy's claim to the status of nonbelligerency was only a belated attempt to save Germany's face. Under the terms of the treaty of military alliance of May 22, 1939, Italy was bound to military intervention on Germany's side immediately after the outbreak of the war. That Italy chose a different course could create the impression that she had betrayed her ally, resulting in a loss of political prestige for the latter at an especially critical moment. It is probably true that at that time Mussolini, not believing in Germany's victory, actually betrayed Hitler. The partners, however, agreed that full disclosure of these facts would have been detrimental for both. As a remedy, it was proclaimed that Italy's conduct was the result of previous agreement and that, though actually not engaged in the war, she was not a neutral, but only a nonbelligerent, that is, she continued her political support of Germany. The expression "nonbelligerency" was therefore intended to justify an extremely ambiguous political situation rather than to define a new legal status.

It has been shown that fascism has taken unscrupulous advantage of the present rules of international law, thus obtaining advantages that they were not intended to grant. Besides, at times it has also openly violated them. However, the structure of totalitarian states would make it exceedingly difficult to adhere to international rules, even if they were willing to do so. Let us consider, for instance, the neutrality rules. They permit certain transactions (for example, sale of war material) between belligerent states and citizens of neutral states, whereas the same transactions are forbidden between neutral and belligerent states. Since transactions performed by citizens of a totalitarian state are imputed to the state itself, the latter, in order to comply with its duties as a neutral, would have to compel its subjects to refrain from any transaction with a belligerent state in which the neutral state could not enter directly. Citizens and government of totalitarian states would then be at a disadvantage with regard to citizens and governments of democratic governments, respectively. Totalitarian states would hardly accept such a situation.

These remarks should not be construed as justification of the conduct of the totalitarian states. They only show the fundamental incompatibility which exists between their structure and some of the existing rules of international law.

This section was written before the fall of the Fascists. It is to be hoped that as a result of her recent change of regime Italy will again revert to her traditional policy of compliance with the precepts of international law.

[24] Kunz, "Neutrality and the European War," 39 Michigan Law Review (1941) 719, 750.

Amicable Settlement

Numerous Italian treaties, even those of recent date, provide for the amicable settlement of disputes resulting from them. In addition, Italy concluded many general treaties of arbitration. About twenty were concluded before 1913. On May 5, 1914, Italy concluded with the United States one of the so-called "Bryan treaties," which was ratified March 19, 1915. Even after the advent of the Fascists, Italy continued to conclude arbitration treaties. Among the most recent are those with Switzerland (September 20, 1924), Spain (August 7, 1926), Germany (December 29, 1926), Chile (February 24, 1927), Hungary (April 5, 1927), Lithuania (September 17, 1927), Turkey (May 30, 1928), Norway (June 17, 1928), Finland (August 21, 1928), Ethiopia (August 2, 1928), Greece (September 23, 1928), Persia (September 5, 1929), Austria (September 6, 1930), Latvia (April 28, 1930), the United States (September 23, 1931), Saudi Arabia (February 10, 1932), Colombia (March 18, 1932), Luxembourg (April 15, 1932), Russia (September 2, 1933), Costa Rica (October 31, 1933), Yemen (September 4, 1937), and Manchukuo (July 5, 1938). These treaties have some common characteristics. They are usually called "treaties of conciliation and judicial settlement," since they contemplate both procedures for the settlement of the disputes to which they refer. Whenever a difference arises, the parties shall first try to settle through diplomatic channels. In case of failure, a mixed conciliation commission will be established. Whenever a settlement cannot be reached through conciliation the parties will resort to arbitration. Many kinds of disputes are not subject to arbitration. In most of these treaties the Permanent Court of International Justice is designated as judge. In 1936 Italy adhered to the optional clause contained in Article 36 of its Statute.

The most comprehensive and technically accurate of these treaties is probably that with Switzerland. All difference of any nature between the two states which cannot be settled through diplomatic channels shall be submitted to a commission of conciliation composed of five members. Unless an extension of time is granted by both parties, the commission shall present a report containing proposals for the settlement of the dispute within five months from the day on which the dispute was submitted to it. If one of the parties rejects the proposals or fails to notify acceptance within a period of six months, each party may request that the case be submitted to the Permanent Court of International Justice. If the court deems that the dispute is not of a legal nature, its decision shall be *ex aequo et bono*. The parties will fulfill in good faith the decision of the Court. During the conciliatory and judicial procedure the parties will refrain from any act which may impair the acceptance of the proposals of the commission or of the decision of the Court. The conclusion of the treaty was made possible by the absence of any probable motive for serious dissent between Italy and Switzerland. Even in the past, disputes between the two states were usually settled through diplomatic channels or arbitration: for example, concerning the Alp of Cravairola (1874, mentioned above), the payment of custom duties (1893),[25] and the interpretation of the Treaty of Commerce of 1904 (1911).[26]

Italy is party to several multilateral conventions for the peaceful settlement of international disputes: for example, the Hague conventions of 1892 and 1907; the Locarno agreements, October 16, 1925; and the Kellogg Pact and the General Act of Geneva of 1928 for the peaceful settlement of international disputes. She is also a member of the Permanent Court of International Arbitration and of the Permanent Court of International Justice.

Although Italy has concluded several treaties providing for the peaceful settlement of international disputes, she has seldom resorted to international arbitration. This procedure was followed mainly in the settlement of disputes originating from claims of Italian citizens against Latin American States, which were usually decided by mixed claims commissions. Mixed arbitral tribunals were established by the peace treaties at the end of the first World War between Italy and her former adversaries.[27] Before the Permanent Court of International Arbitration, Italy was a party to the case of the preferential claims against Venezuela, which was decided in favor of Italy, Great Britain, and Germany on February 22, 1904; to the Canevaro case, concerning claims of Italian citizens and of a corporation against Peru, decided May 3, 1912; [28] and to the cases of Carthage and Manouba against France, decided on May 6, 1913. The latter involved the legitimacy of the detention of two French ships suspected of transporting contraband of war and enemy troops during the war between Italy and Turkey. In both cases Italy was condemned to pay an indemnity. From a legal standpoint the two decisions are of minor importance, since the principal questions arising from the incidents had been already settled by the parties out of court.[29] By *compromis*, November 8, 1912, Italy and France decided to submit to arbitration by the Permanent Court of International Arbitration, the dis-

---

[25] Ralston, *International Arbitration from Athens to Locarno*, p. 93.

[26] The award is published in 6 Riv. dir. int. (1912) 268.

[27] The decisions are published in *Recueil des décisions des tribunaux arbitraux mixtes*, 10 vols.

[28] On the Canevaro case see Anzilotti's "Nota" in 6 Riv. dir. int. (1912) 482 ff.; Kohler, "Die Lehren des Kanevarofalles," 7 Zeitschrift für Völkerrecht (1913) 1 ff.; Boeck, "La Sentence arbitrale de la Cour permanente de la Haye dans l'affaire Canevaro," 20 Rev. gén. dr. int. publ. (1913) 317 ff.

[29] For their analysis see Anzilotti, "Nota," 7 Riv. dir. int. (1913) 200 ff., 398 ff., and 502 ff.

putes arising from the stopping of the "Tavignano," a French ship, and from the firing of some shots against the "Camouna" and the "Gaulois," also French ships, during the war between Italy and Turkey. Later on, the parties appointed a commission of inquiry in order to ascertain the facts. The dispute was finally settled out of court by agreement on May 2, 1913, whereby Italy consented to pay five thousand francs for individual losses.[30] As already recalled, the dispute between Italy and Turkey concerning the delimitation of the territorial waters of Castelrosso, which was to be decided by the Permanent Court of International Justice, was settled by them out of court. In 1936 Italy brought an action against France before the Permanent Court of International Justice, maintaining that the expropriation of some concession of an Italian citizen in Morocco violated the international obligations of France toward Italy concerning that territory (*Case Relating to Phosphates in Morocco*). Italy contended that the Court had jurisdiction on the matter since both parties had accepted the optional clause. By decision of June 14, 1938, the Court decided that the Italian application was not entertainable, since it referred to facts preceding France's acceptance of the optional clause.[31] The Wal-Wal incident of December, 1934, was submitted to arbitration under the terms of the Italo-Ethiopian Treaty of Conciliation of August 2, 1928. A commission of five members was appointed to ascertain which of the two parties was responsible. It decided on September 3, 1935, that neither one was responsible.[32]

Acts Short of War

Italy took part in several collective military operations which were not in the nature of a war: for example, the pacific blockade of Crete (1897–1898); coercive action together with Great Britain and Germany against Venezuela (1902–1903);[33] repression of the Boxer Rebellion in China (1900); blockade of the coasts of Montenegro and northern Albania, together with England, France, Austria, and Germany (1913); blockade of the Greek coast in 1915 and then again in 1916 and 1917 with the other Entente powers.

A recent instance of individual military action other than war on the part of Italy alone was the bombing and occupation of Corfu in 1923, whereas the military operations against Ethiopia in 1935–1936 were in the nature of a real war.

[30] The documents pertaining to the case are published in 9 Riv. dir. int. (1915) 434 ff.
[31] See *supra*, p. 295, and the order of the Perm. Ct. Int. Jus., June 26, 1933, Publ. Ser. A/B, No. 51.
[32] The principal documents concerning the arbitration are published in Potter, *The Wal Wal Arbitration*.
[33] Basdevant, "L'Action coercitive anglo-germano-italienne contre le Venezuela (1902–1903)," 11 Rev. gén. dr. int. publ. (1904) 362 ff.

War

After the occupation of Rome in 1870, the Kingdom of Italy fought four wars; against Ethiopia (1896), Turkey (1911–1912), the Central Powers (1915–1918), and Ethiopia (1935–1936). Their territorial consequences have already been considered. These wars did not result in any important contributions by Italy to the development of international law. In the wars against Ethiopia and Turkey, Italy did not apply new practices; in that against the Central Powers her attitude conformed substantially to that of her allies.

Italo-Abyssinian War of 1896.—This war started without declaration. Notwithstanding her backward civilization, Ethiopia was already an international subject, and the conflict was therefore in the nature of an international war. Difference of civilization between the two countries influenced the conduct of hostilities. Each of the belligerents accused the other of violations of the laws of war. It has been proved conclusively that the Ethiopians killed enemy wounded and subjected Italian prisoners, both white and colored, to inhuman treatment and often to cruel mutilation. Friends of the Ethiopians accused the Italians of cruelty against civilians. These accusations were not true. Mistakes may, however, have been committed because of the difficulty of drawing a distinction between Abyssinian troops, which were not uniformed, and civilians. All able-bodied Ethiopian men took part in the hostilities, since the Negus had declared a holy war. Aside from this, from the point of view of international law the hostilities did not present much interest.[34]

By Royal Decree, August 16, 1896, a prize court was established called *Reale Commissione delle Prede.* The only case decided was that of the Dutch ship "Doelwik," [35] which was captured by an Italian cruiser. The ship carried arms destined for Ethiopia, and since this country had no access to the sea, they were to be unloaded at Jibuti for trans-shipment to the interior. By decision of December 8, 1896, the Prize Court declared lawful the capture of the ship on the basis of the theory of continuous voyage. But since the war had terminated in the meantime, its restitution to the owners was ordered. The war ended by the peace of Addis Ababa of October 26, 1896.

Italo-Turkish War.—This war was preceded by an Italian ultimatum on September 28, 1911, and was begun the following day, after a formal declaration. It was chiefly a colonial conflict between countries of dif-

[34] See Fedozzi, "Le Droit international et les récentes hostilités italo-abyssines," 26 Rev. dr. int. et lég. comp. (1896) 580 ff.
[35] Text in Gaz. Uff., December 15, 1896. On this case see Brusa, "L'Affaire du Doelwik," 4 Rev. gén. dr. int. pub. (1897) 157 ff. For further information on Italian prize courts see Sereni, "Italian Prize Courts (1866–1942)," 37 Am. J. Int. L. (1943) 248 ff.

ferent civilizations.[36] By unilateral resolution Italy decided to confine hostilities to the Turkish possessions in Africa and in the Aegean Sea, excluding European and Asiatic Turkey. Egypt did not participate in the conflict, although under the nominal suzerainty of Turkey. In Libya, Turkey had few contingents of regular troops. The war was fought mainly by irregular Arab formations led by Turkish officers and inspired by religious fanaticism. Even civilians took arms against the Italians as a result of the Sultan's declaration of a holy war. Several acts of cruelty were committed against Italian wounded and prisoners. It does not appear that the Italian troops violated the laws of war. Turkey suspended the capitulations in favor of the Italians and expelled many of them from her territory. These acts gave rise to strong protests on the part of Italy.[37]

The Italian government declared the blockade of the Turkish coasts of Libya [38] and of the Red Sea [39] and of the island of Rhodes.[40] On October 4, 1911, it issued a declaration prohibiting contraband in favor of Turkey either directly by sea or through trans-shipment, or by land. Instructions to the navy framed in accordance with the traditional rules of international law concerning capture and prizes were issued by Royal Decree October 13, 1911, No. 1145.[41] Another decree of the same date, No. 1146, created a prize commission similar to that established during the Abyssinian War. Of the cases decided,[42] few are of legal importance. Some discussion arose as to the capture of the Turkish ship "Kaisserie" for which the status of hospital ship was unsuccessfully claimed.[43] The war ended by the Peace of Ouchy, October 18, 1912.

The World War.—Shortly after the outbreak of the first World War,

[36] See the anonymous article, "La nostra guerra con la Turchia," in 6 Riv. dir. int. (1912) 54 ff., 224 ff., 419 ff. and 533 ff.; 7 Riv. dir. int. (1913) 178 ff.; 8 Riv. dir. int. (1914) 32 ff.; and 9 Riv. dir. int. (1915) 419 ff.; Rapisardi Mirabelli, "La Guerre italo-turque et le droit des gens," 45 Rev. dr. int. et lég. comp. (1912) 159 ff., 411 ff.; 46 Rev. dr. int. et lég. comp. (1913) 85 ff., 523 ff., and 649 ff.; Coquet, "Italie et Turquie-Guerre—Origines et causes du conflit—Déclaration de guerre," in 19 Rev. gén. dr. int. publ. (1912) 370 ff.; 20 Rev. gén. dr. int. publ. (1913) 243 ff., 510 ff., 605 ff.; 21 Rev. gén. dr. int. publ. (1914) 105 ff.; 22 Rev. gén. dr. int. publ. (1915) 242 ff.

[37] Fusinato, "Le Capitolazioni e la guerra," 6 Riv. dir. int. (1912) 389 ff.; Anzilotti, *Corso di diritto internazionale*, 1915, III, 258 ff.

[38] September 29, 1911, modified October 19, 1911.

[39] January 21–22, 1912, widened April 5, 1912.   [40] May 11, 1912.

[41] During the hostilities Italy arrested enemy subjects on board neutral ships. See cases cited by Baty, 33 Am. J. Int. L. (1939) 662.

[42] The decisions of the Commission are published in Commissione delle Prede, *Atti*.

[43] The case went before the prize court because the ship was privately owned and chartered by the Turkish government. By judgment February 21, 1912, the court condemned the Turkish ship "Sabah," which had been captured by an Italian cruiser in a port held by Turkey and escorted her to an Italian port. Anzilotti (6 Riv. dir. int. [1912] 146) contested the legitimacy of the capture on the ground that an enemy ship cannot be captured when in port and not ready to sail. This thesis did not have any following.

Italy declared her neutrality (August 3, 1914).[44] It appeared almost immediately that the sympathies of the Italian people were on the side of the democratic powers. On May 4, 1915, Italy declared that the treaty of Triple Alliance with Austria and Germany was terminated.[45] This was perfectly justified, as has already been seen, by Austria's conduct. On May 23, 1915, Italy declared war on Austria;[46] on August 20, 1915, on Turkey;[47] on October 20, 1915, on Bulgaria;[48] and on August 27, 1916, on Germany.[49]

In the conduct of hostilities and the issuance of provisions concerning warfare Italy availed herself of the previous experience of the Allied Powers. Moreover, many of the steps taken by Italy had been planned with them. Hence, Italian practice during World War I does not present characteristics which distinguish it from that of the other Allied countries. No serious violation of the laws of war was attributed to Italy, whereas many were committed against her by Austria and Germany (aerial bombings and other violences against civilian population; looting; killing of prisoners).[50] Italy's respect for the civilian population on enemy territory occupied during the first period of the war was partly due to the fact that it was mostly composed of Italians. Italy was waging a war of liberation, not of conquest.

In contrast with preceding wars, this time Italy was confronted with the problem of the treatment of enemy citizens and property.

Treatment granted to enemy aliens was on the whole generous. Enemy subjects were usually permitted to continue in their residence, and their civil rights were not excessively curtailed. Regulations concerning economic relations with enemy countries and their subjects were issued with considerable delay. Differences of treatment existed for a long period of time among the subjects of the various enemy states.[51] It was only after the armistice that all these provisions were co-ordinated in an organic body by Decree of November 28, 1918, No. 1829.[52] As a rule,

[44] Gazz. uff., August 4, 1914.
[45] See *supra*, pp. 302 ff. Text of the act of denunciation in 9 Riv. dir. int. (1915) 470.
[46] Text of the declaration in 9 Riv. dir. int. (1915) 182. By Royal decree No. 699, of May 25, 1915, the king appointed a general lieutenant to whom he delegated his ordinary powers, including that of issuing decrees. Decrees issued by the general lieutenant are referred to as "lieutenant's decrees."
[47] Text of the declaration in 9 Riv. dir. int. (1915) 419.
[48] Text of the declaration in 10 Riv. dir. int. (1916) 404.   [49] *Ibid.*, p. 403.
[50] Garner, *International Law and the World War*, I, 451 ff.
[51] For instance, for a long while the Bulgarian subjects conserved the right of suing, which was denied to the subjects of other enemy countries; see Pellizzi, "Condition des sujets ennemis en Italie," 45 Journal du droit international privé (1918) 43.
[52] Gazz. uff., December 7, 1918. The text is published also in 12 Riv. dir. int. (1918) 344, with important notes. Article 45 of this decree contains a list of all the legislative provisions on the subject matter enacted during the war.

provisions issued during the war forbade any transaction with enemy countries and enemy residents abroad, transfer of any interest in real estate, merchandise, or firms in Italy belonging to enemy subjects, and payments to enemy subjects abroad. Enemy firms in Italy were placed under control, and in certain cases sequestrated. The government was granted power to seize all enemy property in Italy. Enemy aliens were not permitted to bring lawsuits.[53] Many of these provisions did not apply to the Austro-Hungarian subjects of Italian nationality and to the Ottoman subjects not of Turkish nationality.[54]

As to enemy ships,[55] an Italian Decree of May 16, 1915, No. 659, suspended application of Articles 211 and 243 of the Code of Merchant Marine for the case of Italy's participation in the war. Article 211 prohibited, upon condition of reciprocity, capture and condemnation of foreign merchant ships. Article 243 permitted enemy merchant ships which were in Italian waters at the outbreak of war to leave for their respective countries with a safe conduct. At the time of the declaration of war against Austria there were in Italian ports thirty-six German and twenty-one Austrian ships, which had taken refuge there to escape capture from the Allies. By Italian Decree of May 30, 1915, No. 814, Austrian ships were sequestrated. Those which could be transformed into auxiliary cruisers, were captured; the others were utilized for transportation (Italian Decree, June 17, 1915, No. 957), and the freights were applied to the payment of damages suffered by Italian civilians in consequence of enemy unlawful acts of war (Decree June 24, 1915, No. 1014).[56] By

[53] On May 21, 1915, when Italy's intervention appeared inevitable, the Italian and German government entered into an international agreement, probably the only one of that kind, concerning the treatment of their subjects and of their property in case of war (text in 24 Rev. gén. dr. int. publ. [1917] 150). The treaty provided for a mutual guarantee with respect to the persons and property of the subjects of each party. They were to be allowed to continue their residence without molestation, except that they might be ordered to reside in designated localities and be subjected to police measure in case the public safety and order should so require. The right of departure from the country was allowed; they were to be subject to no restrictions different from those imposed upon neutral persons sojourning in the country; there was to be no requisition of property; no confiscation of patents or other rights of this character; no abrogation or suspension of contracts or debts; the rules of the Hague convention No. 6 with regard to the status of merchant vessels in port at the outbreak of the war were to be applied by each party. Garner, *International Law and the World War*, I, 81, remarks that Germany treated this treaty, too, as a "scrap of paper." Italy therefore did not apply it.

[54] Austrian corporations controlled or managed by persons of notoriously pro-Italian feelings were exempted from these measures: for example, the *Riunione Adriatica di Sicurtà* an Austrian insurance company established in Trieste.

[55] M.R.W., "Du Régime appliqué par l'Italie pendant la guerre européenne aux bâtiments ennemis refugiés dans ses ports," 24 Rev. gén. dr. int. publ. (1917) 337 ff.

[56] In the case of Austrian ships belonging to persons of pro-Italian feelings, the owners were to be reimbursed for the freight. See Article 4, Lieutenant's decree, June 24, 1915, No. 1014, and judgments of the prize court in the cases of the ships "Salvore," "San Marco," "San Giorgio," "Timavo," and "Grado" (Gazz. uff., January 16, 1920); "F. Meisner" (Gazz. uff., January 16, 1920).

Lieutenant's Decree November 11, 1915, No. 1605, these measures were extended to Germany's ships in Italian ports, though Italy was not as yet at war with Germany. Apart from the capture of ships in national ports, Italy had few opportunities of exercising the right of prize, since during the war enemy merchant navies were practically inactive in the Mediterranean. Some enemy ships were captured in the ports occupied by Italy; other neutrals in consequence of alleged violations of blockade.[57] Shortly after the declaration of war on Austria a prize commission was created by Decree May 30, 1915, No. 807. It issued regulations on June 26, 1915, which were lately slightly modified. By Lieutenant's Decree June 3, 1915, No. 839, the first contraband list was published; this was later repeatedly broadened. The Anglo-French convention of November 9, 1914, concerning maritime prizes was extended to Italy by Lieutenant's Decree February 25, 1917, No. 482. The rules concerning the right of prize during the war were enacted by Lieutenant's Decree March 25, 1917, No. 600.[58]

War against Ethiopia.—On October 2, 1935, the Fascist government ordered the invasion of Ethiopia. It was a real war started by Italy without declaration and fought with particular ferocity.[59] Each of the belligerents accused the other of atrocities—aerial bombings against civilians and use of poison gas on the part of Italy, abominable acts against prisoners and wounded enemies on the part of Ethiopia.[60] The war did not give rise to new important questions of international law.

In view of the almost complete absence of enemy subjects and property in Italy, problems concerning their treatment did not arise. Questions of maritime warfare did not arise either, since Ethiopia had no access to the sea. It does not appear that the Jibuti railroad, which con-

[57] Cases of the Greek ships "Aghios Nicolaos," "Aghios Constantinos," and "Aghios Spiridion," "Platitera," "Aghia Elena," "Aghios Caralambos," "Poseidon," "Evangelina," "Mikail," and "Anthippi." During the first World War Italy declared the blockade of the coasts of Austria (May 26, 1915) ; Northern Albania (May 26, 1915, modified on May 30, 1915, and extended on July 4, 1915, to the coast up to Aspinga) ; Bulgaria (October 20, 1915) and Greece (December 8, 1916). Texts of the declarations in Fauchille and Basdevant, *Jurisprudence italienne en matière de prises maritimes*, and Gazz. uff., July 5, 1915, No. 167.
[58] The principal acts concerning the prize commission and its judgments (in all less than 200) are published in Ministero della Marina, *Sentenze della Commissione delle Prede. Guerra europea 1915–1918.* The Italian legislation concerning maritime warfare during the first World War is collected by De Lella, *Legislazione e regolamentazione italiana in materia di prede marittime durante la guerra 1915–1918.*
[59] On the conduct of the hostilities during the Italo-Ethiopian war, Nostitz-Wallwitz, "Das Kriegsrecht in italienisch-abessinischen Krieg," 6 Zeitschrift für ausslandische öffentliches Recht und Völkerrecht (1937) 680 ff.; Kroell, "Les Pratiques de la guerre aérienne dans le conflict italo-éthiopien," 5 Rev. générale de droit aérien (1936) 178 ff.; Spencer, "Quelques Aspects juridiques de l'emploi des aéreonefs dans la guerre italo-éthiopienne," 7 Revue générale de droit aérien (1938) 7 ff.
[60] Apparently Italy neither admitted nor denied officially employment of poisonous gas. She maintained that she would have been entitled to make use of it as a measure of retaliation against Ethiopian atrocities.

nected Ethiopia with the sea through French Somaliland, had been used for military purposes or the transportation of contraband of war.

The League of Nations declared Italy the aggressor and voted economic and financial sanctions against her.[61] They were put in force on November 18, 1935. Italy reacted by denouncing economic and financial agreements with the states which applied the sanctions. Credits of their citizens in Italy were frozen. The war ended in May, 1936, with the destruction of the Ethiopian Empire. Italy annexed its territory and population. After the end of the conflict the sanctions were revoked, and new economic and financial agreements put an end to their consequences.

[61] Highley, *The First Sanctions Experiment.*

Chapter XVII: DOMESTIC LEGISLATION AND CASES CONCERNING INTERNATIONAL MATTERS

THIS section is devoted to the analysis of subjects regulated by Italian legislation which are of interest to international law.

RELATIONSHIP BETWEEN NATIONAL AND INTERNATIONAL LAW

The principle that international law is a part of the law of the land does not find application in Italy. The opposite principle of absolute separation between international and national law prevails. Italian law alone governs legal relations within the national jurisdiction and is the only law applied by the courts and enforced by state agencies in Italy.[1]

International law, however, has a dual influence on Italian legislation. In the first place, reference to rules and concepts of international law is sometimes made by provisions of the domestic law. Article 553 of the Code of Commerce, which provides that naval blockade justifies the interruption of a ship's voyage, refers to international law for the concept of a naval blockade. The Code for Merchant Marine refers to international law for the definition of piracy.[2] In this case there is no reception of international law as such in the Italian legal system, but the existence of the former is presupposed by the latter. In the second place, rules of international law creating obligations which the Italian state must fulfill within its domestic jurisdiction (for example, concession of certain rights to foreigners and the reduction of customs duties) result necessarily in the enactment of domestic legislation. This is the consequence of the separation between international and domestic law. Since the former does not apply within the state, Italy must enact domestic legislation in order to secure the fulfillment of her international duties within her domestic order. Concession of rights to foreigners and reduction of customs duties can only be provided for by legislative acts.

Various legislative techniques are followed to adapt national law to Italy's international obligations, according to the various types of inter-

---

[1] For references to the Italian practice on the matter see Donati, *I trattati internazionali nel diritto costituzionale*; Leibholz, "Der Abschluss und die Tranformation von Staatverträgen in Italien," 16 Zeitschrift für Völkerrecht (1932) 353 ff.

[2] Reference to concepts of international law is often made by the courts too. See the decision of the Court of Cassation, November 27, 1933, in the "Cogne" case (Gidel, *Le droit international public de la mer*, I, 318), where it was disputed whether the capture of an Italian ship by persons who allegedly acted for the government of the city of Fiume was an act of war or an act of piracy.

national rules from which the obligations derived. Three principal systems are followed.

(a) At times international rules establish only some general principles with which the Italian state has to conform its domestic legislation on certain matters. For instance, the Convention June 15, 1927, concerning sickness insurance for workers in industry and commerce and domestic servants provides (Art. 1):

Each member of the International Labour Organization which ratifies this Convention undertakes to set up a system of compulsory sickness insurance which shall be based on provisions at least equivalent to those contained in this convention.

Compliance with this obligation is provided for by the enactment through the normal legislative channels of a statute inspired by the principles indicated in the convention.

(b) In some cases Italy's obligations arise from customary rules. To provide for the compliance with such duties within the state, Italian legislative acts are issued which prohibit any act inconsistent with such obligations. For instance, customary rules of international law bind Italy to exempt heads and ambassadors of foreign states from penal jurisdiction. To comply with this obligation, a provision of the Penal Code has been enacted (Art. 3) providing that "Italian penal law is binding on all, nationals or foreigners, who are in the territory of the state, saving the exceptions prescribed by the domestic public law or by international law."

The duty of the organs of the Italian state to grant immunity from penal jurisdiction to heads and diplomatic agents of foreign states is not derived directly from international law, but from an Italian rule embodied in the Penal Code. The latter, however, is a blank provision. Its contents is indicated not expressly, but with reference to the international rule.

(c) Most of the international obligations of the Italian state are derived from written instruments such as treaties. In order to adapt Italian law to them, the following procedure is usually followed. An order is enacted providing that "full and entire execution is given in the Kingdom to the treaty." The treaty is published in its entirety as an annex to the order. The name of this act is "order of execution" (*ordine di esecuzione*). It is a normal act of legislation, since it is issued by the authorities entrusted with legislative power. However, it differs from the usual legislative acts, because it does not expressly indicate the rights and duties, powers and burdens, which it creates, but only indirectly by reference to the annexed treaty. The order of execution creates all the rules of Italian law necessary to produce within the scope of the domestic legislation the results desired by the treaty to which it refers; it abrogates all the pre-existing provisions which are incompatible with it. The domestic legislation is so completely adapted to the treaty.

While Italy is internationally bound by a treaty as soon as it is concluded, the treaty as such has no influence upon the Italian legislation in consequence of the absolute separation between international and domestic law. It is only by the enactment of the order of execution that legislation can be changed so as to comply with the provisions of the treaty. Theoretically it could happen that Italy, although internationally bound by a treaty, could not comply with its provisions because the order of execution had not been issued. Italian authorities would be bound to apply legislation inconsistent with the obligations resulting from the treaty, although their conduct would give rise to an international liability for Italy. To prevent this inconvenience, the order of execution is issued before the treaty is in force—immediately after it has been signed by the plenipotentiaries and before it has been ratified. Thus the measures necessary for executing the treaty in the domestic legislative sphere can be taken as soon as the treaty becomes effective from the international point of view. If the order of execution cannot be issued (for example, in consequence of the refusal of Parliament to approve the treaty), Italy will not ratify the treaty, thus avoiding obligations which it could not fulfill.

Since the order of execution is issued in contemplation of the treaty, it is ineffective if the treaty to which it refers does not come into force for lack of ratification or for any other reason. This is a consequence of the very nature of the order of execution, which occurs even in the absence of any express provision to this effect.[3] Termination of the treaty automatically brings the order and its effects in the domestic legislation to an end.

Authority to enter into international treaties and to issue an order of execution with regard to them is not vested in the same organs. As a rule the king alone has the power to bind the state internationally. His power is derived from Article 5 of the Constitution of 1848 which provides that "the king makes the treaties of peace, war, commerce and others. He gives notice thereof to the Parliament as soon as permitted by the interest and security of the state, adding convenient communications."

A treaty signed by the king internationally binds the Italian state, even though the parliament was not consulted or refused its assent. But within the state a treaty is not effective until the order of execution has been is-

[3] Contra, however, Cass. Civ. November 30, 1926, in *Foro delle nuove provincie* (1927) 106; Cass. Civ. May 25, 1927, in *Foro delle nuove provincie* (1928) 120.

sued. Since the order, as has already been stated, is an act of legislation, authority to issue it is vested in the organs entrusted with legislative power (as a rule, the king and the parliament acting together).

Important consequences are derived from the fact that the techniques adapting Italian to international law result in the creation of rules of national law.

1) Since there is no limitation in Italy to the judicial interpretation of legislative acts, even if of a political nature, there is no limitation to the interpretation by the Italian courts of the treaties and other international acts when they are transformed through the above-indicated channels in Italian law.[4]

2) An Italian court will take judicial notice of the changes introduced in the Italian law through the above indicated procedures in order to adapt it to international law.

3) An error of interpretation by a court of the rules of international law so transformed into national law is an error of law from which the parties may appeal whenever appeals are only allowed for mistakes of law.

4) The courts, being free to interpret the law, may give an interpretation of it which is in conflict with the international obligations of Italy. Italian courts generally refuse to recognize the immunity of jurisdiction of foreign diplomatic agents in civil matters, though these decisions are certainly contrary to the international obligations of Italy concerning the treatment of foreign diplomatic agents.

LEGAL STATUS OF FOREIGN STATES

The legal status of foreign states, according to Italian law, is affected by the legal doctrines and rules concerning the status of the Italian state in its own legal order. Besides being the supreme political power, the Italian state is also an entity endowed with legal personality in its own legislation. As such, it is subject to the authority of its own laws and has rights and duties, powers and burdens, only within the limits indicated by them. The state may enter into legal transactions, such as contracts; may own personal and real property; may incur liability for wrongful acts; and may sue and be sued.

Administrative acts of state are divided into acts of government, of dominion, and of management.

1) *Acts of Government (atti di governo)*, or political acts, are acts

---

[4] In Italy the opinion of the political power on the existence of a foreign state or government is not binding on the courts. They are also free to decide which power has control of a foreign territory. C. A. Casale, June 30, 1920, and C. A. Milan, November 24, 1921, in *Foro it.* (1921), I, 209; Tr. Rome, January 26, 1923, in *Mon. trib.* (1923), II, 569; C. A. Genoa, May 7, 1930, in *Mon. trib.* (1930) 178.

performed by the government in the exercise of the political power; for example, a diplomatic protest, a declaration of war, or the proclamation of a state of siege.[5] These acts are manifestations of the exclusive and discretionary power of the government. They may give rise to political consequences and responsibilities (resignation of ministers or a parliamentary vote rejecting a motion of confidence), but they are not subjected to the control of the judicial power (Law on the Council of State, June 26, 1924, No. 1054, Article 31).

2) *Acts of Dominion* (*atti di impero*) are acts performed by the state or other public agencies in the fulfillment of the public activities which constitute their exclusive and particular function.[6] By reason of their nature and purposes these acts (for instance, appointments, revocations, or promotions of public officials) could not be the object of private activities.

3) *Acts of Management* (*atti di gestione*) are similar to those performed by private individuals in the ordinary course of business. Their performance enables the state to fulfill its public activities (purchase of stationery, or lease of a building for a public office).

In performing acts of dominion and of management the state is subject to its own laws and liable in case of their violation. There is no place within the system of Italian law for the theory that the "king can do no wrong." An action against the state for the redress of violation of the law which it has committed in the performance (or nonperformance) of an act of management (for example, action for breach of contract for the purchase of property) must be brought before the courts of ordinary jurisdiction. For the redress of violations of the law committed in the performance (or nonperformance) of acts of dominion, special administrative tribunals have been created, the highest of which is the Council of State. An action against the state for the reinstatement of a public official unlawfully discharged must be brought before such a tribunal.

Italian rules governing the legal status of foreign states presuppose: (1) that in view of the separation between national and international law the legal personality of a foreign state, in the Italian legal system, is independent of its international personality; (2) that the functions and the structure of the foreign state and the Italian state are to some extent similar.

The foreign state is a legal person according to Italian law. This principle has already been recognized by the courts under the Civil Code of 1865, although it did not contain any express provision concerning legal

[5] On the concept of *atto di governo* see Ranelletti and Amorth, "Atti del governo," in *Nuovo digesto italiano*, I, 1108.
[6] On the concepts of *atto di impero* and *atto di gestione* see Ranelletti and Amorth, "Atti amministrativi," in *Nuovo digesto italiano*, I, 109.

personality of foreign states.[7] Implied recognition of the principle is to be found in the Royal Decree August 30, 1925, No. 1621 (now Law July 15, 1926, No. 1263), which regulates measures of execution on property of foreign states in Italy. By recognizing that a foreign state may acquire and own any kind of property in Italy, this decree implies its legal personality. The Civil Code of 1939 provides that foreign legal persons are recognized in Italy upon condition of reciprocity. Foreign states are not expressly mentioned, but the provision obviously applies to them, since they are the most important class of foreign persons. Recognition of their personality in Italy is, then, subject to reciprocal treatment in favor of the Italian state. Foreign states endowed with legal personality may perform every act of management in Italy. They may purchase personal and real property,[8] enter into contracts,[9] acquire property by inheritance.[10] They may also, within certain limits, perform acts of dominion (for example, appoint public officials) [11] and in some extraordinary cases requisition property.[12] The Penal Code, Article 299, punishes offenses committed in Italy against the flag or other emblems of a foreign state.[13] There is some authority for the statement that a nonrecognized state has no legal personality in Italy.[14]

The distinction between various classes of state acts is utilized to determine the limits of the jurisdiction of Italian courts over foreign states. The question usually arises in cases in which the foreign state is the defendant. This situation has been considered by Anzilotti in his essay "Exemption of Foreign States from Jurisdiction," [15] which has deeply

[7] Cass. Turin, November 18, 1882, in Giur. it. (1885), I, 1, 125, and C. A. Genoa, August 6, 1881, in Giur. it. (1882), I, 2, 66.

[8] C. A. Naples, June 10, 1933, in 26 Riv. dir. int. (1934) 110. The Royal Decree Law, May 2, 1925, No. 623, provides that the purchase by foreign states of real property in Italy to be used for residence of embassies and consulates is exempt from taxes upon condition of reciprocity.

[9] If it has mercantile character, the contract is governed by the law merchant (Cass. Civ. February 4, 1932, in *Rivista di diritto internazionale privato e processuale* [1932], p. 386).

[10] See cases in note 7, above. They declared that the Danish state could acquire real property in Italy by inheritance.

[11] C. A. Naples, June 10, 1933, in 26 Riv. dir. int. (1934) 110 (employee of an English national cemetery); C. A. Naples, April 7, 1931, in Mon. trib. (1931) 631 (employee of an American Consulate); Pr. Milan, February 13, 1936, in *Giurisprudenza delle corti regionali* (1936), p. 406, and Cass. Civ., January 18, 1933, in 27 Riv. dir. int. (1933) 241 (employees of the Russian Commercial Representation).

[12] Tr. Savona, July 17, 1936, in *Giurisprudenza delle corti regionali* (1936), p. 588 (requisition of real property by English and French military authorities).

[13] For the salute to foreign flags at sea and maritime ceremonial see *Regolamento sopra le insegne, le bandiere, gli onori e le visite*, approved by decree, June 7, 1934, of the Ministry of the Navy, Rome, 1934.

[14] Fedozzi, *Trattato di diritto internazionale*, p. 198.

[15] 4 Riv. dir. int. (1910) 471 ff. On the exemption of foreign states from jurisdiction see also R. Siotto Pintor, "L'esenzione degli stati esteri dalla giurisdizione nella recente giurisprudenza italiana," in *Festgabe für Fritz Fleiner*, pp. 247 ff.; Bosco, "Lo stato attuale della questione dell'esenzione degli stati esteri dalla giurisdizione interna," 21 Riv dir. int. (1929)

affected both Italian doctrine and Italian practice. Starting on the assumption that there is absolute separation between international and national law, Anzilotti draws a distinction between transactions to which a state is a party as a subject of international law (for example, an alliance) and those to which a state is a party as a subject of national law (for example, a contract between a foreign state and an individual for the purchase of a building). Transactions of the first kind can never form the object of an action before a municipal court. The problem of immunity of a foreign state from jurisdiction can only arise in the second case. Since the state entered into this transaction in its capacity of subject of a municipal system of law, there is no reason why the state should not be subject to the jurisdiction of municipal courts for actions arising from such a transaction. Anzilotti, however, claims that the foreign state enjoys immunity of jurisdiction because of the existence of a customary rule of international law which binds every state to grant immunity of jurisdiction to foreign states. Evidence that such a rule exists is to be found, according to Anzilotti, in the agelong and consistent compliance with it on the part of all the states and in their protests in the few cases in which it was violated.

It is to Anzilotti's credit that he put the question in its exact terms by distinguishing between activities of a state as a subject of international law and of national law. Although accepting Anzilotti's statement of the problem, recent Italian doctrine reaches a different conclusion. Careful research on the part of Bosco and other authors has proved that the customary rule concerning foreign state immunity has now fallen into desuetude. In the absence of any special international obligation to the contrary, a state is not bound to grant immunity of jurisdiction to foreign states. The question is left to the discretion of national legislators. No Italian rule expressly providing whether or not immunity of jurisdiction should be granted to foreign states exists. This explains the uncertainty and contradictions of the courts.

Some courts held that Italian law grants the foreign state absolute immunity of jurisdiction.[16] The majority distinguished between acts of management, which are within the jurisdiction of Italian courts,[17] and

---

35 ff.; Scerni, "Nota," 23 Riv. dir. int. (1931) 562 ff.; Sereni, "Sulla proponibilità innanzi all'autorità giudiziaria italiana di azioni nascenti da rapporti in cui è parte uno stato estero," 24 Riv. dir. int. (1932) 434 ff.; Provinciali, *L'immunità giurisdizionale degli stati esteri;* Cansacchi, "Nota," Temi emiliana (1933), pp. 196 ff.; Morelli, *Il diritto processuale civile internazionale,* pp. 145 ff.

16 Tr. Rome, Feb. 13, 1924, in 17 Riv. dir. int. (1925), 236; Cass. Civ., June 12, 1925, 18 Riv. dir. int. (1926) 249. This judgment, however, recognized the jurisdiction of the Italian court on the assumption that the defendant, the Russian state, had waived its exemption.

17 Jurisdiction has been denied by C. A. Naples, July 16, 1926, 19 Riv. dir. int. (1927) 102 ff.; C. A. Milan, June 4, 1929, *Foro it.* (1929) I, 1145; Tr. Naples, December 31, 1930, *Foro it.* (1931) I, 541; Tr. Genoa, February 17, 1931, 23 Riv. dir. int. (1931) 558; C. A. Rome, March

acts of government and dominion, which are not.[18] The latter rule has been expressed by the Court of Cassation as follows:

According to the law in force in Italy, power of jurisdiction over a foreign state can no longer be contested with regard to relationships of private and patrimonial character, while it must certainly be denied with regard to public activities; i.e., to relationships which the foreign state established as a manifestation of its sovereignty.[19]

In accordance with this principle, Italian courts have declined jurisdiction over those actions to which foreign states were parties, which arose from requisitions, employment contracts, sovereign grants of land, and collection of taxes.[20] Jurisdiction has been maintained over actions arising from contracts for the supply of goods, collision between merchant ships, and, in general, transactions governed by private law. Obviously many borderline cases arise in which it is disputable whether a transaction (for example, purchase of arms for national defense) performed by a foreign state constitutes a private act or a public act.[21]

26, 1931, *Foro it.* (1931) I, 701; C. A. Milan, January 21, 1932, Giurisprudenza comparata di diritto internazionale privato (1932), p. 354; C. A. Milan, January 23, 1932, *Foro it.* (1932) I, 746; Cass. Civ., January 18, 1933, *Foro it.* (1933) I, 1520; Cass. Civ., February 6, 1933, Temi emiliana (1933), p. 266; C. A. Naples, June 10, 1933, 26 Riv. dir. int. (1934) 110 ff.; Cass. Civ., June 26, 1934, *Giur. it.* (1934) I, 1, 977.

[18] Jurisdiction has been retained by C. A. Lucca, March 2, 1886, in *Foro it.* (1886) I, 490; Cass. Naples, March 16, 1886 in *Giur. it.* (1886), p. 228; C. A. Genoa, March 27, 1925, 17 Riv. dir. int. (1925) 236; C. A. Genoa, May 4, 1925, 17 Riv. dir. int. (1925) 540; Cass. Civ., March 13, 1926, 18 Riv. dir. int. (1926) 252; Tr. Rome, June 6, 1928, 20 Riv. dir. int. (1928) 521; C. A. Milan, June 4, 1929, in *Foro it.* (1929) I, 1, 1145; C. A. Milan, February 20, 1934, *Temi lombarda* (1934), p. 396; Tr. Florence, August 3, 1934, 27 Riv. dir. int. (1935) 375; Cass. Civ., August 3, 1935, 27 Riv. dir. int. (1935) 372.

[19] Cass. Civ., January 18, 1933, 25 Riv. dir. int. (1933) 241.

[20] The same doctrine applies to actions against political subdivisions of a foreign state (members of a federal state, provinces). See Tr. Florence, June 8, 1906, in 2 Riv. dir. int. (1907) 379.

[21] It is disputed whether reference should be made to the criteria established by Italian or by foreign states in order to determine whether the act performed by the latter is an act of government or an act of management (see Cansacchi, "Nota," in *Temi emiliana* [1933], p. 265). The question was raised especially with reference to the business transactions of the Russian state which considers all foreign commerce a public activity. The Italian courts held that the question is expressly taken care of by Article 3 of the Italo-Russian treaty of commerce of February 7, 1924. It provides: "Considérant que le commerce extérieur dans l'union des Républiques Soviétiques Socialistes appartient à l'Etat, le gouvernement italien accordera à la représentation commerciale de l'union et à ses organes la possibilité d'exercer, dans le territoire de l'Italie, les fonctions imposées à cette représentation par le Gouvernement de l'union . . . Le Gouvernement de l'Union assume la responsabilité de toutes le négotiations conclues par la représentation commerciale en Italie. En conséquence, le marchandises qui se réfèrent à ces négotiations, ne seront pas assujetties à des mésures judiciaires de caractère préventif."

Italian courts held that by these provisions: (a) Italy acknowledges that the exercise of foreign commerce is a public function of the Russian state; (b) Italy acknowledges that the transactions performed by the Soviet Commercial Representation are of a public nature; (c) the commercial transactions of the Sovietic Representation are, however, expressly subjected to the Italian jurisdiction. Merchandise of the representation is only exempted by sequestration. (Cass. Civ., August 3, 1935, in 27 Riv. dir. int. [1935] 373). The Russian Repre-

Special provisions concerning acts of execution on property of foreign states in Italy have been issued for reason of political convenience by the Decree Law August 30, 1925, No. 1621 (now Law July 15, 1926, No. 1263). Article 1 provides that:

No sequestration, attachment, sale or measure of execution in general may be had with regard to personal or real property, ships, credits, securities, notes or any other things belonging to a foreign state without the authorization of the Ministry of Justice. This provision applies only to those states which admit reciprocity.

It is for the Ministry of Justice to decide if a foreign state grants reciprocity. Acts of execution are not forbidden, but they are conditioned upon authorization. The reports annexed to the draft of the law submitted to the parliament for approval expressly state that in the opinion of the government international law does not in principle prohibit acts of execution against foreign states.[22]

LEGAL STATUS OF THE ORGANS OF FOREIGN STATES

Special treatment is accorded to organs of foreign states (heads of state, diplomatic agents, and consular agents) who by reason of their function frequently come into contact with the Italian legal order.[23]

Heads of States

As a rule the Italian state grants to the heads of foreign states the immunities, exemptions and privileges provided for by international law. The Penal Code punishes offenses against their life (Section 295), liberty (Section 296), honor and prestige (Article 297). These provisions are subject to reciprocity. Heads of foreign states are absolutely exempt from criminal jurisdiction. As to the scope of their exemption from civil jurisdiction, there is a sharp conflict of authority between the doctrine and the courts. Authors are of the opinion that they are subjected to it only in case of controversies concerning counterclaims, real property situated in Italy, and some inheritance questions. Courts, on the contrary, have held that their jurisdiction over the head of a foreign state extends to all actions arising from transactions to which he takes part in his pri-

---

sentation may be sued before the Italian courts for actions arising by a collision in Italian waters between an Italian and a Russian ship, owned by a Russian public corporation and engaged in foreign commerce on behalf of the Russian state (Cass. Civ., July 19, 1938, in *Foro it.* [1938], I, 1216). Actions arising by employment contracts between the Russian Representation and its employees are not within the jurisdiction of the Italian courts (Cass. Civ., January 18, 1933, 25 Riv. dir. int. [1933] 241).

[22] Gazz. uff., September 25, 1925, No. 223. The decree with the reports to the Parliament are published in 18 Riv. dir. int. (1926) 159 ff.

[23] The rules of ceremonial concerning foreign states and their heads have been collected by Toscani, *Norme e consuetudini di cerimoniale.* For the maritime ceremonial see "Regolamento su le insegne, le bandiere, gli onori e le visite," approved by decree of the Navy Minister, June 7, 1934, Rome, 1934.

vate capacity.[24] As to the pope, Article 8 of the Lateran Treaty of February 11, 1929, provides that:

Italy, considering the person of the Sovereign Pontiff as sacred and inviolable, declares that any and every attempt against him, as well as any incitement to commit such, is punishable by the same penalties as attempts against the person of the king or incitement to commit the same. Public offenses or insults committed in Italian territory against the person of the Sovereign Pontiff, whether by deed or by spoken or written word, are punishable by the same penalties as similar offenses against the person of the king.

Diplomatic Agents

Italy accepts the classification of diplomatic agents according to the rank established by the Congresses of Vienna (1815) and Aix-la-Chapelle (1818). Article 12 of the Lateran Treaty provides that the papal nuncio is the dean of the diplomatic corps in Italy. Recently the Italian government has sent abroad an ever-increasing number of officials who enjoy diplomatic privileges and are in charge of particular activities (attachés in charge of press, cultural and labor relations). By reciprocity the Italian government has accepted foreign diplomatic agents with analogous functions. The exchange of some of them is expressly provided for by several international conventions.[25] Italy follows the principle that the appointment of a foreign diplomatic agent is subject to approval.[26] Its refusal needs no explanation and is discretionary.

Immunities, exemptions, and privileges of foreign diplomatic agents accredited to the Italian government are usually established by reference to international law rather than by express provisions.

Personal inviolability is granted to diplomatic agents within the limits established by international law. Special punishment is provided for press offenses (Edict on the Press of 1848, Article 28). Article 298 of the Penal Code extends punishment for offenses against the heads of foreign states (Articles 295–297) to those committed against the heads of diplomatic missions in the performance of their functions. Any offense committed against a diplomatic agent other than the head of the mission is

[24] Cass. Rome, March 11, 1921, in *Giur. it.* (1921), I, 1, 471. This case does not involve a question of immunity from jurisdiction of a foreign state. It refers to acts performed by the head of a foreign state in his individual capacity. The C. A. Rome, May 2, 1939, 31 Riv. dir. int. (1940) 466, held that the Cardinal Secretary of State cannot be compelled to appear before the court in an action against the Holy See.

[25] Article 3 of the labor treaty of September 30, 1919, between Italy and France provides that each party may attach to its embassy a diplomatic agent specialized in labor matters.

[26] The preliminary agreement between Italy and Russia of December 26, 1921, concluded before the *de jure* recognition of the Soviet regime provided (Article 4) that each party might refuse to accept as diplomatic representative anyone who was considered *persona non grata*.

In 1936 Italy refused to receive the French ambassador on the ground that his letters of credence were not addressed to "the king of Italy, *Emperor of Ethiopia.*"

punishable by a more severe sentence, as if it had been committed against an Italian public official (Article 61, subdivision 10, Penal Code).

Inviolability is granted to the residence of diplomatic agents accredited to the Italian government and to the residences of those accredited to the Holy See situated in Italian territory (Article 12 of the Lateran Treaty). In the pre-Fascist period this privilege of foreign legations was scrupulously respected. In 1916, during the Italo-Austrian War, when the Italian government seized Palazzo Venezia, then the seat of the Austrian legation to the Holy See, all necessary precautions were taken to preserve the archives. The removal of the documents lasted two months. It was effected by an official of the Spanish embassy, then in charge of the Austrian interests in Italy, under the safeguard of the Italian police.

The seat of the legations is part of the Italian territory. The Court of Cassation held that a crime in a foreign embassy or consulate in Italy is committed on Italian territory,[27] while crimes in Italian embassies or consulates abroad are committed on foreign territory.[28] Italy does not allow the right of asylum in foreign legations and consulates.

Exemption from personal taxes (for example, income taxes) is granted to foreign diplomatic agents. They are also exempt from customs duties and taxes on pianos, billiards, and servants.[29] The property owned by a foreign state and devoted to the use of its mission is exempt from taxation. Freedom and inviolability of diplomatic correspondence is recognized.

Exemption from jurisdiction of diplomatic agents is absolute in criminal matters. As to civil matters, there has been until recently a sharp conflict of authority.[30] Some judgments were in favor of absolute immunity.[31] The majority however, distinguished between acts performed by the agent in his official capacity and as a private individual. In the latter case exemption was denied.[32] In reality this amounted to a complete denial of the exemption, since acts performed by the agent in his official capacity are acts of the state, and any exemption for these acts is granted to the state, not to the agent. As to the acts performed by the agent in his personal capacity, the Court of Cassation of Rome consistently denied exemption. Its last decision on the matter (January 31,

[27] Cass. Pen., February 11, 1921, in La scuola positiva (1922) II, 18.
[28] Cass. Pen., April 13, 1923, in 16 Riv. dir. int. (1924) 175.
[29] For detailed information on the fiscal exemptions of diplomatic agents, Fedozzi, *Trattato di diritto internazionale*, p. 452.
[30] It is generally held that Italian courts have jurisdiction on diplomatic agents in actions affecting real estate or inheritances in Italy and on counterclaims against them.
[31] C. A. Rome, August 3, 1912, 6 Riv. dir. int. (1912) 612 (approved by Anzilotti); Tr. Rome, January 26, 1927, in 20 Riv. dir. int. (1928) 529 (approved by Bosco).
[32] Cass. Rome, April 20, 1915, 9 Riv. dir. int. (1915) 215 (with a dissenting note of Anzilotti); Cass. Rome, January 31, 1922, 16 Riv. dir. int. (1924) 173 (with a dissenting note of Anzilotti); Tr. Rome, July 3, 1930, 23 Riv. dir. int. (1931) 563 (with a dissenting note of Bosco); Tr. Florence, August 3, 1934, 27 Riv. dir. int. (1935) 375.

1922) provoked a protest from the diplomatic corps.[33] After the merger of the Courts of Cassation [34] the question came up again in 1939.[35] The court held that international usage, consistently respected and confirmed in many recent conventions, binds the state to grant exemption from jurisdiction to foreign diplomatic agents for acts performed in their individual capacity. Presumably the lower courts will follow the trend of the highest jurisdiction, thus eliminating the conflict between the international obligations of the Italian state and the decisions of its courts.

The Italian doctrine contends that diplomatic immunities are granted in order to enable the agent to fulfill his mission without impediments and that they therefore apply even when he is an Italian citizen.[36] There is no precise decision on this point. According to the Italian doctrine, diplomatic immunities extend to all official members of the mission (counselors, secretaries, and so forth), but not to the personnel exercising ministerial functions. On the basis of reciprocity diplomatic immunities are extended to the wives of the members of the mission and to the sons living with them, provided that they are not married and do not exercise an independent profession.[37] They are not granted to the families of the administrative personnel. Cases concerning the immunity of the family and suite of diplomatic agents are in sharp conflict, especially with regard to their exemption from civil [38] and penal [39] jurisdiction. As previ-

[33] The protest is published in 26 Am. J. Int. L. (1932), Supp. *Codification of International Law*, p. 105.

[34] The 5 Courts of Cassation existing in Italy (Turin, Florence, Rome, Naples, and Palermo) were unified in 1922 in the Court of Cassation of Rome.

[35] Cass. Civ. S. U., November 16, 1939, in 32 Riv. dir. int. (1940) 93 (approved by Perassi).

[36] Perassi, *Lezioni di diritto internazionale*, 1937, I, 112; Morelli, "Nota," 26 Riv. dir. int. (1934) 42; Marmo, "Nota," 32 Riv. dir. int. (1940) 54.

[37] See Memorandum of the Italian Foreign Office transmitted by the American Ambassador to the Secretary of State, October 16, 1930, Archives, U. S., Dept. of State, quoted in 26 Am. J. Int. L. (1932), Suppl. (Codification of International Law) 61.

[38] Cass. Rome, April 20, 1915 (exemptions granted to the head of the mission extend to his subordinates only when they exercise the functions of the former); Tr. Rome, January 26, 1927 (exemptions recognized to all the members of the mission); Cass. Civ., Sezioni Unite, November 16, 1939, 32 Riv. dir. int. (1940) 93 (exemptions granted to a member of the mission not the head).

[39] It is especially debated whether immunities are granted to domestic servants of the foreign diplomatic agents. In December, 1879, the Rome Tribunal sentenced the coachman of the German embassy to two months' arrest for disorderly conduct. The judgment was affirmed by the Court of Appeals and the Court of Cassation (November 7, 1881), which enunciated the broad principle that domestic servants of an embassy are not entitled to immunity from criminal jurisdiction. See also Rome Pretor, March 29, 1894 (coachman of the legation of Colombia, convicted for disorderly conduct). In 1908 a criminal information against the driver of the U.S. ambassador was not prosecuted. Cavaglieri, *Lezioni di diritto internazionale* (1934), p. 426; Pujia, "Nota," 3 Riv. dir. int. (1908) 341. Recently the Tr. of Rome (March 25, 1938, in *Giurisprudenza delle Corti* [1938], with note of Sereni) decided that the maid of a secretary of the Swiss legation who had committed infanticide was not subject to the Italian criminal jurisdiction. The court held that immunity would not have been granted if the maid had been Italian. The Italian memorandum to the U.S., Dept. of State, quoted above, takes the position that the immunity is granted to domestic servants not of Italian nationality.

ously mentioned, by the Lateran Treaty of February 11, 1929, Italy recognized the right of active and passive legation to the Holy See. The majority of the legations to the Holy See are in Italian territory. Envoys and legations of foreign governments to the Holy See enjoy in Italy all the immunities and exemptions provided for by international law, even when the foreign states have no diplomatic relations with Italy. The latter's obligation to grant such treatment exists toward the Holy See, not toward the states to whom the diplomatic agents belong.

The Italian government has not officially stated when, in its opinion, the obligation to grant diplomatic immunities first arises. It actually grants them from the moment in which the agent enters Italian territory. It is doubtful whether during the period preceding presentation of credentials they are granted as a matter of duty or of courtesy. No specific rules have been stated concerning their termination in case of the extinction of the foreign government which the agent represents. When the Russian imperial government was overthrown, its diplomatic agents in Italy continued to enjoy immunity for some time, although they were denied representative powers. The practice of the Fascist government has been brutal. When Italy recognized Franco in November, 1936, the ambassador appointed by the Spanish Loyalist government was forced to abandon the legation under threat of ejection *manu militari*. When in 1940 Italy invaded Yugoslavia, Italian authorities claimed the right to expel the Yugoslavian minister to the Holy See from the kingdom and to forbid his entrance into the Vatican state on the grounds that the Kingdom of Yugoslavia no longer existed and that therefore his status did not come under the provisions of the above-mentioned Article 12 of the Lateran Treaty. Strong representations of the Holy See were unsuccessful.

Treatment granted the agents of *de facto* governments is not well established. A decision of the tribunal of Rome (May 20, 1921) denied diplomatic prerogatives to the president of an economic mission sent to Rome by the Bolshevist government, which at that time had not yet been recognized by Italy. The judgment has been criticized by several Italian authors,[40] and with reason. The sending of the mission was the result of an agreement between the Italian and the Bolshevist governments. The latter had been thereby recognized, at least *de facto*. The Italian government, having consented to receive the mission, could not deny its diplomatic status. This position was taken by the Italian Ministry of Foreign Affairs in a note to the tribunal stating in part:

The economic delegation came to Italy pursuant to an agreement between the Royal government and the Moscow government. It has an official character, and therefore treatment of its members must be equivalent, in principle, to that established in favor of foreign diplomatic missions.

[40] Marinoni, *Scritti varii*, pp. 401 ff.; Gemma, "Les Gouvernements de fait," 4 Rec. des cours (1924) 390*n*.

Consuls

Rules concerning functions and treatment of foreign consuls in Italy are chiefly established by treaties.[41] Consular conventions containing detailed provisions on the matter have been concluded by Italy with several states: for example, with Albania (February 29, 1924); Argentina (December 28, 1885); Austria (May 5, 1874); Belgium (July 22, 1878); Bulgaria (February 25–May 1, 1910); Costa Rica (December 12, 1933); Egypt (January 23, 1875); El Salvador (January 25, 1876); France (July 22, 1862); Germany (December 21, 1868); Greece (November 15–27, 1880); Guatemala (November 13, 1905); Latvia (May 11, 1932); the Netherlands (August 13, 1875); Peru (June 11, 1907); Poland (July 10, 1935); Portugal (September 30, 1868); Spain (July 21, 1867); the United States (May 8, 1878); Tunis (September 28, 1896); Turkey (September 9, 1929); and Hungary (May 15, 1874).

Provisions concerning the functions of foreign consuls are contained in many Italian treaties of friendship, establishment, commerce, navigation, labor, judicial assistance, and protection of sailors and indigents. In consequence of the most-favored-nation clause, inserted in most of these treaties, the majority of foreign consuls enjoy uniform treatment in Italy.[42]

The Italian state draws a clear distinction between diplomatic agents who are organs of the state for international relations and the consuls through which a state usually performs activities of a domestic character on foreign territory.[43] However, the Italian consular law of August 15, 1858 (Article 20) provides that "the consuls perform administrative functions and in case of delegation also diplomatic functions."

Due to the extensive immigration of Italians, the administrative functions of Italian consuls are manifold.[44] By reciprocity, equal powers belong to foreign consuls in Italy.[45]

---

[41] On the legal status of Italian consuls abroad and of foreign consuls in Italy see Ferrara, *Manuale di diritto consolare;* Chiovenda, *Manuale di pratica consolare.* Royal Decree, January 8, 1931, No. 164, established the rules concerning the issuance of exequaturs to foreign consuls.

[42] For a collection of consular provisions concerning Italy see Toscani, *Convenzioni consolari e clausole in materia consolare.*

[43] Cass. Civ., April 19, 1933, 25 Riv. dir. int. (1933) 233 ff. (approved by Perassi).

[44] The Court of Cassation, Sezioni Unite, November 17, 1927, 20 Riv. dir. int. (1928) 381, held that the Italian state is under no duty toward its citizens to exercise through its consuls the powers granted to the latter by the consular conventions. An Italian citizen is not entitled, therefore, to sue the Italian state for damages, on the grounds that an Italian consul did not administer the estate of an Italian citizen deceased abroad, although he had that power under a consular convention.

[45] The courts have repressed any attempt by foreign consuls to widen their jurisdiction. The Court of Appeals of Genoa, March 31, 1905, 4 Riv. dir. int. (1909) 259, held that the exclusive jurisdiction granted by some consular conventions to foreign consuls over disputes

They have much more limited immunity than do diplomatic agents, and the tendency of the courts is to further restrict them. Personal inviolability is protected by penal law, which provides that punishment for offenses against a foreign consul is more severe if they are committed when the consul is performing his official duties. Consuls are exempt from customs duties and some taxes.[46] The seat of the consulate is considered Italian territory, and with the exception of the archives, does not enjoy any immunity. Consuls are not exempt from penal or civil jurisdiction; special exemptions resulting from treaties are strictly construed by the courts. The Court of Cassation held that the "personal immunity" secured for French consuls by Article 2 of the Consular Convention between Italy and France and extended to consuls of other nations under the most-favored-nation clause, does not imply absolute exemption from penal jurisdiction, but only from such acts as arrest and protective custody. According to this interpretation the consul of Yugoslavia in Genoa was convicted of manslaughter.[47] In civil matters the foreign consul is subject to the Italian jurisdiction,[48] the exemption being accorded only for official acts which are imputed to the state, not to the consul.[49]

TREATMENT OF CITIZENS AND ALIENS

Citizens

It has been the constant policy of the Italian government to favor preservation of the Italian citizenship of her nationals and their descendants residing abroad. As a rule Italy adopts the principle of *jus sanguinis,* whereby the sons of Italian citizens are considered Italians regardless of their birthplace. Many countries to which Italian immigration is directed, especially American countries, follow the opposite principle, *jus soli,* whereby persons born within the territory of a state are citizens of that state, irrespective of the nationality of their parents. As a consequence of the concurrent application of these two principles, sons of Italian citizens who were born in countries where *jus soli* is in force, have double citizenship. Italy concluded several conventions, especially with Latin American states, for the regulation of conflicts concerning citizenship (Convention Italy-Mexico, August 20, 1888; Italy-Nicaragua, Septem-

---

between the captain and the sailors of their national ships does not extend to disputes between the charterer of the ship and a disembarked sailor.

[46] For a detailed list of the exemptions from taxes and customs granted to foreign consuls in Italy see Fedozzi, *Trattato di diritto internazionale,* I, 460.

[47] Cass. Pen., April 13, 1923, 16 Riv. dir. int. (1924) 175.

[48] Cass. Pen., April 19, 1933, 26 Riv. dir. int. (1934) 234; Cass. Turin, February 10, 1876, *Mon. trib.* (1876), p. 473.

[49] Tr. Naples, December 31, 1930, *Foro it.* (1931), I, 254; C. A. Naples, Oct. 19, 1931, *La Corte d'appello* (1932), p. 232.

ber 20, 1917) or some of the consequences of double citizenship (for instance, Convention Italy-Argentina, August 8, 1938 concerning military service of persons with citizenship of both countries). Provisions concerning citizenship are embodied in many Italian treaties of establishment and commerce. Acquisition of Italian citizenship by former Austrian nationals at the end of the World War is governed by the provision of the Treaty of Peace of San Germain-en-Laye of September 10, 1919. The Treaty of Trianon provides for Hungarian nationals. As to the inhabitants of Fiume, the matter is regulated by the Convention Italy-Yugoslavia, July 20, 1925.

The principal act of domestic legislation concerning citizens is the Law June 13, 1912, No. 555, in which a few changes have been made by subsequent statutes.[50] Italian citizenship (*cittadinanza*) is granted to: (*a*) sons of Italian fathers, regardless of place of birth, through *jus sanguinis;* (*b*) women who marry Italian citizens; (*c*) married women or infants whose respective husbands or fathers acquire Italian citizenship; (*d*) anyone who is naturalized; (*e*) residents of annexed territories.

Italian citizenship is forfeited by: (*a*) Italians who reside abroad, expressly or tacitly renouncing their citizenship; (*b*) women who marry foreign nationals; (*c*) married women or infants whose respective husbands or fathers renounce their Italian citizenship; (*d*) anyone proved to be unworthy of citizenship (*indegnita'*); (*e*) the residents of territories lost by Italy.

The status of a citizen of an Italian colony differs from that of a citizen of the Kingdom of Italy. Citizenship in a colony entitles a person to fewer rights, especially in the political field; it is regulated by the legislation of the different colonies. Metropolitan and colonial citizens are comprised under the general definition of subjects (*sudditi*).

Fascism's political and religious persecutions affected also nationality laws. The Law January 21, 1926, No. 108, provides that Italians abroad who carry on activities detrimental to national interests may be deprived of citizenship. Confiscation of property may follow. The law was never practically applied.[51] Citizenship granted to foreign Jews after January 1, 1919, was revoked by Decree Law September 7 and November 17, 1938. Jews deprived of Italian citizenship have been compelled, with few exceptions, to abandon the metropolitan territory, Libya, and the Aegean Islands, but not Italian East Africa. Jewish persecution ended with fascism according to certain recent statements.

[50] These changes have been brought by the laws, December 31, 1928, No. 3490; December 1, 1934, No. 1997; April 4, 1935, No. 517.
[51] Simpson, *Refugees*, p. 56, reports that fifteen persons disfranchised under that decree were reinstated in the Italian citizenship in October, 1932. It seems that Jews who acquired the Italian citizenship by the peace treaties are entitled to retain it.

Italy has few international obligations concerning treatment of her citizens. Most of them result from labor treaties (for example, for the protection of women, children, and persons employed in certain industries). Political obligations (for example, for the protection of minorities) are very rare. The Treaty of Rome between Italy and Yugoslavia, January 27, 1924 (Article 9), provides that: "the same treatment as that granted to the Italian minorities in Dalmatia by virtue of international agreements in force, will be granted to the Yugoslavian minorities in Fiume." This provision protects not only Yugoslavian citizens but also Italian citizens of Yugoslavian nationality.

Italy does not grant equality of treatment to her own subjects. Metropolitan and colonial citizens have a different status. A new group of metropolitan citizens was recently created, composed of persons of Jewish race, who were subject to specific persecution and legal discrimination. These measures apparently ended with fascism.

The principle accepted by Italy that the state has every power over its subjects has important consequences in international relations. Any attempt to leave the country without authorization is punishable by arrest. If the attempt has a political motive, the punishment is more severe.[52] On the other hand, the state may extradite a citizen, even for a political crime, if provision therefor is made by international convention.[53] The Italian state claims power over its citizens beyond its boundaries. They are subject to military conscription, even if residing abroad.[54] They may be punished in Italy for offenses committed abroad.[55] If they are residents of Italy they must assign to the state their securities, deposits, and credits abroad.[56] They must notify the Italian authorities of changes in their status (marriages, changes of nationality, and so forth) which took place abroad.

The conditions under which a ship is considered Italian are established by Article 40 of the Code for Merchant Marine. Only Italian ships can sail under the Italian flag. Exceptions to this rule are very rare.[57] Italian

[52] *Legge di pubblica sicurezza*, approved by Royal Decree, January 18, 1931, No. 773, Article 58.
[53] Penal Code, Article 13; see Baldassari, "L'estradizione nella nuova legislazione italiana," 23 Riv. dir. int. (1931) 3 ff.
[54] Royal Decree, August 5, 1927, No. 1437, on military conscription.
[55] Penal Code, Articles 7–9. An Italian citizen may be prosecuted for political crimes, or crimes committed against the state abroad. He may be prosecuted for other crimes committed abroad only if he is in Italy; in some cases a special request of the victim or of the district attorney is also required.
[56] Decree Law, May 26, 1934, No. 804 (later, Law, December 31, 1934, No. 2214); Decree of the Ministry of Finance May 26, 1934; Decree Law, December 8, 1934, No. 1943; Decree of the Ministry of Finance, December 8, 1934; Decree Law, August 28, 1935, No. 1615 (later, Law, January 9, 1936, No. 102).
[57] For an interesting case of a foreign ship authorized to sail under Italian flag, Tr. Genoa, May 19, 1922, in Il Diritto Commerciale, 1922, II, 185.

ships in territorial waters and on the high seas are considered part of Italian territory and are subject to national jurisdiction in both civil and criminal matters. In foreign territorial waters they are deemed subject to local jurisdiction except in matters regarding internal discipline. Italian warships are deemed to be exempt from foreign jurisdiction in both civil and criminal matters. Article 4 of the Penal Code provides that to the effects of criminal law "Italian ships and aircrafts are considered territory of the state wherever they are, unless they are subject to foreign jurisdiction according to international law."

Under exceptional circumstances political refugees can be granted asylum on Italian warships in foreign territorial waters. Asylum is never granted to persons guilty of ordinary criminal offenses.

Aliens

Aliens (*stranieri*) are persons to whom Italian law does not grant the status of Italian subjects. Stateless persons (*apolidi*) are as a rule considered aliens, although they have some of the duties of nationals (for example, they are subject to military conscription when residents of Italy).[58] A person with dual nationality, one of which is Italian, is considered an Italian. A person with two foreign nationalities is considered a citizen of that state which in granting him citizenship follows criteria more similar to those adopted by the Italian legislation.[59]

Italy claims some powers over aliens even beyond her boundaries. Aliens may be convicted for serious offenses against the state (for example, making and passing counterfeit money) and political crimes committed abroad (Arts. 7 and 8 of the Penal Code). Aliens may be refused admittance to Italy. Recently (Decree Law October 7, 1938, No. 1931) Jews who were not Italian subjects were forbidden to establish permanent residence in the Kingdom, Libya and the Aegean Islands. Their temporary sojourn is permitted.

Treatment of aliens in Italy is regulated chiefly by the provisions of treaties of establishment and commerce. Uniformity of treatment has resulted from the most-favored-nation clause. Under these treaties aliens are granted almost complete enjoyment of civil rights. The Lateran Treaty, February 11, 1929, grants special rights to the citizens of the Vatican state. Albanian citizens in Italy enjoy the same rights as in their

[58] Stateless persons residing in Italy are subject to the same duties as are Italian citizens. Article 14 of the nationality law provides that "civil rights of a resident of Italy who is not a citizen of Italy or of any other state are governed by the Italian laws." Article 19 of the provisions concerning the application of the laws, which precede the Civil Code, provides: "If a person is stateless the law of his residence governs all his relationships which otherwise would be governed by his national law."

[59] On the legal status of the aliens in Italy see Gianzana, *Le straniero nel diritto civile Italiano*, and Udina, *Elementi di diritto internazionale privato*, to which we refer also for further bibliographical references.

own country. The Treaty of Rome, January 27, 1924, grants a special status to the residents of the city of Fiume who adopted Yugoslavian citizenship. They may use their language freely in their private intercourse, in their religious functions, in public acts, and before the courts. They enjoy freedom of religion. They control their own schools and welfare institutions. They may own real property and exercise almost any profession, including that of lawyer, which is generally reserved for Italian citizens.

In the absence of treaties, the situation of aliens is regulated by national legislation only. As a rule they do not enjoy political rights, and they cannot perform public functions or hold public positions (for example, as members of the army, magistrates, or university professors). Professions are generally open to them, with the exception of those of public or semipublic nature (notary public and attorney) or which may involve important national interests (stockbroker and captain of a ship). Aliens enjoy equality of treatment with citizens under the social laws (workmen's compensation and old-age and invalidity pensions); they may attend schools, sue before Italian courts without giving security, and, if poor, they may sue under the same conditions as do the citizens. They enjoy civil rights, but with certain limitations. Article 3 of the Civil Code of 1865 expressly provided that foreigners were to enjoy the same civil rights as citizens. The Civil Code of 1939 (Article 6 of the provisions for the application of the laws) provides that "the foreigner is entitled to enjoy the same civil rights as the citizen, subject to reciprocity and unless differently provided by special laws."

Foreigners may not own more than one-third of an Italian ship (Article 40 of the Code of the Merchant Marine), nor can they be members of the board of directors of the most important Italian banks, insurance companies, and shipping companies according to the charters of said organizations. They may own real estate. Marriage between an Italian and an alien is subject to state authorization. Marriage between a state official and an alien is forbidden.

Article 6 of the Civil Code of 1939 applies also to foreign legal persons. Their recognition is subject to reciprocity. Foreign corporations are regulated by Articles 230–233 of the Code of Commerce. The activity of many foreign concerns (banks and insurance companies) is subject to important limitations. Several institutions, especially of a religious character, exist in Italy for the benefit of aliens. To many of them Italy grants special privileges in consequence of international agreements. By the treaty with Yugoslavia of July 2, 1924, Italy accords to Serbian-orthodox communities of Zara, Trieste, Fiume, and Peroi, the status of Yugoslavian religious institutions. They enjoy absolute autonomy in their administration, organizations, and economic transactions.

Aliens must notify the police of their address and of any change of address.[60] They may be refused admission to a province, and they may be expelled from the kingdom by administrative measures. By decree-laws, September 7 and November 17, 1938, foreign Jews under 65 who were not married to an Italian citizen or established in Italy before January 1, 1919, were expelled. These inhuman measures provoked protests on the part of many foreign governments. The American ambassador, Phillips, addressed a note to the Italian government October 5, 1938, pointing out that although the treaty of commerce signed in 1871 between the two countries had been abrogated, Italians in the United States were still accorded full protection of their rights. The ambassador concluded:

My government believes therefore, that upon further consideration the Italian government will decide that American citizens lawfully residing in Italy will not be discriminated against on account of race or creed and that they will not be subjected to provisions of the nature of those embodied in the decree laws in question.

The Italian answer failed to promise abstention from religious or racial discrimination, but on December 15, the acting Secretary of State, Sumner Welles, revealed that Italy had finally given assurances that "the rights of American citizens will be fully observed." [61]

Foreign Ships

Italian law defines "foreign ships" as ships which have foreign nationality according to their papers. In principle Italy does not claim any jurisdiction over foreign ships outside her own territorial waters. Italian legislation concerning the status of foreign ships within these waters is far from being accurate. Italy has adhered to the Convention on freedom of transit (Barcelona, April 20, 1921), to the Convention on the international status of maritime ports (Geneva December 9, 1923), and to the Convention for the unification of certain rules relating to the immunity of state-owned vessels (Bruxelles, April 10, 1926) and the supplementary protocol of May 24, 1934. Transit and sojourn of foreign merchant ships in Italian waters is also governed by Federal consular treaties of commerce and navigation and by the Law June 16, 1912, No. 612. As a rule Italy admits inoffensive transit of foreign merchant ships through territorial waters. They may be excluded from certain zones and ports, and their sojourn may be limited. In the absence of treaty provisions to the contrary, they may not engage in fishing within the Italian territorial waters or in cabotage. They are fully subjected to Italian police power and jurisdiction. These rules apply also to state-owned commercial ves-

[60] Legge di Pubblica Sicurezza, Article 147.
[61] Hackworth, 3 *Digest of International Law*, 646, and Pelcovitz and Schneiderman, "Respect for the American Passport" 4 *Contemporary Jewish Record* (1941) 482.

sels in Italian waters.[62] Foreign ships are subject to Italian fiscal laws.[63] They are granted no privilege of extraterritoriality. Transactions performed on board the ship are considered to be performed on Italian territory.[64] The same rule applies to crimes committed on board the ship.[65] All legal acts connected with the ship, including loading and unloading, are governed by Italian substantive law.[66] Italian courts have jurisdiction on foreign ships in civil and criminal cases unless the contrary is specifically provided for in international treaties.[67] Arrests may be made on board.[68] Italian authorities, as a matter of courtesy, refrain from intervening on board foreign ships unless required for the protection of public order.

Sojourn and anchorage of foreign warships in Italian territorial waters during peacetime is regulated by the Royal Decree August 24, 1933, No. 2423.[69] No more than three foreign warships of the same foreign state may visit an Italian port at the same time without special permission. Without a special permit sojourn cannot last more than eight days for any ship. Fiscal, police, and sanitary laws and regulations must be respected. Limitations are imposed on the use of radio and military exercises. Submarines must navigate above water. Armed troops for serv-

[62] C. A. Genoa, March 27, 1925, Giur. it. (1925) I, 2, 271; C. A. Genoa, April 24, 1925, in Temi Genovese (1925) 218; C. A. Naples, December 2, 1925, in *Dor*, XII, 319.
[63] Electricity produced on board a foreign ship is subject to the Italian tax on the production of electricity, C. A. Venice, June 14, 1908, 3 Riv. dir. int. (1908) 396.
[64] The Italian workmen's compensation law applies to an accident on board a foreign ship in an Italian port (the victim was not a member of the crew), C. A. Genoa, September 30, 1898, *La Legge* (1899) I, 446. A collision between foreign ships in Italian territorial waters is governed by the Italian law.
[65] Baldoni, *Il mare territoriale nel diritto internazionale comune*, p. 159.
[66] Consiglio di Stato, Opinion of June 23, 1911, in Fedozzi, "La Condition juridique des navires de commerce," 10 Rec. des cours (1925) 113.
[67] Italian cases on the subject are divided. For many references see Jessup, *The Law of Territorial Waters and Maritime Jurisdiction*, pp. 154–158, and Fedozzi, "La Condition juridique des navires de commerce," 10 Rec. des cours (1925) 210 ff. This author remarks; "Quant à la question de juridiction, les sentences italiennes peuvent se divider en deux catégories, la première comprenant les sentences qui ont prétendu appliquer la théorie française sans rechercher en aucune manière a demonstrer pourquoi et comment cette application devrait se faire; la seconde, comprenant les sentences qui ignorant complètement la doctrine française, ont donné des solutions pratiques en s'inspirant des principes généraux sur la condition juridique des navires marchands étrangers dans les eaux territoriales." The circular of the minister of justice, January 21, 1865, and the instructions of the minister of interior to police officials, April 4, 1867, adopt the doctrine of the French Conseil d'État, while the instructions of the Navy ministry of November 23, 1892, adopt the principle of the absolute subjection of foreign ships in territorial waters to local jurisdiction. All these acts have not the binding force on the courts of legislative measures, but are merely advisory. The Italian practice seems to make no distinction between ships in port and ships in other territorial waters. All parts of territorial waters are equally subjected to the power of the local sovereign.
[68] Cass. Civ., July 2, 1923, in *Foro it.* 1924, II, 6.
[69] Article 2 of said decree defines a foreign warship as a ship flying a war flag and in the service of a foreign state.

ices, ceremonies, and so forth cannot be landed without permission. Admittance and sojourn in territorial waters may at any time be forbidden in the interest of national defense. The decree does not contain any provision concerning jurisdiction of Italian courts on foreign warships. However, Italian authorities would refrain from any police or judicial act on board.[70] Crimes on board are not subject to Italian jurisdiction; foreign criminal law would apply. Foreign authorities may pass and execute judgments on the warship. This is confirmed *a contrario* by a special provision of the above-mentioned decree which forbids execution of death sentences. Criminal offenses committed by members of the crew on land are subject to Italian jurisdiction.[71]

WAR AND NEUTRALITY LAWS

On September 5, 1935, a royal commission of legal and military experts was created for drafting war and neutrality legislation.[72] Its work was completed in April, 1937. By Law May 2, 1938, No. 735, the government was formally authorized to issue new rules concerning "(1) the conduct of war and related problems, with special reference to relations with other belligerents and neutrals; (2) the status of neutrality and related problems with special reference to relations with belligerents." These rules were embodied in the War Law and the Neutrality Law, which were enacted by Royal Decree July 8, 1938, No. 1415.

The two laws are not intended to constitute a complete system of rules governing the whole life of the Italian nation in time of war and neutrality. Many rules concerning these situations are to be found in other acts; for example, the penal codes for the army and the navy and several regulations concerning the organization of the nation for war. The main purpose of the laws is to prescribe the fundamental rules of conduct to which the Italian authorities and armed forces must conform in case of war and of neutrality, in order to comply with the duties and fully avail them-

[70] On July 20, 1863, the Italian police arrested some Italian criminals on board the French ship "Aunis," which had the same status as a warship and was in an Italian port. In the ensuing dispute the Italian foreign minister, Visconti Venosta, took the position that "Il est incontestable, selon le principes le plus reconnus du droit des gens, qu'un bâtiment de guerre ne doit pas pouvoir servir de refuge à des malfaiteurs de la pire espèce." The Italian government, however, made restitution of the two criminals to the French authorities which, in turn, delivered them back to the Italian authorities (*Documenti diplomatici relativi alla cattura eseguita sull'Aunis, 20 luglio 1863*, Firenze, 1863).

[71] In 1902 some sailors of an American warship insulted and assaulted Italian citizens in the city of Venice. The United States government refrained from intervention, and they were sentenced by an Italian court. The sailors were then pardoned by the king. Moore, *Digest of International Law*, II, 587.

[72] On the war and neutrality laws see Commissione per le leggi di guerra e neutralità, *Atti*, Vol. I; Sandiford, "Il diritto marittimo di guerra nelle leggi di guerra e neutralità," 71 Rivista marittima (1938) 231 ff.; Verdross, "Das neue italienische Kriegs-und Neutralitätsrecht," 19 Zeitschrift für öffentliches Recht (1939) 193 ff.; Steiner, "Italian War and Neutrality Legislation," 38 Am. J. Int. Law (1939) 151 ff.

selves of the rights established by international law. Thus the two laws may be considered an official restatement on the part of the Italian government of those which are in its opinion the international rights and duties of the neutrals and the belligerents. The laws drew many provisions from the Hague Conventions of 1907, from the Geneva Conventions of 1906 and 1929 concerning the wounded and sick in the armies at war and the prisoners, and from the Treaty of London, April 22, 1930, concerning submarine warfare. The provisions of the London Declaration of 1909 and the works of the Hague Commission of Jurists to consider and report upon the rules of warfare (1922) are also taken into consideration. On the whole, however, they are original enactments, both in scope and in substance.[73]

War Law

This law is a systematic code divided into seven titles and containing 364 articles. It may be brought into operation in case of war or of a grave and imminent external danger. It may be applied in its entirety or in part. It may extend to the whole territory of the state or to part of it.

Title 1, General Provisions (Articles 1–24). This section defines the territory of the state, the enemy character of individuals and legal persons, the powers of military commanders and those of the government with regard to means of communication and transportation. Requisitioning of neutral means of transportation is conditioned upon payment of material seized. Restitution must be made as soon as possible. The law reserves the right to suspend compliance with obligations arising from international law as a measure of reprisal and to suspend compliance with obligations arising from other sources as a measure of retaliation.

Title 2, Military Operations (Articles 25–131), codifies the accepted rules concerning military espionage, prohibition of bacteriological and chemical warfare, parliamentaries, truces, armistices, capitulations and other military agreements, treatment of sick and wounded or prisoners of war. It also contains some civil-law provisions concerning the form and validity of certain acts (for example, wills) performed in the zone of operation. "Legitimate combatants" are defined, and rules are laid down concerning the conduct of warfare and military occupation. Use of weapons (*mezzi bellici*) is said to be lawful only among those who have the status of legitimate combatants (Article 34). Use of force in war

[73] Steiner, "Italian War and Neutrality Legislation," 38 Am. J. Int. Law (1939) 155. This author remarks that the influence of the American neutrality law is to be observed in Article 9 of the Italian Neutrality Law. It provides: "By royal decree there may be prohibited in whole or in part: (1) dealings in arms and war materials by private individuals for the account of belligerent states; (2) the transit of goods indicated in the preceding section through the territory of the state; and (3) the extension of credits by private individuals to belligerent states or their financial institutions. These prohibitions shall be established in a uniform way for all belligerents."

is always lawful, provided it remains within the limits within which it is justified by military needs and is not contrary to military honor. No superfluous suffering or unnecessary damage and destruction should be inflicted upon the enemy (Article 35). Bombardment is allowed only against military objectives; using it solely against civilians or for the sole purpose of destroying property without military importance is absolutely prohibited (Article 42). Private property in occupied enemy territory must be respected. Civil officials there shall continue in their function unless political, military, or legal exigencies require their resignation.[74] Requisitions are subject to compensation, which must be in proportion to local resources.

Title 3, Special Provisions for Maritime Warfare (Articles 132–227). These follow substantially the universally recognized rules of the international maritime law of war.[75] They deal with the treatment of warships and merchant ships, enemy or neutral. Contraband is limited to seven military items (Article 158). By royal decree and after notification to the neutrals the list may be enlarged, so long as it does not include medical supplies or the materials necessary for the internal operation of the ship on which they are found (Article 160). Contraband is subject to capture and confiscation; the same is true of the ships whose cargo, measured by any standard, is more than half contraband (Article 163). Neutral goods on board enemy ships and enemy goods on board neutral ships are exempt from capture if they do not constitute contraband of war (Article 154). Blockade may be applied only to defined areas and must be effective to be valid. The title contains also rules concerning unneutral service, visit, capture, and destruction of merchant ships. The prize court is organized as a special section of the council of state (Article 218). The prize court applies the internal law of the state, but when a controversy cannot be decided by a definite rule of domestic law, recourse may be made to generally recognized international usages (Article 222).

Title 4, Special Regulations for Aerial Warfare (Articles 228–279). This recognizes the great importance acquired by aircraft in modern warfare. The title applies also to military operations of aircrafts against ships. After war is declared foreign aircraft is not allowed to cross the aerial space over the territory of the state without landing, unless with special permission (Article 228). Enemy and neutral aircraft, public and private, are defined. Public and private enemy aircraft are at all times subject to capture and confiscation (Article 239). Neutral aircraft may be captured and confiscated under eight specified circumstances

---

[74] Article 57: "It is forbidden to compel the population [of the occupied territory] to take an oath of allegiance to the Italian state. The officials who continue to serve may be requested to declare that they will act with loyalty."

[75] The provisions of this title apply also to military operations of ships against airplanes.

(Article 240). The rules concerning control of aerial navigation (treatment of enemy or neutral aircraft and goods, contraband of war, unneutral service, visit and capture, and prize judgment) are along the line of corresponding rules concerning maritime navigation.

Title 5, Treatment of Enemy Nationals and Enemy Goods, and Economic Relations with the Enemy (Articles 280–336). This section deals in large measure with the private law referring to enemy nationals. Persons of enemy nationality retain their full capacity and the free exercise of their rights. They may sue and be sued (Article 280). However, they may be expelled (Article 285), and forbidden from or forced to reside in certain areas (Article 286). They may be interned only if able to carry arms or likely to engage in activities detrimental to the state (Article 284). Enemy property may be requisitioned upon compensation or may be sequestrated. Detailed rules govern sequestration of enemy goods and especially enemy concerns. Persons residing in Italy shall not engage in economic transactions with persons residing in enemy territory or with enemy nationals resident in neutral territory (Article 324). Black lists may be issued.

Title 6 (Articles 337–358), deals with penal sanctions, and Title 7 (Articles 359–364), contains final definitions and established forms of procedure for the issuance and publication of supplementary decrees and regulations.

Neutrality Law

This law applies in case of a war in which Italy remains neutral or whenever particular international situations so require (Article 9, Royal Decree, July 8, 1938). Its operation begins and is terminated by royal decree. The law consists of only thirty-five articles and is much less detailed than the war law. It is inspired by the traditional principles of neutrality. No distinction in favor of or against any belligerent may be made.[76] Hostile acts on the part of the belligerents, including search and capture of ships and aircrafts, are not permitted on the territory of the state. This includes territorial waters, the bed of the sea, and the aerial space under state sovereignty.[77] The same prohibition applies to the passage of belligerent troops or convoys for the transportation of munitions or provisions (Article 3) and the enlistment of troops in favor of belligerents (Article 6).[78] Troops taking refuge in the territory must be interned (Article 4), and their prisoners must be freed (Article 5). The

[76] Ships captured by a belligerent in Italian territorial waters must be freed (Article 15). Foreign prize courts cannot be established on the territory of the state (Article 16), but ships and goods captured can be brought into the ports of the state (Article 19).

[77] This principle runs throughout the law. It is expressly enunciated with regard to the prohibition of transit of belligerent troops through the territory of the state (Article 3).

[78] Members of the Italian armed forces may not enlist in the service of a belligerent state (Article 7).

state administration cannot furnish belligerents with arms, ammunition, or financial aid (Article 8).[79] Italian broadcasting stations may not furnish the belligerents with military information which is not of public dominion (Article 11).

Special provisions regulate maritime neutrality. Inoffensive passage of belligerent warships in territorial waters may be forbidden. Submarines must in any case navigate on the surface (Article 13). No more than three warships of the same belligerent may sojourn at the same time in the same area of territorial waters (Article 17). Belligerent warships must comply with the twenty-four-hour rule unless prevented by weather or damage (Article 18). When warships of different belligerents are found simultaneously in the same port, twenty-four hours shall elapse between the departure of the merchant ships of one belligerent and the warships of the other (Article 21). Belligerent warships may under certain conditions obtain repairs and supplies in Italian ports (Articles 22–24), but they cannot increase their military powers nor obtain military supplies and complete their crew.[80] Aircrafts aboard belligerent warships are considered part of the ship (Article 28).

Some rules concern aerial neutrality. Belligerent aircraft may not pass over the territory of the state unless engaged in the transportation of wounded; belligerent aircraft on national territory at the outbreak of the hostilities must leave within twelve hours, a period which may be extended in case of *force majeure* (Article 31). Aircraft failing to observe these rules are to be rendered incapable of departure during the duration of hostilities (Article 32). Members of belligerent forces rescued beyond the limit of Italian territorial waters by an Italian aircraft are to be interned (Article 30).

Italian war and neutrality laws are among the most complete and important of all the laws enacted on these matters in recent years. They comply substantially with the traditional principles of international law. These are applied in the solution of the new problems arising from the recent developments of military technique, especially of aerial warfare. The experiences of the first World War in the military and economic field have been utilized. Frequent reference to the provision of these Italian laws is made in such classics as Oppenheim's *International Law* and the *Draft Convention of Rights and Duties of Neutral States in Naval and Aerial War*, prepared by the Harvard Law School (Research in International Law).

Undoubtedly the two laws are inspired by a sense of equity and by

[79] As to private individuals, see Article 9, quoted above.
[80] The provisions of the Law, June 16, 1912, No. 612, concerning the transit of foreign merchant ships through Italian territorial waters and of the Royal Decree, August 24, 1933, No. 2433, concerning foreign warships apply in time of war and neutrality unless they are inconsistent with the provisions of the War and Neutrality Law, respectively. In July, 1927, the Navy ministry published "Rules concerning Maritime Law of War."

humanitarian principles. Superfluous suffering or unnecessary damage and destruction are not to be inflicted on the enemy (Article 35). It is forbidden to open fire against enemies escaping from a damaged aircraft by means of parachutes (Article 38). A spy, even when caught *in flagrante delicto,* cannot be punished without a regular trial (Article 23). Enemy population of an occupied territory cannot be punished in case of levies *en masse* if they carry arms openly and respect the laws and customs of war (Article 27). Sick and wounded enemies shall receive the same care as the national soldiers (Article 93). In occupied territory, honor and family rights, life and property of individuals, religious opinion and the exercise of cults must be respected (Article 55). Populations of occupied territories shall not be forced to swear allegiance to the state (Article 57). Requisitions must be in proportion to local resources, and they shall not entail the obligation to take part in military operations against their country (Article 62). No general sanctions may be inflicted on the whole population for individual acts unless the people can be held jointly responsible (Article 65).

The humanitarian spirit of these measures is mostly the consequence of the personal conviction of their authors. The majority of the military experts who took part in the drafting of the law of war did not share the ideas of General Douhet, the Italian forerunner of total war.[81] Some of them, such as Colonel Sandiford, were familiar with international law of war and neutrality.[82] Especially beneficent was the influence of the experts of international law: Giannini, Gemma, Salvioli, and Balladore Pallieri. These men grew up in pre-fascist Italy and were still pervaded by feelings of humanity and justice.

Both laws follow principles obviously opposed to fascist ideologies. The Law of War condemns total warfare, and the Neutrality Law prohibits discrimination in favor of one belligerent. It is no surprise, however, that the fascist government consented to issue these enactments. In the first place, it is always possible to disregard in practice the lofty principles expounded in those laws. Besides, legal loopholes may operate to prevent their operation. As to the Law of War, the government reserves the right to suspend the observance of obligations derived from international law as a measure of reprisal and to suspend obligations derived from other sources as a measure of retaliation. It is easy to maintain, even if arbitrarily, that situations have arisen which justify measures of reprisal or retaliation.[83] As to the Neutrality Law, it comes into operation only if so ordered by royal decree. In case of a war, such a decree may

---

[81] Douhet's ideas are expounded in his books: *Il dominio dell'aria; La difesa nazionale; Probabili aspetti della guerra futura.*

[82] Sandiford has written many works on neutrality and aerial and maritime warfare. The most important are: *Diritto aereonautico di guerra* and *Diritto marittimo di guerra.*

[83] During the Ethiopian War, Italy contended that she was entitled to resort to gas warfare as a measure of retaliation against Abyssinian atrocities.

not be issued. This is what happened at the beginning of the second World War, when Italy claimed the ambiguous status of nonbelligerent.

Whatever may have been the practice of the fascist government in the present war, before and after its intervention in it, one cannot deny that the Italian neutrality and war laws are two important documents. The principles embodied in them are good law. They should be taken into consideration in any future codification of the international law of war and neutrality.

Chapter XVIII: CONTRIBUTION OF CONTEMPORARY ITALY TO INTERNATIONAL LAW

POSITION OF THE ITALIAN DOCTRINE AMONG CONTEMPORARY
THEORIES OF INTERNATIONAL LAW

THE transition from the doctrine of nationalities to the positivist conception is not only a change in legal principles but also an aspect of the general evolution of the Italian life which took place after the political unification of the country. The doctrine of nationalities was the reflection in the field of international law of the lyric and heroic dreams of the Risorgimento. The positivist conception is the manifestation of that realistic spirit which pervaded the new Kingdom of Italy. As a result of it the study of the international organization became more technical and scientific. International lawyers confined their research to strictly legal problems. They devoted their attention to the practice of the states rather than to the moral, political, and philosophical aspects of international relations. By this method of research international law was raised to the dignity of an autonomous system of jurisprudence.

The Italian school of international law still maintains these characteristics. Again and again we want to repeat that Fascist ideologies have not exerted the slightest influence on the Italian conception of international law. The Italian school is completely under the influence of Anzilotti and Donati, Romano and Balladore Pallieri. As we have already pointed out, Anzilotti's extreme and uncompromising attitude has been gradually abandoned by his followers. On the other hand, the followers of Romano and Balladore Pallieri strongly approved the positivist method and accepted many of the conclusions reached by Anzilotti with regard to specific problems. The conflict between the heads of the two schools has almost disappeared in the works of their followers. As a result, a new Italian school of international law has been created. This school has an eclectic character, since it partakes of the conception of the positive school as expounded by Anzilotti and by such opponents as Romano and Balladore Pallieri. Notwithstanding this double derivation, the contemporary Italian conception of international law has some uniform and original characteristics whereby it can be distinguished from other doctrines of international law accepted in different countries. Its principal merits can be named as follows: clear distinction between international law and politics; strictly juridical method of approach to the problems considered and a systematic, comprehensive treatment of them; thorough and exhaustive examination of the fundamental legal principles governing the international community; ability to offer solutions for the specific problems of international law which are consistent with said fundamental principles; use of all the relevant literature in the great languages.

The current statement that the Italian school is strictly positivist is somewhat misleading. As far as the method is concerned, Italian scholars are and intend to remain positivists: that is, they want to consider international relations as they are and not as they should be. It must be hoped that this will not change. For whenever positivist method fails, positive law fails also. On the other hand, young Italian scholars recognize that international law is not based exclusively on the consent of the states; they oppose, however, any undue influence of the doctrines of natural law.

The Italian conception, as has already been seen, has not crystallized into a set of immutable rules. On the contrary, it underwent a considerable revolution, caused in part by foreign influences. While endowed with marked originality, the Italian school is not a closed one. In the field of international law there is no cultural isolation in Italy. Italian writers, or at the least the greatest among them, were able to appreciate the contributions of systems other than the Roman to the development of international law. In commemorating Lord Finlay's contribution to the work of the Permanent Court of International Law, Anzilotti pointed out:

He never failed to help us with the ideas of flexibility and of equity which are the basis and almost the life-breath of the English legal system and which in certain respects are so well suited to fill the gaps and make good the imperfections that exist in international law.[1]

All the most important theories expounded abroad, such as those of Kelsen,[2] Verdross, and Lauterpacht, were the object of accurate analysis. Italian works on every problem of international law evidence in general deep knowledge of the relevant foreign literature on the subject.[3] English

[1] Perm. C. Int. Jus., Publ., Ser. E, No. 5, p. 22.
[2] The theories of the Vienna school have been carefully considered in Italy, both by the positivists and by their opponents. Kunz, 52 Rev. dr. int. et lég. comp. (1925) 557, remarks that the works of Kelsen and of his school are very well known in Italy and that quotations from Kelsen, Verdross, and others can be found frequently in the *Rivista di diritto internazionale*. However, the principles of that school have been rejected by the Italians, who accuse it of exaggerated formalism and of naturalistic tendencies. The Italian scholars unanimously reject the monistic conception. For conclusive criticism against it see Perassi, *Lezioni di diritto internazionale*, 1938, II, 1 ff.; Balladore Pallieri, "Le dottrine di Hans Kelsen e il problema dei rapporti tra diritto interno e diritto internazionale," 27 Riv. dir. int. (1935) 24 ff.; Maggiore, "Ciò che resta del Kelsenismo," in *Studii in onore di Santi Romano*, VI, 213 ff.
[3] Foreign works are generally read in their original language and therefore are seldom translated into Italian.

and American writers especially are referred to with regard to practical matters. Recourse is frequently made to English and American sources for ascertaining the practice of the states.[4]

While Italian writers are usually well informed on foreign theory and practice of international law, Italian works are very little known abroad. This is partly due to the difficulty of the Italian language and the fact that there are no translations available and partly to the strictly legal treatment used by the authors, which makes them of little interest to anyone who prefers different methods of approach to international legal problems. However, the influence of such writers as Anzilotti and Donati is felt beyond Italy; many references to Italian works can be found in the books of Verdross, Lauterpacht, and Guggenheim.

The Italian doctrine exerted some influence on international practice through the participation of Italian jurists in international arbitrations. Sclopis presided at the "Alabama" arbitration: Visconti Venosta was one of the arbitrators in the Behring Sea case; Fusinato in the Casablanca case. The king of Italy decided the British Guiana arbitration between England and Brazil (1901), the Zambese arbitration between England and Portugal (1903), and the Clipperton case between France and Mexico (1931). Through Anzilotti the Italian doctrine exerted a considerable influence on the jurisprudence of the Permanent Court of International Justice, especially in its initial phase. The Court echoes Anzilotti's teaching on the relationship between international and national law in the following affirmation:

From the standpoint of the international law and of the Court which is its organ, municipal laws are merely facts which express the will and constitute the activities of the state in the same manner as do legal decisions and administrative measures.[5]

It accepts his doctrine of the sources of international law in asserting that:

The rules of law binding upon the states emanate from their own free will as expressed in conventions or by usages generally accepted as expressing principles of law.[6]

It follows Anzilotti's conception of the international community by pointing out in the same advisory opinion that the main principle of the international community is freedom of the state to do all that is not forbidden

[4] Balladore Pallieri, in the Preface to his *Diritto internazionale pubblico*, 2d ed., remarks: "The Anglo-Saxon practice is certainly the best known. Often it is the only one to which resort may be made in order to prove or to deny the existence of an international custom. As a result, customary international law tends to be shaped to a large degree as the Anglo-Saxon countries wished. This is a well-deserved award for the industry of their scholars."

[5] Case concerning certain German interests in Polish Upper Silesia (The Merits), May 25, 1926, Perm. Ct. Int. Jus., Publ. Ser. A, No. 7, p. 19.

[6] "Case of the S/S Lotus," September 7, 1927, Perm. Ct. Int. Jus., Publ., Ser. A, No. 10, p. 18.

by rules and that "restrictions upon the independence of the states cannot be presumed." [7] Anzilotti's dissents at the Permanent Court of International Justice have the same historical significance as those of Justice Holmes in the Supreme Court of the United States. The rules of interpretation expounded by Anzilotti in his opinions are in themselves a complete body of doctrines on the subject.[8]

Considerable influence was also exerted by the Italian doctrines in the resolutions of the *Institut de Droit International* and the International Law Association. In international meetings Italian jurists have proved that their judgment is immune from political bias. To conclude, the Italian school has developed a vigorous body of doctrine and familiarity with it is useful to any student of international law. Its qualities should be combined with the great virtues of the American international lawyers: realistic approach to the problems considered; thorough review of the diplomatic practice of the states and of all the relevant cases; full understanding of the exigencies of the practice. The result will be a considerable progress in the study of international law, which will exert also a beneficent influence upon the practice.

INFLUENCE OF THE RECENT ITALIAN PRACTICE ON THE FUTURE
DEVELOPMENT OF INTERNATIONAL LAW

Modern Italian practice of international law is much less important than the doctrine. Its lack of originality during the period preceding the Fascist regime is a merit rather than a defect, since it was chiefly the consequence of Italy's substantial compliance with the precepts of international law.

The Fascist government, on the contrary, frequently departed from the traditional forms of international intercourse. However, it was unable to create new international practices. Rather, the Fascists indulged in violations of international law, which became especially grave and frequent after fascism developed into a totalitarian regime and an active imperialistic policy was adopted. The fundamental incompatibility between the Fascist state and international law then became evident. Fascism aims at world hegemony of one state based upon the enslavement of the other states. International law presupposes the co-existence of independent states.

Fascist practice of international law, however, deserves attention for several reasons. First, because fascism was able in several instances to violate the spirit and purposes of international law while formally complying with their letter. A redefinition of the rules of international law

---

[7] *Ibid.*, p. 19.
[8] Hyde, "Judge Anzilotti and the Interpretation of the Treaties," 27 Am. J. Int. L. (1933) 502 ff.; Dumbauld, "Dissenting Opinions in International Adjudications," 90 University of Pennsylvania Law Review (1942) 929 ff.

which will prevent the repetition of this evil presupposes full knowledge of the devices adopted by the Fascist regime in order to achieve that fraud against international law. Second, because our analysis has proved that a totalitarian state would be unable to comply with the rules of international law even if it were willing to do so. This inability is due to the structure of the totalitarian state, which is based upon the centralization in the state of ever-increasing powers and functions; on the growing subordination of private rights and powers to those of the state; and on the disappearance of any clear distinction between public and private activities, both in the internal and in the international field. This type of state cannot comply with many rules of international law which were created to regulate the intercourse of states endowed with different structure and functions. It should be pointed out, however, that the new type of state which developed in the totalitarian countries is not necessarily a Fascist state. It was adopted by the Fascist governments in its extreme form, because it could be utilized as an instrument for the oppression of the majority by the minority and for the suppression of every individual freedom. A strong state, however, is not necessarily totalitarian; it may also serve democratic purposes—in fact, it can be the best safeguard of individual rights and the best protection of all the citizens. It can equitably distribute rights and duties among all the individuals and secure liberty and justice for all. This type of state is the state of tomorrow. Many symptoms show that there is a trend in all democratic countries toward a stronger state organization which will have greater powers and wider functions. The era of individualism is over. The distinction between private and public activities is disappearing. The present World War will only precipitate this change in the structure of the state, and peace will not bring back the old-fashioned type of state. International law must evolve in order to adapt itself to the changing structure of its subjects, and the analysis of the present practice of the totalitarian countries will help to ascertain what changes will be necessary.

Finally, the analysis of the recent Italian practice of international law is useful from a technical point of view. Twenty years of Fascist preaching of violence and cynicism have not been enough to obliterate the deeply rooted sentiment of justice and the legal ability which the Italian people inherited from Rome. These great qualities of the Italians manifested themselves in many international instruments (for example, treaties of labor, of judicial assistance, and for the recognition of foreign judgments), and in several acts of domestic legislation concerning international relations (for example, the laws of war and neutrality). These acts were drafted by experts of considerable technical experience who were free from any political bias. They should therefore be considered in any future codification of international law.

BIBLIOGRAPHY

WORKS CITED IN THE TEXT

Adair, A. R. The Extraterritoriality of Ambassadors in the Sixteenth and Seventeenth Centuries. London, 1929.

Adami, V. I confini di stato nella legislazione internazionale. Roma, 1913.

—— I magistrati ai confini della Republica veneta. Grottaferrata, 1915.

—— "La magistratura dei confini negli antichi dominii di Casa Savoia," 16 Miscellanea di storia italiana (1916) 24 ff.

—— "La magistratura dei confini nello Stato di Milano," 40 Archivio storico lombardo (1913) 211 ff.

Agnetta Gentile, D. Del principio di nazionalità. Palermo, 1875.

Ago, R. "La colpa nell'illecito internazionale," in Studii in onore di Santi Romano, III, 210.

—— "Illecito commissivo e illecito omissivo nel diritto internazionale," 2 Diritto internazionale (1938) 9 ff.

—— Lezioni di diritto internazionale privato. Milano, 1938.

—— "Sui limiti del mare territoriale," 3 Rivista del diritto della navigazione (1937) 370 ff.

—— "Règles générales des conflits des lois," 58 Rec. des cours (1937) 243 ff.

—— "La regola del previo esaurimento dei ricorsi interni in tema di responsabilità internazionale," 3 Archivio di diritto pubblico (1938) 180 ff.

—— Il requisito dell'effettività dell'occupazione in diritto internazionale. Roma, 1934.

—— "La responsabilità indiretta nel diritto internazionale," 1 Archivio di diritto pubblico (1936) 12 ff.

—— Teoria del diritto internazionale privato. Padova, 1934.

Alberi, E. Relazioni degli ambasciatori veneti al senato. 15 vols. Firenze, 1839–1863.

Alberico da Rosate, Commentaria. 9 vols. Lugduni, 1545–1548.

—— Commentarium de statutis. Reprinted in Ziletti, Tractatus, Vol. II.

Albericus de Rosate, see Alberico da Rosate.

Alberoni, G. "Scheme for Reducing the Turkish Empire to the Obedience of Christian Princes, together with a Scheme of Perpetual Diet for Establishing the Public Tranquillity," 7 Am. J. Int. L. (1913) 83 ff.

Alciati, A. Opera omnia. 4 vols. Basileae, 1582.

Alciatus, A., see Alciati.

Alhadeff, A. L'ordinamento giuridico di Rodi e delle altre isole italiane dell'Egeo. Milano, 1927.

Aloisi, V. "Estradizione," in Nuovo digesto italiano, V, 687 ff.

Ambrosini, G. "Africa orientale italiana," in Nuovo digesto italiano, VI, 737 ff.

Angelo da Perugia. Commentaria. 4 vols. Lugduni, 1561.

—— Opera omnia. 5 vols. Lugduni, 1534.

Angelo de Ubaldis, see Angelo da Perugia.

Anzilotti, D. "L'annessione del Congo," 4 Riv. dir. int. (1909) 237 ff.

—— "L'azione individuale contraria al diritto internazionale," 5 Rivista di diritto internazionale e legislazione comparata (1902) 8 ff.

—— Corso di diritto internazionale, 3d ed. Roma, 1928.

—— Corso di diritto internazionale. Roma, Vol. I, 1914; Vol. III, 1915.

—— Corso di lezioni di diritto internazionale. Roma, 1913. Lectures on international private law.

—— Corso di diritto internazionale privato. Roma, 1919.

—— Corso di diritto internazionale privato. Roma, 1925.

—— Il diritto internazionale nei giudizii interni. Bologna, 1902.

—— "La formazione del Regno d'Italia nei riguardi del diritto internazionale," 6 Riv. dir. int. (1912) 1 ff.

—— "La riconvenzione nella procedura internazionale," 21 Riv. dir. int. (1929) 237 ff.

—— Studii critici di diritto internazionale privato. Rocca San Casciano, 1898.

—— Teoria generale della responsabilità dello stato nel diritto internazionale. Firenze, 1902.

—— "Trattati generali di diritto internazionale," 1 Riv. dir. int. (1906) 34 ff.

Aquinas, T. Opera omnia. 15 vols. Romae, 1882–1930.

Arangio Ruiz, S. Storia costituzionale del Regno d'Italia (1848–1898). Firenze, 1898.

Arias, G. "La base delle rappresaglie nella costituzione economica del medioevo," 9 Atti del Congresso di scienze storiche (Roma, 1906) 347 ff.

—— I trattati commerciali della repubblica fiorentina. Firenze, 1901.

Arias de Valderas, F. Tractatus de belli iustitia iniustitiave. Romae, 1533. Reprinted in Ziletti, Tractatus, Vol. XVI.

Augustinus, A. Opera omnia. 11 vols. Lutetiae Parisiorum, 1841–1842.

Ayala, B. de. De jure et officiis bellicis et disciplina militari libri III. Introduction by J. Westlake. 2 vols. Washington, D.C., 1912. Published by the Carnegie Institution of Washington.

Azo, see Azzo.

Azuni, D. A. Le Droit maritime de l'Europe. 2 vols. Paris, 1798. English translation by W. Johnson: The Maritime Law of Europe. 2 vols. New York, 1806.

—— Origine et progrès du droit et de la législation maritime, avec des observations sur le Consulat de la mer. Paris, 1810.

—— Sistema universale dei principii del diritto marittimo dell'Europa. 2 vols. Firenze, 1795.

Azzo. Summa codicis. Basileae, 1563.

—— Summa institutionum. Basileae, 1566.

Baldassarri, A. Gli effetti della naturalizzazione straniera del cittadino rispetto all'ordinamento giuridico italiano. Roma, 1928.

—— L'estradizione nella nuova legislazione italiana," 23 Riv. dir. int. (1931) 3 ff.

—— Il fondamento giuridico della estradizione. Roma, 1914.

—— Il matrimonio dei cittadini all'estero rispetto all'ordinamento giuridico italiano. Bari, 1931.

—— La neutralizzazione. Roma, 1912.

Baldo degli Ubaldi. Opera omnia in iure civili. 5 vols. Venetiae, 1559.

—— Usus feudorum commentaria. Lugduni, 1585.

Baldoni, C. L'asilo a bordo delle navi private. Padova, 1938.

—— "L'asilo sul proprio territorio e sulle navi in alto mare," 3 Archivio di diritto pubblico (1938) 21 ff.

—— "La Corte permanente di giustizia internazionale e gli Stati Uniti d'America," 19 Riv. dir. int. (1927) 17 ff.

—— Il mare territoriale nel diritto internazionale comune. Padova, 1934.

—— "Les Navires de guerre dans les eaux territoriales étrangères," 65 Rec. des cours (1938) 185 ff.

—— "Gli organi e gli istituti nelle unioni internazionali," 23 Riv. dir. int. (1931) 352 ff.

—— "Le riserve nelle convenzioni collettive," 21 Riv. dir. int. (1929) 356 ff.

—— La Società delle Nazioni. Padova, 1936.

—— "Gli Stati Uniti e la Corte di giustizia internazionale," 21 Riv. dir. int. (1929) 309 ff.

—— "La successione nel tempo delle norme di diritto internazionale privato," 24 Riv. dir. int. (1932) 3 ff.

—— "Le Unioni internazionali di stati," N. S. 6 Rivista italiana per le scienze giuridiche (1931) 475 ff.

Baldus de Ubaldis, see Baldo degli Ubaldi.

Balladore Pallieri, G. "L'Arbitrage privé dans les rapports internationaux," 51 Rec. des cours (1935) 287 ff.

—— La concezione positiva del diritto internazionale. Messina, 1932.

—— Diritto internazionale ecclesiastico. Padova, 1940.

—— Diritto internazionale pubblico. 2d ed. Milano, 1938.

—— "Le dottrine di Hans Kelsen e il problema del rapporti tra diritto interno e diritto internazionale," 27 Riv. dir. int. (1935) 24 ff.

—— "Gli effetti dell'atto illecito internazionale," 23 Rivista di diritto pubblico (1931) 64 ff.

—— L'estinzione di fatto degli stati. Messina, 1931.

—— "La forza obbligatoria della consuetudine internazionale," 20 Riv. dir. int. (1928) 338 ff.

—— La guerra. Padova, 1935.

—— L'intervento come istituto giuridico internazionale. Messina, 1930.

—— "La natura giuridica dell'arbitrato internazionale," 21 Riv. dir. int. (1929) 328 ff.

—— I principii generali di diritto riconosciuti dalle nazioni civili. Torino, 1931.

—— "Due recenti teorie sulla natura giuridica della sentenza internazionale," 5 Annali della R. Università di Messina (1930–1931) 186 ff.

Bar, K. L. von. Theorie und Praxis des internationalen Privatrechts. 2d ed., 2 vols. Hannover, 1889.

Barbarus, H. De officio legati. Manuscript in the Vatican Library, Mi. Vat. Lat. 5392, foll. 50–52,v.

Barbazza (Barbatia, de), A. Tractatus de cardinalibus legatis a latere. Lugduni, 1518. Reprinted in Ziletti, Tractatus, Vol. XIII.

Barcia Trelles, C. "Francisco Suarez (1548–1617); les Théologiens espagnols du XVIᵉ siècle et l'école moderne du droit international," 43 Rec. des cours (1933) 385 ff.

Bartolo da Sassoferrato. Consilia, quaestiones et tractatus. 10 vols. Venetiis, 1602.

—— Opera. 10 vols. Basileae, 1589.

—— Tyberiadis. Tractatus de fluminibus. Bononiae, 1576.

Bartolus de Saxoferrato, see Bartolo da Sassoferrato.

Basdevant, J. "L'Action coercitive anglo-germano-italienne contre le Venezuela (1902–1903)," 11 Rev. gén. dr. int. publ. (1904) 362 ff.

Battaglia, F. "Nazione," 24 Enciclopedia italiana (Roma, 1934), 470 ff.

Battino, R. Les Doctrines juridiques contemporaines en Italie. Paris, 1939.

Bavaj, A. Alberico Gentili. Macerata, 1935.

Beale, J. H. Bartolus and the Conflict of Laws. Cambridge, 1914.

Beaufort, D. La Guerre comme instrument de secours ou de punition. La Haye, 1933.

Belli, P. De re militari et bello tractatus. Publications of the Carnegie endowment for international peace, Division of international law. Introduction by A. Cavaglieri. 2 vols. Oxford, 1936.

Benoit, C. "L'Influence des idées de Machiavel," 9 Rec. des cours (1925) 233 ff.

Bernardi, A. Eversionis singularis certaminis libri XL. Basileae, 1562.

Bertacchini, G. Repertorium juris. Venetiis, 1580.

Bertachinus, J., see Bertacchini, G.

Besta, E. Il diritto pubblico italiano. 3 vols. Padova, 1928–1930.

Besta, E., and P. Fedozzi. "I consolati di Sicilia all'estero e i consolati esteri in Sicilia sino al secolo XIX°," 2 Zeitschrift für Völkerrecht (1908) 119 ff.

Bettanini, A. Lo stile diplomatico. Milano, 1936.

Bex, G. Essai sur l'évolution du droit des gens. Paris, 1910.

Bianchi, F. S. Corso elementare di diritto civile. 2 vols. Parma, 1869.

Biscaretti di Ruffia, P. Contributo alla teoria giuridica della formazione degli stati. Milano, 1938.

Biscottini, G. "L'annessione e la fusione di stati e i loro riflessi sul fenomeno successorio," 32 Riv. dir. int. (1940) 133 ff.

—— "Sulla formazione dello stato," 31 Riv. dir. int. (1939) 378 ff.

Bizzarri, D. Studi di storia del diritto italiano. Torino, 1937.

Bluntschli, J. K. Das moderne Völkerrecht der civilisirten staaten als Rechtsbuch dargestellt. 3d ed. Nördlingen, 1878.

Bodin, J. De republica libri sex. Paris, 1583.

Boeck, C. de. "La Sentence arbitrale de la Cour Permanente de la Haye dans l'affaire Canevaro," 20 Rev. gén. dr. int. publ. (1913) 317 ff.

Bösch, E. E. Beitrag zu den Grundlagen des internationalen Rechts; Recht und Nation bei Giambattista Vico. St. Gallen, 1932.

Bonfante, P. Lezioni di storia del commercio. 2 vols. Milano, 1925.

Bonnet, H. L'Arbre des batailles. Paris, 1883.

Bonolis, G. Il diritto medioevale marittimo dell'Adriatico. Pisa, 1921.

—— Questioni di diritto internazionale in alcuni consigli inediti di Baldo degli Ubaldi. Pisa, 1908.

—— Sulle maone genovesi e una maona fiorentina. Firenze, 1907.

Borchard, E. M. "The Attorney General's Opinion on the Exchange of Destroyers for Naval Bases," 34 Am. J. Int. Law (1940) 690 ff.

—— "The United States as a Factor in the Development of International Relations," in E. A. Walsh, The History and Nature of International Relations (New York, 1922), pp. 229 ff.

Borgo (Burgus), G. B. De dominio serenissimae Genuensis reipublicae in mari Ligustico. Romae, 1641.

Borsi, U. "Le clausole eccettuative di controversie nei trattati italiani di arbitrato obbligatorio," 7 Rev. dir. int. (1913) 155 ff.

—— Diritto coloniale italiano. Padova, 1937.

—— "Il nuovo procedimento conciliativo nelle controversie internazionali," 16 Riv. dir. int. (1924) 1 ff.

—— "Ragione di guerra e stato di necessità nel diritto internazionale," 10 Riv. dir. int. (1916) 175 ff.

Bosco, G. Corso di diritto internazionale privato. Firenze, 1936.

—— "La natura giuridica dell'arbitrato internazionale nella dottrina italiana," 23 Riv. dir. int. (1931) 490 ff.

—— "Le nuove leggi sul matrimonio e il diritto internazionale privato italiano," 22 Riv. dir. int. (1930) 363 ff.

—— Rapporti e conflitti tra giurisdizioni internazionali. Roma, 1932.

—— "Lo stato attuale della questione dell'esenzione degli stati esteri dalla giurisdizione interna," 21 Riv. dir. int. (1929) 35 ff.

Bosdari, F. de. Giovanni da Legnano. Bologna, 1901.

Botero, G. Della ragion di stato e delle cause della grandezza delle città. Introduction by C. Morandi. Bologna, 1930.

Breschi, B. La dottrina della guerra nel diritto internazionale. Roma, 1922.

—— La Società delle Nazioni. Firenze, 1922.

Breyne, E. Le Droit de guerre selon Giovanni da Legnano. Louvain, 1932.

Brière, Y. de la. "Les Droits de la juste victoire selon la tradition des théologiens catholiques," 32 Rev. gén. dr. int. publ. (1925) 366 ff.

—— "Les Étapes de la tradition théologique concernant le droit de juste guerre," 44 Rev. gén. dr. int. publ. (1937) 129 ff.

Brocher, C. A. Cours de droit international privé. 3 vols. Paris, 1882–1885.

—— "Étude sur le traité de droit civil international publié par M. Laurent," 13 Rev. dr. int. et lég. comp. (1881) 531 ff.

Brockhaus, F. Das Legitimitätsprinzip. Leipzig, 1868.

Brown, G. K. Italy and the Reformation to 1550. Oxford, 1933.

Bruccoleri, G. L'opera dei delegati italiani alla Società delle Nazioni. 4 vols. Roma, 1935–1937.

Brunet, C. Consequences juridiques de l'annexion de la Savoie et de Nice à la France. Paris, 1890.

Brusa, E. "L'Affaire du Doelwik," 4 Rev. gén. dr. int. publ. (1897) 157 ff.

Bulmerincq, A. von. Praxis, Theorie und Codification des Völkerrechts. Leipzig, 1874.

Burgus, G. B., see Borgo, G. B.

Butler, G., and S. Maccoby. The Development of International Law. London, 1928.

360 BIBLIOGRAPHY

Buzzati, C. Appunti di diritto internazionale. Pavia, 1900.

—— L'autorità delle leggi straniere relative alla forma degli atti. Torino, 1894.

—— Il rinvio nel diritto internazionale privato. Milano, 1898.

—— Trattato di diritto internazionale privato secondo le Convenzioni dell'Aja. Milano, 1907.

—— L'urto di navi in mare. Padova, 1899.

Cacherano da Osasco, O. Disputatio an principi Christiano fas sit foedus inire cum infidelibus. Taurini, 1569.

Cajetanus, see Tommaso da Vio.

Calderini, G. Consilia. Venetiis, 1582.

Calisse, C. A History of Italian Law. Boston, 1928.

—— Storia del diritto italiano. 3 vols. Firenze, 1902.

Cani, G. J. de'. Tractatus de represaliis. Lugduni, 1593. Reprinted in Ziletti, Tractatus, Vol. XII.

Canibus, J. J. a, see Cani, G. J. de'.

Canis, J. J. de', see Cani, G. J. de'.

Cannonieri, P. A. De legationibus. Antwerp, 1615.

Canonherius, P. A., see Cannonieri, P. A.

Cansacchi, G. L'occupazione dei mari costieri. Torino, 1936.

—— La personalità internazionale del S. M. Ordine Gerosolimitano di Malta. Roma, 1936.

—— "L'unione dell'Italia con l'Albania," 37 Riv. dir. int. (1940) 113 ff.

Cappello, M. "Les Consulats et les bailages de la République de Venise," 29 Rev. dr. int. et lég. comp. (1897) 152 ff.

Carlyle, A. J. A History of Medieval Political Thought in the West. 6 vols. London, 1903–1936.

Carnazza Amari, G. Del blocco marittimo. Catania, 1897.

—— Del rispetto della proprietà privata nelle guerre marittime. Bologna, 1898.

—— "Nouvel Exposé du principe de non-intervention," 5 Rev. dr. int. et lég. comp. (1873) 352 ff.

—— Trattato sul diritto internazionale pubblico di pace. 2 vols. Milano, 1875.

Carnelutti, F. Scuola italiana del diritto. Milano, 1936.

Carutti, D. Principii di libero governo. Torino, 1852.

Casanova, L. Lezioni di diritto internazionale. 3d ed. 2 vols. Firenze, 1876. Introduction and notes by B. Brusa.

Casaregis, G. L. M. Discursus legales de commercio. 2 vols. 2d ed. Firenze, 1719.

Cassandro, G. I. Le rappresaglie e il fallimento a Venezia nei secoli XIII°–XIV°. Torino, 1938.

Castaldi, R. Tractatus de imperatore. Reprinted in Ziletti, Tractatus, Vol. XVI.

Castiglioni, C. Consilia. Venetiis, 1538.

Castrensis, P., see Castro, P. di.

Castro, P. di. Opera omnia. 4 vols. Lugduni, 1554.

Catellani, E. Dei conflitti tra le norme di diritto internazionale privato. Venezia, 1897.

—— Diritto internazionale. Padova, 1929.

—— Il diritto internazionale privato e i suoi recenti progressi. 2d ed. 2 vols. Torino, 1895–1902.

—— "Les Maîtres de l'école italienne du droit international du XIXᵉ siècle," 46 Rec. des cours (1933) 709 ff. Same, in Italian, La dottrina italiana del diritto internazionale nel secolo XIX⁰. Roma, 1935.

—— La navigazione fluviale e la questione del Danubio secondo il diritto delle genti. Torino, 1885.

—— "Ottaviano Maggi," 16 Rev. dr. int. et lég. comp. (1884) 410 ff.

Cavaglieri, A. "Alcune osservazioni sul concetto di rinunzia nel diritto internazionale," 12 Riv. dir. int. (1918) 3 ff.

—— "Belligeranza, neutralità e situazioni giuridiche intermedie," 13 Riv. dir. int. (1919–1920) 66 ff.

—— "La Conception positive de la société internationale," 18 Rev. gén. dr. int. publ. (1911) 259 ff.

—— "Concetto e caratteri del diritto internazionale generale," 14 Riv. dir. int. (1922) 289 ff.

—— La consuetudine giuridica internazionale. Padova, 1907.

—— "Il decorso del tempo e i suoi effetti sui rapporti giuridici internazionali," 18 Riv. dir. int. (1926) 169 ff.

—— I diritti fondamentali degli stati nella società internazionale. Padova, 1909.

—— Il diritto internazionale commerciale. Padova, 1936.

—— La dottrina della successione di stati e il suo valore giuridico. Pisa, 1910.

—— "La funzione della clausola rebus sic stantibus nei rapporti internazionali," 70 Archivio giuridico (1903) 106 ff.

—— L'intervento nella sua definizione giuridica. Bologna, 1913.

—— Lezioni di diritto internazionale. Napoli, 1934.

—— Lezioni di diritto internazionale privato. Napoli, 1932.

—— "La natura giuridica della Corte internazionale delle prede," 7 Riv. dir. int. (1913) 121 ff.

—— "Note in materia di successione da stato a stato," 16 Riv. dir. int. (1924) 26 ff.

—— Nuovi studii sull'intervento. Roma, 1928.

—— "Règles générales du droit de la paix," 26 Rec. des cours (1929) 315 ff.

—— "La situazione giuridica dello stato non riconosciuto," 24 Riv. dir. int. (1932) 305 ff.

—— "I soggetti del diritto internazionale," 17 Riv. dir. int. (1925) 18 ff.

—— "Lo stato di necessità nel diritto internazionale," 60 Rivista italiana per le scienze giuridiche (1917) 367 ff.

Cavazzoni Pederzini, F. Studii sopra le nazioni e sopra l'Italia. Torino, 1862.

Celli, P. Sistema di diritto internazionale. Firenze, 1872.

Cereti, C. Panamericanismo e diritto internazionale. Milano, 1939.

—— La revisione dei trattati. Milano, 1934.

—— La tutela giuridica degli interessi internazionali. Milano, 1929.

Chialvo, G. Pierino Belli. Roma, 1910.

Chiovenda, T. Manuale di pratica consolare. Roma, 1931.

Cicchitti, A. "Saseno nella legislazione italiana," Terzo congresso di studi coloniali, Atti (Firenze, 1937), III, 316 ff.

—— "Tien Tsin nella legislazione italiana," Terzo congresso di studii coloniali, Atti (Firenze, 1937), III, 309 ff.

Cino da Pistoia. Commentaria super codicem. Paviae, 1483.

Clark, J. N. The Seventeenth Century. Oxford, 1929.

Clunet, E. Consultation pour les sociétés étrangères d'assurance sur la vie établies en Italie. Paris, 1912.

Cohn, G. Neo-neutrality. New York, 1939.

Comitato giuridico italo-germanico. Atti del primo convegno. Roma, 1939.

Commissione delle prede. Atti. Roma, 1912.

Commissione per le leggi di guerra e neutralità. Atti. Vol. I. Roma, 1937.

Consolato del mare; with an explanation by G. L. M. Casaregis. Reprinted by O. Sciolla. Torino, 1911. Casaregis (1678–1737) was a celebrated expert on the law merchant; this is the most important Italian commentary on the Consolato.

Contuzzi, F. P. "Arbitrati internazionali," in Digesto italiano, VII, 304 ff.

—— Il codice civile nei rapporti col diritto internazionale privato. Napoli, 1897.

—— Il diritto ereditario internazionale. Milano, 1908.

—— Diritto internazionale privato. Milano, 1911.

—— Diritto internazionale pubblico. Milano, 1905.

—— La istituzione dei consoli e il diritto internazionale europeo nella sua applicazione in Oriente. Napoli, 1885.

—— Trattato teorico-pratico di diritto consolare e diplomatico. 2 vols. Torino, 1910–1911.

Coquet, M. "Italie et Turquie-Guerre-Origines et causes du conflit-Déclaration de guerre," in 19 Rev. gén. dr. int. publ. (1912), 370–413.

Corsi, A. L'occupazione militare in tempo di guerra e le relazioni internazionali che ne derivano. Roma, 1882.

Covarruvias, D. Opera omnia. 2 vols. Francofurti ad M., 1538.

Croce, B. The Philosophy of Giambattista Vico. English translation by R. G. Collingwood. London, 1913.

Crusen, C. "Les Servitudes internationales," 22 Rec. des cours (1928) 1 ff.

Cucinotta, E. L'assistenza giudiziaria nei rapporti internazionali. Milano, 1935.

—— Attività pubbliche dello stato esercitate da organi di uno stato straniero. Milano, 1939.

Cybichowski, S. "La Compétence des tribunaux à raison d'infractions commises hors du territoire," 12 Rec. des cours (1926) 272 ff.

Cyllenius, R. De legato Pontificio. Venetiis, 1558.

Daggett, A. P. "The Regulation of Maritime Fisheries by Treaty," 28 Am. J. Int. L. (1934) 692 ff.

Darby, W. E. International Tribunals. 4th ed. London, 1904.

D'Avack, P. A. Chiesa, Santa Sede e Città del Vaticano. Firenze, 1937.

Deák, F., and P. C. Jessup. Neutrality Laws, Regulations and Treaties. 2 vols. Washington, 1939.

Decretales domini Gregorii papae IX suae integritati una cum glossis restitutis. Venetiis, 1584.

Decretum Gratiani. Lutetiae Parisiorum, 1861.

De Francisci, P., and others. Alberico Gentili. Roma, 1936.

De Gioannis Gianquinto, G. Della confisca per contrabando di guerra. Lucca, 1872.

Degli Azzi Vitelleschi, G. "Le rappresaglie negli statuti perugini," in 5 Annali dell'Università di Perugia (1895) 183 ff.

Del Bon, A. Istituzioni di diritto pubblico internazionale. Padova, 1868.

De Lella, G. Legislazione e regolamentazione italiana in materia di prede marittime durante la guerra 1915–1918. Roma, 1935.

Del Giudice, P., ed. Storia del diritto italiano. 3 vols. Milano, 1923–1927.

Del Vecchio, A., and E. Casanova. Le rappresaglie nei Comuni medioevali e specialmente in Firenze. Bologna, 1894.

Del Vecchio, G. La dichiarazione dei diritti dell'uomo. Genova, 1903.

—— Il fenomeno della guerra e l'idea della pace. Torino, 1911.

—— Lezioni di filosofia del diritto. Città di Castello, 1934.

—— "La Société des Nations au point de vue de la philosophie du droit international," 38 Rec. des cours (1931) 545 ff.

—— Sulla teoria del contratto sociale. Bologna, 1906.

De Michelis, G. L'Italia nell'organizzazione internazionale del lavoro. Roma, 1938.

Depping, G. B. Histoire du commerce entre le Levant et l'Europe. 2 vols. Paris, 1830.

Di Carlo, G. Una polemica tra Gioberti e Padre L. Taparelli intorno alla nazionalità. Palermo, 1919.

Dickinson, E. "The Clipperton Island Case," 27 Am. J. Int. L. (1933) 130 ff.

Diena, G. "Ancora qualche osservazione in tema di riconoscimento di stati," 24 Riv. dir. int. (1932) 405 ff.

—— I diritti reali considerati nel diritto internazionale privato. Torino, 1895.

—— Il fallimento degli stati e il diritto internazionale. Torino, 1898.

—— Principii di diritto internazionale pubblico e privato. 2 vols. Napoli, 1914.

—— Il riconoscimento e i diritti fondamentali degli stati. Torino, 1908.

—— "Le Traité de conciliation et de règlement judiciaire entre l'Italie et la Suisse," 52 Rev. dr. int. et lég. comp. (1925) 1 ff.

—— Trattato di diritto commerciale internazionale. 3 vols. Firenze, 1900–1905.

—— I tribunali delle prede belliche e il loro avvenire. Torino, 1896.

Digesto italiano, Il. 24 vols. Torino, 1884–1921. A legal encyclopedia containing several monographs on topics of international law.

Di Jorio, M. La giurisprudenza del commercio. 4 vols. Napoli, 1799.

Diritto internazionale, Milan. 1937 to date. A yearbook of international law published by Balladore Pallieri for the "Istituto per gli studi di politica internazionale" of Milan.

Domenico di San Gimignano. Lectura prima super sexto libro Decretalium. Venetiis, 1476.

Dominicus de Sancto Geminiano, see Domenico di San Gimignano.

Donati, B. "Lineamenti per una teoria giuridica della nazione," 79 Archivio giuridico (1907) 135 ff.

Donati, D. Atto complesso, autorizzazione e approvazione. Modena, 1903.

—— La Città del Vaticano nella teoria generale dello stato. Padova, 1930.

—— Il problema delle lacune nell'ordinamento giuridico. Milano, 1910.

—— Stato e territorio. Roma, 1924.

—— I trattati internazionali nel diritto costituzionale. Torino, 1906.

Donnedieu de Vabres, L. Essai sur la théorie de l'équilibre. Paris, 1900.

Doren, A. J. Storia economica dell'Italia nel Medioevo. Translated from German by G. Luzzatto. Padova, 1934.

Douhet, E. La difesa nazionale. Milano, 1924.

—— Il dominio dell'aria. Roma, 1924.

—— Probabili aspetti della guerra futura. Palermo, 1928.

Duguit, L. Traité de droit constitutionnel. 2 ed. 5 vols. Paris, 1921–1925.

Dumbauld, E. "Dissenting Opinions in International Adjudications," in 90 University of Pennsylvania Law Review (1942) 929–945.

Dumont, J. Corps universel diplomatique du droit des gens. 8 vols. Amsterdam, 1726–1731.

—— Supplément au Corps universel diplomatique du droit des gens. 5 vols. Amsterdam, 1739.

Dupuis, C. Le Principe de l'équilibre et le concert européen. Paris, 1909.

Durando, G. Della nazionalità italiana; saggio politico e militare. Lausanne, 1846.

Ebner, G. "Compagnie coloniali," in Nuovo digesto italiano, III, 411 ff.

Ehrlich, L. "L'Interpretation des traités," 24 Rec. des cours (1928) 1 ff.

Elbe, J. von. "Evolution of the Concept of the Just War in International Law," 33 Am. J. Int. L. (1939) 665 ff.

Engelmann, W. Die Wiedergeburt der Rechtskultur in Italien durch die wissenschaftliche Lehre. Leipzig, 1938.

Enriques, G. "Considerazioni sulla teoria della guerra nel diritto internazionale," 20 Riv. dir. int. (1928) 27 ff.

—— Lo spazio atmosferico nel diritto internazionale. Padova, 1931.

Epsstein, J. The Catholic Tradition of the Law of Nations. London, 1935.

Era, A. Storia dell'accusa di plagio mossa a Domenico Azuni. Sassari, 1928.

Ercole, F. Da Bartolo all' Altusio. Firenze, 1932.

—— Dal comune al principato. Firenze, 1929.

—— "Le origini francesi di una nota formula bartoliana," in 4 Archivio storico italiano (1915) 241 ff.

Esperson, P. La capacità giuridica dello straniero in Italia. Milano, 1889.

—— Dei diritti d'autore sopra le opere dell'ingegno nel diritto internazionale. Pavia, 1890.

—— Diritto cambiario internazionale. Pavia, 1870.

—— Diritto diplomatico e giurisdizione consolare marittima. 3 vols. Torino-Roma, 1874–1877.

—— "Le Droit international privé dans la législation italienne," 7 Journal du droit international privé (1880) 245 ff.

—— "La Législation fiscale italienne dans ses rapports avec le droit international," 25 Rev. dr. int. et lég. comp. (1893) 286 ff.

—— Il principio di nazionalità applicato alle relazioni civili internazionali. Pavia, 1868.

—— La proprietà industriale nei rapporti internazionali. Pavia, 1890.

Faccio, G. C. Le rappresaglie. Vercelli, 1910.

Falconi, E. de. Tractatus de legato a latere. Reprinted in Ziletti, Tractatus, Vol. XV.

Farnese, C. Proposta di un codice di diritto internazionale. Roma, 1873.

Fauchille, P. "Le Conflit de limites entre le Bresil et la Grande-Bretagne et la sentence arbitrale du roi d'Italie," 12 Rev. gén. dr. int. publ. (1905) 25 ff.

—— Traité de droit international public. 8th ed. 4 vols. Paris, 1921–1926.

Fauchille, P., and J. Basdevant. Jurisprudence italienne en matière de prises maritimes. Paris, 1921.

Fedozzi, P. "Le compagnie coloniali e la politica coloniale italiana," 24 Rivista italiana per le scienze giuridiche (1897) 1 ff.

—— "La Condition juridique des navires de commerce," 10 Rec. des cours (1925) 5 ff.

—— Il diritto amministrativo internazionale. Perugia, 1901.

—— Il diritto internazionale privato. Padova, 1935.

—— "Le Droit international et les récentes hostilités italo-abyssines," 26 Rev. dr. int. et lég. comp. (1896) 580 ff.

—— "De l'efficacité extraterritoriale des lois et des actes de droit public," 27 Rec. des cours (1929) 141 ff.

—— Saggio sul protettorato. Venezia, 1897.

—— Trattato di diritto internazionale; introduzione e parte generale. Padova, 1939.

Fenn, P. T. The Origin of the Right of Fishery in Territorial Waters. Cambridge, 1936.

—— "Origins of the Theory of International Waters," 20 Am. J. Int. L. (1926) 465 ff.

Ferrara, F. Manuale di diritto consolare. Padova, 1936.

Ferrari, G. Corso sugli scrittori politici italiani. Milano, 1862.

—— Histoire de l'idée de la raison d'état. Paris, 1860.

Ferrero Gola, A. Corso di diritto internazionale pubblico, privato e marittimo. 2 vols. Parma, 1868.

Ferretti, G. De belli aquatici praeceptis. Venetiis, 1579.

—— De feriis et induciis militaribus, treuga et pace. Venetiis, 1575.

—— De re et disciplina militari aureus tractatus. Venetiis, 1575. Reprinted in Ziletti, Tractatus, Vol. XVI.

—— "Tractatus de oratoribus seu legatis principum et de eorum fide et officio," in Consilia et tractatus, Venetiis, 1562.

Fieschi, S., see Innocent IV.

Figgis, J. N. The Divine Right of Kings. 2d ed. Cambridge, 1934.

Filippucci Giustiniani, G. La dottrina fascista di diritto internazionale. Roma, 1938.

Finch, G. A. The Sources of Modern International Law. Washington, D.C., 1937.

Fiore, P. Degli agenti diplomatici. Pisa, 1875.

—— Diritto internazionale privato. 3d ed. 5 vols. Torino, 1888.

—— Diritto internazionale pubblico. 4th ed. 3 vols. Torino, 1904–1916.

—— Elementi di diritto internazionale privato. 3d ed. Torino, 1888.

—— Il diritto internazionale codificato e la sua sanzione giuridica. 5th ed. Torino, 1915. English translation by E. M. Borchard, New York, 1918.

—— Del fallimento secondo il diritto internazionale privato. Pisa, 1873.

Fiore, P. Nuovo diritto internazionale pubblico secondo i bisogni della civiltà moderna. Milano, 1865.

Fisher, H. A. L. A History of Europe. London, 1937.

Fitzgibbon, R. H. "Alberoni and International Organization," 17 Social Science (1942) 375 ff.

Foce del Giuba, La. Roma, 1912.

Focherini, A. La dottrina canonica del diritto della guerra da S. Agostino a Balthasar d'Ayala. Modena, 1912.

—— La successione degli stati. Modena, 1910.

—— Problemi di diritto internazionale pubblico. Carpi, 1912.

Foerster, R. B. The Italian Emigration of Our Times. Cambridge, 1919.

Fondateurs du droit international, Les. Paris, 1904.

Fontes juris gentium; Handbuch der diplomatischen Korrespondenz der europäischen Staaten. Series B, Section I. 2 vols. Berlin, 1937–1938.

Foreign Relations of the United States, 1870 to date. Preceded by American State Papers, 1789–1834; Papers Relating to Foreign Affairs and Diplomatic Correspondence, 1861–1868.

Foro italiano, Il. A law review published in Rome since 1876. Leading judicial decisions are printed in it. Official reports of the decisions of the Italian courts are not published. Important decisions are published in law reviews such as Il Foro italiano, la Giurisprudenza italiana, and Il Monitore dei tribunali.

Frangipani, C. Allegatione in jure per la vittoria contro Federico l'Imperatore e atto del Papa Alessandro III° per il dominio della republica veneta del suo golfo. Venezia, 1618.

Frank, H. Il nuovo indirizzo del diritto gèrmanico. Roma, 1936.

Freccia, J. De subfeudis baronum, et investituris feudorum. Venetiis, 1579.

Frey, S. Das öffentliche Schiedsgericht in Oberitalien im 12. und 13. Jahrhundert. Luzern, 1928.

Friedman, W. "The Growth of the State Control over the Individual and Its Effects upon the Rules of State Responsibility," 19 British Year Book of International Law (1938) 118 ff.

Fulgosio, R., and R. de Curris. Consilium per quod declarant Gulphum esse dominium venetum. Venetiis, 1442.

Fusinato, G. "Albinaggio," in Digesto italiano, VII, 630.

—— "Antoine Bernardi," 16 Rev. dr. int. et lég. comp. (1884) 599 ff.

—— "Le Capitolazioni e la guerra," 6 Riv. dir. int. (1912) 389 ff.

—— Dell'esecuzione in Italia dei contratti di borsa stipulati all'estero. Roma, 1894.

—— Scritti giuridici. 2 vols. Torino, 1921.

Gabba, F. C. "L'incident consulaire franco-italien à Florence," 20 Rev. dr. int. et lég. comp. (1888) 229 ff.

—— "Introduzione al diritto civile internazionale," in Atti della R. Accademia dei Lincei (Roma 1906–1908).

Galiani, F. Dialogues sur le commerce des blés. Paris, 1770.

—— Doveri dei principi neutrali verso i principi guerreggianti e di questi verso i neutrali. 2 vols. Napoli, 1782.

—— Della moneta. Napoli, 1751.

Gambaro, P. A. Tractatus de officio atque autoritate legati a latere. Venetiis, 1571. Reprinted in Ziletti, Tractatus, Vol. XIII.

Garati (Garatus), M., see Martino da Lodi.

Garner, J. W. International Law and the World War. 2 vols. London, 1920.

Gazzetta ufficiale del Regno d'Italia. Roma. The official journal of the Kingdom of Italy since its establishment in 1861. Law, decrees, and legal notices issued by the Italian state are published in it.

Gemma, S. Appunti di diritto internazionale pubblico. Bologna, 1923.

—— Il diritto internazionale del lavoro. Roma, 1912.

—— Il diritto internazionale del lavoro. Padova, 1939.

—— "Les Gouvernements de fait," 4 Rec. des cours (1924) 297 ff.

—— La guerra e il diritto internazionale. Bologna, 1893.

—— L'impero britannico. Bologna, 1933.

—— Il moderno concetto di neutralità. Verona, 1907.

—— Il rapporto di belligeranza studiato nei suoi caratteri differenziali. Firenze, 1900.

—— Storia dei trattati nel secolo XIX°. Firenze, 1893.

Genevois, E. Histoire de la juridiction consulaire. Paris, 1866.

Gentili, A. Hispanicae advocationis libri duo. Publications of the Carnegie Endowment for International Peace, Division of International Law. Introduction by F. F. Abbott. 2 vols. New York, 1921.

—— De jure belli libri tres. Publications of the Carnegie Endowment for International Peace, Division of International Law. Introduction by C. Philipson. 2 vols. Oxford, 1933.

—— Laudes academiae Perusinae et Oxoniensis. Hannoviae, 1605.

—— Legalium comitiorum Oxoniensium actio. Londinii, 1582.

—— De legationibus libri tres. Publications of the Carnegie Endowment for International Peace, Division of International Law. Introduction by E. Nys. 2 vols. New York, 1924.

—— De legibus interpretibus dialogi sex. London, 1582.

Ghirardini, C. "La comunità internazionale e il suo diritto," 12 Riv. dir. int. (1919–1920) 3 ff.

—— "Delle cosidette occupazioni qualificate," 6 Riv. dir. int. (1912) 48 ff.

—— "La litispendenza nel diritto processuale civile internazionale," 2 Riv. dir. int. (1907) 229 ff.

—— "A proposito d'intervento," 7 Riv. dir. int. (1915) 89 ff.

—— La sovranità nel diritto internazionale. Cremona, 1913.

Ghiron, M. "Gli effetti della guerra odierna sulle convenzioni per la tutela dei diritti industriali," 10 Riv. dir. int. (1916) 355 ff.

Giannini, A. Le convenzioni internazionali di diritto aereonautico. Roma, 1929.

—— L'Etiopia nella Società delle Nazioni. Roma, 1936.

Giannone, P. Istoria civile del Regno di Napoli. 2 vols. Venezia, 1766.

Gianzana, S. Lo straniero nel diritto civile italiano. 3 vols. Torino, 1884.

Gidel, G. Le Droit international public de la mer. 3 vols. Paris, 1932–1934.

Gioberti, V. Del primato morale e civile degli Italiani. Torino, 1843.

Giovannetti, F. De Romano imperio ac eius jurisdictione. Reprinted in Ziletti, Tractatus, Vol. XVI.

Giovanni da Legnano. Tractatus de bello, de represaliis et de duello. Publications of the Carnegie Endowment for International Peace. Introduction by T. E. Holland. Oxford, 1917.

Giurisprudenza italiana, La. A law review published in Turin since 1848. Leading judicial decisions are printed in it. Official reports of the decisions of the Italian courts are not published. Important decisions are published in law reviews such as La giurisprudenza italiana, Il foro italiano and Il monitore dei tribunali.

Goebel, J. Equality of States. New York, 1923.

Graf, A. Roma nelle immaginazioni e nelle memorie del Medioevo. 2 vols. Torino, 1881–1883.

Grasso, G. Principii di diritto internazionale pubblico e privato. 3d ed. Firenze, 1896.

Grotius, H. De iure belli ac pacis libri tres. Introduction by J. B. Scott. Published by the Carnegie Institution of Washington. 2 vols. Washington, D.C., 1913–1925.

Guarino, C. Le rappresaglie in tempo di pace. Milano, 1910.

Guicciardini, F. Opere inedite. Firenze, 1857.

Gutzwiller, M. "Le Développement historique du droit international privé," 29 Rec. des cours (1929) 287 ff.

—— Der Einfluss Savignys auf die Entwicklung des Internationalprivatrechts. Freiburg i. B., 1923.

Habicht, M. "Le Pouvoir du juge international de statuer ex aequo et bono," 49 Rec. des cours (1934) 277 ff.

Hackworth, G. H. Digest of International Law. 5 vols. Washington, D.C., 1940–1943.

Hauriou, M. Précis de droit constitutionnel. Paris, 1923.

—— Principes de droit public. 2d ed. Paris, 1916.

—— La Théorie de l'institution. Paris, 1925.

Hautefeille, L. B. Des Droits et des devoirs des nations neutrales en temps de guerre. 2d ed. 3 vols. Paris, 1868.

Heffter, A. W. Das europäische Völkerrecht. Berlin, 1873.

Hentschel, F. "Franciscus de Victoria und seine Stellung zum Völkerrecht," 17 Zeitschrift für öffentliches Recht (1937) 388 ff.

Hershey, A. "History of International Law during Antiquity and the Middle Ages," 5 Am. J. Int. L. (1911) 901 ff.

—— "History of International Law since the Peace of Westphalia," 6 Am. J. Int. L. (1912) 30 ff.

Heyd, W. von. Le compagnie coloniali degli Italiani in Oriente nel Medio Evo. Venezia, 1862.

—— Histoire du commerce du Levant au moyen âge. 2 vols. Leipzig, 1885–1886.

Heydte, F. A. von der. "Franciscus de Victoria und seine Völkerrecht," 13 Zeitschrift für öffentliches Recht (1933) 239 ff.

Highley, A. E. The First Sanctions Experiment. Geneva, 1938.

Hindmarsch, A. E. Force in Peace. Cambridge, 1933.

Holland, T. E. Studies in International Law. Oxford, 1898.

Holldack, H. "Die kilikischen Handelsprivilegien der Republiken Genua und Venedig," 7 Zeitschrift für Völkerrecht (1913) 196 ff.

Holtzendorff, F. von. "Die geschichtliche Entwicklung der internationalen Rechts- und Staatsbeziehungen bis zum Westphälischen Frieden," in Handbuch des Völkerrechts (Berlin, 1885), 157 ff.

—— "Le Principe des nationalités et la litterature italienne du droit des gens," 2 Rev. dr. int. et lég. comp. (1870) 93 ff.

Hosack, J. On the Rise and Growth of the Law of Nations. London, 1882.

Hostiensis, In primum librum decretalium commentaria. Venetiis, 1581.

—— Summa super titulis decretalium. Lugduni, 1588.

Hrabar, V. E. "L'Epoque de Bartole (1314–1358) dans l'histoire du droit international," 7 Rev. gén. dr. int. publ. (1900) 732 ff.

—— De legatis et legationibus tractatus varii. Dorpat, 1906. The book contains several excerpts from works of Italian Renaissance authors dealing with ambassadors.

—— De legatorum jure tractatuum catalogus completus ab anno MDCXXV usque ad annum MDCC. Dorpati Livonorum, 1918.

Hudson, M. O. "Languages Used in Treaties," 26 Am. J. Int. L. (1932) 371 ff.

Hyde, C. C. "The Termination of the Treaties of a State in Consequence of Its Absorption by Another," 26 Am. J. Int. L. (1932) 133 ff.

—— "Judge Anzilotti and the Interpretation of Treaties," 27 Am. J. Int. L. (1933) 502 ff.

Hyneman, C. S. The First American Neutrality. Urbana, 1934.

Ingenuis, F. de, see Sarpi, P.

Innocent IV. Decretales in Corpus juris canonici; ed. Freyberg. Leipzig, 1889.

—— Apparatus ad quinque libros decretalium. Venetiis, 1578.

Jellinek, G. Allgemeine Staatslehre. 2d ed. Berlin, 1900.

—— System der subjectiven öffentlichen Rechte, Freiburg, i. B., 1892.

Jemolo, A. C. "Guarentigie pontificie," in Nuovo digesto italiano, VI, 526 ff.

—— "Norme di diritto ecclesiastico nei cinque trattati di pace," 13 Rivista di diritto pubblico (1921) 65 ff.

Jessup, P. C. The Law of Territorial Waters and Maritime Jurisdiction. New York, 1927.

Jessup, P. C., and F. Deák. Neutrality; Its History, Economics and Law. 4 vols. New York, 1935–1936.

Jus gentium. Napoli, 1938 to date. A yearbook of international law.

Kaltenborn und Stachau, C. von. Die Vorlaeufern des Hugo Grotius auf dem Gebiete des jus naturae et gentium. Leipzig, 1848.

Kamp, J. von der. Bartolo da Sassoferrato. Urbino, 1935.

Katchenowski, L. Prize Law. Translated from the Russian by F. T. Pratt. London, 1867.

Kohler, J. "Beiträge zum internationalen Strafrecht. I. Das internationale Strafrecht in den italienischen Stadtrechten," 4 Zeitschrift für internationales Recht (1894) 225 ff.

—— "Beiträge zum internationalen Strafrecht. II. Das internationale Strafrecht bei den italienischen Juristen," 5 Zeitschrift für internationales Recht (1895) 232 ff.

Kohler, J. "Handelsverträge zwischen Genua und Narbonne im 12. und 13. Jahrhunderten," in Juristiche Gesellschaft, Berlin, Festgabe für dr. R. Koch (Berlin, 1903), pp. 275 ff.

—— Internationales Strafrecht. Stuttgart, 1917.

—— "Die Lehren des Kanevarofalles," 7 Zeitschrift für Völkerrecht (1913) 1 ff.

Korff, S. A. "Introduction à l'histoire du droit international," 1 Rec. des cours (1923) 1 ff.

Krauske, O. "Die Entwicklung der ständigen Diplomatie vom fünfzehnten Jahrhundert bis zu den Beschlüssen von 1815," 5 Staats- und sozialwissenschaftliche Forschungen (1885), No. 3.

Kroell, J. "Les Pratiques de la guerre aérienne dans le conflit italo-éthiopien," 5 Revue générale de droit aérien (1936) 178 ff.

Kunz, J. "La Doctrine dualiste chez Balladore Pallieri," 11 Revue internationale de la théorie du droit (1937) 12 ff.

—— "Neutrality and the European War 1939–1940," 39 Michigan Law Review (1940) 719 ff.

—— Die Staatenverbindungen. Stuttgart, 1929.

Laghi, F. Il diritto internazionale privato nei suoi rapporti con le leggi territoriali. Bologna, 1888.

—— Teoria dei trattati internazionale. Parma, 1882.

Lainé, A. Introduction au droit international privé. 2 vols. Paris, 1888.

Lambert, J. Les Déplacements de souveraineté en Italie pendant les guerres du XVIIᵉ siècle. Paris, 1911.

—— Les Occupations militaires en Italie pendant les guerres de Louis XIVᵉ. Paris, 1903.

—— Théorie et pratique de la conquête dans l'ancien droit. Paris, 1902.

Lampredi, G. M. Del commercio dei popoli neutrali in tempo di guerra. 2 vols. Firenze, 1788. French translation by J. Penches, Du Commerce des neutres en temps de guerre. 2 vols. Paris, 1802.

—— Juris publici naturalis sive juris naturae et gentium theoremata. 2 vols. Florentiae 1776–1778.

Landogna, F. "Le rappresaglie negli statuti e nelle carte lucchesi," 8 Rivista di storia del diritto italiano (1935) 65 ff.

Lange, C. L. Histoire de l'internationalisme. Christiania, 1919.

Lapradelle, A. de. "La Guerre italo-abyssine et le respect du droit de la guerre," 5 Revue générale de droit aérien (1936) 31 ff.

Lapradelle, A. de, and N. Politis. Recueil des arbitrages internationaux. 2 vols. Paris, 1905.

Lapradelle, P. de. La Frontière. Paris, 1928.

La Terza, P. L. "Il trattato di conciliazione e di regolamento giudiziario tra l'Italia e la Svizzera," 17 Riv. dir. int. (1925) 257 ff.

Laudensis, M., see Martino da Lodi.

Laurent, F. Droit civil international. 8 vols. Bruxelles, 1880–1881.

Lauterpacht, H. The Function of the Law in the International Community. Oxford, 1933.

—— Private Law Sources and International Law. London, 1927.

—— "Revolutionary Propaganda by Governments," 13 Grotius Society Transactions (1938) 143 ff.

—— "The So-called Anglo-American and Continental Schools of Thought in International Law," 12 British Year Book of International Law (1931) 31 ff.

League of Nations. Treaty Series. Publication of Treaties and International Engagements Registered with the Secretariat of the League. Vols. 1 to date. London, 1920 to date.

Leibholz, G. "Der Abschluss und die Transformation von Staatverträgen in Italien," 16 Zeitschrift für Völkerrecht (1932) 353 ff.

Lenel, W. Die Entstehung der Vorherrschaftes Venedigs an der Adria. Strassburg, 1897.

Lignano, J. de, see Giovanni da Legnano.

Lignanus, see Giovanni da Legnano.

Lioy, D. Del principio di nazionalità dal lato della storia e del diritto pubblico. Napoli, 1861.

Lomonaco, G. Trattato di diritto civile internazionale. Napoli, 1874.

—— Trattato di diritto internazionale pubblico. Napoli, 1905.

Longhena, G. "Regime giuridico per la pesca," in Nuovo digesto italiano, XI, 103 ff.

Lucchesi Palli, G. Diritto pubblico marittimo. Napoli, 1840. French translation by A. de Galiani: Principes du droit public maritime, Paris, 1842.

Lupo (Lupus), G. De bello et bellatoribus. Reprinted in Ziletti, Tractatus, Vol. XVI.

—— De confederatione, pace et conventionibus principum. Argentinae, 1511. Reprinted in Ziletti, Tractatus, Vol. XVI.

M. R. W. "Du régime appliqué par l'Italie pendant la guerre européenne aux bâtiments ennemis refugiés dans ses ports," 24 Rev. gén. dr. int. publ. (1917) 337 ff.

Mably, G. B. de. Le Droit public de l'Europe fondé sur les traités. 2 vols. Amsterdam, 1747.

Macchiavelli, N. Opere. 10 vols. Milano, 1804–1805.

Macdonell, J., and E. Manson, eds. The Great Jurists of the World. Boston, 1914.

Maggi, O. De legato, eius officii et dignitate libri II in quibus multa doctissimaque praecepta de rebus gerendis negotiisque administrandis continentur. Venetiis, 1566.

Maggiore, G. "Ciò che resta del Kelsenismo," in Studii in onore di Santi Romano (Padova, 1940), II, 213 ff.

Maine, H. S. International Law. London, 1887.

Mamiani, T. Di un nuovo diritto pubblico europeo. Torino, 1859. English translation by R. Acton, London, 1860.

Mancini, P. S. Diritto internazionale. Naples, 1873. A collection of Mancini's writings on international law by A. Pierantoni.

Marchi, T. La fondazione storico-giuridica dello stato italiano. Parma, 1924.

Marenco, C., G. Manfroni, and G. B. Pessagro. Il Banco di San Giorgio. Genova, 1911.

Marinoni, M. L'efficacia del diritto internazionale. Firenze, 1916.

Marinoni, M. La rappresentanza di uno stato da parte di un altro e le relazioni giuridiche a cui dà origine. Venezia, 1910.

—— La responsabilità degli stati per gli atti dei loro rappresentanti. Roma, 1914.

—— Scritti varii. Città di Castello, 1933.

Martens, F. F. Das Konsularwesen und die Konsularjurisdiction im Orient. Berlin, 1874.

—— Traité de droit international. French translation by A. Leo. 3 vols. Paris, 1883–1887.

Martens, G. F. von. Nouveau recueil général de traités et autres acts relatifs aux rapports de droit international. 1st series, 20 vols., Göttingen, 1843–1875; 2d series, 35 vols., Göttingen, 1876–1908; 3d series, Vols. 1 to date. Leipzig, 1875 to date.

—— Nouveau recueil de traités d'alliance, de paix, de trêve et de plusieurs autres actes servant à la connaissance des rélations étrangères des puissances de l'Europe depuis 1808 jusqu'à présent. 16 vols. Göttingen, 1817–1841.

—— Nouveaux supplements au Recueil de traités depuis 1761 jusqu'à présent. 3 vols. Göttingen, 1839–1842.

—— Recueil des principaux traités d'alliance, de paix, de trêve . . . conclus par les puissances de l'Europe . . . depuis 1761 jusqu'à présent. 2d ed. 8 vols. Göttingen, 1817–1835.

—— Cours diplomatique. 3 vols. Berlin, 1801.

Martens, K. von. Causes célèbres du droit des gens. 2d ed. 5 vols. Leipzig, 1858–1861.

—— Le Guide diplomatique. 5th ed. 2 vols. Leipzig, 1866.

—— Nouvelles causes célèbres du droit des gens. 2 vols. Leipzig, 1843.

Martino da Lodi. De confederatione, pace et conventionibus principum. Reprinted in Ziletti, Tractatus, Vol. XVI.

—— De principibus. Reprinted in Ziletti, Tractatus, Vol. XVI.

—— Tractatus de legatis maxime principum. Lugduni, 1530. Reprinted in Ziletti, Tractatus, Vol. XVI.

—— Tractatus de represaliis. Lugduni, 1593. Reprinted in Ziletti, Tractatus, Vol. XII.

—— Tractatus de bello cum commentario. Conradi Scleifi. Lovanii, 1648.

Martinus Laudensis, see Martino da Lodi.

Mas Latrie, R. de. Le Droit de marque ou droit de représailles au moyen âge. Paris, 1875.

—— Traités de paix et de commerce et documents divers concernant les rélations des Chrétiens avec les Arabes. Paris, 1865.

Matteacci (Mattheacius), A. De jure Venetorum et jurisdictione maris Adriatici. Venetiis, 1617.

Mattheacius, A., see Matteacci, A.

Maulde de la Clavière, M. La Diplomatie au temps de Machiavel. 3 vols. Paris, 1892–1893.

Mazzini, G. Scritti editi ed inediti. Vol. LXXXIV. Imola, 1907–1940.

Mazzoleni, G. B. L'odierno impero britannico. Milano, 1928.

—— "Servitù internazionali," in Nuovo digesto italiano, XII, 209 ff.

Meijers, E. "L'Histoire des principes fondamentaux du droit international privé à partir du moyen âge," 49 Rec. des cours (1934) 543 ff.

Meili, F. Die geschichtliche Entwicklung des internationalen Konkursrechts. Zürich, 1908.

—— Die hauptsächlichsten Entwicklungsperioden des internationalen Strafrechts. Zürich, 1908.

Meinecke, F. Die Idee der Staatsraison in der neueren Geschichte. München, 1926.

Memoriale italiano sulla situazione dell'Etiopia. Roma, 1935.

Menestrina, F. "Nuove provincie," in Nuovo digesto italiano, VIII, 1179 ff.

Meriggi, L. "Le funzioni consultive della Corte permanente di giustizia internazionale," 22 Riv. dir. int. (1930) 62 ff.

—— "Trattati e convenzioni internazionali," in Nuovo digesto italiano, II, 394 ff.

Mérignhac, A. Traité de droit public international. 3 vols. Paris, 1905–1912.

—— Traité théorique et pratique de l'arbitrage international. Paris, 1895.

Meulen, J. Der Gedanke der internationalen Organisation in seiner Entwicklung. 3 vols. The Hague, 1917–1940.

Miceli, V. "Il problema del riconoscimento in diritto internazionale," 19 Riv. dir. int. (1927) 169 ff.

Miltitz, A. de. Manuel des consuls, 2 vols. London-Berlin, 1837–1841.

Ministero degli Esteri. L'Italiano all'estero e la sua condizione giuridica. Roma, 1934.

—— Trattati e convenzioni tra il Regno d'Italia e gli stati esteri. This collection, started in 1861 and published successively in Turin, Florence, and Rome, should comprise all international agreements between Italy and foreign states. Up to 1940, 53 volumes have been published. The collection is not up to date.

Ministero della Marina. Norme di diritto marittimo di guerra. Roma, 1927.

—— Norme e disposizioni sul mare territoriale. Roma, 1939.

—— Regolamento sopra le insegne, le bandiere, gli onori e le visite. Roma, 1934.

—— Sentenze della Commissione delle Prede. Guerra europea 1915–1918. Roma, 1927.

Missiroli, M. La monarchia socialista. Bologna, 1902.

Mohl, R. von. Staatsrecht, Völkerrecht und Politik. 3 vols. Tübingen, 1860–1869.

Molen, G. van der. Alberico Gentili and the Development of International Law; His Life, Work and Times. Amsterdam, 1937.

Molina, L. De justitia et jure tomi sex. Coloniae, 1614.

Monaco, R. L'ordinamento internazionale in rapporto all'ordinamento statuale. Torino, 1932.

—— "I regolamenti interni degli enti internazionali," 1 Jus gentium (1938) 52 ff.

—— "La responsabilità indiretta dello stato per fatti degli individui," 31 Riv. dir. int. (1939) 3 ff.

Mondaini, G. "Eritrea," in Nuovo digesto italiano, V, 459 ff.

Monitore dei tribunali, Il. A law review published in Milan since 1860. Leading judicial decisions are printed in it. Official reports of the decisions of the Italian court are not published. Important decisions are published in law reviews such as Il monitore dei tribunali, Il foro Italiano and La giurisprudenza italiana.

Moore, J. B. A Digest of International Law. 8 vols. Washington, D.C., 1906.

Moore, J. B. History and Digest of the International Arbitrations to which the United States has been a party. 6 vols. Washington, D.C., 1898.

Morelli, G. "La condizione giuridica degli agenti diplomatici di nazionalità italiana accreditati presso la Santa Sede," 26 Riv. dir. int. (1934) 42 ff.

—— Il diritto processuale civile internazionale. Padova, 1938.

—— "Limiti dell'ordinamento statuale e limiti della giurisdizione," 25 Riv. dir. int. (1933) 383 ff.

—— Norme dispositive di diritto internazionale. Urbino, 1932.

—— "L'ordinamento internazionale di fronte alle nuove situazioni di fatto, 1 Archivio di diritto pubblico (1936) 185 ff.

—— La sentenza internazionale. Padova, 1931.

—— "La Théorie générale du procès international," 61 Rec. des cours (1937) 253 ff.

Morgenthau, H. "Positivism, Functionalism, and International Law," 34 Am. J. Int. L. (1940) 260 ff.

Morpurgo, L. "Sulla condizione giuridica dei forestieri in Italia nei secoli di mezzo," 8 Archivio giuridico (1876) 248 ff.

Mowat, A. A History of European Diplomacy. New York, 1925.

Mulas, E. Pierino Belli da Alba precursore di Grozio. Torino, 1878.

Muratori, L. A. Antiquitates italicae Medii Aevi. 6 vols. Mediolani, 1738–1742.

Myers, D. P. Manual of Collections of Treaties and of Collections Relating to Treaties. Cambridge, 1922. It contains a very useful list of collections of Italian treaties and of documents relating to Italy's international relations.

Neumeyer, K. Die gemeinrechtliche Entwicklung des internationalen Privat- und Strafrechts bis Bartolus. München, 1901–1916.

Neyron, P. J. Essai historique et politique sur les guaranties. Göttingen, 1777.

Nicolini, F. Il pensiero giuridico dell'abate Galiani. Bari, 1908.

Nippold, C. "Le Développement historique du droit international," in 2 Rec. des cours (1924) 1 ff.

Nostitz-Wallwitz, C. von. "Das Kriegsrecht in italienisch-abessinischen Krieg," 6 Zeitschrift für ausländisches öffentliches Recht und Völkerrecht (1937) 680 ff.

"Nostra guerra con la Turchia, La," 6 Riv. dir. int. (1912) 54 ff.

Novacovitch, M. Les Compromis et les arbitrages internationales du XIIe au XVe siècle. Paris, 1905.

Novati, F. L'influsso del pensiero latino sopra la civiltà italiana del medioevo. Milano, 1899.

Nuovo digesto italiano. 13 vols. Torino, 1937–1939. A legal encyclopedia containing several monographs on topics of international law.

Nys, E. "Antoine Bernardi évêque de Caserte," 16 Rev. dr. int. et lég. comp. (1884) 283 ff.

—— Christine de Pisan et ses principales œuvres. La Haye, 1914.

—— "Les Commencements de la diplomatie et le droit d'ambassade jusqu'à Grotius," 15 Rev. dr. int. lég. comp. (1883) 577 ff.

—— "Les Droits et les devoirs des neutres par Galiani," 21 Rev. dr. int. et lég. comp. (1899) 382 ff.

—— "Le Droit de la guerre et les condottieri," 43 Rev. dr. int. et lég. comp. (1911) 217 ff.

—— Le Droit de la guerre et les précurseurs de Grotius. Bruxelles, 1882.

—— "Le Droit international et la Papauté," 10 Rev. dr. int. et lég. comp. (1878) 501 ff.

—— Le Droit international; les principes, les théories, les faits. 3 vols. Bruxelles, 1912.

—— Etudes de droit international et de droit politique. 2 vols. Bruxelles, 1896–1901.

—— Les Origines du droit international. Bruxelles, 1894.

—— "La Papauté et le droit international," 37 Rev. dr. int. et lég. comp. (1905) 150 ff.

—— "Traités de subside et troupes auxiliaires dans l'ancien droit. Politique des subsides," 45 Rev. dr. int. et lég. comp. (1913) 173 ff.

Oakes, A. and R. B. Mowat, The Great European Treaties of the Nineteenth Century. Oxford, 1918.

Ogilvie, P. M. International Waterways. New York, 1920.

Olivi, L. Diritto internazionale pubblico e privato. 2 vols. 3d ed. Milano, 1933–1934.

Ollivier, E. L'Empire liberal. 17 vols. Paris, 1895–1913.

Ompteda, D. H. C. van. Litteratur des gesamten sowohl natürlichen als positiven Völkerrechts. Regensburg, 1785.

Orlando, V. E. "Recenti indirizzi circa i rapporti tra diritto e stato," 18 Rivista di diritto pubblico (1926) 273 ff.

—— Regno d'Italia (Formazione del)," in Nuovo digesto italiano, XI, 311 ff.

Ottolenghi, G. "Il diritto dei neutri secondo la 5a e la 12a Convenzione dell'Aja," 4 Riv. dir. int. (1909) 205 ff.

—— La frode alla legge. Torino, 1909.

—— Nuovi lineamenti del diritto internazionale. Torino, 1929.

—— "Sulla personalità internazionale delle unioni di stati," 17 Riv. dir. int. (1925) 313 ff.

—— "Il principio dell'effettività e la sua funzione nell'ordinamento giuridico internazionale," 28 Riv. dir. int. (1936) 3 ff.

—— Il rapporto di neutralità. Torino, 1907.

Paci, G. Disceptatio de dominio maris Hadriatici. Venetiis, 1619.

Pacius, J., see G. Paci.

Padelletti. "L'Alsace et la Lorraine et le droit des gens," 3 Rev. dr. int. et lég. comp. (1871) 464 ff.

Palma, L. Del principio di nazionalità nella moderna società civile europea. Milano, 1867.

—— Trattati e convenzioni in vigore tra il Regno d'Italia e i governi esteri. 2 vols. Torino, 1879–1890.

Panunzio, S. Principio e diritto di nazionalità. Roma, 1921.

Pardessus, J. M. Collection des lois maritimes antérieures au XVIIIe siècle. 6 vols. Paris, 1828–1845.

Paroldo, C. Saggio di codice del diritto internazionale. Torino, 1858.

Pelcovitz, N. A., and H. Schneiderman. "Respect for the American Passport." 4 Contemporary Jewish Record (1941) 481 ff.

Pellizzi, C. "Condition des sujets ennemis en Italie," 45 Journal du droit international privé (1918) 43 ff.

Perassi, T. "Le assicurazioni sociali nel diritto internazionale," in 4 Atti dell' Istituto Nazionale delle Assicurazioni (1932) 56 ff.

—— Lezioni di diritto internazionale. Napoli, 1922.

—— Lezioni di diritto internazionale. 2 vols. Roma, 1937–1938.

—— "Teoria dommatica delle fonti di norme giuridiche in diritto internazionale," 11 Riv. dir. int. (1917) 195 ff.

—— "Il trattato di arbitrato e di conciliazione tra la Germania e la Svizzera," 14 Riv. dir. int. (1921) 155 ff.

Pertile, A. Storia del diritto italiano. 6 vols. Torino, 1896–1902.

Pertile, G. B. Elementi di diritto internazionale moderno.

Pescatore, M. La logica del diritto. Vol. I. Torino, 1863.

Pieper, A. Zur Enstehungsgeschichte der ständigen Nuntiaturen. Freiburg i. B., 1894.

Pierantoni, A. La capacità delle persone giuridiche straniere in Italia. Roma, 1884.

—— Le dichiarazioni di guerra nella storia. Roma, 1905.

—— I fiumi e la convenzione internazionale di Mannheim. Roma, 1879.

—— "La nullité d'un arbitrage international," 30 Rev. dr. int. et lég. comp. (1898) 445 ff.

—— Storia degli studi del diritto internazionale in Italia. 2d ed. Firenze, 1902. The only attempt at a history of the doctrines of international law in Italy. The book is obsolete and of scant value.

—— Trattato di diritto internazionale. Roma, 1881.

Pilotti, M. "Plurality and Unity of Juridical Orders," 19 Iowa Law Review (1934) 244 ff.

—— "Les Unions d'Etats," 24 Rec. des cours (1928) 447 ff.

Pisanelli, G. Lo stato e la nazione. Napoli, 1862.

Potter, P. B. The Freedom of the Seas in History, Law and Politics. New York, 1924.

—— The Wal Wal Arbitration. Washington, 1938.

Pound, R. "Philosophical Theory and International Law," 1 Bibliotheca Visseriana (The Hague, 1924) 77 ff.

Pozzo, P. del. Tractatus elegans et copiosus de re militari. Mediolani, 1515. Reprinted in Ziletti, Tractatus, Vol. XVI.

Preuss, L. "Some Effects of Governmental Control on Neutral Duties," 31 American Society of International Law, Proceedings (1937) 108 ff.

Previté-Orton, C. W. The Defensor Pacis of Marsilius of Padua. Introduction. Cambridge, 1928.

Provinciali, R. L'immunità giurisdizionale degli stati esteri. Padova, 1933.

Pütter, K. T. Beiträge zur Völkerrechtsgeschichte und Wissenschaft. Leipzig, 1843.

Puteo, P. de, see Pozzo, P. del.

Quadri, R. "Funzione del diritto internazionale privato," 1 Archivio di diritto pubblico (1936) 288 ff.
—— Le navi private nel diritto internazionale. Milano, 1940.
—— "Stato," in Nuovo digesto italiano, XII (part 1) 818 ff.
—— La sudditanza nel diritto internazionale. Padova, 1936.
Raccolta ufficiale delle leggi e dei decreti del Regno d'Italia. Roma. The official collection of the laws and decrees of the Kingdom of Italy since its establishment in 1861.
Raestad, A. La Mer territoriale. Paris, 1913.
Ralston, J. H. International Arbitration from Athens to Locarno. London, 1929.
—— The Law and Procedure of International Tribunals. Stanford, 1926. Supplement, Stanford, 1936.
Randolino, P. Pierino Belli. Torino, 1861.
Ranelletti, O., and A. Amorth. "Atti amministrativi," in Nuovo digesto italiano, 1, 109 ff.
—— "Atti del governo," Nuovo digesto italiano, I, 1108 ff.
Rapisardi Mirabelli, A. "Le Congrès de Westphalie, ses négociations et ses résultats au point de vue de l'histoire du droit des gens," in 8 Bibliotheca Visseriana (1929) 5 ff.
—— Il diritto internazionale amministrativo. Padova, 1939.
—— "La guerre italo-turque et le droit des gens," 45 Rev. dr. int. et lég. comp. (1912) 159 ff.
—— I limiti di efficacia delle norme internazionali. Catania, 1922.
—— L'ordine pubblico nel diritto internazionale. Catania, 1908.
—— Il principio della uguaglianza giuridica degli stati. Catania, 1920.
—— Il significato della guerra nel diritto internazionale. Catania, 1900.
—— Gli stadii dell'organizzazione internazionale. Siena, 1926.
—— "Lo status dell'Italia nella documentazione dei suoi atti costitutivi," 43 Studi senesi (1929) 56 ff.
—— Storia dei trattati e delle relazioni internazionali. Milano, 1940.
—— "Théorie générale des unions internationales," 7 Rec. des cours (1925) 341 ff.
Rashofer, H. "Volk und Staat in der italienischen Rechtstheorie des 19 Jahrhunderts," 6 Zeitschrift für ausländisches öffentliches Recht und Völkerrecht (1936) 538 ff.
Ravndal, G. B. The Origin of the Capitulations and of the Consular Jurisdiction. Washington, D.C., 1921.
Recueil des décisions des tribunaux arbitraux mixtes institués par les traités de paix. 10 vols. Paris, 1922–1930.
Reddie, J. Researches, Historical and Critical, in Maritime International Law. 2 vols. Edinburgh, 1844–1845.
Redslob, R. Histoire des grands principes du droit des gens. Paris, 1923.
Régout, R. La Doctrine de la guerre juste de Saint Augustin à nos jours. Paris, 1934.
Renan, E. Qu'est-ce qu'une nation? Paris, 1882.
Renner, K. Das Selbstbestimmungsrecht der Nationen in besonderer Anwendung auf Oesterreich. Wien, 1918.

Renzi, A. Tecnica degli scambi con l'estero. 2d ed. Milano, 1938.

Repertorio del Foro italiano. A supplement of Il foro italiano. A digest of the most important judicial decisions issued every year.

Repertorio della giurisprudenza italiana. A supplement of La giurisprudenza italiana. A digest of the most important judicial decisions issued every year.

Retortillo y Tornos, A. Compendio de historia del derecho internacional. Madrid, 1909.

Reumont, A. de Della diplomazia italiana del secolo XIII°. Firenze, 1857.

Rey, F. "Un Cas de liberté de navigation d'un fleuve international au moyen âge," 11 Rev. gén. dr. int. publ. (1904) 192 ff.

Rivier, A. Notes sur la littérature du droit des gens avant la publication du Jus belli ac pacis de Grotius (1625). Bruxelles, 1883.

Rivista di diritto internazionale. Roma, 1906. The outstanding Italian review of international law. It was founded by Anzilotti, Ricci Busatti, and Senigallia; published by the former two from 1908 to 1922, then by Anzilotti, Cavaglieri, and Perassi, and by Anzilotti and Perassi after the death of Cavaglieri in 1936.

Rivista di diritto internazionale e di legislazione comparata. Napoli, 1898–1902. The first Italian review of international law; published by Senigallia and Pennetti.

Rivista italiana di diritto internazionale privato e processuale. Padova, 1931–1934. A periodical dealing with problems of conflict of laws, published by Fedozzi.

Rizzo, G. B. "La unione dell'Albania con l'Italia e lo statuto del Regno d'Albania," 31 Rivista di diritto publico (1939) 42 ff.

Rocco, F. Uso e autorità delle leggi del Regno delle Due Sicilie considerate nelle relazioni con le persone e con il territorio degli stranieri. 2 vols. Napoli, 1836. The third edition, Napoli, 1859, is entitled Trattato di diritto civile internazionale.

Rodocanachi, E. La Réforme en Italie. 2 vols. Paris, 1920–1921.

Romagnosi, G. D. Delle prede marittime. Prato, 1840.

—— La scienza delle costituzioni. 2 vols. Roma, 1936–1937.

Romano, S. "I caratteri giuridici della formazione del Regno d'Italia," 6 Riv. dir. int. (1912) 345 ff.

—— Il comune. Milano, 1918.

—— Corso di diritto internazionale. 4th ed. Padova, 1939.

—— L'instauramento di fatto di un ordinamento costituzionale e la sua legittimazione. Modena, 1901.

—— L'ordinamento giuridico. Pisa, 1918.

—— "Di una particolare figura di successione di stati. A proposito dell'annessione di Fiume," 17 Riv. dir. int. (1925) 304 ff.

—— La teoria dei diritti pubblici subbiettivi. Milano, 1898.

Rossi, L. Degli scritti inediti giuridico-politici di Giovanni da Legnano. Bologna, 1898.

Rossi, P. Cours de droit constitutionnel. 4 vols. Paris, 1866–1867.

Ruffini, F. L'insegnamento di Mazzini. Milano, 1917.

Salles, G. L'Institution des consulats, son origine, son développement au moyen-âge, chez les différents peuples. Paris, 1898.

Salvatorelli, L. Sommario della storia d'Italia. Torino, 1938. English translation: A Concise History of Italy. New York, 1940.

Salvioli, Gabriele. "Gli accordi di Locarno," 18 Riv. dir. int. (1926) 429 ff.

—— "Sulla clausola rebus sic stantibus nei trattati internazionali," 8 Riv. dir. int. (1914) 264 ff.

—— "La corte permanente di giustizia internazionale," 15 Riv. dir. int. (1924) 11 ff.

—— "La Jurisprudence de la cour permanente de justice internationale," 12 Rec. des cours (1926) 1 ff.

—— "Motivi di nullità delle sentenze internazionali," 29 Riv. dir. int. (1937) 305 ff.

—— "Principii generali di diritto internazionale," 20 Riv. dir. int. (1928) 571 ff.

—— "Le prove nella procedura internazionale," in Studii in onore di Santi Romano, III, 67 ff.

—— "Les Règles internationales de la paix," 46 Rec. des cours (1933) 1 ff.

—— "La Responsabilité des états et la fixation des dommages-intérêts par les tribunaux internationaux," 28 Rec. des cours (1929) 235 ff.

—— "Il riconoscimento degli stati," 18 Riv. dir. int. (1926) 336 ff.

—— "Studii sui caratteri dell'ordinamento giuridico internazionale," 14 Riv. dir. int. (1921) 20 ff.

—— Sulla teoria dell'accordo in diritto internazionale. Napoli, 1914.

—— "I terzi stati nel diritto internazionale," 12 Riv. dir. int. (1918) 229 ff.

Salvioli, Giuseppe. Le Concept de la guerre juste d'après les écrivains antérieurs à Grotius. Translation by G. Hervo. 2d ed. Paris, 1918.

—— Storia del diritto italiano. Torino, 1921.

Sandiford, R. Diritto aereonautico di guerra. Roma, 1937.

—— Diritto marittimo di guerra. Roma, 1938.

—— "Il diritto marittimo di guerra nelle leggi di guerra e neutralità," 71 Rivista marittima (1938) 231 ff.

—— "Il mare territoriale secondo il diritto positivo italiano," 60 Rivista marittima (1927) 122 ff.

Sandonà, G. Trattato di diritto internazionale moderno. Firenze, 1870.

Sapori, A. "Il commercio internazionale del medioevo," 9 Archivio di studi corporativi (1938) 281 ff.

Saredo, G. Saggio sulla storia del diritto internazionale privato. Firenze, 1873.

Sarpi, P. (F. de Ingenuis). Epistula de jurisdictione Venetae reipublicae in Mare Adriaticum. Venetiis, 1619.

—— Opere varie. 2 vols. Helmstat, 1750.

Sassoferrato, Bartolo da, see Bartolo da Sassoferrato.

Satow, E. M. A Guide to Diplomatic Practice. 3d ed. 2 vols. London, 1932.

Savigny, F. C. von. Geschichte der römischen Rechtes im Mittelalter. 2d ed. 7 vols. Heidelberg, 1834–1851.

Scerni, M. L'abuso di diritto nei rapporti internazionali. Roma, 1930.

—— "Cenni sul diritto processuale della Corte permanente di giustizia internazionale," 29 Riv. dir. int. (1937) 12 ff.

—— Il diritto internazionale privato marittimo e aereonautico. Padova, 1936.

—— I principii generali di diritto riconosciuti dalle nazioni civili nella giurisprudenza della Corte permanente di giustizia internazionale. Padova, 1932.

Scerni, M. "La Procédure de la Cour permanente de justice internationale," 65 Rec. des cours (1938) 561 ff.

—— Saggio sulla natura giuridica delle norme emanate da organi creati con atti internazionali. Genova, 1930.

—— "Di una speciale figura di intervento nella procedura della Corte permanente di giustizia internazionale," in Studi in onore di Santi Romano, III, 213 ff.

Schaube, A. "Zur Entstehungsgeschichte der ständigen Gesandtschaften," 10 Mitteilungen der Institutes für oesterreichische Geschichtsforschung. Innsbruck, 1889.

—— Handelsgeschichte der lateinischen Völker des Mittelmeergebiets bis zum Ende der Kreuzzüge. München, 1906.

—— Das Konsulat des Meeres in Pisa. Leipzig, 1888.

—— "La Proxenie au Moyen Age," 28 Rev. dr. int. et lég. comp. (1896) 524 ff.

Schiattarella, R. Il diritto della neutralità nelle guerre marittime. Sassari, 1874.

—— Organismo e storia del diritto internazionale. Siena, 1879.

—— Propedeutica al diritto internazionale. Firenze, 1881.

Schilling, O. Das Völkerrecht nach Thomas von Aquin. Freiburg i. B., 1919.

Scialoia, A. "Mare," in Nuovo digesto italiano, VIII, 155 ff.

Sclopis, F. Storia della legislazione italiana. 3 vols. Torino, 1863–1864.

Scott, J. B. The Catholic Conception of International Law. Washington, D.C., 1934.

—— Law, the State and the International Community. 2 vols. New York, 1939.

—— The Spanish Origin of International Law. Oxford, 1934.

Seligman, E. "La double imposition et la coopération fiscale internationale," 20 Rec. des cours (1927) 459 ff.

Sereni, A. P. "Agency in International Law," 34 Am. J. Int. L. (1940) 638 ff.

—— "Arbitrato internazionale," in Nuovo digesto italiano, I, 637 ff.

—— "Capitolazione," in Nuovo digesto italiano, II, 835 ff.

—— "Casus foederis," in Nuovo digesto italiano, II, 1118 ff.

—— "La cittadinanza degli enti morali nel diritto internazionale," 26 Riv. dir. int. (1934) 171 ff.

—— "La clausola della nazione più favorita," 24 Riv. dir. int. (1932) 53 ff.

—— "Il diritto internazionale delle minoranze," 21 Riv. dir. int. (1929) 461 ff.

—— "La convenzione di Ginevra per l'esecuzione delle sentenze arbitrali straniere," 23 Riv. dir. int. (1931) 595 ff.

—— "Divorzio," in Nuovo digesto italiano, V, 99 ff.

—— "Il giudizio di delibazione e i provvedimenti stranieri di giurisdizione volontaria," 24 Riv. dir. int. (1932) 509 ff.

—— Italian Private Law Enacted in Contemplation of War. New York, 1941.

—— "Italian Prize Courts (1866–1942)," 37 Am. J. Int. L. (1943) 24 ff.

—— "Legal Problems of Divorce in Italy," 28 Iowa Law Review (1943) 286 ff.

—— "The Legal Status of Albania," 35 American Political Science Review (1940) 311 ff.

—— I marchi di fabbrica e di commercio nel diritto internazionale privato. Milano, 1938.

—— "Panama," in Nuovo digesto italiano, IX, 432 ff.

—— "Piccola Intesa, Intesa balcanica e Unione baltica," 28 Riv. dir. int. (1936) 172 ff.

—— "Problemi nuovi del diritto internazionale delle minoranze," 23 Riv. dir. int. (1931) 216 ff.

—— "Sulla proponibilità innanzi all'autorità giudiziaria italiana di azioni nascenti da rapporti in cui è parte uno stato estero," 24 Riv. dir. int. (1932) 434 ff.

—— La rappresentanza nel diritto internazionale. Padova, 1936.

—— "The Status of Croatia under International Law," 35 American Political Science Review (1940) 1144 ff.

—— "Suez," in Nuovo digesto italiano, XII (Part 1), 1192 ff.

Simpson, J. H. Refugees. London, 1938.

Siotto Pintor, M. "L'esenzione degli stati esteri dalla giurisdizione nella recente giurisprudenza italiana," in Festgabe für Fritz Fleiner. Tübingen, 1927. 247 ff.

—— "Positivisme juridique et droit international," in Al Guanom vai iqtisad (Cairo, 1936–1937), pp. 67 ff.

Solaro della Margherita, C. Traités publics de la Royale Maison de Savoie avec les puissances étrangères depuis la paix de Château-Cambrésis jusqu'à nos jours. 8 vols. Torino, 1836–1861.

Solmi, A. Storia del diritto italiano. Milano, 1930.

Sombart, W. Der moderne Kapitalismus. 6th ed. Vol. I. München, 1924.

Soto, D. Libri decem de justitia et jure. Venetiis, 1568.

Spaventa, B. Le filosofia italiana nelle sue relazioni con la filosofia europea. Reprinted, Bari, 1911.

—— Della nazionalità nella filosofia. Napoli, 1862.

Spencer, J. H. "Quelques Aspects juridiques de l'emploi des aéreonefs dans la guerre italo-éthiopienne," 7 Revue générale de droit aérien (1938) 7 ff.

Steiner, H. A. "Italian War and Neutrality Legislation," 38 Am. J. Int. L. (1939) 151 ff.

Stinzing, R. Ulrich Zasius. Basel, 1857.

Strisower, L. Die italienische Schule des internationalen Privatrechts. Wien, 1881.

Studi in onore di Santi Romano. 4 Vols. Padova, 1940. Volume III comprises monographs on international law problems by leading Italian scholars.

Suarez, F. Tractatus de legibus ac Deo legislatore. 2 vols. Neapoli, 1872.

Tacchino, A. I rapporti diplomatici tra la Serenissima Repubblica di San Marino e il Sovrano Militare Ordine di Malta. Mede, 1937.

Taparelli d'Azeglio, L. Della nazionalità. Genova, 1847.

—— Sintesi del diritto naturale. Reprinted, Bologna, 1940.

Tertullianus, G. S. Opera. 3 vols. Vindobonae, 1890–1939.

Thamm, M. Albericus Gentilis und seine Bedeutung für das Völkerrecht, insbesondere seine Lehre um Gesandtschaftswesen. Strassburg, 1896.

Tommaso da Vio. Scripta philosophica. Romae, 1934.

Toscani, A. Convenzioni consolari e clausole in materia consolare. Roma, 1932.

—— Norme e consuetudini di cerimoniale. Roma, 1933.

Triepel, H. Völkerrecht und Landesrecht. Leipzig, 1899.

Turcotti, L. Introduzione ad un nuovo codice del diritto delle genti. Torino, 1874.

Twiss, Sir T. "Albericus Gentilis on the Law of War," 3 The Law Magazine and Review (1878) 149 ff.

—— The Law of Nations. 2 vols. Oxford, 1875.

Ubaldis, A. de, see Angelo da Perugia.

Ubaldis, B. de, see Baldo degli Ubaldi.

Udina, M. Sui conflitti di legge nelle colonie italiane. Firenze, 1933.

—— "Le Droit international privé de l'Italie," in Repertoire de droit international privé (Paris, 1930), VI, 477 ff.

—— Elementi di diritto internazionale privato. Roma, 1933.

—— L'estinzione dell'impero austro-ungarico nel diritto internazionale. 2d ed. Trieste, 1933.

—— "Fiume (Città di)," in Nuovo digesto italiano, VI, 27 ff.

—— "Isole italiane dell'Egeo," in Nuovo digesto italiano, VII, 217 ff.

—— La posizione giuridica attuale delle isole egee nell'ordinamento giuridico italiano. Modena, 1927.

—— "La Succession des états quant aux obligations internationales autres que les dettes publiques," 44 Rec. des cours (1933) 665 ff.

Valery, J. "Le Pape Alexandre III et la liberté des mers," 14 Rev. gén. dr. int. publ. (1907) 240 ff.

Vanderpol, A. La Doctrine scolastique du droit de guerre. Paris, 1919.

—— Le Droit de guerre d'après les théologiens et les canonistes du moyen-âge. Paris, 1911.

Vasquez, F. Controversiarum illustrium aliarumque usu frequentium libri tres. Francofurti ad M., 1572.

Venturini, G. C. "Le misure càutelari nel diritto internazionale," 111 Archivio giuridico (1938) 318 ff.

Verdross, A. von. "Das neue italienische Kriegs-und Neutralitätsrecht," 19 Zeitschrift für öffentliches Recht (1939) 193 ff.

—— Die Verfassung der Völkerrechtsgemeinschaft. Wien, 1926.

Vesnitch, M. R. "Cardinal Alberoni, an Italian Precursor of Pacifism and International Arbitration," 7 Am. J. Int. L. (1913) 82 ff.

Vico, G. B. La scienza nova. 2 vols. Milano, 1831.

Victoria, F. de. De Indis et de jure belli relectiones. Publications of the Carnegie endowment for international peace. Introduction by E. Nys. 2 vols. Washington, D.C., 1917.

Vidari, E. "Galiani, Lampredi e Azuni," 1 Arch. giur. (1868) 210 ff.

—— Del rispetto della proprietà privata in tempo di guerra. Pavia, 1867.

Vio, T. da, see Tommaso da Vio.

Vitta, C. "Divergenze nella dottrina italiana sui principii fondamentali del diritto internazionale pubblico," 21 Riv. dir. int. (1929) 501 ff.

Vollenhoven, C. van. The Law of Peace. Translated from the Dutch by W. H. Carter. London, 1936.

Volpe, G. Il Medioevo. 2d ed. Firenze, 1933.

—— Medioevo italiano. Firenze, 1923.

—— Movimenti religiosi e sette ereticali nella società medioevale italiana. Firenze, 1926.

Wach, A. Der Arrestprocess in seiner geschichtlichen Entwicklung. Leipzig, 1868.

Waldkirch, E. von. "Neutralitätsrecht," in Handbuch des Völkerrechts (Stuttgart, 1936), VI (Part 5), 1 ff.

Walker, T. A. A History of the Law of Nations. Cambridge, 1899. Vol. I.

Wambaugh, S. A Monograph on Plebiscites, with a Collection of Official Documents. New York, 1920.

Wegner, A. "Geschichte des Völkerrechts," in Handbuch des Völkerrechts (Stuttgart, 1936), I, 3.

Weiss, A. Manuel de droit international privé. 8th ed. Paris, 1920.

—— Traité théorique et pratique de droit international privé. 2d ed. 7 vols. Paris, 1907.

Westlake, F. A. Collected Papers on Public International Law. Cambridge, 1914.

Wheaton, H. Elements of International Law. 6th English ed. 2 vols. London, 1929.

—— Histoire du progrès du droit des gens en Europe et en Amérique depuis la paix de Westphalie jusqu'à nos jours. 2 vols. Leipzig, 1865.

—— History of the Law of Nations in Europe and America. New York, 1845.

Wilson, E. G. International Law. 9th ed. New York, 1935.

Winogradoff, P. "Historical Types of International Law," 1 Bibliotheca Visseriana (The Hague, 1923) 1 ff.

Woolf, C. N. S. Bartolus of Sassoferrato. Cambridge, 1913.

Wright, H. F. Catholic Founders of Modern International Law. Washington, D.C., 1934.

—— Francisci de Victoria De jure belli relectio. Washington, D.C., 1916.

Yver, G. Le Commerce et les marchands dans l'Italie meridionale. Paris, 1903.

Zancla, P. La dottrina della sovranità dello stato e il problema dell'autorità internazionale in Bartolo. Palermo, 1933.

—— La revisione dei trattati. Palermo, 1932.

Ziletti, F. Tractatus universi juris, duce et auspice Gregorio XIII pontifice maximo in unum congesti. 18 vols. Venetiis, 1584. This collection comprises most of the Italian writings dealing with subjects of international law published during the fifteenth and sixteenth centuries. The collection is also known as Tractatus tractatuum and Tractatus illustrium jurisconsultorum.

Zimmermann, M. "La Crise de l'organisation internationale à la fin du moyen âge," 44 Rec. des cours (1933) 315 ff.

INDEX

Abbazia, Pact of, 280
Abyssinia, *see* Ethiopia
Accursio (Accursius), 7
Active solidarity, principle of, 47
Acts of state, classification: acts of government, 324; acts of dominion, 325; acts of management, 325
Addetti Culturali, 306 f.
Addetti Stampa, 306
Addis Ababa, 283, 284
Addis Ababa, Treaty of, 282, 315
Aden, Gulf of, spheres of influence in, 282
Adjacent sea, concept of, 71
Administrative assistance, treaties of, 296
Adriatic Sea, dominion of Venice in, 29, 73-75
Advocatio Hispanica (Gentili), 99; its nature and value, 112-14
Aegean sea, Italian islands of the, *see* Dodecanese islands
Aerial neutrality, 346
Aerial space, 288
Aerial warfare, special regulations for, 344
Aeronautic Convention (Oct. 13, 1919), 288
African colonies, seizure of, 203
Africa Orientale Italiana, 281-84
Agame, 283
Ago, Roberto, 209
Agreement, the only primary source of international rules, 216, 219; between international subjects, 247
Agreements, customary rules not to be confused with tacit, 256; *see also* Treaties
Albania, object of Austrian aspirations, 203; Saseno declared an Italian possession, 281; relations with, 291; Italian intervention in, 309, 310
Albanian Fascist Party, 291
Alberico da Rosate, 87, 101
Alciati, Andrea, 103, 105*n*
Alciatus, *see* Alciati, Andrea
Alexander VII, Pope, 133
Aliens, *see* Foreigners
Alphonse of Este, 39
Alsace-Lorraine, 175, 176
Alto-Adige, agreements aimed at elimination of German minority in, 301
Ambassadors, permanent, 16; status: rules governing, 17, 81 ff.; inviolability, 78, 82;

political functions, 80; demands of European: the right of quarter, 133; *see also* Diplomatic intercourse and agents
Ambassadors, Conference of the, 281
American Revolution, proclamations of neutrality during, 135
Amhara, 284
Anatolia, territorial waters, 288
Andrea d'Isernia, 99
Angary, right of, 32, 53, 138*n*
Anglo-Egyptian Sudan, 290
Anti-Comintern Pact, 300
Anzilotti, Dionisio, 186, 196; quoted, 166, 210, 211, 245, 249*n*, 350; teaching of international law, 208 ff.; basic theories, 213-44; theory of recognition, 232, 245 ff. *passim*; effort to eradicate influence of natural law from doctrine of international law, 244; concept of rule *pacta sunt servanda*, 244 ff. *passim*; reaction against positivist doctrine of, 251-68; origin of concept, 266; reason for uncompromising attitude, 267; did not feel influence of Fascism, 273; re immunity of foreign states, 326; reconciliation of doctrine with those of opposers, 349; influence, 351; dissents at Permanent Court of International Justice, 352
Aquinas, Thomas, 202
Arbitral tribunals, mixed, 313
Arbitration, early resort to, 37-42; so-called, under totalitarianism, 37*n*; the arbitrators: legal procedure, 40; reasons for recourse to: devices to guarantee execution of judgments: decline of, 41; international, 190; progress in field of, 239; in positivist doctrine, 240, 264; treaties of, 312; participation of Italian jurists in international adjudications, 351
Archives, preservation of, 331
Armistices and capitulations, 192
Assab Bay, 281
Asylum, right of, 11, 331, 338
Augustine, Saint, 85, 89
Austin, conception of the law, 214
Austria, domination in Italy, 131, 151, 153, 154, 184, 196; relations with, after Congress of Vienna, 182 ff.; power of supervision, 183; settlement of disputes with, 188, 191; wars, 192 f.; Treaty of St. Germain-en-

www.ingramcontent.com/pod-product-compliance
Lightning Source LLC
Chambersburg PA
CBHW020814300326

41914CB00075B/1765/J